# HALSBURY'S

# Laws of England

FOURTH EDITION
2001 REISSUE

Volume 5(2)

# HALSBURY'S
# Laws of England

FOURTH EDITION
2001 REISSUE

LORD MACKAY OF CLASHFERN
Lord High Chancellor of Great Britain
1987–97

## Volume 5(2)

BUTTERWORTHS

LONDON          2001

**Members of the LexisNexis Group worldwide**

| | |
|---|---|
| United Kingdom | LexisNexis UK, a Division of Reed Elsevier (UK) Ltd, Halsbury House,35 Chancery Lane, LONDON WC2A 1EL and 4 Hill Street, EDINBURGH EH2 3JZ |
| Argentina | LexisNexis Argentina, BUENOS AIRES |
| Australia | LexisNexis Butterworths, CHATSWOOD, New South Wales |
| Austria | LexisNexis Verlag ARD Orac GmbH & Co KG, VIENNA |
| Canada | LexisNexis Butterworths, MARKHAM, Ontario |
| Chile | LexisNexis Chile Ltda, SANTIAGO DE CHILE |
| Czech Republic | Nakladatelství Orac sro, PRAGUE |
| France | Editions du Juris-Classeur SA, PARIS |
| Germany | LexisNexis Deutschland GmbH, FRANKFURT, MÜNSTER |
| Hong Kong | LexisNexis Butterworths, HONG KONG |
| Hungary | HVG-Orac, BUDAPEST |
| India | LexisNexis Butterworths, NEW DELHI |
| Ireland | LexisNexis, DUBLIN |
| Italy | Giuffrè Editore, MILAN |
| Malaysia | Malayan Law Journal Sdn Bhd, KUALA LUMPUR |
| New Zealand | LexisNexis Butterworths, WELLINGTON |
| Poland | Wydawnictwo Prawnicze LexisNexis, WARSAW |
| Singapore | LexisNexis Butterworths, SINGAPORE |
| South Africa | LexisNexis Butterworths, DURBAN |
| Switzerland | Stämpfli Verlag AG, BERNE |
| USA | LexisNexis, DAYTON, Ohio |

FIRST EDITION
*Published in 31 volumes between 1907 and 1917*

SECOND EDITION
*Published in 37 volumes between 1931 and 1942*

THIRD EDITION
*Published in 43 volumes between 1952 and 1964*

FOURTH EDITION
*Published in 56 volumes between 1973 and 1987, with reissues between 1988 and 2003*

A CIP Catalogue record for this book is available from the British Library.

ISBN (complete set, standard binding)  0 406 03400 1
      (this volume, standard binding)  0 406 91504 0

Printed and bound in England by Antony Rowe Ltd, Chippenham, Wiltshire

**Visit LexisNexis UK at www.lexisnexis.co.uk**

# Editor in Chief

THE RIGHT HONOURABLE

## LORD MACKAY OF CLASHFERN

LORD HIGH CHANCELLOR OF GREAT BRITAIN

1987-97

**Editor**

CLAIRE MASSON, MA,
A SOLICITOR OF THE SUPREME COURT

**Senior Sub-editor**

CLARE BYRNE, BA

**Sub-editor**

KIRSTEN HOBKIRK, LLB,
OF THE MIDDLE TEMPLE, BARRISTER

**Editorial Assistant**

CATHERINE CALLEYA, LLB

**Indexer**

PAULA BOUWER, BA, LLB

**Publisher**

SIMON HETHERINGTON, LLB

**Group Publisher**

JAMES BOWMAN, LLB,
A SOLICITOR OF THE SUPREME COURT

**The title Charities has been contributed by:**

HUBERT PICARDA Esq, BCL, MA,
one of Her Majesty's Counsel;
of the Inner Temple, Lincoln's Inn and Gray's Inn;
Profumo Scholar of the Inner Temple
President of the Charity Law Association

The law stated in this volume is in general that in force on 1 April 2001, although subsequent changes
have been included wherever possible.

Any future updating material will be found in the Current Service and annual Cumulative
Supplement to Halsbury's Laws of England.

# TABLE OF CONTENTS

# REFERENCES AND ABBREVIATIONS

| | |
|---|---|
| ACT | Australian Capital Territory |
| AJIL | American Journal of International Law (1907 to date) |
| A-G | Attorney General |
| Adv-Gen | Advocate General |
| affd | affirmed |
| Alta | Alberta |
| affg | affirming |
| App | Appendix |
| art | article |
| Aust | Australia |
| B | Baron |
| BC | British Columbia |
| BYIL | British Yearbook of International Law |
| C | Command Paper (of a series published before 1900) |
| c | chapter number of an Act |
| CA | Court of Appeal |
| CAC | Central Arbitration Committee |
| CA in Ch | Court of Appeal in Chancery |
| CB | Chief Baron |
| CCA | Court of Criminal Appeal |
| CC Fees Order 1982 | County Court Fees Order 1982 (SI 1982/1706) as subsequently amended |
| CCR | County Court Rules 1981 (SI 1981/1687) as subsequently amended |
| CCR | Court for Crown Cases Reserved |
| C-MAC | Courts-Martial Appeal Court |
| CO | Crown Office |
| COD | Crown Office Digest |
| CPR | Civil Procedure Rules 1998 (SI 1998/3132) as subsequently amended (see the Civil Court Practice) |
| Can | Canada |
| Cd | Command Paper (of the series published 1900–18) |
| Cf | compare |
| ch | chapter |
| cl | clause |
| Cm | Command Paper (of the series published 1986 to date) |
| Cmd | Command Paper (of the series published 1919–56) |

| | |
|---|---|
| Cmnd | Command Paper (of the series published 1956–86) |
| Comr | Commissioner |
| Court Forms (2nd Edn) | Atkin's Encyclopaedia of Court Forms in Civil Proceedings, 2nd Edn. See note 2, p *14* post |
| Court Funds Rules 1987 | Court Funds Rules 1987 (SI 1987/821) as subsequently amended |
| DC | Divisional Court |
| DPP | Director of Public Prosecutions |
| EAT | Employment Appeal Tribunal |
| EC | European Community |
| ECJ | Court of Justice of the European Community |
| EComHR | European Commission of Human Rights |
| ECSC | European Coal and Steel Community |
| EEC | European Economic Community |
| EFTA | European Free Trade Association |
| Edn | Edition |
| Env LR | Environmental Law Reports |
| Euratom | European Atomic Energy Community |
| Ex Ch | Court of Exchequer Chamber |
| ex p | ex parte |
| Fed | Federal |
| Forms & Precedents (5th Edn) | Encyclopaedia of Forms and Precedents other than Court Forms, 5th Edn. See note 2, p *14* post |
| GLC | Greater London Council |
| HC | High Court |
| HC | House of Commons |
| HL | House of Lords |
| ILPr | International Litigation Procedure |
| IRC | Inland Revenue Commissioners |
| Ind | India |
| Int Rels | International Relations |
| Ir | Ireland |
| J | Justice |
| JA | Judge of Appeal |
| JC | Justiciary Cases |
| Kan | Kansas |
| LA | Lord Advocate |
| LC | Lord Chancellor |
| LCC | London County Council |
| LCJ | Lord Chief Justice |
| LJ | Lord Justice of Appeal |
| LMELR | Land Management and Environmental Law Reports |
| LoN | League of Nations |
| LRC | Law Reports of the Commonwealth (1985–date) |
| MR | Master of the Rolls |
| Man | Manitoba |
| n | note |
| NB | New Brunswick |
| NI | Northern Ireland |

| | |
|---|---|
| NIJB | Northern Ireland Judgment Bulletin |
| NS | Nova Scotia |
| NSW | New South Wales |
| NZ | New Zealand |
| OJ | The Official Journal of the European Community published by the Office for Official Publications of the European Community |
| Ont | Ontario |
| P | President |
| PC | Judicial Committee of the Privy Council |
| PEI | Prince Edward Island |
| q | question |
| QBD | Queen's Bench Division of the High Court |
| Qld | Queensland |
| Que | Quebec |
| r | rule |
| RDC | Rural District Council |
| RPC | Restrictive Practices Court |
| RSC | Rules of the Supreme Court 1965 (SI 1965/1776) as subsequently amended |
| reg | regulation |
| Res | Resolution |
| revsd | reversed |
| Rly | Railway |
| s | section |
| SA | South Africa |
| S Aust | South Australia |
| SC | Supreme Court |
| SC Fees Order 1980 | Supreme Court Fees Order 1980 (SI 1980/821) as subsequently amended |
| SI | Statutory Instruments published by authority |
| SR & O | Statutory Rules and Orders published by authority |
| SR & O Rev 1904 | Revised Edition comprising all Public and General Statutory Rules and Orders in force on 31 December 1903 |
| SR & O Rev 1948 | Revised Edition comprising all Public and General Statutory Rules and Orders and Statutory Instruments in force on 31 December 1948 |
| SRNI | Statutory Rules of Northern Ireland |
| Sask | Saskatchewan |
| Sch | Schedule |
| Sess | Session |
| Sing | Singapore |
| TS | Treaty Series |
| Tanz | Tanzania |
| Tas | Tasmania |
| UDC | Urban District Council |
| UN | United Nations |
| V-C | Vice-Chancellor |

| | |
|---|---|
| Vict.............................................. | Victoria |
| W Aust ........................................ | Western Australia |
| Zimb............................................ | Zimbabwe |

NOTE 1. A general list of the abbreviations of law reports and other sources used in this work can be found in vol 54 (Reissue) Consolidated Table of Cases at p *v* et seq.

NOTE 2. Where references are made to other publications, the volume number precedes and the page number follows the name of the publication; eg the reference '12 Forms & Precedents (5th Edn) 44' refers to volume 12 of the Encyclopaedia of Forms and Precedents, page 44.

NOTE 3. An English statute is cited by short title or, where there is no short title, by regnal year and chapter number together with the name by which it is commonly known or a description of its subject matter and date. In the case of a foreign statute, the mode of citation generally follows the style of citation in use in the country concerned with the addition, where necessary, of the name of the country in parentheses.

NOTE 4. A statutory instrument is cited by short title, if any, followed by the year and number, or, if unnumbered, the date.

# TABLE OF STATUTES

# TABLE OF STATUTORY INSTRUMENTS

# TABLE OF CIVIL PROCEDURE

## Civil Procedure Rules 1998, SI 1998/3132 (CPR)

# TABLE OF DECISIONS OF THE CHARITY COMMISSIONERS

# TABLE OF CASES

PARA

# C

PARA

# G

# K

PARA

# M

PARA

# O

# T

## Y

# CHARITIES

# 1. CHARITABLE PURPOSES

## (1) ESSENTIALS OF CHARITABLE PURPOSES

**1. Introduction and statutory definition of a 'charity'.** The Charities Act 1993 repeals and consolidates various statutes relating to charities[1], including the Charities Act 1960, which in turn repealed and replaced much of the former statute law on charities[2]. For the purposes of the Charities Act 1993 'charity' means any institution, corporate or not, which is established for charitable purposes and is subject to the control of the High Court in the exercise of its jurisdiction with respect to charities[3]. 'Institution' includes any trust or undertaking; and 'charitable purposes' means purposes which are exclusively charitable according to the law of England and Wales[4]. The question whether purposes are or are not charitable is therefore determined according to the same principles as before the new legislative framework introduced by the Charities Act 1960.

The requirement that an institution be subject to the control of the High Court in the exercise of the court's jurisdiction with respect to charities[5] is satisfied if the institution is subject to that jurisdiction in any significant respect[6]. It does not have to be subject to that jurisdiction which the court exercises only over charities and not over other trusts or other corporate bodies, and it is sufficient if the court is competent to restrain the institution from applying its property ultra vires or in breach of trust[7].

The Charities Act 1960 established a register of charities[8], which is continued by the Charities Act 1993[9], and it is the duty of the charity trustees[10] of any charity which is required to be registered[11] to apply for registration[12]. The effect of registration is that an institution is for all purposes other than rectification of the register conclusively presumed to be or to have been a charity at any time when it is or was on the register of charities[13]. The legislation does not provide, however, that an institution which, if it were a charity, would be required to be registered, but which is not registered, is for that reason not a charity[14].

---

1    The Charities Act 1993 repeals and consolidates the Charitable Trustees Incorporation Act 1872 and, except for certain spent or transitional provisions, the Charities Act 1960 and the Charities Act 1992 Pt I (ss 1–57): see the Charities Act 1993 s 98(2), Sch 7. The Charities Act 1993 came into force on 1 August 1993 (s 99(1)), except for Pt VI (ss 41–49) (as amended) (charity accounts, reports and returns) (see para 307 et seq post), s 69 (investigation of accounts) (see para 502 post) and Sch 6 para 21(3), which came into force on 1 March 1996: Charities Act 1993 (Commencement and Transitional Provisions) Order 1995, SI 1995/2695, art 2. Until such day, transitional provisions applied: Charities Act 1993 s 99(3), Sch 8 Pt I. The Charities Act 1992 made various amendments to the existing law and introduced new provisions.

2    The Charities Act 1960 repealed and replaced statutes including the Charitable Trusts Acts 1853 to 1939 and the Mortmain Acts (see paras 75–76 post) and certain obsolete enactments.

3    Charities Act 1993 s 96(1). Certain ecclesiastical property is excluded by s 96(2): see para 187 post.

4    Ibid s 97(1).

5    As to what is meant by 'the court's jurisdiction with respect to charities' cf ibid s 13(4) (see para 209 post), s 15 (see para 175–176 post), s 33(8) (see para 519 post); and see *Construction Industry Training Board v A-G* [1971] 3 All ER 449, [1971] 1 WLR 1303; affd [1973] Ch 173, [1972] 2 All ER 1339, CA. See also the *Report of the Charity Commissioners for England and Wales for 1990* (HC Paper (1990–91) no 362) App A (a).

6    *Construction Industry Training Board v A-G* [1971] 3 All ER 449, [1971] 1 WLR 1303; affd [1973] Ch 173, [1972] 2 All ER 1339, CA.

7   *Construction Industry Training Board v A-G* [1973] Ch 173, [1972] 2 All ER 1339, CA. For territorial limits on the operation of the Charities Act 1993 see s 100(2)–(6). With limited exceptions, it does not extend to Scotland or Northern Ireland.

8   See the Charities Act 1960 s 4(1) (repealed).

9   See the Charities Act 1993 s 3(1).

10  'Charity trustees' means the persons having the general control and management of the administration of a charity: ibid s 97(1).

11  As to charities which are not required to be registered see ibid s 3(5); and para 383 post.

12  See ibid s 3(7)(a).

13  Ibid s 4(1); *Wynn v Skegness UDC* [1966] 3 All ER 336, [1967] 1 WLR 52; *Re Murawski's Will Trusts, Lloyds Bank Ltd v Royal Society for the Prevention of Cruelty to Animals* [1971] 2 All ER 328, [1971] 1 WLR 707. See para 289 post.

14  See *Over Seventies Housing Association v Westminster City Council* [1974] RA 247; and para 289 post.

## 2. Meaning of 'charity'.

Since the Charities Act 1993 provides no statutory definition of what purposes are and what are not charitable, all the cases previously decided on the subject are still relevant. The legal meaning of 'charitable purposes' is said to be precise and technical, and the phrase is a term of art[1], but it is probably incapable of definition[2]. The popular use of the expressions 'charity', 'charitable', 'charitable objects' and 'charitable purposes' does not coincide with their technical legal meaning according to the law of England[3]. The word 'charitable', when used in its legal sense, covers many objects which a layman might not consider to be included under that word, but it excludes some benevolent or philanthropic activities which a layman might consider charitable[4].

Charitable uses or trusts form a distinct head of equity[5], and it is the court's duty to determine whether particular purposes are charitable[6]. To be charitable a purpose must satisfy certain tests: it must either fall within the list of purposes enumerated in the preamble to the ancient statute of Elizabeth I[7] (sometimes referred to as the Statute of Charitable Uses or the Charitable Uses Act 1601) or within one of the four categories of charitable purposes laid down by Lord Macnaghten and derived from the preamble[8], and in the case of the fourth of those categories it must be within the spirit and intendment of the ancient statute, either directly or by analogy with decided cases on the same point[9], or it must have been declared to be charitable by some other statute[10]. In addition, it must be for the public benefit[11], that is to say it must be both beneficial and available to a sufficient section of the community[12].

References to 'charity' in any Act of Parliament should be construed in their technical legal sense, unless a contrary intention appears from the context[13]. For income tax purposes 'charity' means any body of persons or trust established for charitable purposes only[14]. References in any enactment or document to a charity within the meaning, purview and interpretation of the ancient statute of Elizabeth I, or of the preamble to it, are to be construed as references to a charity within the meaning which the word bears as a legal term according to the law of England and Wales[15].

An activity which is charitable in the legal sense is not any the less charitable because it is being carried on without any regular organisation by a person who may discontinue it at any time[16]. Such an activity would come within the statutory definition of charity as a trust or undertaking[17].

1   *National Anti-Vivisection Society v IRC* [1948] AC 31 at 41, [1947] 2 All ER 217 at 219, HL, per Lord Wright; *Chichester Diocesan Fund and Board of Finance Inc v Simpson* [1944] AC 341 at 368, [1944] 2 All ER 60 at 73, HL, per Lord Simonds. See also *Ashfield Municipal Council v Joyce* [1978] AC 122, [1976] 3 WLR 617, PC.

2   *Re Nottage, Jones v Palmer* [1895] 2 Ch 649 at 656, CA, per Rigby LJ; and see *IRC v Educational Grants Association Ltd* [1967] Ch 993 at 1101, [1967] 2 All ER 893 at 897, CA, per Harman LJ.

3   *Income Tax Special Purposes Comrs v Pemsel* [1891] AC 531 at 580, 583, HL, per Lord Macnaghten. As to the popular meaning see *Income Tax Special Purposes Comrs v Pemsel* supra at 552 per Lord Halsbury LC, at 564 per Lord Bramwell, and at 572 per Lord Herschell; and *Baird's Trustees v Lord Advocate* (1888) 15 R 682, Ct of Sess; *Verge v Somerville* [1924] AC 496 at 502, PC. For the statutory meaning of 'charity' see para 1 ante.

4   *Re Shaw, Public Trustee v Day* [1957] 1 All ER 745 at 752, [1957] 1 WLR 729 at 736, per Harman J.

5   *Income Tax Special Purposes Comrs v Pemsel* [1891] AC 531 at 580, HL, per Lord Macnaghten; cited in *Royal College of Surgeons of England v National Provincial Bank Ltd* [1952] AC 631 at 650, [1952] 1 All ER 984 at 992, HL.

6   *National Anti-Vivisection Society v IRC* [1948] AC 31 at 63, [1947] 2 All ER 217 at 232, HL, per Lord Simonds.

7   43 Eliz 1 c 4 (1601). The statute was repealed by the Mortmain and Charitable Uses Act 1888, which however expressly preserved the preamble (s 13(2)). With the repeal of the 1888 Act by the Charities Act 1960, the preamble is no longer on the statute book, but the preamble never had any statutory operation, and its final repeal does not affect the authority of the cases decided on it nor the principles on which future cases are to be decided: *Incorporated Council of Law Reporting for England and Wales v A-G* [1971] Ch 626 at 644, [1971] 1 All ER 436 at 446 per Foster J; affd [1972] Ch 73, [1971] 3 All ER 1029, CA; see para 12 post.

8   See *Income Tax Special Purposes Comrs v Pemsel* [1891] AC 531 at 583, HL, per Lord Macnaghten: see para 13 post.

9   See *Scottish Burial Reform and Cremation Society Ltd v Glasgow City Corpn* [1968] AC 138 at 158, [1967] 3 All ER 215 at 224, HL, per Lord Wilberforce; *Incorporated Council of Law Reporting for England and Wales v A-G* [1972] Ch 73, [1971] 3 All ER 1029, CA.

10   Eg the Recreational Charities Act 1958: see para 46 post.

11   *National Anti-Vivisection Society v IRC* [1948] AC 31 at 65, [1947] 2 All ER 217 at 233, HL, per Lord Simonds: see para 6 et seq post.

12   See para 8 post.

13   *Income Tax Special Purposes Comrs v Pemsel* [1891] AC 531 at 580, HL, per Lord Macnaghten; *Chesterman v Federal Taxation Comr* [1926] AC 128, PC; *Adamson v Melbourne and Metropolitan Board of Works* [1929] AC 142, PC. See also *Ashfield Municipal Council v Joyce* [1978] AC 122, [1976] 3 WLR 617, PC.

14   Income and Corporation Taxes Act 1988 s 506(1): see para 379 post. See also CAPITAL GAINS TAXATION vol 5(1) (Reissue) para 228; INCOME TAXATION; INHERITANCE TAXATION vol 24 (Reissue) paras 491, 505, 520.

15   Charities Act 1960 s 38(4).

16   *Re Marchant, Weaver v Royal Society for the Prevention of Cruelty to Animals* (1910) 54 Sol Jo 425; *Re Mann, Hardy v A-G* [1903] 1 Ch 232; *Re Webster, Pearson v Webster* [1912] 1 Ch 106; and see *Re Kerin* (1966) Times, 24 May. Cf the position of unincorporated associations established for charitable purposes, as to which see para 55 post.

17   See the Charities Act 1993 ss 96(1) (as amended), 97(1); and para 1 ante.


**3. Meaning of 'charity' in Scotland and Ireland.** In Scotland no technical meaning is attached to the words 'charity' and 'charitable'[1], but the construction put upon the words 'charitable purposes', though in some respects wider[2] and in some narrower[3] than in England, was formerly substantially the same[4]. The expressions 'charity' and 'charitable' at any rate have been said to include there a wider range of objects than such as are of a merely eleemosynary character[5]. The development of the general law as to charities in Scotland and England has since progressed and there is a considerable and growing divergence[6]. The ancient statute of Elizabeth I[7] never applied to Scotland and charities, speaking generally, were not controlled by the Scottish courts[8]. Decisions in those courts do not afford satisfactory guidance on the nature of charities in English law[9]; but for income tax purposes the English law of charities must be regarded as part of the law of Scotland[10].

In Ireland the legal and technical meaning of 'charity' was precisely the same as in England, except perhaps in regard to masses[11], for although the ancient statute of

Elizabeth I[12] did not extend to that country, an Irish statute of Charles I[13] contained a closely similar list of purposes which were regarded as charitable in Ireland[14]. This is still the position in Northern Ireland[15]; but the Republic of Ireland has a different legal system, and the meaning of 'charity' there can no longer be assumed to be identical with its meaning in England.

1   *Miller v Rowan* (1837) 5 Cl & Fin 99 at 109, HL, per Lord Brougham; *Income Tax Special Purposes Comrs v Pemsel* [1891] AC 531 at 582, HL, per Lord Macnaghten; *Blair v Duncan* [1902] AC 37 at 43, HL, per Lord Davey. See also *Baird's Trustees v Lord Advocate* (1888) 15 R 682, Ct of Sess, but the words have a sufficiently precise meaning for a gift to trustees to be applied to such charitable purposes as they think fit not to be void for uncertainty by Scots law: see *Crichton v Grierson* (1828) 3 Wils & S 329, HL; *Miller v Rowan* supra at 109 per Lord Brougham; *Grimond v Grimond* (1904) 6 F 285 at 290, Ct of Sess, per Macdonald JC; *Wordie's Trustees v Wordie* 1915 SC 310 (affd 1916 SC (HL) 126); *Cameron's Trustees v Mackenzie* 1915 SC 313; *Chichester Diocesan Fund and Board of Finance Inc v Simpson* [1944] AC 341 at 351, [1944] 2 All ER 60 at 64, HL, per Lord Macmillan (in Scotland the term 'charitable' has in law a less rigidly technical and artificial meaning than in England).

2   'Charitable and benevolent purposes' were treated as charitable in *Hill v Burns* (1826) 2 Wils & S 80 at 90, HL, per Lord Gifford, approved in *Ewen v Bannerman* (1830) 2 Dow & Cl 74 at 101, HL, per Lord Wynford; see also *Miller v Rowan* (1837) 5 Cl & Fin 99, HL; *Cobb v Cobb's Trustees* (1894) 21 R 638, Ct of Sess. Whether such a gift is charitable in English law (apart from statute) depends on whether it is construed as referring to purposes which are both charitable and benevolent, or to purposes which may be either charitable or benevolent. In the former case the gift is valid (see *Re Sutton, Stone v A-G* (1885) 28 ChD 464; *Re Best, Jarvis v Birmingham Corpn* [1904] 2 Ch 354), but in the latter not, as not being restricted to charitable objects (see *Williams v Kershaw* (1835) 5 Cl & Fin 111n; *Re Eades, Eades v Eades* [1920] 2 Ch 353). But see also the Charitable Trusts (Validation) Act 1954; and paras 90–95 post.

3   A gift for religious purposes was held to be not necessarily charitable in *Grimond v Grimond* (1904) 6 F 285 at 291, Ct of Sess, per Lord Moncreiff (and on appeal [1905] AC 124, HL); *Re Pardoe, McLaughlin v A-G* [1906] 2 Ch 184 at 192 per Kekewich J; cf *Bannerman's Trustees v Bannerman* 1915 SC 398; see also *Income Tax Special Purposes Comrs v Pemsel* [1891] AC 531 at 550, HL.

4   *Dundee Magistrates v Morris* (1858) 3 Macq 134 at 154, HL; *Income Tax Special Purposes Comrs v Pemsel* [1891] AC 531 at 558 HL, per Lord Watson, at 563 per Lord Bramwell, at 573 per Lord Herschell, and at 582 per Lord Macnaghten. Examples of purposes treated as charitable in Scotland are *Ferguson v Marjoribanks* (1853) 15 D 637, Ct of Sess (school); *Aberdeen University v Irvine* (1868) LR 1 Sc & Div 289, HL (bursaries or scholarships); *Andrews v M'Guffog* (1886) 11 App Cas 313, HL (school); *Chalmers' Trustees v Turiff Parish School Board* 1917 SC 676 (educational scheme for the poor).

5   *Blair v Duncan* [1902] AC 37 at 43, HL, per Lord Davey. As to eleemosynary corporations see para 213 post.

6   *IRC v City of Glasgow Police Athletic Association* 1952 SC 102; and see observations on appeal [1953] AC 380, [1953] 1 All ER 747, HL.

7   43 Eliz 1 c 4 (1601): see para 2 note 7 ante.

8   *Chichester Diocesan Fund and Board of Finance Inc v Simpson* [1944] AC 341 at 367, [1944] 2 All ER 60 at 72, HL, per Lord Porter; but see *Hill v Burns* (1826) 2 Wils & S 80 at 91, HL, per Lord Gifford.

9   *Chichester Diocesan Fund and Board of Finance Inc v Simpson* [1944] AC 341 at 367, [1944] 2 All ER 60 at 72, HL, per Lord Porter.

10   *IRC v City of Glasgow Police Athletic Association* [1953] AC 380, [1953] 1 All ER 747, HL; *Guild v IRC* [1992] 2 AC 310, [1992] 2 All ER 10, HL.

11   See *Income Tax Special Purposes Comrs v Pemsel* [1891] AC 531 at 544, HL, per Lord Halsbury LC, at 570 per Lord Herschell, and at 582 per Lord Macnaghten; and see *Arnott v Arnott* [1906] 1 IR 127; *O'Hanlon v Logue* [1906] 1 IR 247. See also 1 ICLQR (April 1952) 203–204. As to masses see paras 31, 57 post.

12   43 Eliz 1 c 4 (1601): see para 2 note 7 ante.

13   10 Car 1 (1634).

14   See *Incorporated Society in Dublin v Richards* (1841) 1 Dr & War 258 at 324 per Lord St Leonards; *Income Tax Special Purposes Comrs v Pemsel* [1891] AC 531 at 544–546, HL, per Lord Halsbury.

15   *Baddeley v IRC* [1953] Ch 504 at 516, [1953] 2 All ER 233 at 237, CA, per Sir Raymond Evershed MR; revsd without affecting his dictum sub nom *IRC v Baddeley* [1955] AC 572, [1955] 1 All ER 525, HL. See also *Re Lord Mayor of Belfast's Air Raid Distress Fund* [1962] NI 161.

**4. Purposes must be exclusively charitable.** To be a charity in law, a trust or institution must be established for purposes which are exclusively charitable[1]; a charitable trust can be enforced by the court at the suit of the Attorney General, for the court knows what are charitable purposes and can apply the trust property accordingly, but a trust for benevolent purposes cannot be so enforced and is therefore void for uncertainty[2]. However, a distinction must be drawn between: (1) the designated purposes of the trust; (2) the designated means of carrying out those purposes; and (3) the consequences of carrying them out. Trust purposes of an otherwise charitable nature do not lose that nature merely because the trustees, by way of furtherance of those purposes, have incidental powers to carry on activities which are not themselves charitable. The distinction is between: (a) those non-charitable activities which are merely subsidiary or incidental to a charitable purpose; and (b) those non-charitable activities so authorised which in themselves form part of the trust purpose. In the latter but not the former case, the reference to non-charitable activities will deprive the trust of its charitable status[3].

1   See the Charities Act 1993 s 97(1). If it is established partly for charitable and partly for non-charitable purposes, it may in some circumstances be validated by the Charitable Trusts (Validation) Act 1954: see paras 90–95 post. In determining whether purposes are charitable it may be necessary to refer not only to the body's constitution but also, in cases of doubt and ambiguity, to extrinsic evidence, including its activities: *Southwood v A-G* [1998] 40 LS Gaz R 37, Times, 26 October; affd [2000] NLJR 1017, Times, 18 July, CA. See also *Incorporated Council of Law Reporting for England and Wales v A-G* [1972] Ch 73 at 91 per Sachs LJ and at 99 per Buckley LJ; *IRC v Oldham Training and Enterprise Council* [1996] STC 1218 at 1234–1235 per Lightman J. On the ambit and relevance of an activities test see Picarda *Law and Practice Relating to Charities* (3rd Edn, 1999) pp 32–34.

2   *Chichester Diocesan Fund and Board of Finance Inc v Simpson* [1944] AC 341 at 371, [1944] 2 All ER 60 at 74, HL, per Lord Simonds; the same case in the Court of Appeal, sub nom *Re Diplock, Wintle v Diplock* [1941] Ch 253 at 259, [1941] 1 All ER 193 at 199, per Sir Wilfrid Greene MR; *Morice v Bishop of Durham* (1804) 9 Ves 399 at 404 per Sir William Gaunt MR (on appeal (1805) 10 Ves 522 at 539 per Lord Eldon LC); *IRC v Broadway Cottages Trust Ltd* [1955] Ch 20 at 29, [1954] 3 All ER 120 at 124, CA, per Jenkins LJ; and see para 58 post.

3   *McGovern v A-G* [1982] Ch 321, [1981] 3 All ER 493. See also *Re Coxen, McCallum v Coxen* [1948] Ch 747, [1948] 2 All ER 492; *Royal College of Surgeons of England v National Provincial Bank Ltd* [1952] AC 631, [1952] 1 All ER 984, HL; *Neville Estates Ltd v Madden* [1962] Ch 832, [1961] 3 All ER 769; *Incorporated Council of Law Reporting for England and Wales v A-G* [1972] Ch 73 at 84, [1971] 3 All ER 1029 at 1033, CA, per Russell LJ; *A-G v Ross* [1985] 3 All ER 334, [1986] 1 WLR 252.

**5. Trading by or on behalf of charities.** There are three main questions relating to trading by or on behalf of charities[1]. These are: (1) whether trading by a charity is permissible; (2) whether charities may properly establish subsidiary or associated non-charitable trading companies for the purpose of raising funds; and (3) whether trading by an institution on a non-profit-making basis for the benefit of a local community can be charitable[2].

As to head (1), a charity may properly engage in trading in the course of carrying out its primary purposes; for example a charity for the relief of the disabled may run shops for the sale of goods made by disabled people employed in that charity's workshops, and a charity for the advancement of the Christian religion may sell bibles[3]. A power to trade otherwise than in carrying out the primary purpose does not necessarily prevent an institution from being a charity[4]. It is a question of degree, and it may not be easy to draw the line between a charity which is merely raising funds and furthering its activities by trading and what is in substance a trading institution wearing a charitable mantle[5].

As to head (2), this is permissible if it is within the investment powers of the charity and as an investment is not too speculative for a charity[6].

As to head (3), although, if the village shop closes down, it may be of benefit to the community to set up a community shop, this is not regarded as being within a category recognised by law as charitable[7].

1   See the *Report of the Charity Commissioners for England and Wales for 1980* (HC Paper (1980–81) no 332) paras 5–12; *Report for 1984* (HC Paper (1984–85) no 394) App C.
2   *Report of the Charity Commissioners for England and Wales for 1980* (HC Paper (1980–81) no 332) para 5; *Report for 1984* (HC Paper (1984–85) no 394) App C.
3   *Report of the Charity Commissioners for England and Wales for 1980* (HC Paper (1980–81) no 332) para 6.
4   *Report of the Charity Commissioners for England and Wales for 1980* (HC Paper (1980–81) no 332) para 7.
5   *Report of the Charity Commissioners for England and Wales for 1980* (HC Paper (1980–81) no 332) para 8.
6   *Report of the Charity Commissioners for England and Wales for 1980* (HC Paper (1980–81) no 332) para 10; *Report of the Charity Commissioners for England and Wales for 1984* (HC Paper (1984–85) no 394) App C. As to the taxation implications see para 379 post; and INCOME TAXATION.
7   See the *Report of the Charity Commissioners for England and Wales for 1980* (HC Paper (1980–81) no 332) para 12.

**6.  Public benefit essential.** It is a clearly established principle of the law of charities that a purpose is not charitable unless it is directed to the public benefit[1], so that the element of public benefit is the necessary condition of legal charity[2]. There are two distinct elements in this requirement: (1) the purpose itself must be beneficial and not harmful to the public[3]; and (2) the benefit of the purpose must be available to a sufficient section of the public[4]. The line of distinction between purposes of a public and a private nature is fine and practically incapable of definition[5].

1   *Oppenheim v Tobacco Securities Trust Co Ltd* [1951] AC 297 at 305, [1951] 1 All ER 31 at 33, HL, per Lord Simonds; *Jones v Williams* (1767) Amb 651 (where 'charity' is defined as a gift to a general public use which extends to the poor as well as to the rich); *Ommanney v Butcher* (1823) Turn & R 260 at 273 per Plumer MR; *Goodman v Saltash Corpn* (1882) 7 App Cas 633 at 650, HL, per Earl Cairns; *Re Christchurch Inclosure Act* (1888) 38 ChD 520 at 532, CA, per Lindley LJ; affd sub nom *A-G v Meyrick* [1893] AC 1, HL. For the meaning of 'private charity' see para 52 post.
2   *Gilmour v Coats* [1949] AC 426 at 446, [1949] 1 All ER 848 at 854, HL, per Lord Simonds. Contrast the decision of the Charity Commissioners in relation to the Society of the Precious Blood: *Report of the Charity Commissioners for England and Wales for 1989* (HC Paper (1989–90) no 343) paras 56–62.
3   See para 7 post.
4   See para 8 post.
5   *Re Drummond, Ashworth v Drummond* [1914] 2 Ch 90 at 96 per Eve J; *A-G v Pearce* (1740) 2 Atk 87; *Hall v Derby Borough Urban Sanitary Authority* (1885) 16 QBD 163, DC; *Shaw v Halifax Corpn* [1915] 2 KB 170 at 182, CA, per Kennedy LJ.

**7.  Proof of public benefit.** In determining what purposes are charitable, the court has always applied the overriding test of public benefit[1]. The question whether a purpose will or may be operative for the public benefit is a question to be answered by the court by forming an opinion on the evidence before it[2], having strict regard to the conditions of the gift[3]. However, a purpose may be so obviously beneficial to the community that to call evidence on the question would be absurd[4], and where the purpose in question is one of a religious nature the court assumes a public benefit unless the contrary is shown[5]. If the purpose of the gift is held to be beneficial to the public, it is not relevant for the court to inquire whether one means or another of achieving that purpose is most effective[6]. However, if the element of public benefit is incapable of proof one way or the other, the court will not recognise the trust as being of a charitable nature[7].

A donor's opinion with regard to whether the gift will be beneficial to the public[8], even when based on religious belief[9], and his motive[10], are both immaterial. The fact that a donor expressly refers to his 'general charitable intention' cannot impose on a gift a general charitable intention or make it charitable if, on the face of it, it has only a particular intention which is not charitable[11]. It is for the court to consider each case upon its own special circumstances[12].

As circumstances differ from age to age, a purpose regarded in one age as for the public benefit and charitable may in another be regarded differently, so that a gift in the will of a testator dying in 1700 might be held valid upon the evidence then before the court but, upon different evidence, held invalid if he died in 1900[13]. The converse may also be possible[14]. This is not to say that a charitable trust, when it has once been established, can ever fail: a charity once established in perpetuity does not die, though its nature may be changed[15].

1   *National Anti-Vivisection Society v IRC* [1948] AC 31 at 65, [1947] 2 All ER 217 at 233, HL, per Lord Simonds.
2   *National Anti-Vivisection Society v IRC* [1948] AC 31 at 44, [1947] 2 All ER 217 at 219, HL, per Lord Wright (approving *Re Hummeltenberg, Beatty v London Spiritualistic Alliance Ltd* [1923] 1 Ch 237, and overruling *Re Foveaux, Cross v London Anti-Vivisection Society* [1895] 2 Ch 501 at 507 per Chitty J); applied in *Re Moss, Hobrough v Harvey* [1949] 1 All ER 495. See also *Re Grove-Grady, Plowden v Lawrence* [1929] 1 Ch 557 at 572, CA, per Lord Hanworth MR, and at 583, 588, per Russell LJ; compromised on appeal sub nom *A-G v Plowden* [1931] WN 89, HL.
3   *Re Pinion, Westminster Bank Ltd v Pinion* [1965] Ch 85, [1964] 1 All ER 890, CA; revsg on this point Wilberforce J [1965] Ch 85, [1963] 2 All ER 1049.
4   *Re Shaw's Will Trusts, National Provincial Bank Ltd v National City Bank Ltd* [1952] Ch 163, [1952] 1 All ER 49; and see para 24 post.
5   *Re Watson, Hobbs v Smith* [1973] 3 All ER 678, [1973] 1 WLR 1472; *Holmes v A-G* (1981) Times, 12 February.
6   *Re Shaw's Will Trusts, National Provincial Bank Ltd v National City Bank Ltd* [1952] Ch 163, [1952] 1 All ER 49.
7   *McGovern v A-G* [1982] Ch 321, [1981] 3 All ER 493.
8   See the cases cited in note 2 supra.
9   *Gilmore v Coats* [1949] AC 426 at 456–457, [1949] 1 All ER 848 at 861, HL, per Lord Reid; *Keren Kayemeth Le Jisroel Ltd v IRC* [1932] AC 650, HL.
10  *Hoare v Osborne* (1866) LR 1 Eq 585 at 588 per Kindersley V-C; *Re Delany, Conoley v Quick* [1902] 2 Ch 642 at 649 per Farwell J; *Re King, Kerr v Bradley* [1923] 1 Ch 243 at 245 per Romer J.
11  *Re Sanders' Will Trusts, Public Trustee v McLaren* [1954] Ch 265, [1954] 1 All ER 667 (appeal settled (1954) Times, 22 July, CA); and see para 83 post.
12  *Re Foveaux, Cross v London Anti-Vivisection Society* [1895] 2 Ch 501 at 504 per Chitty J, cited with approval by Lord Simonds in *National Anti-Vivisection Society v IRC* [1948] AC 31 at 67, [1947] 2 All ER 217 at 234, HL.
13  *National Anti-Vivisection Society v IRC* [1948] AC 31 at 74, [1947] 2 All ER 217 at 238, HL, per Lord Simonds.
14  *Gilmour v Coats* [1949] AC 426 at 443, [1949] 1 All ER 848 at 853, HL, per Lord Simonds.
15  *National Anti-Vivisection Society v IRC* [1948] AC 31 at 74, [1947] 2 All ER 217 at 238, HL, per Lord Simonds. However, a charitable trust may be established for a specific, strictly limited purpose (see *Gibson v South American Stores (Gath and Chaves) Ltd* [1950] Ch 177, [1949] 2 All ER 985, CA) or subject to a gift over on the happening of a certain event, eg the failure of the original charitable purpose (see *Re Cooper's Conveyance Trusts, Crewdson v Bagot* [1956] 3 All ER 28, [1956] 1 WLR 1096); such trusts are not necessarily established in perpetuity and could be said to die, or at least to be potentially mortal. See also para 132 post.

**8. Benefit to sufficient section of community.** To satisfy the test of public benefit[1], a purpose must benefit the community, or an appreciably important class of the community[2], which must be sufficiently defined[3] and identifiable by some quality of a public nature[4], but may be restricted within narrow limits[5]. It may be a community abroad[6].

The question what is a sufficient section of the public must be considered in the light of the particular purpose, for they are interdependent; the argument that what is a sufficient section to support a valid trust in one category must be sufficient to support a valid trust in any other category cannot be accepted[7]. In ascertaining whether a purpose is public or private, the salient point to be considered is whether the class to be benefited, or from which the beneficiaries are to be selected, constitutes a substantial body of the public[8].

The beneficiaries must not be numerically negligible[9], and must not be ascertained or determined by their connection with a private individual or private individuals or with a company or other employer[10]; nor may they be merely particular private individuals pointed out by the donor or a fluctuating class of private individuals[11]. A class of trusts for the relief of poverty, known as the 'poor relations cases', forms an exception to this principle[12]. The fact that funds have been publicly subscribed for a purpose is not a test of whether the purpose is of a public nature, though it may afford some indication[13].

An orphanage for the children of deceased railway employees has been held to be a public charity[14]; a 'seamen's mission' for the benefit of seamen in port in the Port of London and the London dock areas is charitable[15], and a statutory body established to promote and improve the standard of training within the whole of one industry in England, Scotland and Wales has been held to be established for exclusively charitable purposes[16]. But a trust for all members of a trade union which was open to all members of the printing industry, but to which not all members of the industry in fact belonged, was held not to be charitable[17], nor was a society for the relief of the sickness of its own members, who numbered over 400,000, charitable[18].

A trust to provide for the education of children of employees or former employees of a group of companies is private[19]; a contributory fund for the relief of air raid victims among the contributors who were employees of a particular company is private[20]; similarly a trust to contribute to the holiday expenses of the workpeople employed in a certain department of a company's business has been held to be a trust for private individuals, and so not charitable[21]. A gift on trust for the children and remoter issue of Presbyterians living at a certain date and descended from Presbyterian settlers in the colony of New South Wales hailing from or born in the north of Ireland was held not to be for the benefit of a section of the community, in the sense in which these words have been interpreted in the authorities[22]. A gift for the education of descendants of named persons, irrespective of their means, is private[23]. Pupils at a particular school may be a sufficient section of the public[24]. A gift to a named community house, construed as a gift for its purposes, was held charitable, the necessary element of public benefit consisting in the assistance rendered by the community house to members of the public in need[25]. A gift to a class which would be held to be private on this principle may nevertheless be a valid charitable gift if the purposes of the gift are restricted to the relief of poverty[26], and a bequest for the relief of such poor persons as the testator's trustees may choose is charitable[27].

On the other hand, where the choice is to be made from a number of named individuals[28], or where the class of beneficiaries is so restricted that the gift is, in effect, one to particular individuals[29], the gift may be held to be not in the nature of a charitable gift at all, but rather a direct beneficial gift to the individuals in question or some of them[30].

1  See paras 6–7 ante.

2  *Verge v Somerville* [1924] AC 496 at 499, PC; *Oppenheim v Tobacco Securities Trust Co Ltd* [1951] AC 297 at 305, [1951] 1 All ER 31 at 33, HL, per Lord Simonds.

3  *Keren Kayemeth Le Jisroel Ltd v IRC* [1932] AC 650, HL; *Williams' Trustees v IRC* [1947] AC 447 at 457, [1947] 1 All ER 513 at 519, HL, per Lord Simonds; *Northern Ireland Valuation Comr v Lurgan Borough Council* [1968] NI 104 at 153–156, CA, per McVeigh LJ.

4  *Keren Kayemeth Le Jisroel Ltd v IRC* [1932] AC 650, HL; *Williams' Trustees v IRC* [1947] AC 447, [1947] 1 All ER 513, HL; *Re Compton, Powell v Compton* [1945] Ch 123, [1945] 1 All ER 198, CA; *Re Hobourn Aero Components Ltd's Air Raid Distress Fund, Ryan v Forrest* [1946] Ch 194, [1946] 1 All ER 501. CA; see also *Dingle v Turner* [1972] AC 601 at 623, [1972] 1 All ER 878 at 889, HL, per Lord Cross of Chelsea; *Charter v Race Relations Board* [1973] AC 868 at 907, [1973] 1 All ER 512 at 533, HL, per Lord Cross of Chelsea.

5  See the cases cited in notes 14–24 infra; and para 52 post.

6  As to foreign charitable purposes see paras 50–51 post.

7  *IRC v Baddeley* [1955] AC 572 at 615, [1955] 1 All ER 525 at 549, HL, per Lord Somervell of Harrow; *Re Dunlop, Northern Bank Executor and Trustee Co Ltd v A-G for Northern Ireland* [1984] NI 408; cf *Dingle v Turner* [1972] AC 601 at 624, [1972] 1 All ER 878 at 889, HL, per Lord Cross of Chelsea.

8  *Shaw v Halifax Corpn* [1915] 2 KB 170 at 181, CA, per Buckley LJ; *Verge v Somerville* [1924] AC 496 at 499, PC; *A-G v Pearce* (1740) 2 Atk 87; *Hall v Derby Borough Urban Sanitary Authority* (1885) 16 QBD 163, DC.

9  *Oppenheim v Tobacco Securities Trust Co Ltd* [1951] AC 297 at 306, [1951] 1 All ER 31 at 34, HL, per Lord Simonds; but see *Cross v Lloyd-Greame* (1909) 102 LT 163.

10  *Oppenheim v Tobacco Securities Trust Co Ltd* [1951] AC 297, [1951] 1 All ER 31, HL; *Re Compton, Powell v Compton* [1945] Ch 123, [1945] 1 All ER 198, CA; *Caffoor v Income Tax Comr, Colombo* [1961] AC 584, [1961] 2 All ER 436, PC; *Davies v Perpetual Trustee Co Ltd* [1959] AC 439, [1959] 2 All ER 128, PC; and see *IRC v Educational Grants Association Ltd* [1967] Ch 993 at 1009, [1967] 2 All ER 893 at 896, CA, per Lord Denning MR.

11  *A-G v Pearce* (1740) 2 Atk 87; *A-G v Comber* (1824) 2 Sim & St 93; *Goodman v Saltash Corpn* (1882) 7 App Cas 633 at 650, HL, per Earl Cairns; *Re Drummond, Ashworth v Drummond* [1914] 2 Ch 90. See also *Charter v Race Relations Board* [1973] AC 868, [1973] 1 All ER 512, HL; and the cases cited in notes 28–29 infra. As to the difficulty of distinguishing a section of the public from a fluctuating class of individuals cf *Dingle v Turner* [1972] AC 601 at 624, [1972] 1 All ER 878 at 889, HL, per Lord Cross of Chelsea.

12  *Oppenheim v Tobacco Securities Trust Co Ltd* [1951] AC 297 at 305, 308, [1951] 1 All ER 31 at 33, 35, HL, per Lord Simonds. These cases 'stick out like a sore thumb from the general rule': *IRC v Educational Grants Association Ltd* [1967] Ch 993 at 1011, [1967] 2 All ER 893 at 898, CA, per Harman LJ; 'a hallowed, if illogical, exception': *Re Scarisbrick, Cockshott v Public Trustee* [1951] Ch 622 at 639, [1951] 1 All ER 822 at 830, CA, per Sir Raymond Evershed MR. See also *Dingle v Turner* [1972] AC 601, [1972] 1 All ER 878, HL; and see para 21 post.

13  *Shaw v Halifax Corpn* [1915] 2 KB 170, CA; *Hall v Derby Borough Urban Sanitary Authority* (1885) 16 QBD 163, DC (these were decisions on whether a particular foundation was a 'public charity' within the meaning of local Acts); see also *Re Hobourn Aero Components Ltd's Air Raid Distress Fund, Ryan v Forrest* [1946] Ch 194, [1946] 1 All ER 501, CA; *Re Forster, Gellatly v Palmer* [1939] Ch 22, [1938] 3 All ER 767. The funds may be levied by taxation (*A-G v Brown* (1818) 1 Swan 265; *A-G v Dublin Corpn* (1827) 1 Bli NS 312 at 334, 336, HL; *A-G v Eastlake* (1853) 11 Hare 205; *Re St Bride's, Fleet Street, Church or Parish Estate* (1877) 35 ChD 147n; *Re St Botolph Without Bishopsgate Parish Estates* (1887) 35 ChD 142 at 150–151, per North J; see also *A-G v Shrewsbury Corpn* (1843) 6 Beav 220), or given by the Crown (*A-G v Blizard* (1855) 21 Beav 233; contra, *A-G v Galway Corpn* (1829) 1 Mol 95). The trust property may be purchased under statutory authority for public purposes: *Re St Pancras Burial Ground* (1866) LR 3 Eq 173.

14  *Hall v Derby Borough Urban Sanitary Authority* (1885) 16 QBD 163: see note 13 supra.

15  *Finch v Poplar Borough Council* (1967) 66 LGR 324.

16  *Construction Industry Training Board v A-G* [1971] 3 All ER 449, [1971] 1 WLR 1303; affd without dealing with this point [1973] Ch 173, [1972] 2 All ER 1339, CA.

17  *Re Mead's Trust Deed, Briginshaw v National Society of Operative Printers and Assistants* [1961] 2 All ER 836, [1961] 1 WLR 1244.

18   *Waterson v Hendon Borough Council* [1959] 2 All ER 760, [1959] 1 WLR 985; but see *Re Forster, Gellatly v Palmer* [1939] Ch 22, [1938] 3 All ER 767.

19   *Oppenheim v Tobacco Securities Trust Co Ltd* [1951] AC 297, [1951] 1 All ER 31, HL (where the number of employees exceeded 110,000); disapproving *Re Rayner, Cloutman v Regnart* (1920) 89 LJCh 369; and approving *Re Compton, Powell v Compton* [1945] Ch 123, [1945] 1 All ER 198, CA; and *Re Hobourn Aero Components Ltd's Air Raid Distress Fund, Ryan v Forrest* [1946] Ch 194, [1946] 1 All ER 501, CA; *Re Cox, Baker v National Trust Co Ltd* [1955] AC 627, [1955] 2 All ER 550, PC; and *IRC v Educational Grants Association Ltd* [1967] Ch 993, [1967] 2 All ER 893, CA.

20   *Re Hobourn Aero Components Ltd's Air Raid Distress Fund, Ryan v Forrest* [1946] Ch 194, [1946] 1 All ER 501, CA.

21   *Re Drummond, Ashworth v Drummond* [1914] 2 Ch 90 (where the employees concerned numbered between 400 and 500); approved in *Re Compton, Powell v Compton* [1945] Ch 123, [1945] 1 All ER 198, CA.

22   *Davies v Perpetual Trustee Co Ltd* [1959] AC 439, [1959] 2 All ER 128, PC; cf *Re Tree, Idle v Tree* [1945] Ch 325, [1945] 2 All ER 65.

23   *Re Compton, Powell v Compton* [1945] Ch 123, [1945] 1 All ER 198, CA.

24   *Oppenheim v Tobacco Securities Trust Co Ltd* [1951] AC 297 at 306, [1951] 1 All ER 31 at 34, HL, per Lord Simonds, and at 309, 36 per Lord Normand; *Perpetual Trustees Co Ltd v Ferguson* (1951) 51 SR NSW 256, though see, as to the particular schools in question in that case, *Thompson v Federal Taxation Comr* (1959) 102 CLR 315, Aust HC.

25   *Re Banfield, Lloyds Bank Ltd v Smith* [1968] 2 All ER 276, [1968] 1 WLR 846.

26   See para 21 post.

27   *A-G v Pearce* (1740) 2 Atk 87; and see para 116 post.

28   *Liley v Hey* (1842) 1 Hare 580. As to gifts for the benefit of individuals see para 53 post.

29   *A-G v Hughes* (1689) 2 Vern 105, revsg sub nom *A-G v Baxter* (1684) 1 Vern 248, explained in *Moggridge v Thackwell* (1803) 7 Ves 36 at 76 per Lord Eldon LC; affd (1807) 13 Ves 416, HL; *Thomas v Howell* (1874) LR 18 Eq 198.

30   See the cases cited in note 29 supra. If the gifts had been charitable, they would have failed under the law of mortmain (now repealed: see para 76 post).


**9. Preference given to limited class.** Where a trust is held to be primarily for the benefit of a sufficient section of the community, it is not invalidated by a direction to give preference, in applying part of the available income, to a smaller class which would not in itself be a sufficient section of the community[1], such as the employees of a particular company[2] or the descendants of the founder of the charity[3]. Nevertheless, where the preferential direction is mandatory, extends to the whole of the income and is in favour of a class which will almost certainly always exhaust the whole income, the absolute priority of the preferential class prevents the trust from being for the benefit of a sufficient section of the community[4].


1   *Re Koettgen's Will Trusts, Westminster Bank Ltd v Family Welfare Association Trustees Ltd* [1954] Ch 252, [1954] 1 All ER 581.

2   *Re Koettgen's Will Trusts, Westminster Bank Ltd v Family Welfare Association Trustees Ltd* [1954] Ch 252, [1954] 1 All ER 581.

3   The 'Founder's Kin' cases, explained in *Caffoor v Income Tax Comr, Colombo* [1961] AC 584 at 602, [1961] 2 All ER 436 at 444, PC: they should probably be regarded as belonging more to history than to doctrine.

4   *Caffoor v Income Tax Comr, Colombo* [1961] AC 584, [1961] 2 All ER 436, PC (doubting *Re Koettgen's Will Trusts, Westminster Bank Ltd v Family Welfare Association Trustees Ltd* [1954] Ch 252, [1954] 1 All ER 581). See *Re Martin* (1977) 121 Sol Jo 828 (right of residence to testator's daughters in old people's home).

**10. Benefit to rich as well as poor.** An object may be charitable in the legal sense notwithstanding that it will benefit the rich as well as the poor[1], but it is difficult to believe that a trust would be held charitable if the poor were excluded from its benefit[2].

1    *Jones v Williams* (1767) Amb 651; *Income Tax Special Purposes Comrs v Pemsel* [1891] AC 531 at 583, HL, per Lord Macnaghten; *Verge v Somerville* [1924] AC 496 at 499, PC; see also *Re Hillier, Dauncey v Finch and A-G* [1944] 1 All ER 480.
2    *Re Macduff, Macduff v Macduff* [1896] 2 Ch 451 at 464, CA, per Lindley LJ; *A-G v Duke of Northumberland* (1877) 7 ChD 745 at 752 per Jessel MR; and see *Re Resch's Will Trusts, Le Cras v Perpetual Trustee Co Ltd* [1969] 1 AC 514 at 542, [1967] 3 All ER 915 at 923, PC. See *Joseph Rowntree Memorial Trust Housing Association Ltd v A-G* [1983] Ch 159, [1983] 1 All ER 288, where it was said that it is not necessarily fatal to charitable status that the benefit cannot be withdrawn if a beneficiary ceases to qualify.

**11. Charity trading or charging for services.** The provision of benefits to the public may be charitable notwithstanding that a charge is made[1], or that a contribution is required from beneficiaries[2]. An institution may carry on a trade or business in order to achieve its purposes and still be charitable, so long as no part of any profit made can be distributed to members or applied otherwise than for charitable purposes[3]. It is not necessary, for it to be charitable, that a gift for the provision of homes for the aged should provide for all the needs of the beneficiaries[4], and the provision of such accommodation may be charitable even if it is to be let to the beneficiaries at economic rents[5].

1    *Scottish Burial Reform and Cremation Society Ltd v Glasgow Corpn* [1968] AC 138, [1967] 3 All ER 215, HL; *Brighton College v Marriott* [1926] AC 192, HL; *IRC v Falkirk Temperance Cafe Trust* 1927 SC 261; *The Abbey, Malvern Wells, Ltd v Minister of Local Government and Planning* [1951] Ch 728, [1951] 2 All ER 154; *Re Resch's Will Trusts, Le Cras v Perpetual Trustee Co Ltd* [1969] 1 AC 514, [1967] 3 All ER 915, PC; *Incorporated Council of Law Reporting for England and Wales v A-G* [1972] Ch 73, [1971] 3 All ER 1029, CA; *Joseph Rowntree Memorial Trust Housing Association Ltd v A-G* [1983] Ch 159, [1983] 1 All ER 288.
2    *Re Estlin, Prichard v Thomas* (1903) 72 LJCh 687; *Re Clarke, Bracey v Royal National Lifeboat Institution* [1923] 2 Ch 407; *Re Chaplin, Neame v A-G* [1933] Ch 115; *IRC v Peeblesshire Nursing Association* 1927 SC 215; *Re Cottam's Will Trusts, Midland Bank Executor and Trustee Co Ltd v Huddersfield Corpn* [1955] 3 All ER 704, [1955] 1 WLR 1299.
3    *Brighton College v Marriott* [1926] AC 192, HL; *Incorporated Council of Law Reporting for England and Wales v A-G* [1972] Ch 73 at 86, 90, [1971] 3 All ER 1029 at 1034, CA per Russell LJ, and at 1038 per Sachs LJ. See para 5 ante.
4    *Re Payling's Will Trusts, Armstrong v Payling* [1969] 3 All ER 698, [1969] 1 WLR 1595; cf *Re Monk, Giffen v Wedd* [1927] 2 Ch 197, CA.
5    *Re Cottam's Will Trusts, Midland Bank Executor and Trustee Co Ltd v Huddersfield Corpn* [1955] 3 All ER 704, [1955] 1 WLR 1299; *Scottish Burial Reform and Cremation Society Ltd v Glasgow Corpn* [1968] AC 138 at 156, [1967] 3 All ER 215 at 224, HL, per Lord Wilberforce; though see also *IRC v Peeblesshire Nursing Association* 1927 SC 215 at 222 per Lord Sands (provision charitable if at less than cost price).

**12. Not all public purposes charitable.** Not every object which is beneficial to the community is charitable[1]. The preamble to the ancient statute of Elizabeth I[2], contained a varied list of charitable purposes[3], and made it clear that at least those purposes were charitable[4].

The objects enumerated in the preamble were as follows: the relief of aged, impotent and poor people; the maintenance of sick and maimed soldiers and mariners, schools of learning and free schools and scholars of universities; the repair of bridges, ports, havens, causeways, churches, sea banks and highways; the education and preferment of orphans;

the relief, stock or maintenance for houses of correction; marriages of poor maids; supportation, aid and help of young tradesmen, handicraftsmen and persons decayed; the relief or redemption of prisoners or captives; the aid or ease of any poor inhabitants concerning payment of fifteens[5], setting out of soldiers[6] and other taxes.

The list was not exhaustive[7]; but to decide whether a beneficial purpose is beneficial in a way which the law regards as charitable, it has been the practice of the courts to refer to the list in the preamble. The objects there enumerated and all others 'which by analogies are deemed within its spirit and intendment' are charitable in the legal sense[8]. No other objects are in law charitable[9]; however, when a purpose has been proved to be of general public utility or beneficial to the community, it will be held to be charitable unless there is some reason for holding that it is not within the spirit and intendment of the preamble[10]. The purposes named in the preamble, which has received a very wide construction[11], are to be regarded only as instances of charities[12].

Notwithstanding that neither the ancient statute nor the preamble is now on the statute book[13], it is still the general law that a purpose is not charitable unless it is within the spirit and intendment of the preamble[14]. The preamble never had any statutory operation, and the vast body of case law derived from it is unaffected by its repeal[15].

1 *National Anti-Vivisection Society v IRC* [1948] AC 31 at 41, [1947] 2 All ER 217 at 220, HL, per Lord Wright.
2 43 Eliz 1 c 4 (1601) (now wholly repealed: see para 2 note 7 ante).
3 *Income Tax Special Purposes Comrs v Pemsel* [1891] AC 531 at 581, HL, per Lord Macnaghten; *Re Macduff, Macduff v Macduff* [1896] 2 Ch 451 at 467, CA, per Lindley LJ; *Re Foveaux, Cross v London Anti-Vivisection Society* [1895] 2 Ch 501 at 504, per Chitty J; *Re Nottage, Jones v Palmer* [1895] 2 Ch 649 at 656, CA, per Rigby LJ.
4 *National Anti-Vivisection Society v IRC* [1948] AC 31 at 64–65, [1947] 2 All ER 217 at 233, HL, per Lord Simonds.
5 'Fifteens' or 'fifteenths' were taxes on personalty.
6 See para 40 note 21 post.
7 *National Anti-Vivisection Society v IRC* [1948] AC 31 at 64, [1947] 2 All ER 217 at 233, HL, per Lord Simonds.
8 *Morice v Bishop of Durham* (1804) 9 Ves 399 at 405, per Grant MR (on appeal (1805) 10 Ves 522); *Income Tax Special Purposes Comrs v Pemsel* [1891] AC 531 at 581, HL, per Lord Macnaghten; *Re Macduff, Macduff v Macduff* [1896] 2 Ch 451 at 467, CA, per Lindley LJ; *Verge v Somerville* [1924] AC 496 at 502, PC.
9 *Gilmour v Coats* [1949] AC 426 at 442, [1949] 1 All ER 848 at 852, HL, per Lord Simonds (unless they are declared to be so by statute; see eg the Recreational Charities Act 1958; and paras 46–49 post).
10 *Incorporated Council of Law Reporting for England and Wales v A-G* [1972] Ch 73, [1971] 3 All ER 1029, CA. But see *Barralet v A-G* [1980] 3 All ER 918, sub nom *Re South Place Ethical Society, Barralet v A-G* [1980] 1 WLR 1565, where Dillon J cast some doubt on this proposition.
11 *Cocks v Manners* (1871) LR 12 Eq 574 at 585, per Wickens V-C.
12 *London University v Yarrow* (1857) 1 De G & J 72 at 79 per Lord Cranworth LC; *Re Foveaux, Cross v London Anti-Vivisection Society* [1895] 2 Ch 501 at 504 per Chitty J.
13 See para 2 ante.
14 See *Scottish Burial Reform and Cremation Society Ltd v Glasgow Corpn* [1968] AC 138, [1967] 3 All ER 215, HL.
15 *Incorporated Council of Law Reporting for England and Wales v A-G* [1971] Ch 626 at 644, [1971] 1 All ER 436 at 445 per Foster J; affd [1972] Ch 73, [1971] 3 All ER 1029, CA.

**13. Four divisions of charity.** Charitable purposes, in the legal sense, derived from the ancient statute of Elizabeth I[1], have been classified into four principal divisions[2]: (1) the relief of poverty[3]; (2) the advancement of education[4]; (3) the advancement of religion[5]; and (4) other purposes beneficial to the community not falling under any of the preceding heads[6]. In addition, certain purposes are declared to be charitable by the

Recreational Charities Act 1958[7]; these may be regarded as forming part of the fourth category.

All claims to bring a purpose under the head of charity must assert that it comes within one or more of these four divisions[8]. Where a trust is described merely as being for charitable purposes, and a class of objects to be benefited is defined, the purposes of the trust cannot be taken to be confined to that particular charitable purpose which would render a trust for that class valid as a charity, but rather the purposes must be construed as being all the four traditional categories of charitable objects, and the trust must be interpreted in the light of the application of all four categories to the class of objects to be benefited[9].

The test of benefit to the community applies to all the divisions, though as regards the first three it may be assumed unless the contrary appears[10]. There are statutory requirements in relation to cases falling within the Recreational Charities Act 1958[11]. All charitable purposes must fall within one or more of these divisions, though not every institution or trust whose purpose might be brought within one of them is necessarily a charity[12], for it must, further, be publicly beneficial and of a public nature[13].

1   43 Eliz 1 c 4 (1601) (now wholly repealed: see para 2 note 7 ante): see para 12 ante.
2   This is the so-called *Pemsel* classification: see *Income Tax Special Purposes Comrs v Pemsel* [1891] AC 531 at 583, HL, per Lord Macnaghten. The classification was taken from the argument of Sir Samuel Romilly in *Morice v Bishop of Durham* (1805) 10 Ves 522 at 532 per Lord Eldon LC. See also *Re Macduff, Macduff v Macduff* [1896] 2 Ch 451 at 466, CA, per Lindley LJ.
3   See paras 16–23 post.
4   See paras 24–29 post.
5   See paras 30–36 post.
6   See paras 37–45 post.
7   See paras 46–49 post.
8   *National Anti-Vivisection Society v IRC* [1948] AC 31 at 52, [1947] 2 All ER 217 at 226, HL, per Lord Porter. Many charitable purposes do not fit neatly within a single category: *Re Hopkins' Will Trusts, Naish v Francis Bacon Society Inc* [1965] Ch 669 at 678, [1964] 3 All ER 46 at 51 per Wilberforce J; cf *Trustees of City of Belfast YMCA v Northern Ireland Valuation Comr* [1969] NI 3, CA.
9   *Re Cox, Baker v National Trust Co Ltd* [1955] AC 627, [1955] 2 All ER 550, PC.
10  *National Anti-Vivisection Society v IRC* [1948] AC 31 at 42, [1947] 2 All ER 217 at 220, HL, per Lord Wright. In the same case Lord Simonds, at 65, 233, put it rather more widely, saying that the assumption should be made when a purpose appears broadly to fall within one of the familiar categories of charity, adding that the court will not be astute in such a case to defeat upon doubtful evidence the avowed benevolent intention of a donor. See also *Re Watson, Hobbs v Smith* [1973] 3 All ER 678, [1973] 1 WLR 1472; *Re Hetherington* [1990] Ch 1, sub nom *Re Hetherington, Gibbs v McDonnell* [1989] 2 All ER 129. However, the gift failed for this reason in *Gilmour v Coats* [1949] AC 426, [1949] 1 All ER 848, HL.
11  See the Recreational Charities Act 1958 s 1(2). Nothing in s 1 is to be taken as derogating from the principle that to be charitable a trust or institution must be for the public benefit: s 1(1) proviso. See also para 48 post.
12  *Re Macduff, Macduff v Macduff* [1896] 2 Ch 451 at 474, CA, per Rigby LJ.
13  See paras 6–8 ante.

**14. Racial discrimination.** A provision which is contained in a charitable instrument[1] (whenever that instrument took or takes effect) and which provides for conferring benefits on persons of a class defined by reference to colour now takes effect for all purposes as if it provided for conferring the like benefits[2]: (1) on persons of the class which results if the restriction by reference to colour is disregarded[3]; or (2) where the original class is defined by reference to colour only, it takes effect as if it conferred benefits on persons generally[4].

The provisions which make it unlawful to discriminate against a person on the ground of colour, race[5], nationality, or ethnic[6] or national origins in the employment field, education, planning, public authorities and the provision of goods, facilities, services or premises[7] do not affect any provision which is contained in a charitable instrument (whenever that instrument took or takes effect) and which provides for conferring benefits on persons of a class defined otherwise than by reference to colour[8], nor do they render unlawful any act[9] which is done in order to give effect to such a provision[10].

1   For these purposes, 'charitable instrument' means an enactment or other instrument passed or made for charitable purposes, or an enactment or other instrument so far as it relates to charitable purposes: Race Relations Act 1976 s 34(4). For these purposes, 'charitable purposes' means purposes which are exclusively charitable according to the law of England and Wales: s 34(4).
2   Ibid s 34(1). Nothing in this provisions alters the effect of any provision as regards any time before 13 June 1977: see s 34(1).
3   Ibid s 34(1)(a); and see DISCRIMINATION vol 13 (Reissue) para 437.
4   Ibid s 34(1)(b); and see DISCRIMINATION vol 13 (Reissue) para 437.
5   Gipsies have been held to be a racial group: *Commission for Racial Equality v Dutton* [1989] QB 783, [1989] 1 All ER 306, CA.
6   For a group to constitute an ethnic group it must regard itself, and be regarded by others, as a distinct community by virtue of certain characteristics. Of these, two are essential, ie (1) a long shared history; and (2) a cultural tradition of its own. Other common but not essential characteristics include: (3) a common geographical origin; (4) a common language; (5) a common literature; (6) a common religion; and (7) being a minority: *Mandla v Dowell Lee* [1983] 2 AC 548, [1983] 1 All ER 1062, HL. Rastafarians have been held not to be a separate ethnic group: *Dawkins v Department of the Environment* [1993] IRLR 284, CA.
7   Ie the Race Relations Act 1976 Pt II (4–16) (as amended), Pt III (ss 17–27) (as amended), Pt IV (ss 28–33) (as amended): see DISCRIMINATION vol 13 (Reissue) para 405 et seq.
8   Including a class resulting from the operation of ibid s 34(1): s 34(3).
9   'Act' includes a deliberate omission: ibid s 78(1).
10  See ibid s 34(2), (3).

**15. Sex discrimination.** Though in general the Sex Discrimination Act 1975 applies to charities, for example, in advertising for and selecting paid staff, there are two special provisions relating to them. First, it is provided[1] that any provision contained in a charitable instrument[2] and which provides for conferring benefits to persons of one sex only (disregarding any benefits to persons of the opposite sex which are exceptional or are relatively insignificant) is not rendered unlawful by the Sex Discrimination Act 1975[3] and nor is any act[4] which is done in order to give effect to such a provision[5].

Secondly, there are further provisions in relation to educational charities, which apply to any trust deed or other instrument concerning property applicable in connection with the provision of education[6] in specified[7] establishments and in any way restricting the benefits available under the instrument to persons of one sex[8]. In the case of these charities, on the application of the trustees[9] the Secretary of State[10], if satisfied that the removal or modification of the restriction would conduce to the advancement of education without sex discrimination[11], he may by order make such modifications of the instrument as appear to him expedient for removing or modifying the restriction, and for any supplemental and incidental purposes[12]. However, if the trust was created by gift or bequest, no order must be made until 25 years after the date on which the gift or bequest took effect, unless the donor or his personal representatives, or the personal representatives of the testator, have consented in writing to the making of the application for the order[13]. Notice[14] of the application must be published, containing particulars of the proposed order and stating that representations may be made to the Secretary of State within a period specified in the notice[15], which must not be less than one month from the date of the notice[16]. The applicants must publish the notice in such manner as may be specified by the Secretary of State, and the cost of any publication of the notice may be defrayed out of the property of the trust[17]. Before making the order the Secretary of State must take into account any representations duly made in accordance with the notice[18].

1   See the Sex Discrimination Act 1975 s 43 (as amended); and DISCRIMINATION vol 13 (Reissue) para 355.
2   For these purposes, 'charitable instrument' means an enactment or other instrument so far as it relates to charitable purposes: ibid s 43(3) (substituted by the Sex Discrimination Act 1975 (Amendment of Section 43) Order 1977, SI 1977/528). 'Charitable purposes' means purposes which are exclusively charitable according to the law of England and Wales: Sex Discrimination Act 1975 s 43(3) (as so substituted).
3   Ie ibid Pt II (ss 6–20) (as amended), Pt III (ss 22–36) (as amended) and Pt IV (ss 37–42) (as amended): see DISCRIMINATION vol 13 (Reissue) para 326 et seq.
4   'Act' includes a deliberate omission: ibid s 82(1).
5   See ibid s 43(1), (2). Section 43 was held in *Hugh-Jones v St John's College, Cambridge* [1979] ICR 848, EAT, to cover the award of a research fellowship available only to men.
6   'Education' includes any form of training or instruction: Sex Discrimination Act 1975 s 82(1).
7   Ie specified in ibid s 22, Table paras 1–5 (as amended): see DISCRIMINATION vol 13 (Reissue) para 342; and EDUCATION.
8   Ibid s 78(1).
9   Or the responsible body as defined by ibid s 22: see EDUCATION.
10  As to the Secretary of State see para 513 post. In relation to Wales, the functions of the Secretary of State under the Sex Discrimination Act 1975 s 78 are carried out by the National Assembly for Wales: National Assembly for Wales (Transfer of Functions) Order 1999, SI 1999/672, art 2, Sch 1. As to the National Assembly for Wales see CONSTITUTIONAL LAW AND HUMAN RIGHTS.
11  References to sex discrimination refer to any discrimination falling within the Sex Discrimination Act 1975 ss 1, 2 (see DISCRIMINATION vol 13 (Reissue) para 310 et seq): s 5(1)(b).
12  Ibid s 78(2).
13  Ibid s 78(3).
14  'Notice' means a notice in writing: ibid s 82(1).
15  Ibid s 78(4)
16  Ibid s 78(5).
17  Ibid s 78(6).
18  Ibid s 78(7).

# (2)  PARTICULAR CHARITABLE PURPOSES

## (i)  Relief of the Aged, Impotent and Poor

**16.  Purposes to be read separately.** The first division of charitable objects is the relief of poverty[1]. The relief of 'aged, impotent and poor people' is charitable[2]. The words are to be read disjunctively[3], so that the relief of aged people who are not also poor comes within them[4], and the relief of impotence without any element of poverty is a charitable purpose[5]. The word 'relief' implies that the persons in question have a need attributable to their condition as aged, impotent or poor persons which requires alleviating, and which those persons could not alleviate, or would find difficulty in alleviating, themselves from their own resources. The word 'relief' is not synonymous with 'benefit'[6].

1    Ie the first division mentioned by Lord Macnaghten in *Income Tax Special Purposes Comrs v Pemsel* [1891] AC 531 at 583, HL, per Lord Macnaghten: see para 13 ante. As to the four divisions of charitable objects see para 13 ante.

2    Preamble to the ancient statute Elizabeth I 43 Eliz 1 c 4 (1601) (now wholly repealed: see para 2 note 7 ante): see paras 12–13 ante.

3    *Re Glyn's Will Trusts, Public Trustee v A-G* [1950] 2 All ER 1150n; *Re Bradbury, Needham v Reekie* [1950] 2 All ER 1150n; *Re Robinson, Davis v Robinson* [1951] Ch 198, [1950] 2 All ER 1148; *Re Lewis, Public Trustee v Allen* [1955] Ch 104, [1954] 3 All ER 257; *Joseph Rowntree Memorial Trust Housing Association Ltd v A-G* [1983] Ch 159, [1983] 1 All ER 288; *Re Dunlop, Northern Bank Executor and Trustee Co Ltd v A-G for Northern Ireland* [1984] NI 408.

4    *Re Glyn's Will Trusts, Public Trustee v A-G* [1950] 2 All ER 1150n (free cottages for old women of the working classes of the age of 60 or upwards: charitable); *Re Bradbury, Needham v Reekie* [1950] 2 All ER 1150n (maintenance of aged persons in a nursing home: charitable); *Re Robinson, Davis v Robinson* [1951] Ch 198, [1950] 2 All ER 1148 (gifts to the old people over 65 years of a named locality as trustees think best: charitable). It had been doubted whether a gift for the benefit of the aged, unrestricted to poor objects, was charitable: *Re Lucas, Rhys v A-G* [1922] 2 Ch 52; *A-G v Haberdashers' Co* (1834) 1 My & K 420 at 428 per Lord Brougham LC.

5    *Re Roadley, Iveson v Wakefield* [1930] 1 Ch 524 (gifts for patients in named hospitals); and see *Re Elliott, Raven v Nicholson* (1910) 102 LT 528; and *Re Fraser, Yeates v Fraser* (1883) 22 ChD 827 (gifts for the benefit of the blind); *Re Hillier, Dauncey v Finch and A-G* [1944] 1 All ER 480 (gift for the sick and wounded); *Re Lewis, Public Trustee v Allen* [1955] Ch 104, [1954] 3 All ER 257. In relation to charities for the relief of sickness see guidelines of the *Report of Charity Commissioners for England and Wales for 1978* (HC Paper (1979–80) no 94) App B.

6    *Joseph Rowntree Memorial Trust Housing Association Ltd v A-G* [1983] Ch 159, [1983] 1 All ER 288; *Re Dunlop, Northern Bank Executor and Trustee Co Ltd v A-G for Northern Ireland* [1984] NI 408.

**17.  Meaning of 'poor'.** 'Poor' is a relative term, not confined to the destitute[1]. It may be taken as meaning persons who have to 'go short' in the ordinary acceptation of that term, due regard being had to their status in life and so forth[2].

1    *Trustees of Mary Clark Home v Anderson* [1904] 2 KB 645; *Re Estlin, Prichard v Thomas* (1903) 72 LJCh 687; *Re Gardom, Le Page v A-G* [1914] 1 Ch 662, CA (revsd without affecting this point sub nom *Le Page v Gardom* (1915) 84 LJCh 749, HL); *Shaw v Halifax Corpn* [1915] 2 KB 170, CA; *Re Clarke, Bracey v Royal National Lifeboat Institution* [1923] 2 Ch 407; *Re De Carteret, Forster v De Carteret* [1933] Ch 103. Cf *Re Drummond, Ashworth v Drummond* [1914] 2 Ch 90 (persons employed at a weekly wage of 15 shillings held not poor within the meaning of the preamble to the ancient statute of Elizabeth I 43 Eliz 1 c 4 (1601) (now wholly repealed: see para 2 note 7 ante) (see paras 12–13 ante)); and see *Re Central Employment Bureau for Women and Students' Careers Association Inc* [1942] 1 All ER 232; *Spiller v Maude* (1881) 32 ChD 158n (not more than £50 per annum in 1850); *Re Lacy, Royal General Theatrical Fund Association v Kydd* [1899] 2 Ch 149.

2    *Re Coulthurst, Coutts & Co v Coulthurst* [1951] Ch 661 at 666, [1951] 1 All ER 774 at 776, CA, per Sir Raymond Evershed MR; *Re Niyazi's Will Trusts* [1978] 3 All ER 785, [1978] 1 WLR 910. As to the ways in which trustees may be able to give assistance of real value see the guidance of the *Report of Charity Commissioners for England and Wales for 1978* (HC Paper (1979–80) no 94) App A.

**18.  Contribution by beneficiaries.** Relief is charitable where it is given by way of bounty and not by way of bargain[1], but this does not mean that it cannot be charitable if the beneficiaries contribute to the cost of the benefits they receive[2].

1    *IRC v Society for Relief of Widows and Orphans of Medical Men* (1926) 136 LT 60 at 65 per Rowlatt J (relief of distressed widows of the medical profession who paid subscriptions; the chief income was derived from investments, donations and legacies; *Spiller v Maude* (1881) 32 ChD 158n applied); see also *Blair v Duncan* [1902] AC 37, HL; and *Verge v Somerville* [1924] AC 496, PC.

2    *Re Estlin, Prichard v Thomas* (1903) 72 LJCh 687; *Re Clarke, Bracey v Royal National Lifeboat Institution*
     [1923] 2 Ch 407; *Re Chaplin, Neame v A-G* [1933] Ch 115; *Re Cottam's Will Trusts, Midland Bank*
     *Executor and Trustee Co Ltd v Huddersfield Corpn* [1955] 3 All ER 704, [1955] 1 WLR 1299. Cf *IRC v*
     *Peeblesshire Nursing Association* 1927 SC 215 per Lord Sands; *Over Seventies Housing Association v*
     *Westminster City Council* [1974] RA 247; *Joseph Rowntree Memorial Trust Housing Association Ltd v A-G*
     [1983] Ch 159, [1983] 1 All ER 288. See generally para 11 ante.

**19.   General and particular relief.** A gift may be general and indefinite[1] or for the
poor of a particular parish, town or other place[2] or even on a particular estate[3], or for
persons of a particular religious denomination attending a certain chapel[4], or for members
of a particular regiment[5], or for a particular class of poor or the poor of a particular class,
as poor gentlewomen[6], distressed gentlefolk[7], persons of moderate means[8] or widows of
limited means with small dependent children[9], or persons who are not self-supporting[10],
housekeepers[11], tradesmen of a particular kind[12], unsuccessful literary men[13], servants[14],
old and worn-out clerks of a particular firm[15], poor and incapacitated employees of a
company[16] or necessitous employees of a limited company and their dependants[17],
members of a particular club who fall on evil days[18], 'poor struggling youths of merit'[19],
poor pious persons[20], poor emigrants[21] or persons descended from residents of a particular
borough in a particular year needing assistance to improve their condition in life by
emigrating[22], inmates of a workhouse[23] or hospital[24], debtors[25], 50 old men and 50 old
women of a particular place, being 'needy and deserving'[26], the widows and orphans of
poor clergymen[27] or of seamen of a particular port[28] or of the victims of a particular
disaster[29], or widows and orphans living in a particular parish[30], or indigent bachelors and
widowers 'who have shown sympathy with science'[31]. A gift for the working classes,
including those still working, is not, by implication or otherwise, for the relief of poor
people[32], but a gift for the construction of a working men's hostel has been held to be
charitable[33]. A gift for the relief of domestic distress is charitable[34].

1    *A-G v Peacock* (1676) Cas *temp* Finch 245 (for the good of poor people for ever); *A-G v Syderfen* (1683)
     1 Vern 224; *A-G v Rance* (1728) cited in Amb 422; *Nash v Morley* (1842) 5 Beav 177; *Re Darling, Farquhar*
     *v Darling* [1896] 1 Ch 50 (to the poor and the service of God).
2    *Woodford Inhabitants v Parkhurst* (1639) Duke 70; *A-G v Pearce* (1740) 2 Atk 87; *A-G v Clarke* (1762) Amb
     422; *A-G v Exeter Corpn* (1826) 2 Russ 45; subsequent proceedings (1827) 3 Russ 395; *A-G v Bovill*
     (1840) 1 Ph 762; *A-G v Blizard* (1855) 21 Beav 233; *Re Roadley, Iveson v Wakefield* [1930] 1 Ch 524 (poor
     of a parish); *A-G v Wilkinson* (1839) 1 Beav 370; *Russell v Kellett* (1855) 3 Sm & G 264; *Re Lucas, Rhys*
     *v A-G* [1922] 2 Ch 52 (poor of a township); *Re Lousada, Bacon v Bacon* (1887) 82 LT Jo 358 ('London
     poor'); *Salter v Farey* (1843) 7 Jur 831; *Re Lambeth Charities* (1853) 22 LJCh 959; *Re St Alphage, London*
     *Wall* (1888) 59 LT 614.
3    *Bristow v Bristow* (1842) 5 Beav 289; see also *A-G v Persse* (1842) 2 Dr & War 67.
4    *Re Wall, Pomeroy v Willway* (1889) 42 ChD 510.
5    *Re Donald, Moore v Somerset* [1909] 2 Ch 410.
6    *A-G v Power* (1809) 1 Ball & B 145; *Re Estlin, Prichard v Thomas* (1903) 72 LJCh 687; *Trustees of Mary*
     *Clark Home v Anderson* [1904] 2 KB 645; *Re Gardom, Le Page v A-G* [1914] 1 Ch 662, CA (on appeal
     sub nom *Le Page v Gardom* (1915) 84 LJCh 749, HL); *Shaw v Halifax Corpn* [1915] 2 KB 170, CA.
7    *Re Young, Young v Young* [1951] Ch 344, [1950] 2 All ER 1245.
8    *Re Clarke, Bracey v Royal National Lifeboat Institution* [1923] 2 Ch 407.
9    *Re De Carteret, Forster v De Carteret* [1933] Ch 103.
10   *Re Central Employment Bureau for Women and Students' Careers Association Inc* [1942] 1 All ER 232.
11   *A-G v Pearce* (1740) 2 Atk 87.
12   *Re White's Trusts* (1886) 33 ChD 449.
13   *Thompson v Thompson* (1844) 1 Coll 381 at 395 per Knight Bruce V-C.
14   *Reeve v A-G* (1843) 3 Hare 191; *Loscombe v Wintringham* (1850) 13 Beav 87.
15   *Re Gosling, Gosling v Smith* (1900) 48 WR 300.

16  *Re Rayner, Cloutman v Regnart* (1920) 89 LJCh 369.
17  *Dingle v Turner* [1972] AC 601, [1972] 1 All ER 878, HL (poor employees); *Gibson v South American Stores (Gath and Chaves) Ltd* [1950] Ch 177, [1949] 2 All ER 985, CA.
18  *Re Young's Will Trusts, Westminster Bank Ltd v Sterling* [1955] 3 All ER 689, [1955] 1 WLR 1269.
19  *Milne's Executors v Aberdeen University Court* (1905) 7 F 642, Ct of Sess.
20  *Nash v Morley* (1842) 5 Beav 177.
21  *Barclay v Maskelyne* (1858) 32 LTOS 205. See *Re Sidney, Hingeston v Sidney* [1908] 1 Ch 488, CA ('emigration uses' not charitable).
22  *Re Tree, Idle v Tree* [1945] Ch 325, [1945] 2 All ER 65.
23  *A-G v Vint* (1850) 3 De G & Sm 704.
24  *Reading Corpn v Lane* (1601) Duke 81.
25  *A-G v Painter Stainers' Co* (1788) 2 Cox Eq Cas 51; *A-G v Ironmongers' Co* (1834) 2 My & K 576.
26  *Re Reed* (1893) 10 TLR 87; and see *Re Wall, Pomeroy v Willway* (1889) 42 ChD 510.
27  *Waldo v Caley* (1809) 16 Ves 206; see also *Re Friend of the Clergy's Charters, Friend of the Clergy v A-G* [1921] 1 Ch 409.
28  *Powell v A-G* (1817) 3 Mer 48.
29  *Pease v Pattinson* (1886) 32 ChD 154; *Re Hartley Colliery Accident Relief Fund, Plummer v Jordan* (1908) 102 LT 165n; *Cross v Lloyd-Greame* (1909) 102 LT 163 (where the victims were only six in number).
30  *A-G v Comber* (1824) 2 Sim & St 93; *Russell v Kellett* (1855) 3 Sm & G 264.
31  *Weir v Crum-Brown* [1908] AC 162, HL.
32  *Re Sanders' Will Trusts, Public Trustee v McLaren* [1954] Ch 265, [1954] 1 All ER 667; distinguishing *Re Glyn's Will Trusts, Public Trustee v A-G* [1950] 2 All ER 1150n. As to the phrase 'working classes' see *Rodwell v Minister of Health* [1947] KB 404 at 411, [1947] 1 All ER 80 at 82 per Morris J; *HE Green & Sons v Minister of Health (No 2)* [1948] 1 KB 34 at 38, [1947] 2 All ER 469 at 471 per Denning J; *Belcher v Reading Corpn* [1950] Ch 380 at 392, [1949] 2 All ER 969 at 984 per Romer J; *Guinness Trust (London Fund) v Green* [1955] 2 All ER 871 at 873, [1955] 1 WLR 872 at 875, CA, per Denning LJ; *Re Niyazi's Will Trusts* [1978] 3 All ER 785 at 788, [1978] 1 WLR 910 at 915 per Megarry V-C; *Westminster City Council v Duke of Westminster* [1991] 4 All ER 136.
33  *Re Niyazi's Will Trusts* [1978] 3 All ER 785, [1978] 1 WLR 910.
34  *Kendall v Granger* (1842) 5 Beav 300 at 303 per Lord Langdale MR.

**20. Poor of a particular religion.** The relief of the poor of a particular church or religious denomination, such as Jews[1], Presbyterians[2], Moravians[3], Unitarians[4], Irvingites[5] or Methodists[6], is charitable, and has always been so, notwithstanding the law of superstitious uses[7]; so also is a gift for ministers 'persecuted or in poverty' on account of preaching certain doctrines[8].

1  *De Costa v De Paz* (1754) 2 Swan 487n; *Re Haendler, A-G v Revel* (1931) Times, 4 July; and see *A-G v Mathieson, Re Wilkinson and Fell's Contract* [1907] 2 Ch 383 at 392, CA, per Cozens-Hardy MR (Mildmay Mission to the Jews).
2  *A-G v Wansay* (1808) 15 Ves 231.
3  *Income Tax Special Purposes Comrs v Pemsel* [1891] AC 531, HL.
4  *A-G v Shore* (1843) 11 Sim 592; *Shore v Wilson* (1842) 9 Cl & Fin 355 at 507–508, HL, per Maule J.
5  *A-G v Lawes* (1849) 8 Hare 32.
6  *Dawson v Small* (1874) LR 18 Eq 114.
7  See para 56 post.
8  *A-G v Lawes* (1849) 8 Hare 32.

**21. Gifts to poor relations.** Perpetual trusts for the benefit of poor relations or descendants are charitable[1], though the charitable nature of these trusts is, perhaps, anomalous as lacking the necessary public element[2].

Gifts for poor relations intended for immediate distribution are also charitable[3], but some gifts to relations are construed as being intended to be confined to statutory next of kin and these are not charitable, the object then being not to relieve poverty among a class but to benefit specific individuals[4]. Such gifts are confined to the statutory next of kin if all members of the class are entitled to participate[5], but not if the beneficiaries are poor relations to be selected[6], nor if a contrary intention appears from the will[7]. Poor relations who become rich must not participate[8], and a gift for the poorest of the testator's kindred can only be charitable when intended for persons who are actually poor[9].

A gift for the poor, giving a preference to poor relations, is charitable[10]. An inquiry may be directed as to who are poor relations[11].

1   *White v White* (1802) 7 Ves 423 (trust for apprenticing poor relations); *A-G v Price* (1810) 17 Ves 371 (poor kinsmen in a particular place); *Isaac v Defriez* (1754) Amb 595 (poorest relations); *Browne v Whalley* [1866] WN 386; *Gillam v Taylor* (1873) LR 16 Eq 581 (lineal descendants); *Re Drake's Will Trusts, Drake v Drake* [1971] Ch 179, [1970] 3 All ER 32, CA ('male descendants' construed as not limited to males descended solely through males, overruling *Bernal v Bernal* (1838) 3 My & Cr 559); *A-G v Duke of Northumberland* (1877) 7 ChD 745; contra, *Liley v Hey* (1842) 1 Hare 580; *Peek v Peek* (1869) 17 WR 1059.
2   *Re Compton, Powell v Compton* [1945] Ch 123, [1945] 1 All ER 198, CA; approved in *Oppenheim v Tobacco Securities Trust Co Ltd* [1951] AC 297, [1951] 1 All ER 31, HL.
3   *A-G v Buckland (or Bucknall)* (1742) cited in Amb 71n; *Mahon v Savage* (1803) 1 Sch & Lef 111; and see *Re Shepherd, Smithem v Shepherd* (1921) 152 LT Jo 18. In no charitable disposition which is valid because of its public character is there any warrant for distinguishing between trusts maintained for a period and trusts for immediate distribution: *Re Scarisbrick, Cockshott v Public Trustee* [1951] Ch 622 at 639, [1951] 1 All ER 822 at 830, CA, per Sir Raymond Evershed MR.
4   *Re Scarisbrick, Cockshott v Public Trustee* [1951] Ch 622 at 638, [1951] 1 All ER 822 at 828, CA, per Evershed MR.
5   *Re Scarisbrick, Cockshott v Public Trustee* [1951] Ch 622 at 640, [1951] 1 All ER 822 at 831, CA, per Sir Raymond Evershed MR.
6   *Re Scarisbrick, Cockshott v Public Trustee* [1951] Ch 622, [1951] 1 All ER 822, CA ('such relations of my son and daughters as in the opinion of the survivor of my said son and daughters shall be in needy circumstances'); cf *Re Cohen, Cowan v Cohen* [1973] 1 All ER 889, [1973] 1 WLR 415 (relatives in special need).
7   *Carr v Bedford* (1678) 2 Rep Ch 146; *Griffith v Jones* (1686) 2 Rep Ch 394; *Edge v Salisbury* (1749) Amb 70 ('nearest relations'); *Brunsden v Woolredge* (1765) Amb 507 ('mother's poor relations'); *Widmore v Woodroffe* (1766) Amb 636 ('most necessitous of my relations'); *Gower v Mainwaring* (1750) 2 Ves Sen 87 at 110 per Lord Hardwicke LC ('friends and relations' means 'relations'); see also *Roach v Hammond* (1715) Prec Ch 401; *Anon* (1716) 1 P Wms 327 ('poor relations'); *Green v Howard* (1779) 1 Bro CC 31 ('testator's relations'). As to such a bequest's being void for uncertainty when not confined to statutory next of kin see *Widmore v Woodroffe* (1766) Amb 636 at 640 per Lord Hardwicke LC; *Mahon v Savage* (1803) 1 Sch & Lef 111; *Brandon v Brandon* (1819) 3 Swan 312 ('nearest and next of kin').
8   *Mahon v Savage* (1803) 1 Sch & Lef 111.
9   *A-G v Duke of Northumberland* (1877) 7 ChD 745; and see *A-G v Price* (1810) 17 Ves 371.
10  *Waldo v Caley* (1809) 16 Ves 206.
11  *A-G v Price* (1810) 17 Ves 371; *A-G v Sidney Sussex College, Cambridge* (1865) 34 Beav 654; revsd without affecting this point (1866) 21 ChD 514n.

**22.   Gifts to other limited classes of the poor.** By analogy with the poor relations cases[1], it has been held that trusts for the relief of necessitous employees of a limited company and their dependants[2], for the benefit of widows and orphaned children of deceased officers and ex-officers of a bank (the terms of the gift indicating that it was intended for the relief of privation)[3], and for fellow members of a club who may fall on evil days[4], are charitable, despite the lack of a sufficient section of the public as objects of the charity. These trusts would not be valid charitable trusts if not restricted to the relief of poverty[5].

On the same principle, gifts to friendly societies for the relief of poverty among members are charitable[6], though such gifts are not charitable where the purpose is the relief of sickness or distress generally[7]. It may be that the validity of a trust to assist emigration by persons residing in a particular area before a certain date and their descendants depends on the presence of the element of relief of poverty[8].

1 See para 21 ante.

2 *Dingle v Turner* [1972] AC 601, [1972] 1 All ER 878. HL (poor employees); *Gibson v South American Stores (Gath and Chaves) Ltd* [1950] Ch 177, [1949] 2 All ER 985, CA; see also *Re Gosling, Gosling v Smith* (1900) 48 WR 300 (old and worn-out clerks of a banking firm), doubted in *Gibson v South American Stores (Gath and Chaves) Ltd* supra; *Re Rayner, Cloutman v Regnart* (1920) 89 LJCh 369 (poor and incapacitated employees of a company), distinguishing *Re Drummond, Ashworth v Drummond* [1914] 2 Ch 90.

3 *Re Coulthurst, Coutts & Co v Coulthurst* [1951] Ch 661, [1951] 1 All ER 774, CA.

4 *Re Young's Will Trusts, Westminster Bank Ltd v Sterling* [1955] 3 All ER 689, [1955] 1 WLR 1269.

5 See *Re Cox, Baker v National Trust Co Ltd* [1955] AC 627, [1955] 2 All ER 550, PC.

6 *Spiller v Maude* (1881) 32 ChD 158n; *Pease v Pattinson* (1886) 32 ChD 154; *Re Buck, Bruty v Mackey* [1896] 2 Ch 727; *Re Lacy, Royal General Theatrical Fund Association v Kydd* [1899] 2 Ch 149; *IRC v Society for Relief of Widows and Orphans of Medical Men* (1926) 136 LT 60; cf *Dingle v Turner* [1972] AC 601 at 617. [1972] 1 All ER 878 at 883, HL, per Lord Cross.

7 *Re Hobourn Aero Components Ltd's Air Raid Distress Fund, Ryan v Forrest* [1946] Ch 194, [1946] 1 All ER 501, CA; *Waterson v Hendon Borough Council* [1959] 2 All ER 760, [1959] 1 WLR 985; *Re Clark's Trust* (1875) 1 ChD 497; *Cunnack v Edwards* [1896] 2 Ch 679, CA; but cf *Re Forster, Gellatly v Palmer* [1939] Ch 22, [1938] 3 All ER 767.

8 *Re Tree, Idle v Tree* [1945] Ch 325, [1945] 2 All ER 65, as explained in *Davies v Perpetual Trustee Co Ltd* [1959] AC 439, [1959] 2 All ER 128, PC.

**23. Relief of poverty inferred or indirect.** In some cases an unexpressed intention to relieve poverty may be inferred from the nature of the gift[1]. The relief of poverty may also be effected indirectly. Thus, bequests in aid of the granting of allotments[2], the apprenticing of poor children[3], and the distribution of doles[4], are charitable.

Similarly, the following are charitable: the establishment, maintenance and support of institutions or funds for the relief of various forms of poverty or distress, such as soup kitchens[5], hospitals and dispensaries[6] and, as conducive to the work of hospitals, funds for providing accommodation for relatives who come from a distance to visit patients critically ill in hospital[7], funds for homes of rest for nurses[8] and funds to provide extra comforts for nurses at Christmas[9], funds to provide extra amenities for patients in paying beds in hospitals[10], nursing homes or societies for persons of moderate means[11], convalescent homes[12], homes of rest[13], a house to be maintained by the local authority as a children's home[14], asylums[15], almshouses[16], homes for lady teachers[17] or ladies in reduced circumstances[18] or working girls[19], orphanages[20], institutions for the benefit of impoverished actors[21], and the sick and poor funds of a parish church[22]. Neighbourhood law centres formed for the purpose of giving legal aid and advice to poor persons have been registered as charities[23], as have trusts to provide low interest or interest-free loans to assist poor persons to purchase freehold or leasehold housing accommodation[24].

Aged persons have been held proper objects of charity under a gift not containing any express direction or indication of relief[25]; but it does not appear that the element of relief is necessarily implied in any gift to the aged. Persons not under 50 years of age have been held to be aged[26].

A home of rest for those needing it is a provision for the relief of the impotent[27]. The prevention of cruelty to children is charitable, probably as being the relief of the impotent[28]. Faith-healing may be charitable as being for the relief of the impotent[29]. A gift to pay money to the eventual discoverers of the cause of and a cure for cancer was held to be exclusively charitable[30].

Gifts to religious communities having for their object the relief of the sick and poor are charitable[31].

1   See eg *A-G v Comber* (1824) 2 Sim & St 93 (widows and orphans); *Thompson v Corby* (1860) 27 Beav 649 (aged widows and spinsters); *Re Dudgeon, Truman v Pope* (1896) 74 LT 613 (respectable single women over 60 years of age); *Re Wall, Pomeroy v Willway* (1889) 42 ChD 510 (Unitarians of over 50 years of age attending a particular chapel); *Re Gosling, Gosling v Smith* (1900) 48 WR 300 (pensioning old and worn-out clerks); *Re Lucas, Rhys v A-G* [1922] 2 Ch 52 (small weekly payments to oldest respectable inhabitants of named place); *Verge v Somerville* [1924] AC 496, PC (Australian Repatriation Fund); *Re Roadley, Iveson v Wakefield* [1930] 1 Ch 524 (maintenance of patients from named parishes at named hospitals); *Re Coulthurst, Coutts & Co v Coulthurst* [1951] Ch 661, [1951] 1 All ER 774, CA (widows and orphaned children of deceased officers and deceased ex-officers of bank considered by reason of financial circumstances most deserving); *Re Niyazi's Will Trusts* [1978] 3 All ER 785, [1978] 1 WLR 910 (gift for construction of working men's hostel). Cf *Re Sidney, Hingeston v Sidney* [1908] 1 Ch 488, CA (emigration uses: not charitable); *Re Drummond, Ashworth v Drummond* [1914] 2 Ch 90 (holiday fund for employees of a company: not charitable); *A-G for Northern Ireland v Forde* [1932] NI 1, CA (gift to widows of persons resident on estate: not charitable). As to the views of the Charity Commissioners on relief for the unemployed see the *Report of the Charity Commissioners for England and Wales for 1983* (HC Paper (1983–84) no 447) paras 12–13.

2   *Crafton v Frith* (1851) 4 De G & Sm 237. See also the Charities Act 1993 s 79(1); and para 240 post.

3   *A-G v Minshull* (1798) 4 Ves 11; *A-G v Earl Winchelsea* (1791) 3 Bro CC 373; *A-G v Wansay* (1808) 15 Ves 231.

4   *A-G v Minshull* (1798) 4 Ves 11; *A-G v Bovill* (1840) 1 Ph 762; *Thompson v Thompson* (1844) 1 Coll 381 at 392 per Knight Bruce V-C.

5   *Biscoe v Jackson* (1887) 35 ChD 460, CA.

6   *Pelham v Anderson* (1764) 2 Eden 296; *A-G v Gascoigne* (1833) 2 My & K 647; *A-G v Kell* (1840) 2 Beav 575; *Wharton v Masterman* [1895] AC 186, HL; *Re Cox, Cox v Davie* (1877) 7 ChD 204; *Re Garrard, Gordon v Craigie* [1907] 1 Ch 382; *Re Weir Hospital* [1910] 2 Ch 124, CA; *Re Welsh Hospital (Netley) Fund, Thomas v A-G* [1921] 1 Ch 655; *Re Roadley, Iveson v Wakefield* [1930] 1 Ch 524; *Re Resch's Will Trusts, Le Cras v Perpetual Trustee Co Ltd* [1969] 1 AC 514, [1967] 3 All ER 915, PC. Hospitals give in-patients continuous treatment; dispensaries give out-patients occasional medical and surgical aid: *Re Ford* [1945] 1 All ER 288. Not all hospitals are charitable, but a gift in a will may be construed as a gift only to hospitals not run for profit, which are charitable: *Re Smith's Will Trusts, Barclays Bank Ltd v Mercantile Bank Ltd* [1962] 2 All ER 563, [1962] 1 WLR 763, CA.

7   *Re Dean's Will Trusts, Cowan v Board of Governors of St Mary's Hospital, Paddington* [1950] 1 All ER 882.

8   *Re White's Will Trusts, Tindall v Board of Governors of United Sheffield Hospitals* [1951] 1 All ER 528.

9   *Re Bernstein's Will Trusts, National Westminster Bank Ltd v Board of Governors of United Liverpool Hospitals* (1971) 115 Sol Jo 808.

10  *Re Adams, Gee v Barnet Group Hospital Management Committee* [1968] Ch 80, [1967] 3 All ER 285, CA.

11  *Re Clarke, Bracey v Royal National Lifeboat Institution* [1923] 2 Ch 407. Cf *IRC v Peeblesshire Nursing Association* 1927 SC 215.

12  *IRC v Trustees of Roberts Marine Mansions* (1927) 43 TLR 270, CA (seaside home at reduced charges for members of drapery and allied trades requiring rest and change of air for the benefit of their health).

13  *Re Estlin, Prichard v Thomas* (1903) 72 LJCh 687 (home of rest for lady teachers); *Re James, Grenfell v Hamilton* [1932] 2 Ch 25 (home of rest for certain religious sisters and clergy and persons chosen by mother superior); *Re Chaplin, Neame v A-G* [1933] Ch 115 (home of rest to afford means of recuperation from strain).

14  *Re Sahal's Will Trusts, Alliance Assurance Co Ltd v A-G* [1958] 3 All ER 428, [1958] 1 WLR 1243; though see also *Re Cole, Westminster Bank Ltd v Moore* [1958] Ch 877, [1958] 3 All ER 102, CA.

15  *Harbin v Masterman* (1871) LR 12 Eq 559; *Harbin v Masterman* [1894] 2 Ch 184, CA; affd sub nom *Wharton v Masterman* [1895] AC 186, HL (asylum for destitute orphans); *Henshaw v Atkinson* (1818) 3 Madd 306 (blind asylum).

16  *Mayor of London's Case* (1639) Duke 83; *Re Whiteley, Bishop of London v Whiteley* [1910] 1 Ch 600; and see *Chamberlayne v Brockett* (1872) 8 Ch App 206. Cf *Re Brown, Brown v Brown* (1900) 32 OR 323 (luxuries for inmates of poorhouse).

17  *Re Estlin, Prichard v Thomas* (1903) 72 LJCh 687 (the ladies in question paid part of the expenses of board and lodging).

18  *Trustees of Mary Clark Home v Anderson* [1904] 2 KB 645; *Re Gardom, Le Page v A-G* [1914] 1 Ch 662, CA; *Shaw v Halifax Corpn* [1915] 2 KB 170, CA; *Re Armitage, Ellam v Norwich Corpn* [1972] Ch 438, sub nom *Re Armitage's Will Trusts, Ellam v City and County of Norwich* [1972] 1 All ER 708.

19  *Rolls v Miller* (1884) 27 ChD 71, CA.

20  *Hall v Derby Borough Urban Sanitary Authority* (1885) 16 QBD 163, DC; *Harbin v Masterman* [1894] 2 Ch 184, CA (affd sub nom *Wharton v Masterman* [1895] AC 186, HL); *Re Clergy Society* (1856) 2 K & J 615; *Re Douglas, Obert v Barrow* (1887) 35 ChD 472.

21  *Spiller v Maude* (1881) 32 ChD 158n; *Re Lacy, Royal General Theatrical Fund Association v Kydd* [1899] 2 Ch 149.

22  *Re Garrard, Gordon v Craigie* [1907] 1 Ch 382 (conceded in argument).

23  *Report of the Charity Commissioners for England and Wales for 1974* (HC Paper (1974–75) no 381) paras 67–72.

24  *Report of the Charity Commissioners for England and Wales for 1990* (HC Paper (1990–91) no 362) App A (e).

25  *Re Shepherd, Firman v Shepherd* (1952) unreported (trust to divide income equally among the 21 oldest inhabitants of a locality without a means test).

26  *Re Wall, Pomeroy v Willway* (1889) 42 ChD 510. However, the average expectation of life has increased since 1889, and a more advanced age might now be held to be the minimum.

27  Cf the preamble to the ancient statute of Elizabeth I 43 Eliz 1 c 4 (1601) (now wholly repealed: see para 2 note 7 ante): see paras 12–13 ante; and see *Re Estlin, Prichard v Thomas* (1903) 72 LJCh 687; *Re James, Grenfell v Hamilton* [1932] 2 Ch 25; *Re Chaplin, Neame v A-G* [1933] Ch 115; but see *Re Morris' Will Trusts* (1962) Times, 25 January, where a gift to provide a home of rest was held not to be intended to relieve the impotent.

28  *Income Tax Special Purposes Comrs v Pemsel* [1891] AC 531 at 572, HL, where, however, Lord Herschell discusses 'charity' in its popular sense. See also *Re Sahal's Will Trusts, Alliance Assurance Co Ltd v A-G* [1958] 3 All ER 428, [1958] 1 WLR 1243 (gift of house to be maintained by local authority as a children's home). But see *Re Cole, Westminster Bank Ltd v Moore* [1958] Ch 877, [1958] 3 All ER 102, CA.

29  *Re Kerin* (1966) Times, 24 May. However, on appeal the order in this case was wholly set aside by consent.

30  *Re Watson's Settlement Trusts, Dawson v Reid* [1959] 2 All ER 676, [1959] 1 WLR 732.

31  *Cocks v Manners* (1871) LR 12 Eq 574; *Re Delany, Conoley v Quick* [1902] 2 Ch 642, and cases there cited; *Re Banfield, Lloyds Bank Ltd v Smith* [1968] 2 All ER 276, [1968] 1 WLR 846.

## (ii)  Educational Purposes

**24.  Advancement of education and learning.** The second division of charitable objects[1] is the advancement of education. The advancement and propagation of education and learning generally are charitable purposes[2], even in the absence of any element of poverty in the class of beneficiaries[3], but the trust must be for the benefit of a sufficient section of the community[4]. It need not be confined to education by a teacher in a classroom[5], and it need not be connected with teaching or education in the conventional sense[6]. Thus the purposes of a students' union attached to a medical college[7], or a polytechnic[8], have been held to be charitable.

This category of charitable purposes extends to the improvement of a useful branch of human knowledge and its public dissemination[9], though a gift which merely tends to the increase of knowledge is not charitable[10], and research of a private character, for example for the benefit of the members of a particular society, would not normally be charitable[11]. The promotion of academic research may be a charitable purpose if the research is of educational value to the researcher, or if it is so directed as to lead to something which will pass into the store of educational material or to improve the sum of communicable knowledge in an area which education may cover[12]. The principles in relation to research are as follows[13].

(1)    A trust for research will ordinarily qualify as a charitable trust if, but only if: (a) the subject matter of the proposed research is a useful subject of study; and (b) it is contemplated that knowledge acquired as a result of the research will be disseminated to others; and (c) the trust is for the benefit of the public, or a sufficiently important section of the public[14].

(2)    In the absence of a contrary context, however, the court will be readily inclined to construe a trust for research as importing subsequent dissemination of the results thereof[15].

(3)    Furthermore, if a trust for research is to constitute a valid trust for the advancement of education, it is not necessary either: (a) that a teacher/pupil relationship should be in contemplation; or (b) that the persons to benefit from the knowledge to be acquired should be persons who are already in the course of receiving 'education' in the conventional sense[16].

(4)    In any case where the court has to determine whether a bequest for the purposes of research is or is not of a charitable nature, it must pay due regard to any admissible extrinsic evidence which is available to explain the wording of the will in question or the circumstances in which it was made[17].

Where a gift is clearly educational the court does not require evidence of public benefit, nor will it inquire into the efficacy of the method of education advocated[18], but this does not prevent evidence being admissible to enable the court to decide whether there is any educational tendency in the gift[19].

The furtherance of 'religious and mental improvement' is charitable[20], as is the Scout movement, which exists to instruct boys of all classes in the principles of loyalty, discipline and good citizenship[21].

Education in political matters in the interests of one party only is not charitable[22]; nor is adult education with particular reference to the memorandum of one political party[23]. If the essential or dominant purpose is not education but a political object it is not charitable[24].

Many purposes which fall to be considered under this division of charitable purposes may also be considered under the fourth head[25], and may be accepted as falling under either or both of these heads[26].

---

1    Ie the second division mentioned by Lord Macnaghten in *Income Tax Special Purposes Comrs v Pemsel* [1891] AC 531 at 583, HL, per Lord Macnaghten: see para 13 ante. As to the four divisions of charity see para 13 ante.

2    *Whicker v Hume* (1858) 7 HL Cas 124; *President of United States of America v Drummond* (1838) cited in 7 HL Cas 155.

3    *R v Income Tax Special Comrs, ex p University College of North Wales* (1909) 78 LJKB 576 at 578, CA, per Cozens-Hardy MR.

4    See para 8 ante. See also *Oppenheim v Tobacco Securities Trust Co Ltd* [1951] AC 297 at 305, [1951] 1 All ER 31 at 33, HL, per Lord Simonds.

5    *Royal Choral Society v IRC* [1943] 2 All ER 101, CA; *Re Koeppler Will Trusts, Barclays Bank Trust Co Ltd v Slack* [1986] Ch 423, [1985] 2 All ER 869, CA.

6    See *Re Compton, Powell v Compton* [1945] Ch 123 at 127, [1945] 1 All ER 198 at 200, CA, per Lord Greene MR; *Re Hopkins' Will Trusts, Naish v Francis Bacon Society Inc* [1965] Ch 669 at 680, [1964] 3 All ER 46 at 52 per Wilberforce J; *Re Koeppler Will Trusts, Barclays Bank Trust Co Ltd v Slack* [1986] Ch 423, [1985] 2 All ER 869, CA (conferences for highly qualified participants on recognised academic subjects held to be for the advancement of education). But see also *Re Shaw, Public Trustee v Day* [1957] 1 All ER 745, [1957] 1 WLR 729; on appeal [1958] 1 All ER 245n, CA.

7   *London Hospital Medical College v IRC* [1976] 2 All ER 113, [1976] 1 WLR 613 (union existed solely to further educational purposes of college: benefits received by students incidental to implementation of those purposes).

8   *A-G v Ross* [1985] 3 All ER 334, [1986] 1 WLR 252. Note the *Attorney General's Guidance on Expenditure by Student Unions: Report of Charity Commissioners for England and Wales for 1983* (HC Paper (1983–84) no 447) App A. See also the Further and Higher Education Act 1992 s 77 (as amended) (see EDUCATION), which permits the transformation of polytechnics into universities with the consent of the Privy Council.

9   *Incorporated Council of Law Reporting for England and Wales v A-G* [1972] Ch 73 at 102, [1971] 3 All ER 1029 at 1046, CA, per Buckley LJ. See also *Vancouver Society of Immigrant and Visible Minority Women v Minister of National Revenue* (1999) 169 DLR (4th) 34, Can SC (structured transmission of useful information and training).

10  *Re Shaw, Public Trustee v Day* [1957] 1 All ER 745, [1957] 1 WLR 729, following *Whicker v Hume* (1858) 7 HL Cas 124; and *Re Macduff, Macduff v Macduff* [1896] 2 Ch 451, CA.

11  See *Re British School of Egyptian Archaeology, Murray v Public Trustee* [1954] 1 All ER 887 at 890, [1954] 1 WLR 546 at 551 per Harman J; *Re Hopkins' Will Trusts, Naish v Francis Bacon Society Inc* [1965] Ch 669 at 681, [1964] 3 All ER 46 at 53 per Wilberforce J.

12  See *Re Hopkins' Will Trusts, Naish v Francis Bacon Society Inc* [1965] Ch 669 at 680, [1964] 3 All ER 46 at 52 per Wilberforce J. See also *Incorporated Council of Law Reporting for England and Wales v A-G* [1972] Ch 73, [1971] 3 All ER 1029, CA.

13  *Re Besterman's Will Trusts* (21 January 1980, unreported) per Slade J, cited by the same judge in *McGovern v A-G* [1982] Ch 321 at 352–353, [1981] 3 All ER 493 at 518. See also *Re Koeppler Will Trusts, Barclays Bank Trust Co Ltd v Slack* [1986] Ch 423, [1985] 2 All ER 869, CA.

14  *Re Besterman's Will Trusts* (21 January 1980, unreported) per Slade J, cited by the same judge in *McGovern v A-G* [1982] Ch 321 at 352–353, [1981] 3 All ER 493 at 518.

15  *Re Besterman's Will Trusts* (21 January 1980, unreported) per Slade J, cited by the same judge in *McGovern v A-G* [1982] Ch 321 at 352–353, [1981] 3 All ER 493 at 518.

16  *Re Besterman's Will Trusts* (21 January 1980, unreported) per Slade J, cited by the same judge in *McGovern v A-G* [1982] Ch 321 at 352–353, [1981] 3 All ER 493 at 518.

17  *Re Besterman's Will Trusts* (21 January 1980, unreported) per Slade J, cited by the same judge in *McGovern v A-G* [1982] Ch 321 at 352–353, [1981] 3 All ER 493 at 518.

18  *Re Shaw's Will Trusts, National Provincial Bank Ltd v National City Bank Ltd* [1952] Ch 163, [1952] 1 All ER 49.

19  *Re Pinion, Westminster Bank Ltd v Pinion* [1965] Ch 85, [1964] 1 All ER 890, CA; affg on this point [1965] Ch 85, [1963] 2 All ER 1049.

20  *Re Scowcroft, Ormrod v Wilkinson* [1898] 2 Ch 638; *Barralet v A-G* [1980] 3 All ER 918, sub nom *Re South Place Ethical Society, Barralet v A-G* [1980] 1 WLR 1565 (study and dissemination of ethical principles and the cultivation of a rational religious sentiment).

21  *Re Webber, Barclays Bank Ltd v Webber* [1954] 3 All ER 712, [1954] 1 WLR 1500, following *Re Alexander* (1932) Times, 30 June. Presumably, charitable status is by analogy extended to the Guide movement.

22  *Bonar Law Memorial Trust v IRC* (1933) 49 TLR 220.

23  *Re Hopkinson, Lloyds Bank Ltd v Baker* [1949] 1 All ER 346; see also para 60 post.

24  *Re Bushnell, Lloyds Bank Ltd v Murray* [1975] 1 All ER 721, [1975] 1 WLR 1596. See also *Webb v O'Doherty* (1991) 3 Admin LR 731, (1991) Times, 11 February (the funds of a students' union, an educational charity, could not be used to campaign for an end to the Gulf War, a political purpose). Education of the public in the subject of militarism and disarmament was political and not a charitable object: *Southwood v A-G* [1998] 40 LS Gaz R 37, Times, 26 October; affd [2000] NLJR 1017, Times, 18 July, CA.

25  Ie other purposes beneficial to the community: see para 37 et seq post.

26  See eg *Re Shakespeare Memorial Trust, Earl of Lytton v A-G* [1923] 2 Ch 398; *Re Hopkins' Will Trusts, Naish v Francis Bacon Society Inc* [1965] Ch 669, [1964] 3 All ER 46; *Construction Industry Training Board v A-G* [1971] 3 All ER 449, [1971] 1 WLR 1303 (affd without dealing with this point [1973] Ch 173, [1972] 2 All ER 1339, CA); *Incorporated Council of Law Reporting for England and Wales v A-G* [1972] Ch 73, [1971] 3 All ER 1029, CA.

**25.  Education of limited class.** Gifts for the education of special classes of persons forming a section of the community[1], such as women and girls who are not self-supporting[2], or the daughters of missionaries[3], or persons professing particular religious doctrines[4], or the employees in the whole of a particular industry[5], and gifts for educational purposes with a provision for the participation of the founder's kin, are charitable[6].

However, gifts for the education of descendants of named persons[7], or for the education of employees or of children of employees or former employees of a limited company[8], are not charitable, and an institute maintained for the promotion of efficiency, progress and general development among persons engaged or employed in insurance was held to be for the benefit, not of the public, but of the insurance profession[9].

1    See *Oppenheim v Tobacco Securities Trust Co Ltd* [1951] AC 297 at 305, [1951] 1 All ER 31 at 33, HL, per Lord Simonds. As to whether purposes satisfy requirement of benefiting a sufficient section of the community see para 8 ante. For provision as to racial discrimination see para 14 ante, and as to sex discrimination see para 15 ante.
2    *Re Central Employment Bureau for Women and Students' Careers Association Inc* [1942] 1 All ER 232.
3    *German v Chapman* (1877) 7 ChD 271, CA.
4    *Income Tax Special Purposes Comrs v Pemsel* [1891] AC 531, HL; *Walsh v Gladstone* (1843) 1 Ph 290; *Carbery v Cox* (1852) 3 I Ch R 231n (Roman Catholics); *Re Michel's Trust* (1860) 28 Beav 39 (Jews).
5    *Construction Industry Training Board v A-G* [1971] 3 All ER 449, [1971] 1 WLR 1303; affd without dealing with this point [1973] Ch 173, [1972] 2 All ER 1339, CA.
6    *Spencer v All Souls' College* (1762) Wilm 163; *A-G v Sidney Sussex College, Cambridge* (1866) 21 ChD 514n; *Re Lavelle, Concannon v A-G* [1914] 1 IR 194 (explained in *Re Compton, Powell v Compton* [1945] Ch 123, [1945] 1 All ER 198, CA); and see *Re Koettgen's Will Trusts, Westminster Bank Ltd v Family Welfare Association Trustees Ltd* [1954] Ch 252, [1954] 1 All ER 581; and para 9 ante.
7    *Re Compton, Powell v Compton* [1945] Ch 123, [1945] 1 All ER 198, CA. Cf *Laverty v Laverty* [1907] 1 IR 9 (education of 'any boy or man' of a particular surname: not charitable); and see *Davies v Perpetual Trustee Co Ltd* [1959] AC 439, [1959] 2 All ER 128, PC.
8    *Oppenheim v Tobacco Securities Trust Co Ltd* [1951] AC 297, [1951] 1 All ER 31, HL, doubting *Re Rayner, Cloutman v Regnart* (1920) 89 LJCh 369; *Re Leverhulme, Cooper v Leverhulme* [1943] 2 All ER 143. See also *Re Cox, Baker v National Trust Co Ltd* [1955] AC 627, [1955] 2 All ER 550, PC; *IRC v Educational Grants Association Ltd* [1967] Ch 993, [1967] 2 All ER 893, CA.
9    *Chartered Insurance Institute v London Corpn* [1957] 2 All ER 638, [1957] 1 WLR 867, DC (where the question at issue was whether the institute was an organisation whose main objects were concerned with the advancement of education, so as to entitle it to rating relief); but see *Royal College of Nursing v St Marylebone Corpn* [1959] 3 All ER 663, [1959] 1 WLR 1077, CA.

**26.  Education in particular subjects.** The promotion of education in particular subjects, such as art[1], artistic taste[2], the appreciation of the fine arts[3], music[4] or the music of one particular composer[5], choral singing[6], playing the organ[7], drama[8], the arts of social intercourse[9], the Irish language[10], archaeology[11], commercial education[12], training for industrial employment[13], craftsmanship[14], the art and science of government[15], economic and sanitary science[16], psychological healing[17], or Christian knowledge[18], is charitable. But education in the cause of a particular political party is not charitable[19]; nor is the presentation of 'classical, artistic, cultural and educational dramatic works'[20]. A trust whose purpose is the mere increase of knowledge is not charitable in the legal sense[21], and gifts to the Simplified Spelling Society[22] and for investigations into the efficacy of a new alphabet[23] have been held not to be charitable.

1    *Re Allsop, Gell v Carver* (1884) 1 TLR 4 (school of art). A gift to 'encourage artistic pursuits' is not charitable: *Re Ogden, Taylor v Sharp* (1909) 25 TLR 382, CA; and see *Gwynn v Cardon* (c 1800) cited in 10 Ves 533; *Re Bootham Ward Strays, York, IRC v Scott* [1892] 2 QB 152 at 165, CA, per Lord Herschell. The promotion of art is charitable: *Re Town and Country Planning Act 1947, Crystal Palace Trustees v Minister of Town and Country Planning* [1951] Ch 132, [1950] 2 All ER 857n, doubting *Re Ogden, Taylor v Sharp* supra.

2    *Royal Choral Society v IRC* [1943] 2 All ER 101 at 105, CA, per Lord Greene MR; and see *Re Hopkins' Will Trusts, Naish v Francis Bacon Society Inc* [1965] Ch 669, [1964] 3 All ER 46.
3    *Re Shaw's Will Trusts, National Provincial Bank Ltd v National City Bank Ltd* [1952] Ch 163, [1952] 1 All ER 49.
4    *IRC v Glasgow Musical Festival Association* 1926 SC 920 (society engaged in stimulating public interest in music and encouraging those members of the public who have musical gifts to cultivate them); *Shillington v Portadown Urban Council* [1911] 1 IR 247; *Re Henry Wood National Memorial Trust, Armstrong v Moiseiwitsch* (1965) 109 Sol Jo 876 (gift to build a concert hall). A gift to any musical or literary society in a district is not charitable: *Re King, Henderson v Cranmer* [1931] WN 232.
5    *Re Delius, Emanuel v Rosen* [1957] Ch 299, sub nom *Re Delius' Will Trusts, Emanuel v Rosen* [1957] 1 All ER 854.
6    *Royal Choral Society v IRC* [1943] 2 All ER 101, CA; and see *Re Levien, Lloyds Bank Ltd v Worshipful Co of Musicians* [1955] 3 All ER 35, [1955] 1 WLR 964 (individual singer).
7    *Re Levien, Lloyds Bank Ltd v Worshipful Co of Musicians* [1955] 3 All ER 35, [1955] 1 WLR 964.
8    *Re Shakespeare Memorial Trust, Earl of Lytton v A-G* [1923] 2 Ch 398.
9    *Re Shaw's Will Trusts, National Provincial Bank Ltd v National City Bank Ltd* [1952] Ch 163, [1952] 1 All ER 49.
10   *A-G v Flood* (1816) Hayes & Jo App xxi at xxxviii; and see *Brownjohn v Gale* [1869] WN 133.
11   *Yates v University College, London* (1873) 8 Ch App 454 (affd (1875) LR 7 HL 438); *Re British School of Egyptian Archeology, Murray v Public Trustee* [1954] 1 All ER 887, [1954] 1 WLR 546 (Egyptology).
12   *Re Koettgen's Will Trusts, Westminster Bank Ltd v Family Welfare Association Trustees Ltd* [1954] Ch 252, [1954] 1 All ER 581 (conceded).
13   *Construction Industry Training Board v A-G* [1971] 3 All ER 449, [1971] 1 WLR 1303; affd without dealing with this point [1973] Ch 173, [1972] 2 All ER 1339, CA.
14   *IRC v White and A-G* (1980) 55 TC 651.
15   *Re Arthur McDougall Fund Trusts, Thompson v Fitzgerald* [1956] 3 All ER 867, [1957] 1 WLR 81.
16   *Re Berridge, Berridge v Turner* (1890) 63 LT 470, CA.
17   *Re Osmund, Midland Bank Executor and Trustee Co Ltd v A-G* [1944] Ch 206, [1944] 1 All ER 262, CA.
18   *A-G v Stepney* (1804) 10 Ves 22.
19   *Re Hopkinson, Lloyds Bank Ltd v Baker* [1949] 1 All ER 346; *Bonar Law Memorial Trust v IRC* (1933) 49 TLR 220. Education of the public in the subject of militarism and disarmament was political and not a charitable object: *Southwood v A-G* [1998] 40 LS Gaz R 37, Times, 26 October; affd [2000] NLJR 1017, Times, 18 July, CA.
20   *Associated Artists Ltd v IRC* [1956] 2 All ER 583, [1956] 1 WLR 752.
21   See the cases cited in para 24 note 10 ante.
22   *Trustees of Sir GB Hunter (1922) C Trust v IRC* (1929) 45 TLR 344.
23   *Re Shaw, Public Trustee v Day* [1957] 1 All ER 745, [1957] 1 WLR 729; appeal dismissed by consent on terms [1958] 1 All ER 245n, CA.

## 27.  Preservation of objects of educational value.

**27.  Preservation of objects of educational value.** The preservation of objects of historic interest for public inspection is a charitable purpose[1], whether they be specimen buildings[1] or a collection of armour, antiques and articles of virtu[2], but the preservation intact of a collection of paintings, furniture and other objects as a museum to be open to the public is not charitable if the gift, carried out in accordance with the donor's intentions, is shown to have no possible educational value[3].

1    *Re Cranstoun, National Provincial Bank Ltd v Royal Society for the Encouragement of Arts, Manufactures and Commerce* [1932] 1 Ch 537. See the *Report of the Charity Commissioners for England and Wales for 1990* (HC Paper (1990–91) no 362) App A (b) (Settle and Carlisle Railway Trust registered as a charity).
2    *Re Spence, Barclays Bank Ltd v Stockton-on-Tees Corpn* [1938] Ch 96, [1937] 3 All ER 684.
3    *Re Pinion, Westminster Bank Ltd v Pinion* [1965] Ch 85, [1964] 1 All ER 890, CA.

**28.  Educational institutions.** The establishment and support of colleges[1], schools[2], professorships[3], fellowships[4], lectureships[5], scholarships[6] and prizes[7], and the providing of schoolmasters[8], are charitable purposes. Gifts to learned societies and institutions for the advancement of science[9], such as the Royal Society or the Royal Geographical Society[10], the Royal Literary Society[11], the Royal College of Surgeons[12] and the Zoological Society[13], are charitable; but institutions which, on the true construction of their constitutions, are for the benefit of a particular profession are not charitable[14]. A trust to buy books for Trinity College, Oxford, was treated as charitable on the ground that a large, well-assorted library tends to the promotion of education[15]. An institution established for the purpose of publishing material essential for the study of a learned science may be charitable, notwithstanding that the material is directly of use primarily to the members of a profession as a professional tool[16].

1   *Porter's Case* (1592) 1 Co Rep 24 b; *Plate v St John's College* (1638) Duke 77; *A-G v Comber* (1824) 2 Sim & St 93; *Christ's College, Cambridge, Case* (1757) 1 Wm Bl 90; *A-G v Whorwood* (1750) 1 Ves Sen 534 at 536 per Lord Hardwicke LC; *Walsh v Gladstone* (1843) 1 Ph 290 (Roman Catholic college); *R v Income Tax Special Comrs, ex p University College of North Wales* (1909) 78 LJKB 576, CA (college founded to give instruction in all the branches of a liberal education, except theology, and drawing revenue from a government grant, fees from pupils, donations, etc, as well as from investments); *Royal College of Surgeons of England v National Provincial Bank Ltd* [1952] AC 631, [1952] 1 All ER 984, HL (college incorporated for promotion and encouragement of the study and practice of the art and science of surgery); and see *Aberdeen University v Irvine* (1868) LR 1 Sc & Div 289, HL; *Wallis v Solicitor-General for New Zealand* [1903] AC 173, PC. On the other hand, the support of a staff training college for employees of a limited company who attend compulsorily is not charitable: *Re Leverhulme, Cooper v Leverhulme* [1943] 2 All ER 143.

2   *Gibbons v Maltyard* (1592) Poph 6; *Rugby School Case* (1626) Duke 80; *A-G v Nash* (1792) 3 Bro CC 588; *Kirkbank v Hudson* (1819) 7 Price 212; *A-G v Earl of Lonsdale* (1827) 1 Sim 105 at 109 per Leath V-C (school for gentlemen's sons); *Hartshorne v Nicholson* (1858) 26 Beav 58; *Re Sir Robert Peel's School at Tamworth, ex p Charity Comrs* (1868) 3 Ch App 543; *Re Allsop, Gell v Carver* (1884) 1 TLR 4 (school of art); *Re Gilchrist Educational Trust* [1895] 1 Ch 367; *Smith v Kerr* [1902] 1 Ch 774 at 778, CA, per Collins MR (ancient Inns of Chancery); *Re Hawkins, Walrond v Newton* (1906) 22 TLR 521 (school for religious teaching and elementary education); *Brighton College v Marriott* [1926] AC 192 at 204, HL, per Lord Blanesburgh (school for sons of noblemen and gentlemen); *The Abbey, Malvern Wells, Ltd v Ministry of Local Government and Planning* [1951] Ch 728, [1951] 2 All ER 154 (school for girls carried on by private company but dividends bound to be applied under trust deed in promoting work of school), distinguishing *Re Girls' Public Day School Trust Ltd, Girls' Public Day School Trust Ltd v Minister of Town and Country Planning* [1951] Ch 400 (school for girls carried on by private company, but certain shareholders not obliged to apply benefits for purposes of school: not charitable).

3   *Yates v University College, London* (1873) 8 Ch App 454 (affd (1875) LR 7 HL 438 (professorship of archaeology)); *Re Buckland, Buckland v Bennett* (1887) 22 LJNC 7 (professorship of economic fish culture).

4   *Jesus College Case* (1615) Duke 78.

5   *A-G v Cambridge Margaret and Regius Professors* (1682) 1 Vern 55.

6   *R v Newman* (1670) 1 Lev 284; *Re Levitt* (1885) 1 TLR 578; *University College of North Wales v Taylor* [1908] P 140, CA; *Re Williams, Taylor v Wales University* (1908) 24 TLR 716.

7   *Thompson v Thompson* (1844) 1 Coll 381 at 398 per Knight Bruce V-C; *Farrer v St Catharine's College, Cambridge* (1873) LR 16 Eq 19; *Re Mariette, Mariette v Aldenham School Governing Body* [1915] 2 Ch 284; *Chesterman v Federal Taxation Comr* [1926] AC 128, PC.

8   *Hynshaw v Morpeth Corpn* (1629) Duke 69; *A-G v Earl of Winchelsea* (1791) 3 Bro CC 373.

9   'Science' embraces a wide and ascertainable range of subjects: see *Weir v Crum-Brown* [1908] AC 162 at 168–169, HL, per Lord Macnaghten.

10  *Beaumont v Oliveira* (1869) 4 Ch App 309; *Royal Society of London and Thompson* (1881) 17 ChD 407.

11  *Thomas v Howell* (1874) LR 18 Eq 198.

12  *Royal College of Surgeons of England v National Provincial Bank Ltd* [1952] AC 631, [1952] 1 All ER 984, HL (college incorporated to promote study and practice of surgery charitable, although members obtained incidental professional advantages). explaining *Re Royal College of Surgeons of England* [1899] 1 QB 871, CA. See also *Royal College of Nursing v St Marylebone Corpn* [1959] 3 All ER 663, [1959] 1 WLR 1077, CA.

13  *Re Lopes, Bence-Jones v Zoological Society of London* [1931] 2 Ch 130; followed in *North of England Zoological Society v Chester RDC* [1959] 3 All ER 116, [1959] 1 WLR 773, CA.

14  Eg *Chartered Insurance Institute v London Corpn* [1957] 2 All ER 638, [1957] 1 WLR 867.

15  *A-G v Marchant* (1866) LR 3 Eq 424 at 430 per Kindersley V-C; and cf *Re Good, Harington v Watts* [1905] 2 Ch 60.

16  *Incorporated Council of Law Reporting for England and Wales v A-G* [1972] Ch 73, [1971] 3 All ER 1029, CA; though see also, as to law reporting, *Incorporated Council of Law Reporting for State of Queensland v Taxation Comr* (1971) 45 ALJR 552, Aust HC (charitable but not educational), following *Incorporated Council of Law Reporting for the State of Queensland v Federal Taxation Comr* (1924) 34 CLR 580, Aust HC.

**29. Games and tournaments.** The promotion of organised games at a boarding school and the provision of prizes for events in school sports are charitable purposes as being for the advancement of that part of the educational work of the school which has to do with the physical development of the students[1]. This has been extended to a trust to promote the physical education and development of pupils at schools and universities, as an addition to such part of their education as relates to their mental education, by providing facilities and assistance for association football and other games or sports[2]. The promotion of annual chess tournaments with prizes, open to young men resident in a particular city, is charitable, for the game possesses educational value[3].

A trust to provide an annual school treat has been held charitable as tending to the advancement of education[4]; and a trust to provide an annual outing for children of members of an ex-serviceman's club has been held charitable as serving an educational purpose[5]; but a gift to provide a pennyworth of sweets each for all children resident in a parish, unconfined to children who had attended school, has been held not charitable[6].

1  *Re Mariette, Mariette v Aldenham School Governing Body* [1915] 2 Ch 284; and see *Re Gray, Todd v Taylor* [1925] Ch 362 (regimental sporting fund: charitable as promoting efficiency of army). Cf *Re Nottage, Jones v Palmer* [1895] 2 Ch 649, CA (see para 58 post); *Re Harrow School Governors and Murray's Contract* [1927] 1 Ch 556 (provision of school sanatorium an educational purpose within the Education Act 1921 s 117 (repealed)); *Trustees of City of Belfast YMCA v Northern Ireland Valuation Comr* [1969] NI 3, CA.

2  *IRC v McMullen* [1981] AC 1, [1980] 1 All ER 884, HL.

3  *Re Dupree's Deed Trusts, Daley v Lloyds Bank* [1945] Ch 16, [1944] 2 All ER 443.

4  *Re Mellody, Brandwood v Haden* [1918] 1 Ch 228.

5  *Re Ward's Estate, Ward v Ward* (1937) 81 Sol Jo 397.

6  *Re Pleasants, Pleasants v A-G* (1923) 39 TLR 675.

### (iii)  Religious Purposes

**30. Advancement of religion.** The third division of charitable objects[1] is the advancement of religion. The words 'advancement of religion', as used to denote one class of legally charitable objects, mean the promotion of spiritual teaching in a wide sense, and the maintenance of the doctrines on which it rests and of the observances that serve to promote and manifest it[2]. To advance religion means to promote it, to spread its message ever wider among mankind, and to take some positive steps to sustain and increase religious belief; and these things are done in a variety of ways which may be comprehensively described as pastoral and missionary[3]. Religion is concerned with man's relations with God, and two of the essential attributes of religion are faith and worship: faith in a god and worship of that god[4].

1   Ie the third division mentioned by Lord Macnaghten in *Income Tax Special Purposes Comrs v Pemsel* [1891] AC 531 at 583, HL, per Lord Macnaghten: see para 13 ante. As to the four divisions of charity see para 13 ante.

2   *Keren Kayemeth Le Jisroel Ltd v IRC* [1931] 2 KB 465 at 477, CA, per Lord Hanworth MR; affd without defining 'advancement of religion' [1932] AC 650, HL (acquisition of land in Asia Minor for settling Jews: not a religious purpose).

3   *United Grand Lodge of Ancient Free and Accepted Masons of England v Holborn Borough Council* [1957] 3 All ER 281 at 285, [1957] 1 WLR 1080 at 1090 per Donovan J.

4   *Barralet v A-G* [1980] 3 All ER 918 at 924, sub nom *Re South Place Ethical Society, Barralet v A-G* [1980] 1 WLR 1565 at 1571–1572 per Dillon J, who added that, whether or not by way of an exception, Buddhism is accepted as being a religion.

**31. Religious purposes.** Gifts to 'religious societies' or for 'religious purposes' are prima facie charitable[1], but particular religious societies or purposes are not necessarily charitable[2]. A religious society can exist only as an organised body, with a written or oral constitution[3], devoted to promoting the spiritual teaching of that body[4], and is charitable only in so far as its objects serve charitable religious purposes and its powers are limited to ancillary ends, as distinct from subsidiary activities not in themselves religious or charitable[5].

Charitable religious purposes are those which tend directly or indirectly to the instruction or edification of the public[6]. The presence of the necessary element of public benefit is a question of fact to be determined by the court upon proof by means of evidence cognisable by it, and does not depend on doctrinal belief[7]. The celebration of a religious rite, such as the saying of masses, in public has been held to confer a sufficient public benefit because of the edifying and improving effect of such celebration on the members of the public who attend[8]. Moreover, where there is a gift for a religious purpose which could be carried out in a way which is beneficial to the public, but could also be carried out in a way which would not have a sufficient element of public benefit, the gift is to be construed as a gift to be carried out only by the methods that are charitable, all non-charitable methods being excluded[9].

Religious orders and communities are usually unincorporated associations, and unless property held by them is impressed with charitable trusts it is subject to the law relating to unincorporated associations[10]. The general principle that unincorporated associations supported by their members to provide benefits for themselves are not charitable does not apply with full force to associations for religious purposes[11]. A purely contemplative or secluded order or community is not charitable, there being no element of benefit to the public from their activity of which the court will take cognisance[12]; but a gift to a community which is in contact with the general public may satisfy the requirement of public benefit[13].

Gifts which contain a public religious element and are charitable in this way are gifts for 'promoting religion'[14], for the 'worship of God'[15], for the 'spread of the Gospel'[16] or of Christianity[17], or to be used 'in the service of my Lord and Master'[18], or 'for God's work'[19], for purposes 'having regard to the glory of God in the spiritual welfare of His creatures'[20], or for the distribution of Bibles[21] or of other religious books[22], or for organised religious pilgrimages[23], or for the maintenance of institutions formed for the promotion of religion, such as the United Society for the Propagation of the Gospel[24], the Protestant Alliance[25], the Irish Church Mission[26], the Church Missionary Society[27], the Society for Promoting Christian Knowledge[28], the Sunday School Association[29], the Young Men's Christian Association[30], the Church Army[31], the Salvation Army[32], or to 'the following religious societies namely...'[33]. Religion may be promoted by the provision of organised recreational facilities[34].

1  *Re White, White v White* [1893] 2 Ch 41 at 53, CA, per Lindley LJ; *Arnott v Arnott* [1906] 1 IR 127; *Dunne v Byrne* [1912] AC 407 at 411, PC; *Re Ward, Public Trustee v Ward* [1941] Ch 308, sub nom *Re Ward, Public Trustee v Berry* [1941] 2 All ER 125, CA (educational or charitable or religious purposes for Roman Catholics in the British Empire: charitable).

2  *Re White, White v White* [1893] 2 Ch 41 at 51–52, CA, per Lindley LJ; *MacLaughlin v Campbell* [1906] 1 IR 588; *Gilmour v Coats* [1949] AC 426 at 449, [1949] 1 All ER 848 at 856, HL, per Lord Simonds and at 454, 859 per Lord Reid (purposes of convent of strictly cloistered nuns not charitable).

3  *Re Thackrah, Thackrah v Wilson* [1939] 2 All ER 4 (the Oxford Group; a company called The Oxford Group was afterwards incorporated: see *Oxford Group v IRC* [1949] 2 All ER 537, CA; and note 5 infra).

4  *Keren Kayemeth Le Jisroel Ltd v IRC* [1931] 2 KB 465 at 469, CA, per Rowlatt J; approved on appeal [1932] AC 650, HL.

5  *Oxford Group v IRC* [1949] 2 All ER 537, CA (the advancement of the Christian religion in accordance with the principles of the Oxford Group Movement; the maintenance, support and assistance of the Oxford Group Movement in every way: not charitable); *Neville Estates Ltd v Madden* [1962] Ch 832, [1961] 3 All ER 769.

6  *Cocks v Manners* (1871) LR 12 Eq 574 at 585 per Wickens V-C; *Re Delany, Conoley v Quick* [1902] 2 Ch 642 at 648 per Farwell J; *Chesterman v Federal Taxation Comr* [1926] AC 128 at 131, PC; *Re Williams, Public Trustee v Williams* [1927] 2 Ch 283 at 287 per Clauson J; cf *Re Banfield, Lloyds Bank Ltd v Smith* [1968] 2 All ER 276, [1968] 1 WLR 846; *Re Warre's Will Trusts, Wort v Salisbury Diocesan Board of Finance* [1953] 2 All ER 99, [1953] 1 WLR 725. The study and dissemination of ethical principles and the cultivation of a rational religious sentiment is not a charitable religious purpose: *Barralet v A-G* [1980] 3 All ER 918, sub nom *Re South Place Ethical Society, Barralet v A-G* [1980] 1 WLR 1565.

7  *Re Coats' Trusts, Coats v Gilmour* [1948] Ch 340 at 347, [1948] 1 All ER 521 at 526, CA, per Lord Greene MR; on appeal sub nom *Gilmour v Coats* [1949] AC 426 at 446, [1949] 1 All ER 848 at 854, HL, per Lord Simonds. See also para 7 ante.

8  *Re Hetherington* [1990] Ch 1, sub nom *Re Hetherington, Gibbs v McDonnell* [1989] 2 All ER 129 (aliter in the case of the celebration of a religious rite in private); *Re Caus, Lindeboom v Camille* [1934] Ch 162; and see *Gilmour v Coats* [1949] AC 426, [1949] 1 All ER 848, HL.

9  *Re Hetherington* [1990] Ch 1, sub nom *Re Hetherington, Gibbs v McDonnell* [1989] 2 All ER 129.

10  See the extensive discussion in *Leahy v A-G for New South Wales* [1959] AC 457, [1959] 2 All ER 300, PC.

11  *Neville Estates Ltd v Madden* [1962] Ch 832, [1961] 3 All ER 769.

12  *Cocks v Manners* (1871) LR 12 Eq 574; *Gilmour v Coats* [1949] AC 426, [1949] 1 All ER 848, HL.

13  *Cocks v Manners* (1871) LR 12 Eq 574; *Re Braham, Daw v Samuel* (1892) 36 Sol Jo 712; *Re Charlesworth, Robinson v Archdeacon of Cleveland* (1910) 101 LT 908; *Neville Estates Ltd v Madden* [1962] Ch 832, [1961] 3 All ER 769; *Re Banfield, Lloyds Bank Ltd v Smith* [1968] 2 All ER 276, [1968] 1 WLR 846; though see *Re Warre's Will Trusts, Wort v Salisbury Diocesan Board of Finance* [1953] 2 All ER 99, [1953] 1 WLR 725 (sed quaere). See also *Northern Ireland Valuation Comr v Trustees of the Redemptorist Order* [1971] NI 114, CA.

14  *A-G v Stepney* (1804) 10 Ves 22; *Baker v Sutton* (1836) 1 Keen 224; *Wilkinson v Lindgren* (1870) 5 Ch App 570; contra, *Browne v Yeall* (1791) 7 Ves 50n, doubted in *Morice v Bishop of Durham* (1805) 10 Ves 522 at 539 per Lord Eldon LC and in *Re Macduff, Macduff v Macduff* [1896] 2 Ch 451 at 471–472, CA, per Rigby LJ. Cf *Dunne v Byrne* [1912] AC 407, PC, explained in *Re Bain, Public Trustee v Ross* [1930] 1 Ch 224 at 230, CA, per Lord Hanworth MR.

15  *A-G v Pearson* (1817) 3 Mer 353 at 409 per Lord Eldon LC.

16  *Re Lea, Lea v Cooke* (1887) 34 ChD 528.

17  *A-G v Stepney* (1804) 10 Ves 22; *A-G v London Corpn* (1790) 1 Ves 243; *Re Hood, Public Trustee v Hood* [1931] 1 Ch 240, CA (spreading Christian principles and minimising drink traffic).

18  *Powerscourt v Powerscourt* (1824) 1 Mol 616; *Felan v Russell* (1842) 4 I Eq R 701; *Re Darling, Farquhar v Darling* [1896] 1 Ch 50.

19  *Re Barker's Will Trusts, Barker v Crouch* (1948) 64 TLR 273.

20  *Townsend v Carus* (1844) 3 Hare 257.

21  *A-G v Stepney* (1804) 10 Ves 22.

22  *Thornton v Howe* (1862) 31 Beav 14; *Re Watson, Hobbs v Smith* [1973] 3 All ER 678, [1973] 1 WLR 1472.

23  *Re McCarthy* [1958] IR 311. It does not appear that this decision depended on any characteristic peculiar to Irish law.

24   *Re Maguire* (1870) LR 9 Eq 632.

25   *Re Delmar Charitable Trust* [1897] 2 Ch 163 (defence of doctrines of the Reformation).

26   *A-G v Becher* [1910] 2 IR 251 (conversion of Roman Catholics to Protestantism).

27   *Re Clergy Society* (1856) 2 K & J 615.

28   *Re Clergy Society* (1856) 2 K & J 615.

29   *R v Income Tax Special Comrs, ex p Essex Hall* [1911] 2 KB 434, CA.

30   *Trustees of City of Belfast YMCA v Northern Ireland Valuation Comr* [1969] NI 3, CA.

31   *Re Smith, Walker v Battersea General Hospital* (1938) 54 TLR 851; cf *Re Church Army* (1906) 75 LJCh 467,
     CA.

32   *Re Smith, Walker v Battersea General Hospital* (1938) 54 TLR 851; and see *Re Fowler, Fowler v Booth* (1914)
     31 TLR 102, CA.

33   *Re White, White v White* [1893] 2 Ch 41 at 53, CA. See *Re Macduff, Macduff v Macduff* [1896] 2 Ch 451
     at 466, CA, per Lindley LJ, and at 474, per Rigby LJ. See also *Grimond v Grimond* [1905] AC 124, HL
     (but note that this decision was on Scots law, and see the dissenting judgment of Lord Moncreiff in the
     Court of Session, [1905] AC 603n at 607). See also the consideration of *Re White, White v White* supra,
     in *Re Smith's Will Trusts, Barclays Bank Ltd v Mercantile Bank Ltd* [1961] 3 All ER 824, [1961] 1 WLR
     1387; on appeal [1962] 2 All ER 563, [1962] 1 WLR 763, CA.

34   *Trustees of City of Belfast YMCA v Northern Ireland Valuation Comr* [1969] NI 3, CA.


**32. Religious denominations.** There is no distinction in the matter of charity
between one sort of religion and another[1], or between one sect and another[2], or between
the established church and other churches[3]. It does not appear that a polytheistic religion
would be excluded[4]. Gifts to 'the Church of England'[5] or 'the Church of Rome'[6] for its
use are charitable. The advancement of the Roman Catholic and Jewish religions and of
all dissenting denominations, and the maintenance and benefit of their schools and
chapels are also charitable purposes[7]; the promotion of faith-healing is charitable, perhaps
as being for the advancement of religion[8]. However, gifts for denominational institutions
or purposes are not necessarily for religious purposes, and are therefore not charitable[9].


1   In addition to many Christian sects, the Charity Commissioners have registered trusts for the
    advancement of the Hindu, Sikh, Islamic and Buddhist religions. As to the Charity Commissioners see
    paras 486–512 post.

2   *Thornton v Howe* (1862) 31 Beav 14 at 19–20 per Romilly MR; *Re Watson, Hobbs v Smith* [1973] 3 All
    ER 678, [1973] 1 WLR 1472. As to the Unification Church see *Report of the Charity Commissioners for
    England and Wales for 1982* (HC Paper (1982–83) no 370) App C. The Attorney General appealed against
    the refusal of the Charity Commissioners to accede to his request to remove the trusts from the register,
    but the appeal was eventually discontinued: see the statement of the Attorney General in 126 HC Official
    Report (6th Series), 3 February 1988 cols 977–978, and the debate in the House of Lords, 493 HL
    Official Report (5th Series), 10 February 1988, col 247 et seq.

3   *Gilmour v Coats* [1949] AC 426 at 458, [1949] 1 All ER 848 at 862, HL, per Lord Reid.

4   In *Bowman v Secular Society Ltd* [1917] AC 406 at 448–450, HL, Lord Parker said only that a trust for the
    purpose of any kind of monotheistic theism would be a good charitable trust; however, nothing relating
    to polytheistic religion was said or was at issue in the case. *Yeap Cheah Neo v Ong Cheng Neo* (1875) LR
    6 PC 381 was not decided on this point but on the ground that the trust would not be in any way for
    the public benefit; it is analogous to the cases of trusts for the maintenance of tombs, which are not
    charitable: see para 54 post. In *Barralet v A-G* [1980] 3 All ER 918, sub nom *Re South Place Ethical Society,
    Barralet v A-G* [1980] 1 WLR 1565 Dillon J said that Buddhism was accepted by everyone as being a
    religion, though perhaps by way of exception to the proposition that an essential attribute of religion is
    faith in a god.

5   *Re Barnes, Simpson v Barnes* (1922) [1930] 2 Ch 80n.

6   *Re Schoales, Schoales v Schoales* [1930] 2 Ch 75.

7   See *Neville Estates Ltd v Madden* [1962] Ch 832, [1961] 3 All ER 769.

8   *Re Kerin* (1966) Times, 24 May, although on appeal the order in this case was wholly set aside by consent.
    However faith healing even without a religious element has been recognised as charitable: *Re Le Cren
    Clarke, Funnell v Stewart* [1996] 1 All ER 715, [1996] 1 WLR 288. It is doubtful whether the promotion

of spiritualism is charitable (cf *Re Hummeltenberg, Beatty v London Spiritualistic Alliance Ltd* [1923] 1 Ch 237), but the case cited may not be conclusive.

9   *MacLaughlin v Campbell* [1906] 1 IR 588 (Roman Catholic purposes: not charitable); *Re Stratton, Knapman v A-G* [1931] 1 Ch 197, CA (bequest to vicar for time being of parish for parochial institutions or purposes: not charitable); *Re Jackson, Midland Bank Executor and Trustee Co Ltd v Archbishop of Wales* [1930] 2 Ch 389 (bequest to archbishop to be applied in any manner he might think best for helping to carry on the work of the Church in Wales: not charitable); *Trustees of Cookstown Roman Catholic Church v IRC* (1953) 34 TC 350 (religious, educational and other parochial requirements: not charitable).

**33. Missionary purposes.** The expression 'missionary purposes' is ambiguous and may comprise objects which are not charitable[1]; but the context[2] or surrounding circumstances[3] may show that the testator used the expression in the more restricted, popular sense of Christian missionary work, in which sense a gift for missionary purposes is charitable[4].

1   *Re Rees, Jones v Evans* [1920] 2 Ch 59; *Scott v Brownrigg* (1881) 9 LR Ir 246.
2   *Dunne v Duignan* [1908] 1 IR 228 (where, also, the words 'foreign missions' were distinguished from 'missionary purposes'); *Re Hall, Hall v Hall* (1915) 31 TLR 396 (the City Mission in London); *Jackson v A-G* [1917] 1 IR 332 (Presbyterian missions and orphans); *Re Moon's Will Trusts, Foale v Gillians* [1948] 1 All ER 300 (bequest to trustees of named church for mission work in district served by it).
3   *Re Rees, Jones v Evans* [1920] 2 Ch 59; *Re Kenny, Clode v Andrews* (1907) 97 LT 130; *Re Redish, Armfield-Marrow v Bennet* (1909) 26 TLR 42; *Re Moon's Will Trusts, Foale v Gillians* [1948] 1 All ER 300.
4   See the cases cited in notes 2–3 supra; and *A-G v Becher* [1910] 2 IR 251; *Income Tax Special Purposes Comrs v Pemsel* [1891] AC 531, HL.

**34. Support of clergy and church purposes.** The following purposes are charitable: the establishment of a bishopric[1], the provision of clergy[2] or preachers[3], or the increase of their stipends[4], even though conditional upon their preaching certain doctrines[5] or a sermon in commemoration of the testator[6], or permitting free sittings[7], or wearing a black gown in the pulpit[8], or preaching to a particular class of persons such as prisoners[9], or making certain payments[10], or upon condition that the benefice is never held in plurality[11].

A society of clergymen holding meetings to discuss pastoral matters and education is charitable, so that a gift to pay the expenses of the members' dinners, in order to encourage attendance at meetings, was held charitable[12]; as were gifts for the augmentation of livings or for the purchase of advowsons for the spread of particular religious views[13], and trusts for the benefit of parishioners to nominate the parson[14].

A gift for the assistance of the education of candidates for holy orders[15], or of a rentcharge to a vicar so long as he forgoes tithes[16], or for pensioning a perpetual curate, is charitable[17]. A gift to a society for the relief of infirm, sick and aged Roman Catholic secular priests in a particular diocese[18], and a gift for active or retired evangelistic workers, including missionaries, required to be Protestants and to hold certain beliefs, tend to the advancement of religion and are charitable[19]. A gift of cottages to be used as rest homes for retired aged missionaries is charitable[20].

A gift to a parish church is charitable, having been regarded formerly as for the benefit of the parson and parishioners and their successors for ever[21], and latterly as for church purposes, that is, purposes connected with the services of the church[22]. Gifts, also, for such objects connected with a church as the minister shall think fit[23], for church expenses generally[24], or to provide a clerk[25], a sexton[26], an organist[27] or choristers[28], are charitable; but gifts for parish work or purposes[29] are not, and gifts for diocesan purposes[30] may not be, charitable, not being restricted to the advancement of religion. A gift for the benefit of the choir of a parish church serves to maintain and improve the religious services of the church, and so is for the advancement of religion and charitable[31]. In the context of a particular will, a church may be entitled under a gift to charitable institutions[32].

1    *A-G v Bishop of Chester* (1785) 1 Bro CC 444.

2    *Dundee Magistrates v Dundee Presbytery* (1861) 4 Macq 228, HL; *Pennington v Buckley* (1848) 6 Hare 451 at 453 per Wigram V-C (gift for benefit of unbeneficed curates).

3    *Pember v Knighton* (1639) Duke 381; *Penstred v Payer* (1639) Duke 381; *Grieves v Case* (1792) 4 Bro CC 67; cf *Re Braham, Daw v Samuel* (1892) 36 Sol Jo 712 (reader and lecturer for Hebrew congregation).

4    *A-G v Brereton* (1752) 2 Ves Sen 425; *A-G v Sparks* (1753) Amb 201; *Middleton v Clitherow* (1798) 3 Ves 734; *Widmore v Woodroffe* (1766) Amb 636 (Queen Anne's Bounty); *Gibson v Representative Church Body* (1881) 9 LR Ir 1; *Re Maguire* (1870) LR 9 Eq 632 (gift to Additional Curates' Aid Society); *Re Macnamara, Hewitt v Jeans* (1911) 104 LT 771.

5    *A-G v Molland* (1832) 1 You 562.

6    *Durour v Motteux* (1749) 1 Ves Sen 320; *Re Parker's Charity* (1863) 32 Beav 654; cf *Re Arber, Taylor v Shelton* (1919) Times, 13 December (annual payment to church bellringers in consideration of their ringing the bells on the anniversary of testator's death: not charitable).

7    *Re Randell, Randell v Dixon* (1888) 38 ChD 213.

8    *Re Robinson, Wright v Tugwell* [1897] 1 Ch 85, CA. As to subsequent removal of condition see *Re Robinson, Wright v Tugwell* [1923] 2 Ch 332; and para 171 post.

9    *Re Hussey's Charities, Cheyne v Apreece, Symons v Delaval* (1861) 30 LJCh 491.

10   *Re Corcoran, Corcoran v O'Kane* [1913] 1 IR 1.

11   *Re Macnamara, Hewitt v Jeans* (1911) 104 LT 771.

12   *Re Charlesworth, Robinson v Archdeacon of Cleveland* (1910) 101 LT 908.

13   *Re Hunter, Hood v A-G* [1897] 2 Ch 105, CA. However, such gifts are not charitable if no trust of the advowson is declared, on which ground the House of Lords reversed this decision: *Hunter v A-G* [1899] AC 309, HL. The sale of advowsons is now prohibited: see the Patronage (Benefices) Measure 1986 s 3(1); and ECCLESIASTICAL LAW.

14   *Re St Stephen, Coleman Street, Re St Mary the Virgin, Aldermanbury* (1888) 39 ChD 492; *Hunter v A-G* [1899] AC 309 at 322, HL, per Lord Davey; *Foley v A-G* (1721) 7 Bro Parl Cas 249, HL; *A-G v Scott* (1750) 1 Ves Sen 413; *A-G v Webster* (1875) LR 20 Eq 483 at 491 per Jessel MR. Cf on the other hand *A-G v Parker* (1747) 1 Ves Sen 43; *A-G v Forster* (1804) 10 Ves 335 at 340 per Lord Eldon LC; *A-G v Newcombe* (1807) 14 Ves 1 at 10 per Lord Eldon LC, where such a trust was considered valid but not charitable. See also *Edenborough v Archbishop of Canterbury* (1826) 2 Russ 93. However, a trust of an advowson merely to appoint a fit and proper person to fill the vacant living, without any beneficiary, is not charitable: *Re Church Patronage Trust, Laurie v A-G* [1904] 2 Ch 643, CA.

15   *Re Williams, Public Trustee v Williams* [1927] 2 Ch 283.

16   *Milbank v Lambert* (1860) 28 Beav 206. As to tithes see ECCLESIASTICAL LAW vol 14 para 1209 et seq.

17   *A-G v Parker* (1747) 1 Ves Sen 43. See also *A-G v Brereton* (1752) 2 Ves Sen 425 at 426–427 per Lord Hardwicke LC.

18   *Re Forster, Gellatly v Palmer* [1939] Ch 22, [1938] 3 All ER 767. This gift could not be upheld as being for the relief of poverty.

19   *Re Mylne, Potter v Dow* [1941] Ch 204, [1941] 1 All ER 405. Cf *Baptist Union of Ireland (Northern) Corpn Ltd v IRC* [1945] NI 99 (fund for Baptist ministers who paid subscriptions and their widows and orphans: charitable).

20   *Re White's Will Trusts, Barrow v Gillard* [1955] Ch 188, [1954] 2 All ER 620.

21   *Re St Andrew, Holborn* (undated) cited in *Cheeseman v Partridge* (1739) 1 Atk 436 at 437.

22   *Re Gare, Filmer v Carter* [1952] Ch 80, [1951] 2 All ER 863. See further para 111 post.

23   *Re Bain, Public Trustee v Ross* [1930] 1 Ch 224, CA (gift to vicar for such objects connected with the church as he should think fit; church objects and parochial activities distinguished); *Re Martley, Simpson v Cardinal Bourne* (1931) 47 TLR 392 (for the benefit of the work of the cathedral); *Re Eastes, Pain v Paxon* [1948] Ch 257, [1948] 1 All ER 536 (gift to vicar and churchwardens of a particular church for any purposes in connection with the church). However, see also *Re Stratton, Knapman v A-G* [1931] 1 Ch 197, CA (gift to vicar of parish 'for parochial institutions or purposes': not charitable); *Re Davies, Lloyds Bank Ltd v Mostyn* (1932) 49 TLR 5, CA (gift to archbishop for work connected with the Roman Catholic church in the archdiocese: not charitable); *Farley v Westminster Bank Ltd* [1939] AC 430, [1939] 3 All ER 491, HL (gift to vicars and churchwardens of named churches for parish work: not charitable).

24   *Re Scowcroft, Ormrod v Wilkinson* [1898] 2 Ch 638 at 642 per Stirling J.

25  *Durour v Motteux* (1749) 1 Ves Sen 320.

26  *Durour v Motteux* (1749) 1 Ves Sen 320.

27  *A-G v Oakaver* (1736) cited in 1 Ves Sen 536; *Re Scowcroft, Ormrod v Wilkinson* [1898] 2 Ch 638. Cf *Re Arber, Taylor v Shelton* (1919) Times, 13 December (see note 6 supra).

28  *Turner v Ogden* (1787) 1 Cox Eq Cas 316. The contrary decision in *A-G v Oakaver* (1736) cited in 1 Ves Sen 536 was discussed and not followed in *Re Royce, Turner v Wormald* [1940] Ch 514, [1940] 2 All ER 291.

29  *Farley v Westminster Bank Ltd* [1939] AC 430, [1939] 3 All ER 491, HL (work); *Trustees of Cookstown Roman Catholic Church v IRC* (1953) 34 TC 350; *Re Stratton, Knapman v A-G* [1931] 1 Ch 197, CA.

30  *Re Rumball, Sherlock v Allan* [1956] Ch 105, [1955] 3 All ER 71, CA; *Re Van Wart, Ramsay v Bourne* (1911) Times, 17 February (this report is misleading: see the order made in the case, set out at [1956] Ch 119, [1955] 3 All ER 78); *Re Beddy* (1953) (unreported), discussed in *Re Rumball, Sherlock v Allan* supra; *Re Davies, Lloyds Bank Ltd v Mostyn* (1932) 49 TLR 5, CA; contra, *Re Macgregor, Thompson v Ashton* (1932) 32 SR NSW 483 (gift for diocesan purposes charitable).

31  *Re Royce, Turner v Wormald* [1940] Ch 514, [1940] 2 All ER 291; and see *Re Hendry, Watson v Blakeney* (1887) 56 LT 908 (choir fund apparently charitable).

32  *Re Nesbitt's Will Trusts, Dr Barnardo's Homes National Incorporated Association v United Newcastle-upon-Tyne Hospitals Board of Governors* [1953] 1 All ER 936, [1953] 1 WLR 595.

**35. Gifts to holders of religious offices.** If a gift is expressed to be made to the holder of a particular religious office for the time being, it must be determined whether it is intended as a beneficial gift to the person holding that office when the gift takes effect[1], or whether it is to be held by that person and his successors in office as trustees[2].

If the latter is found to be the case, and if the duties and functions of the office are charitable in nature, the gift will be interpreted as a gift on trust for the charitable purposes inherent in the office[3]. Thus the following gifts are charitable: gifts to a minister and his successors[4], to a dissenting minister for the time being[5], to a vicar and churchwardens for the time being to be applied as they think fit, without any specified object[6], to a vicar[7], and to women holding certain offices in a religious order or their successors[8].

Where the gift is not merely expressed to be to the holder of a religious office and other words are added which might themselves indicate the nature of the trusts imposed by the gift, the court has to decide whether the words following the gift are intended merely to indicate that, within the scope of the trusts properly appropriate to the nature of the office by which the donee is described, the discretion is entirely the donee's, or whether by the added words the donor is himself intending to state, or at least to indicate, the trusts on which the donee is to hold the property[9].

In the former case the added words do not render inapplicable the prima facie presumption that the gift is charitable; in the latter case the question is whether the trusts indicated by the added words are themselves exclusively charitable. Thus the following gifts are charitable: gifts to a named vicar for his work[10], to the vicar of a named church to be used for his work in the parish[11], to a Roman Catholic archbishop to be used for such purposes as he should think fit[12], one to be applied as directed by a bishop for the general purposes of his diocese[13], and a gift to the editors of a missionary periodical for such objects as they might think fit, being construed as intended for the benefit of associated missionary activities for which they distributed gifts[14]. On the other hand, a gift to a Roman Catholic archbishop and his successors to be used and expended wholly or in part as he might judge most conducive to religion in the diocese is not charitable[15], for where the trusts of a gift are clearly set out they cannot be modified or limited in scope by reference to the position or character of the trustee[16]. Where the holder of the charitable office in question is not given sole control over the application of the property, the presumption that the purposes of the gift are the charitable purposes of the office does not apply[17].

1   See eg *Re Meehan, Tobin and Tobin v Cohalan and Meehan* [1960] IR 82 (gift to a bishop for the time being absolutely: an 'O'Hagan clause', ie designed to catch any charitable legacies which might fail under the law of mortmain or otherwise, so that the purpose of the clause would be frustrated if it had been held to be a gift on charitable trusts); see also *Re Van Wart, Ramsay v Bourne* (1911) Times, 17 February, as explained in *Re Rumball, Sherlock v Allan* [1956] Ch 105, [1955] 3 All ER 71, CA.

2   In the absence of special considerations such as those indicated in note 1 supra, a gift in virtue of office must be a gift on trust: see *Re Flinn, Public Trustee v Flinn* [1948] Ch 241 at 244, [1948] 1 All ER 541 at 542 per Jenkins J.

3   *Re Flinn, Public Trustee v Flinn* [1948] Ch 241, [1948] 1 All ER 541. The principle is not confined to the holders of religious offices, but most of the cases are in this field. See, however, *Re Spensley's Will Trusts, Barclays Bank Ltd v Staughton* [1954] Ch 233, [1954] 1 All ER 178, CA (National Trust); *Re Endacott, Corpe v Endacott* [1960] Ch 232, [1959] 3 All ER 562, CA (parish council).

4   *A-G v Molland* (1832) 1 You 562; *Thornber v Wilson* (1855) 3 Drew 245 (gift to the Roman Catholic minister of a particular chapel for a period of years); *Re Davies, Lloyd v Cardigan County Council* [1915] 1 Ch 543.

5   *A-G v Cock* (1751) 2 Ves Sen 273; *A-G v Sparks* (1753) Amb 201. The same does not apply to a gift for the particular minister in office: *Doe d Phillips v Aldridge* (1791) 4 Term Rep 264.

6   *Re Garrard, Gordon v Craigie* [1907] 1 Ch 382; see also *Thornber v Wilson* (1855) 3 Drew 245; *Re Delany, Conoley v Quick* [1902] 2 Ch 642 at 646 per Farwell J; and distinguish cases where the gift fails for uncertainty: *Fowler v Fowler* (1864) 33 Beav 616.

7   *Re Simson, Fowler v Tinley* [1946] Ch 299, [1946] 2 All ER 220.

8   *Re Delany, Conoley v Quick* [1902] 2 Ch 642.

9   See *Re Rumball, Sherlock v Allan* [1956] Ch 105 at 115, [1955] 3 All ER 71 at 75, CA, per Lord Evershed MR. See also *Re Spensley's Will Trusts, Barclays Bank Ltd v Staughton* [1954] Ch 233, [1954] 1 All ER 178, CA.

10  See *Re Simson, Fowler v Tinley* [1946] Ch 299, [1946] 2 All ER 220.

11  *Re Simson, Fowler v Tinley* [1946] Ch 299, [1946] 2 All ER 220, distinguishing *Farley v Westminster Bank Ltd* [1939] AC 430, [1939] 3 All ER 491, HL.

12  *Re Flinn, Public Trustee v Flinn* [1948] Ch 241, [1948] 1 All ER 541, distinguishing *Re Davidson, Minty v Bourne* [1909] 1 Ch 567, CA (gift to Roman Catholic archbishop for the time being to be distributed between charitable, religious or other societies, institutions, persons or objects in connection with the Roman Catholic faith in England); *Re Rumball, Sherlock v Allan* [1956] Ch 105, [1955] 3 All ER 71, CA (gift to bishop for the time being to be used as he thinks fit in his diocese: charitable).

13  *Re Money's Will Trusts, Mawdesley v Jerusalem and East Mission* (1965) 109 Sol Jo 68 (where the principle was applied even though the bishop was not the trustee of the fund, since his power to direct the purposes for which the property should be applied was clearly a fiduciary one). See also the comments of Jenkins LJ in *Re Rumball, Sherlock v Allan* [1956] Ch 105 at 124, [1955] 3 All ER 71 at 81, CA, on *Re Beddy* (1953, unreported).

14  *Re Norman, Andrew v Vine* [1947] Ch 349, [1947] 1 All ER 400.

15  *Dunne v Byrne* [1912] AC 407, PC; and see *Re Davidson, Minty v Bourne* [1909] 1 Ch 567, CA; *Re Stratton, Knapman v A-G* [1931] 1 Ch 197, CA; *Re Davies, Lloyds Bank Ltd v Mostyn* (1932) 49 TLR 5, CA; *Farley v Westminster Bank Ltd* [1939] AC 430, [1939] 3 All ER 491, HL.

16  *Dunne v Byrne* [1912] AC 407 at 410, PC, per Lord Macnaghten. Conversely, where the expressed trusts are charitable they cannot be rendered non-charitable by the character of the trustees: *Re Arthur McDougall Fund Trusts, Thompson v Fitzgerald* [1956] 3 All ER 867, [1957] 1 WLR 81; *Construction Industry Training Board v A-G* [1971] 3 All ER 449, [1971] 1 WLR 1303; affd without dealing with this point [1973] Ch 173, [1972] 2 All ER 1339, CA.

17  *Re Spensley's Will Trusts, Barclays Bank Ltd v Staughton* [1954] Ch 233, [1954] 1 All ER 178, CA, disapproving on this point Vaisey J at [1952] Ch 886, [1952] 2 All ER 49.

## 36. Religious buildings and burial grounds. The       following     are     charitable purposes: the provision, maintenance, repair and ornamentation of a parish church[1] or of a church, chapel or meeting house of any particular Christian denomination[2], the upkeep of a chapel and Sunday school, which may include maintaining both the fabric and the

services[3], the provision or repair of a chancel[4], spire[5], organ[6], bells[7], gallery[8], clock[9], stained-glass window[10], or monument in a church[11] and the continuation of the seating in a parish church[12].

Gifts for maintaining or providing a churchyard[13] or cemetery[14], or a burial ground for a particular sect[15], or for headstones to the graves of certain almshouse pensioners[16], are also charitable, as is the repair of a parsonage[17].

A company established to promote cheap and sanitary methods of disposing of the dead, in particular cremation, has been held to be established for charitable purposes by analogy with the cases on burial[18], but this probably falls within the fourth division of charitable objects[19] under the preamble to the ancient statute of Elizabeth I[20] rather than the advancement of religion.

1  *Re Robertson, Colin v Chamberlin* [1930] 2 Ch 71; *Re Parker* (1859) 4 H & N 666; *Clephane v Edinburgh Magistrates* (1864) 4 Macq 603, HL; *A-G v Ruper* (1722) 2 P Wms 125; *A-G v Brown* (1818) 1 Swan 265 at 297 per Lord Eldon LC; *A-G v Vivian* (1826) 1 Russ 226; *A-G v Love* (1857) 23 Beav 499; *Re Donington Church Estate, Re Charitable Trusts Act 1853* (1860) 2 LT 10; *Re Church Estate Charity, Wandsworth* (1871) 6 Ch App 296; *A-G v Dartmouth Corpn* (1883) 48 LT 933; *Re St Alphage, London Wall* (1888) 59 LT 614; *Re Eighmie, Colbourne v Wilks* [1935] Ch 524 (maintenance of parish church and its decorations).
2  *Re Manser, A-G v Lucas* [1905] 1 Ch 68 at 73 per Warrington J; *Re Williams, James v Williams* (1910) 26 TLR 307 (liquidation of debts on Congregational chapels); *Holmes v A-G* (1981) Times, 12 February (meeting room of the Exclusive Brethren, formerly the Plymouth Brethren); *Broxtowe Borough Council v Birch* [1981] RA 215.
3  *Re Strickland's Will Trusts, National Guarantee and Suretyship Association Ltd v Maidment* [1936] 3 All ER 1027.
4  *Hoare v Osborne* (1866) LR 1 Eq 585.
5  *Re Palatine Estate Charity* (1888) 39 ChD 54.
6  *A-G v Oakaver* (1736) cited in 1 Ves Sen 536.
7  *Turner v Ogden* (1787) 1 Cox Eq Cas 316; and see *Re Palatine Estate Charity* (1888) 39 ChD 54 at 59 per Stirling J.
8  *A-G v Day* [1900] 1 Ch 31.
9  *Re Church Estate Charity, Wandsworth* (1871) 6 Ch App 296; *Re Hendry, Watson v Blakeney* (1887) 56 LT 908.
10 *Re King, Kerr v Bradley* [1923] 1 Ch 243.
11 *Hoare v Osborne* (1866) LR 1 Eq 585; *Re Rigley's Trusts* (1866) 36 LJCh 147; *Re Barker, Sherrington v Dean and Chapter of St Paul's Cathedral* (1909) 25 TLR 753. As to tombs and monuments not forming part of a church see para 54 post.
12 *Re Raine, Walton v A-G* [1956] Ch 417, [1956] 1 All ER 355.
13 *Re Vaughan, Vaughan v Thomas* (1886) 33 ChD 187; *Re Douglas, Douglas v Simpson* [1905] 1 Ch 279; *Re Eighmie, Colbourne v Wilks* [1935] Ch 524 (bequest to rector and churchwardens for keeping burial ground and private monument in it in repair; grave and monument in cemetery adjoining churchyard which had been closed for burials).
14 *A-G v Blizard* (1855) 21 Beav 233.
15 *Re Manser, A-G v Lucas* [1905] 1 Ch 68 (bequest for maintenance of Quaker burial ground).
16 *Re Pardoe, McLaughlin v A-G* [1906] 2 Ch 184. As to private tombs see para 54 post.
17 *A-G v Bishop of Chester* (1785) 1 Bro CC 444.
18 *Scottish Burial Reform and Cremation Society Ltd v Glasgow Corpn* [1968] AC 138, [1967] 3 All ER 215, HL.
19 As to the fourth division of charitable objects see para 37 et seq post.
20 43 Eliz 1 c 4 (1601) (now wholly repealed: see para 2 note 7 ante): see paras 12–13 ante.

### (iv)  Other Beneficial Public Purposes

**37. Purposes beneficial to the community.** The fourth division of charitable objects comprises other purposes beneficial to the community[1], or for the advancement of objects of general public utility[2].

Not all such purposes are charitable: to be so, the purposes must fall within the 'spirit and intendment' of the preamble to the statute of Elizabeth I[3]. Historically, in order to find whether a particular purpose came within that spirit and intendment, the courts sought to find an analogy with purposes mentioned in the preamble itself[4], or with purposes previously held to be within its spirit and intendment[5]. It now appears that, even in the absence of such analogy, objects beneficial to the public, or of public utility, are prima facie within the spirit and intendment of the preamble and, in the absence of any ground for holding that they are outside its spirit and intendment, are therefore charitable in law[6]. Establishing that such an object is of actual benefit to the public may involve consideration of cognisable evidence directed to that point[7].

The community must be a definite community or section of the community[8]; it must be identifiable as such[9]; it must be of appreciable importance[10]; and it must not depend on any personal relationship to a particular individual or individuals[11].

1   Ie the fourth division mentioned by Lord Macnaghten in *Income Tax Special Purposes Comrs v Pemsel* [1891] AC 531 at 583, HL, per Lord Macnaghten: see para 13 ante. As to the four divisions of charity see para 13 ante. As to the meaning of 'community' see the text and notes 8–11 infra; and paras 38–39 post.

2   *Morice v Bishop of Durham* (1804) 9 Ves 399; on appeal (1805) 10 Ves 522. The public element is essential: see para 8 ante.

3   43 Eliz 1 c 4 (1601) (now wholly repealed: see para 2 note 7 ante). See *Re Macduff, Macduff v Macduff* [1896] 2 Ch 451 at 466–467, CA, per Lindley LJ, and at 473–475 per Rigby LJ; *Langham v Peterson* (1903) 87 LT 744; *Re Good, Harington v Watts* [1905] 2 Ch 60 at 66 per Farwell J; *A-G v National Provincial and Union Bank of England* [1924] AC 262, HL; *General Medical Council v IRC* (1928) 97 LJKB 578, CA.

4   See para 12 ante.

5   See the cases cited in note 3 supra; and *Williams' Trustees v IRC* [1947] AC 447, [1947] 1 All ER 513, HL; *Re Strakosch, Temperley v A-G* [1949] Ch 529, [1949] 2 All ER 6, CA; *Incorporated Council of Law Reporting for England and Wales v A-G* [1971] Ch 626, [1971] 1 All ER 436.

6   *Incorporated Council of Law Reporting for England and Wales v A-G* [1972] Ch 73 at 88, 95, 104, [1971] 3 All ER 1029 at 1036, CA, per Russell LJ, at 1042 per Sachs LJ, and at 1048 per Buckley LJ; *Scottish Burial Reform and Cremation Society Ltd v Glasgow Corpn* [1968] AC 138, [1967] 3 All ER 215, HL; *IRC v McMullen* [1979] 1 All ER 588, [1979] 1 WLR 130, CA (revsd, without discussing this point [1981] AC 1, [1980] 1 All ER 884, HL). In *Barralet v A-G* [1980] 3 All ER 918, sub nom *Re South Place Ethical Society, Barralet v A-G* [1980] 1 WLR 1565, however, Dillon J doubted whether this more generous approach is permissible in the light of earlier House of Lords decisions such as *Williams' Trustees v IRC* [1947] AC 447, [1947] 1 All ER 513, HL. See also *A-G v Heelis* (1824) 2 Sim & St 67; *Brisbane City Council v A-G for Queensland* [1979] AC 411 at 422, [1978] 3 All ER 30 at 33, PC.

7   See eg *Charitable Status: Public Concern at Work (1993)* Decisions of the Charity Commissioners (1994) vol 2 p 5, where the Charity Commissioners sought views from the Confederation of British Industry, the Securities and Investment Board and such major companies on the question of actual benefit. As to the Charity Commissioners see paras 486–512 post.

8   *Verge v Somerville* [1924] AC 496 at 499, PC.

9   *Keren Kayemeth Le Jisroel Ltd v IRC* [1932] AC 650, HL; *Williams' Trustees v IRC* [1947] AC 447, [1947] 1 All ER 513, HL.

10  *National Anti-Vivisection Society v IRC* [1948] AC 31 at 65, [1947] 2 All ER 217 at 233, HL, per Lord Simonds; *Verge v Somerville* [1924] AC 496 at 499, PC.

11  *Oppenheim v Tobacco Securities Trust Co Ltd* [1951] AC 297 at 306, [1951] 1 All ER 31 at 34, HL, per Lord Simonds; *Re Compton, Powell v Compton* [1945] Ch 123, [1945] 1 All ER 198, CA.

**38. General benefit of community.** A gift in general terms for the benefit of a country or district, not indicating a specific purpose, is charitable, apparently on the principle that it is impliedly for purposes recognised by the law as charitable[1]. Examples are gifts 'to my country England'[2]; and gifts, whether general or for specific purposes, for the benefit of the inhabitants of a county[3], town[4], ward[5] or parish[6], and gifts in general terms for the benefit of the inhabitants, or a class of the inhabitants[7], of particular localities[8], for example a borough[9], city[10], town[11], village[12], or parish[13], or the occupiers of certain cottages on a manor[14], or the free inhabitants of ancient tenements in a particular place[15].

However, a trust for defined purposes which are not charitable is not rendered charitable by the fact that the area of benefit is a particular locality[16].

1   *Williams' Trustees v IRC* [1947] AC 447 at 459, [1947] 1 All ER 513 at 521, HL, per Lord Simonds; and see *Re Strakosch, Temperley v A-G* [1949] Ch 529, [1949] 2 All ER 6, CA. The leading case is *Goodman v Saltash Corpn* (1882) 7 App Cas 633, HL (applied in *Peggs v Lamb* [1994] Ch 172, [1994] 2 All ER 15), the decision in which was later described by Lord Ashbourne in *Harris v Earl of Chesterfield* [1911] AC 623 at 633, HL, as a splendid effort of equitable imagination. See also *Alfred F Beckett Ltd v Lyons* [1967] Ch 449, [1967] 1 All ER 833, CA.

2   *Re Smith, Public Trustee v Smith* [1932] 1 Ch 153, CA, explaining dicta in *A-G v National Provincial and Union Bank of England* [1924] AC 262, HL.

3   *A-G v Earl of Lonsdale* (1827) 1 Sim 105.

4   *Wrexham Corpn v Tamplin* (1873) 21 WR 768; *A-G v Dartmouth Corpn* (1883) 48 LT 933; *Re Baynes, Public Trustee v Leven Corpn* [1944] 2 All ER 597 (gift to Common Good Fund of town council in Scotland); but see para 3 ante.

5   *Baylis v A-G* (1741) 2 Atk 239.

6   *West v Knight* (1669) 1 Cas in Ch 134; *Dolan v Macdermot* (1868) 3 Ch App 676; *A-G v Lord Hotham* (1823) Turn & R 209; *A-G v Earl of Lonsdale* (1827) 1 Sim 105; *A-G v Webster* (1875) LR 20 Eq 483; *Re St Bride's, Fleet Street, Church or Parish Estate* (1877) 35 ChD 147n; *Re St Botolph Without Bishopsgate Parish Estates* (1887) 35 ChD 142; *Re St Alphage, London Wall* (1888) 59 LT 614; *Re St Stephen, Coleman Street, Re St Mary the Virgin, Aldermanbury* (1888) 39 ChD 492; *Re Parish of St Nicholas Acons* (1889) 60 LT 532; *Re Norton's Will Trusts, Lightfoot v Goldson* [1948] 2 All ER 842 (any use trustees think best for benefit of church and parish, but preferably for certain purposes that might, however, prove impracticable).

7   Eg the native inhabitants of Dacca (*Mitford v Reynolds* (1842) 1 Ph 185), the freemen of a borough (*Re Norwich Town Close Estate Charity* (1888) 40 ChD 298, CA), or the schoolchildren of a town (*Re Mellody, Brandwood v Haden* [1918] 1 Ch 228), or, possibly, the 21 oldest inhabitants of a locality without a means test (*Re Shepherd, Firman v Shepherd* (1952) unreported; see para 23 ante).

8   See *Goodman v Saltash Corpn* (1882) 7 App Cas 633 at 642, HL, per Lord Selborne LC; *Peggs v Lamb* [1994] Ch 172, [1994] 2 All ER 15.

9   *Re Norwich Town Close Estate Charity* (1888) 40 ChD 298, CA; and see *Stanley v Norwich Corpn* (1887) 3 TLR 506; but cf *Prestney v Colchester Corpn and A-G* (1882) 21 ChD 111 at 119 per Hall V-C.

10  *A-G v Carlisle Corpn* (1828) 2 Sim 437; *Mitford v Reynolds* (1842) 1 Ph 185.

11  *A-G v Cashel Corpn* (1842) 3 Dr & War 294; *A-G v Galway Corpn* (1829) 1 Mol 95; *Shillington v Portadown Urban Council* [1911] 1 IR 247.

12  *Wright v Hobert* (1723) 9 Mod Rep 64.

13  *Re Mann, Hardy v A-G* [1903] 1 Ch 232.

14  *A-G v Meyrick* [1893] AC 1, HL. In *Wilson v Barnes* (1886) 38 ChD 507, CA, a gift for the benefit of the copyhold tenants of a manor was held charitable; but copyhold tenure has been abolished (see CUSTOM AND USAGE vol 12(1) (Reissue) para 643).

15  *Goodman v Saltash Corpn* (1882) 7 App Cas 633, HL.

16  *Re Sanders' Will Trusts, Public Trustee v McLaren* [1954] Ch 265, [1954] 1 All ER 667; and see *Re Gwyon, Public Trustee v A-G* [1930] 1 Ch 255 at 261 per Eve J, applying Lord Shaw's dictum in the Scottish case of *Houston v Burns* [1918] AC 337 at 349, HL; *Re King, Henderson v Cranmer* [1931] WN 232; *D'Aguiar v Guyana IRC* (1970) 49 ATC 33, PC. However, a gift for public purposes in a town may be charitable even though, in general, public purposes are not exclusively charitable: see *Re Spence, Barclays Bank Ltd v Stockton-on-Tees Corpn* [1938] Ch 96, [1937] 3 All ER 684; *Re Allen, Hargreaves v Taylor* [1905] 2 Ch 400. See also *A-G of the Cayman Islands v Wahr Hansen* [2001] 1 AC 75, [2000] 3 All ER 642, PC.

**39. Benefit of section of community.** The benefit of a charitable trust of this class[1] need not extend to the whole community, provided that the class to be benefited is substantial enough to give the trust a public character[2]. What is a sufficiently substantial class may vary according to the nature of the benefit to be provided[3], and it is particularly important in considering this category to keep in mind the necessary element of general public utility[4].

1   Ie the fourth division mentioned by Lord Macnaghten in *Income Tax Special Purposes Comrs v Pemsel* [1891] AC 531 at 583, HL, per Lord Macnaghten: see para 13 ante.
2   See para 8 ante.
3   *IRC v Baddeley* [1955] AC 572 at 615, [1955] 1 All ER 525 at 549, HL, per Lord Somervell of Harrow.
4   *IRC v Baddeley* [1955] AC 572 at 590, [1955] 1 All ER 525 at 532, HL, per Viscount Simonds.


**40. Objects of practical utility.** Objects of general public utility or benefit of a practical kind mentioned in the preamble to the statute of Elizabeth I[1] include the repair of bridges, ports, highways and similar instances[2]. These, together with many purposes which have been held charitable by analogy, would normally be provided now by some public authority as public works[3], services or facilities[4], and some benefits which would be charitable have been to some extent superseded in other ways[5], but gifts for such purposes do not thereby cease to be charitable. Other facilities the provision of which is charitable include a library[6], museum[7], public hall[8], reading room[9], botanical garden[10], observatory[11], the means for public recreation[12], or a war memorial of a useful character[13], where the facilities are open to the public[14]. To provide a lifeboat[15] is charitable, as are gifts to the Royal National Lifeboat Institution[16] and the Royal Humane Society[17], and funds for the relief of victims of air raids[18] or floods[19]. To improve the efficiency of charities by the provision to charitable organisations of advice and assistance in the field of information technology is also charitable[20].

The preamble to the statute of Elizabeth I includes the aid or ease of poor inhabitants concerning payment of taxes. Analogous cases beneficial to the community, all of which are charitable[21], are gifts for the benefit of the country to be applied by the Chancellor of the Exchequer[22], or for relief of taxes[23], or in reduction of the National Debt[24], or in reduction of rates[25].

1   43 Eliz 1 c 4 (1601) (now wholly repealed: see para 2 note 7 ante).
2   See para 12 ante.
3   As to 'public works' see the view taken earlier in *Dolan v Macdermot* (1867) LR 5 Eq 60 at 62 per Lord Romilly MR; affd (1868) 3 Ch App 676.
4   Eg repairing highways (*A-G v Governors of Harrow School* (1754) 2 Ves Sen 551; *A-G v Day* [1900] 1 Ch 31); building bridges (*Forbes v Forbes* (1854) 18 Beav 552); protecting the sea coast against encroachment (*A-G v Brown* (1818) 1 Swan 265; *Wilson v Barnes* (1886) 38 ChD 507, CA); providing a fire brigade for the benefit of a locality in 1876 (*Re Wokingham Fire Brigade Trusts, Martin v Hawkins* [1951] Ch 373, [1951] 1 All ER 454); providing a town with water (*Jones v Williams* (1767) Amb 651), light (*A-G v Heelis* (1824) 2 Sim & St 67 at 76–77 per Leach V-C; *A-G v Eastlake* (1853) 11 Hare 205), or other improvements (*Howse v Chapman* (1799) 4 Ves 542; *A-G v Heelis* supra; *A-G v Brown* supra), or with fortifications (*A-G v Carlisle Corpn* (1828) 2 Sim 437; *A-G v Dartmouth Corpn* (1883) 48 LT 933); or building a courthouse (Duke on Charitable Uses 109, 136), or workhouse (*A-G v Blizard* (1855) 21 Beav 233; *Re St Botolph Without Bishopsgate Parish Estates* (1887) 35 ChD 142; *Webster v Southey* (1887) 36 ChD 9; but cf *Burnaby v Barsby* (1859) 4 H & N 690); or providing a cemetery (*A-G v Blizard* supra), or cheap and sanitary methods of disposing of the dead (*Scottish Burial Reform and Cremation Society Ltd v Glasgow Corpn* [1968] AC 138, [1967] 3 All ER 215, HL); but see *Auckland Harbour Board v IRC* [1959] NZLR 204. In *Richmond-upon-Thames London Borough Council v A-G* (1982) 81 LGR 156 Warner J declined to decide the question whether the provision of municipal offices or of a town hall could be a valid charitable purpose.
5   The relief of poverty has been a national responsibility since the National Assistance Act 1948 came into force (see SOCIAL SERVICES AND COMMUNITY CARE). See also *Richmond Corpn v A-G* [1965] RA 117; revsd sub nom *Re Richmond Parish Charity Lands* [1965] RA 343, CA.

6    *Abbott v Fraser* (1874) LR 6 PC 96; *Re Scowcroft, Ormrod v Wilkinson* [1898] 2 Ch 638 at 642 per Stirling J.

7    *British Museum Trustees v White* (1826) 2 Sim & St 594; *Re Allsop, Gell v Carver* (1884) 1 TLR 4; *Re Holburne, Coates v Mackillop* (1885) 53 LT 212; and see *Re Scowcroft, Ormrod v Wilkinson* [1898] 2 Ch 638.

8    *Re Spence, Barclays Bank Ltd v Stockton-on-Tees Corpn* [1938] Ch 96, [1937] 3 All ER 684.

9    *Re Scowcroft, Ormrod v Wilkinson* [1898] 2 Ch 638.

10   *Townley v Bedwell* (1801) 6 Ves 194; *Harrison v Southampton Corpn* (1854) 2 Sm & G 387.

11   *Harrison v Southampton Corpn* (1854) 2 Sm & G 387.

12   *Re Hadden, Public Trustee v More* [1932] 1 Ch 133; *Shillington v Portadown Urban Council* [1911] 1 IR 247 (providing the means of obtaining healthy recreation, including, inter alia, music and instruments for the town band); *Re Morgan, Cecil-Williams v A-G* [1955] 2 All ER 632, [1955] 1 WLR 738; and see *IRC v Baddeley* [1955] AC 572 at 589, [1955] 1 All ER 525 at 532, HL, per Viscount Simonds, at 615 and 549 per Lord Somervell of Harrow, and at 594 and 535 per Lord Reid; *Alexandra Park Trustees v Haringey London Borough* (1967) 66 LGR 306; *Brisbane City Council v A-G for Queensland* [1979] AC 411, [1978] 3 All ER 30, PC; *Liverpool City Council v A-G* (1992) Times, 1 May. This may possibly not apply if the facilities are not open air facilities: see *Northern Ireland Valuation Comr v Lurgan Borough Council* [1968] NI 104 at 125, CA, per Lord Macdermott CJ, and see also at 134 per Curran LJ (there cannot be a valid charity for recreation or other leisure-time occupation which does not comply with the Recreational Charities Act 1958 (see paras 46–49 post)). The Charity Commissioners have not accepted the 'open air' point, and have held that the provision of a public ice skating rink is charitable apart from the Recreational Charities Act 1958, and also under it: *Report of the Charity Commissioners for England and Wales for 1984* (HC Paper (1984–85) no 394) paras 19–25.

13   *Murray v Thomas* [1937] 4 All ER 545; cf *Re Lord Mayor of Belfast's Air Raid Distress Fund* [1962] NI 161.

14   This does not, therefore, apply where the intention is to benefit the founder and subscribers only: *Thomson v Shakespear* (1860) John 612 at 616 per Page Wood V-C (affd 1 De GF & J 399 (museum)); *Carne v Long* (1860) 2 De GF & J 75 (library); *Re Prevost, Lloyds Bank Ltd v Barclays Bank Ltd* [1930] 2 Ch 383 (London Library); and see *Re Russell Institution, Figgins v Baghino* [1898] 2 Ch 72 (literary and scientific institution); *Re Jones, Clegg v Ellison* [1898] 2 Ch 83 (horticultural society); *Re Pitt Rivers, Scott v Pitt Rivers* [1902] 1 Ch 403, CA (museum and pleasure ground).

15   *Johnston v Swann* (1818) 3 Madd 457.

16   *Thomas v Howell* (1874) LR 18 Eq 198; *Re Richardson, Shuldham v Royal National Lifeboat Institution* (1887) 56 LJCh 784; *Re David, Buckley v Royal National Lifeboat Institution* (1889) 41 ChD 168 (affd 43 ChD 27, CA).

17   *Beaumont v Oliveira* (1869) 4 Ch App 309.

18   *Re Lord Mayor of Belfast's Air Raid Distress Fund* [1962] NI 161; and see *Re Hobourn Aero Components Ltd's Air Raid Distress Fund, Ryan v Forrest* [1946] Ch 194 at 200, 202, [1946] 1 All ER 501 at 506, 507, CA, obiter per Lord Greene MR.

19   *Re North Devon and West Somerset Relief Fund Trusts, Baron Hylton v Wright* [1953] 2 All ER 1032, [1953] 1 WLR 1260.

20   *Report of the Charity Commissioners for England and Wales for 1990* (HC Paper (1990–91) no 362) App A(f). See also *Report for 1969* (HC Paper (1969–70) no 276) para 20.

21   A similar analogy (to the 'setting out of soldiers' in the preamble to the statute of Elizabeth I: see para 12 ante) was applied in *Re Good, Harington v Watts* [1905] 2 Ch 60 (gift to maintain library and purchase plate for officers' mess).

22   *Nightingale v Goulbourn* (1848) 2 Ph 594.

23   *A-G v Bushby* (1857) 24 Beav 299.

24   *Thellusson v Woodford* (1799) 4 Ves 227 (affd (1805) 11 Ves 112, HL); *Newland v A-G* (1809) 3 Mer 684; *Ashton v Lord Langdale* (1851) 4 De G & Sm 402 at 403 per Shadwell V-C; *Income Tax Special Purposes Comrs v Pemsel* [1891] AC 531 at 544, HL, per Lord Halsbury LC.

25   *Doe d Preece v Howells* (1831) 2 B & Ad 744; and see *A-G v Limerick Corpn* (1817) 6 Dowl 136.

**41. Efficiency of armed forces.** To increase the efficiency of the army confers a public benefit[1], and gifts tending to that end are charitable, such as a gift for the benefit of a volunteer corps[2], for teaching shooting[3], for the maintenance of a library for a regimental officers' mess[4] or for the mess generally[5], to form a regimental fund for the promotion of sport[6], to provide a prize to be competed for by cadets[7], or for the upkeep of bedrooms and attendance for the men of a regiment[8].

Similarly beneficial to the community, and so charitable, are a gift for the training of boys to become officers in the navy or mercantile marine[9] and a gift for promoting the defence of the United Kingdom from attack by hostile aircraft[10], and a gift exclusively for the purpose of promoting the efficiency of the police forces and the preservation of public order would be charitable[11]; but the principle does not extend to a gift that can be applied solely for the benefit of former members of the navy, army or air force[12]. A gift to two institutions, one for sailors, the other for soldiers, has been held to be a charitable gift[13].

1   *Re Good, Harington v Watts* [1905] 2 Ch 60 at 66 per Farwell J.
2   *Re Lord Stratheden and Campbell, Alt v Lord Stratheden and Campbell* [1894] 3 Ch 265. Property given for the use of a volunteer corps may, however, be regulated by statutory provisions, in which case it is not held on charitable trusts: *Re Edis's Trust, Campbell-Smith v Davies* [1972] 2 All ER 769, [1972] 1 WLR 1135.
3   *Re Stephens, Giles v Stephens* (1892) 8 TLR 792. See also *Charitable Status: Rifle and Pistol Clubs for Instruction and Practice in Shooting (The City of London Rifle and Pistol Club and the Burnley Rifle Club)* Decisions of the Charity Commissioners (1993) vol 1 p 4; and see Picarda *The Law and Practice Relating to Charities* (3rd Edn, 1999) p 148.
4   *Re Good, Harington v Watts* [1905] 2 Ch 60. The decision on the facts, though not the ratio, in this case and in *Re Gray, Todd v Taylor* [1925] Ch 362, was doubted by Lord Normand in *IRC v City of Glasgow Police Athletic Association* [1953] AC 380 at 391, [1953] 1 All ER 747 at 749, HL.
5   *Re Donald, Moore v Somerset* [1909] 2 Ch 410 at 422 per Warrington J.
6   *Re Gray, Todd v Taylor* [1925] Ch 362. See note 4 supra.
7   *Re Barker, Sherrington v Dean and Chapter of St Paul's Cathedral* (1909) 25 TLR 753.
8   *Re Barker, Sherrington v Dean and Chapter of St Paul's Cathedral* (1909) 25 TLR 753.
9   *Re Corbyn, Midland Bank Executor and Trustee Co Ltd v A-G* [1941] Ch 400, [1941] 2 All ER 160.
10  *Re Driffill, Harvey v Chamberlain* [1950] Ch 92, [1949] 2 All ER 933.
11  *IRC v City of Glasgow Police Athletic Association* [1953] AC 380 at 391, [1953] 1 All ER 747 at 749, HL, per Lord Normand: the association was held not to be established exclusively for that purpose, and not to be charitable because the recreation of members of the association was one of its main purposes.
12  *Re Good, Harington v Watts* [1905] 2 Ch 60 (gift for old officers of regiment); *Re Meyers, London Life Association v St George's Hospital* [1951] Ch 534, [1951] 1 All ER 538 (gift for welfare, benefit or assistance of members of navy, army or air force, whether past, present or future, or their wives or children).
13  *Re Smith, Blyth v A-G* (1920) 36 TLR 416, CA.

**42. Useful arts and other public purposes.** The promotion of industry, commerce and art for the public benefit is a charitable purpose[1]; and a gift to the National Trust is charitable[2]. Likewise the preservation of the environment including its flora and fauna is a recognised charitable purpose[3]. It is charitable to further the sound development and administration of the law by the dissemination of accurate reports of judicial decisions[4], or to promote the finding of the original manuscripts of plays attributed to Shakespeare[5], or to encourage good domestic servants[6], good housewifery and horticulture[7], to promote agriculture[8] and to preserve animals or vegetables valuable to man[9]. The Charity Commissioners have taken the view that family conciliation services, by analogy with the provision of courthouses and the publication of law reports, can be charitable as advancing the administration of the law[10].

Among funds which have been held to be charitable are funds to promote marriage among the Jews[11], for the repatriation of men from New South Wales who had served in the First World War[12], for reclaiming fallen women[13], for the assistance or support of unmarried mothers[14], for promoting the spiritual and moral welfare of seamen in port[15] and for the relief of refugees[16], and for a community providing a temporary home of rest and the comfort of friendship to those who need it[17].

A gift for a peal of bells to be rung to commemorate the restoration of the monarchy has been held charitable[18]; and the erection of a monument[19], not of the donor[20], or memorial[21] may perhaps be charitable.

The Charity Commissioners have accepted that promoting good race relations, endeavouring to eliminate discrimination on grounds of race and encouraging equality of opportunity between persons of different racial groups are prima facie charitable purposes[22].

1   *Re Town and Country Planning Act 1947, Crystal Palace Trustees v Minister of Town and Country Planning* [1951] Ch 132, [1950] 2 All ER 857n; *IRC v White and A-G* (1980) 55 TC 651.

2   *Re Verrall, National Trust for Places of Historic Interest or Natural Beauty v A-G* [1916] 1 Ch 100; and see *Re Spensley's Will Trusts, Barclays Bank Ltd v Staughton* [1952] Ch 886, [1952] 2 All ER 49; revsd [1954] Ch 233, [1954] 1 All ER 178, CA. As to the National Trust see OPEN SPACES AND ANCIENT MONUMENTS vol 34 (Reissue) para 103 et seq.

3   See Picarda *The Law and Practice Relating to Charities* (3rd Edn, 1999) pp 164–166. See also *Re Centrepoint Community Growth Trust* (2000) 3 ITELR 269, NZ HC, where trusts for the environment and trusts for the establishment of communities were valid charitable purposes.

4   *Incorporated Council of Law Reporting for England and Wales v A-G* [1972] Ch 73, [1971] 3 All ER 1029, CA; *Incorporated Council of Law Reporting for the State of Queensland v Comr of Taxation* (1971) 45 ALJR 552, Aust HC.

5   *Re Hopkins' Will Trusts, Naish v Francis Bacon Society Inc* [1965] Ch 669, [1964] 3 All ER 46 (see also para 26 ante).

6   *Reeve v A-G* (1843) 3 Hare 191; *Loscombe v Wintringham* (1850) 13 Beav 87. Cf *Re Patten, Westminster Bank v Carlyon* [1929] 2 Ch 276 (staff Christmas fund at a club: not charitable).

7   *Re Pleasants, Pleasants v A-G* (1923) 39 TLR 675.

8   *IRC v Yorkshire Agricultural Society* [1928] 1 KB 611, CA; *Re Pleasants, Pleasants v A-G* (1923) 39 TLR 675; *Brisbane City Council v A-G for Queensland* [1979] AC 411, [1978] 3 All ER 30, PC; and see *Re Clifford* as reported in (1912) 81 LJCh 220 at 222 per Swinfen Eady J (restocking of a river with fish might be for the benefit of the community). But a fund to provide cheap loans to assist planters and agriculturalists is not charitable unless the purposes of the loans themselves are restricted to the promotion of agriculture: *Hadaway v Hadaway* [1955] 1 WLR 16, PC.

9   *London University v Yarrow* (1857) 1 De G & J 72.

10  See *Report of the Charity Commissioners for England and Wales for 1983* (HC Paper (1983–84) no 447) paras 28–34. As to the Charity Commissioners see paras 486–512 post.

11  *Re Cohen, National Provincial and Union Bank of England Ltd v Cohen* (1919) 36 TLR 16.

12  *Verge v Somerville* [1924] AC 496, PC.

13  *Mahony v Duggan* (1880) 11 LR Ir 260.

14  *Re Andrae Estate, Sims v Public Trustee* (1967) 61 WWR 182 (Alta).

15  *Finch v Poplar Borough Council* (1967) 66 LGR 324; and see *Wynn v Skegness UDC* [1966] 3 All ER 336, [1967] 1 WLR 52 (holiday centre for miners, their wives and families in need of a change of air).

16  *Re Morrison, Wakefield v Falmouth* (1967) 111 Sol Jo 758.

17  *Re Banfield, Lloyds Bank Ltd v Smith* [1968] 2 All ER 276, [1968] 1 WLR 846.

18  *Re Pardoe, McLaughlin v A-G* [1906] 2 Ch 184. Cf *Re Arber, Taylor v Shelton* (1919) Times, 13 December (in commemoration of testator's death: not charitable).

19  The Charity Commissioners have treated some such cases as charitable, eg the Wellington Monument in Somerset and the Cobden Obelisk at Midhurst. See the comments on the statement on the text made by the Charity Commissioners in their *Report for 1981* (HC Paper (1981–82) no 363) paras 68–70, in relation to registration of the Mountbatten Statue Appeal trust.

20  *Re Endacott, Corpe v Endacott* [1960] Ch 232, [1959] 3 All ER 562, CA. The fact that the memorial was to be useful did not save it. See also para 54 post.

21  The cases were considered in *Re Lord Mayor of Belfast's Air Raid Distress Fund* [1962] NI 161, and the question was also discussed in *Murray v Thomas* [1937] 4 All ER 545. In each of those cases the memorial was to be of a useful character, such as a building or hall, but Clauson J in *Murray v Thomas* supra was inclined to the view that a war memorial might be charitable even though it was not of a useful character.

22  *Report of the Charity Commissioners for England and Wales for 1983* (HC Paper (1983–84) no 447) paras 15–20. This report, prepared before the decision in *Re Koeppler Will Trusts, Barclays Bank Trust Co Ltd v Slack* [1984] Ch 243, [1984] 2 All ER 111 (revsd [1986] Ch 423, [1985] 2 All ER 869, CA), took the view

that the authority of *Re Strakosch, Temperley v A-G* [1949] Ch 529, [1949] 2 All ER 6, CA (see para 58 post) has been undermined by the race relations legislation. The Inland Revenue has indicated that it will not challenge the view of the Charity Commissioners.


**43. Miners' welfare trusts.** Where trusts declared before 17 December 1957 required or purported to require property to be held for the purpose of activities which are social welfare activities within the meaning of the Miners' Welfare Act 1952[1], and at that date the whole or part of the property held on those trusts or of any property held with that property[2] represented an application of money standing to the credit of the miners' welfare fund[3] or money provided by the Coal Industry Social Welfare Organisation[4], those trusts are to be treated as if they were and always had been charitable[5].


1   See the Miners' Welfare Act 1952 s 16(1) (prospectively repealed); and MINES, MINERALS AND QUARRIES vol 31 (Reissue) para 87. Expenditure on the maintenance of existing social welfare activities is eligible expenditure for the purposes of the Coal Industry Act 1987 s 3 (prospectively repealed): see s 3(3)(a), Sch 2 para 3 (prospectively repealed). As to representation of employee organisations amongst trustees see s 5 (as amended); para 186 post; and MINES, MINERALS AND QUARRIES vol 31 (Reissue) para 88.
2   Property held on the same trusts as other property is deemed to be held with it, even though it is vested in different trustees: Recreational Charities Act 1958 s 2(2).
3   This fund was wound up under the provisions of the Miners' Welfare Act 1952 s 2(1) (prospectively repealed): see MINES, MINERALS AND QUARRIES vol 31 (Reissue) para 87.
4   See ibid s 2 (prospectively repealed); and MINES, MINERALS AND QUARRIES vol 31 (Reissue) para 87.
5   Recreational Charities Act 1958 s 2(1). See also MINES, MINERALS AND QUARRIES vol 31 (Reissue) para 87. For savings under s 3 see para 49 post. See also *Wynn v Skegness UDC* [1966] 3 All ER 336, [1967] 1 WLR 52.


**44. Protection of animals.** Trusts for the protection or benefit of animals, whether useful to man or not, are charitable, as being calculated to promote human morality by encouraging kindness, discouraging cruelty and stimulating humane sentiments to the benefit of mankind[1], unless outweighed by consequences detrimental to the public benefit[2].

Accordingly the following gifts are charitable: gifts to such institutions as the RSPCA[3], a home for lost dogs[4] or for starving and forsaken cats[5], a veterinary college[6] and vegetarian societies[7], or to a periodical devoted to propaganda against cruelty to animals[8], or for the welfare of cats and kittens needing care and attention[9], or for the establishment of an animals' hospital[10], humane slaughterhouses[11] or a fund to provide rewards for policemen for helping to bring to justice cases of cruelty to animals[12].


1   *Re Wedgwood, Allen v Wedgwood* [1915] 1 Ch 113, CA; *Re Moss, Hobrough v Harvey* [1949] 1 All ER 495; *Re Green's Will Trusts, Fitzgerald-Hart v A-G* [1985] 3 All ER 455. Cf *Re Grove-Grady, Plowden v Lawrence* [1929] 1 Ch 557, CA (trust to establish a refuge for animals and birds of all kinds held not charitable as not affording any advantage to animals useful to mankind, or any protection from cruelty to animals generally), compromised on appeal sub nom *A-G v Plowden* [1931] WN 89, HL; *Re Joy, Purday v Johnson* (1888) 60 LT 175; and see *A-G v Whorwood* (1750) 1 Ves Sen 534 at 536 per Lord Hardwicke LC (trust to feed sparrows: not charitable). Trusts for the prevention of cruelty to animals abroad are charitable: *Armstrong v Reeves* (1890) 25 LR Ir 325; *Re Jackson, Bell v Adlam* (1910) Times, 11 June. Gifts for the benefit of specific animals are not charitable: *Re Dean, Cooper-Dean v Stevens* (1889) 41 ChD 552; *Re Howard, Oakley v Aldridge* (1908) Times, 30 October. As to the enforceability of such gifts see para 53 note 25 post; and TRUSTS vol 48 (2000 Reissue) para 507.

2    *National Anti-Vivisection Society v IRC* [1948] AC 31 at 41, 49, [1947] 2 All ER 217 at 219, 224, HL, per Lord Wright, and at 72–73 and 237 per Lord Simonds (anti-vivisection society not charitable, overruling *Re Foveaux, Cross v London Anti-Vivisection Society* [1895] 2 Ch 501); applied in *Animal Defence and Anti-Vivisection Society v IRC* (1950) 66 (pt 2) TLR 1091.

3    *Tatham v Drummond* (1864) 4 De GJ & Sm 484; *Armstrong v Reeves* (1890) 25 LR Ir 325 (Society of Carlsruhe for the Protection of Animals).

4    *Re Douglas, Obert v Barrow* (1887) 35 ChD 472, CA; *Adamson v Melbourne and Metropolitan Board of Works* [1929] AC 142 at 148, PC.

5    *Swifte v A-G for Ireland (No 2)* [1912] 1 IR 133.

6    *London University v Yarrow* (1857) 1 De G & J 72 at 80 per Lord Cranworth LC.

7    *Re Cranston, Webb v Oldfield* [1898] 1 IR 431, CA; *Re Slatter, Howard v Lewis* (1905) 21 TLR 295.

8    *Marsh v Means* (1857) 3 Jur NS 790; and see *Re Cranston, Webb v Oldfield* [1898] 1 IR 431 at 443, CA, per Lord Ashbourne LC (lectures).

9    *Re Moss, Hobrough v Harvey* [1949] 1 All ER 495.

10   *London University v Yarrow* (1857) 1 De G & J 72.

11   *Tatham v Drummond* (1864) 4 De GJ & Sm 484; and see *Re Wedgwood, Allen v Wedgwood* [1915] 1 Ch 113 at 116, CA, per Lord Cozens-Hardy MR; *Re Winton* (1953) Times, 31 January.

12   *Re Herrick, Colohan v A-G* (1918) 52 ILT 213. Cf *Re Hollywood, Smyth v A-G* (1917) 52 ILT 51.

**45. Spread of particular doctrines.** The promulgation of particular doctrines or principles not subversive of morality or otherwise pernicious[1], and not in furtherance of the principles of a particular political party[2], nor involving pressure on the legislature to achieve a political object in changing the law of the land[3], nor designed to sway public opinion on controversial social issues[4], may be charitable, as, for instance, Conservative principles combined with mental and moral improvement[5], Socialism[6], kindness to animals[7], temperance[8], 'extending the knowledge of those doctrines in the various branches of literature to which I have turned my attention and pen, in order to ascertain what appeared to be truth, and to teach it to those who would listen'[9], or carrying on the teachings of Rudolf Steiner, which are directed to the mental or moral improvement of man[10]. The promotion of ethical standards of conduct of work and compliance with the law may be a valid charitable purpose[11].

The question whether the promulgation of a particular doctrine or principle will or may benefit the public must be answered by the court by forming an opinion upon the evidence before it[12]. The same consideration applies to the dissemination of information useful to the community[13].

1    See paras 58, 60 post. An inquiry may be ordered into the nature of the doctrines: *Russell v Jackson* (1852) 10 Hare 204.

2    *Bonar Law Memorial Trust v IRC* (1933) 49 TLR 220 (gift to commemorate a Conservative leader by an educational centre for subjects deemed desirable to governing body composed of leader and chairman ex officio and other members of Conservative party: not charitable), distinguishing *Re Scowcroft, Ormrod v Wilkinson* [1898] 2 Ch 638.

3    See para 60 post. See *Re Bushnell, Lloyds Bank Ltd v Murray* [1975] 1 All ER 721, [1975] 1 WLR 1596.

4    See Picarda *The Law and Practice Relating to Charities* (3rd Edn, 1999) pp 177–179.

5    *Re Scowcroft, Ormrod v Wilkinson* [1898] 2 Ch 638 at 642 per Stirling J. Cf *Re Jones, Public Trustee v Earl of Clarendon* (1929) 45 TLR 259 (Primrose League: not a charity).

6    *Russell v Jackson* (1852) 10 Hare 204 (subject to its being found on inquiry not to be illegal; the Socialist party was not formed until 1904). See *Pare v Clegg* (1861) 29 Beav 589.

7    *Marsh v Means* (1857) 3 Jur NS 790.

8    *Re Hood, Public Trustee v Hood* [1931] 1 Ch 240 at 250, CA, per Lord Hanworth MR, and at 252–253, CA, per Romer LJ; *IRC v Falkirk Temperance Café Trust* 1927 SC 261. Distinguish *IRC v Temperance Council of Christian Churches of England and Wales* (1926) 136 LT 27 (promotion of temperance mainly by political means: not charitable).

9    *Thompson v Thompson* (1844) 1 Coll 381 at 395 per Shadwell V-C (where it was admitted that the testator's writings contained nothing irreligious, illegal or immoral).
10    *Re Price, Midland Bank Executor and Trustee Co Ltd v Harwood* [1943] Ch 422, [1943] 2 All ER 505.
11    See *Charitable Status: Public Concern at Work (1993)* Decisions of the Charity Commissioners (1994) vol 2 p 5.
12    *National Anti-Vivisection Society v IRC* [1948] AC 31, [1947] 2 All ER 217, HL; approving observations in *Re Hummeltenberg, Beatty v London Spiritualistic Alliance Ltd* [1923] 1 Ch 237 at 242 per Russell J, which were adopted in *Re Grove-Grady, Plowden v Lawrence* [1929] 1 Ch 557, CA, and overruling the dictum of Chitty J in *Re Foveaux, Cross v London Anti-Vivisection Society* [1895] 2 Ch 501, that where the merits of a particular object are controversial the court stands neutral.
13    See *Re Besterman's Will Trusts* (21 January 1980, unreported); *McGovern v A-G* [1982] Ch 321, [1981] 3 All ER 493; and Picarda *The Law and Practice Relating to Charities* (3rd Edn, 1999) p 164.

## (v) Recreational Charities

**46. Recreation and other leisure-time occupation.** It is deemed by statute to be, and, subject to certain provisions[1], always to have been, charitable to provide, or assist in the provision of, facilities for recreation or other leisure-time occupation, if the facilities are provided in the interests of social welfare[2]. The Recreational Charities Act 1958 applies in particular to the provision of facilities at village halls, community centres and women's institutes, and to the provision and maintenance of grounds and buildings to be used for the purpose of recreation or leisure-time occupation, and extends to the provision of facilities for those purposes by the organising of any activity[3]. The activities do not have to have an educational element[4].

1    Ie subject to the provisions of the Recreational Charities Act 1958: see s 1(1). As to whether trusts for this type of purpose are or can be charitable if they do not comply with the provisions of the Recreational Charities Act 1958 see para 40 note 12 ante; and *Northern Ireland Valuation Comr v Lurgan Borough Council* [1968] NI 104 at 125, 134, 166, CA.
2    Recreational Charities Act 1958 s 1(1). As to the interests of social welfare see s 1(2); and para 47 post. The Recreational Charities Act 1958, which binds the Crown (s 5), is not to be taken to restrict the purposes which are to be regarded as charitable independently of it: s 3(1). As to the application of the Recreational Charities Act 1958 to Scotland and Northern Ireland see s 6(2) (as amended).
3    Ibid s 1(3). There seems to be no reason and little scope for applying the ejusdem generis rule of construction to s 1(1) by reference to this provision, even though it is not expressed to be without prejudice to the generality of s 1(1).
4    See *Charitable Status: Fairfield (Croydon) Ltd—The Recreation Charities Act 1958 (1995)* Decisions of the Charity Commissioners (1997) vol 5 p 7.

**47. The interests of social welfare.** The statutory requirement that the facilities be provided in the interests of social welfare[1] is not to be treated as satisfied unless: (1) the facilities are provided with the object of improving the conditions of life for the persons for whom the facilities are primarily intended[2]; and (2) either those persons have need of such facilities by reason of their youth, age, infirmity or disablement, poverty or social or economic circumstances[3], or the facilities are to be available to the members or female members of the public at large[4].

1    Ie the requirement under the Recreational Charities Act 1958 s 1(1): see para 46 ante. The Recreational Charities Act 1958 contains no definition of 'social welfare'. There are decisions on the words 'social welfare' under the Rating and Valuation (Miscellaneous Provisions) Act 1955 s 8 (repealed; replaced by

the General Rate Act 1967 s 40, (itself repealed and replaced by the Local Government Finance Act 1988 s 47 (as amended)): see para 377 post), but these may be misleading: see *Northern Ireland Valuation Comr v Lurgan Borough Council* [1968] NI 104 at 126, 151, CA.

2   Recreational Charities Act 1958 s 1(2)(a). The subsection appears to contemplate that there may be a primary and a secondary class of beneficiaries: see *Wynn v Skegness UDC* [1966] 3 All ER 336, [1967] 1 WLR 52. The provision was discussed in *IRC v McMullen* [1978] 1 All ER 230, [1978] 1 WLR 664; affd [1979] 1 All ER 588, [1979] 1 WLR 130, CA, but revsd on other grounds [1981] AC 1, [1980] 1 All ER 884, HL. At first instance Walton J said that the persons for whom the facilities are primarily intended must be to some extent and in some way deprived persons, and this view was shared by the majority in the Court of Appeal. The dissenting judgment of Bridge LJ was, however, said to be clearly correct in the Scottish case of *Guild v IRC* [1992] 2 AC 310, [1992] 2 All ER 10, HL (a tax case where the English law of charities was applicable as part of the law of Scotland). It suffices that the facilities are provided with the object of improving the conditions of life for members of the community generally.

  Provision of bar facilities at a rugby club do not improve conditions of life for those for whom the facilities were primarily intended: *Charitable Status: North Tawton Rugby Union Football Club (1995)* Decisions of the Charity Commissioners (1997) vol 5 p 7.

3   Recreational Charities Act 1958 s 1(2)(b)(i).
4   Ibid s 1(2)(b)(ii).

**48. Public benefit and recreational charities.** Nothing in the general provision as to recreational and similar trusts[1] is to be taken to derogate from the principle that, to be charitable, a trust or institution must be for the public benefit[2]. Although the Recreational Charities Act 1958 lays down certain requirements of its own as to the section of the public which is to benefit[3], these do not seem to exclude the application of the test of benefit for a sufficient section of the public, and they operate subject to this overriding principle[4].

1   Ie nothing in the Recreational Charities Act 1958 s 1: see paras 46–47 ante.
2   Ibid s 1(1) proviso. As to the meaning of 'for the public benefit' in this context see *Wynn v Skegness UDC* [1966] 3 All ER 336 at 345, [1967] 1 WLR 52 at 63 per Ungoed-Thomas J.
3   See para 47 ante.
4   See *Charitable Status: North Tawton Rugby Union Football Club (1995)* Decisions of the Charity Commissioners (1997) vol 5 p 7.

**49. Past transactions.** Although the Recreational Charities Act 1958, which came into force on 13 March 1958 when it received the royal assent, is declaratory and therefore retrospective in effect, it does not apply to make charitable any trust, or to validate any disposition, of property if, before 17 December 1957, that property, or any property representing or forming part of it, or any income arising from any such property, has been paid or conveyed to, or applied for the benefit of, the persons entitled by reason of the invalidity of the trust or disposition[1].

  The Act does not affect any order made or judgment given, whether before or after 13 March 1958, in legal proceedings begun before 17 December 1957[2]; and nothing in the Act requires anything properly done before 17 December 1957, or anything done or to be done in pursuance of a contract entered into before that day, to be treated for any purpose as wrongful or ineffectual[3].

  Apart from certain provisions relating to income tax and stamp duty which have been of academic interest only since 13 March 1960[4], nothing in the Act requires anything to be treated, for the purposes of any enactment, as having been charitable at a time before 13 March 1958, so as to invalidate anything done or any determination given before that date[5].

1   Recreational Charities Act 1958 s 3(2)(a).
2   Ibid s 3(2)(b).
3   Ibid s 3(2)(c).
4   See ibid s 3(4), (5).
5   Ibid s 3(3).

### (vi)  Charitable Purposes Abroad

**50.  Choice of law.**  If in an English court the question arises of the validity of a gift by will for purposes which may be charitable but which are to be carried out entirely abroad, the question is determined, in the case of a gift of immovable property, by the law of the country in which the property is situated[1] and, in the case of movable property, by the law of the country in which the testator was domiciled at the date of his death[2]. Formerly the English law as to gifts for superstitious uses[3] was applied to gifts to be applied abroad[4] even though the gifts were valid according to the foreign law[5], but English rules as to mortmain and perpetuities were not so applied[6].

1   *Re Hoyles, Row v Jagg* [1911] 1 Ch 179, CA (mortgages on land in Ontario); *Philipson-Stow v IRC* [1961] AC 727, [1960] 3 All ER 814, HL (land in South Africa). As to the distinction between immovables and movables see CONFLICT OF LAWS vol 8(1) (Reissue) para 902 et seq.
2   *Re Levick's Will Trusts, Ffennell v IRC* [1963] 1 All ER 95, [1963] 1 WLR 311. In some old charity cases the gift has apparently been tested both by English and by foreign law: *Thompson v Thompson* (1844) 1 Coll 381. As to domicile see CONFLICT OF LAWS vol 8(1) (Reissue) para 680 et seq.
3   See para 56 post.
4   *De Garcin v Lawson* (1798) 4 Ves 433n.
5   *Re Elliott, Elliott v Elliott* [1891] WN 9.
6   *Fordyce v Bridges* (1848) 2 Ph 497 at 515 per Lord Cottenham LC (perpetuity); *Oliphant v Hendrie* (1784) 1 Bro CC 571; *Mackintosh v Townsend* (1809) 16 Ves 330 (mortmain); though see also *A-G v Mill* (1827) 3 Russ 328; affd (1831) 2 Dow & Cl 393, HL; and cf *Jewish National Fund Inc v Royal Trust Co and Richter* [1965] SCR 784, 53 DLR (2d) 577, Can SC.

**51.  Test for validity under English law.**  If the validity of a gift falls to be determined under English domestic law, the test is not necessarily the same in all cases as for a gift to be applied in England. It is well established that trusts for the relief of the aged, impotent and poor[1] or for the advancement of education[2] or religion[3] abroad are valid under English law. The fact that the activities of the charity are to be exercised abroad does not make it non-charitable if it otherwise satisfies the tests[4].

However, not all purposes which are charitable in England as being within the fourth head of charitable purposes[5] would be charitable if they were to be carried out abroad[6]. Gifts for some such purposes have been upheld[7], but public policy might prevent the recognition, as being charitable under English domestic law, of a gift for the improvement of the army or the reduction of the national debt of a foreign state[8].

The test which should be applied in these cases has never been formulated by an English court, but in Australia the test is whether the purpose is beneficial to the foreign community and not inimical to the general concept of legal charity as understood by the local law[9].

1    Eg *Ironmongers' Co v A-G* (1844) 10 Cl & Fin 908, HL; *Re Robinson, Besant v German Reich* [1931] 2 Ch 122; *Re Geck, Freund v Steward* (1893) 69 LT 819, CA; *Re Niyazi's Will Trusts* [1978] 3 All ER 785, [1978] 1 WLR 910. This applies even if inhabitants of a country of alien ideology are to benefit: *Re Burnham* (1958) 17 DLR (2d) 298 (BC); and cf *Re Robinson, Besant v German Reich supra* at 128 per Maugham J. As to charitable trusts for the relief of the aged, impotent and poor see paras 16–23 ante.

2    *Re Davis' Trusts* (1889) 61 LT 430; *Re Shaw's Will Trusts, National Provincial Bank Ltd v National City Bank Ltd* [1952] Ch 163, [1952] 1 All ER 49. As to charitable trusts for the advancement of education see paras 24–29 ante.

3    *Income Tax Special Purposes Comrs v Pemsel* [1891] AC 531, HL. As to charitable trusts for the advancement of religion see paras 30–36 ante.

4    *Keren Kayemeth Le Jisroel Ltd v IRC* [1931] 2 KB 465 at 477, CA, per Lord Hanworth MR (affd without considering this point [1932] AC 650, HL); *Re Robinson, Besant v German Reich* [1931] 2 Ch 122.

5    Ie the fourth division mentioned by Lord Macnaghten in *Income Tax Special Purposes Comrs v Pemsel* [1891] AC 531 at 583, HL, per Lord Macnaghten: see para 13 ante. The fourth division comprises other purposes beneficial to the community: see para 37 et seq ante.

6    *Camille and Henry Dreyfus Foundation Inc v IRC* [1954] Ch 672 at 684, [1954] 2 All ER 466 at 471, CA, per Evershed MR, and at 704 and 485 per Jenkins LJ; affd without considering this point [1956] AC 39, [1955] 3 All ER 97, HL.

7    *Re Vagliano, Vagliano v Vagliano* (1905) 75 LJCh 119 (charitable purposes generally); *Armstrong v Reeves* (1890) 25 LR Ir 325 (protection of animals); *Re Lowin* [1967] 2 NSWR 140, NSW CA (revsg [1965] NSWR 1624) (musical competitions in Vienna); *Re Stone, Perpetual Trustee Co Ltd v Stone* (1970) 91 WN NSW 704 (reclamation and afforestation of land in Israel); *Re Jacobs, Westminster Bank Ltd v Chinn* (1970) 114 Sol Jo 515 (see note 9 infra; and *Report of the Charity Commissioners for England and Wales for 1970* (HC Paper (1970–71) no 409) p 28) (improvement and reclamation of land in Israel); although cf *Jewish National Fund Inc v Royal Trust Co and Richter* [1965] SCR 784, 53 DLR (2d) 577, Can SC.

8    *Camille and Henry Dreyfus Foundation Inc v IRC* [1954] Ch 672 at 684, [1954] 2 All ER 466 at 471, CA, per Lord Evershed MR and at 704 and 485 per Jenkins LJ; affd without discussing this point [1956] AC 39, [1955] 3 All ER 97, HL. Cf *Habershon v Vardon* (1851) 4 De G & Sm 467 (gift held non-charitable as contrary to public policy).

9    *Re Stone, Perpetual Trustee Co Ltd v Stone* (1970) 91 WN NSW 704 at 717, applying *Re Lowin* [1967] 2 NSWR 140, NSW CA; and *Camille and Henry Dreyfus Foundation Inc v IRC* [1954] Ch 672, [1954] 2 All ER 466, CA, affd without considering this point [1956] AC 39, [1955] 3 All ER 97, HL. In the absence of binding decisions, the principles on which the Charity Commissioners and the Commissioners of Inland Revenue proceed are set out in the *Report of the Charity Commissioners for England and Wales for 1992* (HC Paper (1992–93) no 651) para 76. See *Re Jacobs, Westminster Bank Ltd v Chinn* (1970) 114 Sol Jo 515, where the point was not discussed in the judgment.

# (3) NON-CHARITABLE PURPOSES

## (i) Gifts for Private Charities or Individuals

**52. 'Private charities'.** Bequests for private charitable purposes[1] are not recognised by the courts as charitable in the legal sense[2], except where, by the use of the word 'private', a testator may be said to have drawn a distinction between charities available for all and charities which are restricted to a special class or administered by individuals without the intervention of any corporate organisation[3].

1    As to the ambiguity of the expression 'private charity' see *A-G v Pearce* (1740) 2 Atk 87 ('each particular object may be private, but it is the extensiveness which will constitute it a public charity'); *Nash v Morley* (1842) 5 Beav 177; *Hall v Derby Sanitary Authority* (1885) 16 QBD 163 at 171 per Manisty J, and at 173 per Smith J; *Re Slevin, Slevin v Hepburn* [1891] 2 Ch 236, CA.

2    *Ommanney v Butcher* (1823) Turn & R 260; *Ellis v Selby* (1836) 1 My & Cr 286 at 292–293 per Lord Cottenham LC; *Nash v Morley* (1842) 5 Beav 177 at 183 per Lord Langdale MR.

3    *Re Sinclair's Trust* (1884) 13 LR Ir 150 at 154 per Porter MR. With this interpretation of the word 'private', it may be possible to reconcile *Waldo v Caley* (1809) 16 Ves 206, where a gift for 'charitable purposes as well of a public as a private nature' was held good; *Johnston v Swann* (1818) 3 Madd 457, where a trust for public and private charities was held good; and *Horde v Earl of Suffolk* (1833) 2 My & K 59, where a trust 'to distribute in charity to private individuals or public institutions' was held good.

**53. Gifts for benefit of individuals.** Gifts for the benefit of particular individuals or a fluctuating body of particular individuals[1], whether named by the testator or to be selected by his trustees[2] or by any other person[3], are never charitable, although they may be upheld as gifts to individuals if the recipients can deal with the capital and income of the gifts as they please[4]. Examples are gifts for persons residing in a particular street[5], for the children of the testator's tenants on a particular estate[6], for a city company whose property was impressed with no charitable trust[7], for the members of a religious community associated only for the purpose of working out their own salvation[8], even though involving intercessory prayer and other spiritual exercises affording edification by example[9], for poor relations limited to statutory next of kin[10], for descendants of named persons[11], for the workpeople employed in a certain department of a company's business[12], for employees of a particular company who give financial subscriptions[13], for all the employees of a public company[14], or for children of past and present employees of a group of companies[15], unless the gifts are to relieve poor employees or past employees of the company or group[16].

The following have also been held not to be charitable: bequests for the benefit of an orphan school kept by an individual substantially at his own expense[17], for the support of any boy or man of a particular surname[18], for keeping a portrait in repair[19], for providing a particular estate with labourers' cottages[20], to a livery company for giving a dinner on the testator's birthday to which certain churchwardens should be invited[21], for a private chapel with chaplain and choristers[22], for a Church of England retreat house[23], for the suppression of cruelty to animals by the private prayers of members of a society[24], for the maintenance of particular animals[25], for a refuge for animals and birds[26], for a sanctuary for birds and wild flowers[27], to feed sparrows[28], a gift of a house to provide a commodious residence for the High Commissioner of Australia for the time being[29], a devise of a house to a college as a residence for a fellow who should 'sometimes give entertainment to the poor'[30], a conveyance of land to be used as a recreation ground for the benefit of the employees of a named company[31], for establishing a hotel for distinguished overseas visitors to Stratford-upon-Avon[32], and a fund to maintain a building of national architectural interest which was used largely for the private purposes of the body to which it belonged[33].

1    *Goodman v Saltash Corpn* (1882) 7 App Cas 633 at 650, HL, per Earl Cairns.

2    *Liley v Hey* (1842) 1 Hare 580; *Thomas v Howell* (1874) LR 18 Eq 198; *Edge v Salisbury* (1749) Amb 70.

3    *A-G v Hughes* (1689) 2 Vern 105.

4    *Cocks v Manners* (1871) LR 12 Eq 574; *Re Clarke, Clarke v Clarke* [1901] 2 Ch 110; *Re Smith, Johnson v Bright-Smith* [1914] 1 Ch 937; *Re Drummond, Ashworth v Drummond* [1914] 2 Ch 90 at 97 per Eve J. See also *Re Taylor, Midland Bank Executor and Trustee Co Ltd v Smith* [1940] Ch 481, [1940] 2 All ER 637; appeal

dismissed by consent [1940] Ch 834, CA (gift to bank staff fund having purposes charitable and non-charitable: not charitable, but valid; *Cocks v Manners* supra and *Re Clarke, Clarke v Clarke* supra applied).

5     *Rogers v Thomas* (1837) 2 Keen 8.

6     *Browne v King* (1885) 17 LR Ir 488; and cf *Bristow v Bristow* (1842) 5 Beav 289.

7     *A-G v Haberdashers' Co* (1834) 1 My & K 420; *Re Meech's Will, Butchers' Co v Rutland* [1910] 1 Ch 426.

8     *Cocks v Manners* (1871) LR 12 Eq 574; *Stewart v Green* (1870) IR 5 Eq 470; *Re Delany* (1881) 9 LR Ir 226. See also *Re Delany, Conoley v Quick* [1902] 2 Ch 642, where the objects of the convent were charitable; *Neville Estates Ltd v Madden* [1962] Ch 832, [1961] 3 All ER 769; *Re Banfield, Lloyds Bank Ltd v Smith* [1968] 2 All ER 276, [1968] 1 WLR 846.

9     *Gilmour v Coats* [1949] AC 426, [1949] 1 All ER 848, HL. See also *Neville Estates Ltd v Madden* [1962] Ch 832, [1961] 3 All ER 769; *Re Banfield, Lloyds Bank Ltd v Smith* [1968] 2 All ER 276, [1968] 1 WLR 846.

10    *Edge v Salisbury* (1749) Amb 70, where 'nearest relations' was construed to mean statutory next of kin; *Brunsden v Woolredge* (1765) Amb 507; *Widmore v Woodroffe* (1766) Amb 636; *Goodinge v Goodinge* (1749) 1 Ves Sen 231; *Doyley v A-G* (1735) 4 Vin Abr 485, pl 16; *Salusbury v Denton* (1857) 3 K & J 529. See also *Gower v Mainwaring* (1750) 2 Ves Sen 87; and para 19 ante.

11    *Re Compton, Powell v Compton* [1945] Ch 123, [1945] 1 All ER 198, CA. See also *Davies v Perpetual Trustee Co Ltd* [1959] AC 439, [1959] 2 All ER 128, PC.

12    *Re Drummond, Ashworth v Drummond* [1914] 2 Ch 90.

13    *Re Hobourn Aero Components Ltd's Air-Raid Distress Fund, Ryan v Forrest* [1946] Ch 194, [1946] 1 All ER 501, CA.

14    *Wernher's Charitable Trust v IRC* [1937] 2 All ER 488. See also *Re Cox, Baker v National Trust Co Ltd* [1955] AC 627, [1955] 2 All ER 550, PC; *Re Koettgen's Will Trusts, Westminster Bank Ltd v Family Welfare Association Trustees Ltd* [1954] Ch 252, [1954] 1 All ER 581; *Caffoor (Trustees of Abdul Gaffoor Trust) v Income Tax Comr, Colombo* [1961] AC 584, [1961] 2 All ER 436, PC.

15    *Oppenheim v Tobacco Securities Trust Co Ltd* [1951] AC 297, [1951] 1 All ER 31, HL.

16    *Gibson v South American Stores (Gath and Chaves) Ltd* [1950] Ch 177, [1949] 2 All ER 985, CA; following *Re Gosling, Gosling v Smith* (1900) 48 WR 300, and *Re Sir Robert Laidlaw's Will Trusts* (1935, unreported).

17    *Clark v Taylor* (1853) 1 Drew 642; cf *Re Marchant, Weaver v Royal Society for the Prevention of Cruelty to Animals* (1910) 54 Sol Jo 425.

18    *Laverty v Laverty* [1907] 1 IR 9.

19    *Re Gassiot, Fladgate v Vintners' Co* (1901) 70 LJCh 242.

20    *Re Tunno, Raikes v Raikes* [1886] WN 154, where the object was the benefit of the owner of the estate.

21    *Re Barnett, Waring v Painter Stainers Co* (1908) 24 TLR 788; but see *Re Coxen, McCallum v Coxen* [1948] Ch 747, [1948] 2 All ER 492 (bequest to provide dinner to charity trustees meeting for trust business: charitable as promoting efficient management of charity).

22    *Hoare v Hoare* (1886) 56 LT 147 at 150 per Chitty J.

23    *Re Warre's Will Trusts, Wort v Salisbury Diocesan Board of Finance* [1953] 2 All ER 99, [1953] 1 WLR 725.

24    *Re Joy, Purday v Johnson* (1888) 60 LT 175 at 178 per Chitty J, where the real object contemplated by the testator was the improvement of the members of the society, not the suppression of cruelty to animals, which is a valid charitable purpose. As to trusts for the protection or benefit of animals see para 44 ante.

25    *Re Dean, Cooper-Dean v Stevens* (1889) 41 ChD 552; *Re Howard, Oakley v Aldridge* (1908) Times, 30 October. If a trust or condition for maintaining specified animals does not violate any rule against remoteness, it is not in itself unlawful. There may be no beneficiary directly interested in seeing to its enforcement; but when a trustee accepts a trust, the execution of which includes a lawful direction, or where an annuitant accepts an annuity subject to a lawful condition, the courts have not abstained from recognising such obligations. In *Pettingall v Pettingall* (1842) 11 LJCh 176 (applied in *Re Thompson, Public Trustee v Lloyd* [1934] Ch 342) the executor was held, upon the construction of the will, to be a beneficial legatee of the surplus of an annual sum which he was directed to apply to the keeping of a mare; the court enforced the obligation by requiring full information to be given when required respecting the animal, by giving liberty to apply, and by an undertaking to maintain the animal comfortably. In *Mitford v Reynolds* (1848) 16 Sim 105 at 116, 120 per Shadwell V-C, there was a charitable bequest, after deducting the annual amount required for the keep of specified horses; the court's order included provision for the horses. In *Re Dean, Cooper-Dean v Stevens* supra, a trust annuity for the maintenance of certain horses and dogs was held valid. A proper way of providing for specified animals has been said to be by giving an annuity to a custodian payable so long as any of them are living: *Re Howard, Oakley v Aldridge* supra. See also *Re Endacott, Corpe v Endacott* [1960] Ch 232, [1959] 3 All ER 562, CA.

26    See para 44 ante.

27    *Re Glyn's Will Trusts* (1953) Times, 28 March.

28   See *A-G v Whorwood* (1750) 1 Ves Sen 534 at 536 per Lord Hardwicke LC.

29   *Re Spensley's Will Trusts, Barclays Bank Ltd v Staughton* [1954] Ch 233, [1954] 1 All ER 178, CA. But see *Re Courtauld-Thomson Trusts* (1954) Times, 18 December, where a gift to apply income, and, if necessary, capital, in defraying the expenses of residence of a minister of the Crown in certain property, the subject matter of another disposition, was held to be a valid charitable trust.

30   *A-G v Whorwood* (1750) 1 Ves Sen 534.

31   *Wernher's Charitable Trust v IRC* [1937] 2 All ER 488.

32   *Re Corelli, Watt v Bridges* [1943] Ch 332, [1943] 2 All ER 519.

33   *Trades House of Glasgow v IRC* 1970 SLT 294.


**54. Monuments and tombs.** Gifts for building, maintaining or repairing a monument or tomb which does not form part of the fabric or ornament of a church[1], whether as a memorial or burying place of the donor alone[2] or of himself and his family[3], cannot be supported as charities, though they may be valid as private trusts if they do not offend the law against perpetuities[4]. However, these cases are anomalous and should not be followed except where the one is exactly like another[5].

Gifts for monuments and tombs may not be construed as charitable even when expressed through a charitable gift to be applied preferably in a particular way 'and a small provision for keeping in repair the graves of my wife's parents'[6]. So, too, a bequest to an infirmary for the purpose of maintaining the testator's grave and headstone is void; and a further bequest of personalty for the general purposes of the infirmary subject to its accepting the prior bequest takes effect free from the condition[7]. However, a bequest for maintaining a burial ground, and in particular the grave of the testator's wife, is good[8], and the direction with regard to the particular grave is merely a special obligation ancillary to the repair of the burial ground and not a separate trust[9].

Where a fund is bequeathed to trustees upon trust out of the income to keep a tomb not forming part of a church[10] in repair, and as to the residue[11], surplus[12], balance[13] or remainder[14], upon trust for charitable objects, the gift is construed as a bequest of the whole fund charged with a gift that fails, and not as a gift of the residue after a void gift[15], and accordingly the whole fund, including the amount necessary to satisfy the invalid object, is applicable to the valid charitable object[16].

As in the case of gifts for the repair of tombs, a condition attaching to a gift, that a tomb which is not part of the fabric of a church be kept in repair, is not charitable but is not of itself illegal. If such a condition is limited within the perpetuity period, so that no remote interest will arise on its determination, it may be a valid condition[17]; and a perpetual condition of this sort attaching to a valid charitable gift, with a gift over on breach of the condition to another charity, has been held valid[18]. However, where the gift over is not to a charity, the condition is void and the original bequest takes effect free from the condition[19], and if the condition attaches to a non–charitable gift, that gift fails and with it the gift over[20].

By contrast, a bequest to trustees of a sum of money upon trust to invest it and pay the income to a cemetery company during such period as the company should keep specified graves in order, and if the graves should not be kept in order to pay the income to charitable organisations entitled to the balance of the testator's residuary income not required for another charitable purpose, has been held not to infringe the rule against perpetuities or the rule against inalienability and to be a valid gift[21].

Local authorities and burial authorities have power to agree with any person to maintain private monuments and memorials in certain circumstances in consideration of the payment of a sum by him, provided that no such agreement imposes on the authority an obligation of maintenance with respect to a period exceeding 99 years from the date of the agreement[22]. A burial authority also has power to agree with any person, on such terms and conditions as it thinks proper, to maintain any grave, vault, tombstone or other memorial in a cemetery for a period not exceeding 100 years from the date of the agreement[23].

1   *Trimmer v Danby* (1856) 25 LJCh 424; *Hoare v Osborne* (1866) LR 1 Eq 585; *Re Rigley's Trusts* (1866) 36 LJCh 147; *Re Barker, Sherrington v Dean and Chapter of St Paul's Cathedral* (1909) 25 TLR 753.

2   *Mellick v Asylum President and Guardians* (1821) Jac 180; *Adnam v Cole* (1843) 6 Beav 353; *Lloyd v Lloyd* (1852) 2 Sim NS 255; *Willis v Brown* (1838) 2 Jur 987.

3   *Gravenor v Hallum* (1767) Amb 643; *Durour v Motteux* (1749) 1 Ves Sen 320; *Doe d Thompson v Pitcher* (1815) 3 M & S 407; *Re Rickard, Rickard v Robson* (1862) 31 Beav 244; *Fowler v Fowler* (1864) 33 Beav 616; *Hoare v Osborne* (1866) LR 1 Eq 585; *Re Rigley's Trusts* (1866) 36 LJCh 147; *Fisk v A-G* (1867) LR 4 Eq 521; *Hunter v Bullock* (1872) LR 14 Eq 45; *Dawson v Small* (1874) LR 18 Eq 114; *Re Williams* (1877) 5 ChD 735; *Re Birkett* (1878) 9 ChD 576; *Yeap Cheah Neo v Ong Cheng Neo* (1875) LR 6 PC 381; *Re Vaughan, Vaughan v Thomas* (1886) 33 ChD 187; *Re Rogerson, Bird v Lee* [1901] 1 Ch 715; *Toole v Hamilton* [1901] 1 IR 383. As to the maintenance of graveyards see para 36 ante.

4   *Mellick v Asylum President and Guardians* (1821) Jac 180; *Trimmer v Danby* (1856) 25 LJCh 424; *Roche v M'Dermott* [1901] 1 IR 394 at 399. A trust in a will to keep up a tomb for as long as the law for the time being permits is valid for 21 years from the time of the testator's death: *Pirbright v Salwey* [1896] WN 86, followed in *Re Hooper, Parker v Ward* [1932] 1 Ch 38. Cf *Re Moore, Prior v Moore* [1901] 1 Ch 936, where the addition of words 'that is to say until the period of twenty-one years from the death of the last survivor of all persons who shall be living at my death' rendered the trust void for uncertainty. But see now the Perpetuities and Accumulations Act 1964; and PERPETUITIES AND ACCUMULATIONS.

5   *Re Endacott, Corpe v Endacott* [1960] Ch 232 at 251, [1959] 3 All ER 562 at 571, CA, per Harman LJ, and at 246 and 568 per Lord Evershed MR.

6   *Re Norton's Will Trusts, Lightfoot v Goldson* [1948] 2 All ER 842.

7   *Re Elliott, Lloyds Bank Ltd v Burton-on-Trent Hospital Management Committee* [1952] Ch 217, [1952] 1 All ER 145, where the prior bequest was admitted to be void as creating a perpetuity and, the condition precedent being therefore illegal, its effect on the further bequest as *malum prohibitum* was decided by reference to the civil law. See also WILLS vol 50 (Reissue) para 369.

8   See *Re Hooper, Parker v Ward* [1932] 1 Ch 38.

9   *Re Manser, A-G v Lucas* [1905] 1 Ch 68.

10  The repair of a tomb forming part of a church is charitable: see para 36 ante.

11  *Fisk v A-G* (1867) LR 4 Eq 521; *Re Vaughan, Vaughan v Thomas* (1886) 33 ChD 187.

12  *Hoare v Osborne* (1866) LR 1 Eq 585; *Dawson v Small* (1874) LR 18 Eq 114; *Re Williams* (1877) 5 ChD 735.

13  *Hunter v Bullock* (1872) LR 14 Eq 45; and cf *Re Taylor, Martin v Freeman* (1888) 58 LT 538, where in a special case a bequest of 'the balance' was not construed as residuary. As to what constitutes a residuary gift to charity see generally *Paice v Archbishop of Canterbury* (1807) 14 Ves 364; *A-G v Goulding* (1788) 2 Bro CC 428; *Harbin v Masterman* (1871) LR 12 Eq 559; *Harbin v Masterman* [1894] 2 Ch 184, CA (affd sub nom *Wharton v Masterman* [1895] AC 186, HL).

14  *Re Birkett* (1878) 9 ChD 576.

15  The principle on which this class of cases is to be distinguished from the class (of which *Mitford v Reynolds* (1842) 1 Ph 185, forms one; see para 79 post), in which the charity took only the surplus after the amount necessary for the invalid object had been ascertained, and not the entire fund, is that the direction for the upkeep of the tomb created only a moral obligation: *Re Rogerson, Bird v Lee* [1901] 1 Ch 715 at 719 per Joyce J; *Re Dalziel, Midland Bank Executor and Trustee Co Ltd v St Bartholomew's Hospital* [1943] Ch 277, [1943] 2 All ER 656, where a gift over showed that no mere moral obligation was intended.

16  *Re Rogerson, Bird v Lee* [1901] 1 Ch 715; and see the cases cited in notes 11–14 supra. Cf *Fowler v Fowler* (1864) 33 Beav 616 (where the gift of the surplus, after a trust to repair a tomb, was held void for uncertainty on the ground that the amount required for repairing a tomb could not be ascertained); *Re Rigley's Trusts* (1866) 36 LJCh 147 (where the court directed an inquiry to ascertain in what proportions a gift valid as to part and invalid as to the other part, namely the repair of a private tomb, should be divided). An affidavit of a competent person as to the cost of such repairs has been accepted: *Re Vaughan, Vaughan v Thomas* (1886) 33 ChD 187; *Re Birkett* (1878) 9 ChD 576 at 579 per Jessel MR. The principle of these 'tomb cases' has been held inapplicable to a somewhat analogous gift for maintaining a memorial masonic temple: *Re Porter, Porter v Porter* [1925] Ch 746.

17  *Lloyd v Lloyd* (1852) 2 Sim NS 255 at 264 per Lord Cranworth V-C; *Re Dean, Cooper-Dean v Stevens* (1889) 41 ChD 552 at 557 per North J; *Pirbright v Salwey* [1896] WN 86. The ratio decidendi of the two

last cited cases is 'anomalous and not easy to explain' (Jarman on Wills (8th Edn, 1951) p 286 note (s)); but *Pirbright v Salwey* supra was followed in *Re Hooper, Parker v Ward* [1932] 1 Ch 38 (Maugham J). In *Lloyd v Lloyd* supra there were two trusts for the repair of tombs: one of the inheritance on a trust to repair a tomb, which the court held void as a perpetuity (*Lloyd v Lloyd* supra at 266 per Lord Cranworth V-C); the other a condition that two annuitants should out of their life estates keep a tomb in repair, which was held binding on the annuitants. In that case, at 264, Kindersley V-C said that he was satisfied that a condition simply for keeping a tomb in repair was not a charitable one, and was not of itself illegal; it might be illegal to vest property in trustees in perpetuity for such a purpose; but the direction that the annuitants should out of their life interests keep the tomb in repair was quite lawful and they were obliged, out of their annuities, to do so according to the direction of the will.

18   *Re Tyler, Tyler v Tyler* [1891] 3 Ch 252, CA. The principle of the decision was that the rule against perpetuities does not apply to a transfer, in certain events, of property from one charity to another. As to the validity of gifts over see para 135 post.

19   *Re Davies, Lloyd v Cardigan County Council* [1915] 1 Ch 543.

20   *Re Dalziel, Midland Bank Executor and Trustee Co Ltd v St Bartholomew's Hospital* [1943] Ch 277, [1943] 2 All ER 656.

21   *Re Chardon, Johnston v Davies* [1928] Ch 464; *Re Chambers' Will Trusts, Official Trustees of Charitable Funds v British Union for Abolition of Vivisection* [1950] Ch 267. Tudor on Charities (5th Edn, 1929) p 701 sets out clauses of the will and the court order omitted from the report of *Re Chardon, Johnston v Davies* supra, and notes that the decision in that case was not affected by the presence of charitable interests. See also the article 'The Upkeep of a Tomb' (1950) 100 L Jo 524, explaining the decision on the basis that the legatees were free to dispose of the income as they pleased so long as the graves were kept in repair. Such a gift would now be affected by the Perpetuities and Accumulations Act 1964 s 12: see para 136 post; and PERPETUITIES AND ACCUMULATIONS vol 35 (Reissue) para 1040.

   On the other hand, a gift of income for an indefinite period to a society for the furtherance of non-charitable purposes is void: *Re Wightwick's Will Trusts, Official Trustees of Charitable Funds v Fielding-Ould* [1950] Ch 260, [1950] 1 All ER 689, citing *Re Dutton, ex p Peake* (1878) 4 ExD 54; *Re Clark's Trust* (1875) 1 ChD 497; *Re Swain, Phillips v Poole* (1908) 99 LT 604; *Cocks v Manners* (1871) LR 12 Eq 574 at 586 per Wickens V-C; *Re Clarke, Clarke v Clarke* [1901] 2 Ch 110; *Re Drummond, Ashworth v Drummond* [1914] 2 Ch 90. See also *Re Elliott, Lloyds Bank Ltd v Burton-on-Trent Hospital Management Committee* [1952] Ch 217, [1952] 1 All ER 145 (see the text and note 7 supra); *Re Conner, Provincial Bank of Ireland Ltd v General Cemetery Co of Dublin and Lucas* [1960] IR 67.

22   See the Parish Councils and Burial Authorities (Miscellaneous Provisions) Act 1970 s 1(1) (as amended); and CREMATION AND BURIAL. As to burial authorities see CREMATION AND BURIAL.

23   Local Authorities' Cemeteries Order 1977, SI 1977/204, art 10(7). See also CREMATION AND BURIAL.


**55. Gifts for associations and perpetual institutions.** An association or institution may benefit its members in the course of carrying out its main charitable purpose, and this alone will not prevent its being a charity[1]. It is a question of fact whether there is so much personal benefit, intellectual or professional, to the members of a society or body as to be incapable of being disregarded[2].

Gifts for associations or institutions whose objects are solely or substantially for the private advantage of their members are not charitable[3], as, for example, gifts to societies for promoting the interests of the members of a profession[4], and gifts for friendly and other mutual benefit societies[5] not requiring poverty as an essential element to entitle a member to the benefits of the society[6], the Corps of Commissionaires[7], a trade union or its benevolent fund[8], a sacred harmonic society[9], a mechanics' institute[10], a library[11], chess club[12], or museum[13], established for subscribers only. However, this principle does not apply with full force to associations established for religious purposes, although it would if they were wholly secluded and contemplative[14].

On the winding up of associations of this kind the funds may be divisible among the members for the time being[15], but, where there is no resulting trust for subscribers and the members are only entitled by their contract of membership to a limited interest in the funds of the association, any surplus after satisfying the contractual rights of members passes to the Crown as bona vacantia[16].

A gift to a perpetual unincorporated non-charitable institution may be construed as a gift to the individual members of the institution for the time being; and may be valid, if it is not, and when paid will not become, subject to any trust which prevents the existing members from spending the money as they please[17]. If, however, the gift is one which, by reason of its own terms or of the constitution of the institution in whose favour it is made, tends to a perpetuity, it is bad[18], except in the case of a gift authorised by the Literary and Scientific Institutions Act 1854[19], notwithstanding that such an institution is perpetual and non-charitable and that the members pay subscriptions[20].

1   See *IRC v Yorkshire Agricultural Society* [1928] 1 KB 611 at 630, CA, per Atkin LJ; and para 28 note 12 ante.

2   *Midland Counties Institution of Engineers v IRC* (1928) 14 TC 285 at 293, CA, per Rowlatt J; *London Hospital Medical College v IRC* [1976] 2 All ER 113 at 122, [1976] 1 WLR 613 at 623 per Brightman J ('a matter of degree').

3   A society engaged in joint operation for the sake of gain may be a partnership, but a society for charitable purposes is not: see PARTNERSHIP vol 35 (Reissue) para 4.

4   *R v Income Tax Special Comrs, ex p Headmasters' Conference, R v Income Tax Special Comrs, ex p Incorporated Association of Preparatory Schools* (1925) 41 TLR 651; *Geologists' Association v IRC* (1928) 14 TC 271, CA (combination of members for scientific purposes and mutual improvement, all the benefits being enjoyed primarily by the members; followed in *Midland Counties Institution of Engineers v IRC* (1928) 14 TC 285, CA (association of persons for mutual improvement in technical and professional knowledge); *Honourable Co of Master Mariners v IRC* (1932) 17 TC 298 (association to foster professional interests); *Chartered Insurance Institute v London Corpn* [1957] 2 All ER 638, [1957] 1 WLR 867, DC. So, too, a body formed to register and regulate the members of a profession is not charitable: *General Medical Council v IRC* (1928) 97 LJKB 578, CA; *General Nursing Council for Scotland v IRC* 1929 SC 664 (council not a body established for charitable purposes only; funds partly benefited professional interest); *General Nursing Council for England and Wales v St Marylebone Borough Council* [1959] AC 540, [1959] 1 All ER 325, HL).

5   *Re Clark's Trust* (1875) 1 ChD 497; *Cunnack v Edwards* [1896] 2 Ch 679, CA; *Re Topham, Public Trustee v Topham* [1938] 1 All ER 181 (club having for object the religious, intellectual, physical and social improvement of its members and associated with a church); *Lord Nuffield v IRC* (1946) 175 LT 465 (trust to organise mutual insurance associations to meet expenditure necessitated by illness, not charitable); and see the cases cited in note 15 infra. The receipt of donations and subscriptions is not sufficient to make a friendly society charitable: *Re Clark's Trust* supra at 500 per Hall V-C; *Re Buck, Bruty v Mackey* [1896] 2 Ch 727 at 733 per Kekewich J; *Braithwaite v A-G* [1909] 1 Ch 510. See, however, *Re Forster, Gellatly v Palmer* [1939] Ch 22, [1938] 3 All ER 767.

6   See the cases cited in para 22 notes 6–7 ante.

7   *Re Clarke, Clarke v Clarke* [1901] 2 Ch 110.

8   *Re Amos, Carrier v Price* [1891] 3 Ch 159. See also *Re Estlin, Prichard v Thomas* (1903) 72 LJCh 687.

9   *Re Allsop, Gell v Carver* (1884) 1 TLR 4; but see *Royal Choral Society v IRC* [1943] 2 All ER 101, CA.

10  *Re Dutton, ex p Peake* (1878) 4 ExD 54; *Re Sheraton's Trusts* [1884] WN 174.

11  *Carne v Long* (1860) 2 De GF & J 75; *Re Swain, Phillips v Poole* (1908) 99 LT 604; *Re Prevost, Lloyds Bank Ltd v Barclays Bank Ltd* [1930] 2 Ch 383.

12  *Re Swain, Phillips v Poole* (1908) 99 LT 604.

13  *Thomson v Shakespear* (1860) 1 De GF & J 399; *Laverty v Laverty* [1907] 1 IR 9; *Re Joy, Purday v Johnson* (1888) 60 LT 175.

14  *Neville Estates Ltd v Madden* [1962] Ch 832, [1961] 3 All ER 769; and see para 31 ante.

15  *Brown v Dale* (1878) 9 ChD 78; *Re Russell Institution, Figgins v Baghino* [1898] 2 Ch 72; *Re Jones, Clegg v Ellison* [1898] 2 Ch 83; *Re Printers and Transferrers Amalgamated Trades Protection Society* [1899] 2 Ch 184; *Re Lead Co's Workmen's Fund Society, Lowes v Governor and Co for Smelting Down Lead with Pit and Sea Coal* [1904] 2 Ch 196; *Re Customs and Excise Officers' Mutual Guarantee Fund, Robson v A-G* [1917] 2 Ch 18; *Re St Andrew's Allotment Association's Trusts, Sargeant v Probert* [1969] 1 All ER 147, [1969] 1 WLR 229; *Re Sick and Funeral Society of St John's Sunday School, Golcar* [1973] Ch 51, [1972] 2 All ER 439; *Re Bucks Constabulary Widows and Orphans Fund Friendly Society (No 2)* [1979] 1 All ER 623, [1979] 1 WLR 936; *Re GKN Bolts and Nuts Ltd Sports and Social Club, Leek v Donkersley* [1982] 2 All ER 855, [1982] 1 WLR 774. Contra, *Re West Sussex Constabulary's Widows, Children and Benevolent (1930) Fund Trusts, Barnett v Ketteringham* [1971] Ch 1, [1970] 1 All ER 544. See also *Re Grant's Will Trusts, Harris v Anderson* [1979] 3 All ER 359, [1980] 1 WLR 360; *Conservative and Unionist Central Office v Burrell (Inspector of*

*Taxes)* [1980] 3 All ER 42 (affd without discussion of this point [1982] 2 All ER 1, [1982] 1 WLR 522, CA).

16 *Cunnack v Edwards* [1896] 2 Ch 679, CA. As to the court's jurisdiction to dissolve such societies on sufficient cause being shown see *Blake v Smither* (1906) 22 TLR 698; and on the question of dissolution generally see *Re William Denby & Son Ltd Sick and Benevolent Fund, Rowling v Wilks* [1971] 2 All ER 1196, [1971] 1 WLR 973. As to bona vacantia see CROWN PROPERTY vol 12(1) (Reissue) para 231 et seq.

17 *Cocks v Manners* (1871) LR 12 Eq 574; *Re Clarke, Clarke v Clarke* [1901] 2 Ch 110 at 114 per Byrne J; *Re Smith, Johnson v Bright-Smith* [1914] 1 Ch 937; *Re Drummond, Ashworth v Drummond* [1914] 2 Ch 90 at 97 per Eve J; *Bourne v Keane* [1919] AC 815 at 874, HL, per Lord Buckmaster, and at 916, per Lord Parmoor; *Re Delany, Conoley v Quick* [1902] 2 Ch 642; *Re Turkington, Owen v Benson* [1937] 4 All ER 501 (gift to local masonic lodge as a fund to build local temple: held that members could not be trustees for themselves); *Re Taylor, Midland Bank Executor and Trustee Co Ltd v Smith* [1940] Ch 481, [1940] 2 All ER 637 (on appeal [1940] Ch 834, CA) (gift for bank staff association fund, formed for purposes only partly charitable, to be administered according to rules of fund under which committee could deal with it as it pleased; on appeal, parties agreed); *Re Price, Midland Bank Executor and Trustee Co Ltd v Harwood* [1943] Ch 422, [1943] 2 All ER 505 (gift to Anthroposophical Society to be used at the discretion of the chairman and executive council for carrying on the teachings of the founder: capital and income being held to be available); *Re Lipinski's Will Trusts, Gosschalk v Levy* [1976] Ch 235, [1977] 1 All ER 33 (a non-charitable purpose trust which is directly or indirectly for the benefit of ascertained individuals is valid). Contrast *Re Grant's Will Trusts, Harris v Anderson* [1979] 3 All ER 359, [1980] 1 WLR 360. See also generally *Leahy v A-G for New South Wales* [1959] AC 457, [1959] 2 All ER 300, PC; *Neville Estates Ltd v Madden* [1962] Ch 832, [1961] 3 All ER 769; *Re Recher's Will Trusts, National Westminster Bank Ltd v National Anti-Vivisection Society* [1972] Ch 526, [1971] 3 All ER 401.

18 *Re Clarke, Clarke v Clarke* [1901] 2 Ch 110 at 114 per Byrne J; *Thomson v Shakespear* (1860) 1 De GF & J 399; *Carne v Long* (1860) 2 De GF & J 75; *Re Dutton, ex p Peake* (1878) 4 ExD 54; *Re Amos, Carrier v Price* [1891] 3 Ch 159; *Re Swain, Phillips v Poole* (1908) 99 LT 604; *Re Clifford, Mallam v McFie* [1912] 1 Ch 29, 81 LJCh 220; *Re Macaulay's Estate, Macaulay v O'Donnell* [1943] Ch 435n, HL (gift to local lodge of Theosophical Society for the maintenance and improvement of the local Theosophical Lodge denotes permanency and endowment). The invalidity of such gifts is not saved by the Perpetuities and Accumulations Act 1964: see s 15(4); and PERPETUITIES AND ACCUMULATIONS vol 35 (Reissue) para 1005.

19 See LIBRARIES AND OTHER SCIENTIFIC AND CULTURAL INSTITUTIONS vol 28 (Reissue) para 483.

20 See the Literary and Scientific Institutions Act 1854 s 30; and LIBRARIES AND OTHER SCIENTIFIC AND CULTURAL INSTITUTIONS vol 28 (Reissue) para 497. See also *Re Badger, Mansell v Viscount Cobham* [1905] 1 Ch 568 at 573 per Buckley J.

### (ii) Superstitious Uses

**56. Superstitious uses.** Certain kinds of gift have in the past been held void as being for superstitious uses, whether or not their validity would otherwise depend on whether they were valid charitable gifts. A superstitious use may be defined as one which has for its object the propagation or the rites of a religion not tolerated by the law[1].

The Act of Uniformity 1558 made all forms of religion other than that of the Church of England illegal, and consequently gifts for the clergy or the buildings of Roman Catholics or Protestant dissenters, or for the propagation of the doctrines and principles of Roman Catholicism or the Jewish religion[2], were held void for superstition upon the common law principle that no disposition of property for purposes which are illegal can effect the intended purposes[3].

The effect of the Act of Uniformity 1558 was, however, alleviated by a succession of relieving Acts[4], and the Act of Uniformity itself has now been almost wholly repealed. The result is that there are now no religions proscribed by law[5]. It has been said that dispositions connected with relics, the veneration of saints or the sustenance of miracle producers might be held invalid despite the relieving Acts[6], but even if these practices were regarded as superstitious, such dispositions would not in themselves fall within the definition of superstitious uses[7]. If they were to be held invalid it might be on the ground that they were not charitable, there being no evidence of public benefit of which the court could take cognisance[8].

1  This is not exhaustive but will serve as a working definition: *Bourne v Keane* [1919] AC 815 at 845, 874, 916, HL, per Lord Birkenhead LC. See also *R v Lady Portington* (1692) 1 Salk 162; Duke on Charitable Uses 106.

2  See eg *Jones' Case* (1690) [1893] 2 Ch 49n, HL; *A-G v Todd* (1837) 1 Keen 803; *Smart v Prujean* (1801) 6 Ves 560; *De Garcin v Lawson* (1798) 4 Ves 433n; *Doe d Wellard v Hawthorn* (1818) 2 B & Ald 96; *Cary v Abbot* (1802) 7 Ves 490; *A-G v Power* (1809) 1 Ball & B 145; *De Themmines v De Bonneval* (1828) 5 Russ 288; *De Costa v De Paz* (1754) 2 Swan 487n.

3  *Bourne v Keane* [1919] AC 815 at 847, HL, per Lord Birkenhead LC.

4  See the Toleration Act 1688 (repealed); the Nonconformist Relief Act 1779 (repealed); the Places of Religious Worship Act 1812 (repealed); the Roman Catholic Relief Act 1829 (see ECCLESIASTICAL LAW vol 14 para 1389 et seq); the Roman Catholic Charities Act 1832 (repealed); the Liberty of Religious Worship Act 1855 (repealed); the Roman Catholic Relief Act 1926 (repealed); the Religious Disabilities Act 1846 (repealed) (Jews). As to the effect of the Toleration Act 1688 see *Evans' Case* (1767) cited in 3 Mer 375n.

5  Cf *Thornton v Howe* (1862) 31 Beav 14; and see para 32 ante.

6  *Bourne v Keane* [1919] AC 815 at 855, HL, per Lord Birkenhead LC.

7  See the text to note 1 supra.

8  Cf *Gilmour v Coats* [1949] AC 426, [1949] 1 All ER 848, HL.

**57. Gifts for masses for the dead.** Gifts for masses were among the gifts void as being for superstitious uses; even after the relieving Acts[1] it was believed that gifts for masses for the dead were void for superstition[2], but this was based on a misunderstanding[3]. It seems that no gifts can now be rendered void on this ground[4]. Such a gift may well be charitable, for it is clearly for the advancement of religion, and the element of public benefit required is satisfied at least where the masses are to be celebrated in public[5].

1  As to the relieving Acts see para 56 text and note 4 ante.

2  See *West v Shuttleworth* (1835) 2 My & K 684.

3  See *Bourne v Keane* [1919] AC 815, HL, overruling *West v Shuttleworth* (1835) 2 My & K 684 and the cases following it.

4  The Roman Catholic Charities Act 1860 (repealed) seems to have assumed that there could still be trusts void for superstition, but it was a remedial Act and, if there could be no such trusts, the remedy is merely superfluous: see *Bourne v Keane* [1919] AC 815 at 856, HL, per Lord Birkenhead LC, and at 896, per Lord Atkinson. Lord Birkenhead LC said in that case, at 860, that the decision did not mean that there are now no superstitious uses, but he did not suggest any, nor have any come to light since 1919.

5  *Re Hetherington* [1990] Ch 1, sub nom *Re Hetherington, Gibbs v McDonnell* [1989] 2 All ER 129, following *Re Caus, Lindeboom v Camille* [1934] Ch 162, notwithstanding doubts expressed in *Gilmour v Coats* [1949] AC 426, [1949] 1 All ER 848, HL. As to the requirement for public benefit see paras 6–8 ante. As to religious purposes see para 31 ante.

## (iii)  Non–Charitable Public Purposes

**58. Non-charitable public objects.** Although purposes beneficial to the public or of public utility are prima facie charitable[1], certain public purposes are not charitable because they do not fall within the spirit and intendment of the preamble to the statute of Elizabeth I[2].

Thus, the following have been held not to be charitable: bequests for purposes of benevolence[3] or benevolence and liberality[4], for patriotic[5], civil or religious[6], philanthropic[7], parochial[8], missionary[9], pious[10], or Roman Catholic[11] purposes, or worthy causes[12], or for parish work[13], or for social or recreational purposes in connection with certain churches[14], or for purposes most conducive to the good of religion in a diocese[15], or for purposes conducive to the attainment of the objects of an association not limited to the advancement of religion[16], or for helping to carry on the work of the Church in Wales[17], or for executing the Papal office[18], or for purposes of hospitality[19] or general utility[20] or for emigration uses[21], or for strengthening the bonds of unity between a Commonwealth country and the mother country or for appeasing racial feeling between sections of a community[22], or for promoting closer understanding between the English and Swedish peoples[23], or for simplifying spelling[24], or for increasing the sum of available knowledge[25], or for the storage of books[26], or for the encouragement of a mere sport or game such as cricket, football, fencing, yachting, bicycling, lawn tennis, or any other healthy exercise and recreation primarily calculated to amuse individuals, even though the sport may be beneficial to the community[27].

Although the provision of the means of public recreation may be charitable[28], trusts for the promotion of religious, social and physical well-being[29], and for religious, moral, social and recreative purposes[30] and for giving aid and advice to the community generally[31] have been held not to be charitable. A gift to provide 'some useful memorial to myself' is not charitable[32]; nor is a gift for the general benefit and welfare of children for the time being in a local authority home[33]. The protection of the interests of holders in the United Kingdom of foreign bonds[34] is not charitable; nor is a pig marketing board[35] or a statutory body set up to administer a harbour[36], and a body established to help the government resist strikes threatening essential public services is also not charitable[37].

1   *Incorporated Council of Law Reporting for England and Wales v A-G* [1972] Ch 73, [1971] 3 All ER 1029, CA; and see para 12 ante.
2   43 Eliz 1 c 4 (1601) (now wholly repealed: see para 2 note 7 ante). See also para 12 ante. A trust to distribute income among organisation or institution operating for the public good was held not exclusively charitable: see *A-G of the Cayman Islands v Wahr Hansen* [2001] 1 AC 75, [2000] 3 All ER 642, PC.
3   *James v Allen* (1817) 3 Mer 17; *Re Jarman's Estate, Leavers v Clayton* (1878) 8 ChD 584; *A-G for New Zealand v Brown* [1917] AC 393, PC; *A-G for New Zealand v New Zealand Insurance Co Ltd* [1936] 3 All ER 888, PC.
4   *Morice v Bishop of Durham* (1805) 10 Ves 522. This is not so in Scotland: *Miller v Rowan* (1837) 5 Cl & Fin 99, HL.
5   *A-G v National Provincial and Union Bank of England* [1924] AC 262, HL.
6   *Re Friends' Free School, Clibborn v O'Brien* [1909] 2 Ch 675.
7   *Re Macduff, Macduff v Macduff* [1896] 2 Ch 451, CA.
8   *Re Stratton, Knapman v A-G* [1931] 1 Ch 197, CA; *Cookstown Roman Catholic Church Trustees v IRC* (1953) 34 TC 350 (parochial requirements).
9   As to missionary purposes see para 33 ante.
10  *Heath v Chapman* (1854) 2 Drew 417 at 425–426 per Page Wood V-C.
11  *MacLaughlin v Campbell* [1906] 1 IR 588; and see *Re Davidson, Minty v Bourne* [1909] 1 Ch 567, CA. Cf *Re Schoales, Schoales v Schoales* [1930] 2 Ch 75 (gift to the Roman Catholic Church for its use: charitable).
12  *Re Gillingham Bus Disaster Fund, Bowman v Official Solicitor* [1958] Ch 300 at 305, [1958] 1 All ER 37 at 39 per Harman J; affd [1959] Ch 62, [1958] 2 All ER 749, CA, where there are dicta arguably supporting the opposite proposition. See *Re Atkinson's Will Trusts, Atkinson v Hall* [1978] 1 All ER 1275, [1978] 1 WLR 586 where the inclusion of 'worthy causes' in the list in the text was approved.

13  *Farley v Westminster Bank Ltd* [1939] AC 430, [1939] 3 All ER 491, HL.

14  *Londonderry Presbyterian Church House Trustees v IRC* [1946] NI 178, CA.

15  *Dunne v Byrne* [1912] AC 407, PC.

16  *Oxford Group v IRC* [1949] 2 All ER 537, CA; followed in *Associated Artists Ltd v IRC* [1956] 2 All ER 583, [1956] 1 WLR 752. See also para 31 note 5 ante.

17  *Re Jackson, Midland Bank Executor and Trustee Co Ltd v Archbishop of Wales* [1930] 2 Ch 389.

18  *Re Moore, Moore v Pope Benedict XV* [1919] 1 IR 316.

19  *Re Hewitt's Estate, Gateshead Corpn v Hudspeth* (1883) 53 LJCh 132; and see *A-G v Whorwood* (1750) 1 Ves Sen 534; and *Re Corelli, Watt v Bridges* [1943] Ch 332, [1943] 2 All ER 519 (hostel for distinguished visitors from far countries).

20  *Kendall v Granger* (1842) 5 Beav 300; *Re Woodgate* (1886) 2 TLR 674.

21  *Re Sidney, Hingeston v Sidney* [1908] 1 Ch 488, CA; *Keren Kayemeth Le Jisroel Ltd v IRC* [1932] AC 650, HL (trust for settlement of Jews in Palestine and elsewhere); but cf *Verge v Somerville* [1924] AC 496, PC (cited in para 42 note 12 ante) and *Re Tree, Idle v Tree* [1945] Ch 325, [1945] 2 All ER 65 (cited in para 22 note 8 ante).

22  *Re Strakosch, Temperley v A-G* [1949] Ch 529, [1949] 2 All ER 6, CA, but see para 42 text and note 21 ante. See also *Re Koeppler Will Trusts, Barclays Bank Trust Co Ltd v Slack* [1984] Ch 243, [1984] 2 All ER 111; revsd [1986] Ch 423, [1985] 2 All ER 869, CA; and para 60 post.

23  *Anglo-Swedish Society v IRC* (1931) 47 TLR 295.

24  *Sir GB Hunter (1922) C Trust (Trustees) v IRC* (1929) 45 TLR 344; *Re Shaw, Public Trustee v Day* [1957] 1 All ER 745, [1957] 1 WLR 729.

25  *Whicker v Hume* (1858) 7 HL Cas 124 at 155 per Lord Chelmsford LC; *Re Macduff, Macduff v Macduff* [1896] 2 Ch 451 at 472–473, CA, per Rigby LJ; *Re Shaw, Public Trustee v Day* [1957] 1 All ER 745, [1957] 1 WLR 729.

26  *Re Hawkins, Walrond v Newton* (1906) 22 TLR 521.

27  *Re Nottage, Jones v Palmer* [1895] 2 Ch 649, CA; *Re Clifford, Mallam v McFie* [1912] 1 Ch 29, 81 LJCh 220 (angling); *Re Patten, Westminster Bank Ltd v Carlyon* [1929] 2 Ch 276 (teaching cricket); *Peterborough Royal Foxhound Show Society v IRC* [1936] 2 KB 497, [1936] 1 All ER 813 (fox hunting). Cf *Re Stephens, Giles v Stephens* (1892) 8 TLR 792 (encouragement of skill in rifle shooting: charitable); *Re Gray, Todd v Taylor* [1925] Ch 362 (gifts for the encouragement of sports tending to increase the efficiency of the army: charitable); *Re Mariette, Mariette v Aldenham School Governing Body* [1915] 2 Ch 284; *Re Lipinski's Will Trusts, Gosschalk v Levy* [1976] Ch 235, [1977] 1 All ER 33 (sports club existing for the benefit of its members; not charitable); *Report of Charity Commissioners for England and Wales for 1989* (HC Paper (1989–90) no 343) paras 42–55 (Birchfield Harriers not charitable); and see the Recreational Charities Act 1958; and paras 46–49 ante. See also *IRC v City of Glasgow Police Athletic Association* [1953] AC 380, [1953] 1 All ER 747, HL. As to games and tournaments see para 29 ante.

28  See the Recreational Charities Act 1958; and paras 46–49 ante.

29  *IRC v Baddeley* [1955] AC 572, [1955] 1 All ER 525, HL.

30  *Londonderry Presbyterian Church House Trustees v IRC* [1946] NI 178, CA.

31  *D'Aguiar v Guyana IRC* (1970) 49 ATC 33, PC.

32  *Re Endacott, Corpe v Endacott* [1960] Ch 232, [1959] 3 All ER 562, CA.

33  *Re Cole, Westminster Bank Ltd v Moore* [1958] Ch 877, [1958] 3 All ER 102, CA; but see *Re Sahal's Will Trusts, Alliance Assurance Co Ltd v A-G* [1958] 3 All ER 428, [1958] 1 WLR 1243.

34  *Foreign Bondholders Corpn v IRC* [1944] 1 KB 403, [1944] 1 All ER 420, CA.

35  *Northern Ireland Pig Marketing Board v IRC* [1945] NI 155.

36  *Auckland Harbour Board v IRC* [1959] NZLR 204.

37  *Trustees for the Roll of Voluntary Workers v IRC* 1942 SC 47.


**59.  Purposes contrary to public policy.** A gift for a purpose not permitted by the law is void and cannot be charitable[1]. Similarly, if the gift is for a purpose contrary to public policy it is not a good charitable gift. Thus, gifts to pay the fines of imprisoned criminals[2], or which tend to promote revolution in a friendly foreign state[3], or for propagating doctrines subversive of morality[4] or disseminating pernicious knowledge[5], may be held void. A gift for a purpose contrary to ecclesiastical law, but not otherwise illegal, is not invalid on that ground[6], and the propagation of doctrines subversive of Christianity is not necessarily contrary to public policy[7].

1  Cf the cases on superstitious uses: see para 56 ante. As to gifts for illegal purposes see GIFTS vol 20 (Reissue) paras 61–62.

2  *Thrupp v Collett* (1858) 26 Beav 125. The reference in the preamble to the statute of Elizabeth I (43 Eliz 1 c 4 (1601) (now wholly repealed: see para 2 note 7 ante)) to the relief and redemption of prisoners or captives (see para 12 ante) may be taken to refer to prisoners of war or Christian captives in Barbary (cf *Ironmongers' Co v A-G* (1844) 10 Cl & Fin 908, HL), or debtors other than those in contempt of court (cf *Re Prison Charities* (1873) LR 16 Eq 129).

3  *Habershon v Vardon* (1851) 4 De G & Sm 467 (political restoration of the Jews to Jerusalem, then under Turkish sovereignty).

4  *Thornton v Howe* (1862) 31 Beav 14; *Thompson v Thompson* (1844) 1 Coll 381 at 397 per Shadwell V-C; and see *Russell v Jackson* (1852) 10 Hare 204 (socialism); *Pare v Clegg* (1861) 29 Beav 589.

5  *Re Macduff, Macduff v Macduff* [1896] 2 Ch 451 at 474, CA, per Rigby LJ.

6  *Re Bowman, Secular Society Ltd v Bowman* [1915] 2 Ch 447 at 470, CA, per Warrington LJ; on appeal sub nom *Bowman v Secular Society Ltd* [1917] AC 406, HL.

7  *Bowman v Secular Society Ltd* [1917] AC 406, HL, overruling *Briggs v Hartley* (1850) 19 LJCh 416, and *Cowan v Milbourn* (1867) LR 2 Exch 230. It seems that this authority extends to doctrines subversive of all religion (see *Bowman v Secular Society Ltd* supra at 420 per Lord Finlay LC), although the House of Lords only treated the society as anti-Christian. See also *Thompson v Thompson* (1844) 1 Coll 381.

**60. Political purposes.** A trust for the attainment of political objects is not charitable, not because it is illegal (for everyone is at liberty to advocate or promote by any lawful means a change in the law), but because the court has no means of judging whether a proposed change in the law will or will not be for the public benefit, and therefore cannot say that a gift to secure the change is a charitable gift[1]. Political purposes include[2]: (1) furthering the interests of a political party; (2) procuring, or opposing[3], changes in the law of this, or a foreign, country; (3) procuring a reversal of government policy or a particular decision of government authority in this, or a foreign, country; (4) attempting to sway public opinion on controversial social issues[4]. Any purpose with the object of influencing the legislature is a political purpose[5]; and a trust for furthering the views of a particular political party, whether under the guise of an educational centre[6] or a fund for adult education on party lines[7], is not charitable; but a trust for a purpose which is charitable is not rendered non-charitable even if the trust instrument envisages the use of political means to achieve the charitable object[8].

1  *Bowman v Secular Society Ltd* [1917] AC 406 at 442, HL, per Lord Parker, dealing with a society advocating the disestablishment of the Church; *National Anti-Vivisection Society v IRC* [1948] AC 31, [1947] 2 All ER 217, HL (society having as its main purpose the compulsory abolition of vivisection by Act of Parliament: not charitable); *Re Jones, Public Trustee v Earl of Clarendon* (1929) 45 TLR 259 (Primrose League: not a charity); *English-Speaking Union v Westminster City Council* (1959) 4 RRC 97, DC; *Re Bushnell, Lloyds Bank Ltd v Murray* [1975] 1 All ER 721, [1975] 1 WLR 1596 (trust for propagation of doctrines of socialist medicine not charitable); *McGovern v A-G* [1982] Ch 321, [1981] 3 All ER 493. See also *IRC v Temperance Council of Christian Churches of England and Wales* (1926) 136 LT 27; *Re Hood, Public Trustee v Hood* [1931] 1 Ch 240 at 250, CA, per Lord Hanworth MR, and at 252 per Lawrence LJ (trust to promote temperance mainly by political means: not charitable, though the advancement of temperance otherwise is charitable).

2  *McGovern v A-G* [1982] Ch 321, [1981] 3 All ER 493. As to where useful arts and other public purposes are charitable see para 42 ante. As to non-charitable public objects see para 58 ante.

3  *Re Koeppler Will Trusts, Barclays Bank Trust Co Ltd v Slack* [1984] Ch 243, [1984] 2 All ER 111; revsd [1986] Ch 423, [1985] 2 All ER 869, CA, without affecting relevant dictum.

4  See eg *Southwood v A-G* [1998] 40 LS Gaz R 37, Times, 26 October; affd [2000] NLJR 1017, Times, 18 July, CA, where a trust to advance education of the public in militarism and disarmament, which defined policies of certain government and challenged them, was political, not charitable.

5  *IRC v Temperance Council of Christian Churches of England and Wales* (1926) 136 LT 27; cf *Re Shaw, Public Trustee v Day* [1957] 1 All ER 745, [1957] 1 WLR 729, where the achievement of the purpose (the promotion of a new alphabet) would have involved legislation (an appeal was dismissed by consent on

terms [1958] 1 All ER 245n, CA). See also *Baldry v Feintuck* [1972] 2 All ER 81 at 85, [1972] 1 WLR 552 at 558 per Brightman J; *Webb v O'Doherty* (1991) 3 Admin LR 731, (1991) Times, 11 February (campaigning in the sense of seeking to influence public opinion on political matters not a charitable activity).

6   *Bonar Law Memorial Trust v IRC* (1933) 49 TLR 220; and see para 45 note 2 ante.

7   *Re Hopkinson, Lloyds Bank Ltd v Baker* [1949] 1 All ER 346.

8   *National Anti-Vivisection Society v IRC* [1948] AC 31 at 51, 61, 76, [1947] 2 All ER 217 at 225, HL, per Lord Wright, at 231 per Lord Simonds, and at 239 per Lord Normand; *Re Hood, Public Trustee v Hood* [1931] 1 Ch 240, CA.

## 2. CREATION OF CHARITABLE TRUSTS

## (1) FORMAL REQUIREMENTS AND RESTRICTIONS

### (i) Creation by Assurance

**61. Realty and personalty.** As a general rule, realty and personalty of all descriptions, including advowsons[1] and easements[2], may be given to a charity by deed or by will.

Since the repeal of the mortmain laws[3], restrictions on the assurance of land in favour of charity exist only in the form of personal and corporate incapacity. Limited owners and persons under disability may make charitable gifts only in accordance with their particular powers or in the manner and form prescribed by enabling statutes. A corporation may only make charitable gifts within the framework of its constitution and for objects contemplated by it[4], if it is created by statute[5] or registered under the Companies Acts[6] or is a municipal corporation[7]. A corporation created by royal charter, however, has prima facie the same power of disposition as a natural person[8].

1   *A-G v Ward* (1829) 7 LJOS Ch 114; *A-G v Archbishop of York* (1853) 17 Beav 495; *A-G v St John's Hospital, Bedford* (1864) 10 Jur NS 897; *Re St Stephen, Coleman Street, Re St Mary the Virgin, Aldermanbury* (1888) 39 ChD 492; *Hunter v A-G* [1899] AC 309 at 322, HL, per Lord Davey; *Re Church Patronage Trust, Laurie v A-G* [1904] 2 Ch 643, CA. But see the Patronage (Benefices) Measure 1986 s 3 (prospectively amended), prohibiting the sale of advowsons; and ECCLESIASTICAL LAW.

2   The contrary was stated in Duke on Charitable Uses, ed Bridgman (1805) 137–138, but there seems to be no reason why such a grant should not be made, and in many cases charities must be entitled to easements (see EASEMENTS AND PROFITS À PRENDRE).

3   See paras 75–76 post.

4   It may not be ultra vires for a company to give away its property to charity, if it is done bona fide in the interests of the company: see *Hutton v West Cork Rly Co* (1883) 23 ChD 654 at 673, CA, per Bowen LJ; *Evans v Brunner, Mond & Co* [1921] 1 Ch 359; *Re Lee, Behrens & Co Ltd* [1932] 2 Ch 46; but see also *Parke v Daily News Ltd* [1962] Ch 927, [1962] 2 All ER 929. Parliament has recognised this by obliging companies to disclose, in directors' reports, charitable donations to a total of more than £200: see the Companies Act 1985 s 235, Sch 7 paras 3–5; and COMPANIES vol 7(2) (1996 Reissue) para 1072.

5   *Baroness Wenlock v River Dee Co* (1883) 36 ChD 675n, CA; on appeal (1885) 10 App Cas 354, HL.

6   As to registration of companies see COMPANIES vol 7(1) (1996 Reissue) para 21 et seq.

7   See LOCAL GOVERNMENT; LONDON GOVERNMENT. See generally GIFTS.

8   See *Sutton's Hospital Case* (1612) 10 Co Rep 1a, 23a at 30b, Ex Ch. As to the limitation of powers of chartered corporations see CORPORATIONS vol 9(2) (Reissue) para 1136; GIFTS vol 20 (Reissue) para 9.

**62. Facilities for giving land, etc to charity.**   The Universities of Oxford, Cambridge and Durham and certain colleges[1], and the Crown Estates Commissioners with the consent of Her Majesty under the royal sign manual[2] may give limited areas of land for certain charitable purpose.

Particular classes of donor have also been given facilities for giving limited areas of land for special charitable purposes. These include any life tenant, a lord of a manor in respect of common land, a beneficiary under a trust, the guardian of a minor, and various corporate or public bodies and trustees holding land in a corporate, public or charitable capacity, who may grant land as a site for a school and certain allied purposes[3], or for enlarging a churchyard or burial ground[4]. Similar provisions apply to assist gifts for the promotion of science, literature and the fine arts, including libraries and reading rooms[5]; or for a place of worship, a minister's residence or a burial place[6].

Former powers for endowing or augmenting a minister's income or providing a church or chapel for a new parish[7] and of corporations, trustees of charitable institutions and persons absolutely entitled for giving to the Church Commissioners[8] land for providing a church, chapel, churchyard or parsonage[9] have been replaced by more extensive powers conferred on any corporation, any trustees for charitable purposes, the Crown Estates Commissioners, the Chancellor of the Duchy of Lancaster, the Duke of Cornwall and government departments to give or convey land to the Church Commissioners for churches, churchyards or burial grounds, residences for incumbents or other ecclesiastical persons, or for providing access to or improving the amenities of any of the foregoing[10].

In some cases the court has allowed subscriptions and donations in favour of charity to be made out of the estate of a mentally disordered person[11], but it can only authorise a gift to a purpose for which the patient might be expected to provide if he were not mentally disordered[12]. A capital sum may in some circumstances be paid to charity under a power of advancement in discharge of the moral obligation of a wealthy beneficiary under a settlement[13].

1   See the Universities and College Estates Act 1925 ss 15, 16 (as amended); and EDUCATION.
2   See the Crown Estate Act 1961 s 4; and CROWN PROPERTY vol 12(1) (Reissue) para 294. As to the Crown Estate Commissioners see CROWN PROPERTY vol 12(1) (Reissue) para 280.
3   See the School Sites Act 1841 s 2 (as amended), s 6 (as amended), s 10 (as amended); and EDUCATION.
4   See the Consecration of Churchyards Act 1867 s 4 (as amended), applying certain provisions of the School Sites Act 1841; and CREMATION AND BURIAL; ECCLESIASTICAL LAW.
5   See the Literary and Scientific Institutions Act 1854; and LIBRARIES AND OTHER SCIENTIFIC AND CULTURAL INSTITUTIONS vol 28 (Reissue) para 476 et seq.
6   See the Places of Worship Sites Act 1873; the Places of Worship Sites Amendment Act 1882; and ECCLESIASTICAL LAW vol 14 para 1065. See also the Reverter of Sites Act 1987 s 1 (as amended), ss 6, 7; and paras 63–64 post.
7   New Parishes Act 1843 s 22 (repealed); New Parishes Act 1844 s 11 (repealed); New Parishes Act 1856 s 4 (repealed). See the New Parishes Measure 1943; and ECCLESIASTICAL LAW.
8   These Commissioners have replaced the Ecclesiastical Commissioners: see the Church Commissioners Measure 1947; and ECCLESIASTICAL LAW vol 14 para 362 et seq.
9   Church Building Act 1818 s 33 (repealed); Church Building Act 1819 (repealed); Church Building Act 1822 ss 2, 3 (both repealed); Church Building Act 1831 ss 2, 7 (both repealed); Church Building Act 1838 ss 6–9 (all repealed). See the New Parishes Measure 1943; and ECCLESIASTICAL LAW.
10  See the New Parishes Measure 1943 ss 13, 14 (as amended); and ECCLESIASTICAL LAW vol 14 paras 1061–1062.
11  *Re Frost* (1870) 5 Ch App 699; *Re Strickland* (1871) 6 Ch App 226.
12  See the Mental Health Act 1983 ss 95(1)(c), 96(1)(d); and MENTAL HEALTH vol 30 (Reissue) paras 1441–1442.
13  *Re Clore's Settlement Trusts, Sainer v Clore* [1966] 2 All ER 272, [1966] 1 WLR 955.

**63. Rights of reverter.** Land granted under the School Sites Act 1841 and the other similar nineteenth century enactments for the establishment of schools and churches and other charitable purposes may now be put to alternative use if, the land being no longer used for the purpose of the grant, the person entitled to the land cannot be traced[1].

Where any relevant enactment provides for land to revert to the ownership of any person at any time, being a time when the land ceases, or has ceased for a specified period, to be used for particular purposes, the enactment has effect, and is deemed always to have had effect[2], as if it provided (instead of for the reverter) for the land to be vested after that time, on the trust arising under this provision, in the persons in whom it was vested immediately before that time[3]. The trust so arising in relation to any land is a trust for the persons who, but for these provisions, would from time to time be entitled to the ownership of the land by virtue of its reverter with a power, without consulting them, to sell the land and to stand possessed of the net proceeds of sale (after payment of costs and expenses) and of the net rents and profits until sale (after payment of rates, taxes, costs of insurance, repairs and other outgoings) in trust for those persons; but they are not be entitled by reason of their interest to occupy the land[4]. Where a trust in relation to any land has arisen or is treated as having arisen[5] and immediately before that time the land was vested in any persons in their capacity as the minister and churchwardens of any parish[6], those persons are treated as having become trustees[7] in that capacity and, accordingly, their interest in the land passes and, if the case so requires, to be treated as having passed to their successors from time to time[8].

These provisions do not confer any right on any person as a beneficiary in relation to any property in respect of which that person's claim was statute-barred[9] before 17 August 1987[10] or in relation to any property derived from any such property or in relation to any rents or profits received, or breach of trust committed, before that date[11]. Where any property is held by any persons as trustees of a trust which has arisen[12] and there are no beneficiaries of that trust[13], the trustees have no power to act in relation to that property except[14]: (1) for the purposes for which they could have acted if these provisions[15] had not been passed[16]; or (2) for the purpose of securing the establishment of a Charity Commissioners' scheme[17] or the making of an order under the special powers[18] as to trusts for religious education[19].

1   See the Reverter of Sites Act 1987; the text and notes 2–19 infra; and para 64 post. The need for reform in this area was identified by the Law Commission in its report *Rights of Reverter* (Cmnd 8410) (1981). Nothing in the Act requires any land which is or has been the subject of any grant, conveyance or other assurance under any relevant enactment to be treated as or as having been settled land: Reverter of Sites Act 1987 s 6(1). The power conferred by the School Sites Act 1841 s 14 (as amended) (power of sale etc) is exercisable at any time in relation to land in relation to which, but for the exercise of the power, a trust might subsequently arise under the Reverter of Sites Act 1987 s 1 (as amended); and the exercise of that power in respect of any land prevents any trust from arising under s 1 (as amended) in relation to that land or any land representing the proceeds of sale of that land: s 6(2); and see EDUCATION. 'Relevant enactment' means any enactment contained in the School Sites Acts (see EDUCATION), the Literary and Scientific Institutions Act 1854 (see LIBRARIES AND OTHER SCIENTIFIC AND CULTURAL INSTITUTIONS vol 28 (Reissue) para 476 et seq) or the Places of Worship Sites Act 1873 (see ECCLESIASTICAL LAW vol 14 para 1065): Reverter of Sites Act 1987 s 7(1). References to land include references to: (1) any part of any land which has been the subject of a grant, conveyance or other assurance under any relevant enactment; and (2) any land an interest in which (including any future or contingent interest arising under any such enactment) belongs to the Crown, the Duchy of Lancaster or the Duchy of Cornwall: s 7(2).

2   Ie subject to ibid s 4 (as amended): see para 64 post.

3   Ibid s 1(1).

4   Ibid s 1(2) (s 1 amended by the Trusts of Land and Appointment of Trustees Act 1996, s 5, Sch 2 para 6). The amendments made by the Trusts of Land and Appointment of Trustees Act 1996 do not affect any entailed interest created before its commencement (1 January 1997): s 25(4). The amendments made by the Trusts of Land and Appointment of Trustees Act 1996 in consequence of the abolition of the doctrine of conversion do not affect a trust created by a will if the testator died before 1 January 1997, and do not affect personal representatives of a person who died before that date: see s 25(5).

5   Ie under the Reverter of Sites Act 1987 s 1(1) (as amended) at such a time as is mentioned in that provision: see the text and notes 2–3 supra.

6    For these purposes, 'churchwardens' include chapel wardens, 'minister' includes a rector, vicar or perpetual curate, and 'parish' includes a parish of the Church in Wales: ibid s 1(6).

7    Ie under ibid s 1 (as amended).

8    Ibid s 1(3) (as amended: see note 4 supra).

9    The reference to a person's claim being statute-barred is a reference to the Limitation Act 1980 providing that no proceedings are brought by that person to recover the property in respect of which the claim subsists: Reverter of Sites Act 1987 s 1(6). As to limitation see further LIMITATION OF ACTIONS.

10    Ie the commencement of the Reverter of Sites Act 1987.

11    Ibid s 1(4) (as amended: see note 4 supra). Anything validly done before 17 August 1987 in relation to any land which by virtue of s 1 (as amended) is deemed to have been held at the time in trust is, if done by the beneficiaries, deemed, so far as necessary for preserving its validity, to have been done by the trustees: s 1(4).

12    See note 7 supra.

13    Ie in consequence the Reverter of Sites Act 1987 s 1(4): see the text and notes 9–11 supra.

14    Ibid s 1(5). See the *Report of the Charity Commissioners for England and Wales for 1988* (HC Paper (1988–89) no 319) paras 78–83.

15    Ie the Reverter of Sites Act 1987.

16    Ibid s 1(5)(a).

17    Ie a scheme under ibid s 2: see para 64 post. As to the Charity Commissioners see paras 486–512 post.

18    Ie under the Education Act 1996 s 554 (as amended): see EDUCATION.

19    Reverter of Sites Act 1987 s 1(5)(b) (amended by the Education Act 1996 s 582(1), Sch 37 para 67). An order made under the Education Act 1996 s 554 (as amended) (see para 176 post) with respect to so much of any endowment as consists of land in relation to which a trust under the Reverter of Sites Act 1987 s 1 (as amended) has arisen or will arise after the land ceased or ceases to be used for particular purposes, or any other property subject to a trust under that provision may extinguish any rights to which a person is or may become entitled as a beneficiary under the trust: s 5(1) (s 5 amended by the Education Act 1996 s 582(1), Sch 37 para 67). The Secretary of State may not by an order under the Education Act 1996 s 554 extinguish any such rights unless he is satisfied that all reasonably practicable steps to trace the persons who are or may become entitled to any of those rights have been taken and that either: (1) there is no claim by any person to be a person who is or may become entitled which is outstanding, or which has at any time been accepted as valid by the trustees or by persons whose acceptance binds or will bind the trustees, or which has been upheld in proceedings that have been concluded; or (2) consent to the making of an order under s 554 (as amended) has been given by every person whose claim to be such a person is outstanding or has been so accepted or upheld: Reverter of Sites Act 1987 s 5(2) (as so amended). A claim by any person to be a beneficiary under a trust is outstanding if it has been notified to the trustees, it has not been withdrawn and proceedings for determining whether it ought to have been upheld have not been commenced or (if commenced) have not been concluded: s 7(3). Proceedings in relation to any person's claim are not treated as concluded where the time for appealing is unexpired or an appeal is pending unless that person has indicated his intention not to appeal or to continue with his appeal: s 7(4).

     Where applications for the extinguishment of the rights of any beneficiaries are made with respect to the same trust property both to the Secretary of State under the Education Act 1996 s 554 (as amended) or to the Charity Commissioners under the Reverter of Sites Act 1987 s 2 (see para 64 post) the Commissioners may not consider or further consider the application made to them unless the Secretary of State either consents to the consideration of the application made to the Charity Commissioners before the application made to him or disposes of the application made to him without extinguishing the rights of one or more of the beneficiaries: s 5(3) (as so amended).

     Trustees of a trust arising under s 1 (as amended) may pay or apply capital money for the purposes of any provision of s 5 (as amended) or the Education Act 1996 s 554 (as amended): Reverter of Sites Act 1987 s 5(4) (as so amended).

     As to the Secretary of State see para 513 post. In relation to Wales, the functions of the Secretary of State under the Reverter of Sites Act 1987 are carried out by the National Assembly for Wales: National Assembly for Wales (Transfer of Functions) Order 1999, SI 1999/672, art 2, Sch 1. As to the National Assembly for Wales see CONSTITUTIONAL LAW AND HUMAN RIGHTS.

## 64. Charity Commissioners' schemes under the Reverter of Sites Act 1987.

Where any persons hold any property as trustees of a trust which has arisen under the provisions of Reverter of Sites Act 1987[1], the Charity Commissioners[2], on the application of the trustees[3], may by order[4] establish a scheme which extinguishes the rights of the beneficiaries under the trust and requires the trustees to hold the property on trust for such charitable purposes as may be specified in the order[5]. The charitable purposes must be as similar in character as the Commissioners think is practicable in all the circumstances to the purposes, whether charitable or not, for which the trustees held the relevant land[6] before the cesser of use in consequence of which the trust arose[7]. However, in determining the character of the latter purposes, if they think it appropriate to do so, the Commissioners may give greater weight to the persons or locality benefited by the purposes than to the nature of the benefit[8].

1 Ie under the Reverter of Sites Act s 1 (as amended): see para 63 ante.
2 As to the Charity Commissioners see paras 486–512 post.
3 As to the application by trustees see para 65 post.
4 As to orders to establish Charity Commissioners' schemes see para 66 post.
5 Reverter of Sites Act 1987 s 2(1). Section 2(1) is expressed to be subject to the provisions of ss 2(2)–(8), 3, 4 (see paras 65–66 post): see s 2(1). An order may contain any such provision as may be contained in an order made by the High Court for establishing a scheme for the administration of a charity and has the same effect as an order so made: s 2(2). As to the general jurisdiction and powers of the court in relation to the settlement of schemes see para 174 et seq post.
6 'Relevant land', in relation to a trust which has arisen under ibid s 1 (as amended) (see para 63 ante), means the land which but for the Reverter of Sites Act 1987 would have reverted to the persons who are the first beneficiaries under the trust: s 7(1).
7 Ibid s 2(3).
8 Ibid s 2(3).

**65. Applications for Charity Commissioners' schemes under the Reverter of Sites Act 1987.** The Charity Commissioners may not make any order[1] establishing a scheme under the Reverter of Sites Act 1987[2] unless the trustees have satisfied the requirements for the making of an application for a scheme. These requirements are satisfied if, before the application is made[3]:

(1) notices[4] have been published in two national newspapers and in a local newspaper circulating in the locality where the relevant land[5] is situated[6];

(2) each of the notices specified a period for the notification to the trustees of claims by beneficiaries, being a period ending not less than three months after the date of publication of the last of those notices to be published[7];

(3) that period has ended[8];

(4) for a period of not less than 21 days during the first month of that period, a copy of one of the notices was affixed to an object on the relevant land in such a positions and manner as, so far as practicable, to make the notice easy for members of the public to see and read it without going on to the land[9]; and

(5) the trustees have considered what other steps could be taken to trace the persons who are or may be beneficiaries and to inform those persons of the application for the scheme and have taken such of the steps considered by them as it was reasonably practicable for them to take[10].

The above requirements do not apply in the case of an application made in respect of any trust if the time when the trust is treated as having arisen was before 17 August 1987[11] and more than 12 years have elapsed since then[12].

The Commissioners must refuse to consider an application by the trustees under these provisions unless it is accompanied by a statutory declaration by the applicants that the requirements for the making of an application[13] are satisfied with respect to the making of the application or, if the declaration so declares, do not apply, and that one of two specified conditions[14] is identified in the declaration and fulfilled[15]. The declaration is conclusive for these purposes of the matters declared in it[16].

1   As to orders to establish Charity Commissioners' schemes see para 66 post. As to the Charity Commissioners see paras 486–512 post.
2   Ie under the Reverter of Sites Act 1987 s 2: see paras 64 ante, 66 post.
3   Ibid s 3(1).
4   A notice must: (1) set out the circumstances that have resulted in a trust's having arisen under the Reverter of Sites Act 1987 s 1 (as amended) (see para 63 ante); (2) state that an application is to be made for the establishment of a scheme with respect to the property subject to the trust; and (3) contain a warning to every beneficiary that, if he wishes to oppose the extinguishment of his rights, he ought to notify his claim to the trustees in the manner, and within the period, specified in the notice: s 3(2).
5   For the meaning of 'relevant land' see para 64 note 6 ante. As to references to land see para 63 note 1 ante.
6   Reverter of Sites Act 1987 s 3(1)(a).
7   Ibid s 3(1)(b).
8   Ibid s 3(1)(c).
9   Ibid s 3(1)(d). Where at the time when the trustees publish a notice for the purposes of s 3(2) (see note 4 supra) the relevant land is not under their control and it is not reasonably practicable for them to arrange for a copy to be affixed as so required, s 3(1)(d) is to be disregarded: s 3(3).
10   Ibid s 3(1)(e).
11   Ie the commencement of the Reverter of Sites Act 1987.
12   Ibid s 3(4).
13   Ie the requirements under ibid s 3: see the text and notes 1–12 supra.
14   Ie one of the conditions in ibid s 2(6): see para 66 head (2) in the text post.
15   Ibid s 2(7).
16   Ibid s 2(7).

**66. Orders of the Charity Commissioners establishing schemes under the Reverter of Sites Act 1987.** The Charity Commissioners[1] may not make any order establishing a scheme under the Reverter of Sites Act 1987[2] unless:

(1)   the requirements[3] for making an application for the order are satisfied or do not apply[4];

(2)   one of the following conditions is fulfilled[5]:

    (a)   there is no claim by any person to be a beneficiary in respect of rights proposed to be extinguished which is outstanding[6] or which has at any time been accepted as valid by the trustees or by persons whose acceptance binds them or which has been upheld in proceedings that have been concluded[7]; or

    (b)   consent to the establishment of such a scheme has been given by every person whose claim to be a beneficiary in respect of those rights is outstanding or has been so accepted or upheld[8];

(3)   public notice of the Commissioners' proposals has been given inviting representations to be made to them within a period specified in the notice, being a period ending not less than a month after the date of the giving of the notice[9]; and

(4)    that period has ended and the Commissioners have taken into consideration any representations which have been made within that period and not withdrawn[10].

An order made on an application[11] with respect to any trust must be so framed as to secure that if a person who, but for the making of the order, would have been a beneficiary under the trust and has not consented to the establishment of a scheme under these provisions, notifies a claim to the trustees within the period of five years after the date of the making of the order, that person may be paid an amount equal to the value of his rights at the time of their extinguishment[12].

Where an order[13] is made by the Commissioners: (i) public notice of it must be given in such manner as they think sufficient and appropriate[14]; and (ii) a copy of the order must, for not less than one month after the date of giving the notice, be available for public inspection at all reasonable times at the Commissioners' office and at some convenient place in the locality where the land is situated[15]. The notice must contain such particulars of the order, or such directions for obtaining information about it, as the Commissioners think sufficient and appropriate[16].

An appeal against an order[17] may be brought in the High Court by any of the following: (A) the Attorney General[18]; (B) the trustees of the trust established under the order[19]; (C) a beneficiary of, or the trustees of, the trust in respect of which the application for the order had been made[20]; (D) any person interested in the purposes for which the last-mentioned trustees or any of their predecessors held the relevant land[21] before the cesser of use in consequence of which the trust arose[22]; (E) or any two or more inhabitants of the locality where that land is situated[23]. Unless it is brought by the Attorney General, an appeal may not be so brought against any order after the end of the three-month period beginning with the day following the date on which public notice of the order is given, or without either a certificate by the Commissioners that it is a proper case for an appeal or the leave of the High Court[24].

Trustees of a trust which has arisen[25] may pay or apply capital money for certain purposes[26] under the Reverter of Sites Act 1987[27].

1    As to the Charity Commissioners see paras 486–512 post.
2    Ie a scheme under the Reverter of Sites Act 1987 s 2: see para 64 ante.
3    Ie the requirements of ibid s 3: see para 65 ante.
4    Ibid s 2(5)(a). The reference in the text to when the requirements for making an application for the order do not apply is a reference to where they do not apply by virtue of s 3(4) (see para 65 ante): see s 2(5)(a).
5    Ibid s 2(5)(b).
6    As to where a claim is outstanding see para 63 note 19 ante.
7    Reverter of Sites Act 1987 s 2(6)(a).
8    Ibid s 2(6)(b).
9    Ibid s 2(5)(c). The notice must contain such particulars of the Commissioners' proposals or such directions for obtaining information about them and must be given in such manner as they think sufficient and appropriate; a further such notice is not required where the Commissioners decide, before proceeding with any proposals of which notice has been given, to modify them: s 2(8).
10   Ibid s 2(5)(d).
11   As to the application by trustees see para 65 ante.
12   Reverter of Sites Act 1987 s 2(4).
13   Ie under ibid s 2: see the text and notes 1–12 supra; and para 64 ante.
14   Ibid s 4(1)(a)
15   Ibid s 4(1)(b).
16   Ibid s 4(1).
17   See note 13 supra.
18   Reverter of Sites Act 1987 s 4(2)(a).
19   Ibid s 4(2)(b).
20   Ibid s 4(2)(c).

21  For the meaning of 'relevant land' see para 64 note 6 ante.

22  Reverter of Sites Act 1987 s 4(2)(d). The reference to the trust arising in the text is a reference to a trust arising under s 1 (as amended) (see para 63 ante): see s 4(2)(d).

23  Ibid s 4(2)(e).

24  Ibid s 4(3). The Charities Act 1993 ss 89, 91, 92 (see paras 492, 493, 549 post) (supplemental provisions with respect to orders and appeals) apply in relation to, and to appeals against, orders under the Reverter of Sites Act 1987 s 2 as they apply in relation to, and to appeals against, orders under the Charities Act 1993: Reverter of Sites Act 1987 s 4(4) (amended by the Charities Act 1993 s 98(1), Sch 6 para 24).

25  Ie under the Reverter of Sites Act 1987 s 1 (as amended): see para 63 ante.

26  Ie for the purposes of ibid s 2 (see the text and notes 1–12 supra), s 3 (see para 65 ante) or s 4 (as amended) (see the text and notes 13–24 supra).

27  Ibid s 4(5).


**67. Writing generally necessary.** Assurances in favour of a charity generally take the form of a conveyance on trust or a declaration of trust; but an express trust is not necessary, since the Crown as parens patriae is the trustee of funds given to charity without trustees or objects selected or without any express trust[1].

Charitable trusts declared in respect of land[2] since 1925 must be manifested and proved by some writing signed by some person who is able to declare the trust or by his will[3], but trusts of personalty are valid without evidence in writing[4].

A charitable trust[5], like a private trust[6], may be created by informal as well as by technical language, provided that the donor's intention to devote the property to charity is clear. Precatory or recommendatory words have frequently been held to create trusts where the testator's intention has been held to be imperative[7]. Similarly, provisions in which the word 'condition' occurs may create trusts[8].

In the case of a charitable gift, the court pays more regard to the intention than to the form of conveyance; for this reason an estate in fee simple might pass to a charity even though the conveyance contained no words of limitation, if it was clear that a gift to charity in perpetuity was intended[9]. A gift which is exclusively charitable made by will may be widened, and so invalidated, by codicil if that is the necessary implication from the words used[10].

A gift may be made to charity by means of a power of appointment[11]. An exercise of a power defective as not complying with the terms of the power will be good if not otherwise invalid[12].

A voluntary conveyance of lands to charity is not avoided by a subsequent conveyance for value unless it was made with the intention of defrauding the purchaser under the subsequent conveyance[13].


1  *Moggridge v Thackwell* (1803) 7 Ves 36 at 69, 83 per Lord Eldon LC (affd (1807) 13 Ves 416, HL); *Morice v Bishop of Durham* (1805) 10 Ves 522 at 541 per Lord Eldon LC; *Ommanney v Butcher* (1823) Turn & R 260 at 271 per Plumer MR: provided there is certainty of intention (see para 76 post). See also para 457 post. As to the law of trusts generally see TRUSTS.

2  For the meaning of 'land' see the Law of Property Act 1925 s 205(1)(ix) (as amended); and REAL PROPERTY vol 39(2) (Reissue) para 77.

3  See ibid s 53(1)(b). In the absence of such writing there would be a resulting trust for the settlor (cf *Hodgson v Marks* [1971] Ch 892, [1971] 2 All ER 684, CA, a non-charity trust case). The requirement of evidence in writing does not apply to resulting, implied or constructive trusts (see the Law of Property Act 1925 s 53(2)) but a charitable trust is hardly likely to arise in these forms. However, see *Re Tyler's Fund Trusts, Graves v King* [1967] 3 All ER 389, [1967] 1 WLR 1269.

4  *Lyell v Kennedy* (1889) 14 App Cas 437 at 457, HL, per Lord Selborne. See further DEEDS AND OTHER INSTRUMENTS vol 13 (Reissue) para 23; TRUSTS vol 48 (2000 Reissue) para 544.

5   *Salusbury v Denton* (1857) 3 K & J 529; *Goodman v Saltash Corpn* (1882) 7 App Cas 633 at 642, HL, where
    Lord Selborne LC said it was immaterial whether the words used were 'trust', 'intent', 'purpose',
    'proviso' or 'condition'

6   *Brown v Higgs* (1803) 8 Ves 561; *Re Williams, Williams v Williams* [1897] 2 Ch 12 at 21–22, CA, per
    Lindley LJ. A private trust is for the benefit of ascertained or ascertainable individuals. As to private trusts
    see TRUSTS vol 48 (2000 Reissue) para 531.

7   *Re Burley, Alexander v Burley* [1910] 1 Ch 215; and see TRUSTS vol 48 (2000 Reissue) para 551. See also
    *A-G v Davies* (1802) 9 Ves 535 at 546 per Lord Eldon LC; *Kirkbank v Hudson* (1819) 7 Price 212; and
    *Pilkington v Boughey* (1841) 12 Sim 114. In those cases the trust was established, but held void as infringing
    the mortmain law then in force. The mortmain statutes have been repealed: see paras 75–76 post.

8   See para 68 post.

9   *A-G v Berwick-upon-Tweed Corpn* (1829) Taml 239 at 246 per Leach MR. If there was no indication that
    a gift to charity in perpetuity was intended, a grant to a person for the benefit of a charity containing no
    words of limitation would, it is conceived, have given the charity the benefit of the grant merely during
    the life of the grantee.

10  *Wheeler v Sheer* (1730) Mos 288, where a gift for such charitable uses as the testator should appoint by
    codicil was followed by a codicil giving the property to such uses and purposes (omitting the word
    'charitable') as he should direct; explained in *Moggridge v Thackwell* (1803) 7 Ves 36 at 79 per Lord Eldon
    LC; *Mills v Farmer* (1815) 1 Mer 55 at 72 per Lord Eldon LC. See also *Charitable Donations Comrs v
    Sullivan* (1841) 1 Dr & War 501 at 507.

11  *Cook v Duckenfield* (1743) 2 Atk 562 at 567 per Lord Hardwicke LC. As to powers of appointment see
    POWERS vol 36(2) (Reissue) para 205 et seq.

12  *Sayer v Sayer, Innes v Sayer* (1849) 7 Hare 377; affd sub nom *Innes v Sayer* (1851) 3 Mac & G 606, where
    a number of authorities are cited. See POWERS vol 36(2) (Reissue) para 362.

13  *Ramsay v Gilchrist* [1892] AC 412, PC. See also the Law of Property Act 1925 s 173; and
    MISREPRESENTATION AND FRAUD vol 31 (Reissue) para 868 et seq. See also *A-G v Newcastle Corpn*
    (1842) 5 Beav 307 at 312 per Lord Langdale MR (affd sub nom *Newcastle-upon-Tyne Corpn v A-G* (1845)
    12 Cl & Fin 402, HL); *Trye v Gloucester Corpn* (1851) 14 Beav 173.

**68.  Condition creating a trust.** A trust is created where the whole of the property is
devoted to purposes which exclude all the donee's beneficial interest, even though the
words used are primarily words of condition[1]; or where property is given upon condition
that a fixed and definite sum, which does not exhaust the entire revenue, shall be applied
in a specified charitable way[2]. On the other hand, where property is given on condition
that an indefinite sum shall be expended for a certain purpose, it is a gift upon condition,
and not a trust; and the donee is entitled to the beneficial interest in the property[3]. It is
a gift upon condition and not a trust where the gift is on condition that, for example, the
donees perform certain duties[4], or a minister preach in a black gown[5].

1   *A-G v Master, Wardens etc of the Wax Chandlers' Co* (1873) LR 6 HL 1 ('for this intent and purpose and
    upon this condition'); *Merchant Taylors' Co v A-G* (1871) 6 Ch App 512 ('to this intent and upon this
    condition'); *Wright v Wilkin* (1862) 2 B & S 259, Ex Ch. See also *Goodman v Saltash Corpn* (1882) 7 App
    Cas 633 at 642, HL, per Lord Selborne LC; *Re Christchurch Inclosure Act* (1888) 38 ChD 520 at 531, CA,
    per Lindley LJ; Duke on Charitable Uses, ed Bridgman (1805) 123–124, 137.

2   *A-G v Grocers' Co* (1843) 6 Beav 526. See also *Re Richardson, Shuldham v Royal National Lifeboat Institution*
    (1887) 56 LJCh 784 (condition to construct and maintain lifeboats attached to a legacy to a charitable
    society construed as a trust).

3   *Jack v Burnett* (1846) 12 Cl & Fin 812, HL (gift to a college on condition that three bursars should be
    maintained); *Re Tyler, Tyler v Tyler* [1891] 3 Ch 252, CA (condition that a tomb should be kept in
    repair); *Re Rosenblum, Rosenblum v Rosenblum* (1924) 131 LT 21.

4   *A-G v Christ's Hospital* (1830) 1 Russ & M 626; *A-G v Cordwainers' Co* (1833) 3 My & K 534 at 543 per
    Leach MR: the imposition of a penalty for non-performance of the condition implies a benefit, if the
    condition be performed, and is inconsistent with any other intention than that the testator meant to

give a beneficial interest to the company upon the terms of complying with the directions contained in his will.

5   *Re Robinson, Wright v Tugwell* [1897] 1 Ch 85, CA; but see *Robinson, Wright v Tugwell* [1923] 2 Ch 332, where this condition was dispensed with.


**69. Charge or trust for charity is binding.** According to the ancient equitable doctrine that no person can acquire an estate with notice of a charitable use without being bound by it, the grantee or devisee of an estate subject to a charge in favour of a charity is a trustee, at any rate until separate trustees of the charge are appointed[1]. If, however, the conveyance or will appoints trustees of the charge, it seems that no fiduciary obligation is imposed on the grantee or devisee[2].

There is a distinction between a charge and a trust in favour of charity[3]. If a devise is made subject to the payment of an annuity to a charitable institution, it is a question of construction[4] whether the devisee is a trustee of the annuity for the charity, or the charity merely has a right to recover the annuity as a charge[5]. A charitable trust may be so limited as to affect part only of the property granted or devised, as where property is given subject to[6], or in trust to make[7], specified charitable payments which do not exhaust the whole estate[8]. In those cases where the donor has not expressed a general intention to devote the whole property to charity, the donee takes beneficially subject only to the specific appropriation[9], unless it appears that he was intended to take only as a trustee, in which case a resulting trust arises in favour of the donor and his successors in title[10].

1   *Charitable Donations and Bequests Comrs v Wybrants* (1845) 2 Jo & Lat 182 at 198 per Lord Sugden LC. See also the non-charity cases of *Hodge v Churchward* (1847) 16 Sim 71, and *Cunningham v Foot* (1878) 3 App Cas 974, HL.
2   *Cunningham v Foot* (1878) 3 App Cas 974 at 987, HL, per Lord Cairns LC.
3   See *Charitable Donations and Bequests Comrs v Wybrants* (1845) 2 Jo & Lat 182 at 198 per Lord Sugden LC.
4   See *Cunningham v Foot* (1878) 3 App Cas 974, HL.
5   The question is of importance in relation to the operation of the Limitation Acts; cf the cases cited in note 1 supra.
6   *Southmolton Corpn v A-G* (1854) 5 HL Cas 1; *A-G v Dean and Canons of Windsor* (1860) 8 HL Cas 369. Cf gifts on condition: see paras 128–129 post.
7   *Beverley Corpn v A-G* (1857) 6 HL Cas 310.
8   *Merchant Taylors' Co v A-G* (1871) 6 Ch App 512 at 520 per James LJ; *A-G v Cordwainers' Co* (1833) 3 My & K 534; *A-G v Trinity College, Cambridge* (1856) 24 Beav 383.
9   *A-G v Bristol Corpn* (1820) 2 Jac & W 294; *A-G v Master, Wardens etc of the Wax Chandlers' Co* (1873) LR 6 HL 1 at 9 per Lord Chelmsford; *A-G v Grocers' Co* (1843) 6 Beav 526; *A-G v Skinners' Co* (1827) 2 Russ 407.
10  *Re Stanford, Cambridge University v A-G* [1924] 1 Ch 73. See also para 163 post.


**70. Equitable doctrines.** The ordinary law as to ademption applies to legacies given to charities[1], as, presumably, do the doctrines of performance, satisfaction and election[2]. Where a legacy is given to the trustees of an endowment fund, it may be adeemed by a gift to the same trustees by the testator during his life[3].

1   *Twining v Powell* (1845) 2 Coll 262; *Makeown v Ardagh* (1876) IR 10 Eq 445. See EQUITY vol 16 (Reissue) para 857 et seq; WILLS vol 50 (Reissue) para 393 et seq.
2   As to election, satisfaction and ademption, and performance see EQUITY vol 16 (Reissue) paras 842 et seq, 857 et seq and 872 et seq respectively.
3   *Re Corbett, Corbett v Lord Cobham* [1903] 2 Ch 326.

## (ii) Creation without an Assurance

**71. Charity established by voluntary subscriptions.** A charity created or established by voluntary subscriptions does not differ from charities established in other ways, provided that a fund exists which is subject to a charitable trust[1].

1   *A-G v Kell* (1840) 2 Beav 575; *Re Welsh Hospital (Netley) Fund, Thomas v A-G* [1921] 1 Ch 655; *Re British Red Cross Balkan Fund, British Red Cross Society v Johnson* [1914] 2 Ch 419; *Re North Devon and West Somerset Relief Fund Trusts, Baron Hylton v Wright* [1953] 2 All ER 1032, [1953] 1 WLR 1260; *Re Lord Mayor of Belfast's Air Raid Distress Fund* [1962] NI 161; cf *Re Gillingham Bus Disaster Fund, Bowman v Official Solicitor* [1959] Ch 62, [1958] 2 All ER 749, CA. As to funds raised by contributions see para 98 post.

**72. Secret trusts.** A donor may make an effective disposition in favour of charity by means of a non-charitable gift affected by a secret trust for charity, whether or not mentioned in the instrument of gift, as by a direction to a donee to use a gift for the charitable purposes agreed between donor and donee[1]. A testator also may make a testamentary disposition to charity subject to a secret trust for non-charitable purposes[2].

The requisites for establishing the existence of a secret trust in favour of charity do not differ from those for other secret trusts[3]. They include the necessity of the testator's intention being communicated to the donee and accepted by him[4], and the admissibility of evidence to prove the terms of a secret charitable trust when its existence is admitted[5]; but where there is no communication in a testator's lifetime of his intention to create a secret trust for charity[6], or where no secret trust is proved[7], the donee takes absolutely, unless it appears that he is a trustee and takes upon a resulting trust[8]. A secret trust is a personal obligation binding the individual donee. If he renounces or disclaims, or dies in the lifetime of the donor, the trust cannot operate[9].

1   *Re Huxtable, Huxtable v Crawfurd* [1902] 2 Ch 793, CA; cf *Re Tyler's Fund Trust, Graves v King* [1967] 3 All ER 389, [1967] 1 WLR 1269.
2   *Re Young, Young v Young* [1951] Ch 344, [1950] 2 All ER 1245.
3   As to secret trusts see further TRUSTS vol 48 (2000 Reissue) para 572 et seq. As to evidence of secret trusts see WILLS vol 50 (Reissue) paras 459–461.
4   *Re Huxtable, Huxtable v Crawfurd* [1902] 2 Ch 793, CA; *Moss v Cooper* (1861) 1 John & H 352.
5   *Edwards v Pike* (1759) 1 Eden 267.
6   *Juniper v Batchellor* (1868) 19 LT 200; *Carter v Green* (1857) 3 K & J 591; *Littledale v Bickersteth* (1876) 24 WR 507.
7   *Re Downing's Residuary Estate* (1888) 60 LT 140; *Baldwin v Baldwin* (1856) 22 Beav 413.
8   *Ommanney v Butcher* (1823) Turn & R 260.
9   *Re Maddock, Llewelyn v Washington* [1902] 2 Ch 220 at 231, CA, per Cozens-Hardy LJ.

## (iii) Establishment not to contravene General Law

**73. Charity constituting nuisance.** Except under statutory authority, a charity or charitable institution may not be established in such manner or place as to constitute a nuisance[1], and an injunction[2] will be granted to restrain the establishment of a charity which, though charitable, will constitute a nuisance[3].

1   As to nuisance see NUISANCE.
2   As to injunctions see INJUNCTIONS.
3   *Baines v Baker* (1752) Amb 158; *Metropolitan Asylum District Managers v Hill* (1881) 6 App Cas 193, HL; *Fleet v Metropolitan Asylums Board* (1886) 2 TLR 361, CA; *Matthews v Sheffield Corpn* (1887) 31 Sol Jo 773; *Bendelow v Wortley Union Guardians* (1887) 57 LJCh 762; *A-G v Manchester Corpn* [1893] 2 Ch 87; *A-G v Nottingham Corpn* [1904] 1 Ch 673. For the class of hospital which has been held to constitute a nuisance see *Tod-Heatly v Benham* (1888) 40 ChD 80, CA.

**74. Charity in breach of restrictive covenant.** Charitable institutions such as hospitals and institutions for educating and lodging girls, may not be established in premises subject to a restrictive covenant for use as a private dwelling house only, and not for the purposes of trade or business; and an injunction will be granted to restrain the establishment of an institution which, though charitable, will constitute a breach of covenant[1].

1   *German v Chapman* (1877) 7 ChD 271, CA (institution for education and lodging of girls); *Bramwell v Lacy* (1879) 10 ChD 691; *Portman v Home Hospitals Association* (1879) 27 ChD 81n; *Frost v King Edward VII Welsh etc Association* [1918] 2 Ch 180 (compromised on appeal 35 TLR 138, CA) (hospitals); *Rolls v Miller* (1884) 27 ChD 71, CA (institution for working girls); and see *Barnard Castle UDC v Wilson* [1901] 2 Ch 813 at 817 per Buckley LJ (carrying on a school is carrying on a business), affd on this point but revsd on other grounds [1902] 2 Ch 746 at 755, CA, per Vaughan Williams LJ, and at 758 per Stirling LJ. Cf *C & G Homes Ltd v Secretary of State for Health* [1991] Ch 365, [1991] 2 All ER 841, CA. As to restrictive covenants generally see EQUITY vol 16 (Reissue) para 787 et seq.

## (iv)  Repeal of Law of Mortmain

**75. Mortmain restrictions.** Before 29 July 1960[1], assurances inter vivos of land, or of personal estate to be laid out in the purchase of land, in favour of charity were, with various exceptions, subject to certain restrictions: they had to take effect in possession; they might be made subject to certain reservations only; if not for valuable consideration, they had to be made not less than a certain period before the death of the donor; and they had to comply with certain provisions as to form and recording. If these restrictions were not complied with, the assurance was void.

Land might be assured by will to charity, but unless the recipient charity was authorised to retain the land by an order of the court or the Charity Commissioners[2], the land had to be sold within one year after the testator's death or such extended period as might be duly determined.

The law of mortmain also prohibited the assurance of land to charitable and other corporations otherwise than under royal licence or statutory authority. Any land assured contrary to this prohibition was forfeit to the Crown[3].

1   Ie the date of the passing of the Charities Act 1960. The various restrictions mentioned in the text were contained principally in the Mortmain and Charitable Uses Act 1888, the Mortmain and Charitable Uses Act 1891 and the Mortmain and Charitable Uses Act Amendment Act 1892, which were all, together with any enactments amending them, repealed by the Charities Act 1960: see s 38(1) (repealed). The full list of mortmain repeals is contained in Sch 7 Pt II (repealed).
2   As to the Charity Commissioners see paras 486–512 post.

**76. Repeal and consequential provisions.** The law of mortmain was repealed by the Charities Act 1960[1]. Various provisions consequential on the repeal were made as follows.

No right or title to any property may be defeated or impugned, and no assurance or disposition of property may be treated as void or voidable, by virtue of any of the enactments relating to mortmain which have been repealed[2], or any other enactment relating to mortmain, if on 29 July 1960 the possession was in accordance with that right or title or with that assurance or disposition, and no step has been taken to assert a claim by virtue of any such enactment[3]. However, this provision does not validate any assurance or disposition so as to defeat a right or title acquired by adverse possession before 29 July 1960[4].

In relation to the wills of persons dying before 29 July 1960, the repeal of the Mortmain and Charitable Uses Act 1891 abrogates any requirement to sell land then unsold, but it does not enable effect to be given to a direction to lay out personal estate in land without an order under that Act, nor does it affect the power to make such an order[5].

1    See the Charities Act 1960 ss 38(1), 48(2), Sch 7 Pt II (all repealed); and para 75 note 1 ante.
2    See para 75 note 1 ante.
3    Charities Act 1960 s 38(2) (repealed).
4    Ibid s 38(2) proviso (repealed).
5    Ibid s 38(3).

# (2) ESSENTIAL REQUIREMENTS

## (i) Imperative Words creating a Trust

**77. Words of trust.** As in the case of an ordinary trust, there must be certainty of intention on the donor's part to make a gift[1]. The words used must be such that on the whole they ought to be construed as imperative[2]; a mere expression of desire or hope will not create a trust of any kind[3]. The word 'trust' itself need not be used[4].

In the absence of a binding contract an expression of intention in a deceased's lifetime to give money to charity is not effective after death[5].

1    As to certainty of intention see TRUSTS vol 48 (2000 Reissue) paras 548–551.
2    *Knight v Knight* (1840) 3 Beav 148 at 173 per Lord Langdale MR. See *Liverpool City Council v A-G* (1992) Times, 1 May.
3    See eg *Re Adams and Kensington Vestry* (1884) 27 ChD 394, CA.
4    As to where writing is generally necessary see para 67 ante. See also TRUSTS vol 48 (2000 Reissue) para 550. As to whether contractual rights and obligations are created by subscribing to a charity see *Brooks v Richardson* [1986] 1 All ER 952, [1986] 1 WLR 385.
5    *Re Hudson, Creed v Henderson* (1885) 54 LJCh 811; *Sinnett v Herbert* (1871) LR 12 Eq 201; *Re Smith, Champ v Marshallsay* (1890) 64 LT 13.

## (ii) Certainty as to Subject Matter

**78. Certainty as to trust fund.** The general rule of equity that a gift will fail if the trust property cannot clearly be identified applies to charitable trusts[1]. Thus, if the amount of a gift purporting to be made in favour of a charity cannot be ascertained, the gift fails[2], although a gift of a sum 'not exceeding' a named figure is construed as a gift of the named sum[3].

1  As to certainty of subject matter in relation to trusts generally see TRUSTS vol 48 (2000 Reissue) para 553 et seq.
2  *Hartshorne v Nicholson* (1858) 26 Beav 58 (where the amount of the gift was left blank). See also *Ewen v Bannerman* (1830) 2 Dow & Cl 74, HL; *Cherry v Mott* (1836) 1 My & Cr 123 (where an amount could only be ascertained by entering into an impossible contract); and the non-charity case of *Asten v Asten* [1894] 3 Ch 260. In *Dundee Magistrates v Morris* (1858) 3 Macq 134, HL (considered in *Fisk v A-G* (1867) LR 4 Eq 521, and *Re Birkett* (1878) 9 ChD 576), a will, in which the testator directed that a hospital for 100 boys should be established in Dundee without stating what amount should be applied to this object, was held to furnish a sufficient means of ascertaining the amount of the legacy. See also *Macduff v Spence's Trustees* 1909 SC 178 (a trust to apply the interest of a fund or so much thereof as the trustees might deem expedient to charitable objects held valid; but this case is probably not good law in England).
3  *Thompson v Thompson* (1844) 1 Coll 381 at 395 per Knight Bruce V-C; *Gough v Bult* (1848) 16 Sim 45. However, see *Coxe v Basset* (1796) 3 Ves 155; and cf *Re Mills, Midland Bank Executor and Trustee Co Ltd v Board of Governors of United Birmingham Hospitals* [1953] 1 All ER 835, [1953] 1 WLR 554; *Re Vernon* (1957) Times, 27 June.

**79. Gift of uncertain surplus.** Where there is a gift of a fund to be applied in the first place to a particular purpose with a gift over of the surplus, then if the first purpose cannot be carried out because it is unlawful, but the amount which would have been required can be reasonably ascertained, the gift to charity of the surplus over that amount is valid[1]. But where the first purpose is so indefinite that the amount required for it cannot be reasonably ascertained, so that there is no ascertainable surplus, the gift fails entirely[2]. The result is the same where the testator, although estimating the cost of effecting the first purpose, gives his executors a discretion to exceed that amount[3]. An inquiry may be directed to ascertain the amount needed to fulfil the primary invalid purpose[4].

However, where a fund is given primarily for a charitable purpose, but is subject to an invalid charge, as, for example, for the perpetual repair of a tomb not forming part of a church, there is no apportionment, for the whole fund goes to charity[5].

1  *Dundee Magistrates v Morris* (1858) 3 Macq 134, HL; *Mitford v Reynolds* (1842) 1 Ph 185. See also *A-G v Parsons* (1803) 8 Ves 186 at 192 per Lord Eldon LC; and *Re Coxen, McCallum v Coxen* [1948] Ch 747 at 752, [1948] 2 All ER 492 at 498 per Jenkins J.
2  *Chapman v Brown* (1801) 6 Ves 404, explained in *Re Birkett* (1878) 9 ChD 576 at 579 per Jessel MR; *Cherry v Mott* (1836) 1 My & Cr 123 at 134 per Lord Langdale MR; *Cramp v Playfoot* (1858) 4 K & J 479; *Peek v Peek* (1869) 17 WR 1059; *Kirkmann v Lewis* (1869) 38 LJCh 570; *Re Taylor, Martin v Freeman* (1888) 58 LT 538; *Re Porter, Porter v Porter* [1925] Ch 746; *Re Dalziel, Midland Bank Executor and Trustee Co Ltd v St Bartholomew's Hospital* [1943] Ch 277, [1943] 2 All ER 656. The principle underlying this rule is that if the entire fund might have been properly applied to the first purpose, if it had been lawful, there would be no ascertainable residue for the second.
3  *Limbrey v Gurr* (1819) 6 Madd 151.
4  *Chapman v Brown* (1801) 6 Ves 404 at 410 per Grant MR; *Mitford v Reynolds* (1842) 1 Ph 185 at 199 per Lord Lyndhurst LC. See also *Dundee Magistrates v Morris* (1858) 3 Macq 134, HL. Where the invalid purpose was the repair of a tomb it was held that the gift failed to the extent of the capital representing the annual amount necessary to keep that tomb in repair, treating the capital as invested in consols: *Re Vaughan, Vaughan v Thomas* (1886) 33 ChD 187 at 194 per North J.
5  *Kelly v A-G* [1917] 1 IR 183; *Re Rogerson, Bird v Lee* [1901] 1 Ch 715, following *Fisk v A-G* (1867) LR 4 Eq 521, *Re Birkett* (1878) 9 ChD 576, and *Re Vaughan, Vaughan v Thomas* (1886) 33 ChD 187. In cases of this kind the obligation to repair the tomb is a moral one and is not legally binding: *Hunter v Bullock* (1872) LR 14 Eq 45; *Dawson v Small* (1874) LR 18 Eq 114 at 118 per Bacon V-C; *Re Williams* (1877)

5 ChD 735; *Re Taylor, Martin v Freeman* (1888) 58 LT 538; *Re Rogerson, Bird v Lee* [1901] 1 Ch 715 at 719 per Joyce J; *Re Manser, A-G v Lucas* [1905] 1 Ch 68 at 75 per Warrington J; *Re Dalziel, Midland Bank Executor and Trustee Co Ltd v St Bartholomew's Hospital* [1943] Ch 277, [1943] 2 All ER 656. As to monuments and tombs see para 54 ante.

**80. Perpetual gift of income.** A gift of income in perpetuity to a charity does not necessarily carry with it the right to capital, as it would in the case of a gift to an individual, unless there is an intention discoverable from the terms of the gift that the capital should go with the income[1].

1  *Re Levy, Barclays Bank Ltd v Board of Guardians and Trustees for Relief of Jewish Poor* [1960] Ch 346, [1960] 1 All ER 42, CA.

**81. Additions to trust property.** When trustees hold an interest in land on charitable trusts and subsequently acquire a further interest in the same land, whether by gift or prescription, the whole is held subject to the original charitable trusts[1]. Similarly, where a right of presentation in connection with a charitable corporation had been exercised for centuries by a municipal corporation, it was held that the municipal corporation held the right on trust for the charitable purposes for which it was originally created[2]. Where trustees of land for charitable purposes acquire neighbouring land and there is no evidence as to the source of the purchase money, it will not necessarily be presumed that the money used came out of the rents and profits of the original land, so that the whole is subject to the original trusts[3].

If land is purchased partly with money belonging to a charity, the charity is entitled to such proportion of the land as the money contributed by the charity bears to the whole price[4]. Where a fund is given to specified charitable objects in fixed proportions, and the fund has increased, the rule is to apportion the accretions pro rata between the different objects[5]. Where the funds of one charity are inextricably mixed with the funds of another charity, both charities are entitled to participate pro rata in the increased value of the aggregate funds[6].

1  *A-G v Cashel Corpn* (1842) 3 Dr & War 294.
2  *A-G v St John's Hospital, Bedford* (1864) 10 Jur NS 897.
3  *A-G v Master, Wardens etc of the Wax Chandlers' Co* (1873) LR 6 HL 1; but see *Re Ambleside Charity* (1870) 18 WR 663. These cases may be reconciled by contrasting the different nature and circumstances of the trustees in question.
4  *A-G v Newcastle Corpn* (1842) 5 Beav 307 (appeal compromised sub nom *Newcastle-upon-Tyne Corpn v A-G* (1845) 12 Cl & Fin 402, HL).
5  *A-G v Marchant* (1866) LR 3 Eq 424 (accretions arising from increased income). As to surplus income see paras 123–127 post.
6  *Edinburgh Corpn v Lord Advocate* (1879) 4 App Cas 823, HL.

### (iii)  Trusts Exclusively Charitable

A.  APART FROM STATUTE

**82. Court must be able to execute trust.** The validity of a charitable trust does not depend on the application of the test of certainty of objects which is applicable to private trusts[1], but as with all trusts its validity does depend on whether it can be executed by the court[2]. Provided a trust is restricted in its objects or purposes to that which the law regards as charitable, it does not fail because the particular objects are not defined[3], for the court can execute a charitable trust by means of a scheme, notwithstanding that the particular objects are not stated[4]. The application of the trust property to charity must be obligatory[5]; and a gift cannot be treated as valid merely because the trustees have always applied the property to charity if they have a discretion under the trust instrument to apply it to non-charitable purposes[6], although some such dispositions were validated by the Charitable Trusts (Validation) Act 1954[7].

1   See *IRC v Broadway Cottages Trust* [1955] Ch 20, [1954] 3 All ER 120, CA; and TRUSTS vol 48 (2000 Reissue) para 555.

2   See *Morice v Bishop of Durham* (1805) 10 Ves 522. A trust of residue for charitable purposes is not rendered void for uncertainty by the fact that the trustees have power to retain investments indefinitely, for that alone cannot prevent the court from having jurisdiction to execute the trust in case of maladministration: *Dick v Audsley* [1908] AC 347, HL.

3   *Morice v Bishop of Durham* (1805) 10 Ves 522 at 527–528 per Lord Eldon LC: if the bequest is in trust for charity, it is no objection that the charity is not particularly defined, neither is it necessary that the testator should use the word 'charity'. See also *Ommanney v Butcher* (1823) Turn & R 260; *Re Douglas, Obert v Barrow* (1887) 35 ChD 472 at 485, CA, per Cotton LJ; *Re Macduff, Macduff v Macduff* [1896] 2 Ch 451 at 463, CA, per Lindley LJ, and at 469–470 per Rigby LJ; *Re Garrard, Gordon v Craigie* [1907] 1 Ch 382; *Chichester Diocesan Fund and Board of Finance Inc v Simpson* [1944] AC 341 at 348, [1944] 2 All ER 60 at 62, HL, per Viscount Simon LC.

4   As to schemes see para 170 et seq post.

5   *Re Macduff, Macduff v Macduff* [1896] 2 Ch 451 at 465, CA, per Lindley LJ, and at 470 per Rigby LJ; and see *A-G v Lawes* (1849) 8 Hare 32 at 42 per Knight Bruce V-C; *Morice v Bishop of Durham* (1805) 10 Ves 522 at 541 per Lord Eldon LC; *James v Allen* (1817) 3 Mer 17 at 19 per Grant MR; *Nash v Morley* (1842) 5 Beav 177 at 183 per Lord Langdale MR; *Re Douglas, Obert v Barrow* (1887) 35 ChD 472 at 482, CA, per Cotton LJ; *Re Davidson, Minty v Bourne* [1909] 1 Ch 567, CA; *Re Warre's Will Trusts, Wort v Salisbury Diocesan Board of Finance* [1953] 2 All ER 99, [1953] 1 WLR 725 (residence for missioners and for a retreat house); *Re Harpur's Will Trusts, Haller v A-G* [1962] Ch 78, [1961] 3 All ER 588, CA. Cases when part is clearly given to charity should be distinguished: see para 87 post.

6   *Re Jarman's Estate, Leavers v Clayton* (1878) 8 ChD 584 at 587 per Hall V-C.

7   As to the Charitable Trusts (Validation) Act 1954 see paras 90–95 post.

**83. Clear charitable intention necessary.** The question whether any particular gift is or is not charitable is not one for speculative reasoning as to what was the donor's intention, even though his general wishes may be discoverable. No gift is to be deemed charitable unless, in express terms or by necessary implication, the donor has signified a clear intention to devote the property to charitable purposes[1]. To ascertain the intention of a testator, a fair interpretation must be put upon the whole will taken together[2].

Purposes or objects which are not defined or indicated are not presumed to be charitable[3], except where a general intention to give to charity is to be gathered from the instrument[4], or where the nature of the gift permits such a presumption[5].

A recital of a charitable intention cannot render charitable a trust whose expressed objects are not charitable[6]; but, if the objects of the trust are ambiguous, the recital may be referred to for the purpose of explaining and ascertaining what was the donor's meaning[7].

Where executors had transferred land to a local authority, which had covenanted to use it as a recreation ground[8] and for no other purpose, it was held that the land was not held on charitable trusts[9]. It was further held that the Attorney General was not entitled to sue the local authority on its personal covenants[10].

1   *Hunter v A-G* [1899] AC 309 at 315, HL, per Earl of Halsbury LC, and at 319 per Lord Shand. Where no charitable intention is manifest, the court will not execute a trust to distribute a fund among such persons or such purposes as may appear just to the trustees: *Harris v Du Pasquier* (1872) 26 LT 689; *Gibbs v Rumsey* (1813) 2 Ves & B 294; *Fowler v Garlike* (1830) 1 Russ & M 232; and see *Buckle v Bristow* (1864) 13 WR 68.

2   *Hunter v A-G* [1899] AC 309 at 320, HL, per Lord Davey.

3   *Buckle v Bristow* (1864) 13 WR 68.

4   *Mills v Farmer* (1815) 1 Mer 55 at 95 per Lord Eldon LC; *Re Willis, Shaw v Willis* [1921] 1 Ch 44, CA.

5   As to the inference of charitable intention see para 84 post. The cases on gifts for the benefit of a particular locality may be regarded as a special example of such a presumption or implication: see para 38 ante.

6   Cf *Re Sanders' Will Trusts, Public Trustee v McLaren* [1954] Ch 265, [1954] 1 All ER 667.

7   *A-G v Jesus College, Oxford* (1861) 29 Beav 163 at 168 per Romilly MR.

8   It was common ground that the provision of a recreation ground was a charitable purpose: see para 40 ante.

9   *Liverpool City Council v A-G* (1992) Times, 1 May.

10  *Liverpool City Council v A-G* (1992) Times, 1 May.


**84. Inference of charitable intention.** A gift to or for the benefit of a charitable society, simpliciter, is construed as a gift for its general purposes[1]. A gift to a charitable corporation is an absolute gift to it and makes the property given applicable for the objects stated in the corporation's memorandum or charter as part of its general corporate property[2].

A gift on trust to the holder of an office whose functions are charitable in nature[3] is not for that reason a charitable gift if express trusts are attached to the gift by the donor; but where no express trusts are declared, it may sometimes be inferred that the trusts of the gift are the charitable trusts of the trustee's office[4].

1   See *Re White, White v White* [1893] 2 Ch 41 at 52, CA, per Lindley LJ; *Green v Rutherforth* (1750) 1 Ves Sen 462 at 472 per Lord Hardwicke LC; *Re Vernon's Will Trusts, Lloyds Bank Ltd v Group 20 Hospital Management Committee (Coventry)* [1972] Ch 300, [1971] 3 All ER 1061n; *Re Finger's Will Trusts, Turner v Ministry of Health* [1972] Ch 286, [1971] 3 All ER 1050. If the association is established for charitable purposes, no objection on the ground of perpetuity can arise. As to gifts to unincorporated associations see para 55 ante.

2   As to the property of charitable corporations see para 224 post.

3   The same applies to a gift on trust to a charitable society: *A-G v Sibthorp* (1830) 2 Russ & M 107; *A-G v Dean and Canons of Windsor* (1858) 24 Beav 679 at 701–702 per Romilly MR (gifts to dean and canons); *Gloucester Corpn v Wood* (1843) 3 Hare 131 (on appeal sub nom *Gloucester Corpn v Osborn* (1847) 1 HL Cas 272) (gift to municipal corporation); and see *Doe d Toone v Copestake* (1805) 6 East 328; *Aston v Wood* (1868) LR 6 Eq 419 (gift to trustees of nonconformist chapel); *Re Freeman, Shilton v Freeman* [1908] 1 Ch 720, CA; *Re Friends' Free School, Clibborn v O'Brien* [1909] 2 Ch 675.

4   Most of the cases on this point arise out of gifts to holders of religious offices. As to gifts to the holders of religious offices see para 35 ante.


**85. Alternative, subsidiary or cumulative purposes.** Gifts expressed in the alternative, such as for 'charitable or other purposes'[1], 'charitable or public purposes'[2], 'charitable or benevolent purposes'[3], or in other alternative terms admitting non-charitable objects[4], are not charitable. Where the word 'or' is used, it must be determined whether it is used exegetically[5] (meaning 'that is to say'; 'in other words') or disjunctively (that is, separating two alternatives)[6].

The word 'and' is similarly ambiguous: gifts for 'charitable and benevolent' purposes[7] and similar gifts[8] have been held charitable on the ground that the objects indicated must possess both characteristics; but where, upon the true construction of a gift, those words create not cumulative characteristics which each object must possess, but cumulative classes of objects, the trust is not charitable[9]. It may sometimes be the case, however, that the context shows that a word which would normally admit non–charitable objects bears in the particular will a restricted meaning admitting only such objects of the kind which it indicates as are also charitable[10].

1  *Ellis v Selby* (1836) 1 My & Cr 286; *Re Chapman, Hales v A-G* [1922] 2 Ch 479, CA.

2  *Vezey v Jamson* (1822) 1 Sim & St 69; *Re Davis, Thomas v Davis* [1923] 1 Ch 225; *Blair v Duncan* [1902] AC 37, HL; *Langham v Peterson* (1903) 87 LT 744.

    Where a gift is 'for the benefit of the schools, and charitable institutions, and poor, and other objects of charity, and any other public objects', the words 'or any other public objects' must be ejusdem generis with the specified ones, and therefore for charitable objects: *Re Bennett, Gibson v A-G* [1920] 1 Ch 305. Cf *A-G of the Cayman Islands v Wahr Hansen* [2001] 1 AC 75, [2000] 3 All ER 642, PC where general statements of benevolent or philanthropic objects were not to be artificially construed so as to be impliedly limited to charitable purposes only when there were clear indications that no such implied limitation had been intended.

3  *Houston v Burns* [1918] AC 337, HL; *Re Jarman's Estate, Leavers v Clayton* (1878) 8 ChD 584; *Re Riland's Estate, Phillips v Robinson* [1881] WN 173; *Chichester Diocesan Fund and Board of Finance Inc v Simpson* [1944] AC 341, [1944] 2 All ER 60, HL; *A-G for New Zealand v Brown* [1917] AC 393, PC.

4  *Shaw's Trustees v Esson's Trustees* (1905) 8 F 52, Ct of Sess (charitable, benevolent or religious objects at discretion of trustees); *Re Davidson, Minty v Bourne* [1909] 1 Ch 567, CA (charitable, religious or other objects in connection with the Roman Catholic faith); *Ellis v IRC* (1949) 31 TC 178, CA; *Re Macduff, Macduff v Macduff* [1896] 2 Ch 451, CA (purposes 'charitable, philanthropic or …'); *Down v Worrall* (1833) 1 My & K 561 (pious and charitable purposes or otherwise); *Thompson v Thompson* (1844) 1 Coll 381 at 399 per Knight Bruce V-C; *Re Sidney, Hingeston v Sidney* [1908] 1 Ch 488, CA (charitable or emigration uses).

5  See *Rickerby v Nicholson* [1912] 1 IR 343 (religious or charitable purposes); *Re Salter, Rea v Crozier* [1911] 1 IR 289 (charitable or religious purposes); *Re Sinclair's Trusts* (1884) 13 LR Ir 150 (any charitable or religious purpose); *McPhee's Trustees v McPhee* 1912 SC 75; *Re Tomkinson, M'Crea and Bell v A-G of Duchy of Lancaster* (1929) 74 Sol Jo 77 (to such charities or to such religious bodies) in which the gifts were held to be valid.

6  See *Chichester Diocesan Fund and Board of Finance Inc v Simpson* [1944] AC 341, [1944] 2 All ER 60, HL, where the possible interpretations are discussed. In view of the technical meaning of the word 'charitable' in English law, there are obvious difficulties in the way of the exegetical construction, for it might tend to widen 'charitable' rather than to restrict 'benevolent'.

7  *Re Best, Jarvis v Birmingham Corpn* [1904] 2 Ch 354; *Caldwell v Caldwell* (1921) 91 LJPC 95, HL; *Jemmit v Verril* (1826) Amb 585n.

8  *A-G v Herrick* (1772) Amb 712 ('charitable and pious uses'); *Re Lloyd, Greame v A-G* (1893) 10 TLR 66 ('religious and benevolent' purposes); *Re Sutton, Stone v A-G* (1885) 28 ChD 464 ('charitable and deserving objects'). See also *Blair v Duncan* [1902] AC 37 at 44, HL, per Lord Davey ('charitable and public purposes'), *Baker v Sutton* (1836) 1 Keen 224 ('religious and charitable institutions and purposes'); *Re Scowcroft, Ormrod v Wilkinson* [1898] 2 Ch 638 ('furtherance of Conservative principles and religious and mental improvement').

9  *Re Eades, Eades v Eades* [1920] 2 Ch 353 ('religious, charitable and philanthropic objects'); *Williams v Williams, Williams v Kershaw* (1835) 5 Cl & Fin 111n ('benevolent, charitable and religious purposes'); *A-G v Dartmouth Corpn* (1883) 48 LT 933 ('charitable, needful and necessary' purposes); and see *A-G v National Provincial and Union Bank of England* [1924] AC 262, HL ('such patriotic purposes or objects and such charitable institution or institutions or charitable object or objects in the British Empire' as trustees should select); *A-G of the Bahamas v Royal Trust Co* [1986] 3 All ER 423, [1986] 1 WLR 1001, PC (education and welfare); and the Scottish case, *Edgar etc v Cassells* 1922 SC 395 ('benevolent, charitable and religious institutions in G' construed distributively, though such construction did not render the gift void by Scottish law). The question is whether the gift is for purposes which are both charitable and benevolent or for charitable purposes and for benevolent purposes. The more numerous the qualifications enumerated, the more likely is the latter conclusion: *Re Eades, Eades v Eades* supra.

10  *Dolan v Macdermot* (1868) 3 Ch App 676; *Re Bennett, Gibson v A-G* [1920] 1 Ch 305; *Re Ludlow, Bence-Jones v A-G* (1923) 93 LJCh 30, CA.

**86. Construction of objects of companies and other bodies.** Similar considerations apply to the objects of companies and other corporate or unincorporated bodies. If a company is formed for a number of objects, some of which, being main objects, permit expenditure on non-charitable activities, or some of which, though subsidiary, are not merely ancillary to the main objects and are not charitable, the company is not formed for charitable purposes only[1]. However, if the non-charitable activities do not represent a collateral or independent purpose, but are incidental to, and consequent upon, the way in which the charitable purpose for which alone the body was formed is carried on, the body is charitable[2]. Where such a body has a written constitution, it is not permissible to look at its activities rather than its specified objects to decide what its objects are[3]. It is, however, permissible to refer to outside evidence in order to decide whether the ascertained objects can be carried out only in a way which is exclusively charitable[4].

1    *Oxford Group Ltd v IRC* [1949] 2 All ER 537, 31 TC 221, CA; *Ellis v IRC* (1949) 31 TC 178 (on appeal 31 TC 178, CA); *Associated Artists Ltd v IRC* [1956] 2 All ER 583, [1956] 1 WLR 752; *IRC v City of Glasgow Police Athletic Association* [1953] AC 380, [1953] 1 All ER 747, HL.

2    *Institution of Civil Engineers v IRC* [1932] 1 KB 149, CA; *Royal College of Surgeons of England v National Provincial Bank Ltd* [1952] AC 631, [1952] 1 All ER 984, HL; *Royal College of Nursing v St Marylebone Corpn* [1959] 3 All ER 663, [1959] 1 WLR 1077, CA; *Neville Estates Ltd v Madden* [1962] Ch 832, [1961] 3 All ER 769.

3    *Bowman v Secular Society Ltd* [1917] AC 406, HL; *Keren Kayemeth Le Jisroel Ltd v IRC* [1931] 2 KB 465, CA; *Tennant Plays Ltd v IRC* [1948] 1 All ER 506, CA; *Berry v St Marylebone Borough Council* [1958] Ch 406, [1957] 3 All ER 677, CA; *Incorporated Council of Law Reporting for England and Wales v A-G* [1972] Ch 73, [1971] 3 All ER 1029, CA; affg [1971] Ch 626, [1971] 1 All ER 436.

4    See *Incorporated Council of Law Reporting for England and Wales v A-G* [1972] Ch 73, [1971] 3 All ER 1029, CA.

**87. Intention to devote part to charity.** Even if some of the objects of a trust are prima facie non-charitable[1], or illegal[2], the gift may be good if there is an overriding intention that some part of the property be applied to charity. If it can be ascertained what are the proper proportions to be attributed to the several objects, the court will direct an inquiry[3], but if from the nature of the gift it appears impracticable to do so the court will divide the fund equally between the different objects[4], and the gift will only fail as to the proportion appropriated to the non-charitable objects. In simple cases the amount sufficient for the non-charitable purpose may be ascertained by affidavit[5].

Apportionment between a void part and a valid part is not, however, possible where on its true construction the gift is one entire gift to an entire class with uncertainty in the criteria specified for the selection of beneficiaries from that class[6].

1    *Hunter v A-G* [1899] AC 309 at 323–324, HL, per Lord Davey; *Wilkinson v Lindgren* (1870) 5 Ch App 570; *Pocock v A-G* (1876) 3 ChD 342, CA; *Re Douglas, Obert v Barrow* (1887) 35 ChD 472, CA; *Re Hurley, Nichols v Pargiter* (1900) 17 TLR 115; *Re Allen, Hargreaves v Taylor* [1905] 2 Ch 400; *Re Hood, Public Trustee v Hood* [1931] 1 Ch 240, CA. See also *A-G v Fletcher* (1835) 5 LJCh 75; *Dolan v Macdermot* (1868) 3 Ch App 676; *Wrexham Corpn v Tamplin* (1873) 21 WR 768; *Adnam v Cole* (1843) 6 Beav 353; *Hoare v Osborne* (1866) LR 1 Eq 585; *Re Rigley's Trusts* (1866) 36 LJCh 147; *Re Vaughan, Vaughan v Thomas* (1886) 33 ChD 187. It is immaterial whether the non-charitable objects are definite or indefinite: *Re Clarke, Bracey v Royal National Lifeboat Institution* [1923] 2 Ch 407.

2    *A-G v Hartley* (1793) 4 Bro CC 412; *Carter v Green* (1857) 3 K & J 591; *Salusbury v Denton* (1857) 3 K & J 529, following *Doyley v A-G* (1735) 4 Vin Abr 485, pl 16, at 486 per Lord Cowper; but distinguish *Down v Worrall* (1833) 1 My & K 561, where the trustees had a discretion to apply a fund either for charitable purposes or for an individual.

3   *Adnam v Cole* (1843) 6 Beav 353; *Hoare v Osborne* (1866) LR 1 Eq 585 at 588 per Kindersley V-C;
    *Re Rigley's Trusts* (1866) 36 LJCh 147; and see *Re Gardom, Le Page v A-G* [1914] 1 Ch 662; revsd on
    another point [1914] 1 Ch 662 at 674, CA, per Cozens-Hardy MR; and affd sub nom *Le Page v Gardom*
    (1915) 84 LJCh 749, HL.
4   *Doyley v A-G* (1735) 4 Vin Abr 485, pl 16, at 486 per Lord Cowper; *Crafton v Frith* (1851) 4 De G &
    Sm 237; *Re Hall's Charity* (1851) 14 Beav 115; *Salusbury v Denton* (1857) 3 K & J 529; *Hoare v Osborne*
    (1866) LR 1 Eq 585 at 588–589 per Kindersley V-C; *A-G v Marchant* (1866) LR 3 Eq 424; *Hunter v
    A-G* [1899] AC 309 at 323–324, HL, per Lord Davey; *Re Clarke, Bracey v Royal National Lifeboat
    Institution* [1923] 2 Ch 407; *Re Gavacan, O'Meara v A-G* [1913] 1 IR 276; *Re King, Henderson v Cranmer*
    [1931] WN 232.
5   *Re Vaughan, Vaughan v Thomas* (1886) 33 ChD 187 at 194 per North J.
6   *Re Wright's Will Trusts* (1982) (1999) 13 TLI 48, CA.


**88. Power to revoke charitable trusts.** If trusts are declared which are charitable,
but there is a power to revoke the trusts and declare new ones which need not necessarily
be charitable, the existence of the unexercised power does not make the original trusts
non-charitable while they last[1].


1   *Gibson v South American Stores (Gath and Chaves) Ltd* [1950] Ch 177, [1949] 2 All ER 985, CA; cf *George
    Drexler Ofrex Foundation Trustees v IRC* [1966] Ch 675, [1965] 3 All ER 529; *Re Sir Robert Peel's School,
    Tamworth, ex p Charity Comrs* (1868) 3 Ch App 543. See also *IRC v Yorkshire Agricultural Society* [1928] 1
    KB 611 at 633, CA, per Atkin LJ. See also para 129 note 17 post.


**89. Incidental non-charitable benefits.** A gift may be charitable notwithstanding
that the attainment of its purposes incidentally produces benefits of a non-charitable
character[1] or that non-charitable benefits are conferred for the purpose of promoting the
principal charitable purpose[2].

The Charity Commissioners[3] do not normally require charity trustees to justify the
inclusion in their governing instrument of a charging clause. However, if it is proposed
that trustees should be paid simply for acting as trustees, the Commissioners need to be
satisfied that the inclusion of the clause does not have the effect of extending the purposes
of the institution so that it is incapable of being a charity since it would exist at least in
part to benefit the trustee or trustees[4].


1   See the cases cited in para 86 note 2 ante.
2   Cf *Re Coxen, MacCallum v Coxen* [1948] Ch 747, [1948] 2 All ER 492 (provision for an annual dinner
    and for payment of fees to trustees for their attendance at meetings, held ancillary to management of large
    fund for the benefit of orthopaedic hospitals). See also *Re Charlesworth, Robinson v Archdeacon of Cleveland*
    (1910) 101 LT 908 (cited in para 34 note 12 ante); *Queen's University of Belfast v A-G for Northern Ireland*
    [1966] NI 115 (provision for payment of annual sum to each of four outside electors, ancillary to
    promotion of research by award of elective studentships).
3   As to the Charity Commissioners see paras 486–512 post.
4   As to the policy of the Charity Commissioners towards remuneration of trustees under the Charities Act
    1993 see *Remuneration of Trustees (1993)* Decisions of the Charity Commissioners (1994) vol 2 p 14.


B.  CHARITABLE TRUSTS (VALIDATION) ACT 1954


**90. Dispositions affected by the Charitable Trusts (Validation) Act 1954.**
Certain dispositions which would have been invalid under the general law as not being
for charitable purposes only were validated retrospectively by the Charitable Trusts
(Validation) Act 1954[1].

The Act applies to any disposition of property to be held or applied for objects declared by an imperfect trust provision[2], and to any covenant[3] to make such a disposition, where apart from the Act the disposition or covenant is invalid under the law of England and Wales, but would be valid if the objects were exclusively charitable[4].

A covenant entered into before 30 July 1954[5] is not, however, enforceable by virtue of the Act unless confirmed by the covenantor after that date, but a disposition made in accordance with such a covenant is to be treated for the purposes of the Act as confirming the covenant and any previous disposition in accordance with it[6]. A disposition in settlement or other disposition creating more than one interest in the same property is treated for the purposes of the Act as a separate disposition in relation to each of the interests created[7].

1   The Charitable Trusts (Validation) Act 1954 does not affect trust instruments coming into operation on or after 16 December 1952: see s 1(2); and para 92 post. The Act binds the Crown: s 6. The ordinary principles as to certainty of object (see para 85 ante) apply to such instruments.
2   For the meaning of 'imperfect trust provision' see para 91 post.
3   'Covenant' includes any agreement, whether under seal or not; and 'covenantor' is to be construed accordingly: Charitable Trusts (Validation) Act 1954 s 1(4).
4   Ibid s 2(1). Cf *Vernon (William Vernon & Sons Ltd Employees Fund Trustees) v IRC* [1956] 3 All ER 14, [1956] 1 WLR 1169, where the trusts, though not exclusively charitable, were apparently not invalid, so that the Charitable Trusts (Validation) Act 1954 did not affect them. The Act does not apply if the invalidity has already been acted upon: see s 2(2); and para 93 post.
5   Ie the commencement of the Charitable Trusts (Validation) Act 1954.
6   Ibid s 3(6).
7   Ibid s 2(3). It was held by a majority of the Court of Appeal that contributions to an appeal fund, whose purposes were defraying funeral expenses of victims of an accident, caring for disabled victims and then to apply the rest of the funds to such worthy cause or causes in memory of the victims, were dispositions to which the Charitable Trusts (Validation) Act 1954 could apply but were not dispositions creating three separate interests in the money given: *Re Gillingham Bus Disaster Fund, Bowman v Official Solicitor* [1959] Ch 62, [1958] 2 All ER 749, CA.

**91. Imperfect trust provisions.** For the purposes of the Charitable Trusts (Validation) Act 1954, 'imperfect trust provision' means any provision declaring objects for which property is to be held or applied, and so describing those objects that, consistently with the terms of the provision, the property could be used exclusively for charitable purposes, but could nevertheless be used for purposes which are not charitable[1]. The trust declared need not be so imperfect as to be invalid[2].

It has been held[3] that a gift for such worthy causes as trustees may think fit is not a disposition to which the Act applies[4], and that the Act was intended to cure dispositions such that the whole of the money could be devoted to charity by excluding words which are too wide or too vague[5]. In a later case, however, it was held that imperfect trust provisions are not solely those which declare the objects of the trust in such a form as to include by express reference some legally charitable purpose as well as some non-charitable purpose[6]. Thus the Act has been held to validate trusts for welfare purposes amongst employees of companies[7] and members of a trade union[8] which would otherwise have failed as being partly for non-charitable purposes, and also because the beneficiaries were not a sufficient section of the public, by limiting the purposes to the relief of poverty among the specified class[9].

The Act does not apply to a trust which is purely a private discretionary trust with no flavour of charity, but which might be validated if the beneficiaries were required to be poor[10]. Similarly it does not apply to a trust with only one expressed object, where that object is not charitable[11]. A trust for 'such purposes as my trustees may think fit' might not be validated by the Act, notwithstanding that the trustees could properly choose charitable objects[12].

The Act does not apply to a gift to be divided between institutions and associations of a particular type, because such a gift does not declare the objects for which property is to be held or applied[13].

1 Charitable Trusts (Validation) Act 1954 s 1(1). Where some of the trust property is *required* to be held for a non-charitable purpose the Act cannot, therefore, apply: *Vernon (William Vernon & Sons Ltd Employees Fund Trustees) v IRC* [1956] 3 All ER 14, [1956] 1 WLR 1169.

2 See *Re Harpur's Will Trusts, Haller v A-G* [1962] Ch 78, [1961] 3 All ER 588, CA.

3 Although Buckley J, in *Re Wykes, Riddington v Spencer* [1961] Ch 229 at 239, sub nom *Re Wykes' Will Trusts, Riddington v Spencer* [1961] 1 All ER 470 at 474, treated this as obiter dictum, it appears that it was an alternative ground for decision: see *Re Harpur's Will Trusts, Haller v A-G* [1962] Ch 78 at 95, [1961] 3 All ER 588 at 594, CA, per Harman LJ; *Re Saxone Shoe Co Ltd's Trust Deed, Re Abbott's Will Trusts, Abbott v Pearson* [1962] 2 All ER 904 at 915, [1962] 1 WLR 943 at 957 per Cross J.

4 *Re Gillingham Bus Disaster Fund, Bowman v Official Solicitor* [1958] Ch 300, [1958] 1 All ER 37; affd [1959] Ch 62, [1958] 2 All ER 749, CA.

5 *Re Gillingham Bus Disaster Fund, Bowman v Official Solicitor* [1958] Ch 300 at 306, [1958] 1 All ER 37 at 40 per Harman J.

6 *Re Wykes, Riddington v Spencer* [1961] Ch 229 at 238, sub nom *Re Wykes' Will Trusts, Riddington v Spencer* [1961] 1 All ER 470 at 477 per Buckley J. In *Re Gillingham Bus Disaster Fund, Bowman v Official Solicitor* [1959] Ch 62 at 80, [1958] 1 All ER 749 at 758, CA, Ormerod LJ was of the same view, and cf Lord Evershed MR at 75, 755. Some persuasive support for this view may be given by *Re McCullough* [1966] NI 73; *Re Ashton, Siddall v Gordon* [1955] NZLR 192, NZ CA; *Leahy v A-G for New South Wales* [1959] AC 457, [1959] 2 All ER 300, PC (all decided on similar statutory provisions).

7 *Re Wykes, Riddington v Spencer* [1961] Ch 229, sub nom *Re Wykes' Will Trusts, Riddington v Spencer* [1961] 1 All ER 470.

8 *Re Mead's Trust Deed, Briginshaw v National Society of Operative Printers and Assistants* [1961] 2 All ER 836, [1961] 1 WLR 1244.

9 As to the relief of poverty among limited classes such as these see para 22 ante.

10 *Re Saxone Shoe Co Ltd's Trust Deed, Re Abbott's Will Trusts, Abbott v Pearson* [1962] 2 All ER 904, [1962] 1 WLR 943. In *Re Wykes, Riddington v Spencer* [1961] Ch 229, sub nom *Re Wykes' Will Trusts, Riddington v Spencer* [1961] 1 All ER 470, the reference to welfare purposes permitted a flavour of charity to be discerned, but Buckley J did not base his decision on that. In *Re McCullough* [1966] NI 73, Lowry J said that no specific indication of a charitable intention was required; but see *Re Ashton, Siddall v Gordon* [1955] NZLR 192, NZ CA.

11 *Buxton v Public Trustee* (1962) 41 TC 235. The object was 'to promote and aid the improvement of international relations and intercourse'.

12 See *Leahy v A-G for New South Wales* [1959] AC 457, [1959] 2 All ER 300, PC, approving *Re Hollole* [1945] VLR 295 (a gift to a trustee to be disposed by him as he may deem best). See also *Re Wykes, Riddington v Spencer* [1961] Ch 229 at 243, sub nom *Re Wykes' Will Trusts, Riddington v Spencer* [1961] 1 All ER 470 at 476 per Buckley J.

13 *Re Harpur's Will Trusts, Haller v A-G* [1961] Ch 38, [1960] 3 All ER 237; affd [1962] Ch 78, [1961] 3 All ER 588, CA.

**92. Effect of the Charitable Trusts (Validation) Act 1954.** The effect of the Charitable Trusts (Validation) Act 1954 is that any imperfect trust provision[1] contained in an instrument taking effect before 16 December 1952[2] has, and is deemed to have had, effect, in relation to any disposition or covenant[3] to which the Act applies[4]: (1) as respects the period before 30 July 1954[5], as if the whole of the declared objects were charitable[6]; and (2) as respects the period thereafter, as if the provision had required the property to be held or applied for the declared objects in so far only as they authorise use for charitable purposes[7]. A document inviting gifts of property to be held or applied for objects declared by the document is treated for these purposes as an instrument taking effect when it is first issued[8].

Thus the imperfect trust provision itself is not validated, unless it is also the disposition; and there may well be provisions for purposes which would fall within the definition of imperfect trust provision but which would not be invalid as dispositions, and would therefore not be affected[9], because they do not have effect in relation to any disposition to which the Act applies[10].

1　　For the meaning of 'imperfect trust provision' see para 91 ante.
2　　Ie the date of publication of the *Report of the Committee on the Law and Practice relating to Charitable Trusts* Cmd 8710 (1952) (the Nathan Report) and it was made known that the government would introduce legislation enacted by the Charitable Trusts (Validation) Act 1954: see 179 HL Official Report (5th series), 16 December 1952, col 998; and 509 HC Official Report (5th series), 8 December 1952, written answers col *154.*
3　　For the meaning of 'covenant' see para 90 note 3 ante.
4　　Charitable Trusts (Validation) Act 1954 s 1(2). As to dispositions and covenants to which the Charitable Trusts (Validation) Act 1954 applies see paras 90 ante, 93 post.
5　　Ie the date of the commencement of the Charitable Trusts (Validation) Act 1954.
6　　Ibid s 1(2)(a).
7　　Ibid s 1(2)(b).
8　　Ibid s 1(3). In *Re Gillingham Bus Disaster Fund, Bowman v Official Solicitor* [1958] Ch 300, [1958] 1 All ER 37; affd [1959] Ch 62, [1958] 2 All ER 749, CA, a letter published in a newspaper, announcing the establishment of the fund, was held to be a document within this provision.
9　　Ie by the Charitable Trusts (Validation) Act 1954 s 2(1): see para 90 ante.
10　See *Harpur's Will Trusts, Haller v A-G* [1962] Ch 78 at 91, [1961] 3 All ER 588 at 592, CA, per Lord Evershed MR.

## 93. Savings: dispositions already treated as invalid.

The Charitable Trusts (Validation) Act 1954 does not apply to any disposition if, before 16 December 1952[1], property comprised in, or representing that comprised in, the disposition in question or another disposition made for the objects declared by the same imperfect trust provision, or income arising from any such property, has been paid or conveyed to, or applied for the benefit of, the persons entitled by reason of the invalidity of the disposition in question or the other disposition, as the case may be[2].

1　　Ie the date of publication of the *Report of the Committee on the Law and Practice relating to Charitable Trusts* Cmd 8710 (1952) (the Nathan Report) and it was made known that the government would introduce legislation enacted by the Charitable Trusts (Validation) Act 1954: see 179 HL Official Report (5th series), 16 December 1952, col 998; and 509 HC Official Report (5th series), 8 December 1952, written answers col *154.*
2　　Charitable Trusts (Validation) Act 1954 s 2(2).

## 94. Transitional provisions in relation to legal proceedings and tax payments.

The Charitable Trusts (Validation) Act 1954 contained transitional provisions enabling effect to be given to its provisions in legal proceedings begun before the commencement of the Act on 30 July 1954, as well as those begun afterwards[1], and even enabling certain judgments and orders[2] to be varied in accordance with the provisions of the Act[3].

The operation of the Act did not affect retrospectively any liability to tax, nor did it invalidate anything done or any determination given before the commencement of the Act[4].

1   Charitable Trusts (Validation) Act 1954 s 4(1).
2   This did not, however, include orders or judgments made or given before the commencement of the Charitable Trusts (Validation) Act 1954 in proceedings begun before 16 December 1952 (the date of publication of the *Report of the Committee on the Law and Practice relating to Charitable Trusts* (Cmd 8710) (1952) (the Nathan Report) and it was made known that the government would introduce legislation enacted by the Charitable Trusts (Validation) Act 1954: see 179 HL Official Report (5th series), 16 December 1952, col 998; and 509 HC Official Report (5th series), 8 December 1952, written answers col *154*): see the Charitable Trusts (Validation) Act 1954 s 4(2).
3   See ibid s 4(3).
4   See ibid s 4(4).


**95. Savings: adverse claims.** No proceedings may be begun by any person to enforce his right to any property[1] comprised in, or representing that comprised in a disposition to which the Charitable Trusts (Validation) Act 1954 applies[2] after 30 July 1955[3] or after the expiration of one year beginning with the date on which the right first accrues to him or to some person through whom he claims, whichever is the later, unless before or after its accrual, the right either[4]: (1) has been concealed by the fraud of some person administering the imperfect trust provision[5] or his agent[6]; or (2) or has been acknowledged by some such person or his agent by means of a written acknowledgment given to the person having the right or his agent and signed by the person making it, or by means of a payment or transfer of property in respect of the right[7]. If the period prescribed for any person to bring proceedings to recover any property expires without his having recovered the property or begun proceedings to do so, his title to the property is extinguished[8].

Subject to the limitation period set out above, where a disposition to which the Charitable Trusts (Validation) Act 1954 applies was made before, and is not confirmed[9] after, 30 July 1954, the Act does not prejudice a person's right, by reason of the invalidity of the disposition, to property comprised in, or representing that comprised in, the disposition as against the persons administering the imperfect trust provision or the persons on whose behalf they do so, unless the right accrued to him or some person through whom he claims before 16 December 1946[10]. However, the persons administering the imperfect trust provision, and any trustee for them or for the persons on whose behalf they do so, are entitled, as against a person whose right to the property is saved by this last provision, to deal with the property as if his right to the property had not been so saved, unless they have express notice of a claim by him to enforce his right to the property[11].

For the purposes of these provisions, a right by reason of the invalidity of a disposition to property comprised in, or representing that comprised in, the disposition is deemed not to accrue to anyone so long as he is under a disability or has a future interest only, or so long as the disposition is subject to another disposition made by the same person, and the whole of the property or the income arising from it is held or applied for the purposes of that disposition[12]. The other disposition may be a disposition deemed to be separate by virtue of the Act itself[13].

1   Ie the right by virtue of the Charitable Trusts (Validation) Act 1954 s 3(1): see the text and notes 9–11 infra.
2   As to dispositions to which the Charitable Trusts (Validation) Act 1954 applies see paras 90, 93 ante.

3   Ie after the expiration of one year beginning with 30 July 1954 ie the commencement of the Charitable Trusts (Validation) Act 1954.
4   Ibid s 3(2).
5   For the meaning of 'imperfect trust provision' see para 91 ante.
6   Charitable Trusts (Validation) Act 1954 s 3(2)(a).
7   Ibid s 3(2)(b).
8   Ibid s 3(2). This provision is not to be taken as extending the time for bringing any proceedings beyond the period of limitation prescribed by any other statute: s 3(2). The Limitation Act 1980 s 38(2)–(6) (see LIMITATION OF ACTIONS vol 28 (Reissue) paras 928, 1068) applies for the purposes of the Charitable Trusts (Validation) Act 1954 as it does for the purposes of the Limitation Act 1980 to define the circumstances in which a person is deemed to be under a disability or to claim through another person: Charitable Trusts (Validation) Act 1954 s 3(4) (amended by the Limitation Act 1980 s 40(2), Sch 3 para 4). Rights may accrue to a person for the purposes of this provision notwithstanding that the person or persons to whom they accrue are not ascertained: *Re Harpur's Will Trusts, Haller v A-G* [1961] Ch 38 at 49, [1960] 3 All ER 237 at 243 per Cross J.
9   See para 90 text to note 5 ante.
10  Charitable Trusts (Validation) Act 1954 s 3(1). As to claiming through another person see note 8 supra.
11  Ibid s 3(1). There is also provision for the preservation of the right of a person, whose rights are saved by s 3(1), by virtue of his interest in the property to damages or other relief in respect of any dealing with the property, if the person dealing with the property had at the time express notice of a claim by him to enforce his right to the property: see s 3(5).
12  Ibid s 3(3).
13  *Re Chitty's Will Trust, Thomas's Will Trusts, Ransford v Lloyds Bank Ltd* [1970] Ch 254, [1969] 3 All ER 1492. As to what are deemed to be separate dispositions see para 90 ante.

C. POWERS OF APPOINTMENT IN FAVOUR OF CHARITY

**96. Test for validity of power of appointment.** Powers of appointment, whether mere powers or trust powers, are subject to a different test as to certainty of objects from that applicable to trusts as such[1]. The test for powers is whether it can be said of any person or institution whether he or it is or is not an object of the power as defined in the instrument creating the power[2]. Therefore, although the court will not establish a charitable trust where the testator has merely given power to trustees to distribute an indefinite sum in charity[3], a power in a will to distribute income to charitable institutions or 'such other organisation or body not registered as a charity but in the opinion of my trustees having charitable objects' is not invalid, though a trust in those terms would be[4].

A power to appoint to charitable and non-charitable indefinite objects is as invalid as a gift to such objects, and consequently, if a testator makes a gift to charitable and non-charitable objects in such shares and proportions as another person may nominate, the power of appointment is invalid and the subject matter of the gift is divided equally between the objects, the gift failing as to the proportions attributable to the non-charitable objects[5]. However, the inclusion of definite non-charitable institutions together with charity generally as discretionary objects under a trust which does not involve a perpetuity does not render the trust uncertain as to its objects[6].

1   As to powers of appointment see generally POWERS; TRUSTS; WILLS.
2   See *Whishaw v Stephens* [1970] AC 508, sub nom *Re Gulbenkian's Settlement Trusts, Whishaw v Stephens* [1968] 3 All ER 785, HL; *McPhail v Doulton* [1971] AC 424, [1970] 2 All ER 228, HL.
3   *Coxe v Basset* (1796) 3 Ves 155 (power given to trustees to continue charities and benefactions or to bestow any other).
4   *Re Wootton's Will Trusts, Trotter v Duffin* [1968] 2 All ER 618, [1968] 1 WLR 681.
5   *Re Clarke, Bracey v Royal National Lifeboat Institution* [1923] 2 Ch 407.
6   *Re Douglas, Obert v Barrow* (1887) 35 ChD 472, CA.

# (3) ASCERTAINMENT OF OBJECTS OF THE TRUST

## (i) Construction in general

**97. Benignant construction of charitable bequests.** A benignant construction is placed on charitable bequests[1]. If a testator declares his intention to give the whole of his estate to charity, but specifically appropriates part only, the general intention in favour of charity prevails, and the proportion not appropriated by him will be appropriated by the court to charity[2]. Similarly, precatory recommendations in favour of particular charities do not prevent partial application in other ways[3].

The court infers from very slight circumstances that a testator means to give the whole of an estate to charitable purposes[4]; but no such inference is made if the testator is aware that the specific charitable payments which he directs do not exhaust the property given to the trustee[5]; nor can a charitable intention be inferred from the mere fact that the trustees are a charitable society and are given a wide discretion[6]. The court's leniency towards charitable gifts is also exemplified by the cases in which gifts apparently to charitable institutions have been construed as gifts for charitable purposes carried on by the institutions[7].

A gift to a legatee 'for the charitable purposes agreed upon between us' does not imply a general charitable intention, but only a limited charitable intention for the purposes agreed[8], and evidence is admissible to show what these purposes are, but not to limit the amount of the gift[9].

1   *Weir v Crum-Brown* [1908] AC 162 at 167, HL, per Lord Loreburn LC; *IRC v McMullen* [1981] AC 1 at 11, [1980] 1 All ER 884 at 890, HL, per Lord Hailsham of St Marylebone LC, with whom three other Law Lords expressly agreed; *Guild v IRC* [1992] 2 AC 310, [1992] 2 All ER 10, HL; but note *Scottish Burial Reform and Cremation Society Ltd v Glasgow City Corpn* [1968] AC 138 at 153, [1967] 3 All ER 215 at 222, HL, per Lord Upjohn. Thus, where a gift is capable of two constructions, one which would make it void and the other which would render it effectual, the latter must be adopted: *Bruce v Deer Presbytery* (1867) LR 1 Sc & Div 96 at 97, HL, per Lord Chelmsford LC; *Houston v Burns* [1918] AC 337 at 341–342, HL, per Lord Finlay LC; and see *Re Bain, Public Trustee v Ross* [1930] 1 Ch 224 at 230, CA, per Lord Hanworth MR. Compare the similar maxim of civil law that where there is an ambiguity, a benignant construction should be given if possible (*semper in dubiis benigniora praeferenda sunt*): Dig, lib 1 tit xvii s 56. See also *Dundee Magistrates v Morris* (1858) 3 Macq 134 at 155, HL, per Lord Chelmsford LC, and at 166 per Lord Cranworth. Cf *A-G of the Cayman Islands v Wahr Hansen* [2001] 1 AC 75, [2000] 3 All ER 642, PC (benignant construction of inter vivos settlement negatived by contrary indications).
2   *Beverley Corpn v A-G* (1857) 6 HL Cas 310 at 318 per Lord Cranworth LC, approving the doctrine laid down in *Arnold v A-G* (1698) Show Parl Cas 22, HL, and in *A-G v Johnson* (1753) Amb 190.
3   *Moggridge v Thackwell* (1803) 7 Ves 36; affd (1807) 13 Ves 416, HL.
4   *A-G v Skinners' Co* (1827) 2 Russ 407.
5   *Beverley Corpn v A-G* (1857) 6 HL Cas 310 at 320 per Lord Cranworth LC. See *A-G v Bristol Corpn* (1820) 2 Jac & W 294; *A-G v Drapers' Co* (1840) 2 Beav 508; *A-G v Dean and Canons of Windsor* (1860) 8 HL Cas 369. See also para 123 post.
6   *Re Freeman, Shilton v Freeman* [1908] 1 Ch 720, CA; but see also para 82 ante.
7   This is important when there is a question as to whether the stated objects of the gift have failed: see generally para 139 et seq post.
8   *Re Huxtable, Huxtable v Crawfurd* [1902] 2 Ch 793 at 796, CA, per Vaughan Williams LJ.
9   *Re Huxtable, Huxtable v Crawfurd* [1902] 2 Ch 793 at 796, CA, per Vaughan Williams LJ; *Re Blackwell, Blackwell v Blackwell* [1929] AC 318, HL. As to secret trusts see para 72 ante; and TRUSTS vol 48 (2000 Reissue) paras 572–577.

**98. Fund raised by contributions.** When a fund raised from numerous contributories for somewhat indefinite purposes is vested in trustees, the trustees have prima facie implied authority to declare the trusts; and trusts so declared will be binding until set aside at the instance of the Attorney General or of one or more of the donors[1].

The precise ambit of this rule is unclear; it cannot be used to widen the purposes of a gift for a specific charitable purpose so as to defeat the claim of a donor by way of resulting trust on initial failure of the purpose[2].

1    *A-G v Mathieson, Re Wilkinson and Fell's Contract* [1907] 2 Ch 383 at 394, CA, per Cozens-Hardy MR; *A-G v Clapham* (1855) 4 De GM & G 591 at 626 per Lord Cranworth LC; *Re Lord Mayor of Belfast's Air Raid Distress Fund* [1962] NI 161; *Re Henry Wood National Memorial Trust, Armstrong v Moiseiwitsch* [1967] 1 All ER 238n, [1966] 1 WLR 1601.
2    Cf *Re Henry Wood National Memorial Trust, Armstrong v Moiseiwitsch* [1967] 1 All ER 238n, [1966] 1 WLR 1601.

## (ii) Extrinsic Evidence

**99. Contemporaneous evidence.** Evidence is admissible of contemporaneous documents and usage[1], of the circumstances attending the execution of the trust document[2], of the donor's contemporaneous acts[3], of the early application or distribution of the fund[4], and of the construction placed on doubtful questions which arose in the early administration of the trust[5]. The donee's contemporaneous acts are of little value for the purpose of placing a construction upon any instrument of gift executed by a donor; they only show the intention and the view with which the donee accepted the gift[6].

1    *Shore v Wilson* (1842) 9 Cl & Fin 355, HL; *Drummond v A-G for Ireland* (1849) 2 HL Cas 837 at 857 per Lord Brougham; *Aberdeen University v Irvine* (1868) LR 1 Sc & Div 289, HL; *A-G v Anderson* (1888) 57 LJCh 543. As to the presumption of a charitable trust from usage see para 104 post.
2    *A-G v Anderson* (1888) 57 LJCh 543.
3    *A-G v Trinity College, Cambridge* (1856) 24 Beav 383 at 399 per Romilly MR; *A-G v Dean and Canons of Windsor* (1860) 8 HL Cas 369 at 402 per Lord Campbell LC; *A-G v Dartmouth Corpn* (1883) 48 LT 933.
4    *Shore v Wilson* (1842) 9 Cl & Fin 355 at 569, HL, per Tindal LJ; *A-G v Brazen Nose College* (1834) 2 Cl & Fin 295, HL.
5    *A-G v Caius College* (1837) 2 Keen 150.
6    *A-G v Trinity College, Cambridge* (1856) 24 Beav 383. It is not so where the trusts are accepted conditionally or subject to certain qualifications, which the court may collect from contemporaneous transactions as evidenced by documents or usage: *A-G v Drapers' Co, Howell's Charity* (1843) 6 Beav 382 at 386 per Lord Langdale MR and cases there cited.

**100. Inadmissible evidence.** Parol evidence is not admissible for the purpose of interpreting a patent ambiguity, as where a blank is left in a trust deed or will[1], though it may be admitted to cure a latent ambiguity, that is to say, to ascertain the meaning the testator affixed to the expressions he used[2].

Evidence of intention is not admissible to cure an error in description[3]. Nor is evidence of counsel's opinion given at or prior to the execution of a trust deed admissible on its construction, because it merely amounts to evidence of the intention of the party executing it and to admit it would be a breach of the parol evidence rule[4].

Where the document of trust is lost, the court will take into consideration existing copies[5].

1   *Baylis v A-G* (1741) 2 Atk 239. As to ambiguities see DEEDS AND OTHER INSTRUMENTS vol 13 (Reissue) para 207; WILLS vol 50 (Reissue) paras 458.

2   *Shore v Wilson* (1842) 9 Cl & Fin 355 at 390, HL, per Lord Lyndhurst ('godly preachers of Christ's holy Gospel'); *Drummond v A-G for Ireland* (1849) 2 HL Cas 837 at 862 per Lord Brougham ('Protestant dissenters'); *A-G v Clapham* (1855) 4 De GM & G 591 at 627 per Lord Cranworth LC; *A-G v Beverley Corpn* (1855) 6 De GM & G 256 at 268 per Turner LJ; *A-G v Dartmouth Corpn* (1883) 48 LT 933 ('charitable, needful, and necessary uses'); *Edge v Salisbury* (1749) Amb 70 ('relations'); *Re Kenny, Clode v Andrews* (1907) 97 LT 130; *Re Rees, Jones v Evans* [1920] 2 Ch 59 ('missionary'). See also *Re Kilvert's Trusts* (1871) 7 Ch App 170 at 173 per James LJ; *Re How, How v How* [1930] 1 Ch 66; *Re Moon's Will Trusts, Foale v Gillians* [1948] 1 All ER 300; and see para 101 post.

3   *National Society for the Prevention of Cruelty to Children v Scottish National Society for the Prevention of Cruelty to Children* [1915] AC 207 at 214, HL, per Lord Dunedin; *British Home and Hospital for Incurables v Royal Hospital for Incurables* (1903) 89 LT 495; revsd on other grounds (1904) 90 LT 601, CA.

4   *Rabin v Gerson Berger Association Ltd* [1986] 1 All ER 374, [1986] 1 WLR 526, CA. As to the admission of extrinsic evidence see DEEDS AND OTHER INSTRUMENTS vol 13 (Reissue) para 184 et seq.

5   *A-G v Cashel Corpn* (1842) 3 Dr & War 294; *A-G v Archbishop of York* (1853) 17 Beav 495; and see *A-G v Boultbee* (1794) 2 Ves 380; affd (1796) 3 Ves 220.

**101. Extrinsic evidence to explain latent ambiguity.** Extrinsic evidence is admissible in the case of latent ambiguity, as where a description in a will applies equally to more than one institution[1], to determine which institution the testator had in his mind[2]. Examples of admissible extrinsic evidence are to show that one of the institutions which claimed the legacy did not exist when the testator was resident in the locality[3], or that the testator was interested in[4], or had declared he would leave a legacy to[5], or had subscribed to[6] and referred in his books in a particular way to[7], a particular charity.

The fact that a dissolved charity satisfied the description given by the testator better than an existing society does not prevent an existing society, which satisfies the description sufficiently, from taking the legacy[8].

1   The fact that an existing institution is accurately described does not preclude all possibility of there being ambiguity: *National Society for the Prevention of Cruelty to Children v Scottish National Society for the Prevention of Cruelty to Children* [1915] AC 207 at 212, HL, per Lord Loreburn, and at 214 per Lord Dunedin. There is no absolute rule that a person, whether juridical or natural, answering the description in the will must have the gift whatever other considerations arise: *Re Meyers, London Life Association v St George's Hospital* [1951] Ch 534, [1951] 1 All ER 538. As to ambiguities see DEEDS AND OTHER INSTRUMENTS vol 13 (Reissue) para 207; WILLS vol 50 (Reissue) paras 458.

2   *Middleton v Clitherow* (1798) 3 Ves 734; *Wilson v Squire* (1842) 1 Y & C Ch Cas 654 at 656 per Wigram V-C; *Re Briscoe's Trusts* (1872) 26 LT 149; *Re Fearn's Will* (1879) 27 WR 392; *Re Raven, Spencer v National Association for the Prevention of Consumption and other Forms of Tuberculosis* [1915] 1 Ch 673 at 681 per Warrington J; *Re King, King v Long* (1918) 53 ILT 60; *Re Satterthwaite's Will Trusts, Midland Bank Executor and Trustee Co Ltd v Royal Veterinary College* [1966] 1 All ER 919, [1966] 1 WLR 227, CA; *Re Nesbitt's Will Trusts, Dr Barnardo's Homes National Incorporated Association v United Newcastle-upon-Tyne Hospitals Board of Governors* [1953] 1 All ER 936, [1953] 1 WLR 595. An inquiry may be directed to decide which the testator intended to benefit: *Middleton v Clitherow* supra; *Re Dymond, Dymond v A-G* (1906) Times, 2 April. See also the non-charity cases *Charter v Charter* (1874) LR 7 HL 364 at 370–371 per Lord Chelmsford, and at 376 per Lord Hatherley; *Re Beale, Beale v Royal Hospital for Incurables* (1890) 6 TLR 308, CA; and para 100 ante.

3   *King's College Hospital v Wheildon* (1854) 18 Beav 30.

4   *Gibson v Coleman* (1868) 18 LT 236.

5   *A-G v Hudson* (1720) 1 P Wms 674.

6   *Bunting v Marriott* (1854) 19 Beav 163; *Re Kilvert's Trusts* (1871) 7 Ch App 170 at 173 per James LJ; *Makeown v Ardagh* (1876) IR 10 Eq 445; *Re Fearn's Will* (1879) 27 WR 392; *Re Bradley, Oldershaw v Governesses' Benevolent Institution* (1887) 3 TLR 668; *Re Howard, Crofton v Lord's Day Observance Society* (1899) 43 Sol Jo 380.

7   *British Home and Hospital for Incurables v Royal Hospital for Incurables* (1904) 90 LT 601, CA.

8   *Coldwell v Holme* (1854) 2 Sm & G 31; *Re Magrath, Histed v Queen's University of Belfast* [1913] 2 Ch 331 (where the existing institution was in effect the defunct institution reconstituted).


**102.  Trivial error in description.** A trivial error in describing the legatee does not invalidate the gift if the testator's intention is clear[1]; and where an institution is accurately described, a direction as to the use to be made of the money not applicable to the circumstances is immaterial[2].

The context of the will is also important, and may show that the description of a charity is exact, and not loose[3] or that the testator did not intend to benefit institutions of a particular character[4].

In short, the course to be adopted to find what legatee answers the description given in a will is the same in the case of a legacy to a charity as in the case of a legacy to an ordinary legatee[5].


1   *Makeown v Ardagh* (1876) IR 10 Eq 445. Examples are a vicar who is described as a rector (*Hopkinson v Ellis* (1842) 5 Beav 34), or a society which had changed its name but not its objects (*Re Kilvert's Trusts* (1871) 7 Ch App 170). As to the misdescription of property or persons see WILLS vol 50 (Reissue) para 507 et seq.

2   *Smith v Ruger* (1859) 5 Jur NS 905.

3   *Bradshaw v Thompson* (1843) 2 Y & C Ch Cas 295, where the description was ambiguous, and a general hospital was held entitled to take a legacy in preference to an ophthalmic hospital, because in other gifts in the same will, where the testator intended to benefit institutions for particular complaints, he had said so in express terms; *Re Alchin's Trusts, ex p Furley, ex p Earl Romney* (1872) LR 14 Eq 230; and see *Wallace v A-G* (1864) 33 Beav 384 at 392 per Romilly MR; *British Home and Hospital for Incurables v Royal Hospital for Incurables* (1904) 90 LT 601, CA.

4   Eg rate-supported institutions: *Lechmere v Curtler* (1855) 24 LJCh 647; *Re Davies' Trusts* (1872) 21 WR 154.

5   *Re Kilvert's Trusts* (1871) 7 Ch App 170 at 174 per Mellish LJ. See WILLS.


**103.  Usage in construction of trust instrument.** The true construction of ancient instruments of trust may be aided by evidence of long usage and acquiescence[1], and where such instruments may be construed in two ways the court inclines, if possible, to the one supported by long usage[2] rather than assumes that a breach of trust has been committed[3]. But usage cannot be held to sanction a clear breach of trust[4], nor as a rule can evidence of long usage be admitted to vary a trust the terms of which are unambiguous[5].


1   *A-G v Bristol Corpn* (1820) 2 Jac & W 294 at 321 per Lord Eldon LC; *A-G v Smythies* (1833) 2 Russ & M 717 at 749 per Lord Brougham LC. As to the interpretation of deeds and the principles of construction see DEEDS AND OTHER INSTRUMENTS vol 13 (Reissue) para 163 et seq.

2   See the cases cited in note 1 supra; and *A-G v Rochester Corpn* (1854) 5 De GM & G 797 at 822 per Turmer LJ.

3   *A-G v Sidney Sussex College* (1869) 4 Ch App 722 at 732 per Lord Hatherley LC. See also *Bruce v Deer Presbytery* (1867) LR 1 Sc & Div 96, HL.

4   *A-G v Bristol Corpn* (1820) 2 Jac & W 294 at 321 per Lord Eldon LC; *Drummond v A-G for Ireland* (1849) 2 HL Cas 837 at 861 per Lord Brougham; *A-G v Rochester Corpn* (1854) 5 De GM & G 797 at 822 per Turner LJ: *A-G v St John's Hospital, Bedford* (1865) 2 De GJ & Sm 621; and see *Re Swansea Free Grammar School* [1894] AC 252, PC. In some cases, however, a legal origin for long usage inconsistent with the instrument of trust has been presumed: *Queen's College, Cambridge, Case* (1821) Jac 1; *A-G v Middleton*

(1751) 2 Ves Sen 327 at 330 per Lord Hardwicke LC; *Re Parish of St Nicholas Acons* (1889) 60 LT 532; *A-G v Dalton* (1851) 13 Beav 141.

5   *A-G v Calvert* (1857) 23 Beav 248 at 263 per Romilly MR; *A-G v St Cross Hospital* (1853) 17 Beav 435; *A-G v Gould* (1860) 28 Beav 485 at 501 per Romilly MR; *A-G v West* (1858) 27 LJCh 789; *A-G v Ewelme Hospital* (1853) 17 Beav 366.

## (iii)  Presumption of Charitable Trust from Usage

**104.  Presumption from usage.** In the absence of any document declaring the trusts of a fund, their nature may be determined by usage[1]. Where property has been held from time immemorial for the use and repair of what originally was the only church in a parish, the money is not applicable for the purposes of a new church in the same parish[2]. The trustees' accounts showing the application of the income of a fund for a long period may determine the charitable purposes on which the fund is held[3]. However, where trustees remain in adverse possession of the trust property after the legal title has reverted to the grantors, they do so on the trusts of the original grant, and cannot themselves declare fresh trusts of the property[4].

The court will presume whatever may be necessary, even an Act of Parliament[5], to give long standing usage a legal origin and render it valid[6]; it will be guided by the earliest evidence of usage, and will if possible presume that what was then done and long afterwards continued was rightly done[7]; but when the deed of foundation is produced, and is clear, nothing can be presumed to the contrary of what it established[8].

1   *A-G v St Cross Hospital* (1853) 17 Beav 435 at 464–465 per Romilly MR; *A-G v Bishop of Worcester* (1851) 9 Hare 328 at 359 per Turner V-C; and see *A-G v Boultbee* (1794) 2 Ves 380 (where regard was had to the terms of an entry in an ancient book kept by the trustees for entering their proceedings); *Goodman v Saltash Corpn* (1882) 7 App Cas 633, HL.

2   *Re Church Estate Charity, Wandsworth* (1871) 6 Ch App 296; but see para 81 ante.

3   *Re St Bride's, Fleet Street, Church or Parish Estate* (1877) 35 ChD 147n.

4   *Re Ingleton Charity, Croft v A-G* [1956] Ch 585, [1956] 2 All ER 881 (the reverter in that case was automatic, under the School Sites Act 1841).

5   *A-G v Ewelme Hospital* (1853) 17 Beav 366; *A-G v Mercers' Co, Re St Paul's School* (1870) 18 WR 448 at 449 per James V-C.

6   *A-G v Mercers' Co, Re St Paul's School* (1870) 18 WR 448; *Cocksedge v Fanshaw* (1779) 1 Doug KB 119; *Goodman v Saltash Corpn* (1882) 7 App Cas 633 at 640, 644, HL, per Lord Selborne LC (where from long enjoyment by free inhabitants of a borough of a right of fishery a charitable trust in their favour under a lost grant to the corporation was presumed); *Haigh v West* [1893] 2 QB 19 at 26, CA, per Charles J (where enrolment of a lost grant was presumed); and see *Lord Fitzhardinge v Purcell* [1908] 2 Ch 139 at 165 per Parker J; *Harris v Earl of Chesterfield* [1911] AC 623, HL.

7   *A-G v Dalton* (1851) 13 Beav 141 at 142 per Lord Langdale MR.

8   *A-G v St Cross Hospital* (1853) 17 Beav 435; *A-G v Ewelme Hospital* (1853) 17 Beav 366; *A-G v Gould* (1860) 28 Beav 485; and see *Edinburgh Corpn v Lord Advocate* (1879) 4 App Cas 823, HL.

**105.  Instances of usage.** A charitable trust may be presumed from such circumstances as the receipt for a long period of a rentcharge by a charity[1], or the letting of certain rights of pasturage by a parish vestry[2], or the exercise by the free inhabitants of a borough of a right of oyster fishery[3].

Various periods of uninterrupted usage have been held sufficient to establish charitable trusts[4]. Statutes now repealed prescribed various periods of usage for the establishment of the trusts of Roman Catholic and dissenting charities, in the absence of written instruments[5].

1   *A-G v West* (1858) 27 LJCh 789; and see *Stanley v Norwich Corpn* (1887) 3 TLR 506 (where certain rents had been paid to freemen of a city for a long period).

2   *Haigh v West* [1893] 2 QB 19 at 26, CA, per Charles J; and see *A-G v Cashel Corpn* (1842) 3 Dr & War 294.

3   *Goodman v Saltash Corpn* (1882) 7 App Cas 633, HL; and cf *Lord Fitzhardinge v Purcell* [1908] 2 Ch 139 at 165 per Parker J.

4   *A-G v West* (1858) 27 LJCh 789 (30 years); *A-G v Moor* (1855) 20 Beav 119 (100 years); *Re Parker's Charity* (1863) 32 Beav 654 (100 years); *Bunting v Sargent* (1879) 13 ChD 330 at 336 (105 years) per Jessel MR; *Robinson v Smith* (1908) 24 TLR 573 (over 100 years); *Re Parish of St Nicholas Acons* (1889) 60 LT 532 (200 years); *Queen's College, Cambridge, Case* (1821) Jac 1 (250 years); *Re St Alphage, London Wall* (1888) 59 LT 614 (300 years); *A-G v Mercers' Co, Re St Paul's School* (1870) 18 WR 448 (350 years).

5   See the Roman Catholic Charities Act 1860 s 5 and the Nonconformists' Chapels Act 1844 s 2. Both were repealed by the Charities Act 1960 s 39(1), Sch 5 (repealed), but not so as to affect the operation of charities which took effect before the passing of the two Acts: see s 39(2). As to the beneficiaries of religious trusts and the form of worship intended see para 110 post.

## (iv) Beneficiaries of Religious Trusts

**106. Denomination intended by founder to be followed.** One principle applicable to all charities without exception is that the founder's intentions are to be carried into effect so far as they are capable of being so, and so far as they are not contrary to law or morality. If, therefore, the founder has directed that only persons conforming to particular religious doctrines shall be recipients of his bounty, his will must be followed[1].

1   *A-G v Calvert* (1857) 23 Beav 248 at 255 per Romilly MR; *Re Malling Abbey Trusts, Beaumont v Dale* (1915) 31 TLR 397, CA (Church of England); *Craigdallie v Aikman* (1820) 2 Bli 529, HL (Scottish seceders); *A-G v Pearson* (1817) 3 Mer 353 at 410 per Lord Eldon LC; *Milligan v Mitchell* (1837) 3 My & Cr 72 (Scottish dissenters).

**107. Presumptions as to particular denominations.** A trust for the purpose of building a church or otherwise for maintaining and propagating the worship of God, containing no more precise expression of intention, is construed as a trust for the advancement of the established religion of the country[1]. Where the instrument of foundation was made before the Reformation, it was construed as though made after that event[2]. The expression 'Presbyterian' does not denote any particular doctrine or mode of worship[3]. In the absence of express direction, there is a presumption, in the case of eleemosynary[4] and educational charities[5], against the founder's intention being that the recipients must be persons holding a particular form of religious belief. Thus, in eleemosynary charities the founder's religious opinions and tenets are wholly to be disregarded. The presumption is that he intended to include persons of all persuasions, and the burden of proof lies on those who seek to exclude any[6].

In gifts to educational charities the founder's opinions are only of value where some ·directions may have been given by him relative to the religious instruction to be given to the pupils to be taught, and then only for the purpose of explaining and elucidating any obscurity or ambiguity which may be found in such direction[7].

1   *A-G v Pearson* (1817) 3 Mer 353 at 409 per Lord Eldon LC; *A-G v Calvert* (1857) 23 Beav 248 at 258
    per Romilly MR.
2   *A-G v Calvert* (1857) 23 Beav 248 at 260 per Romilly MR; and see *Glasgow College v A-G* (1848) 1 HL
    Cas 800.
3   *A-G v Bunce* (1868) LR 6 Eq 563 at 574 per Malins V-C. With regard to Presbyterian trusts see *Westwood
    v McKie* (1869) 21 LT 165; *General Assembly of the Free Church of Scotland v Lord Overtoun, Macalister v
    Young* [1904] AC 515, HL.
4   As to eleemosynary corporations see para 213 post.
5   As to educational charities see EDUCATION.
6   *A-G v Calvert* (1857) 23 Beav 248 at 259 per Romilly MR; *A-G v St John's Hospital, Bath* (1876) 2 ChD
    554.
7   *A-G v Calvert* (1857) 23 Beav 248 at 258–259 per Romilly MR; *A-G v Clifton* (1863) 32 Beav 596; and
    see *Re St Leonard, Shoreditch, Parochial Schools* (1884) 10 App Cas 304, PC.

**108. Presumptions in case of gift expressly for religious purpose.** In the case of a charity for the support of a religious establishment generally, or the purpose of religious instruction, two presumptions arise: first, that the founder intended to support an establishment belonging to some particular form of religion, and that he intended some particular doctrine of religion to be taught; and secondly, that this establishment and doctrine were those which he himself supported and professed; the court will look carefully at his course of life and conduct and spell out expressions, not merely in the instrument of foundation, but in his will and works, to ascertain what were the doctrines and opinions entertained and professed by him[1].

1   *A-G v Calvert* (1857) 23 Beav 248 at 256 per Romilly MR; *Shore v Wilson* (1842) 9 Cl & Fin 355, HL;
    *General Assembly of the Free Church of Scotland v Lord Overtoun, Macalister v Young* [1904] AC 515 at 613,
    HL, per Earl of Halsbury LC.

**109. Ascertainment of founder's intention.** The founder's intention is a question of fact[1], not always easily ascertained[2]. Where there is no expressed intention[3], or where the language is ambiguous[4], and in those cases only, the objects and mode of executing the trust may be ascertained from a consideration of extrinsic circumstances. Thus, where vague expressions, such as 'Protestant dissenters', are used, extrinsic evidence is admissible to show what denominations are intended to be included[5].

Nevertheless, evidence is not admissible to contradict an express trust[6], or to sanction a breach of trust[7], or to show the sense in which words were used by particular individuals[8], other than the authors of the trusts in question[9].

Reference also may be made to contemporaneous statutes to see in what sense the words were used in the age in which the deeds were executed[10], to contemporaneous deeds relating to the same chapel[11], or to a contemporaneous declaration of trust[12], or to the ecclesiastical history of the period[13]; and where the trust is for the benefit of an existing congregation of dissenters, the character of the congregation may be made the subject of inquiry[14].

The founder's meaning may be explained by evidence as to the character of the congregation for whose benefit the gift was made[15].

1   *Shore v Wilson* (1842) 9 Cl & Fin 355, HL.
2   *Foley v Wontner* (1820) 2 Jac & W 245.
3   *A-G v Murdoch* (1849) 7 Hare 445; affd (1852) 1 De GM & G 86.

4    *A-G v Calvert* (1857) 23 Beav 248 at 263 per Romilly MR; *A-G v Gould* (1860) 28 Beav 485.

5    *Shore v Wilson* (1842) 9 Cl & Fin 355 at 390, HL, per Lord Lyndhurst. In some cases Unitarians were held not entitled to participate; but it has been said that upon most occasions they would now be considered to be Protestant dissenters (*Drummond v A-G for Ireland* (1849) 2 HL Cas 837 at 863 per Lord Campbell); and see *Re Hutchinson's Trusts* [1914] 1 IR 271. As to presumption arising from usage see also paras 104–105 ante.

6    *A-G v Clapham* (1855) 4 De GM & G 591.

7    *Drummond v A-G for Ireland* (1849) 2 HL Cas 837.

8    *Drummond v A-G for Ireland* (1849) 2 HL Cas 837 at 863 per Lord Campbell; *Re How, How v How* [1930] 1 Ch 66.

9    *Drummond v A-G for Ireland* (1849) 2 HL Cas 837 at 858 per Lord Brougham; and see para 100 ante.

10   *Drummond v A-G for Ireland* (1849) 2 HL Cas 837 at 863 per Lord Campbell; *Shore v Wilson* (1842) 9 Cl & Fin 355 at 413, HL, per Campbell A-G. See also para 100 ante.

11   *A-G v Anderson* (1888) 57 LJCh 543.

12   *A-G v Clapham* (1855) 4 De GM & G 591 at 626 per Lord Cranworth LC.

13   *A-G v Bunce* (1868) LR 6 Eq 563 at 571–572 per Malins V-C.

14   *A-G v Murdoch* (1849) 7 Hare 445; affd (1852) 1 De GM & G 86; and see *Dill v Watson* (1836) 2 Jo Ex Ir 48. Many denominations of dissenters, in order to secure uniformity in the trusts of their chapels, schools and other property, use model deeds which are in fact carefully prepared deeds relating to particular chapels, schools, etc, by reference to which the trusts of other chapels, etc can be declared. Denominations which use such model deeds include the Methodist Church, the Baptists, the United Reformed Church, the Fellowship of Independent Evangelical Churches, Unitarians, the Calvinistic Methodist or Presbyterian Church of Wales.

15   *A-G v Molland* (1832) 1 You 562, where teaching 'the Gospel of Christ under the name of orthodoxy' was so explained.

**110. Form of worship intended.** It is not essential for the trusts of religious charities to be in writing in order that they may be enforced by the court[1]. The court may ascertain what form of religious worship was intended from the established usage of the congregation[2].

It was provided by statute that, in the case of Nonconformist chapels where there was no written instrument specifying particular forms of worship or opinions, 25 years' usage was to be taken as conclusive evidence of what might be taught or observed there[3]; and that in the case of Roman Catholic charities, if the trusts of the charity were not ascertained by means of any written document, 20 years' consistent usage was deemed conclusive evidence of the trusts on which the property was settled[4]. These provisions have now been repealed, but without prejudice to their operation as applied to charities taking effect before the repeals[5].

1    See also para 67 ante.

2    *A-G v Pearson* (1817) 3 Mer 353 at 400 per Lord Eldon LC; *A-G v Murdoch* (1849) 7 Hare 445; affd (1852) 1 De GM & G 86; *Drummond v A-G for Ireland* (1849) 2 HL Cas 837. For a form of order directing an inquiry as to usage see *A-G v Pearson* supra at 420 per Lord Eldon LC. As to usage being presumptive evidence of trusts see para 104 ante.

3    Nonconformists' Chapels Act 1844 s 2 (repealed).

4    Roman Catholic Charities Act 1860 s 5 (repealed).

5    See the Charities Act 1960 s 39(1), (2), Sch 5 (s 39(1), Sch 5 repealed).

**111. Gifts for benefit of a church.** A fund given for the 'reparation' of a church may in a proper case be applied in the erection of new buildings[1] and paying the salaries of persons who look after the fabric or ornaments of the building[2].

The income of a fund directed to be employed by the churchwardens of a parish 'about the parish church' is applicable to general expenditure about the church as a whole, including repairs to the chancel, although the churchwardens are not concerned with chancel repairs, which formerly fell on the rector as owner of the great tithes[3].

The endowment of a church means that the income only of the fund is to be applied for the benefit of the incumbent[4].

A gift to a parish church may be construed to be a gift to the parson and parishioners and their successors for ever[5], for their benefit, intended to be devoted to purposes in the parish connected with the services of the church, such purposes now being activities properly directed by the parochial church council[6]. Gifts to a vicar[7] and a dissenting minister[8] may also be gifts for the benefit of the office, and not merely personal legacies to the holder of the office at the date of the gift.

A charitable bequest to a bishop 'to be applied by him for such general or special purposes in connection with' a named cathedral church 'as he in his absolute and uncontrolled discretion may think fit' may be applied in paying the stipend of an honorary canon having a stall in the cathedral, even though his main work lies outside the parish in which the cathedral is situated, or of a canon missioner with duties inside the cathedral, even though he is liable to be employed in the diocese outside the parish, but not of a canon missioner with general diocesan duties and having only an honorary stall in the cathedral[9].

1   *Re Palatine Estate Charity* (1888) 39 ChD 54. See *A-G v Master, Wardens etc of the Wax Chandlers' Co* (1873) LR 6 HL 1; *Re Booth's Charities* (1866) 14 WR 761.
2   *Re Palatine Estate Charity* (1888) 39 ChD 54 (this includes the verger or organ tuner, but not the organist).
3   *A-G v Parr* [1920] 1 Ch 339. Tithes have been abolished: see the Tithe Act 1936; and ECCLESIASTICAL LAW vol 14 para 1209 et seq. As to chancel repairs see ECCLESIASTICAL LAW vol 14 para 1100 et seq.
4   *Re Robinson, Wright v Tugwell* [1892] 1 Ch 95 at 100 per North J; on appeal [1897] 1 Ch 85, CA.
5   *Cheeseman v Partridge* (1739) 1 Atk 436. As to gifts to holders of religious offices see para 35 ante.
6   *Re Gare, Filmer v Carter* [1952] Ch 80, [1951] 2 All ER 863.
7   *Re Parker's Charity* (1863) 32 Beav 654. See also *Re Garrard, Gordon v Craigie* [1907] 1 Ch 382.
8   *A-G v Cock* (1751) 2 Ves Sen 273; and see *Cheeseman v Partridge* (1739) 1 Atk 436 (schoolmaster).
9   *Re Whitehead* (1908) Times, 14 October.

## (v)   Gifts for Institutions, Parishioners or Parishes

**112.   Gifts for institutions.** Where gifts are made to an existing charitable institution or to its governors or treasurer, generally[1] or for promoting certain definite objects which are in fact the objects of that institution[2], the gifts are applicable by the trustees, governors, or other officials for the general purposes of the institution.

A gift to an existing institution for a purpose which is in fact within the objects of the institution is prima facie a gift for the performance of that purpose by the institution in the course of its own activities. Thus, a gift of a fund to a city company to be employed in apprenticing young men should prima facie be applicable for apprenticing them in the craft in which the corporate body was engaged[3]; and where there is a gift to a college for the purpose of educating the descendants of a testator[4], education at that particular college, and not elsewhere, is presumed to be intended[5].

1   *Green v Rutherforth* (1750) 1 Ves Sen 462 at 472 per Lord Hardwicke LC (a gift to a college); *Re White, White v White* [1893] 2 Ch 41 at 52, CA, per Lindley LJ.
2   *Incorporated Society in Dublin v Richards* (1841) 1 Dr & War 258 at 294, 332 per Lord Sugden LC.
3   *A-G v Sidney Sussex College* (1869) 4 Ch App 722 at 730 per Lord Hatherley LC.
4   A gift for the education of descendants of named persons would now be regarded as a family trust and not charitable: *Re Compton, Powell v Compton* [1945] Ch 123 at 136, [1945] 1 All ER 198 at 205, CA, per Lord Greene MR.
5   *A-G v Sidney Sussex College* (1869) 4 Ch App 722 at 731 per Lord Hatherley LC.


**113. Gifts for parishioners or for the poor.** Where children of parishioners of a certain parish are alone eligible as objects of a charity, the word 'parishioner' has hitherto been taken in its ordinary sense of a person occupying premises liable to be rated in the parish[1].

A charity for the poor of a parish was not to be applied in such a way as to relieve those who had otherwise to support the poor by means of the poor rate[2]; but this principle did not apply to a gift which was intended in aid of poor rate[3].

1   *Etherington v Wilson* (1875) 1 ChD 160, CA. See also *A-G v Parker* (1747) 3 Atk 576; *Edenborough v Archbishop of Canterbury* (1826) 2 Russ 93; *A-G v Rutter, Sellon v Nicholls* (1768) 2 Russ 101n ('inhabitants and parishioners'); *Carter v Cropley* (1857) 8 De GM & G 680 at 687 per Bruce LJ; *Kensit v Rector of St Ethelburga, Bishopsgate Within* [1900] P 80. For a detailed analysis of the cases relating to 'parishioners' or 'inhabitants' see Tudor on Charities (7th Edn, 1984) p 210 et seq.
        The effect of the Local Government Finance Act 1988, which abolished domestic rates and replaced them by the community charge, which was then subsequently replaced by the council tax in 1993 (see the Local Government Finance Act 1992; and RATING AND COUNCIL TAX vol 39(1) (Reissue) para 602) has not been considered by the courts.
2   This principle was established in cases deciding that persons receiving poor law relief were not proper objects of such a charity: see *A-G v Leage* [1881] WN 167; *A-G v Bovill* (1840) 1 Ph 762; *Deptford Churchwardens v Sketchley* (1847) 8 QB 394 at 405 per Lord Denman CJ; *A-G v Wilkinson* (1839) 1 Beav 370; *A-G v Exeter Corpn* (1827) 3 Russ 395. See also *A-G v Price* (1744) 3 Atk 108; *A-G v Gutch* (1830) cited in Shelford on Mortmain (1836) 628; *A-G v Clarke* (1762) Amb 422; *Bishop of Hereford v Adams* (1802) 7 Ves 324; *A-G v Rochester Corpn* (1854) 5 De GM & G 797; *Re Sekforde's Charity* (1861) 4 LT 321. The poor law has been replaced by the modern social security system: see SOCIAL SECURITY AND PENSIONS vol 44(2) (Reissue) paras 2–6.
3   *A-G v Blizard* (1855) 21 Beav 233; *Re Richmond Parish Charity Lands, Richmond Corpn v Morell* (1965) 11 RRC 89; revsd on appeal on some points (1965) 11 RRC 283, CA (the same charity as in *A-G v Blizard* supra, after the abolition of the poor rate). See also para 40 ante.


### (vi)  Uncertainty of Objects


**114. Uncertainty of objects in general.** Where a clear charitable intention is expressed, a gift which is otherwise valid is never allowed to fail on account of the uncertainty of the object, but the particular mode of application will be directed by the Crown in some cases, and by the court in others[1].

Effect will therefore be given to bequests for charitable purposes generally[2], or for the relief of poverty[3], or for the advancement of education[4] or religion[5] generally, and to charitable gifts where the testator has indicated the class of objects to be benefited, such as the poor of a particular place[6] or the clergy of a particular sect[7], without prescribing the particular way in which his intention is to be carried into effect. In all of these cases the law supplies the mode of effectuating the intention[8].

1   *Moggridge v Thackwell* (1803) 7 Ves 36, where Lord Eldon considered the earlier cases; *Morice v Bishop of Durham* (1804) 9 Ves 399 at 404 per Grant MR (on appeal (1805) 10 Ves 522); *Mills v Farmer* (1815) 1 Mer 55; *Re White, White v White* [1893] 2 Ch 41 at 53, CA, per Lindley LJ; *Re Forester, Jervis v Forester* (1897) 13 TLR 555; *Re Pyne, Lilley v A-G* [1903] 1 Ch 83; *Re Bennett, Sucker v A-G* [1960] Ch 18, [1959] 3 All ER 295. Where the court has jurisdiction, schemes may also be directed by the Charity Commissioners: see the Charities Act 1993 s 16(1); and para 180 post. As to the Charity Commissioners see paras 486–512 post.
2   *A-G v Herrick* (1772) Amb 712; *Morice v Bishop of Durham* (1805) 10 Ves 522 at 54 Lord Eldon LC; *Miller v Rowan* (1837) 5 Cl & Fin 99 at 109, HL, per Lord Brougham. As to where no trust is created and property is given to charity generally see para 457 post.
3   *A-G v Rance* (1728) cited in Amb 422. As to the relief of poverty see para 16 et seq ante.
4   *Whicker v Hume* (1858) 7 HL Cas 124. As to the advancement of education see para 24 et seq ante.
5   *Re White, White v White* [1893] 2 Ch 41 at 52, CA, per Lindley LJ. As to the advancement of religion see para 30 et seq ante.
6   *A-G v Wilkinson* (1839) 1 Beav 370.
7   *A-G v Hickman* (1732) 2 Eq Cas Abr 193 pl 14; *A-G v Gladstone* (1842) 13 Sim 7.
8   *Mills v Farmer* (1815) 1 Mer 55 at 95 per Lord Eldon LC. See also paras 457, 478 post.

**115. Description by locality.** In case of ambiguity, where the testator describes the institution he intends to benefit as being in a particular locality, prima facie[1] the legacy will go to an institution situated in the locality named, though the name used is more like that of an institution in another locality[2]. On the other hand, a legacy to the hospitals of London was not limited to hospitals within the City of London[3]; while a gift to 'all and every the hospitals', without further description, was confined to hospitals in the locality where the testatrix resided[4].

1   For cases in which other indications in the will contradictory to the description by locality have been followed see *Re Morgan, Marriott v Society for Abolition of Vivisection* (1909) 25 TLR 303; *British Home and Hospital for Incurables v Royal Hospital for Incurables* (1904) 90 LT 601, CA.
2   *Wilson v Squire* (1842) 1 Y & C Ch Cas 654; *Re Lycett, Riley v King's College Hospital* (1897) 13 TLR 373 (where the 'King's Cross Hospital' was construed to mean the Great Northern Hospital, King's Cross, in preference to the King's Cross Hospital at Dundee); *Bradshaw v Thompson* (1843) 2 Y & C Ch Cas 295 (where the 'Westminster Hospital, Charing Cross' was construed to mean the Charing Cross Hospital rather than the Westminster Hospital or the Royal Westminster Ophthalmic Hospital). See also *General Lying-in Hospital v Knight* (1851) 21 LJCh 537; *Re Kilvert's Trusts* (1871) 7 Ch App 170 at 173 per James LJ; *Re Clergy Society* (1856) 2 K & J 615; *Buxton v Blakiston* (1886) 2 TLR 293; *Re Glubb, Barnfield v Rogers* (1897) 14 TLR 66.
3   *Wallace v A-G* (1864) 33 Beav 384; and see *Ditcham v Chivis* (1828) 4 Bing 706; *Beckford v Crutwell* (1832) 5 C & P 242.
4   *Masters v Masters* (1718) 1 P Wms 421 at 425.

## (vii) Delegation of Ascertainment of Objects

**116. Power to determine object.** Power to determine the particular object to be benefited may be delegated[1], so long as charitable and no other objects may benefit[2]. Thus, a direction to trustees to divide a fund at their discretion among such charitable institutions or objects as they think expedient is valid[3]; so, too, a bequest to such charitable objects of a definite class as the trustees select is valid and not void for uncertainty[4]. Whether the discretion extends to the whole gift or only to part of it is a question of construction[5], as is the question whether the trustees may appoint capital or only income to the selected objects[6].

The court will modify an apportionment which is not in accordance with the testator's wishes[7]. Where, however, trustees are given the widest possible discretion within certain limits in the choice of objects, they need not exercise their discretion in accordance with the known views of the testator[8].

Where the power to determine the particular object is delegated to a person who fails to exercise the power, the gift to charity does not fail on that account. Thus, a gift is not invalidated by a trustee neglecting to appoint[9] or an executor renouncing[10], or by the appointment of an executor being revoked[11], or by the death in the testator's lifetime of any person entrusted with the nomination of the particular object[12], or by the name of the intended nominator being left blank[13], or by the trustees declining to act[14] or dying without exercising the discretion[15]. In such cases the court will distribute the money after an inquiry[16].

A direction to trustees to apply residue for such charitable institutions or such other charitable objects as they might in their absolute discretion select does not enable them to set up and distribute the residue to a charitable foundation having a permanent existence[17].

1   *A-G v National Provincial and Union Bank of England* [1924] AC 262 at 264, HL, per Lord Cave LC. As to who may exercise discretionary power see para 328 post.

2   *Chichester Diocesan Fund and Board of Finance Inc v Simpson* [1944] AC 341 at 371, [1944] 2 All ER 60 at 74, HL, per Lord Simonds; see also at 348, 62 per Viscount Simon LC, at 350, 63 per Lord Macmillan, and at 356, 66 per Lord Wright.

3   *Waldo v Caley* (1809) 16 Ves 206; *Horde v Earl of Suffolk* (1833) 2 My & K 59; *Re Lea, Lea v Cooke* (1887) 34 ChD 528; *Cleland's Trustees v Cleland* 1907 SC 591; *Dick's Trustees v Dick* 1907 SC 953; affd sub nom *Dick v Audsley* [1908] AC 347, HL. See also the cases on cumulative purposes cited in para 85 ante, and cf the cases on alternative purposes there cited, where the bequests were held void for uncertainty.

4   See *Re Garrard, Gordon v Craigie* [1907] 1 Ch 382; *Re Bennett, Gibson v A-G* [1920] 1 Ch 305; *Re Bain, Public Trustee v Ross* [1930] 1 Ch 224, CA; *Re Norman, Andrew v Vine* [1947] Ch 349, [1947] 1 All ER 400; *Re Flinn, Public Trustee v Flinn* [1948] Ch 241, [1948] 1 All ER 541; *Re Eastes, Pain v Paxon* [1948] Ch 257, [1948] 1 All ER 536.

5   See eg *Re Hall's Charity* (1851) 14 Beav 115.

6   *Re Beesty's Will Trusts, Farrar v Royal Alfred Merchant Seamen's Society* [1966] Ch 223, [1964] 3 All ER 82.

7   *A-G v Buller* (1822) Jac 407. See also *A-G v Rochester Corpn* (1676) Cas *temp* Finch 193; *A-G v Rochester Corpn* (1833) 6 Sim 273.

8   *Re Squire's Trusts, Chester and Flower v Oxford and Cambridge Universities and A-G* (1901) 17 TLR 724.

9   *A-G v Boultbee* (1796) 3 Ves 220; *Re Douglas, Obert v Barrow* (1887) 35 ChD 472 at 485, CA, per Cotton LJ.

10  *A-G v Fletcher* (1835) 5 LJCh 75. A power for executors to nominate is not exercisable by trustees subsequently appointed: *Hibbard v Lamb* (1756) Amb 309.

11  *White v White* (1778) 1 Bro CC 12; *Moggridge v Thackwell* (1803) 7 Ves 36 at 78 per Lord Eldon LC.

12  *Moggridge v Thackwell* (1803) 7 Ves 36 (affd (1807) 13 Ves 416, HL); *Re Willis, Shaw v Willis* [1921] 1 Ch 44, CA.

13  *Baylis v A-G* (1741) 2 Atk 239.

14  *Doyley v A-G* (1735) 2 Eq Cas Abr 194.

15  *A-G v Bucknall* (1742) 2 Atk 328.

16  *Doyley v A-G* (1735) 2 Eq Cas Abr 194.

17  *Re Muller's Estate* (22 June 1990, unreported): *Report of the Charity Commissioners for England and Wales for 1990* (HC Paper (1990–91) no 362) App D(a).

**117. Founder's right to nominate beneficiaries.** The right of nominating the beneficiaries of a charity belongs naturally to the founder and his heirs or nominees[1], until forfeited by neglect or improper use[2].

This right of nomination, while capable of alienation[3], does not necessarily pass upon the alienation of land to which it is attached. Thus, the owner of a manor to which a right of patronage is attached can alienate the manor without parting with the right of patronage[4].

1    *A-G v Leigh* (1721) 3 P Wms 145n (inmates of almshouses); *Green v Rutherforth* (1750) 1 Ves Sen 462; *Philips v Bury* (1694) 2 Term Rep 346 at 352–353, HL, per Holt CJ. It is not clear what effect the abolition of descent to the heir has upon rights of patronage. As to the old rules of descent see EXECUTORS AND ADMINISTRATORS vol 17(2) (Reissue) para 584.

2    *A-G v Leigh* (1721) 3 P Wms 145n; Tudor on Charities (7th Edn, 1984) p 405.

3    *A-G v Brentwood School* (1832) 3 B & Ad 59; *A-G v Boucherett* (1858) 25 Beav 116 (cases of school patronage); *Re Church Patronage Trust, Laurie v A-G* [1904] 2 Ch 643, CA (advowson).

4    *A-G v Ewelme Hospital* (1853) 17 Beav 366. Where the owner of lands granted out of them a perpetual rentcharge in support of a charity, and subsequently conveyed away the fee simple, it was held that his heir was not thereby deprived of the right of nominating the objects of the charity: *A-G v Rigby* (1732) 3 P Wms 145. Descent to the heir has been abolished: see note 1 supra.

**118. Right vested in trustees or others.** Trustees to whom a testator gives the direction and management of a school provided by him are entitled to nominate and appoint the scholars[1]. The transfer to local authorities of the powers of vestries[2] has not affected any right of electing almsmen vested by deed in the minister, churchwardens, overseers and ratepayers of a parish[3] or any right vested in trustees of electing the minister of a parish[4].

1    *A-G v Dean and Canons of Christ Church* (1822) Jac 474 at 486 per Plumer MR (revsd on another point (1826) 2 Russ 321); and see *A-G v Scott* (1750) 1 Ves Sen 413.

2    See LOCAL GOVERNMENT.

3    *A-G v Drapers' Co* (1858) 4 Drew 299. Overseers were abolished by the Rating and Valuation Act 1925 s 62 (repealed) and their powers transferred to the rating authorities, or to such other local authorities or persons as were mentioned in the Overseers Order 1927, SR & O 1927/55 (as amended). Domestic rates were abolished by the Local Government Finance Act 1988 and replaced by the community charge, itself replaced by the council tax in 1993: see the Local Government Finance Act 1992; RATING AND COUNCIL TAX vol 39(1) (Reissue) para 602; and LOCAL GOVERNMENT.

4    *Carter v Cropley* (1857) 8 De GM & G 680. See also *Shaw v Thompson* (1876) 3 ChD 233; and cf *Re Hayle's Estate* (1862) 31 LJCh 612. As to transfer to the parochial church council see ECCLESIASTICAL LAW vol 14 para 575.

**119. Church Commissioners' powers.** In orders made by them under the Bishops Trusts Substitution Act 1858[1], the Charity Commissioners[2] are not entitled to make any order in relation to any advowson or right of patronage or presentation, part of the possessions of a see, which might be exchanged or otherwise disposed of by scheme of the Church Commissioners; nor may any orders relating to any ecclesiastical patronage be made under that Act without the consent of the Church Commissioners[3].

1    See para 243 post.

2    As to the Charity Commissioners see paras 486–512 post.

3    See the Bishops Trusts Substitution Act 1858 s 2 (as amended); and para 243 post. As to the Church Commissioners see ECCLESIASTICAL LAW vol 14 paras 361–383.

**120. Beneficiaries' qualifications.** Where by the instrument establishing a charity the beneficiaries are required to possess certain qualifications, as, for example, to be parishioners of a certain parish[1], or to have been pupils for a number of years at a certain school[2], or where, other things being equal, preference is to be given to freemen of a certain town[3], the conditions imposed by the instrument must be complied with. However, the parties exercising the right of nomination need not take into consideration the motives with which the proposed beneficiaries secured the necessary qualifications[4]; and where compliance with certain religious forms is annexed as a condition to a charitable gift no further religious test can properly be required[5].

1    *Etherington v Wilson* (1875) 1 ChD 160, CA. As to the effect of a union of benefices upon charitable trusts relating to the united parishes see the Pastoral Measure 1983 Sch 3 para 11 (as amended); and para 242 post.

2    *Re Storie's University Gift* (1860) 2 De GF & J 529.

3    *Re Nettle's Charity* (1872) LR 14 Eq 434 (election to scholarship).

4    *Etherington v Wilson* (1875) 1 ChD 160, CA, where the proposed beneficiary had become a parishioner temporarily to obtain the required qualification.

5    *A-G v Calvert* (1857) 23 Beav 248.

**121. Nomination by subscribers' votes.** Subscribers to a charity who are entitled to votes in proportion to the amount of their subscriptions may vote for any candidate they please. There is nothing illegal in a bargain between two subscribers by which the candidate of one is to be given the votes of both at an election in consideration of the candidate of the other having similar treatment at another election, and such a contract is enforceable at law[1].

1    *Bolton v Madden* (1873) LR 9 QB 55.

**122. Improper nomination.** A nomination which fails to comply with the directions of the instrument establishing the charity may be set aside[1], unless it is made in good faith under a mistaken construction of a scheme[2]. On setting aside an improper nomination the court has no jurisdiction to nominate proper beneficiaries, where by the charity's constitution the nomination rests with the trustees[3].

No application to the court to set aside the election of any person may be made by any other person who claims to be the proper object of a charity unless the making of the application is authorised by the Charity Commissioners[4].

Where the objects of a charity have been nominated for many years by the wrong persons, the court will not compel them to account for the payments made[5].

1    *Re Nettle's Charity* (1872) LR 14 Eq 434.

2    *Re Storie's University Gift* (1860) 30 LJCh 193 at 199 per Turner LJ.

3    *Re Storie's University Gift* (1860) 30 LJCh 193 at 198 per Turner LJ.

4    See the Charities Act 1993 s 33(2); and para 521 post. As to the Charity Commissioners see paras 486–512 post.

5    *A-G v Rigby* (1732) 3 P Wms 145.

## (4) SURPLUS INCOME

**123. Whole property given: surplus and later accretion.** Where, at the date of the bequest, the property given is more than sufficient to satisfy the purposes specified in the will, and it also appears that the testator intended to give the whole property to charity, but was mistaken only as to the quantum, the whole is applicable to increase the charities specified or cy-près[1].

Where, however, it appears on the face of a will that the testator knew that the value of his estate was or might be more than the amount of the specific appropriation, and he has expressed no intention of devoting the whole to charity, the surplus does not go to charity, but either goes beneficially to the donees to whom the property is given in trust for the charitable purposes[2] or results to the testator and those claiming under him[3].

Where there is a direction to make specific charitable payments out of the income, it is a question of construction in each case whether the intention is to devote the whole property to charity[4]. Where the surplus income is directed to be applied in repairing the premises given to the charity, the whole property is held to have been devoted to charity[5].

If property, or the whole of the income arising from it[6], as, for example, a rentcharge equal to the annual value of the land charged[7], is given to charity any subsequent increase in the value of the property accrues to the charity[8].

A gift of income to a charity in perpetuity does not necessarily carry with it a right to the capital; it depends on the terms of the gift[9].

1   *Re Monk, Giffen v Wedd* [1927] 2 Ch 197, CA; *A-G v Earl of Winchelsea* (1791) 3 Bro CC 373; *A-G v Minshull* (1798) 4 Ves 11; *Arnold v A-G* (1698) Show Parl Cas 22, HL. For cases on surplus capital see para 163 post. Surplus income may in these circumstances be applied by a scheme under the Charities Act 1993 s 13(1)(b) (see para 206 post). As to cy-près applications by scheme see para 201 et seq post.
2   *A-G v Skinners' Co* (1827) 2 Russ 407 at 443 per Lord Eldon LC; *A-G v Skinners' Co* (1833) 5 Sim 596. See also *Re Jordeyn's Charity* (1833) 1 My & K 416; *A-G v Trinity College, Cambridge* (1856) 24 Beav 383; and the cases cited in para 125 note 4 post.
3   *Re Stanford, Cambridge University v A-G* [1924] 1 Ch 73.
4   *A-G v Bristol Corpn* (1820) 2 Jac & W 294 at 315, 318 per Lord Eldon LC; *Beverley Corpn v A-G* (1857) 6 HL Cas 310 at 333 per Lord Wensleydale; *A-G v Dean and Canons of Windsor* (1860) 8 HL Cas 369 at 393–394 per Lord Campbell LC, and at 406 per Lord Cranworth.
5   *Beverley Corpn v A-G* (1857) 6 HL Cas 310 at 324 per Lord Chelmsford LC; *Merchant Taylors' Co v A-G* (1871) 6 Ch App 512; *A-G v Master, Wardens etc of the Wax Chandlers' Co* (1873) LR 6 HL 1.
6   *A-G v Skinners' Co* (1827) 2 Russ 407 at 411 per Lord Eldon LC (gift of rents and profits equivalent to gift of the lands themselves); *Southmolton Corpn v A-G* (1854) 5 HL Cas 1 at 31–32 per Lord St Leonards; *Beverley Corpn v A-G* (1857) 6 HL Cas 310.
7   *Kennington Hastings Case* (1612) Duke 71; *Hynshaw v Morpeth Corpn* (1629) Duke 69; *Eltham Inhabitants v Warreyn* (1634) Duke 67; *Sutton Colefield Case* (1635) Duke 68.
8   *Ex p Jortin* (1802) 7 Ves 340; *A-G v Bristol Corpn* (1820) 2 Jac & W 294; *A-G v Wilson* (1834) 3 My & K 362.
9   *Re Levy, Barclays Bank Ltd v Board of Guardians and Trustees for the Relief of the Jewish Poor* [1960] Ch 346, [1960] 1 All ER 42, CA.

**124. Gift of surplus: surplus and later accretion.** If a testator gives particular sums, not exhausting the entire income, for specified charitable purposes, and gives the remainder of the income for other charitable purposes, a question of construction arises whether any increase in the income is divisible pro rata among the specified objects and the objects entitled to the residue[1], or whether the whole residue of the augmented income passes to the objects entitled to the residue[2].

If there is an express gift of surplus income of the donee who is charged with the payments, this may be interpreted in two ways: either (1) as a gift of the residue, whatever it may amount to, in which case the residuary donee is entitled to any increased income[3]; or (2) as a gift of an aliquot proportion of the whole, in which case the donee shares rateably with the other donees in any increase[4]. The question into which of these two classes a gift falls is a matter of construction, to be solved in each particular case by considering the instrument of foundation as a whole[5]. The court is not entitled to take a broad view of the parties' rights based on the donor's supposed intention[6]. Such words as 'overplus', 'surplus', or 'residue' do not necessarily indicate that the gift is residuary[7]. An express gift of surplus will be disregarded where, if effect were given to it, the donor's intention would be defeated[8].

1   *A-G v Caius College* (1837) 2 Keen 150. See *A-G v Coopers' Co* (1812) 19 Ves 187; *A-G v Solly* (1835) 5 LJCh 5.

2   *Re Avenon's Charity, A-G v Pelly* (1912) 56 Sol Jo 241, reported on further consideration [1913] 2 Ch 261 (where the surplus, having exceeded what was necessary for the residuary purpose, was all applied cy-près to the residuary purpose); *Re Lepton's Charity, Ambler v Thomas* [1972] Ch 276, [1971] 1 All ER 799.

3   *Southmolton Corpn v A-G* (1854) 5 HL Cas 1; *Beverley Corpn v A-G* (1857) 6 HL Cas 310 at 326 per Lord Chelmsford LC; *Re Rowe, Merchant Taylors' Co v London Corpn* (1914) 30 TLR 528.

4   *A-G v Drapers' Co, Kendrick's Charity* (1841) 4 Beav 67; *A-G v Jesus College, Oxford* (1861) 29 Beav 163; and see the cases cited in note 3 supra.

5   *A-G v Dean and Canons of Windsor* (1860) 8 HL Cas 369 at 405–406 per Lord Cranworth.

6   *Re Lepton's Charity, Ambler v Thomas* [1972] Ch 276, [1971] 1 All ER 799, where the disparity resulting from the increase of income was alleviated by the application of the Charities Act 1960 s 13(1)(a)(ii), (e)(iii) (repealed) (see now the Charities Act 1993 s 13; and para 206 post).

7   *Beverley Corpn v A-G* (1857) 6 HL Cas 310; *Southmolton Corpn v A-G* (1854) 5 HL Cas 1 at 25–26 per Lord Cranworth LC. As to the expression 'or thereabouts' see also *A-G v Trinity College, Cambridge* (1856) 24 Beav 383 at 392–393 per Romilly MR. No difficulty arises where the instrument expressly directs the surplus income (*Re Jordeyn's Charity* (1833) 1 My & K 416; *Southmolton Corpn v A-G* supra at 5 per Lord Cranworth LC), or any subsequent increase (*Charitable Donations and Bequests Comrs v Baroness De Clifford* (1841) 1 Dr & War 245), to be applied for charitable or other purposes or for the benefit of the donees (*A-G v Gascoigne* (1833) 2 My & K 647, where the executors took beneficially; *A-G v Skinners' Co* (1827) 2 Russ 407; *A-G v Drapers' Co, Kendrick's Charity* (1841) 4 Beav 67).

8   *Re Ashton's Charity* (1859) 27 Beav 115 (gift of surplus to six 'almswomen', who would have ceased to be almswomen if they received the whole of the largely increased surplus income, treated as a gift to charity generally).

**125. No gift of surplus: surplus and later accretion.** If, at the time of the gift, the specific payments do not exhaust the whole income, and there is no express gift of the surplus, but there is a clear intention, whether express or implied, to attach a charitable trust to the whole property, the surplus will be devoted to charity, however deficient may be the appropriation of the whole income, for the general charitable intention will prevail[1].

In such a case the donees will not be entitled to the surplus or increase unless they are themselves a charity[2], or there are other circumstances from which a contrary intention can be inferred[3]. If, however, there is no general intention to devote the whole to charity, the surplus income belongs to the parties charged with making the payments, and not to the charities[4], notwithstanding that such specific payments, by lapse of time or change of circumstances, have become insufficient to satisfy the purposes for which they were originally made[5]; for the absence of any disposition of the surplus is prima facie an indication of an intention to benefit the donee[6].

This rule has been frequently applied in the case of gifts to corporations such as colleges[7], city companies[8], or local authorities[9], or a dean and canons[10], subject to or charged with specific charitable payments which do not exhaust the income; but the principle is not confined to gifts to such bodies[11].

1   *Arnold v A-G* (1698) Show Parl Cas 22, HL; *A-G v Sparks* (1753) Amb 201; *A-G v Painter Stainers' Co* (1788) 2 Cox Eq Cas 51; *A-G v Haberdashers' Co* (1792) 4 Bro CC 103; *A-G v Bristol Corpn* (1820) 2 Jac & W 294 at 318 per Lord Eldon LC; *A-G v Skinners' Co* (1827) 2 Russ 407 at 442 per Lord Eldon LC; *Mystery of Mercers v A-G* (1828) 2 Bli NS 165, HL; *A-G v Drapers' Co* (1840) 2 Beav 508; *A-G v Coopers' Co* (1840) 3 Beav 29; *A-G v Grocers' Co* (1843) 6 Beav 526 at 546 per Lord Langdale MR; *Southmolton Corpn v A-G* (1854) 5 HL Cas 1 at 32 per Lord St Leonards; *Beverley Corpn v A-G* (1857) 6 HL Cas 310 at 318 per Lord Chelmsford LC; *A-G v Dean and Canons of Windsor* (1860) 8 HL Cas 369; *Shepherd v Bristol Corpn* (1818) 3 Madd 319 at 352 per Leach V-C; affd on this point but revsd on other grounds sub nom *A-G v Bristol Corpn* supra at 318 per Lord Eldon LC.

2   *A-G v Trinity College, Cambridge* (1856) 24 Beav 383 at 399 per Romilly MR; and see *A-G v Bristol Corpn* (1820) 2 Jac & W 294.

3   *A-G v Drapers' Co* (1840) 2 Beav 508.

4   *A-G v Bristol Corpn* (1820) 2 Jac & W 294 at 307 per Lord Eldon LC; *A-G v Skinners' Co* (1827) 2 Russ 407 at 443 per Lord Eldon LC; *A-G v Cordwainers' Co* (1833) 3 My & K 534; *A-G v Brazen Nose College* (1834) 2 Cl & Fin 295, HL; *A-G v Fishmongers' Co, Kneseworth's Will* (1841) 5 My & Cr 11; *A-G v Grocers' Co* (1843) 6 Beav 526; *Jack v Burnett* (1846) 12 Cl & Fin 812, HL; *Southmolton Corpn v A-G* (1854) 5 HL Cas 1 at 34 per Lord St Leonards; *A-G v Trinity College, Cambridge* (1856) 24 Beav 383; *A-G v Dean and Canons of Windsor* (1860) 8 HL Cas 369; *Merchant Taylors' Co v A-G* (1871) 6 Ch App 512 at 519 per James LJ.

5   *A-G v Gascoigne* (1833) 2 My & K 647; *Charitable Donations and Bequests Comrs v Baroness De Clifford* (1841) 1 Dr & War 245.

6   *A-G v Trinity College, Cambridge* (1856) 24 Beav 383 at 392 per Romilly MR. See also *A-G v Master, Wardens etc of the Wax Chandlers' Co* (1873) LR 6 HL 1 at 19 et seq.

7   *A-G v Catherine Hall, Cambridge* (1820) Jac 381; *A-G v Brazen Nose College* (1834) 2 Cl & Fin 295, HL; *Jack v Burnett* (1846) 12 Cl & Fin 812, HL; *A-G v Trinity College, Cambridge* (1856) 24 Beav 383; *A-G v Sidney Sussex College* (1869) 4 Ch App 722; *Re Lavelle, Concannon v A-G* [1914] 1 IR 194.

8   *A-G v Cordwainers' Co* (1833) 3 My & K 534; *A-G v Fishmongers' Co, Kneseworth's Will* (1841) 5 My & Cr 11; *A-G v Grocers' Co* (1843) 6 Beav 526; *A-G v Master, Wardens etc of the Wax Chandlers' Co* (1873) LR 6 HL 1 at 9 per Lord Chelmsford, and at 19 per Lord Cairns.

9   *A-G v Bristol Corpn* (1820) 2 Jac & W 294; *Southmolton Corpn v A-G* (1854) 5 HL Cas 1 at 34 per Lord St Leonards; *Beverley Corpn v A-G* (1857) 6 HL Cas 310.

10  *A-G v Dean and Canons of Windsor* (1860) 8 HL Cas 369.

11  *Merchant Taylors' Co v A-G* (1871) 6 Ch App 512 at 519 per James LJ. See *A-G v Smythies* (1833) 2 Russ & M 717 at 741 per Lord Brougham LC (master of an almshouse); and cf *A-G v Master of Brentwood School* (1833) 1 My & K 376; *A-G v Governors of Atherstone Free School* (1834) 3 My & K 544.

**126. No gift of surplus: no surplus but later accretion.** If there is no express gift of surplus income, but the specific payments exhaust the entire income at the time of the gift, any subsequent increase[1] in the income is applicable to similar purposes and prima facie in similar proportions[2]. The deficiency in case of a decrease in the income is apportionable in the same way[3]. However, the court may, within certain limits, vary the proportions[4].

This rule is equally applicable whether the donor thought at the time that he was disposing of the entire income[5], or there are words that might have been interpreted as limiting the extent of the benevolent purpose had they stood alone, but such words are coupled with other words which show that the benevolent purpose operates to the extent of the whole fund[6].

1   *Southmolton Corpn v A-G* (1854) 5 HL Cas 1 at 32 per Lord St Leonards.
2   *Thetford School Case* (1609) 8 Co Rep 130b.
3   *Thetford School Case* (1609) 8 Co Rep 130b; *Sutton Colefield Case* (1635) Duke 68; *A-G v Townsend*
    (1670) Duke 34; *Arnold v A-G* (1698) Show Parl Cas 22, HL; *A-G v Coventry Corpn* (1702) Colles 280,
    HL; *A-G v Johnson* (1753) Amb 190; *A-G Haberdashers' Co* (1792) 4 Bro CC 103; *A-G v Coopers' Co*
    (1812) 19 Ves 187; *A-G v Bristol Corpn* (1820) 2 Jac & W 294 at 315, 317–318, 322 per Lord Eldon LC;
    *Mystery of Mercers v A-G* (1828) 2 Bli NS 165, HL; *A-G v Wilson* (1834) 3 My & K 362; *A-G v Brazen*
    *Nose College* (1834) 2 Cl & Fin 295 at 328, HL, per Lord Brougham LC; *A-G v Barham* (1835) 4 LJCh
    128; *A-G v Coopers' Co* (1840) 3 Beav 29; *A-G v Christ's Hospital* (1841) 4 Beav 73; *A-G v Gilbert* (1847)
    10 Beav 517; *Southmolton Corpn v A-G* (1854) 5 HL Cas 1; *Beverley Corpn v A-G* (1857) 6 HL Cas 310
    at 320 per Lord Chelmsford LC; *A-G v Master, Wardens etc of the Wax Chandlers' Co* (1873) LR 6 HL 1.
4   *A-G v Dean and Canons of Windsor* (1860) 8 HL Cas 369 at 452 per Lord Kingsdown; *A-G v Marchant*
    (1866) LR 3 Eq 424 at 430 per Kindersley V-C.
5   *A-G v Marchant* (1866) LR 3 Eq 424 at 430 per Kindersley V-C; and see *A-G v Bristol Corpn* (1820) 2
    Jac & W 294 at 332 per Lord Eldon.
6   *A-G v Painter Stainers' Co* (1788) 2 Cox Eq Cas 51 at 55.

**127. Whether donees take surplus and increase.** The donees are entitled to the surplus where it has been charged with the expense of repairs[1], or where they have bound themselves by penalties or covenanted to pay fixed sums to charity whether the income of the property is sufficient or not[2].

Donees will not take beneficially where there has been long usage to the contrary, or where by the instrument of foundation they are given power to regulate the charity[3].

Speaking generally, the increase will belong to the donee, first, if the gift be to the donee subject to certain payments to others; secondly, if the gift be upon condition of making certain payments subject to a forfeiture upon non-performance of the condition; or, thirdly, if the donee might be a loser by the insufficiency of the fund[4].

In the case of a gift to a particular body for the benefit of the body with a provision that certain members or officials are to receive specific annual sums, the body is entitled to the bulk of the property with the full increase, and the particular members or officers are entitled only to the sums specifically given them[5]. Thus, where property is given not for purposes of individual benefit, but for the performance of duties, any increase of income exceeding reasonable remuneration for the performance of those duties will be applied to other charitable purposes[6].

A gift of the income of property to maintain poor scholars, each having so much a day, is a gift to them of the whole, and entitles them to the surplus[7].

1   *A-G v Skinners' Co* (1827) 2 Russ 407; *A-G v Coopers' Co* (1840) 3 Beav 29.
2   *Jack v Burnett* (1846) 12 Cl & Fin 812 at 828, HL, per Lord Cottenham LC. See also *A-G v Bristol Corpn*
    (1820) 2 Jac & W 294 at 303 per Lord Eldon LC; and cf *A-G v Merchant Venturers' Co, Bristol* (1848) 17
    LJCh 137.
3   *A-G v Mercers' Co, Re St Paul's School* (1870) 18 WR 448.
4   *Jack v Burnett* (1846) 12 Cl & Fin 812 at 828, HL, per Lord Cottenham.
5   *Southmolton Corpn v A-G* (1854) 5 HL Cas 1 at 32–33 per Lord St Leonards; and see *A-G v Bristol Corpn*
    (1820) 2 Jac & W 294 at 317 per Lord Eldon LC. In the case of a gift to a corporation consisting of a
    master and almsmen, with a direction that the almsmen should receive fixed stipends, the almsmen were
    not allowed to share rateably with the master in the increased income: *A-G v Smythies* (1833) 2 Russ &
    M 717 at 747–748 per Lord Brougham LC; *Re Ashton's Charity* (1859) 27 Beav 115, where the increased
    income was applied to charity generally.
6   *Thetford School Case* (1609) 8 Co Rep 130b; *A-G v Bristol Corpn* (1820) 2 Jac & W 294; *A-G v Smythies*
    (1833) 2 Russ & M 717 at 747 per Lord Brougham LC. Distinguish the case of a gift to a college for its
    maintenance with a provision that each scholar should have a certain sum, in which case the scholars are
    not entitled to share in any increased income: *A-G v Smythies* supra at 747 per Lord Brougham LC.
7   *A-G v Master of Brentwood School* (1833) 1 My & K 376 at 394 per Leach MR; and see *A-G v Governors*
    *of Atherstone Free School* (1834) 3 My & K 544 at 555 per Lord Brougham LC.

## (5) CONDITIONAL AND LIMITED INTERESTS

**128. Conditions precedent.** A charitable gift may be made subject to conditions precedent, for example, that the gift shall take effect only if the testator's estate is sufficient for the intended object[1] or amounts to a certain sum[2]. Gifts to hospitals have frequently been made subject to conditions precedent relating to nationalisation[3].

A legacy to a fund raised for the purpose of effecting a particular charitable object may be construed as a gift on condition that the particular object proves to be practicable[4]; and a gift may be made for a particular charitable purpose on condition that other property is given for the same object[5].

Such gifts of realty fail if the condition is not[6], or cannot be[7], fulfilled or offends against the rule against perpetuities[8], unless the fulfilment of the condition is not essential to the gift[9]. In the case of gifts of personalty subject to conditions precedent which are illegal, a distinction is drawn between illegality involving that which is inherently wrong[10] and that which is wrong only because it is prohibited by law[11]; in the latter case the invalidity of the condition does not avoid the gift and the donee takes free from the condition[12].

Cases of gifts subject to conditions precedent are to be distinguished from cases in which there is an immediate outright gift to charity but the particular application directed is postponed and may depend on the occurrence of events contingent and uncertain[13].

1   *Cherry v Mott* (1836) 1 My & Cr 123.
2   *Thomas v Howell* (1874) LR 18 Eq 198; and see *Re Swain, Monckton v Hands* [1905] 1 Ch 669, CA.
3   *Re Frere, Kidd v Farnham Group Hospital Management Committee* [1951] Ch 27, [1950] 2 All ER 513; *Re Buzzacott, Munday v King's College Hospital* [1953] Ch 28, [1952] 2 All ER 1011; *Connell's Trustees v Milngavie District Nursing Association* 1953 SC 230; *Re Lowry's Will Trusts, Barclays Bank Ltd v United Newcastle-upon-Tyne Hospitals Board of Governors of* [1967] Ch 638, [1966] 3 All ER 955.
4   *Re London University Medical Sciences Institute Fund, Fowler v A-G* [1909] 2 Ch 1, CA.
5   *McCormick v Queen's University of Belfast* [1958] NI 1.
6   *Cherry v Mott* (1836) 1 My & Cr 123.
7   *Re Emson, Grain v Grain* (1905) 74 LJCh 565.
8   See para 134 post.
9   *Re Selinger's Will Trusts, Midland Bank Executor and Trustee Co Ltd v Levy* [1959] 1 All ER 407, [1959] 1 WLR 217 (a suitable charity to be found within one year of testator's death; if none found legacy to be revoked; held only to be intended to prevent delay in administration, so that where administration was delayed for other reasons, the gift took effect, even though a recipient was not found until two years after the death).
10  Ie *malum in se.*
11  Ie *malum prohibitum.* See *Re Piper, Dodd v Piper* [1946] 2 All ER 503 at 505, where Romer J observed: 'the difference between *malum prohibitum* and *malum in se* has never been very precisely defined or considered'.
12  *Re Elliott, Lloyds Bank Ltd v Burton-on-Trent Hospital Management Committee* [1952] Ch 217, [1952] 1 All ER 145 (condition relating to upkeep of a grave, involving only *malum prohibitum*); *Re Hepplewhite's Will Trusts* (1977) Times, 21 January (gift subject to several conditions, some valid, some invalid: gift good subject only to valid conditions). As to distinctions between various types of impossibility see *Re Moore, Trafford v Maconochie* (1888) 39 ChD 116, CA.
13  *Chamberlayne v Brockett* (1872) 8 Ch App 206; *Re Swain, Monckton v Hands* [1905] 1 Ch 669, CA.

**129. Conditions subsequent.** Charitable gifts may be made subject to conditions subsequent which come into effect if, after the gift has taken effect, some act is omitted to be done[1] or some act is done[2]. However, a mere intention to make the enjoyment of the gift conditional is inoperative unless it is actually carried out[3]. There have been many examples of conditions subsequent relating to the nationalisation of charitable institutions[4].

Conditions subsequent include: (1) common law conditions[5], a breach of which involves forfeiture to the grantor or his representatives[6]; (2) conditions enforceable in equity[7]; and (3) conditions followed by executory limitations or gifts over[8].

If the condition infringes the rule against perpetuities[9], or is illegal[10], or involves a breach of trust[11], or is repugnant to the gift[12], or is void for uncertainty[13], the charity takes the gift discharged from the condition and, if there is a gift over, that also fails[14]. Where trustees are given a discretionary power to exclude certain institutions from benefit under a charitable gift, the validity of that power is governed by the same principles as a gift over[15]; thus if the power involves perpetuity and is not restricted to charity it is bad and the initial gift to charity is unfettered[16].

Charitable trusts have sometimes been declared subject to express powers of revocation, but there has apparently been no decision on the validity of such a power except as regards the rule against perpetuities[17].

However, if the condition itself is not bad but the gift over cannot take effect because it is to a person who is not an object of the power which is exercised by the gift[18], or because of the mortmain laws[19], the prior estate is defeated on the fulfilment of the condition and the property is held upon a resulting trust or falls into residue.

---

1   *A-G v Christ's Hospital* (1790) 3 Bro CC 165 (children from particular parish to be maintained); *Re Tyler, Tyler v Tyler* [1891] 3 Ch 252, CA (keeping a tomb in repair); *Re Conington's Will* (1860) 6 Jur NS 992 (incumbent of particular church to be maintained and special services to be held); *Re Robinson, Wright v Tugwell* [1892] 1 Ch 95 (approved [1897] 1 Ch 85, CA) (black gown to be worn in pulpit; but see *Re Robinson, Wright v Tugwell* [1923] 2 Ch 332, where this condition was dispensed with); *Re Parker's Charity* (1863) 32 Beav 654 (anniversary sermon).

2   *Milbank v Lambert* (1860) 28 Beav 206 (vicar not to collect tithes); *Re Barrett's Trusts, Dyson v Sheffield Corpn* (1910) 26 TLR 330.

3   *Yates v University College, London* (1875) LR 7 HL 438 (where the testator omitted to make rules compliance with which was required by the gift); *University College of North Wales v Taylor* [1908] P 140, CA (where the condition intended to be attached to the gift was contained in a memorandum excluded from probate as not being sufficiently referred to in the will for identification).

4   Eg *Royal College of Surgeons of England v National Provincial Bank Ltd* [1952] AC 631, [1952] 1 All ER 984, HL; *Re Bawden's Settlement, Besant v London Hospital Board of Governors* [1953] 2 All ER 1235, [1954] 1 WLR 33n; *Mollison's Trustees v Aberdeen General Hospitals Board of Management* 1953 SC 264.

5   *Re Hollis' Hospital Trustees and Hague's Contract* [1899] 2 Ch 540; *Re Da Costa, Clarke v Church of England Collegiate School of St Peter* [1912] 1 Ch 337.

6   Shep Touch 117, 119, 120; Co Litt 201a.

7   See the cases cited in para 68 ante (where words of condition created a trust). See also the cases where charities accepting property subject to conditions were held bound to perform them, eg *A-G v Caius College* (1837) 2 Keen 150 at 163 per Lord Langdale MR; and para 130 post.

8   See *Christ's Hospital v Grainger* (1849) 1 Mac & G 460; *Re Conington's Will* (1860) 6 Jur NS 992; *Re Tyler, Tyler v Tyler* [1891] 3 Ch 252, CA; *Royal College of Surgeons of England v National Provincial Bank Ltd* [1952] AC 631, [1952] 1 All ER 984, HL.

9   *Re Talbot, Jubb v Sheard* [1933] Ch 895; *Re Bawden's Settlement, Besant v London Hospital Board of Governors* [1953] 2 All ER 1235, [1954] 1 WLR 33n.

10  *Re Amos, Carrier v Price* [1891] 3 Ch 159 at 167 per North J (contrary to the Mortmain Acts).

11  *Re Tyler, Tyler v Tyler* [1891] 3 Ch 252, CA.

12  *Lydiatt v Foach* (1700) 2 Vern 410; *Watson v Hinsworth Hospital* (1707) 2 Vern 596 (condition that rent of property given to charity should never be raised); *A-G v Catherine Hall, Cambridge* (1820) Jac 381 at 395 per Lord Eldon LC; *A-G v Greenhill* (1863) 33 Beav 193 (conditions restricting alienation); *Re Restell, Royal Hospital for Incurables v Restell* (1901) 17 TLR 395; *Hope v Gloucester Corpn* (1855) 7 De GM & G 647. See also the cases cited in para 154 note 11 post.

13  See *Re Hayes' Will Trusts, Dobie v National Hospital Board of Governors* [1953] 2 All ER 1242, [1954] 1
    WLR 22 (gift to 29 institutions with power to trustees to exclude any if impracticable or inequitable that
    they should share). The requirement of certainty is stricter for a condition subsequent than for a
    condition precedent: *Blathwayt v Baron Cawley* [1976] AC 397, [1975] 3 All ER 625, HL; *Re Barlow's
    Will Trusts* [1979] 1 All ER 296, [1979] 1 WLR 278.

14  See *Yates v University College, London* (1875) LR 7 HL 438, followed in *Re Barnett, Waring v Painter-
    Stainers' Co* (1908) 24 TLR 788; *Re Barker, Sherrington v Dean and Chapter of St Paul's Cathedral* (1909)
    25 TLR 753; *Re Dalziel, Midland Bank Executor and Trustee Co Ltd v St Bartholomew's Hospital* [1943] Ch
    277, [1943] 2 All ER 656. Conversely, gifts to individuals subject to conditions which infringed the
    mortmain laws were taken by the legatee free from the condition: *Doe d Burdett v Wrighte* (1819) 2 B &
    Ald 710; *Poor v Mial* (1821) 6 Madd 32; *Henchman v A-G* (1834) 3 My & K 485.

15  *Re Hayes' Will Trusts, Dobie v National Hospital Board of Governors* [1953] 2 All ER 1242, [1954] 1 WLR
    22; *George Drexler Ofrex Foundation Trustees v IRC* [1966] Ch 675, [1965] 3 All ER 529.

16  *Re Bawden's Settlement, Besant v London Hospital Board of Governors* [1953] 2 All ER 1235, [1954] 1 WLR
    33n. The condition upon which a gift over effected under such a power would take effect would be the
    trustees' decision to exercise the power; since they cannot effect it if the power is bad, the condition can
    never occur.

17  In *Re Sir Robert Peel's School at Tamworth, ex p Charity Comrs* (1868) 3 Ch App 543, the validity of the
    power was assumed but the decision turned on a quite different point; in *Gibson v South American Stores
    (Gath and Chaves) Ltd* [1950] Ch 177, [1949] 2 All ER 985, CA, the validity of the power was not in
    issue. In *Re Watson's Settlement Trusts, Dawson v Reid* [1959] 2 All ER 676, [1959] 1 WLR 732 the power
    of revocation was not limited to the perpetuity period and permitted new non-charitable trusts to be
    declared; accordingly it was held to be invalid. Under the mortmain laws such a power, if attached to a
    gift of realty, would have rendered the gift void. Apparently the perpetuity period in the case of a
    revocable settlement by deed runs from the moment when it is no longer revocable: Morris and Leach
    *Rule against Perpetuities* (2nd Edn, 1962) p 57. As to the rule against perpetuities see para 134 post. As to
    the repeal of the law of mortmain see paras 75–76 ante.

18  *Doe d Blomfield v Eyre* (1848) 5 CB 713.

19  *Robinson v Wood* (1858) 27 LJCh 726.

**130. Acceptance of conditional gift.** Where a gift subject to a condition is
accepted, the condition must be fulfilled, whether or not the subject matter of the gift is
adequate for the purpose[1]. The subsequent abandonment of the benefit of a gift to which
a condition is attached does not relieve the party who accepted it from the burden of
fulfilling the condition[2]. Trustees are not bound to accept property subject to a special
trust or condition[3].

As a rule, donees who accept conditional gifts are entitled to have the property vested
in them[4]. Where the condition is a continuing one and there are no special trustees to
hold the fund, it may be retained in court and the income paid out so long as the
conditions are performed[5].

1  *A-G v Christ's Hospital* (1790) 3 Bro CC 165; *A-G v Andrew* (1798) 3 Ves 633 at 646 per Lord Eldon
   LC; *A-G v Caius College* (1837) 2 Keen 150; *Jack v Burnett* (1846) 12 Cl & Fin 812 at 828, HL, per Lord
   Cottenham LC; *A-G v Master, Wardens etc of the Wax Chandlers' Co* (1873) LR 6 HL 1 at 19 per Lord
   Cairns; *Re Richardson, Shuldham v Royal National Lifeboat Institution* (1887) 56 LJCh 784; and see *A-G v
   Merchant Venturers' Co, Bristol* (1848) 17 LJCh 137.

2  *A-G v Christ's Hospital* (1830) 1 Russ & M 626.

3  *A-G v Andrew* (1798) 3 Ves 633 (affd sub nom *Andrew v Master and Wardens of Merchant Taylors' Co* (1800)
   7 Ves 223, HL); *A-G v Caius College* (1837) 2 Keen 150.

4  *A-G v Christ's Hospital* (1790) 3 Bro CC 165; *Re Richardson, Shuldham v Royal National Lifeboat Institution*
   (1887) 56 LJCh 784. See also *Re Lopes, Bence-Jones v Zoological Society of London* [1931] 2 Ch 130; *Re
   Restell, Royal Hospital for Incurables v Restell* (1901) 17 TLR 395.

5  *Re Robinson, Wright v Tugwell* [1892] 1 Ch 95; approved [1897] 1 Ch 85, CA.

**131. Condition with gift over strictly enforced.** The rule of equity under which relief is given against a forfeiture on breach of condition[1] does not apply where there is a gift over on breach[2]. Thus, where property is given upon certain charitable trusts, with a proviso that in certain events it is to be transferred and held upon other charitable trusts, the property will pass upon the happening of the particular event[3]. If the event be the trustees' neglect of the terms of their trust, the gift over will take effect notwithstanding the general rule that a charitable purpose is not defeated by the trustee's failure or neglect or the failure of trust machinery[4], and that the position of one beneficiary under a trust ought not to be prejudiced as against other beneficiaries by any neglect on the trustee's part[5]. However, even in such a case, the court has power to make a scheme which will defeat the gift over and preserve the substance of the prior gift[6].

On the other hand, where the gift over is to be considered as a collateral remedy to secure the testator's charitable intention expressed in the prior gift, the trustee's neglect to observe a condition[7] or perform a trust in strict accordance with the directions in the will[8] may not occasion a forfeiture. The dividing line between the two classes of case is very difficult to find.

The onus of proof on the question whether a forfeiture has taken place lies on the party alleging it[9]. The court construes forfeiture clauses strictly[10].

If the right of a beneficiary entitled under a gift over or forfeiture becomes barred by limitation[11], the trustees or the beneficiaries under the prior gift hold the property free from the gift over, but on the trusts of the original gift[12]. They cannot themselves declare new trusts of the property[13].

1  *Cage v Russel* (1681) 2 Vent 352; *Hollinrake v Lister* (1826) 1 Russ 500 at 508 per Lord Gifford MR. See WILLS vol 50 (Reissue) para 388.
2  *Simpson v Vickers* (1807) 14 Ves 341.
3  *Re Malling Abbey Trusts, Beaumont v Dale* (1915) 31 TLR 397, CA; *Royal College of Surgeons of England v National Provincial Bank Ltd* [1952] AC 631, [1952] 1 All ER 984, HL.
4  *Brown v Higgs* (1803) 8 Ves 561 at 574 per Lord Eldon LC.
5  *Re Jones, Williams v Rowlands* [1948] Ch 67, [1947] 2 All ER 716.
6  *Re Hanbey's Will Trusts, Cutlers' Co v President and Governors of Christ's Hospital, London* [1956] Ch 264, [1955] 3 All ER 874, where no scheme was ordered, however, owing to the prolonged though honest breaches of trust and the difficulty of settling any useful scheme which would apply the trust properly cy-près with the objects the testator had in mind in his will.
7  *A-G v Christ's Hospital* (1830) 1 Russ & M 626. See also *Re Selinger's Will Trusts, Midland Bank Executor and Trustee Co Ltd v Levy* [1959] 1 All ER 407, [1959] 1 WLR 217 (condition as to time, held not to be of the essence of the gift and non-fulfilment of the condition not to cause a forfeiture).
8  *Re Hanbey's Will Trusts, Cutlers' Co v President and Governors of Christ's Hospital, London* [1956] Ch 264, [1955] 3 All ER 874; *Re Parish of Upton Warren* (1833) 1 My & K 410; *Re Richardson's Will* (1887) 58 LT 45.
9  *Re Hartshill Endowment* (1861) 30 Beav 130; and see *Re Conington's Will* (1860) 6 Jur NS 992. In both these cases the question was whether a condition requiring the performance of the Church of England service had been satisfied.
10  *Re Jones, Williams v Rowlands* [1948] Ch 67, [1947] 2 All ER 716 (where a condition relating to the time within which certain buildings were to be erected was held not to have come into operation either because the trustees could not be said to have failed to complete what they had not been allowed to begin or because the condition was subject to an overriding condition which had not been fulfilled). See also *Re Beard's Trusts, Butlin v Harris* [1904] 1 Ch 270 (where a gift over on a school's becoming subject to a school board was held not to take effect on the school's coming under the control of a county council, and no forfeiture took place); *Re Gregory, How v Charrington* (1935) 52 TLR 130 (where a gift over if an orphanage was taken over for or subsidised by the state or by any public or local authority was held not to take effect although the school belonging to the orphanage was recognised as a public elementary school and received grants from a local authority in aid of teachers' salaries); and *Re Blunt's Trusts, Wigan v Clinch* [1904] 2 Ch 767 (where a forfeiture was held to have taken place, inasmuch as there was a

bequest of an annuity for the support of national schools with a gift over if funds necessary for carrying on the schools should be raised under any statutory powers).

11  See *Re Trustees of Orchard Street Schools* [1878] WN 211. See also the Limitation Act 1980; and LIMITATION OF ACTIONS. As to the time limit for actions in respect of trust property see s 21; and LIMITATION OF ACTIONS vol 28 (Reissue) para 1037 et seq.

12  *Re Ingleton Charity, Croft v A-G* [1956] Ch 585, [1956] 2 All ER 881 (a case of automatic reverter under the School Sites Act 1841). See also *Re Trustees of Orchard Street Schools* [1878] WN 211.

13  *Re Ingleton Charity, Croft v A-G* [1956] Ch 585, [1956] 2 All ER 881.

**132. Gifts of limited interests.** There may be a gift to charity of less than an absolute interest in property and, subject to the application of the rule against perpetuities[1], the interest given may be an interest determinable upon the happening of some event which is contingent and may never occur[2]. Thus, income may be given for the support of a school so long as it should continue to be carried on according to the trusts of its original deed[3], or to an incumbent so long as sittings in the parish church were free of pew-rents[4], or there may be a gift to a society during such time as it maintains two graves[5]. Similarly, there may be a gift to charity limited not to take effect until the occurrence of a particular event[6].

In such cases, the interest which is not disposed of belongs to the donor, and devolves as part of his estate[7].

1  There is doubt as to whether the rule applies to these interests at common law; it does apply in relation to dispositions taking effect after 15 July 1964: see para 136 post.

2  *Lyons Corpn v Advocate-General of Bengal* (1876) 1 App Cas 91, PC; *Re Randell, Randell v Dixon* (1888) 38 ChD 213; *Re Hartshill Endowment* (1861) 30 Beav 130; *A-G v Molland* (1832) 1 You 562; *A-G v Pyle* (1738) 1 Atk 435. As to gifts of limited duration see para 165 post.

3  *Re Blunt's Trusts, Wigan v Clinch* [1904] 2 Ch 767.

4  *Re Randell, Randell v Dixon* (1888) 38 ChD 213. See also *Re Cooper's Conveyance Trusts, Crewdson v Bagot* [1956] 3 All ER 28, [1956] 1 WLR 1096.

5  *Re Chardon, Johnston v Davies* [1928] Ch 464 (a fuller account of the will, and the court's order, in this case are set out in Tudor on Charities (5th Edn, 1929) p 701); *Re Chambers' Will Trusts, Official Trustees of Charitable Funds v British Union for the Abolition of Vivisection* [1950] Ch 267 (distinguished in *Re Wightwick's Will Trusts, Official Trustees of Charitable Funds v Fielding-Ould* [1950] Ch 260, [1950] 1 All ER 689, where the limited gift was a gift on trust for non-charitable purposes and involved a perpetuity, and so failed).

6  *A-G v Earl of Craven* (1856) 21 Beav 392 at 400 per Romilly MR; *Yates v University College, London* (1875) LR 7 HL 438; *Re Roberts, Repington v Roberts-Gawen* (1881) 19 ChD 520, CA.

7  *A-G v Pyle* (1738) 1 Atk 435; *Re Randell, Randell v Dixon* (1888) 38 ChD 213; *Re Blunt's Trusts, Wigan v Clinch* [1904] 2 Ch 767.

## (6) RULES AGAINST REMOTENESS

**133. Rule against perpetual trusts.** Charitable trusts are exempt from the rule that a gift is void if its terms preclude the alienation of the capital of the fund for a period which may last longer than the perpetuity period[1], whereas a perpetual trust for a non-charitable purpose is void[2] and not less so because the trustee is a charitable society[3].

A charitable trust may, therefore, be made to last for any period, whether perpetual, indefinite or limited[4], and for the same reason a gift of income to a charity in perpetuity does not necessarily carry with it the capital, as it would in the case of a gift to an individual[5].

1   This is the rule referred to as the rule against perpetuities in eg *Chamberlayne v Brockett* (1872) 8 Ch App 206 at 211 per Lord Selborne LC; *A-G v Webster* (1875) LR 20 Eq 483 at 491 per Jessel MR; *Income Tax Special Purposes Comrs v Pemsel* [1891] AC 531 at 581–582, HL, per Lord Macnaghten. It has also been referred to as the rule against inalienability: *Re Chardon, Johnston v Davies* [1928] Ch 464; *Re Wightwick's Will Trusts, Official Trustees of Charitable Funds v Fielding-Ould* [1950] Ch 260, [1950] 1 All ER 689. It is to be distinguished from the rule against remoteness of vesting, commonly known as the rule against perpetuities (see para 134 post). It has not been affected by the Perpetuities and Accumulations Act 1964: see s 15(4). As to the perpetuity period see para 134 note 4 post; and PERPETUITIES AND ACCUMULATIONS vol 35 (Reissue) para 1012.
2   *Thomson v Shakespear* (1860) 1 De GF & J 399; *Carne v Long* (1860) 2 De GF & J 75; *Re Rickard, Rickard v Robson* (1862) 31 Beav 244; *Re Dutton, ex p Peake* (1878) 4 Ex D 54; *Re St Stephen, Coleman Street, Re St Mary the Virgin, Aldermanbury* (1888) 39 ChD 492 at 503 per Jay J; *Re Norwich Town Close Estate Charity* (1888) 40 ChD 298 at 307, CA, per Cotton LJ; *Income Tax Special Purposes Comrs v Pemsel* [1891] AC 531 at 581, HL, per Lord Macnaghten; and see para 55 ante, especially the cases there cited on gifts to unincorporated associations. See also *A-G of the Cayman Islands v Wahr-Hansen* [2001] 1 AC 75, [2000] 3 All ER 642, PC.
3   *Re Tyler, Tyler v Tyler* [1891] 3 Ch 252 at 258, CA, per Lindley LJ; and see *Re Freeman, Shilton v Freeman* [1908] 1 Ch 720, CA. As to trusts for repairing tombs see para 54 ante.
4   *Re Randell, Randell v Dixon* (1888) 38 ChD 213; *Re Bowen, Lloyd Phillips v Davis* [1893] 2 Ch 491.
5   *Re Levy, Barclays Bank Ltd v Board of Guardians and Trustees for the Relief of the Jewish Poor* [1960] Ch 346, [1960] 1 All ER 42, CA; *Re Beesty's Will Trusts, Farrar v Royal Alfred Merchant Seamen's Society* [1966] Ch 223, [1964] 3 All ER 82.

**134. Rule against perpetuities.** Charitable trusts are subject to the rule against perpetuities, which prevents the creation of interests in property which are to vest at too remote a time, in the same way as any other trust[1] except in one respect, that being the case of a gift over from one charity to another[2].

In the case of a disposition under an instrument taking effect before 16 July 1964[3], a charitable trust which need not take effect within the perpetuity period is void[4]. Thus, trusts for the benefit of charity limited to take effect after an indefinite failure of issue[5], or upon alienation[6], or upon the election of the next lieutenant-colonel of a regiment[7], or upon some other condition precedent which might not be fulfilled within the perpetuity period[8], failed[9].

In its application to dispositions under instruments taking effect after 15 July 1964[10], the rule was modified by the Perpetuities and Accumulations Act 1964[11]. The changes most relevant to charitable gifts are that, instead of a period of lives in being plus 21 years, the perpetuity period in relation to a disposition may be a period specified as such of up to 80 years[12], and that a disposition which is void at common law is to be treated as valid until it becomes established that the vesting of the disposition must occur, if at all, after the end of the perpetuity period[13]. Changes were also made in relation to possibilities of reverter and of resulting trusts[14]. Many of the decisions under the old law would have been different under the statute.

1   *Chamberlayne v Brockett* (1872) 8 Ch App 206. Thus an option to purchase land given to a charity is subject to the ordinary law as to perpetuities: *Worthing Corpn v Heather* [1906] 2 Ch 532.
2   This exception is discussed in para 135 post.
3   Ie the commencement date of the Perpetuities and Accumulations Act 1964. This Act affects instruments taking effect after 15 July 1964: see s 15(5); and PERPETUITIES AND ACCUMULATIONS vol 35 (Reissue) para 1009. Dispositions made after that date but pursuant to an instrument taking effect before 16 July 1964 are not affected: see s 8(2); and PERPETUITIES AND ACCUMULATIONS vol 35 (Reissue) para 1034. Where a disposition is made otherwise than by instrument, the Act applies as if it had been contained in an instrument taking effect when the disposition was made: s 15(6).
4   Ie unless the prior limitation is in favour of charity: see para 135 post. The perpetuity period is defined as lives in being, plus 21 years: see PERPETUITIES AND ACCUMULATIONS vol 35 (Reissue) para 1012.

5    *Charitable Donations and Bequests Comrs v Baroness De Clifford* (1841) 1 Dr & War 245; *Re Johnson's Trusts* (1866) LR 2 Eq 716 at 720 per Page Wood V-C; and see *Re Roberts, Repington v Roberts-Gawen* (1881) 19 ChD 520, CA.

6    *Pewterers' Co v Governors of Christ's Hospital* (1683) 1 Vern 161.

7    *Re Lord Stratheden and Campbell, Alt v Lord Stratheden and Campbell* [1894] 3 Ch 265.

8    *Chamberlayne v Brockett* (1872) 8 Ch App 206; *Re White's Trusts* (1886) 33 ChD 449; *Re Wightwick's Will Trusts, Official Trustees of Charitable Funds v Fielding-Ould* [1950] Ch 260, [1950] 1 All ER 689; *Re Mander, Westminster Bank Ltd v Mander* [1950] Ch 547, [1950] 2 All ER 191; *Re Cooper's Conveyance Trusts, Crewdson v Bagot* [1956] 3 All ER 28, [1956] 1 WLR 1096; *Re Watson's Settlement Trusts, Dawson v Reid* [1959] 2 All ER 676, [1959] 1 WLR 732; *George Drexler Ofrex Foundation Trustees v IRC* [1966] Ch 675, [1965] 3 All ER 529.

9    These cases are to be distinguished from those in which there is an immediate effective gift to charity, but the particular application directed may not be possible until some time in the future: see eg *Chamberlayne v Brockett* (1872) 8 Ch App 206; *Re Swain, Monckton v Hands* [1905] 1 Ch 669, CA.

10    See note 3 supra.

11    As to the Perpetuities and Accumulations Act 1964 generally see PERPETUITIES AND ACCUMULATIONS.

12    See ibid s 1; and PERPETUITIES AND ACCUMULATIONS vol 35 (Reissue) para 1010.

13    See ibid s 3(1); and PERPETUITIES AND ACCUMULATIONS vol 35 (Reissue) para 1009. How the perpetuity period is to be determined under this wait-and-see provision is governed by s 3(4), (5): see PERPETUITIES AND ACCUMULATIONS vol 35 (Reissue) para 1011. Under s 3(5), the only permissible lives in being in relation to a charitable gift are likely to be those of the settlor (see s 3(5)(a)) and of any person entitled to a prior interest (see s 3(5)(d)).

14    See ibid s 12; para 136 post; and PERPETUITIES AND ACCUMULATIONS vol 35 (Reissue) para 1040.

**135. Validity of gifts over.** An interest which is contingent upon the occurrence of an event which will cause a gift over to take effect is subject to the rule against perpetuities, so that, under the common law, if the event need not necessarily, or, under the Perpetuities and Accumulations Act 1964[1], if it does not, happen within the perpetuity period, the gift over is void.

However, this is subject to an exception in the case of a gift over from one charity to another on a certain event[2], whether the event is one which has any connection with the charitable purposes of the gift or not[3]. This exception does not extend to a non–charitable gift followed by a gift over in favour of charity, nor to a charitable gift with a gift over to private individuals[4] or in favour of purposes which need not necessarily be charitable[5].

Express gifts over to residue have generally been held not to be subject to the rule against perpetuities on the ground that they do no more than state the result which the law would imply in the absence of an express provision[6].

1    As to the Perpetuities and Accumulations Act 1964 generally see PERPETUITIES AND ACCUMULATIONS.

2    *Christ's Hospital v Grainger* (1849) 1 Mac & G 460; *Re Tyler, Tyler v Tyler* [1891] 3 Ch 252, CA; *Royal College of Surgeons of England v National Provincial Bank Ltd* [1952] AC 631, [1952] 1 All ER 984, HL, where it was decided that there was no difference where the gift over is to a charity incorporated by royal charter.

3    In *Re Tyler, Tyler v Tyler* [1891] 3 Ch 252, CA, the event was failure to keep a family vault in good repair. Although a trust to apply part of the money to the repair of the vault would have been void, the court held that a condition creating a perpetual inducement to do a lawful act was not void. In *Re Martin, Barclays Bank Ltd v Board of Governors of St Bartholomew's Hospital* [1952] WN 339, there was a gift of income upon a similar condition, and if ever the gravestones were not in good repair, a gift over to another charity; the condition attached to the gift of income was void but the condition which gave rise to the gift over was held nevertheless to be valid. See also *Re Lopes, Bence-Jones v Zoological Society of London* [1931] 2 Ch 130 and, for cases in which the condition did relate to the purposes of the gift, see *Re Parish of Upton Warren* (1833) 1 My & K 410; *Christ's Hospital v Grainger* (1849) 1 Mac & G 460; *Re Hanbey's Will Trusts, Cutlers' Co v President and Governors of Christ's Hospital, London* [1956] Ch 264, [1955] 3 All ER 874. In *Royal College of Surgeons of England v National Provincial Bank Ltd* [1952] AC 631,

[1952] 1 All ER 984, HL, the condition related to nationalisation of the hospital to which the prior gift was made.

4    *Re Bowen, Lloyd Phillips v Davis* [1893] 2 Ch 491 at 494 per Stirling J; *Re Barnett, Waring v Painter Stainers' Co* (1908) 24 TLR 788; *Re Peel's Release* [1921] 2 Ch 218; *Re Talbot, Jubb v Sheard* [1933] Ch 895; *Gibson v South American Stores (Gath and Chaves) Ltd* [1950] Ch 177, [1949] 2 All ER 985, CA; *Re Cooper's Conveyance Trusts, Crewdson v Bagot* [1956] 3 All ER 28, [1956] 1 WLR 1096; and see *Chamberlayne v Brockett* (1872) 8 Ch App 206 at 211 per Lord Selborne LC; *Worthing Corpn v Heather* [1906] 2 Ch 532; *Re Davies, Lloyd v Cardigan County Council* [1915] 1 Ch 543; *Re Wightwick's Will Trusts, Official Trustees of Charitable Funds v Fielding-Ould* [1950] Ch 260, [1950] 1 All ER 689.

5    *Re Friends' Free School, Clibborn v O'Brien* [1909] 2 Ch 675; *Re Da Costa, Clarke v Church of England Collegiate School of St Peter* [1912] 1 Ch 337; and see *Re Beard's Trusts, Butlin v Harris* [1904] 1 Ch 270 (where on construction it was held that there had been no forfeiture under the gift over). It has been held that where a gift to a charity is conditional on the performance of acts (not relating to the subject matter of the gift) extending to a possibly remote period, the charity is not bound by the condition, and is entitled to a clean conveyance, free from the condition, unless there is a gift over to another charity: *Re Da Costa, Clarke v Church of England Collegiate School of St Peter* supra; *Re Tyler, Tyler v Tyler* [1891] 3 Ch 252, CA. As to the ordinary rule that gifts subject to a condition must be accepted with whatever disadvantage that condition may carry see *A-G v Christ's Hospital* (1790) 3 Bro CC 165; *A-G v Christ's Hospital* (1830) 1 Russ & M 626 at 628 per Leach MR. For an example of an alternative ultimate trust for charity see *Re Davey, Prisk v Mitchell* [1915] 1 Ch 837, CA.

6    *Re Randell, Randell v Dixon* (1888) 38 ChD 213. But see *Re Engels, National Provincial Bank Ltd v Mayer* [1943] 1 All ER 506. This accordingly depends on the application of the rule against perpetuities to possibilities of reverter and of resulting trusts: see para 136 post.

**136. Limited gifts and undisposed interests.** The rule against perpetuities[1] is concerned only with the commencement of interests, not with their duration[2]. Thus, where a sum of money was given to a school so long as it should continue endowed, it was held to be given only for that period, so that when the school ceased to be endowed the gift fell into residue[3]. Where property would fall into residue by operation of law, the interest disposed of having come to an end, an express direction that it should do so will not bring the case within the rule against perpetuities[4]. However, the interest which may arise by forfeiture on breach of a common law condition is subject to the rule[5].

In relation to dispositions taking effect after 15 July 1964[6], possibilities of reverter on the determinable estate in fee simple and possibilities of a resulting trust on the determination of any other determinable interest in property are subject to the rule against perpetuities as if they were rights of re-entry or similar rights arising on breach of a condition subsequent[7]. If the provision in that form would be void at common law, it is necessary to wait until it is established that the condition cannot be satisfied within the relevant perpetuity period[8]. If the provision falls to be treated as void for remoteness, the determinable interest becomes an absolute interest[9]. These statutory provisions apply not only to gifts expressed to last so long as some state of affairs persists[10], but also to limited gifts for charitable purposes which subsequently fail[11].

1    See para 134 ante.
2    *Re Chardon, Johnston v Davies* [1928] Ch 464.
3    *A-G v Pyle* (1738) 1 Atk 435, where, however, the rule against perpetuities was not mentioned.
4    *Re Randell, Randell v Dixon* (1888) 38 ChD 213; *Re Blunt's Trusts, Wigan v Clinch* [1904] 2 Ch 767; and see *Lyons Corpn v Advocate-General of Bengal* (1876) 1 App Cas 91, PC; *Walsh v Secretary of State for India* (1863) 10 HL Cas 367. But see, contra, *Re Engels, National Provincial Bank Ltd v Mayer* [1943] 1 All ER 506.
5    *Re Trustees of Hollis' Hospital and Hague's Contract* [1899] 2 Ch 540; *Re Da Costa, Clarke v Church of England Collegiate School of St Peter* [1912] 1 Ch 337. See also *Hopper v Liverpool Corpn* (1943) 88 Sol Jo 213.
6    See para 134 note 3 ante.

7	See the Perpetuities and Accumulations Act 1964 s 12(1); and PERPETUITIES AND ACCUMULATIONS vol 35 (Reissue) para 1040.
8	See ibid s 3; para 134 ante; and PERPETUITIES AND ACCUMULATIONS vol 35 (Reissue) paras 1009, 1011.
9	See ibid s 12(1).
10	Eg *Re Chardon, Johnston v Davies* [1928] Ch 464.
11	Eg *Re Cooper's Conveyance Trusts, Crewdson v Bagot* [1956] 3 All ER 28, [1956] 1 WLR 1096. This type of gift is almost invariably accompanied by some express direction or condition relating to failure of the purpose. As to gifts of limited duration see para 165 post.

**137. Accumulations.** The statutory restriction on accumulations[1] is applicable to charitable funds which are directed to be accumulated beyond the time permitted by the statute[2]. If an accumulation is directed of a fund the capital and income of which are given absolutely to a charity, the charity is entitled to stop the accumulation and demand immediate payment of the fund[3].

1	See the Law of Property Act 1925 s 164; the Perpetuities and Accumulations Act 1964 s 13; and PERPETUITIES AND ACCUMULATIONS vol 35 (Reissue) para 1119 et seq.
2	*Martin v Maugham* (1844) 14 Sim 230; *Re Bradwell, Goode v Board of Trustees for Methodist Church Purposes* [1952] Ch 575, [1952] 2 All ER 286.
3	*Wharton v Masterman* [1895] AC 186, HL; *Re Travis, Frost v Greatorex* [1900] 2 Ch 541, CA. The trust amounts to a directory provision of a kind which the trustees ought prima facie to bear in mind and carry out: *Re Knapp, Spreckley v A-G* [1929] 1 Ch 341 at 344 per Maugham J.

# (7) FINALITY

**138. Alteration of trusts.** When a charitable trust has once been declared and established, the trusts cannot be varied or added to by the founder, whether an individual[1] or a body of subscribers[2], or by the trustees[3], unless a valid power of appointment or revocation[4] was reserved at the time the trusts were declared. In general, only the court or the Charity Commissioners[5] in the exercise of the jurisdiction to make cy-près schemes[6] can alter charitable trusts once they are declared[7]. Exceptionally, in respect of certain small charities, the charity trustees themselves have power, with the concurrence of the Charity Commissioners, to modify the trusts of the charity[8].

1	*Re Hartshill Endowment* (1861) 30 Beav 130.
2	*A-G v Kell* (1840) 2 Beav 575; *A-G v Bovill* (1840) 1 Ph 762.
3	See *Cross v Lloyd-Greame* (1909) 102 LT 163; *Baldry v Feintuck* [1972] 2 All ER 81, [1972] 1 WLR 552. Note, however, the principle of *A-G v Mathieson, Re Wilkinson and Fell's Contract* [1907] 2 Ch 383, CA, that where funds are subscribed by the public for some charitable purpose and later the trustees declare the trusts on which the funds are held, that declaration of trust is binding unless and until rectified at the suit of the Attorney General: see para 98 ante.
4	As to the validity of powers of revocation see paras 88, 129 note 17 ante. See also *Re Holloway's Trusts, Greenwell v Ryan* (1909) 26 TLR 62 (express power to vary the trusts); *Re Harrison, Harrison v A-G* (1915) 85 LJCh 77; *Re Jewish Orphanage Endowment Trusts, Sebag-Montefiore v Rothschild Executor and Trustee Co* [1960] 1 All ER 764, [1960] 1 WLR 344 (power to modify contained in a scheme). Even if there is power to alter the trusts, it may be expressly or impliedly limited: *Baldry v Feintuck* [1972] 2 All ER 81, [1972] 1 WLR 552 (attempt to alter purposes of students' union of a university to permit application of funds partly for charitable purposes not connected with education and partly for non-charitable purposes).
5	See the Charities Act 1993 s 16; and para 180 post. As to the Charity Commissioners see paras 486–512 post.

6   Alternatively, jurisdiction may be exercised under the Variation of Trusts Act 1958. Such cases can rarely arise, but in *Re Roberts' Settlement Trusts* [1961] TR 401, the court approved, on behalf of the settlor's future wives, an arrangement excluding the settlor and any wife of his from benefit under a charitable trust. As to the Variation of Trusts Act 1958 generally see TRUSTS vol 48 (2000 Reissue) paras 958–959.

7   See para 204 post. As to cy-près schemes generally see para 201 et seq post. The duty of the court is to construe the trust instrument and carry out its charitable directions. If the conditions for cy-près application are not satisfied the court has no jurisdiction (apart from the Variation of Trusts Act 1958 (see note 6 supra); and the Charities Act 1993 s 74 (see the text and note 8 infra)) to alter the terms of the trust, no matter how beneficial such alterations may be: *Re Weir Hospital* [1910] 2 Ch 124, CA; *Oldham Borough Council v A-G* [1993] Ch 210, [1993] 2 All ER 432, CA.

8   See the Charities Act 1993 s 74; and paras 210–211 post.

# 3. FAILURE OF STATED CHARITABLE OBJECTS

## (1) FAILURE OF STATED OBJECTS GENERALLY

### (i) Introduction

**139. In general.** In many cases it is impossible to carry out the charitable objects specified by the donor. This impossibility may extend to some only of the provisions of the gift, or to the whole gift: for example, there may be gifts to a charitable institution which has either ceased to exist[1] or changed its nature[2], or gifts which are insufficient[3] or more than sufficient[4] to carry out the stated purposes.

In considering these cases the first problem is to ascertain what are the objects of the gift. Owing to the leniency with which the court treats charitable gifts, it does not follow that, because the actual objects stated in the instrument cannot strictly be carried out, the stated object has failed. For example, gifts to an unincorporated charitable association are normally construed as gifts for the purposes of that institution, and therefore the object of the gift does not necessarily fail if the institution itself ceases to exist: the object of the gift is the purpose, not the institution[5].

Having ascertained the object of the gift, the next problem is to decide whether it has failed[6]. Again the court adopts a lenient view in deciding whether there has been a failure. Thus, a gift to a perpetually endowed charitable institution does not fail if the institution is dissolved, provided that some of its funds remain held on charitable trusts, which may not necessarily be the same trusts[7].

Even when the object of the gift has been ascertained and it has been shown that the object has failed, the gift itself will not necessarily fail. In certain cases the gift can be applied cy-près for charitable purposes similar to those which have failed[8]. However, in cases of initial failure, a cy-près application can normally only be made where the donor has shown a general charitable intention[9], since the justification for a cy-près application is that the court is giving effect to the presumed intention of the donor.

1   See para 143 post.
2   See paras 144–148 post.
3   See para 154 post.
4   See para 156 post.
5   See para 141 post.
6   See para 143 post. For a view of the law which equates this question with the question of the existence of a general charitable intention see para 159 post.
7   See para 143 et seq post.
8   As to cy-près applications see generally para 201 et seq post.
9   As to general charitable intention see para 159 post.

### (ii) Gifts to Charitable Institutions

A. IN GENERAL

**140. Lapse of charitable gifts by will.** Problems on gifts to non-existent institutions have always arisen in relation to gifts by will. In such cases, under the general law, the gift will lapse if the legatee 'predeceases' the testator[1]. Therefore two problems have to be considered: (1) was the object of the testator's bounty the institution itself, or rather the purposes it carried on; and (2) has either the institution itself ceased to exist or, if it be a purpose gift, the purpose ceased to be practicable[2] before the date of death.

1   As to the doctrine of lapse see WILLS vol 50 (Reissue) para 398 et seq.
2   As to whether purposes are still practicable see para 142 post.

B. WHERE THE INSTITUTION CEASED TO EXIST BEFORE THE GIFT TOOK EFFECT

*(A)   Gifts for Purposes or for the Institution*

**141. Construction.** In principle, gifts to named charitable institutions must be construed in exactly the same way as gifts to non-charitable institutions or to individuals. However, because charitable institutions are established for some charitable purpose or purposes, it may be possible for the court to decide that on its true construction a particular gift is for the work carried on by the institution, and not simply for the institution itself. However, this will not save the gift if the purpose itself has ceased to exist[1].

The authorities establish that there is a distinction between incorporated and unincorporated bodies in this context[2]. A gift to an incorporated body is not a gift upon trust for its purposes unless there is something in the context which shows that it is[3]; but a gift to an unincorporated association established for charitable purposes is a gift upon trust for those purposes unless there is something in the gift to show that the continued existence of the association is of the essence of the gift[4].

Where the gift is not to the institution itself by its proper name but to, say, a 'home' or 'hospital', the conclusion that a purpose gift is intended is almost, if not absolutely, inescapable[5]. It has been held that the gift is a gift for purposes in some cases where the named institution has once existed but has ceased to exist before the gift takes effect[6], or where the named institution was in fact merely an informal establishment carried on by the testatrix herself for charitable work[7]. In other cases, however, even where the gift was clearly intended for the benefit of the work carried on by the named institution, it has been held not to be a gift for purposes but solely a gift to the institution[8]. Again, a gift may be construed as one not to augment generally the endowment of a charity running, inter alia, a specified home, but exclusively for the benefit of patients at that home[9]. Where the existence of the institution itself is essential to the gift, the gift cannot be treated as a gift simply for its purposes[10].

Where the institution has ceased to exist, but has been replaced by another carrying on the identical work and functions, the gift may be construed as a misdescription of the latter institution[11].

1   *Re Spence, Ogden v Shackleton* [1979] Ch 483, sub nom *Re Spence's Will Trusts, Ogden v Shackleton* [1978] 3 All ER 92; *Re Prescott* [1990] 2 IR 342.
2   *Re Finger's Will Trusts, Turner v Ministry of Health* [1972] Ch 286, [1971] 3 All ER 1050; *Re Vernon's Will Trusts, Lloyds Bank Ltd v Group 20 Hospital Management Committee (Coventry)* [1972] Ch 300n, [1971] 3 All ER 1061n.
3   *Re Finger's Will Trusts, Turner v Ministry of Health* [1972] Ch 286, [1971] 3 All ER 1050; *Bowman v Secular Society Ltd* [1917] AC 406 at 442, HL, per Lord Finlay LC; *Re Cain, National Trustees Executors and Agency Co of Australasia Ltd v Jeffrey* [1950] VLR 382 at 389 per Dean J. For a case in which there was such an

indication in the context see *Re Meyers, London Life Association v St George's Hospital* [1951] Ch 534, [1951] 1 All ER 538.

4   *Re Vernon's Will Trusts, Lloyds Bank Ltd v Group 20 Hospital Management Committee (Coventry)* [1972] Ch 300n, [1971] 3 All ER 1061n; *Re Finger's Will Trusts, Turner v Ministry of Health* [1972] Ch 286, [1971] 3 All ER 1050. Some unincorporated associations are enabled by statute to hold property for purposes without the interposition of any trust, charitable or otherwise: see *Re Edis's Trusts, Campbell-Smith v Davies* [1972] 2 All ER 769, [1972] 1 WLR 1135.

5   *Re Finger's Will Trusts, Turner v Ministry of Health* [1972] Ch 286 at 296, [1971] 3 All ER 1050 at 1058 per Goff J.

6   *Re Souter, Brook v Talbot* (1907) Times, 24 January; *Re Withall, Withall v Cobb* [1932] 2 Ch 236; *Re Watt, Hicks v Hill* [1932] 2 Ch 243n, CA; *Re Morgan's Will Trusts, Lewarne v Minister of Health* [1950] Ch 637, [1950] 1 All ER 1097; *Re Glass, Public Trustee v South-West Middlesex Hospital Management Committee* [1950] Ch 643n, [1950] 2 All ER 953n; *Re Meyers, London Life Association v St George's Hospital* [1951] Ch 534, [1951] 1 All ER 538; *Re Hutchinson's Will Trusts, Gibbons v Nottingham Area No 1 Hospital Management Committee* [1953] Ch 387, [1953] 1 All ER 996; *Re Griffiths, Powell v Griffiths* (23 July 1958, unreported), cited in [1963] 1 All ER 680n; *Re Morrison, Wakefield v Falmouth* (1967) 111 Sol Jo 758; *Re Finger's Will Trusts, Turner v Ministry of Health* [1972] Ch 286, [1971] 3 All ER 1050.

7   *Re Webster, Pearson v Webster* [1912] 1 Ch 106.

8   *Re Goldney, Goldney v Queen Elizabeth Hospital for Children* (1946) 115 LJCh 337; *Re Pochin, Midland Bank Executor and Trustee Co v Godkin* [1948] Ch 182n.

9   *Re Spence, Ogden v Shackleton* [1979] Ch 483, sub nom *Re Spence's Will Trusts, Ogden v Shackleton* [1978] 3 All ER 92, distinguishing *Re Lucas, Sheard v Mellor* [1948] Ch 424, [1948] 2 All ER 22, CA.

10  See *Clark v Taylor* (1853) 1 Drew 642 (as explained in *Re Slevin, Slevin v Hepburn* [1891] 2 Ch 236, CA); *Langford v Gowland* (1862) 3 Giff 617; *Fisk v A-G* (1867) LR 4 Eq 521; *Makeown v Ardagh* (1876) IR 10 Eq 445; *Re Ovey, Broadbent v Barrow* (1885) 29 ChD 560; *Re Rymer, Rymer v Stanfield* [1895] 1 Ch 19, CA; *Re Brightwen, Shelly v Shelly* (1907) Times, 7 February; *Re Harwood, Coleman v Innes* [1936] Ch 285; *Re Stemson's Will Trusts, Carpenter v Treasury Solicitor* [1970] Ch 16, [1969] 2 All ER 517; and see the cases cited in note 8 supra.

11  *Re Magrath, Histed v Queen's University of Belfast* [1913] 2 Ch 331; following *Coldwell v Holme* (1854) 2 Sm & G 31.

**142. Purposes still practicable.** If the gift is construed as a gift for purposes, it appears that the gift will not lapse, notwithstanding the disappearance of the institution itself, if the purposes of the former institution are still being carried on by some other body; the gift is applicable by way of scheme for those purposes[1]. It has been held that if the institution has ceased to exist and there is no longer any need to carry on its purposes, the purposes have ceased to exist and the object has failed[2].

1   See the cases cited in para 141 note 6 ante.
2   *Re Slatter's Will Trusts, Turner v Turner* [1964] Ch 512, [1964] 2 All ER 469; *Re Spence, Ogden v Shackleton* [1979] Ch 483, sub nom *Re Spence's Will Trusts, Ogden v Shackleton* [1978] 3 All ER 92. The case of an institution becoming redundant because its purposes have been fulfilled is one of failure through impracticability: see para 154 text to note 1 post.

*(B)  Tests for Non-existence of the Institution*

**143. In general.** If the gift is construed as being to the institution itself, the question is whether that institution, as a charity, has ceased to exist. It may be still in existence even though its operations are diminished[1], and even if its continued existence is precarious[2], but not if it is merely nugatory[3]. The closure of one branch of a large charity does not affect the validity of a gift to the charity[4] unless the gift can only be construed as a gift to that particular branch[5]. The non-existence of an institution which was intended to be a trustee for charitable purposes which can still be effected does not affect the validity of the gift[6].

Apart from factual problems, there is a general rule that a perpetual charity endowed with funds can never cease to exist so long as it has endowments, however much its constitution may have been altered[7]. Particular instances are dealt with in the following paragraphs.

1   *Re Buck, Bruty v Mackey* [1896] 2 Ch 727; *Re Waring, Hayward v A-G* [1907] 1 Ch 166.
2   *Re Roberts, Stenton v Hardy* [1963] 1 All ER 674, [1963] 1 WLR 406.
3   *Re Meyers, London Life Association v St George's Hospital* [1951] Ch 534, [1951] 1 All ER 538; *Connell's Trustees v Milngavie District Nursing Association* 1953 SC 230.
4   *Re Bradfield, Bradfield v Hancock* (1892) 36 Sol Jo 646.
5   *Re Slatter's Will Trusts, Turner v Turner* [1964] Ch 512, [1964] 2 All ER 469.
6   *Marsh v A-G* (1860) 2 John & H 61. As to failure of or disclaimer by trustees see para 155 post.
7   *Re Faraker, Faraker v Durell* [1912] 2 Ch 488, CA; *Re Lucas, Sheard v Mellor* [1948] Ch 424, [1948] 2 All ER 22, CA; *Re Vernon's Will Trusts, Lloyds Bank Ltd v Group 20 Hospital Management Committee (Coventry)* [1972] Ch 300n, [1971] 3 All ER 1061n.

**144. Alteration by scheme.** If, before the gift takes effect, a named charity has been consolidated with others under a scheme made by the Charity Commissioners[1], it is nevertheless still in existence and the gift is payable to the trustees of the consolidated funds[2]. Similarly if, under a scheme for the administration of the assets of the named charity, a new charity is established elsewhere for similar purposes, the gift may be payable to the trustees of the new charity[3].

1   As to the Charity Commissioners see paras 486–512 post. As to schemes see para 170 et seq post.
2   *Re Faraker, Faraker v Durell* [1912] 2 Ch 488, CA.
3   *Re Lucas, Sheard v Mellor* [1948] Ch 424, [1948] 2 All ER 22, CA; and see *Re Vernon's Will Trusts, Lloyds Bank Ltd v Group 20 Hospital Management Committee (Coventry)* [1972] Ch 300n, [1971] 3 All ER 1061n.

**145. Alteration of objects by the institution itself.** If a named charity, having power to do so, alters its name and objects so as to include further charitable objects before a gift to it takes effect, the gift is nevertheless payable to it under its new name[1].

1   *Re Bagshaw, Westminster Bank Ltd v Taylor* [1954] 1 All ER 227, [1954] 1 WLR 238.

**146. Dissolution of institution under power in its constitution.** Where a company established for charitable purposes is wound up[1], or an unincorporated association is dissolved under powers contained in its own constitution[2], it is no longer in existence, notwithstanding that its assets cannot be devoted to any purposes that are not charitable[3]. But where the assets and functions of a company had been transferred under the National Health Service Act 1946, a gift in augmentation of those assets was held to be payable to the body to which the assets had been transferred, despite the subsequent dissolution of the company before the death of the testator[4].

1   *Re Stemson's Will Trusts, Carpenter v Treasury Solicitor* [1970] Ch 16, [1969] 2 All ER 517; followed in *Re Finger's Will Trusts, Turner v Ministry of Health* [1972] Ch 286, [1971] 3 All ER 1050.

2   *Re Finger's Will Trusts, Turner v Ministry of Health* [1972] Ch 286, [1971] 3 All ER 1050.
3   Such a company will not be restored to the register of companies under the Companies Act 1985 s 651 in order to take a legacy on a death after the dissolution: *Re Servers of the Blind League* [1960] 2 All ER 298, [1960] 1 WLR 564 (decided under earlier legislation).
4   *Re Vernon's Will Trusts, Lloyds Bank Ltd v Group 20 Hospital Management Committee (Coventry)* [1972] Ch 300n, [1971] 3 All ER 1061n.


**147. Alteration of objects and amalgamation under statute.** If an amalgamation or change of constitution is effected by or under a statute, the consequences may depend upon the construction of the statute[1]. The fact that hospitals became nationalised under the National Health Service Act 1946 did not mean that they ceased to be charitable[2], nor did they cease to be eligible as objects of a gift divisible among hospitals which, in the trustees' opinion, were most in need of it[3]. Gifts to or for the benefit of voluntary hospitals which, before the testator's death, had become vested in the Minister of Health or in a specially constituted board of governors, were upheld as being for the purposes of the charitable work of the voluntary hospitals still being carried on by the nationalised hospitals[4].

1   Cf *Re Donald, Moore v Somerset* [1909] 2 Ch 410.
2   *Re Dean's Will Trusts, Cowan v Board of Governors of St Mary's Hospital, Paddington* [1950] 1 All ER 882, 94 Sol Jo 239.
3   *Re Perreyman, National Provincial Bank Ltd v Perreyman* [1953] 1 All ER 223, 96 Sol Jo 851.
4   *Re Morgan's Will Trusts, Lewarne v Minister of Health* [1950] Ch 637, [1950] 1 All ER 1097; *Re Glass, Public Trustee v South-West Middlesex Hospital Management Committee* [1950] Ch 643n, [1950] 2 All ER 953n; *Re Frere, Kidd v Farnham Group Hospital Management Committee* [1951] Ch 27, [1950] 2 All ER 513; *Re Meyers, London Life Association v St George's Hospital* [1951] Ch 534, [1951] 1 All ER 538. See also para 141 ante.


**148. Informal amalgamation.** Gifts to two named societies which, before the gifts took effect, merged with one another were held both to be payable to the united society[1]. A gift to a society which amalgamated with another to which the testatrix later subscribed was held to be payable to the new society[2]. Where a legacy is construed as being for the benefit of a particular charitable activity which, at the date of the will, is carried on by one organisation but, at the date of the testator's death, is carried on by another, the change of machinery does not affect the validity of the gift[3]. Similarly, a change in the constitution of a named institution does not affect the validity of a gift to it on trust for some special charitable purpose[4].

1   *Re Joy, Purday v Johnson* (1888) 60 LT 175; cf *Re Wilson, Wardle v Lemon* (1909) 25 TLR 465 (legacy to fund formerly used for benefit of two villages, but before testator's death restricted to one of them, the other starting its own separate fund: legacy divided between the two funds in proportion to the population of the two villages).
2   *Re Pritt, Morton v National Church League* (1915) 85 LJCh 166.
3   *Re Wedgwood, Sweet v Cotton* [1914] 2 Ch 245. See also *Re Adams, Harle v Adams* (1888) 4 TLR 757; *Re Dawson's Will Trusts, National Provincial Bank Ltd v National Council of the YMCA Inc* [1957] 1 All ER 177, [1957] 1 WLR 391.
4   *Re Dean's Will Trusts, Cowan v Board of Governors of St Mary's Hospital, Paddington* [1950] 1 All ER 882, 94 Sol Jo 239; *Re White's Will Trusts, Tindall v Board of Governors of United Sheffield Hospitals* [1951] 1 All ER 528, 95 Sol Jo 205.

C. OTHER CASES

**149. Gift where institution never existed.** Where the named institution has never existed, the stated object has normally failed. The gift will, therefore, lapse unless there is a general charitable intention which enables it to be applied cy-près[1].

1   *Re Davis, Hannen v Hillyer* [1902] 1 Ch 876; and see para 161 post. In *Re Parkes, Cottrell v Parkes* (1909) 25 TLR 523, it was held in such a case that the donor's intention was to benefit certain purposes, rather than a particular institution: cf para 141 ante. As to cy-près schemes see para 201 et seq post.

**150. Gift where institution ceased to exist after gift took effect.** A legacy to an orphanage which was in existence at the date of the testator's death but which closed before the estate was distributed was held to have vested in the orphanage absolutely on the testator's death, and not to have been divested on the closure of the orphanage[1]. The same principle was applied in the case of a reversionary legacy for a school which closed during the prior life interest[2].

A gift to a company established for charitable purposes from a person who dies after the company goes into liquidation but before it is formally dissolved need not fail according to its terms[3].

1   *Re Slevin, Slevin v Hepburn* [1891] 2 Ch 236, CA; following *Hayter v Trego* (1830) 5 Russ 113. See also *Re Buck, Bruty v Mackey* [1896] 2 Ch 727; *Re Hunter, Lloyds Bank Ltd v Mistress and Governors of Girton College, Cambridge* [1951] Ch 190, [1951] 1 All ER 58.
2   *Re Soley, Grover v Drapers' Co* (1900) 17 TLR 118.
3   *Re ARMS (Multiple Sclerosis Research) Ltd, Alleyne v A-G* [1997] 2 All ER 679, [1997] 1 WLR 877 (where the property was in the event distributable among the creditors).

**151. Gift where institution unascertainable.** If a gift is made to a named institution whose identity cannot be ascertained, then, depending on the testator's apparent intention, the court may hold that a particular institution was intended to take but that it has not been shown to exist or to have existed[1], or that no particular institution was intended[2]. In the latter case the gift is treated as a gift for the indicated charitable purposes. On the other hand, a particular institution may have been intended, but it may be impossible to decide which of various possible claimants is the one intended by the testator[3]. In such a case the principle applicable is that uncertainty of objects does not invalidate a gift that is clearly charitable[4].

1   *Re Goldschmidt, Commercial Union Assurance Co Ltd v Central British Fund for Jewish Relief and Rehabilitation* [1957] 1 All ER 513, [1957] 1 WLR 524; cf *Re Tharp, Longrigg v People's Dispensary for Sick Animals of the Poor Inc* [1942] 2 All ER 358; revsd [1943] 1 All ER 257, CA, on the construction of the gift. As to gifts where the institution never existed see para 149 ante.
2   *Simon v Barber* (1829) 3 Hare 195n.
3   See *Bennett v Hayter* (1839) 2 Beav 81; *Gibson v Coleman* (1868) 18 LT 236; *Re Alchin's Trust, ex p Furley, ex p Earl Romney* (1872) LR 14 Eq 230; *Re Songest, Mayger v Forces' Help Society and Lord Roberts' Workshops* [1956] 2 All ER 765, [1956] 1 WLR 897, CA (for the eventual outcome of this case see [1956]

3 All ER 489n, [1956] 1 WLR 1311, CA); *Re Satterthwaite's Will Trusts, Midland Bank Executor and Trustee Co Ltd v Royal Veterinary College* [1966] 1 All ER 919, [1966] 1 WLR 277, CA.

4   See para 82 ante. The property will be applied by scheme, usually by division between some or all of the claimants likely to have been intended: see para 198 post.


**152. Disclaimer of gift.** A gift on trust cannot be invalidated by the trustee's refusal to accept the trusts[1] unless it is of the essence of the gift that the named trustee should act[2]. Where a gift is to a charitable institution absolutely, however, and the institution disclaims, the gift fails in the same way as would an absolute gift to an individual[3].

1   See para 155 post.
2   See *Re Lysaght, Hill v Royal College of Surgeons* [1966] Ch 191, [1965] 2 All ER 888.
3   See *Re Slevin, Slevin v Hepburn* [1891] 2 Ch 236 at 242, CA, per Kay LJ. In one case such a gift has been held not to fail: *Denyer v Druce* (1829) Taml 32; and see dicta in *Simon v Barber* (1829) 3 Hare 195n.


### (iii)   Other Cases where Object fails


**153. Gift to be applied in illegal manner.** If the purpose of a gift is illegal or contrary to public policy, the gift cannot be charitable and will not be allowed to take effect[1]. But if the purpose is charitable, and only the particular manner of effecting it is illegal, then the court will give effect to the gift despite the failure of the intended manner of application[2].

The same is true where income is directed to be accumulated for an excessive period and then to be applied for charitable purposes[3]: the direction to accumulate is treated as mere machinery, the failure of which cannot prevent the property from being devoted to charity[4]. Similarly, if a gift is initially valid, the fact that a subsequent statute makes it illegal to carry it out exactly as directed does not cause any part of the gift to lapse[5].

If property is given for charitable purposes and the trustees have a discretion to apply it in various ways, they may not apply it in an illegal manner, and the fact that the donor has purported to permit an illegal as well as a legal mode of application does not cause any kind of failure[6].

1   *Thrupp v Collett* (1858) 26 Beav 125; *Sims v Quinlan* (1865) 17 I Ch R 43. As to purposes contrary to public policy see para 59 ante.
2   *A-G v Vint* (1850) 3 De G & Sm 704. See also cases of gifts void as being for superstitious uses but nevertheless charitable, eg *De Costa v De Paz* (1754) 2 Swan 487n; *Cary v Abbot* (1802) 7 Ves 490. As to superstitious uses see para 56 ante.
3   *Martin v Maugham* (1844) 14 Sim 230; followed reluctantly in *Re Bradwell, Goode v Board of Trustees for Methodist Church Purposes* [1952] Ch 575, [1952] 2 All ER 286; distinguished in *Re Lushington, Wynyard v A-G* [1963] NZLR 313; on appeal sub nom *Re Lushington, Manukau County v Wynyard* [1964] NZLR 161, NZ CA, where there was held to be no general charitable intention.
4   *Re Bradwell, Goode v Board of Trustees for Methodist Church Purposes* [1952] Ch 575, [1952] 2 All ER 286.
5   *A-G v Green* (1789) 2 Bro CC 492.
6   See eg *Sorresby v Hollins* (1740) 9 Mod Rep 221; *Faversham Corpn v Ryder* (1854) 5 De GM & G 350; *Salusbury v Denton* (1857) 3 K & J 529; *Sinnett v Herbert* (1871) LR 12 Eq 201 (on appeal (1872) 7 Ch App 232).

**154. Impracticable gifts.** The purpose for which a charitable gift is made may fail because it has already been fulfilled[1], or because it is impossible to carry it out at all[2], as where the gift postulates the existence of an institution[3] or a state of affairs[4] or class of objects[5] which does not exist or ceases to exist[6]. The purpose of a gift may also be impracticable because insufficient money has been given[7], or because the property given and intended to be used is unsuitable[8], or because no suitable site can be found[9]. The donor may have attached conditions to the gift which render it unlikely or impossible that the purposes can ever be achieved[10], or conditions which are repugnant to the fulfilment of the primary charitable purpose so that, as it stands, the gift is self-defeating[11].

When the fund given is inadequate for the intended purpose at the date when it ought to be applied to that purpose according to the terms of the gift, it should not be retained and accumulated until it is sufficient, but should be dealt with there and then[12]. In some cases where inadequate funds were given the gift has been construed as conditional upon sufficient funds becoming available, so that if they do not become available the gift never takes effect at all[13].

The intended purpose need not be immediately practicable[14]; the question is whether at the relevant date[15] it is practicable to carry the donor's intentions into effect, or whether at that date there is any reasonable prospect that it will be practicable to do so at some future time[16].

The burden of proof in relation to impracticability lies on the party who alleges that the gift has failed through impracticability[17].

1  *Corbyn v French* (1799) 4 Ves 418; *Bunting v Marriott* (1854) 19 Beav 163.
2  See *A-G v Bishop of Oxford* (1785) 1 Bro CC 444n, discussed in *Corbyn v French* (1799) 4 Ves 418; *Re Welstead* (1858) 25 Beav 612; *A-G v Combe* (1679) 2 Cas in Ch 18; *Brantham v East Burgold* (circa 1790) cited 2 Ves 388; and cf *New v Bonaker* (1867) LR 4 Eq 655.
3  Eg a particular school: *Incorporated Society v Price* (1844) 1 Jo & Lat 498; *Re Templemoyle Agricultural School* (1869) IR 4 Eq 295; cf *Marsh v Means* (1857) 3 Jur NS 790 (for continuing publication of a certain periodical which was not published after the date of the will).
4  Eg that property given as a burial ground will continue to be available for the purpose (*Campbell v Liverpool Corpn* (1870) LR 9 Eq 579; and cf *Re St Pancras Burial Ground* (1866) LR 3 Eq 173; *A-G v Glyn* (1841) 12 Sim 84); or that certain public services will continue to be available on a voluntary basis only (*Re Mackenzie, Moir v Angus County Council* [1962] 2 All ER 890, [1962] 1 WLR 880 (education); though see also *Re Leitch* [1965] VR 204, decided on a similar bequest; *Re Hillier, Hillier v A-G* [1954] 2 All ER 59, [1954] 1 WLR 700, CA (hospital buildings); *Re Wokingham Fire Brigade Trusts, Martin v Hawkins* [1951] Ch 373, [1951] 1 All ER 454 (local fire brigade); see also *Richmond Corpn v A-G* [1965] RA 117; revsd sub nom *Re Richmond Parish Charity Lands* [1965] RA 343, CA (gift in aid of the poor rate)).
5  *A-G v London Corpn* (1790) 1 Ves 243 (infidels in Virginia); *A-G v Hicks* (1810) 3 Bro CC 166n as noted in 29 ER 468 (leprous patients); *A-G v Ironmongers' Co* (1834) 2 My & K 576 (British slaves in Barbary); *A-G v Lawes* (1849) 8 Hare 32 (persecuted ministers of a particular sect); *A-G v Bunce* (1868) LR 6 Eq 563 (Presbyterians at Devizes); *Re Prison Charities* (1873) LR 16 Eq 129 (poor persons imprisoned for debt); *Re Geikie, Robson v Paterson* (1911) 27 TLR 484 (members of a particular church); *Re Welsh Hospital (Netley) Fund, Thomas v A-G* [1921] 1 Ch 655 (sick and wounded Welsh soldiers); *Re Colonial Bishoprics Fund 1841* [1935] Ch 148 (bishops in South Africa in connection with the Church of England). But see also *A-G v Earl of Craven* (1856) 21 Beav 392 (poor infected by plague).
6  However, a temporary absence of objects will not cause a failure, or even a temporary failure: *Aylet v Dodd* (1741) 2 Atk 238.
7  Eg *Cherry v Mott* (1836) 1 My & Cr 123; *Re Queen's School, Chester* [1910] 1 Ch 796; *Re Good's Will Trusts, Oliver v Batten* [1950] 2 All ER 653; *Re Whittaker, Nobel v A-G* [1951] 2 TLR 955; *Re Winton* (1953) Times, 31 January; *Re Dover's Battle of Britain Memorial Hospital Fund* (1955) Times, 29 June; *Re Ulverston and District New Hospital Building Trusts, Birkett v Barrow and Furness Hospital Management Committee* [1956] Ch 622, [1956] 3 All ER 164, CA.
8  *Re Packe, Sanders v A-G* [1918] 1 Ch 437 (appeal settled sub nom *Re Packe, Campion v A-G* (1918) 145 LT Jo 111, CA); *A-G for New South Wales v Perpetual Trustee Co Ltd* (1940) 63 CLR 209, Aust HC;

*Hay v Murdoch* [1952] WN 145, HL. See also *A-G v Earl of Lonsdale* (1827) 1 Sim 105 (land given inter vivos to charitable trustees by tenant for life; trusts impracticable after his death); and *McCormick v Queen's University of Belfast* [1958] NI 1.

9   *Chamberlayne v Brockett* (1872) 8 Ch App 206; *Re White's Trusts* (1886) 33 ChD 449; *Biscoe v Jackson* (1887) 35 ChD 460, CA.

10   *Re Wilson, Twentyman v Simpson* [1913] 1 Ch 314; *Re Mitchell's Will Trusts, Jago v A-G* (1966) 110 Sol Jo 291. Cf *A-G v Minshull* (1798) 4 Ves 11 (gift to apprentice poor children, with a maximum of £10 for each child which became impracticably small); *Re Stewart's Will Trusts* [1983] NI 283.

11   *Re Richardson's Will* (1887) 58 LT 45; *Re Robinson, Wright v Tugwell* [1923] 2 Ch 332 (condition that preacher wear black gown in pulpit, which would alienate congregation); *Re Dominion Students' Hall Trust, Dominion Students' Hall Trust v A-G* [1947] Ch 183 (colour bar condition incompatible with primary object of promoting community among all members of Commonwealth); *Re Lysaght, Hill v Royal College of Surgeons* [1966] Ch 191, [1965] 2 All ER 888 (condition excluding Catholics and Jews; the trustee, essential to the gift, would not accept the gift subject to the condition); cf *Re Meres' Will Trusts* (1957) Times, 4 May (condition that only males of pure English, Irish or Scottish parentage be eligible to benefit: void for uncertainty, but the main gift held valid); *Harris v Sharp* (7 December 1987, unreported), ChD, discussed [1988] Conv (NS) 288 (D Partington).

12   *Re Whittaker, Nobel v A-G* [1951] 2 TLR 955.

13   Eg see *Re London University Medical Sciences Institute Fund, Fowler v A-G* [1909] 2 Ch 1, CA; and para 166 post.

14   See *A-G v Bishop of Chester* (1785) 1 Bro CC 444; *Re Villers-Wilkes, Bower v Goodman* (1895) 11 TLR 250; *Chamberlayne v Brockett* (1872) 8 Ch App 206; *Biscoe v Jackson* (1887) 35 ChD 460, CA; *Sinnett v Herbert* (1872) 7 Ch App 232; *A-G v Lady Downing* (1767) Wilm 1; *A-G v Bowyer* (1798) 3 Ves 714 at 728 per Lord Hardwicke LC; *Re Swain, Monckton v Hands* [1905] 1 Ch 669, CA.

15   Ie in the case of a will, the date of the testator's death; and in the case of an inter vivos gift, the date of the gift: *Re Moon's Will Trusts, Foale v Gillians* [1948] 1 All ER 300; *Re Wright, Blizard v Lockhart* [1954] Ch 347, [1954] 2 All ER 98, CA; and see para 158 post.

16   See the inquiry directed in *Re White's Will Trusts, Barrow v Gillard* [1955] Ch 188, [1954] 2 All ER 620.

17   *Re Tacon, Public Trustee v Tacon* [1958] Ch 447 at 454, [1958] 1 All ER 163 at 164, CA, per Lord Evershed MR.

**155. Failure of or disclaimer by trustee.** Following the general rule that equity does not want for a trustee, the fact that the intended trustee of a gift for charitable purposes[1], or a person to whom a power of selection is given[2], dies before the testator does not generally cause a failure of the gift, for the identity of the trustee is normally regarded as mere machinery[3], and in the exercise of its general jurisdiction over the administration of trusts the court can always remedy failures of machinery[4].

The same is true if an executor is given a power of selection but the appointment is later revoked[5]. If substantially the whole of a small estate is given on trust for a charitable institution and there is no executor who proves, letters of administration with the will annexed may properly be granted to an officer of the institution[6].

Similarly, the refusal of the intended trustee to accept the gift[7] does not constitute a failure of the gift unless it is of the essence of the gift that the intended trustee should act[8], or unless the gift is impracticable if the intended trustee does not act[9]. Again, the gift will not fail if the intended trustee is incapable in law of accepting the trust[10], or if there is no person able to give a good receipt for the gift[11].

A gift upon trust will not normally fail by reason of the default or neglect of the trustees[12], but this principle cannot be applied when that default or neglect is the condition upon which a gift over is expressed to operate[13].

1   *Moggridge v Thackwell* (1792) 1 Ves 464 per Lord Thurlow; reheard by Lord Eldon (1803) 7 Ves 36; affd (1807) 13 Ves 416, HL; *A-G v Hickman* (1732) 2 Eq Cas Abr 193 pl 14; *A-G v Lady Downing* (1767) Wilm 1; *A-G v Gladstone* (1842) 13 Sim 7; *A-G v Sturge* (1854) 19 Beav 597.

2   *Re Willis, Shaw v Willis* [1921] 1 Ch 44, CA; *A-G v Hickman* (1732) 2 Eq Cas Abr 193 pl 14.

3   See eg *Re Morrison, Wakefield v Falmouth* (1967) 111 Sol Jo 758; but for an exceptional case see *Re Lysaght, Hill v Royal College of Surgeons* [1966] Ch 191, [1965] 2 All ER 888.

4   If necessary a scheme will be directed for the administration of the trusts. As to administrative schemes see para 171 post.

5   *White v White* (1778) 1 Bro CC 12.

6   *Re M'Auliffe's Goods* [1895] P 290; followed in *Re Lalor's Goods* (1901) 85 LT 643. See also *Walsh v Gladstone* (1843) 1 Ph 290 (legacy to person who predeceased testator 'to be applied to the use of 'a named college: held, on the evidence, that it would be proper to pay the legacy over to the president of the college).

7   *Doyley v A-G* (1735) 4 Vin Abr 485 pl 16; *A-G v Andrew* (1798) 3 Ves 633 (affd sub nom *Andrew v Master and Wardens of the Merchant Taylors' Co* (1800) 7 Ves 223, HL); *Denyer v Druce* (1829) Taml 32; *A-G v Fletcher* (1835) 5 LJCh 75; *Reeve v A-G* (1843) 3 Hare 191; *Barclay v Maskelyne* (1858) 32 LTOS 205; *Re Burley, Alexander v Burley* [1910] 1 Ch 215; *Re Wilson-Barkworth, Burstall v Deck* (1933) 50 TLR 82; *Re Lawton, Gartside v A-G* [1936] 3 All ER 378.

8   *Re Lysaght, Hill v Royal College of Surgeons* [1966] Ch 191, [1965] 2 All ER 888; and cf *Marquess of Bute's Trustees v Marquess of Bute* (1905) 7 F 49, Ct of Sess.

9   *New v Bonaker* (1867) LR 4 Eq 655 (gift to the President and Vice-President of the United States and the Governor of Pennsylvania).

10  *Re Hampton, Public Trustee v Hampton* (1918) 88 LJCh 103 (the Public Trustee cannot act as trustee of any charitable trust); *Tufnell v Constable* (1838) 7 Ad & El 798 (churchwardens); *Re Woolnough's Will Trusts* (1959) Times, 22 October; *Re Armitage, Ellam v Norwich Corpn* [1972] Ch 438, [1972] 1 All ER 708 (local authorities: see para 229 text and note 4 post). Formerly gifts to corporations were sometimes void under the mortmain laws (repealed: see paras 75–76 ante); but gifts to corporations on trust were sometimes upheld as to the trust, though the corporation could not act as a trustee: see *Sonley v Clock-makers' Co* (1780) 1 Bro CC 81 (private trust); *Incorporated Society in Dublin v Richards* (1841) 1 Dr & War 258. But there were conflicting decisions: see eg *A-G v Flood* (1816) Hayes & Jo App xxi; affd (1817) Hayes 611.

11  *Re Meyers, London Life Association v St George's Hospital* [1951] Ch 534, [1951] 1 All ER 538.

12  *A-G v Boultbee* (1794) 2 Ves 380; affd (1796) 3 Ves 220. This applies even if there is a gift over: *Re Parish of Upton Warren* (1833) 1 My & K 410; and see *A-G v Leigh* (1721) 3 P Wms 145n.

13  *Christ's Hospital v Grainger* (1849) 1 Mac & G 460; *Re Hanbey's Will Trusts, Cutlers' Co v President and Governors of Christ's Hospital, London* [1956] Ch 264, [1955] 3 All ER 874.

**156. Gift of more than is needed for purpose.** If a gift for a specific purpose is of an amount of capital more than is required or appropriate for the purpose, then, as to the surplus, the donor has failed to devote his gift to a specified charitable purpose which can be carried out, and in that sense there is a failure of objects[1]. The same applies to gifts in response to public appeals, where the total sum subscribed is more than can be used for the specified purpose[2]. The question may also arise where the income of a fund subject to a continuing trust for charity is, from the start, greater than is necessary for the specified purpose[3], or becomes so in the course of time by reason of an increase in the income[4] or the decay of the particular charity named[5].

1   *Re Connolly, Walton v Connolly* (1914) 110 LT 688, CA; *Re King, Kerr v Bradley* [1923] 1 Ch 243; *Re Stanford, Cambridge University v A-G* [1924] 1 Ch 73; *Re Monk, Giffen v Wedd* [1927] 2 Ch 197, CA; *Re Royce, Turner v Wormald* [1940] Ch 514, [1940] 2 All ER 291; *Re Raine, Walton v A-G* [1956] Ch 417, [1956] 1 All ER 355. As to whether the surplus is held on resulting trust or is applicable cy-près see para 163 post.

2   Eg *Re North Devon and West Somerset Relief Fund Trusts, Hylton v Wright* [1953] 2 All ER 1032, [1953] 1 WLR 1260. For cases where the sum raised is too small to be used for the specified purpose see para 154 text and note 7 ante.

3   Eg *Arnold v A-G* (1698) Show Parl Cas 22, HL.

4   *A-G v Coopers' Co* (1812) 19 Ves 187.

5   *A-G v Ironmongers' Co* (1834) 2 My & K 576; *Re Slevin, Slevin v Hepburn* [1891] 2 Ch 236 at 240, CA, per Kay LJ. As to surplus income see paras 123–127 ante.

# (2)  CONSEQUENCES OF FAILURE OF STATED OBJECTS

## (i)  In general

**157.  Failure of gift or application cy-près.** If it is established that the stated objects of a charitable gift fail, there are two possible consequences: either the property can be applied cy-près[1] for a charitable purpose similar to the original object, or the whole gift fails. In general, no cy-près application is possible unless the donor has shown a general charitable intention[2], but there are three exceptions to this requirement: (1) where the gift has taken effect but has failed subsequently[3]; (2) where the amount of the gift is, from the outset, surplus to what is required to achieve the stated object, but the donor has shown an intention to devote the property wholly to charity[4]; and (3) in the case of public subscriptions[5]. In all such cases of cy-près application, the application is made by way of scheme[6]. If no cy-près application is possible, the gift fails and will result to the donor.

1　As the cy-près doctrine see para 201 et seq post.
2　See para 159 post.
3　As to subsequent failure see paras 164–165 post.
4　See para 163 post.
5　Ie by virtue, in part, of the Charities Act 1993 s 14: see paras 167–168 post. As to the failure of public appeals for charitable purposes see para 166 et seq post.
6　As to the making of cy-près schemes see para 201 et seq post.

## (ii)  Initial Failure

**158.  When ascertained.** For the purpose of deciding whether a charitable gift can take effect in the first place, the situation must be considered as at the date when the gift first vests in interest in charity, whether in possession[1] or in reversion[2], and whether the gift is to an institution or for a purpose[3]. If the reversionary gift is defeasible, the possibility that it will be divested is to be ignored[4]; the question must be decided by reference to the value of the whole fund at the relevant date, not the value at that date of the reversionary interest[5].

1　*Re Slevin, Slevin v Hepburn* [1891] 2 Ch 236, CA.
2　*Re Moon's Will Trusts, Foale v Gillians* [1948] 1 All ER 300; *Re Wright, Blizard v Lockhart* [1954] Ch 347, [1954] 2 All ER 98, CA; *Re Woodhams, Lloyds Bank Ltd v London College of Music* [1981] 1 All ER 202, [1981] 1 WLR 493.
3　*Re Wright, Blizard v Lockhart* [1954] Ch 347, [1954] 2 All ER 98, CA. See *Harris v Sharp* (7 December 1987, unreported), ChD, discussed [1988] Conv (NS) 288 (D Partington).
4　*Re Tacon, Public Trustee v Tacon* [1958] Ch 447, [1958] 1 All ER 163, CA: the position in relation to a true contingent gift is undecided.
5　*Re Tacon, Public Trustee v Tacon* [1958] Ch 447, [1958] 1 All ER 163, CA. See *Re Martin* (1977) 121 Sol Jo 828 (inflation taken into account, applying *Re Tacon* supra). See also the form of inquiry directed in *Re White's Will Trusts, Barrow v Gillard* [1955] Ch 188, [1954] 2 All ER 620.

**159. General charitable intention.** A gift will not lapse if, although the indicated purpose of the gift has failed at the moment when the gift should take effect, the court can find an intention on the donor's part more general than a bare intention that the impracticable direction be carried into execution as an indispensable part of the trust declared[1]. 'General charitable intention' means a paramount intention to give the property in the first instance for a general charitable purpose rather than a particular charitable purpose and to graft on to the general gift a direction as to the donor's intentions as to the manner in which the general gift is to be carried into effect[2]. The general charitable purpose may be directed to a particular form of charity rather than to charity generally[3].

The process of ascertaining whether there is a general charitable intention may involve considering whether one or more of the directions given by the donor were essential to his intended purpose[4], and this may be decided by construing the gift[5]. Often, however, the words used give little assistance, and more is to be gained from an examination of the nature of the charitable trust itself and what is involved in the project[6]. The fact that a donor refers expressly to his general charitable intention cannot give to the gift a general charitable character when, on the face of it, it is particular and non-charitable[7]. It has been held that the court cannot find a general charitable intention in relation to a gift which is for a non-charitable purpose[8]; and it cannot construct a general charitable intention from mere guesswork[9].

The meaning of 'general charitable intention' has more recently been restated in terms of paramount charitable intention[10]. Under this restatement, the question whether the specified objects have failed and the question of the presence of a general charitable intention are merged into one question, namely whether the impossibility of performing part of the expressed trusts defeats the essential charitable purpose of the donor, or whether this essential purpose can be carried out in a modified way. If the essential purpose of the gift can still be carried out in a modified way, the general or paramount charitable intention takes effect and the court can give effect to it by means of a cy-près scheme[11].

---

1   For this formulation of the meaning of a general charitable intention see *A-G for New South Wales v Perpetual Trustee Co Ltd* (1940) 63 CLR 209 at 225, Aust HC, per Dixon and Evatt JJ.

2   *Re Wilson, Twentyman v Simpson* [1913] 1 Ch 314 at 320–321 per Parker J (the locus classicus on the point). See also *Re Templemoyle Agricultural School* (1869) IR 4 Eq 295 at 301 per Chatterton V-C.

3   See *Re Taylor, Martin v Freeman* (1888) 58 LT 538 at 542 per Kay J.

4   See *Re Lysaght, Hill v Royal College of Surgeons* [1966] Ch 191, [1965] 2 All ER 888, where the gift contained two incompatible directions: the Royal College of Surgeons was to act as trustee but refused to do so if the gift remained subject to a condition relating to religious discrimination. It was held that the trusteeship of the college was essential to the gift, and that the condition as to religious discrimination was not.

5   *A-G for New South Wales v Perpetual Trustee Co Ltd* (1940) 63 CLR 209 at 227, Aust HC, and see at 225–228 generally.

6   *A-G for New South Wales v Perpetual Trustee Co Ltd* (1940) 63 CLR 209 at 227, Aust HC.

7   *Re Sanders' Will Trusts, Public Trustee v McLaren* [1954] Ch 265, [1954] 1 All ER 667 (appeal settled (1954) Times, 22 July, CA).

8   *Re Jenkins' Will Trusts, Public Trustee v British Union for the Abolition of Vivisection* [1966] Ch 249, [1966] 1 All ER 926. Cf *Re Satterthwaite's Will Trusts, Midland Bank Executor and Trustee Co Ltd v Royal Veterinary College* [1966] 1 All ER 919, [1966] 1 WLR 277, CA.

9   *Re Crowe, National Westminster Bank Ltd v Balfour* (1979, unreported); noted in *Report of the Charity Commissioners for England and Wales for 1979* (HC Paper (1979–80) no 608) paras 40–45.

10  *Re Lysaght, Hill v Royal College of Surgeons* [1966] Ch 191, [1965] 2 All ER 888.

11  As to cy-près schemes see para 201 et seq post.

**160. Examples of general charitable intention.** A general charitable intention has been found where a deed contained alternative gifts, all related to one general purpose[1], and where a legacy was one of nine to institutions concerned with animal welfare[2], and where the bulk of an estate after a life interest was specifically dedicated to charity and the particular institution which had ceased to exist was mainly only a co-ordinating body[3]. Where residue is divided between charitable purposes or institutions and the gift of one share fails as to its stated objects, it may be relatively easy to find a general charitable intention[4]. There is no rule that, where a legacy to charity fails and residue is also given to charity, there can be no general charitable intention in relation to the legacy[5]. In most cases the question of whether there is or is not a general charitable intention depends upon the construction of the particular will, and no general principle can be derived from them[6].

Sometimes where the failure is caused by the donor's attaching some impracticable condition to his gift, the condition is held to be an inessential part of the gift and the donor's general charitable intention to be directed towards only the essential elements in the gift[7]. Similarly, when the precise direction, as distinct from the general purpose, is illegal, it may be regarded as inessential[8].

A general charitable intention may be manifested not only in a gift by deed or will, but also in a gift in response to a public appeal[9], but these cases are more often approached on the basis of an intention to make an outright, or only a limited, gift of property to charity, whether or not the purpose of the appeal can be effected[10].

Very slight indications of a general charitable intention will suffice where there is a gift to an institution, apparently charitable[11], which has never existed[12]. It is difficult[13], though not impossible[14], to find a general charitable intention where there is a gift to a particular institution which ceased to exist before the gift took effect, and a parallel principle applies where a particular purpose has become impracticable or impossible of accomplishment before the gift took effect[15].

1  *Re Templemoyle Agricultural School* (1869) IR 4 Eq 295. See also *Re Tyler's Fund Trusts, Graves v King* [1967] 3 All ER 389, [1967] 1 WLR 1269 (gift by deed for charitable institutions to be named in a later document).

2  *Re Satterthwaite's Will Trusts, Midland Bank Executor and Trustee Co Ltd v Royal Veterinary College* [1966] 1 All ER 919, [1966] 1 WLR 277, CA. Cf *Re Jenkins' Will Trusts, Public Trustee v British Union for the Abolition of Vivisection* [1966] Ch 249, [1966] 1 All ER 926.

3  *Re Finger's Will Trusts, Turner v Ministry of Health* [1972] Ch 286, [1971] 3 All ER 1050.

4  *Re Whittaker, Nobel v A-G* [1951] 2 TLR 955; *Re Griffiths, Powell v Griffiths* (23 July 1958, unreported) cited in [1963] 1 All ER 680n.

5  *Lyons Corpn v Advocate-General of Bengal* (1876) 1 App Cas 91, PC; and see para 162 text and note 8 post.

6  See eg *Biscoe v Jackson* (1887) 35 ChD 460, CA (gift to establish cottage hospital and soup kitchen: general charitable intention of benefiting poor of parish); *Re Winton* (1953) Times, 31 January (gift for building humane slaughterhouse for horses: held not limited to that specific purpose); *Re Currie* [1985] NI 299.

7  *Re Lysaght, Hill v Royal College of Surgeons* [1966] Ch 191, [1965] 2 All ER 888, cited in para 159 note 4 ante; *A-G for New South Wales v Perpetual Trustee Co Ltd* (1940) 63 CLR 209, Aust HC; *Re Bloomfield's Bequest* (1920) 54 ILT 213; *Re Robinson, Wright v Tugwell* [1923] 2 Ch 332; *Brantham v East Burgold* (circa 1790) cited 2 Ves 388; *Re Woodhams, Lloyds Bank Ltd v London College of Music* [1981] 1 All ER 202, [1981] 1 WLR 493 (music college refused to accept gift for scholarships restricted to orphans; restriction inessential part of gift and general charitable intention prevailed).

8  *A-G v Vint* (1850) 3 De G & Sm 704. As to where gifts are to be applied in an illegal manner see para 153 ante.

9  Eg *Re North Devon and West Somerset Relief Fund Trusts, Hylton v Wright* [1953] 2 All ER 1032, [1953] 1 WLR 1260.

10   As to the failure of gifts in relation to general or limited charitable purposes see para 167 post. Since the Charities Act 1960 s 14 (repealed; now the Charities Act 1993 s 14) the question has become less important: see paras 166–169 post.

11   Its description or the context may show that it would have been charitable: *Re Maguire* (1870) LR 9 Eq 632; *Re Clergy Society* (1856) 2 K & J 615; *Re Knox, Fleming v Carmichael* [1937] Ch 109, [1936] 3 All ER 623.

12   *Re Davis, Hannen v Hillyer* [1902] 1 Ch 876. See also *Re Bailey, Bailey v Working Ladies' Guild* (1931) 75 Sol Jo 415 (no indication of more general intention from context, but gift applied cy-près); *Re Barnard, Majendie v Duke of Northumberland* (1890) 7 TLR 73.

13   *Re Harwood, Coleman v Innes* [1936] Ch 285. See also *Re Hunter, Genn v A-G of British Columbia* [1973] 3 WWR 197 (BC SC).

14   *Re Finger's Will Trusts, Turner v Ministry of Health* [1972] Ch 286, [1971] 3 All ER 1050.

15   *Re Spence, Ogden v Shackleton* [1979] Ch 483, sub nom *Re Spence's Will Trusts, Ogden v Shackleton* [1978] 3 All ER 92.

**161. Effect of general charitable intention.** If a general charitable intention[1] is found, failure of the particular directions in the gift will not cause the gift itself to fail, for the donor's true intention may still be carried out, and where necessary a scheme will be directed[2] or the property applied by the Attorney General, to whom the power of the Crown to dispose of charitable gifts under the sign manual has been delegated[3].

If a gift to a non-existent institution is saved by the presence of a general charitable intention, the person or authority administering the purposes of the gift under a scheme may be entitled to a share of residue divisible between institutions which are beneficiaries under the instrument[4].

1   As to general charitable intention see paras 159–160 ante.
2   As to cy-près schemes see para 201 et seq post.
3   As to the jurisdiction of the Crown over charities see paras 456–457 post.
4   *Re Davis, Hannen v Hillyer* [1902] 1 Ch 876.

**162. Intention to benefit particular charity only.** In other cases it has been held that every element in the gift was essential to the donor's intention and that, if the particular directions fail, an application of the property in any other way would be contrary to the donor's intention[1]. Frequently an intention to benefit charity only in a particular form appears from the fact that the donor has laid down detailed directions or conditions[2], or has expressly made the conditions of the essence of the gift[3].

In the case of a legacy to a correctly named, known institution which ceased to exist before the date of the testator's death, it may be difficult to find a general charitable intention[4], the more so if the gift is expressed to be 'for the benefit of that institution'[5], or if the testator placed particular reliance on the institution named carrying out his wishes[6]. A gift to an institution which has never existed may be held to be limited in intention to the supposed institution, and to lapse in consequence[7].

It has been said that, where residue is given to charity, it is difficult to find a general charitable intention in relation to a legacy whose objects fail[8]. If a legacy which is only for a particular charitable purpose fails at the moment of the testator's death, it falls into residue or passes as on an intestacy.

When gifts of realty for charitable purposes were void under the mortmain laws[9], ancillary gifts of personalty were held to fail also, as being dependent on the validity of the gift of realty[10], unless they could be construed as being for an independent purpose, whether private[11] or charitable[12].

1   *A-G v Bishop of Oxford* (1786) 1 Bro CC 444n, as explained in *Corbyn v French* (1799) 4 Ves 418.

2   *Re Wilson, Twentyman v Simpson* [1913] 1 Ch 314; *Russell v Kellett* (1855) 3 Sm & G 264; *Re Good's Will Trusts, Oliver v Batten* [1950] 2 All ER 653; *Hay v Murdoch* [1952] WN 145, HL.

3   Eg by a direction that if they are not fulfilled the gift is to fall into residue: *Re Randell, Randell v Dixon* (1888) 38 ChD 213. See also *Re Cooper's Conveyance Trusts, Crewdson v Bagot* [1956] 3 All ER 28, [1956] 1 WLR 1096; *Re Peel's Release* [1921] 2 Ch 218; and para 165 post.

4   *Re Harwood, Coleman v Innes* [1936] Ch 285; *Re Rymer, Rymer v Stanfield* [1895] 1 Ch 19, CA; but see *Re Finger's Will Trusts, Turner v Ministry of Health* [1972] Ch 286, [1971] 3 All ER 1050, citing *Re Roberts, Stenton v Hardy* [1963] 1 All ER 674 at 681, [1963] 1 WLR 406 at 416 per Wilberforce J.

5   *Langford v Gowland* (1862) 3 Giff 617. See also *Re Spence, Ogden v Shackleton* [1979] Ch 483, sub nom *Re Spence's Will Trusts, Ogden v Shackleton* [1978] 3 All ER 92 (gift to defunct old people's home expressed with particularity showed no general charitable intention).

6   *Re Stemson's Will Trusts, Carpenter v Treasury Solicitor* [1970] Ch 16, [1969] 2 All ER 517. For other cases in which gifts to charitable institutions which had ceased to exist were held not to show a general charitable intention see *Clark v Taylor* (1853) 1 Drew 642; *Re Ovey, Broadbent v Barrow* (1885) 29 ChD 560.

7   See *Re Tharp, Longrigg v People's Dispensary for Sick Animals of the Poor Inc* [1942] 2 All ER 358; revsd [1943] 1 All ER 257, CA, on the ground that the named institution was a misdescription of an existing body.

8   *Re Goldschmidt, Commercial Union Assurance Co Ltd v Central British Fund for Jewish Relief and Rehabilitation* [1957] 1 All ER 513, [1957] 1 WLR 524; but see *Lyons Corpn v Advocate-General of Bengal* (1876) 1 App Cas 91, PC; and para 160 note 5 ante.

9   As to the repeal of the mortmain laws see paras 75–76 ante.

10  See eg *A-G v Whitchurch* (1796) 3 Ves 141; *A-G v Hinxman* (1820) 2 Jac & W 270; *Re Taylor, Martin v Freeman* (1888) 58 LT 538.

11  *Blandford v Thackerell* (1793) 2 Ves 238.

12  *A-G v Stepney* (1804) 10 Ves 22.

**163. Surplus: intention to devote whole to charity.** In a number of cases where the property given is more than is needed for the specified charitable purpose, it has been held that the gift is a valid charitable gift as to the whole, and that the surplus should be applied cy-près[1], sometimes on the basis that there was a general charitable intention[2]. In other cases this result has been achieved on the basis that the donor intended to devote to charity the whole of the property given[3]. However, if the donor's intention was to limit his gift to the amount necessary for the particular purpose named, any surplus is held on a resulting trust, or falls into residue, or passes as on an intestacy, as the case may be[4].

1   As to cy-près schemes see para 201 et seq post.

2   *Re Royce, Turner v Wormald* [1940] Ch 514, [1940] 2 All ER 291. As to general charitable intention see para 160 et seq ante.

3   *Re Douglas, Douglas v Simpson* [1905] 1 Ch 279; *Re King, Kerr v Bradley* [1923] 1 Ch 243; *Re Monk, Giffen v Wedd* [1927] 2 Ch 197, CA (where the principle applied was explained by Sargant LJ at 211 as an application of the rule in *Lassence v Tierney* (1849) 1 Mac & G 551, on the basis of an absolute gift of the whole to trustees for charity, followed by a specific direction as to the application of part only of the property); *Re Robertson, Colin v Chamberlin* [1930] 2 Ch 71; *Re Raine, Walton v A-G* [1956] Ch 417, [1956] 1 All ER 355 (where there was held to be no general charitable intention but nevertheless an intention to give the property outright to charity, and the property did not pass as on an intestacy). Each of these cases concerned a gift of residue. See also cases on surplus income (see paras 123–127 ante); and cases on outright gifts in relation to subsequent failure (see para 164 post).

4   *Re Stanford, Cambridge University v A-G* [1924] 1 Ch 73.

## (iii) Subsequent Failure

**164. Outright gift.** A donor may give the whole interest in the property to charity or only an interest of limited duration[1]. Whether or not the gift is outright is a matter of construction[2]. If it is shown that the donor intended to part with his whole interest in the property, and therefore to make an outright gift, the question of general charitable intention is irrelevant[3]. A charity once established does not die and its property, being irrevocably devoted to charity, is applied for other charitable purposes[4]. Thus property given outright by will or inter vivos[5] to a charitable institution[6] or for charitable purposes[7] which vests effectively in charity does not fall into residue if, later, the institution closes[8] or the purposes become impracticable[9].

1　As to gifts of limited duration see para 165 post.

2　See also para 165 note 2 post.

3　*Re Wokingham Fire Brigade Trusts, Martin v Hawkins* [1951] Ch 373, [1951] 1 All ER 454 (approved in *Re Ulverston and District New Hospital Building Trusts, Birkett v Barrow and Furness Hospital Management Committee* [1956] Ch 622, [1956] 3 All ER 164, CA); *Re British School of Egyptian Archaeology, Murray v Public Trustee* [1954] 1 All ER 887, [1954] 1 WLR 546. See also *Campbell v Liverpool Corpn* (1870) LR 9 Eq 579; *Re St Pancras Burial Ground* (1866) LR 3 Eq 173; *Wallis v Solicitor-General for New Zealand* [1903] AC 173, PC. The same is true in Scots law: *Anderson's Trustees v Scott* 1914 SC 942; *Davidson's Trustees v Arnott* 1951 SC 42. In some cases of subsequent failure, the court has considered the question of general charitable intention (*Re Welsh Hospital (Netley) Fund, Thomas v A-G* [1921] 1 Ch 655; *Re North Devon and West Somerset Relief Fund Trusts, Hylton v Wright* [1953] 2 All ER 1032, [1953] 1 WLR 1260; *Re British School of Egyptian Archaeology, Murray v Public Trustee* supra, although as to this, see *Re Ulverston and District New Hospital Building Trusts* supra), but there seem to be no cases of gifts by will in which this has been considered relevant, apart from the special category of cases on capital surplus (see *Re Monk, Giffen v Wedd* [1927] 2 Ch 197, CA; and para 163 ante). There are possibly ambiguous observations in *Re Cunningham, Dulcken v Cunningham* [1914] 1 Ch 427; *Incorporated Society v Price* (1844) 1 Jo & Lat 498; *Lyons Corpn v Advocate-General of Bengal* (1876) 1 App Cas 91, PC, although see the same case at 111 per Sir Montague E Smith ('an absolute charitable gift, capable of being applied cy-près').

4　Cf *National Anti-Vivisection Society v IRC* [1948] AC 31 at 74, [1947] 2 All ER 217 at 238, HL, per Lord Simonds.

5　In theory there is no difference between gifts inter vivos and gifts by will, but the principle established by *Re Slevin, Slevin v Hepburn* [1891] 2 Ch 236, CA, is not easy to apply to gifts inter vivos: see *Re British School of Egyptian Archaeology, Murray v Public Trustee* [1954] 1 All ER 887 at 891, [1954] 1 WLR 546 at 552 per Harman J.

6　*Re Slevin, Slevin v Hepburn* [1891] 2 Ch 236, CA; *Re Soley, Grover v Drapers' Co* (1900) 17 TLR 118.

7　*Re Geikie, Robson v Paterson* (1911) 27 TLR 484; *Re Moon's Will Trusts, Foale v Gillians* [1948] 1 All ER 300; *Re Wright, Blizard v Lockhart* [1954] Ch 347, [1954] 2 All ER 98, CA.

8　See note 6 supra.

9　See note 7 supra.

**165. Gift of limited duration.** If a gift is only for a specific charitable purpose and is limited to that purpose, and the donor parts with his interest in the property only to the extent necessary for the achievement of that purpose, a subsequent failure of that purpose brings to an end the charity's interest in the property given, so that what remains of it is held upon resulting trust for the donor or falls into residue[1]. The question is one of the construction of the gift and may, therefore, turn only on the drafting[2]. In the cases in which a limited gift has been found, there has generally been an express condition or direction relating to failure of the purpose[3], and the efficacy of that direction has depended also on its validity as regards the rule against perpetuities[4]. However, the limited intention may perhaps be inferred from the circumstances of the gift[5].

1   The possibility of such cases was recognised in *Re Slevin, Slevin v Hepburn* [1891] 2 Ch 236 at 239, CA, per Kay LJ.

2   Cf *Re Peel's Release* [1921] 2 Ch 218 (gift to be used 'for ever thereafter' for a charitable purpose with a reverter condition if it should cease to be so used: held to be an initial outright gift to charity, subject to gift over which was void for remoteness) with *Re Cooper's Conveyance Trusts, Crewdson v Bagot* [1956] 3 All ER 28, [1956] 1 WLR 1096 (conveyance on trust for a charitable purpose 'and for no other purpose whatsoever' with provision as to the event of a failure of the purpose: held to be only a limited gift to charity, which reverted, on failure of the purpose, to the grantor's heirs). See also *Bath and Wells Diocesan Board of Finance v Jenkinson* (2000) Times, 6 September, [2000] All ER (D) 1142.

3   *Re Randell, Randell v Dixon* (1888) 38 ChD 213 (gift to endure so long as sittings in a particular church were free from pew-rents); *Re Blunt's Trusts, Wigan v Clinch* [1904] 2 Ch 767 (annuity for support of a school so long as it was carried on on the trusts of its original trust deed); *Re Cooper's Conveyance Trusts, Crewdson v Bagot* [1956] 3 All ER 28, [1956] 1 WLR 1096. See also *Christ's Hospital v Grainger* (1849) 1 Mac & G 460; *Re Hanbey's Will Trusts, Cutlers' Co v President and Governors of Christ's Hospital, London* [1956] Ch 264, [1955] 3 All ER 874. Cf gifts of land as sites for schools subject to reverter under the School Sites Acts, eg *Bankes v Salisbury Diocesan Council of Education Inc* [1960] Ch 631, [1960] 2 All ER 372; and see EDUCATION.

4   See *Re Bowen, Lloyd Phillips v Davis* [1893] 2 Ch 491; *Re Peel's Release* [1921] 2 Ch 218; *Re Talbot, Jubb v Sheard* [1933] Ch 895. As to the rule against perpetuities see para 134 ante. As to the application of the rule against perpetuities to gifts of this kind see para 136 ante.

5   *Gibson v South American Stores (Gath and Chaves) Ltd* [1950] Ch 177, [1949] 2 All ER 985, CA (revsg on this point [1949] Ch 572, [1949] 2 All ER 18). Although it was there said that there was no general charitable intention, the court appears to have held also that there was only a limited gift in the sense indicated above: see *Gibson v South American Stores (Gath and Chaves) Ltd*, CA, supra at 201 and at 998–999 per Lord Evershed MR. The presence of a power of revocation may have had the same effect as the express gift over in the cases cited in note 3 supra. *Burgess' Trustees v Crawford* 1912 SC 387 cannot now be regarded as good authority in England, in the light of *Re Wright, Blizard v Lockhart* [1954] Ch 347, [1954] 2 All ER 98, CA.

## (iv)  Failure of Public Appeals for Charitable Purposes

**166.  Types of failure.** The question of the failure of a charitable purpose frequently has to be considered in relation to property given by the public in different ways in response to an appeal; the appeal may be for a temporary purpose which requires less money than is given for it[1], or it may be for a purpose which cannot be achieved at all because of the lack of money subscribed[2].

Strictly speaking, it may be that where money is subscribed over a period of time and only at the end of the period does it become clear that the purpose is impracticable, the case is one of subsequent failure, for it could not have been said at the moment of each gift that there was no reasonable prospect that the purpose would at some future time be practicable[3]; but in practice such cases are treated as cases of initial failure[4], or of gifts upon a condition that the purpose be found practicable[5].

Furthermore, the courts do not always make a distinction between cases of initial failure in this sense and context and cases where a surplus is left after satisfying the objects of the appeal[6]. The cases establish that different considerations apply to property received from different sources, and this has been partly recognised and partly modified by statute[7].

1   *Re Hartley Colliery Accident Relief Fund, Plummer v Jordan* (1908) 102 LT 165n; *Re Welsh Hospital (Netley) Fund, Thomas v A-G* [1921] 1 Ch 655; *Re North Devon and West Somerset Relief Fund Trusts, Hylton v Wright* [1953] 2 All ER 1032, [1953] 1 WLR 1260 (the Lynmouth flood disaster).

2   *Re Ulverston and District New Hospital Building Trusts, Birkett v Barrow and Furness Hospital Management Committee* [1956] Ch 622, [1956] 3 All ER 164, CA; *Re Hillier, Hillier v A-G* [1954] 2 All ER 59, [1954] 1 WLR 700, CA.

3   See the form of inquiry ordered in *Re White's Will Trusts, Barrow v Gillard* [1955] Ch 188, [1954] 2 All ER 620; and para 158 ante.

4   Eg in the cases cited in note 2 supra. The distinction which is sometimes made is between the case in which the purpose is never capable of achievement at all, and that in which the question arises after the purpose has to some extent been achieved: see *Re Ulverston and District New Hospital Building Trusts, Birkett v Barrow and Furness Hospital Management Committee* [1956] Ch 622 at 635–636, [1956] 3 All ER 164 at 171, CA, per Jenkins LJ. As to initial failure see paras 158–163 ante.

5   *Re London University Medical Sciences Institute Fund, Fowler v A-G* [1909] 2 Ch 1, CA; see also para 128 ante.

6   Eg in *Re North Devon and West Somerset Relief Fund Trusts, Hylton v Wright* [1953] 2 All ER 1032, [1953] 1 WLR 1260.

7   See the Charities Act 1993 s 14; and paras 167–169 post.

**167. General or limited purpose: anonymous gifts.** If the circumstances of the gift are such that a general charitable intention[1] may be found, the failure of the purpose will not cause a failure of the gift, whether it is initially impracticable[2] or, a fortiori, an unapplied surplus is left[3].

However, if the purpose of the appeal was only a limited charitable purpose and that purpose failed, it had been established that anonymous gifts and money collected by way of whist drives, raffles and similar activities were devoted irrevocably to charity[4], and this was confirmed by statute[5]. Property given for specific charitable purposes[6] which fail are applicable cy-près[7] as if given for charitable purposes generally, where it belongs to a donor[8] who cannot be identified[9]. Property is conclusively presumed, without any advertisement or inquiry, to belong to donors who cannot be identified, in so far as it consists[10]: of (1) the proceeds of cash collections made by means of collecting boxes or by other means not adapted for distinguishing one gift from another[11]; or (2) the proceeds of any lottery, competition, entertainment, sale or similar money-raising activity, after allowing for property given to provide prizes or articles for sale or otherwise to enable the activity to be undertaken[12].

1   As to general charitable intention see para 159 et seq ante.

2   *Re Hillier, Hillier v A-G* [1954] 2 All ER 59, [1954] 1 WLR 700, CA.

3   *Re North Devon and West Somerset Relief Fund Trusts, Hylton v Wright* [1953] 2 All ER 1032, [1953] 1 WLR 1260.

4   See *Re Hillier, Hillier v A-G* [1953] 2 All ER 1547, [1954] 1 WLR 9; and compare the non-charity case *Re West Sussex Constabulary's Widows, Children and Benevolent (1930) Fund Trusts, Barnett v Ketteringham* [1971] Ch 1, [1970] 1 All ER 544 (contributions by way of raffles etc are made outright, for the relationship is one of contract not of trust; anonymous gifts are presumed to be given outright, for it would be absurd to impute any other intention to the donors; both therefore became bona vacantia). In *Re Ulverston and District New Hospital Building Trusts, Birkett v Barrow and Furness Hospital Management Committee* [1956] Ch 622, [1956] 3 All ER 164, CA, Jenkins LJ conceived it possible that any anonymous donor might prove by positive evidence that he only had a limited intention in making his gift. This possibility may now be left out of account by reason of the statutory provisions.

5   See the Charities Act 1993 s 14(3); and the text to notes 6–12 infra.

6   For the meaning of 'charitable purposes' see para 1 ante.

7   As to cy-près schemes see para 201 et seq post.

8   For these purposes, references to 'donor' include persons claiming through or under the original donor: Charities Act 1993 s 14(10).

9 See ibid s 14(1)(a); and para 168 post.
10 Ibid s 14(3). See para 168 post.
11 Ibid s 14(3)(a).
12 Ibid s 14(3)(b).

## 168. Limited purpose: gifts irrevocable or resulting trust.

It was sometimes held that, where identifiable donors could be presumed to have made outright gifts, the gift might not fail even though the particular purpose of the gift had failed[1]. This principle has been given some statutory recognition. Where property given[2] for a specific charitable purpose[3] which fails[4] belongs to a donor[5] who has executed in the prescribed form[6] a disclaimer of his right to have the property returned[7], it is applicable cy-près as if given for charitable purposes generally[8].

Further, property given for specific charitable purposes which fail is applicable cy-près as if given for charitable purposes generally, where it belongs to a donor who after the prescribed advertisements[9] and inquiries have been published and made, and the prescribed period beginning with the publication of those advertisements has expired, cannot be identified or cannot be found[10]. Where the prescribed advertisements and inquiries have been published and made by or on behalf of trustees with respect to any such property, the trustees are not liable to any person in respect of the property if no claim by him to be interested in it is received by them before the expiry of the prescribed period[11]. The court[12] may by order direct certain property[13] be treated, without any advertisement or inquiry, as belonging to donors who cannot be identified where it appears to the court either[14]: (1) that it would be unreasonable, having regard to the amounts likely to be returned to the donors, to incur expense with a view to returning the property[15]; or (2) that it would be unreasonable, having regard to the nature, circumstances and amounts of the gifts, and to the lapse of time since the gifts were made, for the donors to expect the property to be returned[16].

Subject to these statutory provisions, which apply to property whenever given[17], property given for specific charitable purposes which fail from the first with no general charitable intention, so far as it was given by identifiable donors, is held upon resulting trust for them[18] rateably in the proportion that each donor's gift bore to the whole sum given[19].

1 *Re Dover's Battle of Britain Memorial Fund* (1955) Times, 29 June. But in so far as this case depended on assuming that all donors gave on the same terms, it must be read in the light of *Re Ulverston and District New Hospital Building Trusts, Birkett v Barrow and Furness Hospital Management Committee* [1956] Ch 622, [1956] 3 All ER 164, CA. See also *Re British School of Egyptian Archaeology, Murray v Public Trustee* [1954] 1 All ER 887, [1954] 1 WLR 546; *Munster and Leinster Bank v A-G* (1954) 91 ILT 34.
2 For these purposes, references to 'property given' include property for the time being representing property originally given or property derived from it: Charities Act 1993 s 14(10).
3 For the meaning of 'charitable purpose' see para 1 ante.
4 For these purposes, a charitable purpose is deemed to 'fail' where any difficulty in applying property to those purposes makes that property or the part not applicable cy-près available to be returned to the donors: Charities Act 1993 s 14(7). As to cy-près schemes see para 201 et seq post.
5 As to the meaning of 'donor' see para 167 note 8 ante.
6 For these purposes, 'prescribed' means prescribed by regulations made by the Charity Commissioners, which they must publish in such manner as they think fit: Charities Act 1993 s 14(8), (9). As to the Charity Commissioners see paras 486–512 post.
7 A donor who disclaims is deemed to have parted with all his interest at the time the gift was made: see ibid s 14(1)(b), (5); and note 19 infra.
8 Ibid s 14(1)(b).

9   As respects the advertisements which are to be published, regulations may make provision as to the form and content of such advertisements as well as the manner in which they are to be published: ibid s 14(8).

10  Ibid s 14(1)(a). See para 167 ante.

11  Ibid s 14(2). The prescribed period referred to in the text is the period mentioned in s 14(1)(a) (see the text and note 10 supra): see s 14(2).

12  'The court' means the High Court and, within the limits of its jurisdiction, any other court in England and Wales having a jurisdiction in respect of charities concurrent (within any limit of area or amount) with that of the High Court, and includes any judge or officer of the court exercising the jurisdiction of the court: ibid s 97(1).

13  Ie property not falling within ibid s 14(3) (which is so treated without any order or any advertisement or inquiry): see para 167 text and notes 10–12 ante. The significance of s 14(3), (4) is that property falling within those subsections is applicable cy-près without the expense of advertisements and inquiries.

14  Ibid s 14(4).

15  Ibid s 14(4)(a).

16  Ibid s 14(4)(b).

17  These provisions apply to property given for charitable purposes, notwithstanding that it was so given before the commencement of the Charities Act 1993: s 14(11).

18  *Re Henry Wood National Memorial Trust, Armstrong v Moiseiwitsch* (1965) 109 Sol Jo 876.

19  *Re British Red Cross Balkan Fund, British Red Cross Society v Johnson* [1914] 2 Ch 419. The rule in *Clayton's Case* (1816) 1 Mer 572 (see EQUITY vol 16 (Reissue) para 913) does not apply to the fund that is left for distribution. Where property is applied cy-près by the Charities Act 1993 s 14, the donor is deemed to have parted with all his interest at the time when the gift was made; but where property is so applied as belonging to donors who cannot be identified or cannot be found, and is not so applied by virtue s 14(3) (see para 167 ante) or s 14(4): (1) the scheme must specify the total amount of that property; and (2) the donor of any part of that amount is entitled, if he makes a claim not later than six months after the date on which the scheme is made, to recover from the charity for which the property is applied a sum equal to that part, less any expenses properly incurred by the charity trustees after that date in connection with claims relating to his gift; and (3) the scheme may include directions as to the provision to be made for meeting any such claim: s 14(5). Where:

(a)  any sum is, in accordance with any such directions, set aside for meeting any such claims (s 14(6)(a)); but

(b)  the aggregate amount of any such claims actually made exceeds the relevant amount (s 14(6)(b));

then, if the Commissioners so direct, each of the donors in question is entitled only to such proportion of the relevant amount as the amount of his claim bears to the aggregate amount referred to in head (b) supra: s 14(6). For these purposes 'the relevant amount' means the amount of the sum so set aside after deduction of any expenses properly incurred by the charity trustees in connection with claims relating to the donors' gifts: s 14(6). For the meaning of 'charity' see para 1 ante. For the meaning of 'charity trustees' see para 1 note 10 ante. As to directions given by the Commissioners see paras 492–493 post. As to schemes see para 170 et seq post.

**169.  Cy-près application on subsequent failure.** Independently of the statutory provisions[1], where property has been given in response to a public appeal and a surplus was left after the purposes had been carried out so far as possible, the property has generally been held to be applicable cy-près[2], even without regard to the question of general charitable intention[3]. In any case of subsequent failure in which, under the general law, the surplus assets are not applicable cy-près[4], the statutory provisions would now operate to make the surplus applicable cy-près so far as it belongs to unidentifiable donors or donors who have disclaimed[5].

1   Ie the Charities Act 1993 s 14: see paras 167–168 ante.

2   *Re Hartley Colliery Accident Relief Fund, Plummer v Jordan* (1908) 102 LT 165n; *Re Welsh Hospital (Netley) Fund, Thomas v A-G* [1921] 1 Ch 655; *Re North Devon and West Somerset Relief Fund Trusts, Hylton v Wright* [1953] 2 All ER 1032, [1953] 1 WLR 1260.

3   *Re Wokingham Fire Brigade Trusts, Martin v Hawkins* [1951] Ch 373, [1951] 1 All ER 454, approved in *Re Ulverston and District New Hospital Building Trusts, Birkett v Barrow and Furness Hospital Management Committee* [1956] Ch 622, [1956] 3 All ER 164, CA, where Jenkins LJ said that the question of general charitable intention could also have been ignored in *Re North Devon and West Somerset Relief Fund Trusts,*

*Hylton v Wright* [1953] 2 All ER 1032, [1953] 1 WLR 1260. See also *Re British School of Egyptian Archaeology, Murray v Public Trustee* [1954] 1 All ER 887 at 892, [1954] 1 WLR 546 at 553, where Harman J compared the questions of general charitable intention and out and out gift to charity. The only case in which such a surplus after subsequent failure has been held on resulting trust appears to be *Re British Red Cross Balkan Fund, British Red Cross Society v Johnson* [1914] 2 Ch 419; it is there stated to have been admitted, but the Attorney General was not a party and the concession may not have been correctly made or binding on him. As to cy-près schemes see para 201 et seq post.

4    Alternatively, where they do not pass as bona vacantia; the distinction is academic, but is adverted to in *Re Hillier, Hillier v A-G* [1953] 2 All ER 1547, [1954] 1 WLR 9, and in *Re Ulverston and District New Hospital Building Trusts, Birkett v Barrow and Furness Hospital Management Committee* [1956] Ch 622, [1956] 3 All ER 164, CA. For the cases in which property reverts to the donor on a subsequent failure of the charitable purposes see para 165 ante.

5    The provisions of the Charities Act 1993 s 14(4)(b), (7) (see para 168 ante) indicate that the provision applies to subsequent as well as to initial failure.

# 4. SCHEMES AND THE CY-PRÈS DOCTRINE

## (1) SCHEMES

### (i) Direction of Schemes

**170. Jurisdiction.** When it is necessary to define the objects or regulate the mode of administration of a charity, a scheme is usually directed either by the court[1] or by the Charity Commissioners[2]. Where, however, there is a gift to charity generally, without the interposition of any trust, and it is necessary to apply the gift to some specific charitable purposes, the application is directed by the Attorney General, to whom the power of the Crown to dispose of charitable gifts under the sign manual has been delegated[3].

1 See para 174 et seq post.
2 See para 180 et seq post. As to the Charity Commissioners see paras 486–512 post.
3 See para 457 post.

**171. General principles for direction of schemes.** A scheme is the method generally employed by the court in administering a charitable trust and is not necessarily, or generally, a scheme for the application of the fund cy-près[1]. It may be used to give effect to the donor's intention, for example by dealing not only with the method of administration but also with the substance of the trust, and by defining it[2]. A scheme will be directed where the trusts of the instrument of foundation are ambiguous or insufficient, or where no particular objects are defined[3], or where there are no trustees, or the trustees are dead[4] or refuse to act[5], or where there has been an increase in the revenue of the charity[6], or the persons managing the charity have misapplied its property[7], or where the charity's investment powers have become inadequate in changed economic circumstances[8], or where a legacy to a charity is to be confined to a particular part of its activities[9], or where for any other reason it is thought expedient to regulate the administration of the charity[10], or to remove or modify conditions or directions imposed in the trust[11].

Schemes may be directed even where there is an unlimited discretion as to distribution left to trustees[12], but in such a case the scheme is framed as far as possible to meet the trustees' wishes[13].

Where legacies[14] or annual sums[15] are given to be distributed in charity at the discretion of private individuals or public institutions, and no permanent trust is intended, schemes for the application of the money are not essential, though in many cases they are directed by the court[16].

A scheme is generally necessary on any application of a charitable fund cy-près[17], unless the trust is altered only in detail[18].

Under a scheme sanctioned by the court containing general terms without any reference to any foreign country, a charity must be administered and the trusts of the scheme carried into effect within the jurisdiction[19].

A scheme may confer upon the trustees or governors of the charity power to alter some of its provisions[20].

1   *Re Robinson, Besant v German Reich* [1931] 2 Ch 122 at 128 per Maugham J. As to the cy-près doctrine see para 201 et seq post.

2   *Re Gott, Glazebrook v Leeds University* [1944] Ch 193, [1944] 1 All ER 293.

3   *A-G v Clarke* (1762) Amb 422; *Re White, White v White* [1893] 2 Ch 41, CA. See *Re Mason's Orphanage and London and North-Western Rly Co* (1895) 65 LJCh 32 at 34 per Stirling J (on appeal [1896] 1 Ch 596, CA); and para 201 post.

4   *Moggridge v Thackwell* (1803) 7 Ves 36 (affd (1807) 13 Ves 416, HL); *A-G v Gladstone* (1842) 13 Sim 7; *Re Stanes' Will, Re Trustee Relief Act* (1853) 21 LTOS 261. As to the failure of trustees see para 199 post.

5   *Reeve v A-G* (1843) 3 Hare 191; and see para 199 post.

6   Eg *A-G v Caius College* (1837) 2 Keen 150; *A-G v Warden etc of Louth Free School* (1851) 14 Beav 201; *Re Campden Charities* (1881) 18 ChD 310, CA.

7   *A-G v Coopers' Co* (1812) 19 Ves 187.

8   *Re Royal Society's Charitable Trusts* [1956] Ch 87, [1955] 3 All ER 14, where the court's functions in relation to administrative schemes are considered; *Steel v Wellcome Custodian Trustees Ltd* [1988] 1 WLR 167 (exceptional case where foundation of scheme was a perfectly general power to apply the fund in the acquisition of any property whatsoever as if the trustees were absolutely and beneficially entitled). See also *Re Shipwrecked Fishermen and Mariners' Royal Benevolent Society Charity* [1959] Ch 220, [1958] 3 All ER 465; *Re Royal Naval and Royal Marine Children's Homes, Portsmouth, Lloyds Bank Ltd v A-G* [1959] 2 All ER 716, [1959] 1 WLR 755; *Re University of London Charitable Trusts* [1964] Ch 282, [1963] 3 All ER 859. As to the investment powers of charities generally and the power to make common investment schemes see paras 363, 366 post.

9   *Re Spence, Ogden v Shackleton* [1979] Ch 483, sub nom *Re Spence's Will Trusts, Ogden v Shackleton* [1978] 3 All ER 92.

10  See *A-G v St Olave's Grammar School, Southwark* (1837) Coop Pr Cas 267; *A-G v Dedham School* (1857) 23 Beav 350; *Re Forbes, Forbes v Forbes* (1910) 27 TLR 27.

11  *Re Robinson, Wright v Tugwell* [1923] 2 Ch 332 (removing 'abiding' condition that a black gown should be worn in the pulpit); *Re Dominion Students' Hall Trust* [1947] Ch 183 (removing colour bar from trust for Dominion students); *Re Lysaght, Hill v Royal College of Surgeons* [1966] Ch 191, [1965] 2 All ER 888 (removing provision for religious discrimination); *Re Woodhams, Lloyds Bank Ltd v London College of Music* [1981] 1 All ER 202, [1981] 1 WLR 493 (modifying restrictions on beneficiaries); *Re JW Laing Trust, Steward's Co Ltd v A-G* [1984] Ch 143, [1984] 1 All ER 50 (obligation to distribute whole of capital and income within ten years of settlor's death removed where trust fund set up in 1922 with £15,000 and worth £24m at time of application); *Re Stewart's Will Trusts* [1983] NI 283.

12  *A-G v Stepney* (1804) 10 Ves 22; *Waldo v Caley* (1809) 16 Ves 206 at 211 per Grant MR; *Jemmit v Verril* (1826) Amb 585n; *Barclay v Maskelyne* (1858) 32 LTOS 205; *Re Hurley, Nichols v Pargiter* (1900) 17 TLR 115; and cf *Re Barnett* (1860) 29 LJCh 871; *Dick v Audsley* [1908] AC 347 at 351, HL, per Lord Loreburn LC.

13  *Bennett v Honywood* (1772) Amb 708 at 710 per Lord Apsley LC; *A-G v Gaskell* (1831) 9 LJOS Ch 188; *Re Delmar Charitable Trust* [1897] 2 Ch 163 at 168 per Stirling J.

14  *A-G v Glegg* (1738) Amb 584; *Johnston v Swann* (1818) 3 Madd 457; *Re Barnett* (1860) 29 LJCh 871; *Re Lea, Lea v Cooke* (1887) 34 ChD 528; and see *Re Garrard, Gordon v Craigie* [1907] 1 Ch 382.

15  *Horde v Earl of Suffolk* (1833) 2 My & K 59. See also *Waldo v Caley* (1809) 16 Ves 206; *Powerscourt v Powerscourt* (1824) 1 Mol 616; *Shrewsbury v Hornby* (1846) 5 Hare 406; *Mahon v Savage* (1803) 1 Sch & Lef 111; *Re Lea, Lea v Cooke* (1887) 34 ChD 528.

16  *Doyley v Doyley* (1735) 7 Ves 58n; *A-G v Stepney* (1804) 10 Ves 22; *Paice v Archbishop of Canterbury* (1807) 14 Ves 364; *Baker v Sutton* (1836) 1 Keen 224; *Pocock v A-G* (1876) 3 ChD 342, CA; *Re Hurley, Nichols v Pargiter* (1900) 17 TLR 115.

17  *Martin v Maugham* (1844) 14 Sim 230; *Biscoe v Jackson* (1887) 35 ChD 460, CA; *Re Bradwell, Goode v Board of Trustees for Methodist Church Purposes* [1952] Ch 575, [1952] 2 All ER 286.

18  *Re Richardson, Shuldham v Royal National Lifeboat Institution* (1887) 56 LJCh 784.

19  *Re Mirrlees' Charity, Mitchell v A-G* [1910] 1 Ch 163.

20  *Re Jewish Orphanage Endowment Trusts, Sebag-Montefiore v Rothschild Executor and Trustee Co* [1960] 1 All ER 764, [1960] 1 WLR 344.

**172. Where a scheme is not required.** Legacies to or for the benefit of established institutions, whether incorporated[1] or not[2], or to their presidents[3], trustees, treasurers or officers[4], as part of their general funds or upon similar trusts to those upon which the general funds are held, may be paid without a scheme being directed[5]. A gift to an individual engaged in a charitable activity for the purposes of that activity may also be paid to that individual without a scheme[6]. Similarly, unless the Attorney General objects, a gift for the purposes of an institution which has ceased to exist may be paid, without a formal scheme, to another institution carrying on the same work[7]; and a legacy may be paid to a trustee without a scheme upon an undertaking to apply the legacy to the charitable purposes of the bequest and render accounts to the Attorney General[8].

On the same principle, legacies for the benefit of a parish church[9], or a Roman Catholic[10] or dissenters'[11] chapel, may be paid to the churchwardens and trustees respectively.

A scheme is not necessary in the case of a gift to an institution for its general purposes but subject to special conditions, as, for example, that certain lifeboats should be maintained[12], or that a particular person should have rights of nomination to a hospital[13].

1   *Emery v Hill* (1826) 1 Russ 112; *Society for the Propagation of the Gospel v A-G* (1826) 3 Russ 142; *A-G v Christ's Hospital* (1830) 1 Russ & M 626; *Re Richardson, Shuldham v Royal National Lifeboat Institution* (1887) 56 LJCh 784.
2   *Re M'Auliffe's Goods* [1895] P 290. See also *Re Lalor's Goods* (1901) 85 LT 643.
3   *Walsh v Gladstone* (1843) 1 Ph 290 (president of a college).
4   *Wellbeloved v Jones* (1822) 1 Sim & St 40 at 43 per Leach V-C; *Emery v Hill* (1826) 1 Russ 112.
5   See also *Minet v Vulliamy* (1819) cited in 1 Russ 113n; *Carter v Green* (1857) 3 K & J 591; and *Re Surfleet's Estate, Rawlings v Smith* (1911) 105 LT 582 (where the gifts were to institutions whose objects included the purchase of land); *Makeown v Ardagh* (1876) IR 10 Eq 445. Cf *Wellbeloved v Jones* (1822) 1 Sim & St 40; *Sons of the Clergy Corpn v Mose* (1839) 9 Sim 610 (where the gifts were on trusts not identical with the purposes of the institutions).
6   *Re Rees, Jones v Evans* [1920] 2 Ch 59.
7   See eg *Re Finger's Will Trusts, Turner v Ministry of Health* [1972] Ch 286, [1971] 3 All ER 1050.
8   *Re Reddish, Penton v Waters* [1934] WN 198. See *Re Wedgwood, Sweet v Cotton* [1914] 2 Ch 245.
9   *A-G v Ruper* (1722) 2 P Wms 125.
10  *De Windt v De Windt* (1854) 23 LJCh 776.
11  *Bunting v Marriott* (1854) 19 Beav 163.
12  *Re Richardson, Shuldham v Royal National Lifeboat Institution* (1887) 56 LJCh 784.
13  *A-G v Christ's Hospital* (1830) 1 Russ & M 626. Cf *Re Lopes, Bence-Jones v Zoological Society of London* [1931] 2 Ch 130, where there was a scheme.

**173. Property situated or payable abroad.** The court will not direct a scheme to be settled where the charity's property is out of the jurisdiction, or is a fund payable to trustees out of the jurisdiction[1]. In such a case the court may direct an inquiry whether the trust can be carried into effect according to the law of the particular country[2], and may pay the money to the persons selected by the testator as the instruments of his benevolence, if they are proper persons to act as trustees[3], but not otherwise[4], or may appoint new trustees for the purpose[5], or may retain the fund in court and direct payment of the dividends to the persons entrusted by the testator with the application of them[6], or may retain the fund in court to await the result of an application to the foreign court[7], or may give liberty to carry into effect a scheme to be settled by the foreign court[8].

The court may direct a scheme to be settled where trusts, which have been established within the jurisdiction for the endowment of a charitable object out of the jurisdiction, become impracticable but the fund and the trustees are within the jurisdiction[9].

Where a scheme became necessary, for lack of objects, in relation to funds administered by an institution which had become subject to a foreign state, the court refused to allow the institution to continue to administer the trusts[10].

---

1    Eg in Scotland (*Edinburgh Corpn v Aubery* (1753) Amb 236; *A-G v Lepine* (1818) 2 Swan 181; *Emery v Hill* (1826) 1 Russ 112; *Re Marr's Will Trusts, Walker v A-G* [1936] Ch 671); Switzerland (*Minet v Vulliamy* (1819) cited in 1 Russ 113n); France (*Martin v Paxton* (1824) cited in 1 Russ 116); United States of America (*Society for the Propagation of the Gospel v A-G* (1826) 3 Russ 142; *New v Bonaker* (1867) LR 4 Eq 655); Germany (*Re Robinson, Besant v German Reich* [1931] 2 Ch 122 at 129 per Maugham J).
2    *Thompson v Thompson* (1844) 1 Coll 381 at 394 per Shadwell V-C (Scotland). See *New v Bonaker* (1867) LR 4 Eq 655 (United States of America).
3    *Edinburgh Corpn v Aubery* (1753) Amb 236; *A-G v Lepine* (1818) 2 Swan 181; *Minet v Vulliamy* (1819) cited in 1 Russ 113n; *Martin v Paxton* (1824) cited in 1 Russ 116; *Emery v Hill* (1826) 1 Russ 112; *Collyer v Burnett* (1829) Taml 79; *Mitford v Reynolds* (1842) 1 Ph 185 at 197 per Lord Lyndhurst LC. See also *New v Bonaker* (1867) LR 4 Eq 655; *Lyons Corpn v Advocate-General of Bengal* (1876) 1 App Cas 91, PC.
4    *Lyons Corpn v East India Co* (1836) 1 Moo PCC 175.
5    *A-G v Stephens* (1834) 3 My & K 347. See also *A-G v Fraunces* [1866] WN 280, where a fund given to a school in a parish in the United States of America was directed to be paid to the governors of another school in the same parish, the original school having disappeared.
6    *A-G v Lepine* (1818) 2 Swan 181. See also *A-G v Sturge* (1854) 19 Beav 597, where the official charged by the testator with the distribution of a fund had died, and the court directed payment to be made to the holder of the office for the time being.
7    *Forbes v Forbes* (1854) 18 Beav 552; *Re Fraser, Yeates v Fraser* (1883) 22 ChD 827.
8    *Re Marr's Will Trusts, Walker v A-G* [1936] Ch 671. Cf *Re Lipton's Trustees* 1943 SC 521; *Re Neech's Executors* 1947 SC 119.
9    *Re Colonial Bishoprics Fund 1841* [1935] Ch 148.
10   *A-G v London Corpn* (1790) 3 Bro CC 171. The charity had been administered in the United States of America, but the founder's will did not confine its scope to America.

---

## (ii)  Settlement of Schemes by the Court

**174. General jurisdiction and powers.** In general the court has jurisdiction in every case to make schemes to regulate the administration of a charity, and the Charity Commissioners have equal concurrent jurisdiction with the court[1].

However, the court now normally makes schemes only in contentious cases or cases which involve special complexities or difficult question of law or fact[2]. Formerly it was the rule that the court would make a scheme if it became necessary in the course of an administration action or any charitable proceedings[3].

Where the court undertakes the execution of charitable trusts it will not retain the funds under its direct control but will direct a scheme in accordance with which the trustees will administer the funds[4].

The court may make a scheme supplemental to the original trusts and temporary in effect[5], or a scheme effective only until the happening of a certain event[6].

If the original trusts are altered by a scheme, a gift over on alteration or non-compliance with the trusts will not take effect[7].

---

1    See the Charities Act 1993 s 16(1); and para 180 post. As to the jurisdiction of the court and the Commissioners in relation to ecclesiastical charities see para 187 post. In most cases an application to the court for a scheme may only be made with the leave of the Commissioners: see para 521 post. As to the

Charity Commissioners see paras 486–512 post.

2    See ibid s 16(10); and para 180 post. Section 16(10) substantially re-enacts the Charitable Trusts Act 1860
     s 5, under which it was decided that the Commissioners were not precluded from exercising jurisdiction
     in contentious cases: *Re Burnham National Schools* (1873) LR 17 Eq 241, not following dictum in
     *Re Hackney Charities, ex p Nicholls* (1864) 34 LJCh 169; on appeal (1865) 4 De GJ & Sm 588.

3    See eg *Re Huxtable, Huxtable v Crawfurd* [1902] 2 Ch 793, CA; *Wellbeloved v Jones* (1822) 1 Sim & St 40;
     *A-G v Haberdashers' Co* (1852) 15 Beav 397. Now it is usual to refer the matter to the Commissioners
     under the Charities Act 1993 s 16(2) for them to settle a scheme: see para 182 post.

4    *A-G v Solly* (1835) 5 LJCh 5; *A-G v Haberdashers' Co* (1791) 1 Ves 295; *A-G v Haberdashers' Co* (1852)
     15 Beav 397 at 406 per Romilly MR. See *A-G v Governors of Harrow School* (1754) 2 Ves Sen 551; *A-G v
     Townley* (1829) Shelford's Law of Mortmain 442.

5    See *A-G v Price* (1908) 24 TLR 761; revsd [1912] 1 Ch 667, CA; on appeal sub nom *Price v A-G* [1914]
     AC 20, HL. Cf *A-G v Edalji* (1907) 97 LT 292.

6    *Re Royal Naval and Royal Marine Children's Homes, Portsmouth, Lloyds Bank Ltd v A-G* [1959] 2 All ER
     716n, [1959] 1 WLR 755.

7    *Re Bacon's Charity* (7 December 1878, unreported) per Jessel MR; a report of the case is on the files of
     the Charity Commissioners and it is noted at Tudor on Charities (4th Edn, 1906) 187 note (q). See also
     *Re Parish of Upton Warren* (1833) 1 My & K 410; *Christ's Hospital v Grainger* (1849) 1 Mac & G 460 at
     464 per Lord Cottenham LC; *Re Trustees of the Orchard Street Schools* [1878] WN 211; *Re Hanbey's Will
     Trusts, Cutlers' Co v President and Governors of Christ's Hospital, London* [1956] Ch 264, [1955] 3 All ER
     874. Quaere whether the court would make a scheme having the effect of defeating a resulting trust (as
     distinct from a gift over to another charity) on non-compliance with the trusts and whether, if the event
     on which the resulting trust was to arise had already happened, there would be jurisdiction to make such
     a scheme.

**175. Schemes in relation to chartered charities.** Before 1961 the court and the
Charity Commissioners[1] had only very limited jurisdiction over charities established by
royal charter[2], and the appropriate procedure for any substantial alteration was the grant
and acceptance of a new charter, although it was doubtful whether this could alter the
purposes for which funds already held could be applied, at least in the case of an
eleemosynary corporation. Now, however, where a royal charter establishing or
regulating a body corporate is amendable by the grant and acceptance of a further charter,
a scheme relating to the body corporate or to the administration of property held by the
body (including a scheme for the cy-près application[3] of any such property) may be made
by the court[4] under the court's jurisdiction with respect to charities notwithstanding that
the scheme cannot take effect without the alteration of the charter[5]. The scheme must
be so framed that it, or such part of it as cannot take effect without the alteration of the
charter, does not purport to come into operation unless or until Her Majesty thinks fit
to amend the charter in such manner as will permit the scheme or that part of it to have
effect[6].

Where under the court's jurisdiction with respect to charities, or under powers
conferred by the Charities Act 1993, a scheme is made with respect to a body corporate,
and it appears to Her Majesty expedient, having regard to the scheme, to amend any
royal charter relating to that body, Her Majesty may, on the application of that body,
amend the charter accordingly by Order in Council in any way in which the charter
could be amended by the grant and acceptance of a further charter[7]. Any such Order in
Council may be revoked or varied in like manner as the charter it amends[8].

1    As to the Charity Commissioners see paras 486–512 post.
2    See *Re Whitworth Art Gallery Trusts, Manchester Whitworth Institute v Victoria University of Manchester* [1958]
     Ch 461, [1958] 1 All ER 176.
3    As to cy-près applications see para 201 et seq post.
4    For the meaning of 'the court' see para 168 note 12 ante.

5    Charities Act 1993 s 15(1). The powers conferred by s 15(1), (2) have been extensively used: see the *Report of the Charity Commissioners for England and Wales for 1965* (HC Paper (1966–67) no 108) pp 8–9; *Report of the Charity Commissioners for England and Wales for 1967* (HC Paper (1967–68) no 261) pp 15–18.
6    Charities Act 1993 s 15(1).
7    See ibid s 15(2). See eg the Royal College of Ophthalmologists (Charter Amendment) Order 1998, SI 1998/2552; the Royal College of Physicians (Charter Amendment) Order 1999, SI 1999/667; the Licensed Victuallers' National Homes (Charter Amendment) Order 2000, SI 2000/1348.
8    Charities Act 1993 s 15(2).

**176. Schemes in relation to certain statutory charities.** The court has no inherent jurisdiction to alter such of the trusts of a charity as are established by or by virtue of a statute[1]. However, the Charities Act 1993 provides that the jurisdiction of the court[2] with respect to charities[3] is not to be restricted or excluded in relation to certain classes of charities by the statutes by or under which they are established[4]. The specified classes are as follows:

(1)    charities established or regulated by any provision of the Seamen's Fund Winding-up Act 1851[5];

(2)    charities established or regulated by schemes under statutory provisions relating to endowed schools and elementary education[6];

(3)    fuel allotments[7];

(4)    charities established or regulated under any provision of the Municipal Corporations Act 1883 or by any scheme under any such provision[8];

(5)    charities regulated by schemes under the London Government Act 1899[9];

(6)    charities established or regulated by orders or regulations under certain provisions[10] of the Regimental Charitable Funds Act 1935[11];

(7)    parochial charities regulated by the Charities Act 1993[12].

A scheme established for any such charity may modify or supersede in relation to it the provision made by any such enactment or instrument as if made by a scheme of the court, and may also make any such authorised[13] provision[14].

1    *Re Shrewsbury Grammar School* (1849) 1 Mac & G 324 at 333 per Lord Cottenham LC; *A-G v Governors of Christ's Hospital* [1896] 1 Ch 879; *Trustees of the London Parochial Charities v A-G* [1955] 1 All ER 1, [1955] 1 WLR 42. See also *Warren v Clancy* [1898] 1 IR 127, CA; *Re Imprisoned Debtors Discharge Society's Act 1856* (1912) 28 TLR 477, CA. As to the amendment of statutes establishing or regulating charities see also para 184 post.
2    For the meaning of 'the court' see para 168 note 12 ante.
3    For the meaning of 'charity' see para 1 ante.
4    See the Charities Act 1993 s 15(3).
5    Ibid s 15(3), Sch 4 para 1(a). The Seamen's Fund Winding-up Act 1851 was repealed by the Charities Act 1960 s 39(1), Sch 5 (repealed).
6    Charities Act 1993 Sch 4 para 1(b). The statutory provisions referred to in the text are the Endowed Schools Act 1869, the Endowed Schools Act 1873, the Endowed Schools Act 1874, the Welsh Intermediate Education Act 1889, the Endowed Schools (Masters) Act 1908, the Education (Miscellaneous Provisions) Act 1948 s 2, Sch 1 Pt II, the Elementary Education Act 1870 s 75, the Education Act 1973 s 2 (all repealed) and the Education Act 1996 s 554 (as amended): Charities Act 1993 Sch 4 para 1(b) (amended by the Education Act 1996 s 582(1), Sch 37 para 121). As to schemes under the Endowed Schools Acts and power to make new provision as to the use of endowments see the Education Act 1996 ss 553, 554 (as amended), 555, 556 (as amended); and EDUCATION. As to rights of reverter see para 63 ante.
7    Charities Act 1993 Sch 4 para 1(d), which defines 'fuel allotments' as land which under any enactment relating to inclosure or any instrument having an effect under any such enactment, is vested in trustees

upon trust that the land or the rents and profits of the land be used for the purpose of providing poor persons with fuel. Notwithstanding anything in the Commons Act 1876 s 19, a scheme for the administration of a fuel allotment may contain certain provisions for the disposal or exchange of the allotment or for its use for any purposes specified in the scheme: see the Charities Act 1993 Sch 4 para 2; and ALLOTMENTS AND SMALLHOLDINGS. As to other types of allotment under the Inclosure Acts see para 186 post.

8 Charities Act 1993 Sch 4 para 1(e). The relevant provisions of the Municipal Corporations Act 1883 were repealed by the Charities Act 1960 s 39(1), Sch 5 (repealed).

9 Charities Act 1993 Sch 4 para 1(f). The relevant provisions of the London Government Act 1899 have been repealed.

10 Ie the Regimental Charitable Funds Act 1935 s 2 (as amended): see ROYAL FORCES.

11 Charities Act 1993 Sch 4 para 1(g).

12 Ibid Sch 4 para 1(h). As to the regulation of parochial charities see s 79 (as amended) and orders made under it: see paras 240–242 post.

13 Ie authorised by ibid Sch 4: see the text and notes 2–12 supra.

14 Ibid s 15(3).


**177. Attorney General's consent.** The application or consent of the Attorney General is probably necessary to an alteration of a scheme by the court[1]. In a proper case it is his duty to make the necessary application[2].

The court will not, upon the motion of one of the interested parties[3], alter a scheme which it has settled with the approval of the Attorney General.

1 *A-G v Stewart* (1872) LR 14 Eq 17; and see *A-G v Hall* (1875) 3 Seton's Form of Decrees, Judgments and Orders (7th Edn, 1912) 1259. See also *Re Royal Society's Charitable Trusts* [1956] Ch 87, [1955] 3 All ER 14.

2 *A-G v Bishop of Worcester* (1851) 9 Hare 328 at 360 per Turner V-C.

3 *Re Sekeford's Charity* (1861) 5 LT 488.


**178. Alteration of schemes settled by court.** A scheme settled by the court for the administration of a charity can be altered by the court if the lapse of time and change of circumstances render it in the interest of the charity that the alteration should be made[1]. Schemes so settled are not altered except upon substantial grounds, and upon clear evidence, not only that the existing scheme does not operate beneficially, but that it can be made to do so consistently with the object of the foundation[2]. A scheme for applying the income of a charity remains in force only until further order or the establishment of a new scheme[3].

If the trusts of a scheme settled by the court are later shown not to be charitable in law, the scheme must be corrected by a further scheme[4]. A scheme making an unfair distribution among the objects of a charity may be altered[5].

1 *A-G v St John's Hospital, Bath* (1865) 1 Ch App 92 at 106 per Turner LJ; *Glasgow College v A-G* (1848) 1 HL Cas 800; and see *A-G v London Corpn* (1790) 3 Bro CC 171; *A-G v Bovill* (1840) 1 Ph 762; *A-G v Rochester Corpn* (1854) 5 De GM & G 797; *Re Hussey's Charities, Cheyne v Apreece, Symons v Delaval* (1861) 7 Jur NS 325 (where a gift to a clergyman for prisoners was divided on the formation of a second prison); *A-G v Hankey* (1867) LR 16 Eq 140n. As to the alteration of a scheme of a charity abroad see *A-G v London Corpn* (1790) 3 Bro CC 171; *Lyons Corpn v Advocate-General of Bengal* (1876) 1 App Cas 91 at 110, PC. As to the procedure for settling schemes see paras 545–547 post.

For special statutory provisions for the alteration of schemes affecting schools see eg the Education Act 1973 ss 1(2), 2 (repealed). Previously the Endowed Schools Acts 1869 to 1948 (repealed) (see para 176 note 4 ante) had contained special provisions for the alteration of schemes. As to schemes under the Endowed Schools Acts and power to make new provision as to the use of endowments see the Education

Act 1996 ss 553, 554 (as amended), 555, 556 (as amended); and EDUCATION. As to rights of reverter see para 63 ante.

2    *A-G v Bishop of Worcester* (1851) 9 Hare 328; and see *Re Sekeford's Charity* (1861) 5 LT 488; *A-G v Stewart* (1872) LR 14 Eq 17.

3    *Re Betton's Charity* [1908] 1 Ch 205.

4    See *Vernon v IRC* [1956] 3 All ER 14, [1956] 1 WLR 1169.

5    *A-G v Buller* (1822) Jac 407. Other types of provision which have been altered include those relating to religious instruction (*A-G v St John's Hospital, Bath* (1876) 2 ChD 554), the number of governors (*Re Browne's Hospital v Stamford* (1889) 60 LT 288), and the granting of building leases (*Re Henry Smith's Charity, Hartlepool* (1882) 20 ChD 516, CA).

**179. Court's powers where scheme not directed.** Where the matter is before the court, and it is not thought necessary to direct a scheme, the court may, as the case requires, refer the apportionment of funds to the master[1], or retain a measure of control by giving any of the parties leave to apply if necessary[2], or order the person applying the fund to account for its distribution[3], or direct payment of the capital into court and payment of the dividends to the person entrusted with their distribution[4].

1    *White v White* (1778) 1 Bro CC 12; *Re Hyde's Trusts* (1873) 22 WR 69.

2    *Waldo v Caley* (1809) 16 Ves 206 at 211 per Grant MR; *Horde v Earl of Suffolk* (1833) 2 My & K 59; *Re Lea, Lea v Cooke* (1887) 34 ChD 528 at 535 per North J.

3    *A-G v Glegg* (1738) Amb 584; *A-G v Governors etc of Sherborne Grammar School* (1854) 18 Beav 256.

4    *M'Coll v Atherton* (1848) 12 Jur 1042. As to where a scheme is not required see para 172 ante.

### (iii) Settlement of Schemes by the Charity Commissioners

**180. General jurisdiction.** The Charity Commissioners[1] may by order exercise the same jurisdiction and powers as are exercisable by the High Court in charity proceedings for the following purposes[2]: (1) establishing a scheme for the administration of a charity[3]; (2) appointing, discharging or removing a charity trustee[4] or trustee for a charity, or removing an officer or employee[5]; (3) vesting or transferring property, or requiring or entitling any person to call for or make any transfer of property or any payment[6].

In relation to a charity, other than an exempt charity[7], whose income from all sources does not in the aggregate exceed £500 a year[8], the Commissioners may exercise their jurisdiction to make schemes on the application of any one or more of the charity trustees or of any person interested in the charity[9] or, if it is a local charity[10], of any two or more inhabitants of the area of the charity[11]. In relation to any other charity, the Commissioners may not normally[12] exercise their jurisdiction to make schemes except on the application of the charity[13] or on a reference to them by the court for the purpose[14] or, in the case of a charity other than an exempt charity, on the application of the Attorney General[15].

Unless the scheme is made under a court order, the Commissioners must give notice of their intention to act to each of the charity trustees, except any that cannot be found or has no known address in the United Kingdom[16] or who is party or privy to the application for the exercise of the jurisdiction[17].

The Commissioners do not have jurisdiction to try or determine the title in law or in equity to any property as between a charity or trustee for a charity and a person holding or claiming the property or an interest in it adversely to the charity, or to try or determine any question as to the existence or extent of any charge or trust[18].

1   As to the Charity Commissioners see paras 486–512 post.
2   Charities Act 1993 s 16(1). The Commissioners must not exercise their jurisdiction under s 16 in any case (not referred to them by order of the court) which, by reason of its contentious character, or of any special question of law or of fact which it may involve, or for other reasons, the Commissioners may consider more fit to be adjudicated on by the court: s 16(10). Some of the guidance given by the Charity Commissioners to their staff is set out in the *Report of the Charity Commissioners for England and Wales for 1989* (HC Paper (1989–90) no 343) paras 73–75. As to the jurisdiction of the courts in relation to charities see para 477 et seq post.
3   Charities Act 1993 s 16(1)(a). For the meaning of 'charity' see para 1 ante.
4   For the meaning of 'charity trustees' see para 1 note 10 ante.
5   Charities Act 1993 s 16(1)(b).
6   Ibid s 16(1)(c). A person guilty of disobedience to an order of the Commissioners under s 16 requiring a transfer of property or payment to be called for or made, may on the application of the Commissioners to the High Court be dealt with as for disobedience to an order of the High Court: see s 88; and para 494 post.
    No vesting or transfer of any property in pursuance of any provision of Pt IV (ss 13–35) (as amended) or Pt IX (ss 70–83) operates as a breach of a covenant or condition against alienation or give rise to a forfeiture: s 97(3).
7   As to exempt charities see para 293 post.
8   References in the Charities Act 1993 to a charity whose income from all sources does not in aggregate amount to more than a specified amount are to be construed: (1) by reference to the gross revenues of the charity; or (2) if the Commissioners so determine, by reference to the amount which they estimate to be the likely amount of those revenues, but without (in either case) bringing into account anything for the yearly value of land occupied by the charity apart from the pecuniary income (if any) received from that land; and any question as to the application of any such reference to a charity must be determined by the Commissioners, whose decision is final: s 96(4).
    If the Secretary of State thinks it expedient to do so: (a) in consequence of changes in the value of money; or (b) with a view to increasing the number of charities in respect of which the Commissioners may exercise their jurisdiction under s 16 in accordance with s 16(5), he may by order amend that provision by substituting a different sum for the sum for the time being specified there: s 16(15). At the date at which this volume states the law no such orders had been made. As to the making of orders generally see s 86 (as amended); and para 517 post. As to the Secretary of State see para 513 post.
9   As the meaning of 'interested in the charity' see para 520 note 4 post.
10  'Local charity' means, in relation to any area, a charity established for purposes which are by their nature or by the trusts of the charity directed wholly or mainly to the benefit of that area or of part of it: Charities Act 1993 s 96(1).
11  Ibid s 16(5).
12  See, however, paras 183, 186 post.
13  The application must be made by all or a majority of the charity trustees. Once an application has been made, it cannot effectively be withdrawn: *Re Poor's Lands Charity, Bethnal Green* [1891] 3 Ch 400.
14  Ie under the Charities Act 1993 s 16(2): see para 182 post. As to ecclesiastical charities see also para 187 post.
15  Ibid s 16(4).
16  'United Kingdom' means Great Britain and Northern Ireland: Interpretation Act 1978 s 5, Sch 1. 'Great Britain' means England, Scotland and Wales: Union with Scotland Act 1706, preamble art I; Interpretation Act 1978 s 22(1), Sch 2 para 5(a). Neither the Channel Islands nor the Isle of Man are within the United Kingdom. See further CONSTITUTIONAL LAW AND HUMAN RIGHTS vol 8(2) (Reissue) para 3.
17  Charities Act 1993 s 16(9). Notice may be given by post, addressed to the recipient's last known address in the United Kingdom: s 16(9).
18  Ibid s 16(3).

**181. Public notice.** The Charity Commissioners[1] may not make any order to establish a scheme for the administration of a charity, or submit such a scheme to the court[2] or the

Secretary of State[3] for an order giving it effect, unless not less than one month previously there has been given public notice of their proposals[4], inviting representations to be made to them within a time specified in the notice, being not less than one month from the date of such notice[5]. Where notice is given of any proposals as required[6], the Commissioners must take into consideration any representations made to them about the proposals within the time specified in the notice, and may, without further notice, proceed with the proposals either without modification or with such modifications as appear to them to be desirable[7].

Certain orders made by the Commissioners[8] must be published either by giving public notice of them or by giving notice of them to all persons entitled to appeal against them, as the Commissioners think fit[9].

Where the Commissioners make an order to establish a scheme for the administration of a charity, a copy of the order must, for not less than one month after the order is published, be available for public inspection at all reasonable times at the Commissioners' office and also at some convenient place in the area of the charity, if it is a local charity[10].

1   As to the Charity Commissioners see paras 486–512 post.
2   For the meaning of 'the court' see para 168 note 12 ante.
3   As to the Secretary of State see para 513 post.
4   Any notice to be given of any proposals or order must give such particulars of the proposals or order, or such directions for obtaining information about them, as the Commissioners think sufficient and appropriate, and any public notice must be given in such manner as they think sufficient and appropriate: Charities Act 1993 s 20(7).
5   Ibid s 20(1). In the case of a scheme relating to a local charity, other than on ecclesiastical charity, in a parish or, in Wales, a community, a draft of the scheme must be communicated to the parish or community council or, in the case of a parish not having a council, to the chairman of the parish meeting: s 20(1). For the meaning of 'local charity' see para 180 note 10 ante. For the meaning of 'ecclesiastical charity' see para 240 note 4 post.
6   Ie required by ibid s 20(1), (2), (3): see the text and notes 1–4 supra; and para 270 post.
7   Ibid s 20(4).
8   Ie orders which are subject to appeal under ibid s 16(12): see para 190 post.
9   Ibid s 20(5).
10  Ibid s 20(6). As to the supply of copies see para 282 note 9 post.

**182. Schemes on reference by the court.** Where the court[1] directs a scheme for the administration of a charity[2] to be established, it may by order refer the matter to the Charity Commissioners[3] for them to prepare or settle a scheme in accordance with such directions, if any, as the court sees fit to give[4]. Any such order may provide for the scheme to be put into effect by order of the Commissioners[5] without any further court order[6].

1   For the meaning of 'the court' see para 168 note 12 ante.
2   For the meaning of 'charity' see para 1 ante.
3   As to the Charity Commissioners see paras 486–512 post.
4   Charities Act 1993 s 16(2).
5   Ie as if prepared under ibid s 16(1): see para 180 ante.
6   Ibid s 16(2).

**183. Powers on trustees' refusal or inability to apply for scheme.** Where   the Charity Commissioners[1] are satisfied with regard to any charity[2], other than an exempt charity[3], that the charity trustees[4] ought in the interests of the charity to apply for a scheme, but have unreasonably refused or neglected to do so, and the Commissioners have given the charity trustees an opportunity to make representations to them, the Commissioners may proceed as if an application for a scheme had been made by the charity[5].

The purposes of a charity may not be altered under this provision unless 40 years have elapsed since the date of its foundation[6].

Where a charity cannot apply to the Commissioners for a scheme by reason of any vacancy among the charity trustees or the absence or incapacity of any of them, but such an application is made by such number of the charity trustees as the Commissioners consider appropriate in the circumstances of the case, the Commissioners may nevertheless proceed as if the application were an application made by the charity[7].

1    As to the Charity Commissioners see paras 486–512 post.
2    For the meaning of 'charity' see para 1 ante.
3    As to exempt charities see para 293 post.
4    For the meaning of 'charity trustees' see para 1 note 10 ante.
5    Charities Act 1993 s 16(6).
6    Ibid s 16(6).
7    Ibid s 16(7).


**184. Schemes amending statutory provisions.** Where it appears to the Charity Commissioners[1] that a scheme for the administration of a charity[2] should be established, but also that it is necessary or desirable for the scheme to alter some statutory provision establishing or regulating the charity or to make some other provision which is beyond the Commissioners' normal powers, or where it appears to them that it is for any reason proper for the scheme to be subject to parliamentary review, they may settle a scheme[3], and effect may be given to it by an order of the Secretary of State[4], a draft of which must be laid before Parliament[5]. Where the scheme goes beyond the powers otherwise exercisable in altering the provisions of a public general Act, the order may not be made unless the draft is approved by resolution of each House of Parliament[6]. Any provision of a scheme brought into effect under this procedure may be modified or superseded by the court[7] or the Commissioners as if it were a scheme brought into effect by order of the Commissioners[8] in the exercise of their ordinary powers[9].

The Commissioners must not proceed under these provisions without the like application, and the like notice to the charity trustees[10], as would be required if they were proceeding (without an order of the court) under their ordinary jurisdiction[11]; but on any application for a scheme, or in a case where they act because the charity trustees have unreasonably refused or neglected to act[12], or are unable to do so[13], they may proceed under these provisions or under their ordinary powers[14], as appears to them to be appropriate[15].

1    As to the Charity Commissioners see paras 486–512 post.
2    For the meaning of 'charity' see para 1 ante.
3    Charities Act 1993 s 17(1).
4    As to the Secretary of State see para 513 post.
5    Charities Act 1993 s 17(2). Such orders of the Secretary of State must be made by statutory instrument: s 86(1)(a). Orders of the Secretary of State under s 17(2) are not subject to annulment in pursuance of a resolution of either House of Parliament: see s 86(1)(b), (2)(a) (as amended); and para 517 post. As to the making of orders generally see s 86 (as amended); and para 517 post. The power under s 17(2) has been

used extensively: examples are referred to in the Annual Reports of the Charity Commissioners (see para 490 note 1 post). For examples of orders that have been made see the Charities (The Hundred Acres Charity, Enfield) Order 1974, SI 1974/1839; the Charities (National Trust for Places of Historic Interest or Natural Beauty) Order 1975, SI 1975/1155; the Charities (The Marine Society) Order 1976, SI 1976/147; the Charities (Cheltenham College) Order 1976, SI 1976/1809; the Charities (The New College of Cobham) Order 1978, SI 1978/1155; the Charities (Booth Charities) Order 1985, SI 1985/1935; the Charities (William Lambe (London) Trust) Order 1986, SI 1986/2003; the Charities (University of Liverpool) Order 1988, SI 1988/1068; the Charities (Borough Lands Charity, Chippenham) Order 1990, SI 1990/843; the Charities (Royal Russell School) Order 1998, SI 1998/2883; the Charities (Seamen's Hospital Society) Order 1999, SI 1999/73. Formerly a special Act was necessary; now expenditure of charity money on promoting legislation is restricted by the Charities Act 1993 s 17 except in the case of exempt charities: see s 17(7); and para 293 post.

6 Ibid s 17(3). This provision is expressed to be subject to the operation of the Statutory Instruments Act 1946 s 6 (see STATUTES vol 44(1) (Reissue) para 1517): see the Charities Act 1993 s 17(3).
7 For the meaning of 'the court' see para 12 note 12 ante.
8 Ie under the Charities Act 1993 s 16: see paras 180, 182–183 ante, 271 post.
9 Ibid s 17(4). However, where a scheme requires the positive approval of Parliament (see the text to note 6 supra), the order giving effect to it may direct that the scheme must not be modified or superseded by a scheme brought into effect otherwise than under s 17, and may also direct that any modifying or superseding scheme is subject to the same limitation: see s 17(5).
10 For the meaning of 'charity trustees' see para 1 note 10 ante.
11 See note 8 supra.
12 See the Charities Act 1993 s 16(6); and para 183 ante.
13 See ibid s 16(7); and para 183 ante.
14 See note 8 supra.
15 Charities Act 1993 s 17(6).

**185. Interim order in lieu of scheme.** If the Charity Commissioners[1] are satisfied: (1) that in existing circumstances the whole of the income of a charity cannot be effectively applied for the purposes of the charity[2]; and (2) that if those circumstances continue a scheme might be made for applying the surplus cy-près[3]; and (3) that for any reason it is not yet desirable to make such a scheme[4], they may by order authorise the charity trustees[5] at their discretion, though subject to any conditions imposed by the order, to apply accrued or accruing income[6] for any purposes for which it might be made applicable by such a scheme[7]. Any application authorised by the order is deemed to be within the purposes of the charity[8].

1 As to the Charity Commissioners see paras 486–512 post.
2 Charities Act 1993 s 17(8)(a). For the meaning of 'charity' see para 1 ante.
3 Ibid s 17(8)(b).
4 Ibid s 17(8)(c).
5 For the meaning of 'charity trustees' see para 1 note 10 ante.
6 The order may not, however, extend to more than £300 out of income accrued before the date of the order, nor to income accruing more than three years after that date, nor to more than £100 out of the income accruing in any of those three years: Charities Act 1993 s 17(9).
7 Ibid s 17(8).
8 Ibid s 17(8).

**186. Special jurisdiction.** There may be special cases in which, by virtue of some statutory provision, the Charity Commissioners[1] have jurisdiction to modify schemes that the court cannot modify[2].

Provisions with respect to allotments for recreation grounds, field gardens or other public or parochial purposes contained in any Inclosure Act, award or order made thereunder, and any provisions with respect to the management of any such allotments contained in any such Act, order, or award, may, on the application of any district or parish council interested in the allotment, be dealt with by a scheme of the Charity Commissioners in the exercise of their ordinary jurisdiction as if the provisions had been established by the founder in the case of a charity having a founder[3].

Any employee organisation[4] in the coal industry where members or members and their dependants constitute a substantial proportion of the beneficiaries under a relevant trust[5] and where neither the organisation nor its members are entitled to appoint any of the trustees of that trust, may apply to the Charity Commissioners for a scheme making such amendments to the provisions regulating the trust as the Commissioners consider appropriate for the purpose of securing fair representation amongst the trustees of those persons employed in the coal industry who may benefit under the trust[6]. These provisions apply to any trust for purposes which are exclusively charitable: (1) which is a trust of property wholly or partly representing an application of money from the miners' welfare fund constituted under the Mining Industry Act 1920[7] or the body known as the Coal Industry Social Welfare Organisation[8]; (2) which is a trust expressed to be for the benefit of (a) persons currently or formerly employed in the coal industry or any class of such persons or their dependants[9]; or (b) members of the mining community in general or of the mining community of a particular area, whether or not any other persons are also beneficiaries[10]; or (3) under the terms of which all or a majority of the trustees are appointed by the body mentioned in head (1) above or are appointed by the British Coal Corporation and an employee organisation[11].

1   As to the Charity Commissioners see paras 486–512 post.
2   See eg *Trustees of the London Parochial Charities v A-G* [1955] 1 All ER 1, [1955] 1 WLR 42. The Charities Act 1993 s 17 (see paras 184–185 ante) provides for a similar situation.
3   Commons Act 1899 s 18. For the purposes of s 18 the Broads Authority is treated as a district council: s 18 (amended by the Norfolk and Suffolk Broads Act 1988 s 21, Sch 6 para 1). As to the Broads Authority see OPEN SPACES AND ANCIENT MONUMENTS vol 34 (Reissue) para 130. As to field gardens see ALLOTMENTS AND SMALLHOLDINGS vol 2 (Reissue) paras 65–68.
       A national park authority has the same power to make an application under the Commons Act 1899 s 18 (as amended) as a local authority: Environment Act 1995 s 70, Sch 9 para 1(4). As to national park authorities see OPEN SPACES AND ANCIENT MONUMENTS vol 34 (Reissue) para 157 et seq.
4   For these purposes, 'an employee organisation' means any organisation appearing to the Charity Commissioners to represent in respect of their employment a substantial number of persons whose employers are licensed operators within the meaning of the Coal Industry Act 1994, or who are all employed by the same licensed operator: Coal Industry Act 1987 s 5(4) (substituted by the Coal Industry Act 1994 s 67, Sch 9 para 36(b)).
5   Ie a trust to which the Coal Industry Act 1987 s 5 applies: see the text and notes 8–11 infra.
6   Ibid s 5(1). See also MINES, MINERALS AND QUARRIES vol 31 (Reissue) para 88.
7   Ie the Mining Industry Act 1920 s 20 (repealed).
8   Coal Industry Act 1987 s 5(3)(a). As to provisions relating to the Coal Industry Social Welfare Organisation see the Miners' Welfare Act 1952 s 12 (prospectively repealed); and MINES, MINERALS AND QUARRIES vol 31 (Reissue) para 87.
9   Coal Industry Act 1987 s 5(3)(b)(i).
10  Ibid s 5(3)(b)(ii).
11  Ibid ss 5(3)(c), 9 (prospectively repealed). As to the British Coal Corporation see MINES, MINERALS AND QUARRIES vol 31 (Reissue) paras 2–3, 89.

**187. Schemes in relation to ecclesiastical charities.** The definition of 'charity' in the Charities Act 1993[1] does not apply to any ecclesiastical corporation[2] in respect of the corporate property of the corporation[3] or to any trust of property for purposes for which the property has been consecrated[4]. Nor is it applicable to any diocesan board of finance within the meaning of the Endowments and Glebe Measure 1976 for any diocese in respect of the diocesan glebe land of that diocese within the meaning of that Measure[5]. This notwithstanding, the power of the court[6] to make schemes in its charity jurisdiction, and the Charity Commissioners' jurisdiction to make schemes[7], extend to the making of schemes with respect to consecrated chapels belonging to charities[8] which are no longer needed for the purposes of the charity[9]. Such schemes may provide for the demolition of the chapel or disposal of the material arising from the demolition, for the sale or other disposal of the chapel or site of it and the application of the proceeds, for its appropriation to such uses as may be specified or generally described in the scheme, and for supplementary and incidental matters[10].

In relation to a charity established for ecclesiastical purposes of the Church of England, being a charity whose administration or purposes are affected by a pastoral scheme or order[11], the Charity Commissioners' powers to make schemes[12] may be exercised on the application of the diocesan board of finance for the relevant diocese[13]. This power also extends to charities affected by a redundancy scheme under the Pastoral Measure 1983[14].

Nothing in the New Parishes Measure 1943 enables the Church Commissioners[15] to deal with the endowment of a charity within the meaning of the Charities Act 1993 without the consent of the Charity Commissioners[16].

1   See the Charities Act 1993 s 96(1); and para 1 ante.
2   Ie any corporation in the Church of England, whether sole or aggregate, which is established for spiritual purposes: ibid s 96(2)(a). As to ecclesiastical matters see further ECCLESIASTICAL LAW.
3   Ibid s 96(2)(a). However, in respect of a corporation aggregate having some non-ecclesiastical purposes, the definition of 'charity' does extend to its corporate property held for those purposes: see s 96(2)(a).
4   See ibid s 96(2)(c).
5   Ibid s 96(2)(b). As from a day to be appointed the definition of 'charity' in the Charities Act 1993 does not apply to any subsidiary of any diocesan board of finance: s 96(2)(b) (prospectively amended by the Church of England (Miscellaneous Provisions) Measure 2000 s 11). As to diocesan boards of finance see ECCLESIASTICAL LAW vol 14 paras 517–518.
6   Ie under the Charities Act 1993: see para 174 et seq ante.
7   Ie under ibid s 16: see para 180 ante. As to the Charity Commissioners see paras 486–512 post.
8   For these purposes, a consecrated chapel held on charitable trusts for the purpose of religious worship by the beneficiaries and staff of a charity and not by the general public is deemed to belong to that charity, notwithstanding that the trusts on which the chapel is held are separate from those of the charity, but this does not apply to a chapel held on separate trusts relating to the use thereof for religious worship: Pastoral Measure 1983 s 55(4). For the meaning of 'charity' see para 1 ante; definition applied by s 87(1) (definition amended by the Charities Act 1993 s 98(1), Sch 6 para 18(4)).
9   Pastoral Measure 1983 s 55(1) (amended by the Charities Act 1993 s 98(1), Sch 6 para 18(1), (2)). Where a scheme is made under the Pastoral Measure 1983, the bishop may, if he thinks it proper to do so, by order under his seal direct that s 61(1) and s 65, if applicable, apply to the chapel as they apply to the buildings mentioned in those provisions, and those provisions then apply accordingly: s 55(2). The scheme, so far as it relates to the chapel, does not have effect unless and until such an order is made, or the bishop directs that the scheme may have effect without such an order: s 55(2). 'The bishop' means the bishop of the diocese concerned: s 87(1).
10  Ibid s 55(3).
11  As to such schemes and orders see the Pastoral Measure 1983; and ECCLESIASTICAL LAW.
12  Ie under the Charities Act 1993 s 16: see para 180 ante.
13  Pastoral Measure 1983 s 40, Sch 3 para 11(6) (amended by the Charities Act 1993 Sch 6 para 18(5)). They may also be exercised on the application of any of the persons specified in the Charities Act 1993 s 16 (see para 180 ante): Pastoral Measure 1983 Sch 3 para 11(6) (as so amended). Any schemes or orders made by the Charity Commissioners for purposes arising in connection with a pastoral scheme or order may be made before the date on which the pastoral scheme or order comes into operation, but not so as to take effect before that date: Sch 3 para 11(7).

14  See ibid s 63(3); and ECCLESIASTICAL LAW.

15  As to the Church Commissioners see ECCLESIASTICAL LAW vol 14 para 363 et seq.

16  New Parishes Measure 1943 s 31 (amended by the Charities Act 1960 s 48, Sch 6; the Education Act 1973 s 1(4), (5), Sch 2 Pt III; and the Charities Act 1993 Sch 6 para 3(1), (4)).


**188. Schemes in relation to redundant places of worship.** Statutory provision is made with respect to the transfer of certain redundant places of worship[1]. These provisions apply in relation to any premises[2] if the premises are held by or in trust for a charity ('the relevant charity'), and the whole or part of the premises has been used as a place of public worship, but the premises are not a church subject to the provisions of the Pastoral Measure 1983[3].

If the court[4] is satisfied, with respect to any relevant premises: (1) that those premises are no longer required, whether wholly or in part, for use as a place of public worship[5]; and (2) that either the Secretary of State, the Historic Buildings and Monuments Commission of England, or a prescribed charity, is willing to enter into an agreement to acquire those premises by way of gift or for a consideration other than full consideration[6]; but (3) that it is not within the powers of the persons in whom those premises are vested to carry out such an agreement except by virtue of these provisions[7], it may, under its jurisdiction with respect to charities, establish a scheme for the making and carrying out of such an agreement[8]. The Charity Commissioners have the same jurisdiction and powers in relation to the establishment of such a scheme[9].

If it appears to the court proper to do so, such a scheme may provide for the acquirer of the relevant premises[10] also to acquire (whether by gift or for a consideration other than full consideration or otherwise) any land held by or in trust for the relevant charity which is contiguous or adjacent to those premises and any objects which are or have been ordinarily kept on those premises[11]. The scheme may also provide for conferring on the acquirer of the relevant premises: (a) such rights of way over any land held by or in trust for the relevant charity as appear to the court to be necessary for the purpose of the discharge of the acquirer's functions in relation to those premises or to any land acquired under the scheme, or for giving to the public reasonable access to those premises or to any such land[12]; and (b) so far as is necessary for the purpose of the discharge of such functions or the giving of such access, any rights of way enjoyed by persons attending services at those premises[13].

The Charity Commissioners may, on the application of the acquirer of the relevant premises, by order establish a scheme[14] making provision for the restoration of the relevant premises, or part of them, to use as a place of public worship[15]. The Charity Commissioners may so establish any such scheme notwithstanding the limit on jurisdiction to make schemes for the protection of charities[16] or that the relevant charity has ceased to exist, and if the relevant charity has ceased to exist, any such scheme may provide for the constitution of a charity by or in trust for which the relevant premises are to be held on the restoration of those premises, or part of them, to use as a place of public worship[17].

Where any relevant premises are acquired by the Secretary of State, the Historic Buildings and Monuments Commission of England or a prescribed charity, any property of a charity whose purposes include (i) the repair and maintenance of those premises[18]; or (ii) the provision of objects for keeping on those premises[19]; or (iii) the maintenance of objects ordinarily kept there[20], continues to be applicable for that purpose so long as the premises remain vested in the Secretary of State, the Commission or the prescribed charity, as the case may be[21].

1 See the Redundant Churches and Other Religious Buildings Act 1969 ss 4, 5 (both as substituted); and ECCLESIASTICAL LAW vol 14 para 1134.

2 'Premises' includes a part of a building: ibid s 4(13) (s 4 substituted by the Charities Act 1992 s 49, Sch 5 para 1).

3 Redundant Churches and Other Religious Buildings Act 1969 s 4(1) (as substituted: see note 2 supra). In relation to the Historic Buildings and Monuments Commission of England, the Redundant Churches and Other Religious Buildings Act 1969 s 4 (as substituted) only applies to any premises falling within s 4(1) (as substituted) if they are situated in England, and references in s 4 (as substituted) to land are references only to land situated in England: s 4(9) (as so substituted). In relation to a prescribed charity, s 4 (as substituted) only applies to any premises falling within s 4(1) (as substituted) if they constitute either a listed building within the meaning of the Planning (Listed Buildings and Conservation Areas) Act 1990, or a scheduled monument within the meaning of the Ancient Monuments and Archaeological Areas Act 1979 (see OPEN SPACES AND ANCIENT MONUMENTS vol 34 (Reissue) para 357): Redundant Churches and Other Religious Buildings Act 1969 s 4(10) (as so substituted). The Secretary of State may direct that any charity specified in the direction is a prescribed charity for these purposes; and any such direction may be varied or revoked by a further direction given by the Secretary of State: s 4(11) (as so substituted). As to the Secretary of State see para 513 post. As to the Historic Buildings and Monuments Commission for England see OPEN SPACES AND ANCIENT MONUMENTS vol 34 (Reissue) para 133 et seq.

4 For the meaning of 'the court' see para 168 note 12 ante; definition applied by ibid s 4(13) (as substituted (see note 2 supra); and s 4(6), (7), (8), (13) (as substituted) amended by the Charities Act 1993 Sch 6 para 10). As to the court's jurisdiction over charities see para 477 et seq post.

5 Redundant Churches and Other Religious Buildings Act 1969 s 4(2)(a) (as substituted: see note 2 supra).

6 Ibid s 4(2)(b) (as substituted: see note 2 supra). For the purposes of s 4(2), (3) (as substituted), in relation to the acquisition of the relevant premises or the acquisition of any land or object: (1) references to acquisition by the Secretary of State are references to acquisition by him under the Historic Buildings and Ancient Monuments Act 1953 s 5 (acquisition by him of buildings of historic or architectural interest) (as amended) (see TOWN AND COUNTRY PLANNING vol 46 (Reissue) para 997); and (2) references to acquisition by the Historic Buildings and Monuments Commission for England are references to acquisition by them under s 5A (as added and amended) (acquisition by them of buildings of historic or architectural interest) (see TOWN AND COUNTRY PLANNING vol 46 (Reissue) para 998): Redundant Churches and Other Religious Buildings Act 1969 s 4(4) (as so substituted). In relation to Wales, the functions of the Secretary of State under the Historic Buildings and Ancient Monuments Act 1953 are carried out by the National Assembly for Wales: National Assembly for Wales (Transfer of Functions) Order 1999, SI 1999/672, art 2, Sch 1. As to the National Assembly for Wales see CONSTITUTIONAL LAW AND HUMAN RIGHTS.

7 Redundant Churches and Other Religious Buildings Act 1969 s 4(2)(c) (as substituted: see note 2 supra).

8 Ibid s 4(2) (as substituted: see note 2 supra).

9 The Charity Commissioners have the same jurisdiction and powers in relation to the establishment of a scheme under ibid s 4(2) (as substituted) as they have under the provisions of the Charities Act 1993 s 16 (except s 16(6)) (see paras 180, 182–183 ante, 271 post) in relation to the establishment of a scheme for the administration of a charity; and s 20 (publicity for proceedings under s 16) (see paras 181, 270 ante, 508 post) accordingly has effect in relation to the establishment of a scheme under the Redundant Churches and Other Religious Buildings Act 1969 s 4(2) (as substituted) as it has effect in relation to the establishment of a scheme for the administration of a charity: s 4(8) (as so substituted; and as amended (see note 4 supra)). As to the Charity Commissioners see paras 486–512 post.

10 For these purposes, references to the acquirer of the relevant premises are references to the person or body acquiring those premises by virtue of a scheme established under ibid s 4(2) (as substituted): s 4(12) (as substituted: see note 2 supra).

11 Ibid s 4(3) (as substituted: see note 2 supra).

12 Ibid s 4(5)(a) (as substituted: see note 2 supra).

13 Ibid s 4(5)(b) (as substituted: see note 2 supra).

14 Ie under the provisions relating to the Commissioners' concurrent jurisdiction with the High Court for certain purposes: see the Charities Act 1993 s 16; and paras 180, 182–183 ante, 271 post.

15 Redundant Churches and Other Religious Buildings Act 1969 s 4(6) (as substituted (see note 2 supra); and as amended (see note 4 supra)).

16 Ie under the Charities Act 1993 s 16(4): see para 180 ante.

17  Redundant Churches and Other Religious Buildings Act 1969 s 4(7) (as substituted (see note 2 supra); and as amended (see note 4 supra)).
18  Ibid s 5(1)(a) (s 5 substituted by the Charities Act 1992 s 49, Sch 5 para 2).
19  Redundant Churches and Other Religious Buildings Act 1969 s 5(1)(b) (as substituted: see note 18 supra).
20  Ibid s 5(1)(c) (as substituted: see note 18 supra).
21  Ibid s 5(1) (as substituted: see note 18 supra). If so provided by the scheme under which the agreement for the acquisition of any such premises is made, s 5(1) (as substituted) has effect in relation to the premises subject to and in accordance with any specified provisions of the scheme: s 5(2) (as so substituted).


**189. Schemes in relation to reserve forces charities.** Statutory provision is made for the treatment of charitable property held for purposes of any body of a reserve force which has been, or is to be, disbanded or amalgamated with another body[1].

A warrant of Her Majesty may designate[2] any unit of a reserve force[3] as the successor to any unit or other body of the same or any other reserve force which has been or is to be disbanded[4]. The Secretary of State[5] must send a copy of any such warrant to the Charity Commissioners[6], the Department of Health and Social Services for Northern Ireland, and a trustee of each charity[7] in England and Wales or Northern Ireland, or a person concerned in the management or control of each recognised body[8], affected by the warrant[9].

The effect of designating the successor to a disbanded unit is that on and after the day on which a warrant comes into force, any charitable property[10] which is held for the purposes of the disbanded unit in question is to be held for the corresponding purposes, or most nearly corresponding purposes, of the successor unit designated by the warrant[11]. If the Charity Commissioners consider that this effect[12] should not apply to all or any of the charitable property held for the purposes of a disbanded unit, they may make an order[13] providing that it does not apply or ceases to apply to that property or part[14]. If a charity affected by a warrant or any trustee of, or person interested in, such a charity considers that this effect[15] should not apply to all or any of the property held by the charity for the purposes of the disbanded unit in question, then the charity, trustee or person interested, as the case may be, may apply to the court[16] for an order providing that it will cease to apply to that property or part[17].

In any case where (1) the Secretary of State requests the Charity Commissioners to make provision with respect to any charitable property which is held for the purposes of a unit of a reserve force that has been or is to be disbanded[18]; or (2) an order is made as to the exclusion of charitable property from the effect of designation of a successor to the disbanded unit[19] the Commissioners may, notwithstanding the limit on jurisdiction to make schemes for the protection of charities[20], exercise such jurisdiction with respect to the property to which the request or order relates[21].

These provisions[22] do not apply to any property held by a charity for the purposes of a unit that has been or is to be disbanded if, under the terms on which the property is so held[23]: (a) any interest of the charity in the property is determined on the disbanding of that unit[24]; and (b) any other person or charity has an interest in the property contingent upon the determination of the interest of the charity[25].


1  See the Reserve Forces Act 1996 s 120. As to the succession to charitable property in relation to Scotland see s 120, Sch 5 Pt III paras 9–14 (amended by virtue of the Transfer of Functions (Lord Advocate and Secretary of State) Order 1999, SI 1999/678, art 2(1), Schedule). As to the succession to charitable property in relation to Northern Ireland see the Reserve Forces Act 1996 Sch 5 Pt IV paras 15–20. See also ROYAL FORCES.

2 'Warrant' means a warrant making such a designation: ibid Sch 5 para 2.

3 'Reserve forces' means the following forces: (1) the Royal Fleet Reserve, the Royal Naval Reserve and the Royal Marines Reserve; (2) the Army Reserve and the Territorial Army; and (3) the Air Force Reserve and the Royal Auxiliary Air Force: ibid s 1(2). Any reference in the Reserve Forces Act 1996 to a reserve force, to two or more of the reserve forces or to all the reserve forces is, unless the context otherwise requires, to be construed as a reference to the whole of the force, or of each force, concerned, including any transitional members: s 129, Sch 9 para 7(1). See ROYAL FORCES.

4 Ibid Sch 5 para 1(1). 'Disbanded unit' means a unit for which a successor is designated under Sch 5 para 1: Sch 5 para 2. References to disbandment of a body of a reserve force (however expressed) include references to its amalgamation with another unit or body: Sch 5 para 2.

5 As to the Secretary of State see para 513 post.

6 As to the Charity Commissioners see paras 486–512 post.

7 For the meaning of 'charity' see para 1 ante; definition applied by the Reserve Forces Act 1996 Sch 5 para 2.

8 'Recognised body' has the same meaning as in the Law Reform (Miscellaneous Provisions) (Scotland) Act 1990 Pt I: Reserve Forces Act 1996 Sch 5 para 2.

9 Ibid Sch 5 para 1(2) (amended by the Transfer of Functions (Lord Advocate and Secretary of State) Order 1999, SI 1999/678 art 5). A copy of such a warrant may be sent by post; and any such copy must be sent so as to arrive on or before the day on which the warrant comes into force and, in any event, not more than 14 days from the day on which the warrant is made: Reserve Forces Act 1996 Sch 5 para 1(3).

10 For these purposes, 'charitable property' means any property belonging to a charity: ibid Sch 5 para 3(2).

11 Ibid Sch 5 para 3(1). The same jurisdiction and powers are exercisable in relation to any charity owning property to which Sch 4 para 3(1) applies as would be exercisable if that were not a provision of an Act of Parliament regulating that charity: Sch 5 para 3(3).

12 Ie the effect of ibid Sch 5 para 3(1): see the text and notes 10–11 supra.

13 Any such order may be made at any time within the period of six months beginning with the day on which the warrant is made: ibid Sch 5 para 4(2).

14 Ibid Sch 5 para 4(1). Neither a warrant nor any order under Sch 5 para 4 or Sch 5 para 5 (see the text and notes 15–17 infra) affects the validity of anything done or omitted with respect to any property affected by the warrant or order before a copy of the warrant or order is received by a trustee of the charity in question: Sch 5 para 7.

15 See note 12 supra.

16 For meaning of 'the court' for these purposes see para 168 note 12 ante; definition applied by the Reserve Forces Act 1996 Sch 5 para 5(3).

17 Ibid Sch 5 para 5(1). Such an application (1) may be made at any time within the period of six months beginning with the day on which the warrant comes into force; and (2) is subject to the Charities Act 1993 s 33(2)–(5) (proceedings not to be begun without the consent of the Charity Commissioners or leave of a judge of the High Court) (see para 521 post), and for the purposes of s 33(5) an application for an order of the Commissioners authorising proceedings under the Reserve Forces Act 1996 Sch 5 para 5 is deemed to be refused if it is not granted during the period of one month beginning with the day on which the application is received by the Commissioners: Sch 5 para 5(2). See also note 14 supra.

18 Ibid Sch 5 para 6(a).

19 Ibid Sch 5 para 6(b). The reference in the text to an order is a reference to an order made under Sch 5 para 4 or Sch 5 para 5 (see the text and notes 12–17 supra) excluding any charitable property from the operation of Sch 5 para 3(1) (see the text and notes 10–11 supra): see Sch 5 para 6(b).

20 Ie under the Charities Act 1993 s 16(4): see para 180 ante.

21 Reserve Forces Act 1996 Sch 5 para 6.

22 Ie ibid Sch 5 paras 3–7: see the text and notes 10–21 supra.

23 Ibid Sch 5 para 8.

24 Ibid Sch 5 para 8(a).

25 Ibid Sch 5 para 8(b).

## (iv) Appeals

**190. Right of appeal from orders of Charity Commissioners.** Where the Charity Commissioners[1] by order exercise the same jurisdiction and powers as are exercisable by the High Court in charity proceedings[2], an appeal against any such order may be brought in the High Court by the Attorney General[3]. Such an appeal may also, at any time within three months beginning with the day following that on which the order is published[4], be brought in the High Court by the charity[5], or any of the charity trustees[6], or by any person removed[7] from any office or employment by the order[8]. Where an order of the Commissioners establishes a scheme for the administration of a charity, any person interested in the charity[9] has the like right of appeal as a charity trustee, and so have, in the case of a charity which is a local charity[10] in any area, any two or more inhabitants of the area and the council of any parish or, in Wales, any community comprising the area or any part of it[11].

In any case except that of an appeal by the Attorney General, no appeal may be brought except with a certificate of the Commissioners that it is a proper case for an appeal, or with the leave of one of the judges of the High Court attached to the Chancery Division[12].

1 As to the Charity Commissioners see paras 486–512 post.
2 Ie under the Charities Act 1993 s 16(1): see para 180 ante.
3 Ibid s 16(11).
4 As to the requirement of public notice see para 181 ante; and cf *Re Diptford Parish Lands* [1934] Ch 151.
5 For the meaning of 'charity' see para 1 ante.
6 For the meaning of 'charity trustees' see para 1 note 10 ante.
7 Ie unless he is removed with the concurrence of the charity trustees or with the approval of the special visitor, if any, of the charity: see the Charities Act 1993 s 16(12).
8 Ibid s 16(12).
9 As the meaning of 'person interested in a charity' see para 520 note 4 post.
10 For the meaning of 'local charity' see para 180 note 10 ante.
11 Charities Act 1993 s 16(14).
12 Ibid s 16(13). Requiring a certificate or leave applies equally to an appeal brought under s 16(12) and to one brought under s 16(14): *Childs v A-G* [1973] 2 All ER 108, [1973] 1 WLR 497 (on the corresponding provisions of the Charities Act 1960 (repealed)). As to the procedure on an appeal see para 549 post.

**191. When court will interfere with scheme.** Apart from cases in which, by reason of lapse of time and changed circumstances, the provisions of a scheme are no longer practicable[1], the court will only interfere with a scheme settled by the Charity Commissioners[2] where they have acted ultra vires or the scheme contains something wrong in principle[3].

1 As to the alteration of schemes settled by court in these circumstances see para 178 ante.
2 As to the Charity Commissioners see paras 486–512 post.
3 *Re Campden Charities* (1881) 18 ChD 310, CA; *Re Campden Charities (No 2)* (1883) 24 ChD 213; *Re Weir Hospital* [1910] 2 Ch 124 at 134, CA, per Cozens-Hardy MR. See also *Re Shaftoe's Charity* (1878) 3 App Cas 872, PC; *Re Sutton Coldfield Grammar School* (1881) 7 App Cas 91, PC; *Re Faraker, Faraker v Durell* [1912] 2 Ch 488, CA.

# (2) SCHEMES WHERE DONOR'S DIRECTIONS INADEQUATE

**192. Particular purpose not defined.** Where the mode of executing a charitable gift is originally undefined, it is impossible, of course, to select an object cy-près to that which has failed[1]. However, the donor's intention will be carried out as far as possible by the application of the gift to charitable objects to be nominated by the Crown, the court[2] or the Charity Commissioners[3], as the case may be.

1    *Barclay v Maskelyne* (1858) 4 Jur NS 1294 at 1297 per Wood V-C.
2    *White v White* (1778) 1 Bro CC 12; *Mills v Farmer* (1815) 1 Mer 55 at 96, 102 per Lord Eldon LC. As to the nomination of charitable objects by the Crown or the court see paras 457, 477 post. Whether the selection of objects is by the Crown or the court, the same principles apply: *Moggridge v Thackwell* (1803) 7 Ves 36 at 87 per Lord Eldon LC; *A-G v Wansay* (1808) 15 Ves 231 at 233 per Lord Eldon LC; *Re Slevin, Slevin v Hepburn* [1891] 2 Ch 236 at 243, CA, per Kay LJ.
3    See the Charities Act 1993 s 16; and paras 180, 182–183 ante, 271 post. As to the Charity Commissioners see paras 486–512 post.

**193. Indications of donor's intention.** In cases where no particular purpose is named by the donor any indications throwing light on the donor's intentions will be considered[1], for example his religious opinions[2], his interest in a particular locality[3], the nature of other charitable bequests in the same will[4], precatory directions in favour of a certain class[5], or even wishes expressed in an unattested codicil[6].

If no indication can be gathered as to his particular intention, the donor's general intention must be considered. Thus, a gift for the poor generally could not properly be applied for a purpose unconnected with the relief of poverty, such as the rebuilding of a church[7].

1    *Cook v Duckenfield* (1743) 2 Atk 562; *Ironmongers' Co v A-G* (1844) 10 Cl & Fin 908 at 922, 924–929, HL.
2    *Re Ashton's Charity* (1859) 27 Beav 115 at 120 per Romilly MR. See also *Ironmongers' Co v A-G* (1844) 10 Cl & Fin 908 at 922, 924–929, HL.
3    *Re Mann, Hardy v A-G* [1903] 1 Ch 232. A gift to 'the ward of Bread Street' was directed to be disposed of as the aldermen of the ward thought fit: *Baylis v A-G* (1741) 2 Atk 239.
4    *Mills v Farmer* (1815) 1 Mer 55 at 103, 722 per Lord Eldon LC; *Ironmongers' Co v A-G* (1844) 10 Cl & Fin 908, HL; *Lyons Corpn v Advocate-General of Bengal* (1876) 1 App Cas 91 at 114, PC.
5    Eg 'clergymen who have large families and good characters': *Moggridge v Thackwell* (1803) 7 Ves 36. See also *A-G v London Corpn* (1790) 3 Bro CC 171.
6    *A-G v Madden* (1843) 2 Con & Law 519.
7    *A-G v Peacock* (1676) Cas *temp* Finch 245.

**194. Court's discretion.** If no particular charitable purpose is indicated, and if the general charitable intention is subject to no restrictions, express or implied, the court's discretion in the application of the fund in what seems the most expedient manner is unlimited[1]. Thus, gifts for charity generally may be applied for the benefit of hospitals[2], schools[3] or other charitable institutions[4]; while bequests for the poor may be used for educational purposes[5], for the benefit of scholars at a particular school[6], for the testator's poor relations[7], or for poor foreign refugees of whom the testator himself had been one[8].

Similarly, where the name of the charity legatee is left blank, the gift is applied under a scheme[9].

1    *Philpott v St George's Hospital* (1859) 27 Beav 107; *Re Ashton's Charity* (1859) 27 Beav 115. See also *Mills v Farmer* (1815) 1 Mer 55.
2    *Legge v Asgill* (1818) 3 Hare 194n; affd Turn & R 265n.
3    *A-G v Syderfen* (1683) 1 Vern 224. See also *Pieschel v Paris* (1825) 2 Sim & St 384; *Re Campden Charities* (1881) 18 ChD 310, CA.
4    *Re Dickason* (1837) 3 Hare 195n.

5   *Bishop of Hereford v Adams* (1802) 7 Ves 324; *Wilkinson v Malin* (1832) 2 Cr & J 636; *A-G v Bovill* (1840) 1 Ph 762; *London School Board v Faulconer* (1878) 8 ChD 571. See, however, *Re Lambeth Charities* (1853) 22 LJCh 959; *A-G v Duke of Northumberland* (1889) 5 TLR 719, CA.

6   *A-G v Peacock* (1676) Cas *temp* Finch 245 (Christ's Hospital).

7   *Ware v A-G* (1824) 3 Hare 194n; contra *Sanford v Gibbons* (1829) 3 Hare 195n.

8   *A-G v Rance* (1728) cited in Amb 422.

9   *Pieschel v Paris* (1825) 2 Sim & St 384; *Re White, White v White* [1893] 2 Ch 41, CA; and see *Re Macduff, Macduff v Macduff* [1896] 2 Ch 451, CA.


**195. Failure of machinery for ascertaining objects.** A scheme will also be directed where the machinery for ascertaining the intended objects of a charitable trust breaks down, as where the bequest is for charitable and non-charitable purposes in shares to be determined by persons who fail to make the necessary apportionment[1], or where objects are intended to be, but are not, named by the donor[2] or others[3], or where a fund is to be divided among a particular class at the discretion of persons who fail to make the division[4].

1   *Doyley v A-G* (1735) 4 Vin Abr 485 pl 16; *Salusbury v Denton* (1857) 3 K & J 529.

2   *A-G v Syderfen* (1683) 1 Vern 224; *Mills v Farmer* (1815) 1 Mer 55; and see *Charitable Donations Comrs v Sullivan* (1841) 1 Dr & War 501.

3   *White v White* (1778) 1 Bro CC 12; *A-G v Boultbee* (1796) 3 Ves 220; *Moggridge v Thackwell* (1803) 7 Ves 36; *A-G v Fletcher* (1835) 5 LJCh 75; *Pocock v A-G* (1876) 3 ChD 342, CA; *Re Willis, Shaw v Willis* [1921] 1 Ch 44, CA.

4   *A-G v Gladstone* (1842) 13 Sim 7; and see *A-G v Wansay* (1808) 15 Ves 231; *Pease v Pattinson* (1886) 32 ChD 154.


**196. Continuing charitable trust.** Where a donor's intention was to establish a continuing charitable trust[1], the execution of which he committed to trustees other than an existing charitable institution engaged in that particular charitable purpose, or an officer or officers of such an institution[2], a scheme will generally be directed if the donor has not prescribed all the details of administration, even though such details are expressly confined to the trustees' discretion[3]. In a simple case a scheme may not be necessary[4]. The principle is that, wherever a permanent charitable trust was intended, the court will not part with a fund of which it has once obtained control without seeing that a proper trust is established[5].

1   A scheme is not usually directed where immediate distribution is authorised: see para 200 post.

2   See paras 171–172 ante.

3   *Wellbeloved v Jones* (1822) 1 Sim & St 40; *Sons of the Clergy Corpn v Mose* (1839) 9 Sim 610; *A-G v Stepney* (1804) 10 Ves 22; *Re Mann, Hardy v A-G* [1903] 1 Ch 232; *Re Webster, Pearson v Webster* [1912] 1 Ch 106; and see para 172 ante.

4   *Nash v Morley* (1842) 5 Beav 177 at 185 per Lord Langdale MR.

5   *Wellbeloved v Jones* (1822) 1 Sim & St 40.


**197. Institutions which cannot be identified.** If a gift is made to a named institution and the testator appears to have intended a particular institution to take, but it cannot be decided which of two or more existing institutions was intended, the gift will be applied by way of scheme[1], usually by being divided between the possible claimants[2].

1    As to schemes generally see para 170 et seq ante.
2    *Re Songest, Mayger v Forces Help Society and Lord Roberts' Workshops* [1956] 2 All ER 765, [1956] 1 WLR 897, CA; *Simon v Barber* (1829) 3 Hare 195n; *Bunting v Marriott* (1854) 19 Beav 163; *Re Hussey's Charities, Cheyne v Apreece, Symons v Delaval* (1861) 30 LJCh 491; and see the cases cited in the notes to para 151 ante. As to gifts to institutions which have never existed see para 149 ante.

**198.   Institutions which do not exist.** If a gift is made to an institution which has never existed or which has ceased to exist before the gift takes effect, but is made in such circumstances that the non-existence of the institution does not cause the gift to fail[1], a scheme[2] is necessary to apply the gift for the same purposes as those of the named institution[3].

1    For the considerations which govern the efficacy of a gift to such an institution see paras 141–142, 149, 161 ante.
2    As to schemes generally see para 170 et seq ante.
3    *Re Clergy Society* (1856) 2 K & J 615; *Re Davis, Hannen v Hillyer* [1902] 1 Ch 876; *Re Finger's Will Trusts, Turner v Ministry of Health* [1972] Ch 286, [1971] 3 All ER 1050, and the cases cited in the notes to para 141 ante. As to whether this is properly called a cy-près application see *Re Robinson, Besant v German Reich* [1931] 2 Ch 122 at 128–129 per Maugham J.

**199.   Failure of trustees.** A scheme[1] has been directed if the trustees died or, being an institution, ceased to exist, or refused to act, whether or not the trust authorised an immediate distribution[2]. Where the trustee appointed was appointed in the capacity of holder of an office which ceased to exist before the testator's death, the matter was referred to the master to approve a proper person to be trustee in place of that officer[3].

1    As to schemes generally see para 170 et seq ante.
2    *Moggridge v Thackwell* (1803) 7 Ves 36; *A-G v Gladstone* (1842) 13 Sim 7; *Reeve v A-G* (1843) 3 Hare 191; *A-G v Lawes* (1849) 8 Hare 32; *Re Stanes' Will, Re Trustee Relief Act* (1853) 21 LTOS 261; *Re Fraser, Yeates v Fraser* (1883) 22 ChD 827; *Re Wilson-Barkworth, Burstall v Deck* (1933) 50 TLR 82; and see para 195 note 3 ante.
3    *A-G v Stephens* (1834) 3 My & K 347.

**200.   Immediate distribution not requiring scheme.** A scheme[1] will not usually be directed where the donor has authorised an immediate distribution[2] or a distribution at intervals for a limited period[3] and the trustees are in existence and accept the trust[4].

1    As to schemes generally see para 170 et seq ante.
2    *Re Barnett* (1860) 29 LJCh 871.
3    *Waldo v Caley* (1809) 16 Ves 206; *Powerscourt v Powerscourt* (1824) 1 Mol 616; *Horde v Earl of Suffolk* (1833) 2 My & K 59.
4    For such cases in which a scheme has been directed see para 171 ante.

# (3) CY-PRÈS SCHEMES

## (i) In general

**201. The cy-près doctrine.** Where a clear charitable intention is expressed, it will not be permitted to fail because the mode, if specified, cannot be executed, but the law will substitute another mode cy-près[1], that is, as near as possible to the mode specified by the donor[2].

An application cy-près results from the exercise of the court's ordinary jurisdiction to administer a charitable trust of which the particular mode of application has not been defined by the donor[3]. Where he has in fact prescribed a particular mode of application and that mode is incapable of being performed, but he had a charitable intention which transcended the particular mode of application prescribed, the court, in the exercise of this jurisdiction, can carry out the charitable intention as though the particular direction had not been expressed at all[4].

However, where the particular mode of application prescribed by the donor was the essence of his intention, which may be shown by a condition[5] or by particularity of language[6], and that mode is incapable of being performed, there is nothing left upon which the court can found its jurisdiction, so that in such circumstances the court has no power to direct any other charitable application in place of that which has failed[7].

Where the particular mode of application does not exhaust a gift, these principles apply to the surplus[8].

There can be no question under English law of a cy-près application of property subject to trusts which are not charitable in law[9].

---

1   See *Moggridge v Thackwell* (1803) 7 Ves 36 at 69 per Lord Eldon LC (affd (1807) 13 Ves 416, HL); *Mills v Farmer* (1815) 1 Mer 55; *A-G v Bristol Corpn* (1820) 2 Jac & W 294 at 308 per Lord Eldon LC; *Chamberlayne v Brockett* (1872) 8 Ch App 206.

2   See the cases cited in note 1 supra. See also *A-G v Whitchurch* (1796) 3 Ves 141 at 144 per Arden MR; *Cary v Abbot* (1802) 7 Ves 490; *Clephane v Edinburgh Corpn* (1869) LR 1 Sc & Div 417 at 421, HL, per Lord Westbury; *Ironmongers' Co v A-G* (1844) 10 Cl & Fin 908 at 922, HL, per Lord Campbell; *Re Avenon's Charity, A-G v Pelly* (1912) 106 LT 295, reported on further consideration [1913] 2 Ch 261.

3   See paras 171, 192 ante.

4   *Re Wilson, Twentyman v Simpson* [1913] 1 Ch 314 at 321 per Parker J; and see *Re Monk, Giffen v Wedd* [1927] 2 Ch 197, CA. See also *Re JW Laing Trust, Steward's Co Ltd v A-G* [1984] Ch 143, [1984] 1 All ER 50 (obligation to distribute capital assets of trust fund within a certain time became inexpedient: scheme approved to remove obligation).

5   *Re Wilson, Twentyman v Simpson* [1913] 1 Ch 314.

6   *Re Good's Will Trusts, Oliver v Batten* [1950] 2 All ER 653.

7   *Re Good's Will Trusts, Oliver v Batten* [1950] 2 All ER 653.

8   See paras 123, 163 ante.

9   *A-G v Haberdashers' Co* (1834) 1 My & K 420; *Thomson v Shakespear* (1860) 1 De G F & J 399; *Carne v Long* (1860) 2 De G F & J 75; *Re Clark's Trust* (1875) 1 ChD 497; and see *Pease v Pattinson* (1886) 32 ChD 154.

---

**202. Cy-près and gifts to institutions.** In the case of a gift to a non-existent institution which does not lapse by reason of the non-existence of the institution[1], the court, having held that the donor's benevolence is not restricted to the named institution, gives effect to that benevolence by applying the gift for the purposes carried on by a defunct institution or, in the case of one which has never existed, for the purposes indicated by the donor so far as ascertainable. This may not necessarily be a cy-près application[2], but it sometimes appears to fall within the cy-près doctrine[3].

1 As to when such a gift does or does not lapse see paras 141–142, 160 ante.
2 See para 198 note 3 ante.
3 As to the cy-près doctrine see para 201 ante.

**203. What objects are cy-près.** The primary rule to be observed in the application of the cy-près doctrine is that the donor's intention must be observed as far as possible. Thus, if the donor names a particular object which is capable of taking effect, any application cy-près that becomes necessary must be restricted within the limits of that object[1], and the mode of application must as far as possible coincide with his wishes[2].

A charity may be cy-près to the original object even though it seems to have no trace of resemblance to it[3], if no other can be found which has a nearer connection[4]; but objects nearer the donor's intention will always be selected in preference to those more remote[5].

Objects already adequately provided for should not be chosen for the purpose of an application cy-près[6], nor should the application be made in such a way as merely to relieve the rates[7], taxes or other public funds.

Where a testator intends to benefit several charitable objects, one of which fails, the fund must not be distributed among the other objects if the one that fails bears no resemblance to the others[8].

When trusts have been altered by a scheme, and the trusts of the scheme become impossible so that a new cy-près scheme is required, the trusts of the new scheme must be as close as possible to the original trusts of the gift[9].

1 *Ironmongers' Co v A-G* (1844) 10 Cl & Fin 908 at 924, HL, per Lord Lyndhurst LC; *Clephane v Edinburgh Corpn* (1869) LR 1 Sc & Div 417 at 421, HL, per Lord Westbury; *Re Prison Charities* (1873) LR 16 Eq 129 at 146 per Bacon V-C.
2 See *Re Lambeth Charities* (1853) 22 LJCh 959; *A-G v Price* (1908) 24 TLR 761 at 763 per Swinfen Eady J (on appeal [1912] 1 Ch 667, CA; on further appeal sub nom *Price v A-G* [1914] AC 20, HL, discharging previous orders and substituting a new scheme by consent). Where a testatrix left property on trust for the foundation of an orphanage school, the establishment of a school where orphans were educated free and pupils who were not orphans were admitted upon payment of fees was held not to be contrary to the testatrix's intentions: *Re De Noailles, Clouston v Tufnell* (1916) 85 LJCh 807.
3 *A-G v Boultbee* (1794) 2 Ves 380 (affd (1796) 3 Ves 220); *Clephane v Edinburgh Corpn* (1869) LR 1 Sc & Div 417 at 421, HL, per Lord Westbury.
4 *A-G v Ironmongers' Co* (1841) Cr & Ph 208 at 227 per Lord Brougham; affd sub nom *Ironmongers' Co v A-G* (1844) 10 Cl & Fin 908, HL (but the will in that case was so phrased that the only proper application of the fund whose objects had failed was to one of the other purposes benefited under the same will).
5 See *Re Bridewell Hospital* (1860) 30 LJCh 99; *Re Prison Charities* (1873) LR 16 Eq 129; *A-G v Duke of Northumberland* (1889) 5 TLR 237; varied on appeal 5 TLR 719, CA. It is submitted that the dictum of Cozens-Hardy MR in *Re Weir Hospital* [1910] 2 Ch 124 at 132, CA, that, wherever the cy-près doctrine has to be applied, the court may consider the comparative advantages of various charitable objects and adopt, by the scheme, the one which seems most beneficial, was intended to apply only to charitable objects equally near to the testator's intention.
6 *Re Prison Charities* (1873) LR 16 Eq 129.
7 *Re Prison Charities* (1873) LR 16 Eq 129; *Re Poplar and Blackwall Free School* (1878) 8 ChD 543; *A-G v Duke of Northumberland* (1889) 5 TLR 237; varied on appeal 5 TLR 719, CA.

8   *Ironmongers' Co v A-G* (1844) 10 Cl & Fin 908 at 927, HL, per Lord Lyndhurst LC (though see note 4
    supra); and see *Lyons Corpn v Advocate-General of Bengal* (1876) 1 App Cas 91, PC.
9   *Re Lambeth Charities* (1853) 22 LJCh 959.

**204. No application cy-près without a scheme.** However desirable it may be, in
no circumstances can trustees of a charity apply the trust funds cy-près on their own
initiative, without the direction of the court or of the Charity Commissioners[1]. The
Commissioners may make interim orders in lieu of a cy-près scheme for a limited
period[2]. Where the case permits and requires the property or some part of it to be applied
cy-près, a trust for charitable purposes[3] places a trustee under a duty to secure its effective
use for charity[4] by taking steps to enable it to be so applied[5].

1   *A-G v Coopers' Co* (1812) 19 Ves 187; *A-G v Vivian* (1826) 1 Russ 226; *A-G v Kell* (1840) 2 Beav 575;
    *A-G v Bushby* (1857) 24 Beav 299; *Ward v Hipwell* (1862) 3 Giff 547; *Re Campden Charities* (1881) 18
    ChD 310 at 328–329, CA, per Jessel MR; *Cross v Lloyd-Greame* (1909) 102 LT 163; and see *Re Weir
    Hospital* [1910] 2 Ch 124 at 133, CA, per Cozens-Hardy MR. See also paras 138 ante, 304 post. As to
    the Charity Commissioners see paras 486–512 post.
2   See the Charities Act 1993 s 17(8); and para 185 ante.
3   For the meaning of 'charitable purposes' see para 1 ante.
4   For the meaning of 'charity' see para 1 ante.
5   Charities Act 1993 s 13(5). This provision is declaratory.

## (ii) When Property may be applied Cy-près

**205. Failure of stated charitable objects.** Before the Charities Act 1960 came into
force no property could be applied cy-près unless it was clearly established that the
donor's directions could not be carried into effect at all[1]. The specified purpose might be
impracticable or impossible[2] for a number of reasons, such as that it had already been
fulfilled[3], or that its objects had ceased to exist[4], or that insufficient money was available[5].
The purpose might be an illegal mode of achieving a lawful purpose[6], or the gift might
be dependent on named trustees accepting the trust[7], or might be connected with
another gift which was void[8]. Alternatively the property available might be more than
could be used for the specified purpose[9].

   The question of a cy-près application may also arise in connection with gifts to
charitable institutions, as where the named institution has never existed[10], or has ceased
to exist before the gift takes effect[11].

1   *A-G v Boultbee* (1794) 2 Ves 380 at 387 per Arden MR (affd (1796) 3 Ves 220); *Re Weir Hospital* [1910]
    2 Ch 124, CA.
2   As to impracticable gifts see para 154 ante.
3   *Bunting v Marriott* (1854) 19 Beav 163; and see para 154 note 1 ante.
4   *A-G v London Corpn* (1790) 3 Bro CC 171; and see para 154 note 5 ante.
5   *Cherry v Mott* (1836) 1 My & Cr 123; and see para 154 note 7 ante.
6   *A-G v Vint* (1850) 3 De G & Sm 704. As to where gifts are to be applied in an illegal manner see para
    153 ante.
7   *Re Lysaght, Hill v Royal College of Surgeons* [1966] Ch 191, [1965] 2 All ER 888; and see para 155 ante.
    See also para 206 note 3 post.
8   *A-G v Whitchurch* (1796) 3 Ves 141; and see para 162 ante.
9   *Re King, Kerr v Bradley* [1923] 1 Ch 243; and see para 156 ante.

10  *Re Davis, Hannen v Hillyer* [1902] 1 Ch 876; and see para 149 ante.
11  *Re Finger's Will Trusts, Turner v Ministry of Health* [1972] Ch 286, [1971] 3 All ER 1050; and see para 141 ante. As to whether in the case of gifts to institutions the application is always correctly described as a cy-près application see para 198 note 3 ante.


**206. Statutory conditions for cy-près application.** The Charities Act 1993 specifies the circumstances in which the original purposes[1] of a charitable gift can be altered to allow the property given or part of it to be applied cy-près[2]. They are as follows:

(1)  where the original purposes, in whole or in part: (a) have been, as far as may be, fulfilled[3]; or (b) cannot be carried out, or cannot be carried out according to the directions given and to the spirit of the gift[4];

(2)  where the original purposes provide a use for part only of the property available by virtue of the gift[5];

(3)  where the property available by virtue of the gift and other property applicable for similar purposes can be more effectively used in conjunction, and to that end can suitably be made applicable to common purposes, regard being had to the spirit of the gift[6];

(4)  where the original purposes were laid down by reference to an area which then was, but has since ceased to be, a unit for some other purpose, or by reference to a class of persons or to an area which has for any reason ceased to be suitable, regard being had to the spirit of the gift, or to be practical in administering the gift[7];

(5)  where the original purposes, in whole or in part, have, since they were laid down: (a) been adequately provided for by other means[8]; or (b) ceased, as being useless or harmful to the community or for other reasons, to be in law charitable[9]; or (c) ceased in any other way to provide a suitable and effective method of using the property available by virtue of the gift, regard being had to the spirit of the gift[10].

These statutory conditions appear to supersede completely the old law on failure of stated objects as an occasion for a cy-près application[11].

If the above requirements are not satisfied the court has no jurisdiction to alter the terms of a charitable gift[12].

1  Where the application of the property given has been altered or regulated by a scheme or otherwise, references to the original purposes of a gift are to be construed as referring to the purposes for which the property is for the time being applicable: Charities Act 1993 s 13(3). See also *Re JW Laing Trust, Steward's Co Ltd v A-G* [1984] Ch 143, [1984] 1 All ER 50 (clause relating to distribution of capital assets within a certain time not an original purpose under what is now the Charities Act 1993 s 13).

2  Charities Act 1993 s 13(1). The section only affects the conditions which must be satisfied in so far as they require a failure of the original purposes: see s 13(2); and para 207 post.

3  Ibid s 13(1)(a)(i). The cases on impossibility and impracticability (see para 154 ante) are included within these categories.

4  Ibid s 13(1)(a)(ii). 'The spirit of the gift' means the basic intention underlying the gift, that intention being ascertainable from the terms of the relevant instrument read in the light of admissible evidence: see *Re Lepton's Charity, Ambler v Thomas* [1972] Ch 276 at 285 per Pennycuick V-C, sub nom *Re Lepton's Will Trusts, Re Lepton's Charity, Ambler v Thomas* [1971] 1 All ER 799 at 803 per Pennycuick V-C. Under the old law (see para 205 ante) it was only the letter of the gift that could be considered.

*Re Lysaght, Hill v Royal College of Surgeons* [1966] Ch 191, [1965] 3 All ER 888, appears to fall within the Charities Act 1993 s 13(1)(a)(ii), although the statutory provision from which it is derived is not mentioned in the report, the argument having centred on whether there was any form of general charitable intention.

5    Ibid s 13(1)(b). This comprises the cases on surplus capital and income: see paras 123 et seq, 156 ante.

6    Ibid s 13(1)(c).

7    Ibid s 13(1)(d); applied in *Peggs v Lamb* [1994] Ch 172, [1994] 2 All ER 15. Cf the power to make schemes enlarging the area of local charities under the Charities Act 1993 s 13(4) (see para 209 post), and the provisions as to dissolution and alteration of parishes (see para 242 post). See also *Richmond Corpn v A-G* [1965] RA 117; on appeal sub nom *Re Richmond Parish Charity Lands* [1965] RA 343, CA.

8    Charities Act 1993 s 13(1)(e)(i).

9    Ibid s 13(1)(e)(ii). Cf *National Anti-Vivisection Society v IRC* [1948] AC 31, [1947] 2 All ER 217, HL.

10   Charities Act 1993 s 13(1)(e)(iii). In *Re Lepton's Charity, Ambler v Thomas* [1972] Ch 276, sub nom *Re Lepton's Will Trusts, Re Lepton's Charity, Ambler v Thomas* [1971] 1 All ER 799, a testator gave £3 a year out of a fund to a minister and the residue (originally £2 a year) to the poor; since his death the income had risen so that the poor received almost £800. The 'original purposes' of the gift were held to refer to the gift as a whole, and not to the two parts of the gift separately. As to the meaning of 'the spirit of the gift' see note 4 supra. See also *Re Royal Kilmainham Hospital* [1966] IR 451 (decided under similar Republic of Ireland legislation); *Varsani v Jesani* [1999] Ch 219, [1998] 3 All ER 273, CA (charity established to promote interests of religious sect which later split into two factions).

11   See para 205 ante.

12   See *Re Weir Hospital* [1910] 2 Ch 124, CA; *Oldham Borough Council v A-G* [1993] Ch 210, [1993] 2 All ER 432, CA. As to alteration of trusts see para 138 ante.

**207. Necessity for general charitable intention.** On an initial failure[1] of the stated objects of a charitable gift, the property may only be applied cy-près if the donor had a general charitable intention[2] or, in the case of a surplus, if the donor intended to devote to charity the whole of the property given[3]. Where the failure occurs after the gift has once taken effect, the property will be applied cy-près unless the gift was expressly limited to the particular purpose which has failed[4]. The statutory conditions for cy-près applications[5] do not dispense with the necessity for considering these factors[6].

1    As to what constitutes initial failure see para 158 et seq ante. As to the failure of stated charitable objects generally see para 205 ante.

2    As to general charitable intention see paras 159–163 ante.

3    See para 163 ante.

4    As to what constitutes subsequent failure see paras 164–165 ante.

5    See para 206 ante.

6    See the Charities Act 1993 s 13(2); and *Re JW Laing Trust, Steward's Co Ltd v A-G* [1984] Ch 143, [1984] 1 All ER 50; *Oldham Borough Council v A-G* (1992) Times, 13 April (revsd [1993] Ch 210, [1993] 2 All ER 432, CA); cf *Re Lysaght, Hill v Royal College of Surgeons* [1966] Ch 191, [1965] 3 All ER 888.

**208. Property of unidentifiable or disclaiming donors.** Under the law as it stood before the Charities Act 1960, property given for a specific charitable purpose was not necessarily applicable cy-près if that purpose was or became impracticable, unless a general charitable intention could be shown[1]. Now, however, such property may be applied cy-près as if given for charitable purposes generally, where it belongs to a donor who cannot be found or identified after the prescribed advertisements and inquiries have been published and made and the prescribed period beginning with the publication of those advertisements has expired; or where it belongs to a donor who has executed a disclaimer in the prescribed form of his right to have the property returned[2].

1   See eg *Re Hillier, Hillier v A-G* [1954] 2 All ER 59, [1954] 1 WLR 700, CA; and paras 166–169 ante.

2   See the Charities Act 1993 s 14 (which derives from the Charities Act 1960 s 14 (as amended) (now repealed); and paras 167–168 ante. In certain cases, advertisements and inquiries are unnecessary (see the Charities Act 1993 s 14(3)) or may be dispensed with by the court (see s 14(4)). The scheme must specify the amount of any property applied as belonging to donors who cannot be identified or found otherwise than under s 14(3) or (4), and may make provision for meeting any claim by any such donor: see s 14(5). Schemes have been made by virtue of these provisions in a number of cases: see the *Report of the Charity Commissioners for England and Wales for 1965* (HC Paper (1966–67) no 108) p 8; *Report of the Charity Commissioners for England and Wales for 1969* (HC Paper (1969–70) no 276) p 20.

# (4) SCHEMES EXTENDING AREA OF LOCAL CHARITIES

**209. Schemes extending area of local charities.** Where property is held for charitable purposes which are laid down by reference to one of certain types of area, the court[1] may by scheme made under the court's jurisdiction with respect to charities[2], provide for enlarging the area to another specified area[3].

This power is without prejudice to the court's powers to make true cy-près schemes in similar cases[4].

1   For the meaning of 'the court' see para 168 note 12 ante.

2   As to the court's jurisdiction with respect to charities see para 477 et seq post.

3   Charities Act 1993 s 13(4). This provision is expressed to be without prejudice to s 13(1) (see para 206 ante): s 13(4).

   Where the existing area is Greater London, the permissible enlargement is any area comprising Greater London: s 13(4), Sch 3 para 1.

   Where the existing area is any area in Greater London and not in, or partly in, the City of London the permissible enlargements are: (1) any area in Greater London and not in, or partly in the City of London; (2) the area of Greater London, exclusive of the City of London; (3) any area comprising the area of Greater London, exclusive of the City of London; (4) any area partly in Greater London and partly in any adjacent parish or parishes (civil or ecclesiastical) and not partly in the City of London: Sch 3 para 2.

   Where the existing area is a district, the permissible enlargement is any area comprising the district: Sch 3 para 3.

   Where the existing area is a Welsh county or county borough the permissible enlargement is any area comprising that county or county borough: Sch 3 para 3A (added by the Local Government (Wales) Act 1994 s 66(6), Sch 16 para 101(5), (6)).

   Where the existing area is any area in a district, the permissible enlargement is: (a) any area in the district; (b) the district; (c) any area comprising the district; (d) any area partly in the district and partly in any adjacent district: Charities Act 1993 Sch 3 para 4 (amended by the Local Government (Wales) Act 1994 Sch 16 para 101(6)).

   Where the existing area is any area in a Welsh county or county borough, the permissible enlargements are: (i) any area in the county or county borough; (ii) the county or county borough; (iii) any area comprising the county or county borough; (iv) any area partly in the county or county borough and partly in any adjacent Welsh county or county borough or in any adjacent district: Charities Act 1993 Sch 3 para 4A (added by the Local Government (Wales) Act 1994 Sch 16 para 101(5), (6)).

   Where the existing area is a parish (civil or ecclesiastical), or two or more parishes, or an area in a parish, or partly in each of two or more parishes, the permissible enlargement is any area not extending beyond the parish or parishes comprising or adjacent to the existing area: Charities Act 1993 Sch 3 para 5.

   In Wales, where the exiting area is a community, or two or more communities, or an area in a community, or partly in each of two or more communities, the permissible enlargement is any area not extending beyond the community or communities comprising or adjacent to the existing area: Sch 3 para 6.

   As to areas and authorities in England and Wales see LOCAL GOVERNMENT.

4   Ibid s 13(4). For the conditions in which cy-près schemes may be made see para 207 ante. Note also the provisions as to alteration or dissolution of parishes (as to which see para 242 post).

## (5) SPECIAL PROVISIONS FOR SMALL CHARITIES

**210. Small charities: power to transfer property.** The Charities Act 1993 makes provision for a small charity to transfer its property[1]. For a charity to fall within this provision, its gross income[2] in its last financial year[3] must not have exceeded £5,000[4], and the charity must not hold any land on trusts[5] which stipulate that the land is to be used for the purposes, or any particular purposes, of the charity[6]. The provisions do not apply to either an exempt charity[7] or a charitable company[8].

The charity trustees[9] of a charity which comes within these provisions may resolve[10] that all the property of the charity should be transferred to such other charity[11], or be divided between two or more other charities[12], as is or are specified in the resolution[13]. Each charity specified must be either a registered charity or one not required to be registered[14]. Such a resolution can be passed only if the trustees are satisfied that the existing purposes of the charity have ceased to be conducive to a suitable or effective application of the charity's resources, and that the purposes of the charity or charities specified in the resolution are as similar in character to the purposes of the transferor charity as is reasonably practicable[15]. Further, before passing any such resolution the charity trustees must have received from the charity trustees of the specified transferee charity, or each of them if more than one, written confirmation that they are willing to accept a transfer of the property[16].

Where any one of the resolutions mentioned above has been passed by the charity trustees, they must give public notice of the resolution in such manner as they think reasonable in the circumstances, and send a copy to the Charity Commissioners[17] together with a statement of their reasons for passing it[18]. When considering the resolution, the Commissioners may require the charity trustees to provide additional information or explanation as to the circumstances in and by reference to which they determined to act, or relating to their compliance with the statutory[19] requirements[20]. Further, they must take into account any representations made to them within the specified period[21] by persons appearing to them to be interested in the charity[22].

Within three months of receiving a copy of a resolution complying with the statutory requirements the Commissioners must notify the trustees in writing that they either do, or do not, concur with the resolution[23]. Where the Commissioners notify their concurrence with the resolution, the charity trustees must arrange for the charity property to be transferred in accordance with the resolution and on terms that the property so transferred will be held and applied by the transferee charity for the purposes of that charity, but will, as property of the transferee charity, nevertheless be subject to any restrictions on expenditure to which it was subject as property of the transferor charity[24].

1   See the Charities Act 1993 s 74: and the text and notes 2–23 infra.
2   'Gross income', in relation to a charity, means its gross recorded income from all sources, including special trusts: ibid s 97(1). 'Special trust' means property which is held and administered by or on behalf of a charity for any special purposes of the charity, and is so held and administered on separate trusts relating only to that property but a special trust does not, by itself, constitute a charity for the purposes of Pt VI (ss 41–49): s 97(1). For the meaning of 'charity' see para 1 ante.
3   'Financial year' is to be construed, in relation to a charity which is a company, in accordance with the Companies Act 1985 s 223 (as substituted) (see COMPANIES vol 7(2) (1996 Reissue) para 806), and, in relation to any other charity, in accordance with regulations made under the Charities Act 1993 s 42(2) (see the Charities (Accounts and Reports) Regulations 1995, SI 1995/2724, reg 5; and para 309 note 4

post): Charities Act 1993 s 97(1). Prior to the coming into force of the Charities (Accounts and Reports) Regulations 1995, SI 1995/2724, transitional provisions provided for the definition of 'financial year': see the Charities Act 1993 s 99(4), Sch 8 Pt II.

4   The Secretary of State may by order amend ibid s 74(1) by substituting a different sum for the sum for the time being specified there: s 74(11). At the date at which this volume states the law no such order had been made. As to the Secretary of State see para 513 post. As to the making of orders generally see s 86 (as amended); and para 517 post.

5   'Trusts', in relation to a charity, means the provisions establishing it as a charity and regulating its purposes and administration, whether those provisions take effect by way of trust or not, and in relation to other institutions has a corresponding meaning: ibid s 97(1).

6   Ibid s 74(1).

7   As to exempt charities see para 293 post.

8   Charities Act 1993 s 74(1). For these purposes, 'charitable company' means a charity which is a company or other body corporate: s 74(12)(a). For the meaning of 'company' see para 216 post.

9   For the meaning of 'charity trustees' see para 1 note 10 ante.

10  Any resolution must be passed by a majority of not less than two-thirds of the charity trustees voting on the resolution: Charities Act 1993 s 74(3).

11  For these purposes, references to the transfer of property to a charity are references to its transfer to the charity trustees, or to any trustee for the charity, or to a person nominated by the charity trustees to hold it in trust for the charity, as the charity trustees may determine: ibid s 74(12)(b).

12  Ie in such manner as is specified in the resolution: ibid s 74(2)(b).

13  Ibid s 74(2)(a), (b). Such a transfer of any property does not operate as a breach of any covenant or condition against alienation or give rise to a forfeiture: see para 180 note 6 ante.

14  Ibid s 74(2)(a), (b). As to the register see para 282 et seq post.

15  Ibid s 74(4).

16  Ibid s 74(4).

17  As to the Charity Commissioners see paras 486–512 post.

18  Charities Act 1993 s 74(6).

19  Ie those under ibid s 74.

20  Ibid s 74(7).

21  Ie six weeks beginning with the date when the Commissioners received a copy of the resolution: ibid s 74(7).

22  Ibid s 74(7). As to who is a person interested in a charity see para 520 post.

23  Ibid s 74(8).

24  Ibid s 74(9)(a). The Commissioners have power, at the request of the charity trustees, to make orders vesting any property of the transferor charity in the charity trustees of the transferee charity or in any trustee for that charity, or in any other person nominated by those charity trustees to hold the property in trusts: s 74(10).

**211. Small charities: power to modify objects.** A charity which has power to transfer its property[1] has power to modify its objects. First, the charity trustees[2] may resolve[3] that the trusts of the charity[4] should be modified by replacing all or any of the purposes of the charity with such other charitable purposes[5] as are specified in the resolution[6]. Such a resolution can be passed only where the charity trustees are satisfied that the existing purposes of the charity, or such of them as it is proposed to replace, have ceased to be conducive to a suitable and effective application of the charity's resources, and that the purposes specified in the resolution are as similar in character to those existing purposes as is practical in the circumstances[7].

Secondly, the charity trustees may resolve[8] that any provision of the trusts of the charity relating to any of the powers exercisable by the charity trustees in the administration of the charity, or regulating the procedure to be followed in any respect in connection with its administration, should be modified in the manner specified in the resolution[9].

The procedure, if a resolution is passed, is exactly the same as in the case of a resolution to transfer the charity property[10], and if the Charity Commissioners[11] concur with the resolutions the trusts of the charity are deemed to have been modified in accordance with the terms of the resolution as from the date specified in the notification[12].

1   Ie one falling within the Charities Act 1993 s 74(1): see para 210 ante.
2   For the meaning of 'charity trustees' see para 1 note 10 ante.
3   Any resolution must be passed by a majority of not less than two-thirds of the charity trustees voting on the resolution: Charities Act 1993 s 74(3).
4   For the meaning of 'charity' see para 1 ante.
5   For the meaning of 'charitable purposes' see para 1 ante.
6   Charities Act 1993 s 74(2)(c).
7   Ibid s 74(5).
8   See note 3 supra.
9   Charities Act 1993 s 74(2)(d).
10  See ibid s 74(6)–(9); and para 210 ante.
11  As to the Charity Commissioners see paras 486–512 post.
12  Charities Act 1993 s 74(9)(b).

**212. Very small charities: power to spend capital.** The Charities Act 1993 makes provision for a very small charity to spend its capital[1]. For a charity[2] to fall within this provision, its gross income[3] in its last financial year[4] must not have exceeded £1,000[5], and it must have a permanent endowment[6] which does not consist of or comprise any land[7]. This provision does not apply to either an exempt charity[8] or a charitable company[9].

Where they are of the opinion that the property of the charity is too small, in relation to its purposes, for any useful purpose to be achieved by the expenditure of income alone, the charity trustees[10] of a charity which comes within this provision may resolve[11] that the charity ought to be freed from the restrictions with respect to expenditure of capital to which its permanent endowment is subject[12]. Before passing such a resolution the charity trustees must consider whether any reasonable possibility exists of effecting a transfer or division of all the charity's property[13] to another charity or charities[14]. Where the charity trustees have passed such a resolution, they must give public notice of the resolution in such manner as they think reasonable in the circumstances, and send a copy to the Charity Commissioners[15] together with a statement of their reasons for passing it[16].

When considering the resolution, the Commissioners may require the charity trustees to provide additional information or explanation as to the circumstances in or by reference to which they determined to act, or relating to their compliance with the statutory[17] requirements[18]. Further, they must take into account any representations made to them within the specified period[19] by persons appearing to them to be interested in the charity[20]. Within three months of receiving a copy of the resolution complying with the statutory requirements, the Commissioners must notify the trustees in writing that they either do, or do not, concur with the resolution[21]. Where the Commissioners notify their concurrence with the resolution, the charity trustees have, as from the date specified in the notification, power to expend any of the property of the charity without regard to any restrictions with respect to expenditure of capital to which its permanent endowment is subject[22].

1   See the Charities Act 1993 s 75.
2   For the meaning of 'charity' see para 1 ante.
3   For the meaning of 'gross income' see para 210 note 2 ante.

4 For the meaning of 'financial year' see paras 210 note 3 ante, 309 note 4 post.

5 The Secretary of State may by order amend the Charities Act 1993 s 75(1) by substituting a different sum for the sum for the time being specified there: s 75(9). At the date at which this volume states the law no such order had been made. As to the Secretary of State see para 513 post. As to the making of orders generally see s 86 (as amended); and para 517 post.

6 For the meaning of 'permanent endowment' see para 283 note 3 post.

7 Charities Act 1993 s 75(1).

8 As to exempt charities see para 293 post.

9 Charities Act 1993 s 75(1). For these purposes, 'charitable company' means a charity which is a company or other body corporate: s 75(10). For the meaning of 'company' see para 216 post.

10 For the meaning of 'charity trustees' see para 1 note 10 ante.

11 Any resolution must be passed by a majority of not less than two-thirds of the charity trustees voting on the resolution: Charities Act 1993 s 75(3).

12 Ibid s 75(2).

13 Ie under ibid s 74: see paras 210–211 ante.

14 Ibid s 75(4). The trustees must disregard any transfer or division which would impose on the charity an unacceptable burden of costs: s 75(4).

15 As to the Charity Commissioners see paras 486–512 post.

16 Charities Act 1993 s 75(5).

17 Ie those under ibid s 75.

18 Ibid s 75(6)(a), (b).

19 Ie six weeks beginning with the date when the Commissioners received a copy of the resolution: ibid s 75(6).

20 Ibid s 75(6).

21 Ibid s 75(7).

22 Ibid s 75(8).

# 5.  CHARITABLE CORPORATIONS

## (1)  WHAT CORPORATIONS ARE CHARITABLE
## CORPORATIONS

**213.  Meaning of 'charitable corporation' and 'eleemosynary corporation'.** A charitable corporation is one whose corporate purpose is charitable. An eleemosynary corporation is a corporation established for the perpetual distribution of the free alms or bounty of the founder[1].

---

1   1 Bl Com 459; 1 Kyd on Corporations 25; Shelford's Law of Mortmain 23; and see para 230 post. See also the definition of a charity for the purposes of the Charities Act 1993 in s 96(1): para 1 ante. Corporations which are wholly ecclesiastical are taken out of that definition by s 96(2) (as amended) (see para 187 ante). As to what are eleemosynary charities see *Re Armitage, Ellam v Norwich Corpn* [1972] Ch 438, sub nom *Re Armitage's Will Trusts* [1972] 1 All ER 708. As to the different classes of corporation, and as to the powers of corporations generally, see CORPORATIONS. As to the incorporation of charity trustees see para 236 post.

**214.  Colleges and hospitals.** The two principal kinds of charitable corporations used to be hospitals and colleges, the former being created for the maintenance and relief of the poor and impotent, and the latter for the promotion of learning and the support of persons engaged in literary pursuits[1].

Colleges and hospitals, in the strict legal sense of the latter term, are both institutions where the persons benefited by the charity are themselves incorporated[2]. The colleges of Oxford and Cambridge are eleemosynary corporations[3], but the halls are not[4]. The universities of Oxford and Cambridge are civil and not eleemosynary corporations[5]. More modern universities have been founded by royal charter and are eleemosynary corporations[6].

In other than the strict legal sense[7], however, the expression 'hospital' has been used to denote various kinds of corporate institutions[8] for the relief of the poor or infirm, such as corporations where the estate of inheritance only is vested in the master or warden[9], or hospitals managed by an incorporated body of governors or trustees[10].

Hospitals for the sick did not cease to be charities merely because of the coming into effect of the National Health Service Act 1946[11]; and the chartered corporation of a hospital was not automatically dissolved thereby[12], but the Minister of Health was given power to dissolve the original corporation of a hospital which had been nationalised[13].

---

1   1 Kyd on Corporations 25; *Philips v Bury* (1694) Skin 447 at 484, HL.
2   Shelford's Law of Mortmain (1836) 24; *Philips v Bury* (1694) Skin 447 at 484, HL ('if in an hospital the master and poor are incorporated, it is a college, having a common seal to act by, although it hath not the name of a college'). See also *A-G v Wyggeston's Hospital* (1853) 16 Beav 313; *A-G v St Cross Hospital* (1853) 17 Beav 435; *A-G v St John's Hospital, Bedford* (1865) 2 De GJ & Sm 621; *Sutton's Hospital Case* (1612) 10 Co Rep 1a at 23a, 31a, Ex Ch; *Lord Colchester v Kewney* (1866) 35 LJ Ex 204 at 206 per Channell B (affd (1867) LR 2 Exch 253).
3   *R v Vice-Chancellor of Cambridge* (1765) 3 Burr 1647 at 1652, 1656 per Lord Aston CJ; and see *Parkinson's Case* (1689) Carth 92 at 93 per Lord King LC; *Anon* (1698) 12 Mod Rep 232; *Philips v Bury* (1694) Skin 447 at 494, HL; *Patel v University of Bradford Senate* [1978] 3 All ER 841, [1978] 1 WLR 1488 (affd [1979]

2 All ER 582, [1979] 1 WLR 1066, CA). As to the meaning of 'eleemosynary corporation' see para 213 ante.

4   *R v Hertford College* (1878) 3 QBD 693 at 694, CA, per Lord Coleridge CJ.

5   *R v Vice-Chancellor of Cambridge* (1765) 3 Burr 1647; *Patel v University of Bradford Senate* [1978] 3 All ER 841, [1978] 1 WLR 1488 (affd [1979] 2 All ER 582, [1979] 1 WLR 1066, CA); Shelford's Law of Mortmain 25.

6   The charters normally, probably always, provide that inter alios, the members of the academic staff and all the undergraduates are members of the university: see *Patel v University of Bradford Senate* [1978] 3 All ER 841, [1978] 1 WLR 1488 (affd [1979] 2 All ER 582, [1979] 1 WLR 1066, CA).

7   See *Sutton's Hospital Case* (1612) 10 Co Rep 1a at 31a; Shelford's Law of Mortmain 24.

8   *Moses v Marsland* [1901] 1 KB 668, DC; and see *Dean and Chapter of York v Middleborough* (1828) 2 Y & J 196 at 216 per Alexander LCB.

9   Co Litt 342a; Shelford's Law of Mortmain 24.

10   There were formerly many hospitals of this kind. The Charterhouse and Sutton's Hospital are ancient examples of this class (see *Sutton's Hospital Case* (1612) 10 Co Rep 1a). The word 'hospital' is, of course, used also in reference to unincorporated institutions or hospitals managed by unincorporated bodies of governors or trustees. Some modern hospitals are of this latter kind, especially those which have no endowment and are supported by voluntary subscriptions. For a discussion of the various meanings of the word 'hospital' see *Trustees of the Mary Clark Home v Anderson* [1904] 2 KB 645 at 653 per Channell J. As to hospitals see further NATIONAL HEALTH SERVICE.

11   *Re Frere, Kidd v Farnham Group Hospital Management Committee* [1951] Ch 27, [1950] 2 All ER 513. As to the history of the national health legislation see NATIONAL HEALTH SERVICE vol 33 (Reissue) para 3 et seq. As to the effect of nationalisation on gifts to hospitals see para 147 ante.

12   *Re Kellner's Will Trusts, Blundell v Royal Cancer Hospital* [1950] Ch 46, [1949] 2 All ER 774, CA.

13   See the National Health Service Act 1977 s 129, Sch 14 para 6; and NATIONAL HEALTH SERVICE.

**215. Hospitals supported partly by fees.** Not all hospitals are charitable institutions[1], some hospitals are managed commercially[2], with a view to the profit of private individuals, and there are hospitals the services of which are not available to a sufficient section of the public[3]. However, the mere fact that a hospital is supported by the payment of fees does not prevent its being a charitable corporation[4], and the same is true of schools[5]. Furthermore, the Charity Commissioners have power to authorise the committee of management of a voluntary hospital to provide facilities for paying patients in certain circumstances[6].

1   See *Re Smith's Will Trusts, Barclays Bank Ltd v Mercantile Bank Ltd* [1962] 2 All ER 563, [1962] 1 WLR 763, CA (revsg [1961] 3 All ER 824, [1961] 1 WLR 1387); *Re Resch's Will Trusts, Le Cras v Perpetual Trustee Co Ltd* [1969] 1 AC 514, [1967] 3 All ER 915, PC.

2   *Re Resch's Will Trusts, Le Cras v Perpetual Trustee Co Ltd* [1969] 1 AC 514 at 540, [1967] 3 All ER 915 at 921, PC.

3   As to the requirement of benefit to a sufficient section of the community see para 8 ante.

4   *Re Resch's Will Trusts, Le Cras v Perpetual Trustee Co Ltd* [1969] 1 AC 514, [1967] 3 All ER 915, PC. As to the meaning of 'charitable corporation' see para 213 ante. As to contributions by beneficiaries of charity see para 11 ante.

5   *The Abbey, Malvern Wells, Ltd v Ministry of Local Government and Planning* [1951] Ch 728, [1951] 2 All ER 154.

6   See the Voluntary Hospitals (Paying Patients) Act 1936; and para 511 post. As to the Charity Commissioners see paras 486–512 post.

**216. Other charitable corporations.** Besides colleges and hospitals, there are other corporations created solely for the fulfilment of charitable purposes, as where charity trustees[1], governors[2], or the schoolmaster[3], or the schoolmaster and usher[4], have been respectively incorporated for charitable or educational objects. Charitable corporations have also in many cases been created by Act of Parliament[5], or by registration under the Companies Acts, and by charter, to carry into effect various charitable purposes.

In the Charities Act 1993, 'company' means a company formed and registered under the Companies Act 1985, or to which the provisions of that Act apply as they apply to such a company[6].

1   See para 236 post.
2   *Eden v Foster* (1726) 2 P Wms 325 (grammar school).
3   *Whiston v Dean and Chapter of Rochester* (1849) 7 Hare 532 (cathedral school).
4   *A-G v Price* (1744) 3 Atk 108 at 109 per Lord Hardwicke LC (free school); *Re Chelmsford Grammar School* (1855) 1 K & J 543 at 561 per Page-Wood V-C.
5   Eg the Royal Patriotic Fund Corporation (see the Patriotic Fund Reorganisation Act 1903; and ROYAL FORCES).
6   Charities Act 1993 s 97(1); see further COMPANIES.

**217. Local authorities.** Local authorities are trustees of their corporate property for public purposes for the benefit of the ratepayers[1], and as such they are subject to the court's trust jurisdiction[2] and are charity trustees[3]; but they do not come within the definition of charitable corporations because they are not established exclusively for charitable purposes[4].

1   *A-G v Aspinall* (1837) 2 My & Cr 613, approved in *Parr v A-G* (1842) 8 Cl & Fin 409, HL; and see *Re Brown's Mortgage, Wallasey Corpn v A-G* [1945] Ch 166, [1945] 1 All ER 397.
2   *A-G v Wilson* (1840) Cr & Ph 1; *A-G v Lichfield Corpn* (1848) 11 Beav 120; *A-G v De Winton* [1906] 2 Ch 106. See also *A-G v Newcastle-upon-Tyne Corpn and North-Eastern Rly Co* (1889) 23 QBD 492, CA. In *A-G v Aspinall* (1837) 2 My & Cr 613, the argument that the statutory remedies under the Municipal Corporations Act 1835 (repealed) ousted the court's equitable jurisdiction over breaches of trust was rejected.
3   *A-G v Dublin Corpn* (1827) 1 Bli NS 312, HL; *A-G v Liverpool Corpn* (1835) 1 My & Cr 171 at 201 per Pepys MR; *A-G v Stafford Corpn* [1878] WN 74.
4   See para 213 ante. As to the transfer of powers on local government reorganisation see paras 244–245 post. As to local government reorganisation generally see further LOCAL GOVERNMENT.

## (2) FOUNDATION AND DISSOLUTION

**218. Meaning of 'foundation'.** The expression 'foundation' as applied to the establishment of charitable corporations is used in two distinct senses. It denotes: (1) the incorporation of a body of persons (*fundatio incipiens*); and (2) the original endowment of the incorporated body (*fundatio perficiens*)[1].

1   Shelford's Law of Mortmain 323–324; *Sutton's Hospital Case* (1612) 10 Co Rep 1a at 23a, 33a. As to the meaning of 'charitable corporation' see para 213 ante.

**219. Modes of creation.** A charitable corporation may be created: (1) by royal charter[1]; (2) by royal charter giving authority to the holder of an office to create corporations indefinitely[2]; (3) by persons acting under royal licence[3]; (4) by special Act of Parliament[4]; (5) under the Companies Act 1985[5]; and (6) by the Charity Commissioners under the Charities Act 1993[6].

No particular form of words need be used for the creation of a corporation by charter or Act of Parliament, provided the intention to incorporate is clear[7].

The Crown can establish or found a corporation which has had no previous embryonic existence as an unincorporated body of persons, but as a matter of history and of practice this never occurs[8].

1 This was the most usual form of incorporation. For examples see *Re Clergy Society* (1856) 2 K & J 615, and modern universities.

2 'In this manner the Chancellor of the University of Oxford has power by charter to erect corporations and has actually often exerted it' (1 Bl Com 474).

3 For examples see *Sutton's Hospital Case* (1612) 10 Co Rep 1a at 23a, 31a; *Ex p Kirkby Ravensworth Hospital* (1808) 15 Ves 305; *A-G v Dulwich College* (1841) 4 Beav 255.

4 Eg the Church Building Society, the Construction Industry Training Board and the other Industrial Training Boards: see *Construction Industry Training Board v A-G* [1973] Ch 173, [1972] 2 All ER 1339, CA.

5 See generally COMPANIES. For examples see *Re St Hilda's Incorporated College, Cheltenham* [1901] 1 Ch 556; *Incorporated Council of Law Reporting for England and Wales v A-G* [1972] Ch 73, [1971] 3 All ER 1029, CA.

6 See the Charities Act 1993 Pt VII (ss 50–62). The powers conferred by that Act replace those under the Charitable Trustees Incorporation Act 1872 (repealed). It was formerly often found more convenient to make use of the corporate capacity of the official custodian, but this use has been restricted by the Charities Act 1992: see paras 273–281 post. As to corporations formed in this way see para 236 post. As to the Charity Commissioners see paras 486–512 post.

7 *Sutton's Hospital Case* (1612) 10 Co Rep 1a at 23a, 28a; Shelford's Law of Mortmain 27.

8 *A-G v National Hospital for the Relief and Cure of the Paralysed and Epileptic* [1904] 2 Ch 252 at 256 per Kekewich J.

**220. The founder.** The person providing the original endowment is usually regarded as the founder, rather than the person performing the act of incorporation[1].

If the Monarch joins with an individual in endowing a corporation, the Monarch alone is founder[2], but if two or more private individuals contribute to the original endowment, they together constitute the founder[3]. A private individual who has founded a charitable corporation does not cease to be founder by reason of the corporation being subsequently endowed by the Monarch[4].

Where a charity is established by subscriptions the original subscribers alone are the founders. Additional contributions do not constitute a new foundation[5].

1 *Sutton's Hospital Case* (1612) 10 Co Rep 1a at 23a, 33a; *Anon* (1698) 12 Mod Rep 232. See also *St John's College, Cambridge v Todington* (1757) 1 Burr 158 at 200 per Lord Mansfield; and Tudor on Charities (7th Edn, 1984) p 317.

2 2 Co Inst 68.

3 *Re St Leonard, Shoreditch, Parochial Schools* (1884) 10 App Cas 304 at 308, PC.

4 2 Co Inst 68.

5 *Re St Leonard, Shoreditch, Parochial Schools* (1884) 10 App Cas 304, PC.

**221. Founder's right to provide for government and administration.** A charitable corporation, in so far as it is charitable, is the 'creature of the founder'[1]. The founder may accordingly provide for the government and administration of his 'creature' and the application in perpetuity of the revenues[2]. Moreover, he and his appointees have the perpetual right of patronage and visitation[3].

However, he may not alter the corporation's constitution by increasing the number of corporators, or vary the trusts or application of the endowment or revenues[4], unless special powers for this purpose are reserved by the charter of incorporation[5].

It appears that if the number of members of the corporation is not originally fixed, the corporation itself may add to the number[6].

1   *St John's College, Cambridge v Todington* (1757) 1 Burr 158. As to the meaning of 'charitable corporation' see para 213 ante. As to who is the founder see para 220 ante.
2   *Green v Rutherforth* (1750) 1 Ves Sen 462 at 472 per Lord Hardwicke LC; *Philips v Bury* (1694) Skin 447 at 482–483, HL.
3   As to patronage see para 117 ante; and ECCLESIASTICAL LAW vol 14 para 776 et seq. As to visitation see para 458 et seq post.
4   *A-G v Dulwich College* (1841) 4 Beav 255; and see *Ex p Bolton* (1789) 2 Bro CC 662.
5   *R v Vice-Chancellor of Cambridge* (1765) 3 Burr 1647 at 1656 per Lord Mansfield; *St John's College, Cambridge v Todington* (1757) 1 Burr 158. A power to alter the corporation's statutes or byelaws does not imply a power to alter its objects or constitution: *Ex p Bolton* (1789) 2 Bro CC 662; *A-G v Dulwich College* (1841) 4 Beav 255 at 266 per Lord Langdale MR.
6   *A-G v Talbot* (1748) 3 Atk 662 at 675 per Lord Hardwicke LC.

**222. Control over chartered corporations.** Although charitable corporations created by royal charter are the 'creatures of the Crown', yet so long as they exist and are capable of discharging their functions, they are not subject to control by the Crown except such control as is reserved by the charter[1]. However, when a corporation is dissolved, or an integral part of it is gone, the Crown may grant a new charter[2], or on failure of objects the court may dispose of the funds cy-près[3]; the court also has jurisdiction to regulate and control by scheme a charity founded by royal charter[4].

1   *R v Pasmore* (1789) 3 Term Rep 199. See, however, *Queen's College, Cambridge, Case* (1821) Jac 1 at 20–21 per Lord Eldon LC, where it was held that, in the case of a royal foundation, the Crown had an implied power to dispense with the statutes. As to the meaning of 'charitable corporation' see para 213 ante. As to creation by royal charter see para 219 ante.
2   *R v Pasmore* (1789) 3 Term Rep 199.
3   *A-G v Hicks* (1810) 3 Bro CC 166n as noted in 29 ER 468. See also the Charities Act 1993 s 15(1); and para 175 ante. As to the cy-près doctrine see para 201 ante.
4   *Re Whitworth Art Gallery Trusts, Manchester Whitworth Institute v Victoria University of Manchester* [1958] Ch 461, [1958] 1 All ER 176.

**223. Dissolution of charitable corporation.** A charitable corporation may be dissolved in the same way as any other corporation[1]. When a charitable corporation has been dissolved, it is no longer in existence, notwithstanding that all its assets are still traceable and may not be applied for any other than charitable purposes[2].

A charitable company[3] may be wound up both on the petition of any creditor or contributory or itself[4], and also on the petition of the Attorney General[5]. Further, a petition may be presented by the Charity Commissioners if, after they have instituted an inquiry[6], they are satisfied that there is or has been misconduct or mismanagement in the administration of the charity, or that it is necessary or desirable to act for the purpose of protecting the property of the charity or securing a proper application for the purposes of the charity of that property or of property coming to the charity[7]. Where a charitable company[8] is dissolved, the Commissioners may apply to the court[9] for an order declaring the dissolution of the company void[10], and where the name of a charitable company, as being a defunct company, has been struck off[11] the register of companies, the Commissioners may apply[12] for an order restoring the company's name to the register[13]. The powers exercisable by the Commissioners under these provisions are exercisable by them of their own motion, but only with the agreement of the Attorney General on each occasion[14].

A charitable company which has been dissolved and struck off the register will not be restored to the register in order to take a legacy on a death after the date of dissolution[15]. On the other hand bequests received after a charitable company has gone into liquidation but before it is formally dissolved are, unless the terms of the bequest otherwise provide, available for distribution amongst the creditors[16].

1   See COMPANIES vol 7(3) (1996 Reissue) para 2190 et seq; CORPORATIONS vol 9(2) (Reissue) para 1196 et seq. As to the meaning of 'charitable corporation' see para 213 ante.
2   *Re Stemson's Will Trusts, Carpenter v Treasury Solicitor* [1970] Ch 16, [1969] 2 All ER 517; but see *Re Vernon's Will Trusts, Lloyds Bank Ltd v Group 20 Hospital Management Committee (Coventry)* [1972] Ch 300n, [1971] 3 All ER 1061n. See also para 145 ante.
3   For the meaning of 'company' in the Charities Act 1993 see para 216 ante.
4   See the Insolvency Act 1986 s 124 (as amended); and COMPANIES vol 7(3) (1996 Reissue) para 3002.
5   Charities Act 1993 s 63(1). The powers given to the Charity Commissioners by s 32 (see para 496 post) to take legal proceedings do not extend to presenting a petition for the winding up of a charitable company: s 32(2). The affairs of the first company to be wound up under s 63(1) (as originally enacted in the Charities Act 1960 s 30(1) (repealed)) came before the court in *Liverpool and District Hospital for Diseases of the Heart v A-G* [1981] Ch 193, [1981] 1 All ER 994. As to the Charity Commissioners see paras 486–512 post.
6   Ie under the Charities Act 1993 s 8: see para 497 post.
7   Ibid ss 18(1)(a), (b), 63(2).
8   'Charitable company' means a company which is a charity: ibid s 63(6).
9   Ie under the Companies Act 1985 s 651 (as amended): see COMPANIES vol 7(3) (1996 Reissue) para 2696. In relation to a charitable company, s 651(1) (as amended) has effect as if the reference to the liquidator of the company included a reference to the commissioners: Charities Act 1993 s 63(3).
10  Ibid s 63(3).
11  Ie under the Companies Act 1985 s 652: see COMPANIES vol 7(2) (1996 Reissue) para 1496 et seq.
12  Ie under ibid s 653(2): see COMPANIES vol 7(2) (1996 Reissue) para 1504. In relation to a charitable company the reference in s 653(2) to a person aggrieved includes a reference to the Commissioners: Charities Act 1993 s 63(4).
13  Ibid s 63(4).
14  Ibid s 63(5).
15  *Re Servers of the Blind League* [1960] 2 All ER 298, [1960] 1 WLR 564.
16  *Re ARMS (Multiple Sclerosis Research) Ltd, Alleyne v A-G* [1997] 2 All ER 679, [1997] 1 WLR 877.

## (3) CORPORATE PROPERTY

**224. Property is held on trust.** As charitable corporations exist solely for the accomplishment of charitable purposes, they are sometimes said to be but trustees for charity[1], whether the beneficiaries are members of the corporation, as in the case of hospitals[2] and colleges[3], or not[4]. It has accordingly been held that, in the absence of special powers, corporate property may only be invested in the manner permitted by law in respect of trust funds[5], and the governors or directors of the corporation, though not strictly trustees themselves, are in a fiduciary position and may not receive remuneration for work done[6].

In other cases the courts have refused to interfere with the property or affairs of a charitable corporation in the absence of a special trust[7], but the court has jurisdiction to restrain such a corporation from applying its property in unauthorised ways, and may have other jurisdiction over its internal affairs[8]. Perhaps the true meaning of the so-called rule that the court's jurisdiction to intervene in the affairs of a charity depends on the existence of a trust is that the court has no jurisdiction to intervene unless there has been placed on the holder of the assets in question a legally binding restriction, arising either by way of trust in the strict traditional sense or, in the case of a corporate body, under the terms of its constitution, which obliges him or it to apply the assets in question for exclusively charitable purposes; for the jurisdiction of the court necessarily depends on the existence of a person or body who is subject to such obligation and against whom the court can act in personam so far as necessary for the purposes of enforcement[9].

1    *Lydiatt v Foach* (1700) 2 Vern 410; and see *Construction Industry Training Board v A-G* [1973] Ch 173 at 187, [1972] 2 All ER 1339 at 1348, CA, per Buckley LJ. The property of non-charitable corporations is not held on trust: *Bowman v Secular Society Ltd* [1917] AC 406 at 440, HL, per Lord Parker. As to the meaning of 'charitable corporation' see para 213 ante.

2    *Lydiatt v Foach* (1700) 2 Vern 410; *A-G v Wyggeston's Hospital* (1853) 16 Beav 313; *A-G v St Cross Hospital* (1853) 17 Beav 435.

3    *Thetford School Case* (1609) 8 Co Rep 130b; but see *A-G v Whorwood* (1750) 1 Ves Sen 534 at 536 obiter per Lord Hardwicke LC.

4    *Re Manchester Royal Infirmary, Manchester Royal Infirmary v A-G* (1889) 43 ChD 420; *Re Dominion Students' Hall Trust, Dominion Students' Hall Trust v A-G* [1947] Ch 183; *Soldiers', Sailors' and Airmen's Families Association v A-G* [1968] 1 All ER 448n, [1968] 1 WLR 313. See also *Re Church Army* (1906) 75 LJCh 467, CA; *The Abbey, Malvern Wells, Ltd v Ministry of Local Government and Planning* [1951] Ch 728, [1951] 2 All ER 154; and the cases cited in para 216 ante.

5    *Re Manchester Royal Infirmary, Manchester Royal Infirmary v A-G* (1889) 43 ChD 420; *Soldiers', Sailors' and Airmen's Families Association v A-G* [1968] 1 All ER 448n, [1968] 1 WLR 313. In the former case, but not in the latter, the decision was based partly on the fact that the funds had been held on trust before becoming vested in the corporation.

6    *Re French Protestant Hospital* [1951] Ch 567, [1951] 1 All ER 938.

7    *A-G v Magdalen College, Oxford* (1847) 10 Beav 402, decided on the principle that matters of internal regulation were entrusted by the founder to the jurisdiction of the visitor.

8    Cf *Construction Industry Training Board v A-G* [1973] Ch 173, [1972] 2 All ER 1339, CA; affg [1971] 3 All ER 449, [1971] 1 WLR 1303. The court's jurisdiction has always been said to depend on the existence of a trust, but a limited company or other corporation is capable of being subject to the court's charity jurisdiction and therefore of being a charity for the purpose of the Charities Act 1993: see ss 63, 96(1); and para 1 note 2 ante.

9    *Liverpool and District Hospital for Diseases of the Heart v A-G* [1981] Ch 193 at 214, [1981] 1 All ER 994 at 1009–1010 per Slade J. Even when these conditions are fulfilled, the particular terms of the trust or constitution in question may operate substantially or partially to oust the jurisdiction of the court: see the Charities Act 1993 s 96(1); *Construction Industry Training Board v A-G* [1973] Ch 173 at 181–182, [1972] 2 All ER 1339 at 1343–1344, CA, per Russell LJ; *A-G v Magdalen College, Oxford* (1847) 10 Beav 402.

# (4) REGULATION OF CHARITABLE COMPANIES

**225. Exemption from requirement of 'limited' as part of name.** Certain companies[1] established for charitable purposes are exempt from the statutory requirements[2] relating to the use of 'limited'[3] as part of the company name. The exemption is restricted to, first, a private company limited by guarantee, and, secondly, a company which on 25 February 1982 was a private company limited by shares with a name which, by virtue of a licence under the Companies Act 1948[4], did not include 'limited' as part of its name[5].

Charitable companies falling within this exemption are exempt from the requirement to send lists of members to the registrar of companies[6], but are no longer[7] exempt from the requirement that the name of the company must appear in all correspondence and other specified documents[8].

1 For the meaning of 'company' see para 216 ante.
2 See the Companies Act 1985 ss 25, 687; and COMPANIES vol 7(1) (1996 Reissue) paras 79, 154 et seq.
3 For companies registered in Wales the equivalent in Welsh ('cyfyngedig') is permitted: see ibid ss 25(2)(b), 30(6); and COMPANIES vol 7(1) (1996 Reissue) paras 112, 154. Certain abbreviations are also allowed: see s 27; and COMPANIES vol 7(1) (1996 Reissue) para 155.
4 Ie under the Companies Act 1948 s 19. This section, under which there had to be an individual application to the Department of Trade and Industry for a dispensation, was repealed by the Companies Act 1981 s 119, Sch 4.
5 Companies Act 1985 s 30(1), (2). The requirements that have to be complied with are set out in s 30(3)–(5): see COMPANIES vol 7(1) (1996 Reissue) para 112.
6 See ibid s 363(1) (as substituted), s 364A(4) (as added), s 30(7); and COMPANIES vol 7(1) (1996 Reissue) para 112; COMPANIES vol 7(2) (1996 Reissue) paras 1062, 1064.
7 Ie since the coming into force on 1 January 1993 of the (now repealed) Charities Act 1960 s 30BB (added by the Charities Act 1992 s 42).
8 Charities Act 1993 s 67 (derived from the Charities Act 1960 s 30BB (repealed)). For these requirements see the Companies Act 1985 s 349(1); and COMPANIES vol 7(2) (1996 Reissue) para 1134.

**226. Status of charitable company to appear on correspondence.** Where a company is a charity and its name does not include the word 'charity' or the word 'charitable'[1], the fact that the company is a charity must be stated in English in legible characters[2] (1) in all business letters of the company; (2) in all its notices and other official publications; (3) in all bills of exchange, promissory notes, endorsements, cheques and orders for money or goods purporting to be signed on behalf of the company; (4) in all conveyances[3] purporting to be executed by the company; and (5) in all bills rendered by it and in all its invoices, receipts and letters of credit[4]. Contravention of these requirements is an offence[5].

1 This is subject to the Charities Act 1993 s 68(1A) (as added) (see note 4 infra): s 68(1) (amended by the Welsh Language Act 1993 s 33(2)).
2 Charities Act 1993 s 68(1) (amended by the Welsh Language Act 1993 s 35, Sch 2).
3 'Conveyance' means any instrument creating, transferring, varying or extinguishing an interest in land: Charities Act 1993 s 68(2).
4 Ibid s 68(1) (as amended: see notes 1, 2 supra). Where a company's name includes the word 'elusen' or the word 'elusennol' (the Welsh equivalents of the words 'charity' and 'charitable'), s 68(1) does not apply in relation to any document which is wholly in Welsh: s 68(1A) (s 68(1A), (1B) added by the Welsh Language Act 1993 s 33(3)). The statement required by the Charities Act 1993 s 68(1) (as amended) must be in English, except that, in the case of a document which is otherwise wholly in Welsh, the statement may be in Welsh if it consists of or includes the word 'elusen' or the word 'elusennol': s 68(1B) (as so added).
See also s 5 (as amended); and para 286 post.
5 Ibid s 68(3), applying the Companies Act 1985 s 349(2)–(4) (see COMPANIES vol 7(2) (1996 Reissue) para 1134). The offence is punishable on summary conviction by a fine of one-fifth of the statutory maximum: s 730, Sch 24. The 'statutory maximum', with reference to a fine or penalty on summary conviction for an offence, is the prescribed sum within the meaning of the Magistrates' Courts Act 1980 s 32 (as amended): see the Interpretation Act 1978 s 5, Sch 1 (definition added by the Criminal Justice Act 1988 s 170(1), Sch 15 para 58); and CRIMINAL LAW, EVIDENCE AND PROCEDURE vol 11(2) (Reissue) para 806; MAGISTRATES. The 'prescribed sum' means £5,000 or such sum as is for the time being substituted in this definition by order under the Magistrates' Courts Act 1980 s 143(1) (as substituted): see s 32(9) (amended by the Criminal Justice Act 1991 s 17(2)); and CRIMINAL LAW,

EVIDENCE AND PROCEDURE vol 11(2) (Reissue) para 807; MAGISTRATES. As to the determination of the amount of the fine actually imposed, as distinct from the level on the standard scale which it may not exceed, see the Powers of Criminal Courts (Sentencing) Act 2000 s 128; and MAGISTRATES.

**227. Trusts not affected by alteration of objects.** A charitable company or other corporation which has power to alter its constitution cannot, by altering its objects so that it ceases to be charitable, affect the application of: (1) any property acquired under any disposition or agreement previously made otherwise than for full consideration in money or money's worth, or any property representing property so acquired; (2) any property representing income which has accrued before the alteration is made; or (3) the income from any such property[1].

Where a charity is a company, any alteration by it of the objects clause in its memorandum of association, or of any other provision in its memorandum of association or articles of association which is a provision directing or restricting the manner in which property of the company may be used or applied, is ineffective without the prior written consent of the Charity Commissioners[2]. Where such an alteration has been made and in connection therewith the company is required[3] to deliver to the registrar of companies a printed copy of its memorandum, as altered, or is required[4] to forward to him a printed or other copy of the special resolution effecting the alteration, the copy so delivered or forwarded by the company must be accompanied by a copy of the Commissioners' consent[5].

1   See the Charities Act 1993 s 64(1). See also *IRC v Yorkshire Agricultural Society* [1928] 1 KB 611 at 633, CA; and *Baldry v Feintuck* [1972] 2 All ER 81, [1972] 1 WLR 552, as to unincorporated associations.
2   Charities Act 1993 s 64(2). As to the Charity Commissioners see paras 486–512 post.
3   Ie by the Companies Act 1985 s 6(1) or s 17(3): see COMPANIES vol 7(1) (1996 Reissue) para 542; COMPANIES vol 7(2) (1996 Reissue) para 1186.
4   Ie by ibid s 380(1): see COMPANIES vol 7(1) (1996 Reissue) para 691.
5   Charities Act 1993 s 64(3). The provisions of the Companies Act 1985 s 6(3) (offences) are applied to defaults by a company under the Charities Act 1993 s 64 as they apply to any such default mentioned in the Companies Act 1985 s 6(3) (see COMPANIES vol 7(1) (1996 Reissue) para 542): Charities Act 1993 s 64(4).

**228. Invalidity of certain transactions of charitable companies.** The provisions of the Companies Act 1985 which provide that the validity of an act done by a company cannot be called into question on the ground of lack of capacity by reason of anything in the company's memorandum[1] and that, in favour of a person dealing with a company in good faith, the power of the board of directors to bind the company, or authorise others to do so, is to be deemed to be free of any limitation under the company's constitution[2], do not apply to the acts of a company which is a charity except in favour of a person who (1) gives full consideration in money or money's worth in relation to the act in question, and does not know that the act is not permitted by the company's memorandum or, as the case may be, is beyond the powers of the directors; or (2) does not know at the time the act is done that the company is a charity[3]. In any proceedings the burden of proving (a) that a person knew that an act was not permitted by the company's memorandum or was beyond the powers of the directors; or (b) that a person knew that the company was a charity, lies on the person making that allegation[4].

However, where a charitable company purports to transfer or grant an interest in property, the fact that the act was not permitted by the company's memorandum or, as the case may be, that the directors in connection with the act exceeded any limitation on their powers under the company's constitution, does not affect the title of a person who subsequently acquires the property or any interest in it for full consideration without actual notice of any such circumstances affecting the validity of the company's act[5].

Where a company is a charity, the ratification of an act which but for statute[6] would be ultra vires the company, or the ratification of certain transactions to which directors or their associates are parties[7], is ineffective without the prior written consent of the Charity Commissioners[8].

1   See the Companies Act 1985 s 35(1) (substituted by the Companies Act 1989 s 108(1)); and COMPANIES vol 7(2) (1996 Reissue) para 1107.
2   See the Companies Act 1985 s 35A(1) (s 35A added by the Companies Act 1989 s 108(1)); and COMPANIES vol 7(2) (1996 Reissue) para 1108.
3   Charities Act 1993 s 65(1); Companies Act 1985 ss 35(4), 35A(6) (as substituted and added respectively: see notes 1–2 supra; both amended by the Charities Act 1993 s 98(1), Sch 6 para 20(1), (2)).
4   Charities Act 1993 s 65(3).
5   Ibid s 65(2).
6   See the Companies Act 1985 s 35(1) (as substituted); the text and note 1 supra; and COMPANIES vol 7(2) (1996 Reissue) para 1107.
7   See ibid s 322A (added by the Companies Act 1989 s 109(1)); and COMPANIES vol 7(1) (1996 Reissue) para 613.
8   Charities Act 1993 s 65(4).

**229. Requirement of consent of Charity Commissioners to certain acts.**
Where a company is a charity, any approval given by it for the following specified purposes is ineffective without the prior written consent of the Charity Commissioners. The specified purposes are those of the provisions of the Companies Act 1985 relating to: (1) payment to a director in respect of loss of office or retirement[2]; (2) payment to a director in respect of loss of office or retirement made in connection with the transfer of the undertaking or property of the company[3]; (3) incorporation in a director's service contract of a term whereby his employment will or may continue for more than five years[4]; (4) an arrangement whereby assets are acquired by or from a director or a person connected with him[5]; and (5) the provision of funds to meet certain expenses incurred by the director[6].

The prior written consent of the Commissioners is likewise required in the case of the affirmation by the company of voidable arrangements under which assets are acquired by or from a director or a person connected with him[7].

1   Charities Act 1993 s 66(1)(a). The purposes specified are those listed in s 66(2): see heads (1)–(5) in the text. As to the Charity Commissioners see paras 486–512 post.
2   Ie the Companies Act 1985 s 312: see COMPANIES vol 7(1) (1996 Reissue) para 608.
3   Ie ibid s 313(1): see COMPANIES vol 7(1) (1996 Reissue) para 609.
4   Ie ibid s 319(3): see COMPANIES vol 7(1) (1996 Reissue) para 563.
5   Ie ibid s 320(1): see COMPANIES vol 7(1) (1996 Reissue) para 611.
6   Ie ibid s 337(3)(a) (as amended): see COMPANIES vol 7(1) (1996 Reissue) para 600.
7   Charities Act 1993 s 66(1)(b); Companies Act 1985 s 322(2)(c); and see COMPANIES vol 7(1) (1996 Reissue) para 612.

# 6. TRUSTEES

# (1) CORPORATIONS AND QUASI-CORPORATIONS AS TRUSTEES

**230. Eleemosynary and civil corporations.** Corporations, no less than individuals, may as a rule be trustees for charitable purposes[1].

Eleemosynary corporations are trustees of their corporate property, whether their members participate in the charity or not[2]. They may also undertake the execution of special trusts connected with the objects of their foundation[3].

Civil corporations, as, for example, livery companies of the City of London[4] and municipal corporations[5], are in many cases also trustees of charities. Local authorities are also trustees of the municipal property[6], and may hold property on special trusts, for example for the benefit of the borough freemen[7].

1　*Flood's Case* (1616) Hob 136; *A-G v Tancred* (1757) 1 Eden 10 at 14 per Henley, Lord Keeper; *A-G v Master of Brentwood School* (1833) 1 My & K 376 at 390 per Leach MR; *A-G v Liverpool Corpn* (1835) 1 My & Cr 171 at 201 per Pepys MR; *Incorporated Society in Dublin v Richards* (1841) 1 Dr & War 258 at 302–303, 307, 331 per Lord Sugden LC. For other instances of corporations acting as trustees for charities see also *Bene't (or Corpus Christi) College, Cambridge v Bishop of London* (1778) 2 Wm Bl 1182 (devise to college for charitable use); *A-G v Landerfield* (1743) 9 Mod Rep 286 (devise to hospital); *Society for Propagation of the Gospel v A-G* (1826) 3 Russ 142; *Re Manchester Royal Infirmary, Manchester Royal Infirmary v A-G* (1889) 43 ChD 420. As to the incorporation of charity trustees see para 236 post. As to the capacity of a corporation to be a trustee jointly with an individual or individuals see the Bodies Corporate (Joint Tenancy) Act 1899; *Re Thompson's Settlement Trusts, Thompson v Alexander* [1905] 1 Ch 229; and TRUSTS vol 48 (2000 Reissue) paras 509, 758; CORPORATIONS vol 9(2) (Reissue) para 1151.

2　*Lydiatt v Foach* (1700) 2 Vern 410 at 412 per North, Lord Keeper. As to eleemosynary corporations see para 213 ante. As to where the property of charitable corporations is held on trust see para 224 ante.

3　Eg in the case of educational foundations, trusts for additional fellowships (*A-G v Talbot* (1748) 3 Atk 662; *A-G v Whorwood* (1750) 1 Ves Sen 534 at 537 per Lord Hardwicke LC; *A-G v Flood* (1816) Hayes & Jo App xxi at p xxxv per Lord Brougham LC; *Re Catharine Hall, ex p Inge* (1831) 2 Russ & M 590 at 596 per Lord Eldon LC; and as to the necessity for the visitor's consent see *A-G v Master and Fellows of Catharine Hall, Cambridge* (1820) Jac 381 at 400 per Lord Eldon LC); for scholarships or prizes (*A-G v Talbot* supra); for maintenance of schools connected with the foundation (*A-G v Caius College* (1837) 2 Keen 150); for presentation to livings connected with the foundation (*Green v Rutherforth* (1750) 1 Ves Sen 462 at 473 per Lord Hardwicke LC).

4　*A-G v Grocers' Co* (1843) 6 Beav 526.

5　See the Municipal Corporations Act 1882 s 133; and *Colchester Corpn v Lowten* (1813) 1 Ves & B 226; *A-G v Shrewsbury Corpn* (1843) 6 Beav 220; *Viscount Gort v A-G* (1817) 6 Dow 136, HL; *Christ's Hospital v Grainger* (1848) 16 Sim 83 (on appeal (1849) 1 Mac & G 460); *Re Ludlow Charities* (1837) 3 My & Cr 262. For the position under the Municipal Corporations Act 1835 (repealed) see *A-G v Exeter Corpn* (1852) 2 De GM & G 507 at 515 per Lord St Leonards LC; and Tudor on Charities (7th Edn, 1984) pp 313, 362. See also the Charitable Trusts Act 1853 s 65 (repealed by the Municipal Corporations Act 1882 s 5, Sch 1: and see s 133); and *Re Huntingdon Municipal Charities* (1859) 27 Beav 214.

6　See para 217 ante.

7　*Goodman v Saltash Corpn* (1882) 7 App Cas 633, HL; *Prestney v Colchester Corpn and A-G* (1882) 21 ChD 111.

**231. Corporations with limited capacity.** Corporations may have only a limited capacity for holding property on trust[1]. A corporation created by or under statute[2] or otherwise[3] for a particular purpose has no capacity beyond the object for which it was established. Local authorities may not act as trustees for an ecclesiastical charity or a charity for the relief of poverty[4].

Real or personal property vested in a corporation passes automatically to the corporation's successors, and statutory provision has been made to deal with the problem of vacancies[5].

1  Tudor on Charities (7th Edn, 1984) pp 362–363. It is sometimes said that colleges in universities cannot undertake trusts inconsistent with their foundation, but the cases cited as authority (*A-G v Whorwood* (1750) 1 Ves Sen 534; *A-G v Tancred* (1757) 1 Eden 10 at 15 per Henley, Lord Keeper) do not appear to justify the proposition.

2  See *National Guaranteed Manure Co v Donald* (1859) 28 LJEx 185 at 188; *Putney Overseers v London and South Western Rly Co* (1891) 60 LJQB 438 at 439 per Lord Esher MR, CA, per Lord Esher MR.

3  See *Incorporated Society v Price* (1844) 1 Jo & Lat 498. The Chamberlain of the City of London is a corporation sole for the purpose of taking recognisances, obligations, etc, in trust for the portions of orphans: *Fulwood's Case* (1591) 4 Co Rep 64b, 65a; *Byrd v Wilford* (1596) Cro Eliz 464, Ex Ch.

4  Local Government Act 1972 s 139(3). 'Eleemosynary charity' (the term used in the Local Government Act 1933 s 268 (repealed) in place of 'charity for the relief of poverty') includes all charities directed to the relief of individual distress: *Re Armitage, Ellam v Norwich Corpn* [1972] Ch 438, [1972] 1 All ER 708. Gifts to local authorities on trust for such a charity do not fail owing to the trustee's incapacity: see *Re Woolnough's Will Trusts* (1959) Times, 22 October; *Re Armitage, Ellam v Norwich Corpn* supra. Some local authorities have special statutory powers enabling them to act as trustees of such trusts.

5  See the Law of Property Act 1925 s 180; and CORPORATIONS vol 9(2) (Reissue) paras 1151, 1154–1155. Formerly personalty could not be vested in a corporation sole as such; there is a possible doubt, on the strict construction of s 180(1), as to whether it is effective as apparently intended: see CORPORATIONS vol 9(2) (Reissue) paras 1154. A parson, seised of property in right of his church, may be in a different position: see *Duke of Marlborough v St John* (1852) 5 De G & Sm 174; *Ecclesiastical Comrs v Wodehouse* [1895] 1 Ch 552; Littleton s 644; 1 Co Inst 300b, 341b; and cf *Power v Banks* [1901] 2 Ch 487.

**232. Churchwardens and incumbents.** Churchwardens possess a quasi-corporate capacity to hold personalty[1], but not realty[2], for church purposes[3].

Under the School Sites Acts grants of land might formerly be made to the minister, churchwardens and overseers of the poor[4], and may still, in certain circumstances, be made to the minister and churchwardens alone[5], and their successors, as a corporation, for the charitable purposes mentioned in the Acts. Otherwise a minister and churchwardens do not, as a rule, form a corporation[6].

Certain property[7], that is to say certain real property held on charitable trusts for ecclesiastical purposes of the Church of England, and personal property held on permanent trusts[8], if it is vested in an incumbent or churchwardens[9] or in an ecclesiastical corporation sole acting as joint trustee with an incumbent or churchwardens[10] or if the presently acting trustee is the parochial church council but not validly appointed[11], must be brought to the attention of the diocesan authority[12], with a view to being vested in the board as custodian trustee[13]. Subject to objections and representations received, the board must make a vesting declaration[14] vesting the property in itself as custodian trustee[15], and also a scheme for the charity's management, limited to the establishment or continuance of managing trustees[16]. The exercise of these powers is without prejudice to the jurisdiction of the court and the Charity Commissioners to make administrative schemes[17].

Incumbents and churchwardens no longer[18] have the capacity to acquire interests in land or personalty to which the Incumbents and Churchwardens (Trusts) Measure 1964 applies[19], except an interest in personalty by gift or under a will, without the consent of the diocesan authority[20].

1    Shelford's Law of Mortmain 28; *A-G v Ruper* (1722) 2 P Wms 125; and see *Tufnell v Constable* (1838) 7 Ad & El 798.
2    Shelford's Law of Mortmain 29; *A-G v Ruper* (1722) 2 P Wms 125; *Gravenor v Hallum* (1767) Amb 643 at 644 per Lord Camden LC; *Withnell v Gartham* (1795) 6 Term Rep 388 at 396 per Lord Kenyon CJ. It is otherwise in the City of London: *Fell v Official Trustee of Charity Lands* [1898] 2 Ch 44 at 51, CA, per Lindley MR. In some early cases it appears that churchwardens were created corporations by letters patent with power to hold land: Shelford's Law of Mortmain 29; 1 Kyd on Corporations 31. As to actions by and against the churchwardens see ECCLESIASTICAL LAW vol 14 para 550.
3    Property vested in churchwardens alone was not affected by the Local Government Act 1894 (repealed) or by the Overseers Order 1927, SR & O 1927/55; nor did those enactments interfere with their powers, duties and liabilities, so far as they related to the affairs of the church or to charities generally. The Parochial Church Councils (Powers) Measure 1956 s 4 (see ECCLESIASTICAL LAW vol 14 para 575 et seq) gives to parochial church councils certain of the powers, duties and liabilities which the churchwardens formerly had. As to churchwardens generally see ECCLESIASTICAL LAW vol 14 para 542 et seq.
4    See the School Sites Act 1841 s 7. Overseers were abolished by the Rating and Valuation Act 1925 s 62 (as originally enacted), and their functions transferred to rating or other local authorities by s 1(2); and the Overseers Order 1927, SR & O 1927/55. See LOCAL GOVERNMENT; RATING AND COUNCIL TAX. As to charities of which overseers, as such, were, immediately before 1 April 1927, trustees either alone or jointly with any other persons, see arts 9–11 (revoked).
5    See the School Sites Act 1844 ss 4, 5.
6    In the City of London the minister and churchwardens may by custom be a corporation for the execution of charitable trusts (see Tudor on Charities (4th Edn, 1906) p 264 note (f); *A-G v Leage* [1881] WN 167, set out in Tudor on Charities (4th Edn, 1906) p 1041), or may be incorporated for such purposes by a private Act, as in the case of the vicar and churchwardens of St Martin's-in-the-Fields (1 Anne, sess 2, c xxi (1702)).
7    There are various exceptions: glebe and similar property, church movables and ornaments etc, property vested in the official custodian for charities, church educational endowments (defined in the Diocesan Education Committees Measure 1955 s 3 (repealed), see now the Diocesan Boards of Education Measure 1991 s 10 (as amended)), land acquired as sites of proposed churches, parsonage houses etc under the New Parishes Measure 1943 s 16(1), (2) (as substituted and amended), s 17 (as substituted and amended) (see ECCLESIASTICAL LAW vol 14 paras 1081, 1110–1111), land held on a yearly tenancy or term certain of a year or less: see the Incumbents and Churchwardens (Trusts) Measure 1964 s 2(2) (amended by the Endowments and Glebe Measure 1976 s 47(4), Sch 8)).
8    'Permanent trusts' means any trust of property which is a permanent endowment within the meaning of the Charities Act 1993 s 96(3) (see para 283 note 3 post): Incumbents and Churchwardens (Trusts) Measure 1964 s 1 (definition amended by the Charities Act 1993 s 98(1), Sch 6 para 7).
9    'Incumbent' includes any minister with a separate cure of souls but does not include a curate in charge of a conventional district: Incumbents and Churchwardens (Trusts) Measure 1964 s 1. 'Incumbent or churchwardens' means any incumbent and the churchwardens of the parish comprising the benefice of that incumbent or of any parish comprised in any united benefice of that incumbent and is deemed to refer to them or any of them jointly or severally: s 1.
10   Ie either where no present or past trustee, other than the personal representatives of a sole surviving trustee, is or has been any person other than those specified (ibid s 2(1)(a)) or where the presently acting trustees, whether or not validly appointed, are the persons specified, unless they are so acting in contravention of the terms of the trust (s 2(1)(b)).
11   Ie if immediately previously the trusts have been administered by an incumbent or churchwardens with or without an ecclesiastical corporation sole as joint trustee, unless they were acting in contravention of the terms of the trust: ibid s 2(1)(c).
12   'Diocesan authority' means the diocesan board of finance, or any existing or future body appointed by the diocesan synod to act as trustees of diocesan trust property: ibid s 1 (definition amended by the Synodical Government Measure 1969 s 4(7)). As to diocesan boards of finance see ECCLESIASTICAL LAW vol 14 paras 517–518.
13   See the Incumbents and Churchwardens (Trusts) Measure 1964 ss 2(1), (2) (as amended: see note 7 supra), 3(1), (2); and ECCLESIASTICAL LAW vol 14 para 1230. 'Custodian trustee' has the same meaning as in the Public Trustee Act 1906 (see TRUSTS vol 48 (2000 Reissue) para 687 et seq): Incumbents and Churchwardens (Trusts) Measure 1964 s 1. The duties of the board of finance on its becoming aware of

the existence of property falling within those provisions are laid down in the Incumbents and Churchwardens (Trusts) Measure 1964 s 3(2), Schedule. The board must give notice to persons interested, including the Charity Commissioners, of the proposal as to vesting: see Schedule para 2. As to the Charity Commissioners see paras 486–512 post.

14  This has the effect specified in the Trustee Act 1925 s 40(1)(b) (see TRUSTS vol 48 (2000 Reissue) para 760): see the Incumbents and Churchwardens (Trusts) Measure 1964 s 3(3). Any person in whom is vested an interest to which the Measure applies but which cannot be vested in the board by a vesting declaration alone is under a duty to transfer it to the board: see s 3(4).

15  See ibid s 3(2). The vesting declaration will vest subject to all trusts, charges etc affecting it: see ibid s 3(5).

16  Ibid Schedule para 6. The trustees should be the incumbent or churchwardens jointly with, where appropriate, an ecclesiastical corporation sole: Schedule para 6. '

17  See ibid s 3(6). For the jurisdiction to make administrative schemes see paras 170, 180 ante.

18  Ie since 1 January 1965 (the commencement of the Incumbents and Churchwardens (Trusts) Measure 1964).

19  See text and note 7 supra.

20  Incumbents and Churchwardens (Trusts) Measure 1964 s 4.


**233. Local education authorities.** A local education authority may be constituted trustee for any educational endowment or charity for purposes connected with education[1].

1  See the Education Act 1996 s 529 (as amended); and EDUCATION. It appears that education authorities' statutory functions do not give them ipso facto an interest in the establishment of independent educational charities in their areas: *Re Belling, London Borough of Enfield v Public Trustee* [1967] Ch 425, [1967] 1 All ER 105. As to the transfer of the property of registered educational charities following the coming into force of the Local Government Act 1972 see paras 244–245 post.


**234. Public Trustee and custodian trustees.** The Public Trustee may not accept any trust exclusively for religious or charitable purposes[1] or involving the selection of charitable objects of a settlor's bounty[2], but this does not extend to bodies corporate entitled to act as custodian trustees under the Public Trustee Act 1906[3].

1  Public Trustee Act 1906 s 2(5). As to the Public Trustee see TRUSTS vol 48 (2000 Reissue) para 661 et seq. The offices of the Public Trustee and the Official Solicitor were merged on 1 April 2001: see Making Changes: The Future of the Public Trust Office (The Way Forward and an Analysis of the Consultation) (available at www.publictrust.gov.uk).

2  *Re Hampton, Public Trustee v Hampton* (1918) 88 LJCh 103.

3  See the Public Trustee Act 1906 s 4(3); and TRUSTS vol 48 (2000 Reissue) para 688. See also *Re Cherry's Trusts, Robinson v Wesleyan Methodist Chapel Purposes Trustees* [1914] 1 Ch 83. As to corporations entitled to act as custodian trustees see the Public Trustee Rules 1912, SR & O 1912/348, r 30 (as substituted and amended); and TRUSTS vol 48 (2000 Reissue) para 689.


**235. Non-corporate bodies.** A Roman Catholic bishop[1], a dissenting minister[2], a principal of a college, a mayor or bailiff of a city[3], or the officers of a corporate body[4], and their respective successors, are not recognised by the law as corporations, and consequently cannot be trustees for charitable purposes in a corporate capacity, though the particular individuals named may act as trustees[5].

1  *A-G v Power* (1809) 1 Ball & B 145 at 149 per Lord Manners LC; and see *Re Lalor's goods* (1901) 85 LT 643.

2  *A-G for Ireland v Lee* (1869) IR 4 Eq 84.

3    *A-G v Gilbert* (1847) 10 Beav 517.
4    *A-G v Tancred* (1757) 1 Eden 10 at 14 per Henley, Lord Keeper.
5    See the cases cited in notes 2–4 supra.


**236. Certificates of incorporation of charity trustees as a body corporate.**
Where the trustees[1] of a charity apply[2] to the Charity Commissioners for a certificate of
incorporation of the trustees as a body corporate, and the Commissioners consider that
the incorporation of the trustees would be in the interests of the charity, the
Commissioners may grant such a certificate, subject to such conditions or directions[3] as
they think fit to insert in it[4]. The Commissioners must not, however, grant such a
certificate in a case where the charity appears to them to be required to be registered[5] but
is not so registered[6]. On the grant of such a certificate the trustees of the charity become
a body corporate by such name as is specified in the certificate and any relevant rights or
liabilities of those trustees become[7] rights or liabilities of that body[8]. A certificate of
incorporation is conclusive evidence that all the preliminary requirements for
incorporation[9] have been complied with, and the date of incorporation mentioned in the
certificate is deemed to be the date at which incorporation has taken place[10].

The certificate of incorporation vests in the body corporate all real and personal
estate, of whatever nature or tenure, belonging to or held by any person or persons in
trust for the charity, and thereupon any person or persons in whose name or names any
stocks, funds or securities are standing in trust for the charity, must transfer them into the
name of the body corporate, but this does not apply to property vested in the official
custodian[11].

After their incorporation the trustees may sue and be sued in their corporate name,
and have the same powers, and are subject to the same restrictions and limitations, as
respects the holding, acquisition and disposal of property for or in connection with the
purposes of the charity as they had or were subject to while unincorporated[12]. Any
relevant legal proceedings[13] that might have been continued or commenced by or against
the trustees may be continued or commenced by or against them in their corporate
name[14]. After a certificate of incorporation has been granted all trustees of the charity,
notwithstanding their incorporation, are chargeable for such property as comes into their
hands, and are answerable and accountable for their own acts, receipts, neglects, and
defaults, and for the due administration of the charity and its property, in the same
manner and to the same extent as if no such incorporation had been effected[15]. After the
incorporation of the trustees of any charity, every donation, gift and disposition of
property, real or personal, lawfully made before the incorporation but not having actually
taken effect, or thereafter lawfully made, by deed, will or otherwise to or in favour of the
charity, or the trustees of the charity, or otherwise for the purposes of the charity, take
effect as if made to or in favour of the incorporated body[16] or otherwise for the like
purposes[17].

The Commissioners may amend a certificate of incorporation either on the
application of the incorporated body to which it relates or of their own motion[18]. Before
making any such amendment of their own motion, the Commissioners must by notice
in writing inform the trustees of the relevant charity[19] of their proposals, and invite those
trustees to make representations to them within a time specified in the notice, being not
less than one month from the date of the notice[20]. The Commissioners must take into
consideration any representations made by those trustees within the time so specified,
and may then (without further notice) proceed with their proposals either without

modification or with such modifications as appear to them to be desirable[21]. The Commissioners may amend a certificate of incorporation either by making an order specifying the amendment or by issuing a new certificate of incorporation taking account of the amendment[22].

The Commissioners must keep a record of all applications for, and certificates of, incorporation and must preserve all documents sent to them under these provisions[23].

1   For the purposes of the Charities Act 1993 Pt VII (ss 50–62), 'the trustees' means the charity trustees (see para 1 note 10 ante): s 62.

2   Every application to the Charity Commissioners for a certificate of incorporation must be in writing and signed by the trustees of the charity concerned and be accompanied by such documents or information as the Commissioners may require for the purpose of the application: ibid s 52(1). The Commissioners may require any statement contained in any such application, or any document or information so supplied to be verified in such manner as they may specify: s 52(2). 'Document' includes information recorded in any form, and, in relation to information recorded otherwise than in legible form, any reference to its production is to be construed as a reference to the furnishing of a copy of it in legible form, and any reference to the furnishing of a copy of, or extract from, it is accordingly to be construed as a reference to the furnishing of a copy of, or extract from, it in legible form: s 97(2). As to the Charity Commissioners see paras 486–512 post. For the meaning of 'charity' see para 1 ante.

    Before a certificate of incorporation is granted, trustees of the charity must have been effectually appointed to the satisfaction of the Commissioners: s 53(1).

3   All conditions and directions inserted in any certificate of incorporation are binding upon and performed or observed by the trustees as trusts of the charity, and ibid s 88 (see para 494 post) (enforcement of orders of the Commissioners) applies to any trustee who fails to perform or observe any such condition or direction as it applies to a person guilty of disobedience to any such order of the Commissioners as is mentioned in that provision: s 58.

4   Ibid s 50(1).

5   Under ibid s 3: see para 282 et seq post.

6   Ibid s 50(2).

7   Ie without prejudice to ibid s 54: see the text and note 15 infra.

8   Ibid s 50(3). 'Relevant rights or liabilities' means rights or liabilities in connection with any property vesting in the body corporate under s 51 (see the text and note 11 infra): s 50(6). A body incorporated under s 50 need not have a common seal: s 50(5).

    Where a certificate of incorporation is granted vacancies in the number of the trustees of the charity must from time to time be filled up so far as required by the constitution or settlement of the charity, or by any conditions or directions in the certificate, by such legal means as would have been available for the appointment of new trustees of the charity if no certificate of incorporation had been granted, or otherwise as required by such conditions or directions: s 53(2).

9   Ie under ibid Pt VII.

10   Ibid s 55.

11   Ibid s 51. As to the official custodian see para 273 et seq post.

12   Ibid s 50(4)(a), (b).

13   For these purposes, 'relevant legal proceedings' means legal proceedings in connection with any property vesting in the body corporate under ibid s 51 (see the text and note 11 supra): s 50(6).

14   Ibid s 50(4).

15   Ibid s 54.

16   For these purposes, 'incorporated body' means a body incorporated under ibid s 50 (see the text and notes 1–8, 12–14 supra): s 62.

17   Ibid s 59.

18   Ibid s 56(1).

19   For these purposes, 'relevant charity', in relation to an incorporated body, means the charity the trustees of which have been incorporated as that body: ibid s 62.

20   Ibid s 56(2).

21   Ibid s 56(3).

22   Ibid s 56(4).

23   Ibid s 57(1). Any person may inspect such documents, under the direction of the Commissioners, and any person may require a copy or extract of any such document to be certified by a certificate signed by the secretary of the Commissioners: s 57(2).

**237. Execution of documents by incorporated body.** There are provisions
which have effect as respects the execution of documents by an incorporated body[1].

If an incorporated body has a common seal, a document[2] may be executed by the
body by the affixing of its common seal[3].

Whether or not it has a common seal, a document may be executed by an
incorporated body either: (1) by being signed by a majority of the trustees of the relevant
charity and expressed, in whatever form of words, to be executed by the body[4]; or (2)
by being executed in pursuance of an authority conferred[5] by the trustees of the relevant
charity[6]. Such an authority (a) suffices for any document if it is given in writing or by
resolution of a meeting of the trustees of the relevant charity, notwithstanding the want
of any formality that would otherwise[7] be required in giving an authority[8]; (b) may be
given so as to make the powers conferred exercisable by any of the trustees, or may be
restricted to named persons or in any other way[9]; (c) subject to any such restriction, and
until it is revoked has effect, notwithstanding any change in the trustees of the relevant
charity, as a continuing authority given by the trustees from time to time of the charity
and exercisable by such trustees[10].

A document duly executed by an incorporated body which makes it clear on its face
that it is intended by the person or persons making it to be a deed has effect, upon
delivery, as a deed; and it is to be presumed, unless a contrary intention is proved, to be
delivered upon its being so executed[11].

In favour of a purchaser[12] a document is deemed to have been duly executed by such
a body if it purports to be signed by a majority of the trustees of the relevant charity, or
by such of the trustees of the relevant charity as are authorised by the trustees of that
charity to execute it in the name and on behalf of the body[13]. Where the document
makes it clear on its face that it is intended by the person or persons making it to be a
deed, it is deemed to have been delivered upon its being executed[14].

1   Charities Act 1993 s 60(1). For the meaning of 'incorporated body' see para 236 note 16 ante.
2   For the meaning of 'document' see para 236 note 2 ante.
3   Charities Act 1993 s 60(2).
4   Ibid s 60(3)(a).
5   The trustees of the relevant charity in the case of an incorporated body may, subject to the trusts of the
    charity, confer on any two or more of their number a general authority, or an authority limited in such
    manner as the trustees think fit, to execute in the name and on behalf of the body documents for giving
    effect to transactions to which the body is a party: ibid s 60(4). In any such authority to execute a
    document in the name and on behalf of an incorporated body there is, unless the contrary intention
    appears, implied authority also to execute it for the body in the name and on behalf of the official
    custodian or of any other person, in any case in which the trustees could do so: s 60(6). For the meaning
    of 'trusts' see para 210 note 5 ante. For the meaning of 'the trustees' see para 236 note 1 ante. For the
    meaning of 'relevant charity' see para 236 note 19 ante. As to the official custodian see para 273 et seq
    post.
6   Ibid s 60(3)(b).
7   Ie apart from ibid s 60(4): see note 5 supra.
8   Ibid s 60(5)(a).
9   Ibid s 60(5)(b).
10  Ibid s 60(5)(c).
11  Ibid s 60(7).
12  For these purposes, 'purchaser' means a purchaser in good faith for valuable consideration and includes
    a lessee, mortgagee or other person who for valuable consideration acquires an interest in property: ibid
    s 60(8).
13  Ibid s 60(8).
14  Ibid s 60(8).

**238. Power of Charity Commissioners to dissolve incorporated body.** Where the Charity Commissioners[1] are satisfied: (1) that an incorporated body[2] has no assets or does not operate[3]; or (2) that the relevant charity[4] in the case of an incorporated body has ceased to exist[5]; or (3) that the institution[6] previously constituting, or treated by them as constituting, any such charity has ceased to be, or, as the case may be, was not at the time of the body's incorporation, a charity[7]; or (4) that the purposes of the relevant charity in the case of an incorporated body have been achieved so far as is possible or are in practice incapable of being achieved[8], they may of their own motion make an order dissolving the body as from such date as is specified in the order[9].

Where the Commissioners are satisfied, on the application of the trustees[10] of the relevant charity in the case of an incorporated body, that it would be in the interests of the charity for that body to be dissolved, the Commissioners may make an order dissolving the body as from such date as is specified in the order[11].

An order made under these provisions with respect to an incorporated body has the effect of vesting in the trustees of the relevant charity, in trust for that charity, all property for the time being vested in the body, or in any other person, apart from the official custodian[12], in trust for that charity[13]. If the Commissioners so direct in the order (a) all or any specified[14] part of that property vests, instead of vesting in the trustees of the relevant charity, in a specified person as trustee for, or nominee of, that charity, or in such persons (other than the trustees of the relevant charity) as may be specified[15]; (b) any specified investments, or any specified class or description of investments, held by any person in trust for the relevant charity must be transferred to the trustees of that charity, or to any such person or persons as is or are mentioned in head (a) above[16].

In relation to certain orders[17] which are made with respect to an incorporated body, any rights or liabilities of the body become rights or liabilities of the trustees of the relevant charity, and any legal proceedings that might have been continued or commenced by or against the body may be continued or commenced by or against those trustees[18].

Any order made by the Commissioners under these provisions may be varied or revoked by a further order so made[19].

1  As to the Charity Commissioners see paras 486–512 post.
2  For the meaning of 'incorporated body' see para 236 note 16 ante.
3  Charities Act 1993 s 61(1)(a).
4  For the meaning of 'relevant charity' see para 236 note 19 ante.
5  Charities Act 1993 s 61(1)(b).
6  For the meaning of 'institution' see para 1 ante.
7  Charities Act 1993 s 61(1)(c).
8  Ibid s 61(1)(d).
9  Ibid s 61(1). A person guilty of disobedience to an order of the Commissioners under s 61 may on the application of the Commissioners to the High Court be dealt with as for disobedience to an order of the High Court: s 88(a). The power of the Commissioners to discharge an order at any time within 12 months after it has been made does not apply to orders under s 61: see s 89(3); and para 492 post. As to orders of the Commissioners generally see s 89; and para 492 post.
10  For the meaning of 'trustees' see para 236 note 1 ante.
11  Charities Act 1993 s 61(2).
12  As to the official custodian see para 273 et seq post.
13  Charities Act 1993 s 61(3).
14  For these purposes, 'specified' means specified by the Commissioners in the order: ibid s 61(4).
15  Ibid s 61(4)(a).
16  Ibid s 61(4)(b).
17  Ie any order under ibid s 61 by virtue of which: (1) any property vested as mentioned in s 61(3) (see the text and notes 12–13 supra) is vested in the trustees of the relevant charity, or in any person as trustee

for, or nominee of, that charity; or (2) any investments held by any person in trust for the relevant charity are required to be transferred to the trustees of that charity, or to any person as trustee for, or nominee of, that charity: s 61(6).

18  Ibid s 61(5).
19  Ibid s 61(7).

# (2)  TRUSTEES OF PAROCHIAL AND DIOCESAN CHARITIES

**239. Parochial recreation grounds and allotments.** Trustees who hold property for the purposes of a public recreation ground or of allotments for the benefit of the inhabitants of a parish[1] having a parish council[2] or for other charitable purposes (except those of an ecclesiastical charity[3]) connected with such a parish may transfer the property to the parish council or to persons appointed by the council, provided that the Charity Commissioners[4] approve and the council consents[5]. The council or its appointees take the property on the same trusts and subject to the same conditions as the trustees did[6].

1  Or, in Wales, a community: Charities Act 1993 s 79(7)(a). As to areas and authorities in England and Wales see LOCAL GOVERNMENT.
2  Or, in Wales, a community council: ibid s 79(7)(a).
3  For the meaning of 'ecclesiastical charity' see para 240 note 4 post.
4  As to the Charity Commissioners see paras 486–512 post.
5  Charities Act 1993 s 79(1). This provision applies to property held for any public purposes as it applies to property held for charitable purposes: s 79(1). Such a transfer of any property does not operate as a breach of any covenant or condition against alienation or give rise to a forfeiture: see para 180 note 6 ante.
       Section 79 (as amended) does not affect the trusteeship, control or management of any foundation or voluntary school within the meaning of the School Standards and Framework Act 1998: Charities Act 1993 s 79(9) (substituted by Education Act 1996 s 582(1), Sch 37 para 119; and amended by the School Standards and Framework Act 1998 s 140(1), Sch 39 para 49). See EDUCATION. As to limitations on the provisions of the Charities Act 1993 s 79 see s 79(10); and para 241 note 2 post.
6  Ibid s 79(1).

**240. Local representatives as trustees of rural parochial charities.** If the charity trustees[1] of a parochial charity[2] in a parish[3], other than an ecclesiastical charity[4] or one founded less than 40 years previously, do not include persons elected by the local government electors, ratepayers[5] or parish inhabitants or appointed by the parish council[6] or meeting, the council or meeting may appoint additional charity trustees to such number as the Charity Commissioners may allow[7]. If there is only a sole charity trustee of such a charity and he is not so elected or appointed, the Commissioners may approve the increase of the number of trustees to three, of whom one may be nominated by the person holding the office of the sole trustee and one by the council or meeting[8].

Trustees appointed under this provision hold office for four years and are eligible for reappointment on retiring[9].

1  For the meaning of 'charity trustees' see para 1 note 10 ante.
2  'Parochial charity' means, in relation to any parish or, in Wales, community, a charity the benefits of which are, or the separate distribution of the benefits of which is, confined to the inhabitants of the parish or community, or of a single ancient ecclesiastical parish which included that parish or community or part of it, or of an area consisting of that parish or community with not more than four neighbouring parishes or communities: Charities Act 1993 s 96(1).

3    Or, in Wales, a community: ibid s 79(7)(a). As to areas and authorities in England and Wales see LOCAL
     GOVERNMENT.
4    'Ecclesiastical charity' includes a charity the endowment of which is held for one or more of the
     following purposes: (1) for any spiritual purpose which is a legal purpose; or (2) for the benefit of any
     spiritual person or ecclesiastical officer as such; or (3) for use (if a building) as a church, chapel, mission
     room or Sunday school or otherwise by any particular church or denomination, and any building which
     in the Charity Commissioners' opinion has been erected or provided within 40 years before 5 March
     1894 mainly by or at the cost of members of any particular church or denomination; or (4) for the
     maintenance, repair or improvement of any such building or for the maintenance of divine service in it;
     (5) otherwise for the benefit of any particular church or denomination or any of its members as such:
     Local Government Act 1894 s 75(2); applied by the Charities Act 1993 s 96(1). Where any endowment
     of a charity, other than a building held for any of the above purposes, is held in part only for some of the
     above purposes, the charity is an ecclesiastical charity so far as that endowment is concerned: Local
     Government Act 1894 s 75(2) proviso (as so applied).
5    Domestic rates were abolished by the Local Government Finance Act 1988 and replaced by the
     community charge, itself replaced by the council tax in 1993: see the Local Government Finance Act
     1992; and RATING AND COUNCIL TAX vol 39(1) (Reissue) para 602.
6    Or, in Wales, the community council: Charities Act 1993 s 79(7)(a).
7    Ibid s 79(2). Section 79 (as amended) does not affect the trusteeship, control or management of any
     foundation or voluntary school: see para 239 note 5 ante. As to limitations on the provisions of the
     Charities Act 1993 s 79 see s 79(10); and para 241 note 2 post.
8    Ibid s 79(2).
9    Ibid s 79(8). If no previous appointment has been made under s 79(2) or the corresponding provision of
     the Local Government Act 1894 or the Charities Act 1960, and more than one trustee is appointed, half
     of those appointed must be appointed for a term of two years: Charities Act 1993 s 79(8)(a).
     Appointments to fill casual vacancies are for the remainder of the term of the previous appointment:
     s 79(8)(b).

**241. Appointment of trustees of parochial charities.** Before the passing of the
Local Government Act 1894, the inhabitants of a rural parish, in vestry or not, or a select
vestry were sometimes entitled to appoint charity trustees[1] for, or trustees or beneficiaries
of, a charity[2]. In such a case (other than as regards ecclesiastical charities[3]) where the
parish[4] has a parish council[5], the appointment is now to be made by the parish council[6]
or, in the case of beneficiaries, by persons appointed by the parish council[7], and where
the parish[8] does not have a parish council[9], the appointment is to be made by the parish
meeting[10].

In some cases, before the passing of the Local Government Act 1894, overseers as such
or churchwardens as such were charity trustees of or trustees for parochial charities in rural
parishes, alone or jointly with others[11]. In such a case (other than as regards ecclesiastical
charities) the former overseer or churchwarden trustees are replaced by trustees appointed
by the parish council[12] or, if there is no parish council[13], by the parish meeting[14], to a
number not greater than that of the former overseer or churchwarden trustees[15].

If, before 1 April 1927[16], outside Greater London (other than the outer London
boroughs) overseers of a parish as such were charity trustees of or trustees for any charity,
alone or jointly, they are replaced by trustees appointed by the parish council[17] or, if there
is none, by the parish meeting[18], to a number not greater than that of the former overseer
trustees[19]. Where after 1 April 1974 an existing urban parish is not comprised in a parish,
the power of appointing trustees rests with the district council[20].

Charity trustees and trustees for a charity appointed under these provisions must be
appointed for four years, but are eligible for reappointment on retiring[21].

1    For the meaning of 'charity trustees' see para 1 note 10 ante.
2    Charities Act 1993 s 79(3). For the meaning of 'charity' see para 1 ante.

Section 79 (as amended) does not affect the trusteeship, control or management of any foundation or voluntary school: see para 239 note 5 ante. It does not extend to the Isles of Scilly, and they have effect subject to orders made under any enactment relating to local government with respect to local government areas or to the powers of local authorities: s 79(10).

3    For the meaning of 'ecclesiastical charity' see para 240 note 4 ante.

4    Or, in Wales, a community: see the Charities Act 1993 s 79(7)(b). As to areas and authorities in England and Wales see LOCAL GOVERNMENT.

5    Or, in Wales a community council: see ibid s 79(7)(b).

6    See note 5 supra.

7    See note 5 supra.

8    See note 5 supra.

9    See note 5 supra.

10   Charities Act 1993 s 79(3), (11). In relation to Wales, the reference to the parish council in the text is substituted with a reference to council of the county or, as the case may be, county borough: s 79(7)(b) (amended by the Local Government (Wales) Act 1994 s 66(6), Sch 16 para 101(4)). In other cases persons such as the rector and the lord of the manor were trustees, together with overseers or churchwardens; in such cases they seem to continue as trustees, together with persons appointed by the parish council in place of the churchwardens or overseers.

11   Charities Act 1993 s 79(4).

12   Or, in Wales, a community council: ibid s 79(7)(c).

13   See note 12 supra.

14   Or, in Wales, council of the county or, as the case may be, county borough: Charities Act 1993 s 79(7)(c) (amended by the Local Government (Wales) Act 1994 s 66(6), Sch 16 para 101(4)).

15   Charities Act 1993 s 79(4), (11).

16   Ie the date on which overseers were abolished by the Rating and Valuation Act 1925 s 62 (as originally enacted), and their functions transferred to rating or other local authorities by s 1(2); and the Overseers Order 1927, SR & O 1927/55. See LOCAL GOVERNMENT; RATING AND COUNCIL TAX.

17   See note 12 supra.

18   See note 14 supra.

19   Charities Act 1993 s 79(5).

20   Ibid s 79(6).

21   Ibid s 79(8). However, an appointment to fill a casual vacancy must be for the remainder of the term of the previous appointment: s 79(8)(b).

**242. Dissolution of parishes: ecclesiastical charities.** If a benefice is dissolved by a pastoral scheme[1], and any property of a charity established for ecclesiastical purposes of the Church of England is vested in or under the management or control of the incumbent of that benefice or a corporation of which he is a member, the trusts of the charity or the constitution of the corporation have effect with the substitution of the incumbent of the new benefice created by the union or, as the case may be, of a benefice, incorporating part of the area of the dissolved benefice, specified by order of the Charity Commissioners[2]. Corresponding provision is made in the case of the churchwardens and parochial church council of a dissolved benefice[3] and where a team ministry is established by a pastoral scheme for an area comprising the whole or a major part of the area of a benefice[4]. Changes in the vesting of property under these provisions take effect without any conveyance or other assurance[5].

If a pastoral scheme unites one parish with another or alters the area of a parish, the purposes of a charity defined by reference to the area of one of the parishes are altered by the substitution of a reference to the united or altered parish, and the trusts of the charity have effect accordingly[6].

If there is a condition of any benefaction as to attendance at or the performance of divine service or any other act at a church, and the church ceases to be used for divine service by virtue of a declaration of redundancy made by a pastoral scheme, the condition is to be taken as referring to the parish church of the parish in which the church originally specified or its site is situated[7].

Where any property of a charity established for ecclesiastical purposes of the Church of England is vested in or under the management or control of the incumbent of a benefice and the benefice becomes vacant or the bishop declares a suspension period in respect of the benefice, then, during the period of the vacancy or suspension, at the case may be, the trusts of the charity have effect, without any conveyance or other assurance, with the substitution for the incumbent of that benefice of the priest in charge of that benefice[8].

1    Ie under the Pastoral Measure 1983: see ECCLESIASTICAL LAW vol 14 para 856 et seq.
2    Ibid s 40, Sch 3 para 11(1). As to the Charity Commissioners see paras 486–512 post. These provisions do not apply to any fund or property for which provision is made under s 63 (as amended) (trusts for the repair etc of redundant buildings and contents) (see ECCLESIASTICAL LAW): Sch 3 para 11(10).
3    See ibid Sch 3 para 11(2). Unless otherwise dealt with by Sch 3 para 11, property held by or on behalf of the parochial church council of a dissolved parish vests in or is held on behalf of the parochial church council of the parish in which the parish church of the dissolved parish is situated: see Sch 3 para 11(8).
4    See ibid Sch 3 para 11(3) (amended by the Team and Group Ministries Measure 1995 s 6(4)).
5    Pastoral Measure 1983 Sch 3 para 11(4), (8).
6    See ibid Sch 3 para 11(5).
7    Ibid Sch 3 para 11(9). See also s 63(4), where similar provisions apply in relation to giving sermons in church affected by a declaration of redundancy, with the proviso that the sermons may be given in such other church as the bishop may, with the Charity Commissioners' approval, direct.
8    Ibid s 74(1), (2).

**243. Alteration of diocesan boundaries: bishops as trustees.** Upon the application of the bishops concerned, or one of them, the Charity Commissioners[1] may make orders vesting charity property held upon trust by the bishop of one diocese in the bishop of another diocese, and substituting one bishop for another as trustee, in cases where the limits of dioceses have been altered[2].

1    As to the Charity Commissioners see paras 486–512 post.
2    See the Bishops Trusts Substitution Act 1858 ss 1, 2; and ECCLESIASTICAL LAW vol 14 para 801. The order may not deal with advowsons or similar rights which could be dealt with by a scheme of the Church Commissioners, nor may it deal with any ecclesiastical patronage or similar right without the consent of the Church Commissioners: see s 2 (amended by virtue of the Church Commissioners Measure 1947 ss 1, 2, 18(2)). The order may not affect trusts of a visitatorial or any other nature or character relating to the halls or colleges of Oxford or Cambridge Universities or to the colleges of Winchester, Eton or Westminster: see the Bishops Trusts Substitution Act 1858 s 4; and para 465 post. The Act does not extend to endowments of an eleemosynary or any other character governed by a specific Act of Parliament: s 5. Any costs necessarily incident to effecting the transfers are to be defrayed by order of the Charity Commissioners out of the property, real or personal, as they may direct, which are to be transferred: see s 3. As to the Church Commissioners see ECCLESIASTICAL LAW vol 14 para 363 et seq.

# (3)  TRUSTEES OF LOCAL AUTHORITY CHARITIES

**244.  Transfer of local authority charities outside London.** In  consequence  of the reorganisation of local government outside Greater London effected by the Local

Government Act 1972[1], property held on charitable trusts by existing local authorities was transferred to the new authorities established by that Act.

On 1 April 1974, where any property was held, as sole trustee, exclusively for charitable purposes[2] by an existing[3] local authority[4] for an area outside Greater London[5], other than the parish council, parish meeting or representative body of an existing rural parish in England[6], but including the corporation of a borough included in a rural district, that property vested[7], on the same trusts[8], in a new[9] local authority[10].

Where property was held by one of the existing authority in heads (1) to (4) below, and so held for the benefit of, or of the inhabitants of, or of any particular class or body of persons in, a specified area, the property vested in the new authority specified in heads (1) to (4) below, the area of which comprises the whole or the greater part of that specified area[11]. Where the property was so held but was not held for such a benefit, it vested in the new authority specified in heads (1) to (4) below, the area of which comprises the whole or the greater part of the area of the existing authority, that is to say[12]:

(1)  where the existing authority was a county[13] council, the new authority is the council of the new county[14];

(2)  where the existing authority was the council of a borough or urban district in England, the new authority is the council of the parish constituted by reference to existing urban district and borough boundaries[15] or, where there was no such parish, the council of the district[16];

(3)  where the existing authority was the council of a borough or urban district in Wales, the new authority is the council of the community or, where there is no such council, the council of the district[17]; and

(4)  where the existing authority was a rural district council, then, if the rural district is co-extensive with a parish, the new authority is the parish council, and in any other case the new authority is the council of the district[18].

Where the property was held by an existing county council or county borough council for the purposes of a registered educational charity[19] then: (a) if the property was so held for the benefit of, or of the inhabitants of, or of any particular class or body of persons in, a specified area, the property vested in the new authority which is the local education authority for the whole or the greater part of that specified area[20]; and (b) in any other case, the property vested in the new authority which is the local education authority for the whole or the greater part of the area of the existing county council or county borough council by which the property is held[21].

Further, where the property was held by the corporation of a borough included in a rural district, it vested in the parish council for the parish consisting of the area of the existing borough[22].

Where the property was held by the parish council, parish meeting or representative body of an existing rural parish in Wales, then: (i) in the case of property held by an existing parish council, the property vested in the community council for the community or group of communities, the area or areas of which are co-extensive with the area of the parish or parishes for which the existing parish council act[23]; (ii) in the case of property held by the parish meeting or representative body of an existing parish the area of which is comprised in a community for which there is a community council, the property vested in that community council[24]; and (iii) in any other case, the property vested in the council of the district which comprises the area of the existing rural parish[25].

Where, on 1 April 1974, any power with respect to a charity[26] (not being a charity incorporated under the Companies Acts or by charter[27]) was under the trusts of the charity or by virtue of any enactment vested in, or in the holder of an office connected with, certain existing local authorities[28], that power vested in, or in the holder of the corresponding office connected with, or (if there is no such office) the proper officer[29] of, the corresponding[30] new authority[31].

Nothing in these provisions affects any power of Her Majesty, the court[32] or any other person to alter the trusts of any charity and nor do they apply in a case to which the provisions relating to Welsh Church funds apply[33].

1   See further LOCAL GOVERNMENT.
2   For the meaning of 'charitable purposes' see para 1 ante; definition applied by the Local Government Act 1972 s 210(11); Interpretation Act 1978 s 17(2)(a).
3   'Existing', in relation to a local government or other area or a local authority or other body means that area or body as it existed immediately before 26 October 1972 (the passing of the Local Government Act 1972): s 270(1).
4   'Local authority' means a county council, a district council, a London borough council or a parish council but, in relation to Wales, means a county council, county borough council or community: ibid s 270(1) (definition amended by the Local Government Act 1985 s 102, Sch 16 para 8, Sch 17; and the Local Government (Wales) Act 1994 s 1(5)). For these purposes, 'local authority', in relation to a parish, includes a parish meeting and the representative body of a parish: Local Government Act 1972 s 210(11).
5   As to the transfer of powers on local government reorganisation in Greater London see paras 244–245 post.
6   'Wales' means the combined area of the preserved counties, and 'England' does not include any area which is included in any of the preserved counties: Local Government Act 1972 s 269 (substituted by the Local Government (Wales) Act 1994 s 1(3), Sch 2 para 8).
7   Ie in accordance with the Local Government Act 1972 s 210(2)–(5): see the text and notes 11–25 infra.
8   For the meaning of 'trusts' see para 210 note 5 ante; definition applied by ibid s 210(11); Interpretation Act 1978 s 17(2)(a).
9   'New', in relation to any area or authority, means an area or authority established by or under the Local Government Act 1972, including one established by virtue of any provision of the Local Government (Wales) Act 1994: Local Government Act 1972 s 270(1) (amended by the Local Government (Wales) Act 1994 s 66(5), Sch 15 para 57).
10  Local Government Act 1972 s 210(1). As to areas and authorities in England and Wales see LOCAL GOVERNMENT.
11  Ibid s 210(2).
12  Ibid s 210(2).
13  'County', without more, means, in relation to England, a metropolitan county or a non-metropolitan county, but in the expression 'county council' means, in relation to England, a non-metropolitan county only: ibid s 270(1) (amended by the Local Government Act 1985 s 102, Sch 16 para 8).
14  Local Government Act 1972 s 210(2)(a).
15  Ie the council of the parish constituted under ibid s 1, Sch 1 Pt V: see LOCAL GOVERNMENT.
16  Ibid s 210(2)(b). 'District', without more, means, in relation to England, a metropolitan district or a non-metropolitan district: s 270(1).
17  Ibid s 210(2)(c).
18  Ibid s 210(2)(d).
19  Ie established under the Charities Act 1960 s 4 (repealed: now re-enacted in the Charities Act 1993 s 3 (see para 282 et seq post)) in any part of that register maintained by the Secretary of State by virtue of the Charities Act 1960 s 2 (repealed) (educational charities): Local Government Act 1972 s 210(3). For the meaning of 'charity' see para 1 ante; definition applied by the Local Government Act 1972 s 210(11); Interpretation Act 1978 s 17(2)(a).
20  Local Government Act 1972 s 210(3)(a).
21  Ibid s 210(3)(b).
22  Ibid s 210(4).
23  Ibid s 210(5)(a). As to property held by a Welsh borough or urban district council see the text to note 16 supra.
24  Ibid s 210(5)(b).
25  Ibid s 210(5)(c).

26 References in ibid s 210(6) to a power with respect to a charity do not include references to a power of any person by virtue of being a charity trustee of it; but where under the trusts of any charity, not being a charity incorporated under the Companies Acts or by charter, the charity trustees on 1 April 1974 included either an existing local authority to which the Local Government Act 1972 s 210(1) (see the text and notes 1–10 supra) applies or the holder of an office connected with such an existing local authority, those trustees instead included the corresponding new authority as defined in s 210(6) or, as the case may require, the holder of the corresponding office connected with, or (if there is no such office) the proper officer of, that authority: s 210(7). For the meaning of 'charity trustees' see para 1 note 10 ante; definition applied by s 210(11); Interpretation Act 1978 s 17(2)(a).

27 As to modes of creation of charitable corporations see para 219 ante.

28 Ie existing authorities to which the Local Government Act 1972 s 210(1) applies: see the text and notes 1–10 supra.

29 Any reference in the Local Government Act 1972 to a proper officer is, in relation to any purpose and any local authority or other body or any area, to be construed as a reference to an officer appointed for that purpose by that body or for that area, as the case may be: s 270(3).

30 Ie the new authority in which, had the property of the charity been vested in the existing local authority, that property would have been vested under ibid s 210(2)–(5) (see the text and notes 11–25 supra): see s 210(6).

31 Ibid s 210(6).

32 For the meaning of 'the court' see para 168 note 12 ante; definition applied by the Local Government Act 1972 s 210(11); Interpretation Act 1978 s 17(2)(a).

33 Local Government Act 1972 s 210(10). The reference in the text to the provisions relating to Welsh Church funds is a reference to s 211 (see LOCAL GOVERNMENT): see s 210(10).

**245. Transfer of local authority charities in London.** In consequence of the reorganisation of local government administration in and around London under the London Government Act 1963, it became necessary to transfer property held on charitable trusts by the London and Middlesex County Councils and the councils of metropolitan and county boroughs within Greater London, and to transfer powers in respect of a charity vested in those councils or certain others or in the holders of offices connected with such a council. Such property and powers were accordingly vested in either the Greater London Council or the Inner London Education Authority, or in one of the London borough councils, or in the holder of the appropriate office connected with the appropriate council[1]. Apart from those provisions, the Secretary of State for the Environment[2] had power by order to make such incidental, consequential, transitional or supplementary provision as appeared necessary or proper[3].

Under further reorganisation by the Local Government Act 1985 the Greater London Council was abolished[4] and a new Inner London Education Authority was established[5]. It was provided that where, immediately before the abolition date, any property was held exclusively for charitable purposes by the Greater London Council, and the Inner London Education Authority was the charity trustee of the charity to which the property related, that property should on that date vest in the new Inner London Education Authority[6]. Subject to this it was further provided that the Home Secretary could by order make such provision in relation to any charity as appeared to him necessary or expedient in consequence of the abolition of the Greater London Council[7].

Subsequently the new Inner London Education Authority was abolished by the Education Reform Act 1988[8]. Where, immediately before the abolition date, any property was held exclusively for charitable purposes by the Inner London Education Authority as sole trustee and the charity was primarily for the benefit of the area of a single inner London council[9], that property became vested on that date for the like purposes in that council[10]. In other areas where property was held exclusively for charitable purposes by the Inner London Education Authority as sole trustee, that property became vested on that date for the like purposes in the London Residuary Body[11] or in such other person as the Charity Commissioners should before that date appoint[12].

1    For details of the provisions transferring property and powers in respect of charities see the London Government Act 1963 s 81(1) (repealed) (property held by the London or Middlesex County Council), s 81(2) (repealed) (property held by borough councils), s 81(3) (repealed) (powers with respect to a charity vested in such a council or in the holder of an office connected with it), s 81(4) (repealed) (powers with respect to a charity established wholly or mainly for the benefit of an area within Greater London, vested in various county councils), s 81(6) (repealed) (powers with respect to other charities). See also s 81(7) (repealed) (charity trustees, including the holder of an office connected with a borough council within the Greater London area), and s 81(5) (repealed) (power for the Inner London Education Authority to nominate an inner London borough council, or the holder of an office connected with it, in whom powers with respect to a charity were to vest).

2    See the Secretary of State for the Environment Order 1970, SI 1970/1681 (as amended).

3    See the London Government Act 1963 s 84(1); and LONDON GOVERNMENT.
        For an example of the exercise of this power and its interaction with transitional provisions of s 81 (repealed) see *Re Alexandra Park and Palace Acts, Alexandra Park Trustees v Haringey London Borough Council* (1967) 66 LGR 306.

4    See the Local Government Act 1985 s 1(1). The abolition date was 1 April 1986: s 1(2).

5    Ie as from the abolition date (see note 4 supra): ibid s 18 (repealed).

6    Ibid s 90(1) (repealed).

7    Ibid s 90(2) (as amended).

8    Education Reform Act 1988 s 162(1). The abolition date was 1 April 1990: s 162(1), (2).

9    For these purposes, a charity is a charity primarily for the benefit of the area of a single inner London council if the charity is established for purposes which are by their nature or by the trusts of the charity directed wholly or mainly to the benefit of an area which falls wholly or mainly within that council's area: ibid s 192(9).
        'Inner London council' means the council of an inner London borough or (in its capacity as a local authority) the Common Council of the City of London: s 163(2). For the meaning of 'charity' see para 1 ante; and for the meaning of 'trusts' see para 210 note 5 ante; definitions applied by s 192(11) (amended by the Charities Act 1993 s 98(1), Sch 6 para 30).

10   Education Reform Act 1988 s 192(1). See further EDUCATION.
        Powers vested in officers of the Inner London Education Authority vested in the corresponding inner London council officer, if any, and otherwise in an officer appointed, with his consent and that of the council, by the Charity Commissioners: see s 192(2), (3). The appointment was to be made within two years of the abolition date, and in the meantime the London Residuary Body was to be treated as having been appointed: see s 192(7).
        As to the Charity Commissioners see paras 486–512 post.

11   As to the London Residuary Body see EDUCATION.

12   See Education Reform Act 1988 s 192(4).
        Powers with respect to such charities vested in, or in the holder of any office connected with, the Inner London Education Authority, became vested in the London Residuary Body or in such other person as the Charity Commissioners might appoint: see s 192(5). The appointment was to be made within two years of the abolition date, and in the meantime the London Residuary Body was to be treated as having been appointed: see s 192(7). References in s 192(1)–(5) to a power with respect to a charity do not include references to any power of any person by virtue of being a charity trustee of that charity: see s 192(6).
        There is provision for the replacement of charity trustees where they included the Inner London Education Authority or the holder of an office connected with the Inner London Education Authority: see s 192(6). For the meaning of 'charity trustees' see para 1 note 10 ante; definition applied by s 192(11) (amended by the Charities Act 1993 s 98(1), Sch 6 para 30).

# (4) APPOINTMENT OF TRUSTEES

### (i)  Initial Appointment

**246.  Donor's failure to appoint trustee.** The appointment of the first trustees of a charity rests with the donor, but a charitable gift is not defeated by his failure to provide machinery for carrying his charitable purpose into effect[1]. Where money is given to charity generally and indefinitely without trustees or objects selected, the Crown, as parens patriae, is the constitutional trustee, and disposes of the fund under the sign manual[2]. Where there is a devise for such charity as the testator has by writing appointed, and no writing is to be found, the Crown will appoint[3]. Where the donor intends to create a trust, but appoints no trustee, the court disposes of the fund by means of a scheme[4].

1   As to the failure of or disclaimer by trustee see para 155 ante.
2   *Moggridge v Thackwell* (1803) 7 Ves 36 at 83, 86 per Lord Eldon LC; *Cary v Abbot* (1802) 7 Ves 490; *Morice v Bishop of Durham* (1805) 10 Ves 522 at 541 per Lord Eldon LC; *Ommanney v Butcher* (1823) Turn & R 260 at 271 per Plumer MR. As to the Crown's jurisdiction over charities see paras 456–457 post.
3   *A-G v Syderfen* (1683) 1 Vern 224.
4   *Mills v Farmer* (1815) 1 Mer 55 at 94–95 per Lord Eldon LC; *Reeve v A-G* (1843) 3 Hare 191 at 196–197 per Shadwell V-C. As to general principles for the direction of schemes see para 171 ante.

**247.  Who is the initial trustee.** In general, no problem arises in determining who has been appointed trustee and who should act, and if any question does arise it is determined by a process of construction[1]. However, where the gift is to a local branch of a large charitable institution, the byelaws of the institution may require the gift to be transferred to the main institution, although its application may be restricted to the area of the branch[2]. Such byelaws do not extend to gifts which the local branch is to hold on special trusts, not for the general purposes of the institution[3].

1   See eg *Re Lavers* (1908) Times, 7 November, where property was to be vested in trustees 'commonly called the X Trustees (the same who have the right of presentation of the vicarage of Y)'. The right of presentation was not vested in the X Trustees, and it was held that the testator intended to appoint those in whom it was vested.
2   *Royal National Lifeboat Institution v Turver* (1915) 31 TLR 340.
3   *Royal National Lifeboat Institution v Turver* (1915) 31 TLR 340.

### (ii)  Who may or should be appointed New Trustees

**248.  General principles.** Vacancies among trustees should be filled by persons who are likely best to discharge the duties imposed upon them by the trust[1].

The fact that three new trustees are appointed, of whom two hold opposite views on an important matter affecting the charity, is not sufficient reason for upsetting an appointment[2]; but a suspicion that former trustees have used their powers for political ends is sufficient to prevent their re-appointment[3]. There is no objection to trustees being related to one another[4].

1 *Baker v Lee* (1860) 8 HL Cas 495 at 513 per Lord Cranworth.
2 *Re Burnham National Schools* (1873) LR 17 Eq 241 at 250 per Jessel MR.
3 *Re Norwich Charities* (1837) 2 My & Cr 275.
4 *Re Lancaster Charities, Re Charitable Trusts Act 1853* (1860) 3 LT 582. However, the Charity Commissioners sometimes take objection in cases of charities in small parishes, with small bodies of trustees, to a preponderance of members of one family if the trustees co-opt one another. As to the Charity Commissioners see paras 486–512 post.

**249. Disqualification for acting as charity trustee.** A person is disqualified for being a charity trustee[1] or trustee for a charity[2] if:

(1) he has been convicted of any offence involving dishonesty or deception[3];

(2) he has been adjudged bankrupt or sequestration of his estate has been awarded and (in either case) he has not been discharged[4], unless leave has been granted under the Company Directors Disqualification Act 1986[5] for him to act as director of the charity[6];

(3) he has made a composition or arrangement with, or granted a trust deed for, his creditors and has not been discharged in respect of it[7];

(4) he has been removed from the office of charity trustee or trustee for a charity by an order made by the Charity Commissioners[8], or by the High Court, on the grounds of any misconduct or mismanagement in the administration of the charity for which he was responsible or to which he was privy, or which he by his conduct contributed to or facilitated[9];

(5) he has been removed under the Law Reform (Miscellaneous Provisions) (Scotland) Act 1990[10] from being concerned in the management or control of any body[11];

(6) he is subject to a disqualification order or disqualification undertaking under the Company Directors Disqualification Act 1986, to a disqualification order under Part II of the Companies (Northern Ireland) Order 1989[12] or to an order made under the Insolvency Act 1986[13] on failure to pay under a county court administration order[14].

On the application of a disqualified person, with certain exceptions[15], the Commissioners may waive his disqualification either generally or in relation to a particular charity or a particular class of charities[16]. Any such waiver must be notified in writing to the person concerned[17].

1 For the meaning of 'charity trustees' see para 1 note 10 ante.
2 For the meaning of 'charity' see para 1 ante.
3 Charities Act 1993 s 72(1)(a). This applies whether the conviction occurred before or after 1 August 1993 (the commencement of s 72(1)), but does not apply to any conviction which is a spent conviction under the Rehabilitation of Offenders Act 1974: Charities Act 1993 s 72(2)(a). As to spent convictions and the Rehabilitation of Offenders Act 1974 see CRIMINAL LAW, EVIDENCE AND PROCEDURE vol 11(2) (Reissue) para 1566 et seq.
4 Charities Act 1993 s 72(1)(b). This applies whether the adjudication of bankruptcy or the sequestration occurred before or after 1 August 1993 (the commencement of s 72(1)): s 72(2)(b). See BANKRUPTCY AND INSOLVENCY.

5   Ie under the Company Directors Disqualification Act 1986 s 11: see BANKRUPTCY AND INSOLVENCY
    vol 3(2) (Reissue) para 688 et seq.
6   Charities Act 1993 s 72(3).
7   Ibid s 72(1)(c). This applies whether the composition or arrangement was made, or the trust deed was
    granted, before or after the commencement of s 72(1): s 72(2)(c). See BANKRUPTCY AND INSOLVENCY.
8   Ie under the Charities Act 1993 s 18(2)(i) (see para 503 ante); or under the Charities Act 1960 s 20(1A)(i)
    (added by the Charities Act 1992 s 8) (but now repealed); or under the Charities Act 1960 s 20(1)(i) (now
    repealed) before 1 November 1992 (ie the commencement of the Charities Act 1992 s 8): see the
    Charities Act 1993 s 72(1)(d). The Charities Act 1992 s 18 replaces the Charities Act 1960 s 20. As to
    the Charity Commissioners see paras 486–512 post.
9   Charities Act 1993 s 72(1)(d). This applies in relation to orders made and removals effected before or
    after 1 August 1993 (the commencement of s 72(1)): s 72(2)(d). The Commissioners must keep, in such
    manner as they think fit, a register of all persons who have been removed from office as mentioned in
    s 72(1)(d) either by an order of the Commissioners made before or after the commencement of s 72(1)
    or by an order of the High Court made after 1 January 1993 (the commencement of the Charities Act
    1992 s 45(1)): Charities Act 1993 s 72(6). Where any person is removed by the High Court, the court
    must notify the Commissioners of his removal: s 72(6). Entries in the register must be available for public
    inspection in legible form at all reasonable times: s 72(7).
10  Ie the Law Reform (Miscellaneous Provisions) (Scotland) Act 1990 s 7 (powers of Court of Session to
    deal with management of charities).
11  Charities Act 1993 s 72(1)(e). This applies in relation to orders made and removals effected before or
    after 1 August 1993 (the commencement of s 72(1)): s 72(2)(d).
12  Ie the Companies (Northern Ireland) Order 1989, SI 1989/2404, Pt II.
13  Ie under the Insolvency Act 1986 s 429(2)(b) (failure to pay under county court administration order):
    see BANKRUPTCY AND INSOLVENCY vol 3(2) (Reissue) para 877).
14  Ibid s 72(1)(f) (amended by the Insolvency Act 2000 s 8, Sch 4 Pt II para 18(a)). This applies in relation
    to orders made and removals effected before or after 1 August 1993 (the commencement of the Charities
    Act 1993 s 72(1)): s 72(2)(d). A person is not, however, disqualified under s 72(1)(f) if:
    (1)   in the case of a person subject to a disqualification order or disqualification undertaking under the
          Company Directors Disqualification Act 1986, leave for the purposes of s 1(1)(a) (as substituted)
          or 1A(1)(a) (as added) (see COMPANIES vol 7(2) (1996 Reissue) para 1417 et seq) has been granted
          for him to act as director of the charity (Charities Act 1993 s 72(3)(a) (substituted by the
          Insolvency Act 2000 s 8, Sch 4 Pt II para 18(b));
    (2)   in the case of a person subject to a disqualification order under the Companies (Northern Ireland)
          Order 1989, SI 1989/2404, Pt II leave has been granted by the High Court in Northern Ireland
          for him to act as director of the charity (Charities Act 1993 s 72(3)(aa) (added by the Insolvency
          Act 2000 s 8, Sch 4 Pt II para 18(b)); or
    (3)   in the case of a person subject to an order under the Insolvency Act 1986 s 429(2)(b) (see
          BANKRUPTCY AND INSOLVENCY vol 3(2) (Reissue) para 877), leave has been granted by the
          court which made the order for him so to act (Charities Act 1993 s 72(3)(b)).
15  No waiver can be granted in relation to any charity which is a company if the person concerned is for
    the time being prohibited by virtue of a disqualification order or disqualification undertaking under the
    Company Directors Disqualification Act 1986, or of s 11(1), 12(2) or 12A (as added) of that Act
    (COMPANIES vol 7(2) (1996 Reissue) paras 1423–1424), from acting as director of the charity, and leave
    has not been granted for him to act as director of any other company: Charities Act 1993 s 72(4)(a), (b)
    (s 72(4)(a) amended by the Insolvency Act 2000 s 8, Sch 4 Pt II para 18(c)). For the meaning of
    'company' see para 216 ante.
16  Ibid s 72(4). As to the criteria likely to be applied by the Charity Commissioners when considering
    applications for a waiver from undischarged bankrupts or a persons who have made compositions or
    arrangements with their creditors see the *Effect on Disqualification for Acting as Charity Trustee and Criteria
    for Grant of Waiver (1993)* Decisions of the Charity Commissioners (1994) vol 2 p 11 at pp 12–13.
17  Charities Act 1993 s 72(5).

**250.  Person acting as a charity trustee while disqualified.** Any person who acts
as a charity trustee[1] or trustee for a charity[2] while he is disqualified for being such a trustee
by virtue of the relevant provisions of the Charities Act 1993[3] is guilty of an offence[4],
except where the charity concerned is a company[5] and the disqualified person is
disqualified by virtue only of certain specified matters[6] relating to insolvency[7]. However,

no proceedings may be instituted except by or with the consent of the Director of Public Prosecutions[8]. Acts done as charity trustee or trustee for a charity by a person disqualified by virtue of the relevant provisions of the Charities Act 1993[9] are not invalid by reason only of that disqualification[10].

Where the Charity Commissioners[11] are satisfied that any person has acted as charity trustee or trustee for a charity (other than an exempt charity[12]) while disqualified for being such a trustee[13], and that, while so acting he has received from the charity any sums by way of remuneration or expenses, or any benefit in kind, in connection with his acting as charity trustee or trustee for the charity, they may by order direct him to repay to the charity the whole or part of any such sums, or (as the case may be) to pay to the charity the whole or part of the monetary value, as determined by them, of any such benefit[14]. This does not apply to any sums received by way of remuneration or expenses in respect of any time when the person concerned was not disqualified for being a charity trustee or trustee for the charity[15].

1    For the meaning of 'charity trustees' see para 1 note 10 ante.
2    For the meaning of 'charity' see para 1 ante.
3    Ie under the Charities Act 1993 s 72: see para 249 ante.
4    Ibid s 73(1). A person guilty of such an offence is liable on summary conviction to imprisonment for a term not exceeding six months or a fine not exceeding the statutory maximum, or both; and on conviction on indictment to imprisonment for a term not exceeding two years or a fine, or both: s 73(1). As to the statutory maximum see para 226 note 5 ante.
5    For the meaning of 'company' see para 216 ante.
6    Ie where he is disqualified by virtue only of the Charities Act 1993 s 72(1)(b) or (f): see para 249 heads (2), (6) ante.
7    Ibid s 73(2).
8    Ibid s 94(1), (2)(e). As to the Director of Public Prosecutions see CRIMINAL LAW, EVIDENCE AND PROCEDURE vol 11(1) Reissue para 637 et seq.
9    See note 3 supra.
10   Charities Act 1993 s 73(3).
11   As to the Charity Commissioners see paras 486–512 post.
12   As to exempt charities see para 293 post.
13   See note 3 supra.
14   Charities Act 1993 s 73(4). A person guilty of disobedience to any order made by the Commissioners under s 73 may on the application of the Commissioners to the High Court be dealt with as for disobedience to an order of the High Court: s 88; and see para 494 post.
15   Ibid s 73(5).

**251. Qualification under trust instrument necessary.** In selecting trustees, regard must be had to any directions contained in the scheme[1] or other instrument[2] regulating the charity. Thus, where trustees are required to be residents in a certain locality, persons not possessing the necessary qualification should not be appointed[3], although in special circumstances the residential area may be extended[4]. In the absence of express direction in the instrument regulating the charity, new trustees who reside at a distance from the charitable institution may be appointed[5], but as a rule it is expedient to appoint trustees from the neighbourhood[6].

1    *Foord v Baker* (1859) 27 Beav 193, where the scheme provided that no person who had a beneficial interest in the charity estate should act as a trustee. As to schemes see para 170 et seq ante.
2    *A-G v Earl of Stamford* (1843) 1 Ph 737 at 748, 755 per Lord Cottenham LC, where a residential qualification was required by the trust deed. See also *A-G v Pearson* (1817) 3 Mer 353 at 403 per Lord Eldon LC, where, however, the trust deed was silent on this point.

3    *A-G v Cowper* (1785) 1 Bro CC 439; *A-G v France* (1780) cited in *A-G v Cowper* (1785) 1 Bro CC 439;
     *A-G v Earl of Stamford* (1843) 1 Ph 737. See also *A-G v Earl of Devon* (1846) 16 LJCh 34 at 45 per
     Shadwell V-C, where the trustees were to be 'near inhabiting'. In *A-G v Earl of Stamford* (1849) 16 Sim
     453, the requirement that trustees be supplied from within a parish was held to be satisfied by persons
     whose daily work was within the parish, but who resided a short distance outside.

4    *Re Sekforde's Charity* (1861) 4 LT 321 (radius of six miles from charitable institution).

5    *Re Lancaster Charities, Re Charitable Trusts Act 1853* (1860) 7 Jur NS 96: 'it is not always desirable to
     entrust the management of charities to a purely local interest'.

6    *A-G v Moises* (1879) reported in Tudor on Charities (4th Edn, 1906) pp 1036, 1038.


**252. Religious opinions of trustees.** Where a charity is established exclusively for
the benefit of members of the Church of England or for the instruction of children on
Church of England lines, then, independently of any express provision[1] in the instrument
regulating the charity, only members of that church should be appointed trustees[2]. The
same principle applies in the case of charities for the exclusive benefit of dissenting sects[3].

Where a charity is established for purposes connected with a parish church, it is
proper, though of course not necessary, to appoint the parson and the churchwardens as
trustees[4].

It is the practice of the Charity Commissioners to insert in any scheme relating to a
parochial ecclesiastical charity a provision giving the parochial church council of the
parish some direct representation on the governing body of the charity[5].

Where a charity is substantially eleemosynary in character, the religious opinions of
proposed trustees or governors must not be taken into consideration[6].


1    For an example of express provision see *Re Church Patronage Trust, Laurie v A-G* [1904] 2 Ch 643, CA.

2    *Re Norwich Charities* (1837) 2 My & Cr 275 at 305 per Lord Cottenham LC; *Re Scarborough Corpn* (1837)
     1 Jur 36; *Re Stafford Charities* (1857) 25 Beav 28; *Baker v Lee* (1860) 8 HL Cas 495 at 513 per Lord
     Cranworth; *A-G v Clifton* (1863) 32 Beav 596; *Re Burnham National Schools* (1873) LR 17 Eq 241 at 247;
     *A-G v Bishop of Limerick* (1870) 18 WR 1192; and see *Re Hodgson's School* (1878) 3 App Cas 857 at 866,
     PC.

3    *A-G v Pearson* (1817) 3 Mer 353; *Shore v Wilson* (1842) 9 Cl & Fin 355 at 389, HL, per Alderson B; *Re
     Drogheda Charitable and Trust Estates* (1846) 2 Jo & Lat 422; *A-G v Calvert* (1857) 23 Beav 248; *Baker v
     Lee* (1860) 8 HL Cas 495; *A-G v St John's Hospital, Bath* (1876) 2 ChD 554 at 565–566 per Malins V-C.

4    *Re Donington Church Estate, Re Charitable Trusts Act 1853* (1860) 2 LT 10 (in this case the court declined
     to appoint the overseers of the poor and the surveyor of highways as trustees, apparently on the ground
     that they would probably be dissenters, and because the rector and churchwardens objected to their
     appointment). In one case in Ireland the Ecclesiastical Commissioners for Ireland were made trustees: see
     *Re Bishop Gore's Charity* (1844) Drury *temp* Sug 536.

5    As to non-ecclesiastical charities see also the Charities Act 1993 s 79(2); and para 240 ante. As to the
     Charity Commissioners see paras 486–512 post.

6    *Re Norwich Charities* (1837) 2 My & Cr 275; *A-G v Calvert* (1857) 23 Beav 248; *Baker v Lee* (1860) 8 HL
     Cas 495 at 513 per Lord Cranworth; *A-G v Tottenham* (1870) IR 5 Eq 241; *A-G v St John's Hospital, Bath*
     (1876) 2 ChD 554.


**253. No restriction on number.** The statutory limitation on the number of trustees
of settlements of land does not apply in the case of land vested in trustees for charitable,
ecclesiastical or public purposes, or where the net proceeds of the sale of the land are held
for those purposes[1].


1    See the Trustee Act 1925 s 34(3); and TRUSTS vol 48 (2000 Reissue) paras 699, 717.

## (iii)  Appointment under Express Powers

**254.  Strict and directory powers.** Express powers for the appointment of new trustees contained in the instrument or scheme founding or regulating a charity may be construed by the court as being in character either strict powers or directory powers. Strict powers can only be exercised in accordance with the exact circumstances prescribed by the settlement[1]; but non-fulfilment of the prescribed conditions does not prevent the execution of a directory power[2]. The same principle of construction applies also to directions contained in decrees of the court[3] and Acts of Parliament[4]. Appointments under express powers are now rare, since in almost all cases a statutory power is available[5].

1   For a case where a power was apparently construed as strict see *Foley v Wontner* (1820) 2 Jac & W 245.
2   *A-G v Floyer* (1716) 2 Vern 748 (where there was a direction in a will that, when six trustees were reduced to three, others should be appointed, and the sole surviving trustee was allowed to appoint others); and see TRUSTS vol 48 (2000 Reissue) para 713 et seq. See also *A-G v Bishop of Litchfield* (1801) 5 Ves 825; *A-G v Cuming* (1843) 2 Y & C Ch Cas 139; *Doe d Dupleix v Roe* (1794) 1 Anst 86 at 91 per Eyre CB (new trustees validly appointed before number reduced to figure named in trust deed); *A-G v Cowper* (1785) 1 Bro CC 439 (residential qualification construed as directory).
3   *A-G v Scott* (1750) 1 Ves Sen 413 at 415 per Lord Hardwicke LC.
4   *Doe d Read v Godwin* (1822) 1 Dow & Ry KB 259.
5   As to the statutory power of appointment see para 258 post. As to powers generally see POWERS.

**255.  Court's powers.** The court may sanction the appointment of an association registered under the Companies Acts as sole trustee in place of retiring trustees, notwithstanding that the trust deed does not authorise the appointment of a sole trustee[1].

Where the court is administering a charitable trust, trustees ought not to exercise any power they may have of appointing new trustees without the sanction of the court[2]. However, if proper persons are selected, the appointment is valid[3].

Where the trust instrument is lost, but there have been many appointments in the past, the court presumes that the earliest usage was in accordance with the terms of the lost instrument[4]. Where the instrument is not explicit the court may direct an inquiry as to who are entitled to appoint new trustees[5].

1   *Re Barnardo* (1907) Times, 14 June.
2   *A-G v Clack* (1839) 1 Beav 467.
3   *A-G v Lawson* (1866) 36 LJCh 130 at 135 per Kindersley V-C.
4   *A-G v Dalton* (1851) 20 LJCh 569 at 573–574 per Romilly MR. As to usage see *A-G v Pearson* (1817) 3 Mer 353 at 403 per Lord Eldon LC; *A-G v St Cross Hospital* (1853) 17 Beav 435.
5   *Davis v Jenkins* (1814) 3 Ves & B 151 at 155, 159 per Lord Eldon LC.

**256.  Vesting of property in new trustees.** Where, under the trusts of a charity[1], trustees of property held for the purposes of the charity may be appointed or discharged by resolution of a meeting of the charity trustees[2] or other persons, a memorandum declaring a trustee to have been so appointed or discharged, is sufficient evidence of the fact if the memorandum is signed by the person presiding at the meeting or in some other manner directed by the meeting, and attested by two persons present at the meeting[3]. Such a memorandum, if executed as a deed, has the same effect as the statutory provisions which relate to vesting declarations as respects trust property in deeds appointing or discharging trustees[4], as if the appointment or discharge were effected by the deed[5].

The court has power under the Trustee Act 1925 to vest any interest in land, stock or thing in action in any trustee of a charity over which the court would have jurisdiction upon action duly instituted, whether the trustee was appointed under an express power or by the court[6].

1    For the meaning of 'trusts' in this context see para 210 note 5 ante.
2    For the meaning of 'charity trustees' see para 1 note 10 ante.
3    Charities Act 1993 s 83(1). This provision applies to a memorandum made at any time: s 83(4). Section 83 applies in relation to any institution to which the Literary and Scientific Institutions Act 1854 applies (see LIBRARIES AND OTHER SCIENTIFIC AND CULTURAL INSTITUTIONS vol 28 (Reissue) para 477) as it applies in relation to a charity: Charities Act 1993 s 83(5).
4    Ie the Trustee Act 1925 s 40 (as amended): see TRUSTS vol 48 (2000 Reissue) para 760.
5    Charities Act 1993 s 83(2). This only applies to memoranda made after 1 January 1961 (ie the commencement of the Charities Act 1960): Charities Act 1993 s 83(4). The similar provisions of the Trustee Appointment Act 1850, the Trustee Appointment Act 1869, the Trustees Appointment Act 1890 (and, so far as it applied those Acts, the School Sites Act 1852) were repealed by the Charities Act 1960, but where at 1 January 1961 (the commencement of the Charities Act 1960) the provisions of those Acts as to the appointment of trustees applied in relation to any land, they continue to have effect as if they were declared as part of the trusts on which the land is held: s 35(6).
6    See the Trustee Act 1925 s 52; and TRUSTS vol 48 (2000 Reissue) para 764. As to the procedure for applying for a vesting order see TRUSTS vol 48 (2000 Reissue) para 765.

**257. Evidence of vesting.** A duly signed and attested[1] memorandum declaring a trustee to be appointed or discharged by resolution of a meeting of charity trustees, is sufficient evidence of the fact of the appointment or discharge[2]. On proof of the signature, whether by evidence or presumption, the document is presumed to have been duly signed and attested unless the contrary is shown[3].

1    For the requirements as to signature and attestation, and the cases in which these provisions are applicable to appointments and discharges see para 256 ante.
2    Charities Act 1993 s 83(1). This applies to a memorandum made at any time: s 83(4). Section 83 applies in relation to any institution to which the Literary and Scientific Institutions Act 1854 applies (see LIBRARIES AND OTHER SCIENTIFIC AND CULTURAL INSTITUTIONS vol 28 (Reissue) para 477) as it applies in relation to a charity: Charities Act 1993 s 83(5). For the meaning of 'charity trustees' see para 1 note 10 ante.
3    Ibid s 83(3). This provision applies to a memorandum made at any time: s 83(4).

## (iv) Appointment under Statutory Powers

**258. Appointment of trustees under the Trustee Act 1925.** The general provisions of the Trustee Act 1925 as to the appointment of new trustees[1] and the vesting of trust property in new or continuing trustees[2] apply to charitable trusts as much as to any others[3].

1    See the Trustee Act 1925 s 36 (as amended); and TRUSTS vol 48 (2000 Reissue) para 730 et seq. As to the appointment of new trustees generally see TRUSTS vol 48 (2000 Reissue) para 713 et seq.

2   Ibid s 40 (as amended): see TRUSTS vol 48 (2000 Reissue) paras 760–761.
3   Cf *Re Coates to Parsons* (1886) 34 ChD 370.

**259. Trustees of religious or educational societies and church trusts.** Various statutes[1] gave powers of appointment of new trustees to congregations, societies and bodies in relation to trusts of land for various religious or educational purposes. These provisions have been repealed[2], but their operation is preserved in the cases where they applied in relation to any land at the commencement of the Charities Act 1960[3].

1   See the Trustee Appointment Act 1850, the Trustee Appointment Act 1869, the Trustees Appointment Act 1890, and, so far as it applied to any of those Acts, the School Sites Act 1852.
2   Ie by the Charities Act 1960 48(2), Sch 7 Pt I.
3   See ibid s 35(6); and para 256 ante. The Charities Act 1960 commenced on 1 January 1961.

**260. Parochial charities: reorganisation of parishes, etc.** Special statutory provision is made in relation to the appointment of trustees of non-ecclesiastical parochial charities[1], and to cope with the consequences of changes of local secular[2] and ecclesiastical[3] organisation[4].

1   See the Charities Act 1993 s 79(2); and para 240 ante.
2   See ibid s 79; and para 240 ante.
3   See in particular the Pastoral Measure 1983 Sch 3 para 11 (as amended); and para 242 ante. See also the City of London (Guild Churches) Act 1952 s 28; and ECCLESIASTICAL LAW vol 14 para 597 et seq.
4   See generally paras 242–243 ante.

### (v) Appointment by the Court

**261. Court's general jurisdiction.** Apart from any statutory jurisdiction, the High Court has an inherent jurisdiction to appoint new trustees of charities[1], even where there is in existence a power of appointment capable of being executed[2], and under this jurisdiction can appoint additional trustees[3].

The court has no power to appoint judicial trustees for any charity[4].

1   *A-G v London Corpn* (1790) 3 Bro CC 171; *A-G v Stephens* (1834) 3 My & K 347.
2   *A-G v Clack* (1839) 1 Beav 467. It is not proper to apply to the court in ordinary cases where a power of appointment is capable of being exercised: *Re Gibbon's Trusts* (1882) 45 LT 756; *Re Higginbottom* [1892] 3 Ch 132.
3   *Re Burnham National Schools* (1873) LR 17 Eq 241 at 246; *Re Browne's Hospital v Stamford* (1889) 60 LT 288.
4   See the Judicial Trustees Act 1896 s 6(2); and TRUSTS vol 48 (2000 Reissue) para 652 et seq.

**262. Jurisdiction under the Trustee Act 1925.** Whenever it is expedient to appoint a new trustee or new trustees of any trust, whether charitable or otherwise, and it is found inexpedient, difficult or impracticable to do so without the court's assistance, the court may make an order for the appointment of a new trustee either in substitution for or in addition to any existing trustee or trustees, although there is no existing trustee[1], and for vesting the property in the new trustee or trustees without any conveyance[2].

Thus, the court may appoint new trustees of charities where the old trustees have died[3], where a trustee corporation is in liquidation or has been dissolved[4], where an official person nominated as trustee no longer exists in his official character[5], and where the trustees disclaim or decline to act[6], or are abroad[7], are removed for misconduct[8], are incapable by reason of mental disorder[9], or are bankrupt[10].

1   See the Trustee Act 1925 s 41(1) (as amended); and TRUSTS vol 48 (2000 Reissue) para 743. The Trustee Act 1925 applies to charities: see *Re Coates to Parsons* (1886) 34 ChD 370, a case decided on the corresponding provision of the Conveyancing Act 1881 s 31 (repealed). As to the procedure for applying for a vesting order see TRUSTS vol 48 (2000 Reissue) para 765. The consent of the Charity Commissioners may be necessary before proceedings are begun: see the Charities Act 1993 s 33; and para 521 post. As to the Charity Commissioners see paras 486–512 post.

2   See the Trustee Act 1925 ss 44–52 (s 51 as amended), s 58; and TRUSTS vol 48 (2000 Reissue) para 769 et seq. See also *A-G v Langham* (1887) 82 LT Jo 246 (where the court vested charity lands in the Attorney General, the trustee being a person mentally disordered).

3   *Re Nightingale's Charity* (1844) 3 Hare 336. As to the principles upon which the court proceeds in appointing trustees see generally *Re Tempest* (1866) 1 Ch App 485.

4   See the Trustee Act 1925 s 41(1); and TRUSTS vol 48 (2000 Reissue) para 750. See also *Re Yarm Free Grammar School* (1853) 10 Hare, App I, V; *Re No 9 Bomore Road* [1906] 1 Ch 359; *Re Nos 56, 58, Albert Road, Norwood* [1916] 1 Ch 289. Cf the Law of Property Act 1925 s 181 (as amended) (see CORPORATIONS vol 9(2) (Reissue) para 1204) and the Companies Act 1985 s 654 (see COMPANIES vol 7(3) (1996 Reissue) para 2692).

5   *A-G v Stephens* (1834) 3 My & K 347.

6   *Re Beverley Grammar School* (1839) 9 LJCh 91; and see *Re Lincoln Primitive Methodist Chapel, Re Charitable Trusts Act 1853 and Trustee Act 1850* (1855) 1 Jur NS 1011, where the court confirmed the appointment of the new trustees.

7   See *Re Lincoln Primitive Methodist Chapel, Re Charitable Trusts Act 1853 and Trustee Act 1850* (1855) 1 Jur NS 1011.

8   *Ex p Greenhouse* (1815) 1 Madd 92.

9   See the Trustee Act 1925 s 41(1) (as amended); and TRUSTS vol 48 (2000 Reissue) para 750. See also the Trustee Act 1925 s 36(9) (as substituted and amended), s 54 (as substituted and amended); Court of Protection Rules 1994, SI 1994/3046, rr 17, 18; and MENTAL HEALTH vol 30 (Reissue) paras 1415, 1477 et seq; TRUSTS vol 48 (2000 Reissue) paras 732, 745.

10   See the Trustee Act 1925 s 41(1) (as amended); and TRUSTS vol 48 (2000 Reissue) para 750.

**263. Filling of vacancies.** Where it was not intended that the whole number of trustees originally appointed should always be kept up, the court, before filling vacancies, requires to be satisfied that the number of the existing trustees is insufficient[1]. Thus the court has refused to appoint new trustees at the expense of the charity where 10 trustees out of 15[2], and 11 out of 13[3], remained to execute the trusts. In other cases where two-thirds or three-quarters of the trustees remained[4], or where the intention was that the full number should be kept up[5], the court has filled up the vacancies.

1   *Re Worcester Charities* (1847) 2 Ph 284; *Re Shrewsbury Charities* (1849) 1 Mac & G 84; and see *Re Hereford Charities, Re Gloucester Charities* (1842) 6 Jur 289. Jessel MR apparently considered that, where the appointment was by donees of a power, it was the rule in charity cases to keep up the full number of trustees: *Re Cunningham and Bradley and Wilson* [1877] WN 258.

2   *Re Worcester Charities* (1847) 2 Ph 284. See also *Re Hereford Charities, Re Gloucester Charities* (1842) 6 Jur 289; *Re Coates to Parsons* (1886) 34 ChD 370 at 377–378 per North J.

3   *Re Marlborough School* (1843) 13 LJCh 2.

4   *Re Hereford Charities, Re Gloucester Charities* (1842) 6 Jur 289; *Re Bedford Charity* (undated) cited in 10 Hare App I, IVn.

5   *Davis v Jenkins* (1814) 3 Ves & B 151 at 158–159 per Lord Eldon LC. As to the number of new trustees appointed by the court see TRUSTS vol 48 (2000 Reissue) para 744.

**264. Provision for future appointments.** In making an order appointing new trustees[1], or on the settlement of a scheme, the court may give directions or provide for future appointments, and may allow the trustees to appoint others as occasion requires[2].

1   *Re East Bergholt Town Lands* (1853) 2 Eq Rep 90.
2   *Re Puckering's Charity* (1854) Seton's Judgments and Orders (7th Edn) 1264.

## (vi) Appointment by the Charity Commissioners

**265. Jurisdiction.** The Charity Commissioners[1] have the same jurisdiction and powers as the court in relation to the appointment of a charity trustee[2] or trustee for a charity[3], and as to vesting or transferring property and requiring or entitling persons to call for or make transfers of property or payments[4]. They may only exercise their jurisdiction on an application for that purpose such as would be required for the exercise of their jurisdiction to make schemes[5], and generally the same provisions as to notice, contentious matters, appeals and otherwise apply[6].

1   As to the Charity Commissioners see paras 486–512 post.
2   For the meaning of 'charity trustees' see para 1 note 10 ante.
3   For the meaning of 'charity' see para 1 ante.
4   See the Charities Act 1993 s 16(1)(b), (c); and para 180 ante.
5   See ibid s 16(4), (5); and para 180 ante.
6   Ie ibid ss 16(9)–(12), 18, 20(2), (5), (7), (8): see paras 180–181, 190 ante, 270, 503 et seq post.

**266. Practice.** When appointing trustees on the settlement of a scheme[1], the Charity Commissioners'[2] practice is to introduce a representative element, and to arrange in suitable cases that the representative element shall constitute a majority of the trustees. In framing new schemes, they sometimes increase the number of the trustees, and sometimes reduce it. Provision is also frequently made for ex officio and co-optative trustees.

1   As to schemes see para 170 et seq ante.
2   As to the Charity Commissioners see paras 486–512 post.

# (5)  REMOVAL AND DISCHARGE OF TRUSTEES

## (i)  Removal by the Court

**267.  Court's general jurisdiction.** In all cases which may require such a remedy the court has jurisdiction to remove existing trustees and substitute new ones. This jurisdiction is merely ancillary to the court's principal duty, which is the protection of trusts[1], and does not depend upon the existence in the instrument of foundation of an express power of removal[2].

1   *Letterstedt v Broers* (1884) 9 App Cas 371 at 386, PC. For a form of decree removing a trustee see *A-G v Drummond* (1842) 3 Dr & War 162.
2   As to the exercise of express powers of removal see *A-G v Pearson* (1817) 3 Mer 353 at 412–415 per Lord Eldon LC.

**268.  Removal of trustee for breach of trust.** The court has removed trustees who have wilfully committed breaches of trust, as by converting a dissenting chapel to the use of a sect contrary to the founder's wishes[1], transferring the property of one charity to another[2], misapplying increased revenues[3], or allowing Unitarians to participate in a charity founded for Protestant dissenters[4]. A trustee who was lessee of part of a charity estate in defiance of the provisions of the scheme was ordered to resign his office or give up his lease[5]. Corporations who are trustees of charities may similarly be removed for breaches of trust[6]. However, charity trustees are not necessarily removed where they have innocently committed a breach of trust[7].

Trustees who, having committed breaches of trust, refuse to retire voluntarily, may be made to pay the costs of proceedings necessary for the appointment of other trustees[8].

Where inconvenience as regards the receipt of dividends arose from the trustees' being holders of annual offices, the court appointed others to hold the funds, but allowed the office-holders to retain certain rights of nomination[9].

1   *A-G v Pearson* (1835) 7 Sim 290 at 309 per Shadwell V-C; *A-G v Aust* (1865) 13 LT 235. See also *A-G v Munro* (1848) 2 De G & Sm 122 (where a minister of the Established Church of Scotland seceded from that body to the Free Church, and was removed from his charge); *A-G v Anderson* (1888) 57 LJCh 543.
2   *Newsome v Flowers* (1861) 30 Beav 461.
3   *Coventry Corpn v A-G* (1720) 7 Bro Parl Cas 235, HL.
4   *Shore v Wilson* (1842) 9 Cl & Fin 355, HL; *Drummond v A-G for Ireland* (1849) 2 HL Cas 837 at 861 per Lord Brougham.
5   *Foord v Baker* (1859) 27 Beav 193.
6   *A-G v Earl of Clarendon* (1810) 17 Ves 491 at 499 per Grant MR. See also *A-G v Governors of Foundling Hospital* (1793) 2 Ves 42 at 46 per Lord Commissioner Eyre; *A-G v Dixie, ex p Bosworth School* (1805) 13 Ves 519; *Ex p Kirkby Ravensworth Hospital* (1808) 15 Ves 305 at 314 per Lord Eldon LC; *Ex p Greenhouse* (1815) 1 Madd 92.
7   *A-G v Stafford Corpn* (1740) Barn Ch 33; *A-G v Caius College* (1837) 2 Keen 150.
8   *A-G v Murdoch* (1856) 2 K & J 571.
9   *Re Taylor's Charity, ex p Blackburne* (1820) 1 Jac & W 297.

**269. Removal of trustees on other grounds.** A reason sufficient to prevent the appointment of a trustee is not necessarily a sufficient ground for removing an existing trustee[1]. Where no breach of trust has been committed, trustees, if otherwise unexceptionable, are not removed merely on the ground of not possessing the required religious[2] or residential[3] qualification, or on the ground of temporary absence from the United Kingdom[4], or because they were appointed irregularly[5]. Bankruptcy is not necessarily[6], though it is usually[7], a ground for removal.

1  *A-G v Clapham* (1853) 10 Hare 540 at 613 per Page Wood V-C (trustees of a chapel); revsd on appeal without affecting this point (1855) 4 De GM & G 591; and see (1855) 4 De GM & G at 632 per Lord Cranworth LC.

2  *Baker v Lee* (1860) 8 HL Cas 495 at 513 per Lord Cranworth; *A-G v Clifton* (1863) 32 Beav 596 at 601 per Romilly MR; *A-G v Bishop of Limerick* (1870) 18 WR 1192.

3  *A-G v Earl of Clarendon* (1810) 17 Ves 491; *A-G v Earl of Stamford* (1843) 1 Ph 737 at 747–748 per Lord Cottenham LC; and see *A-G v Clifton* (1863) 32 Beav 596 at 601 per Romilly MR.

4  *Re Moravian Society* (1858) 4 Jur NS 703.

5  *A-G v Cuming* (1843) 2 Y & C Ch Cas 139 at 150–151 per Shadwell V-C; *A-G v Daugars* (1864) 33 Beav 621.

6  *Archbold v Ireland Charitable Bequests Comrs* (1849) 2 HL Cas 440.

7  *Bainbrigge v Blair* (1839) 1 Beav 495; *Re Roche* (1842) 1 Con & Law 306; *Re Barker's Trusts* (1875) 1 ChD 43.

### (ii) Removal by the Charity Commissioners

**270. Jurisdiction.** The Charity Commissioners[1] have the same jurisdiction and powers as the High Court to discharge or remove a charity trustee[2] or trustee for a charity[3], or to remove an officer or employee[4]. The jurisdiction is exercisable upon and subject to the same conditions as the jurisdiction to appoint new trustees[5]. They also have jurisdiction to remove charity trustees and other persons where it is necessary for the protection of the charity[6].

1  As to the Charity Commissioners see paras 486–512 post.

2  For the meaning of 'charity trustees' see para 1 note 10 ante.

3  For the meaning of 'charity' see para 1 ante.

4  See the Charities Act 1993 s 16(1)(b); and para 180 ante.

5  See para 266 ante. The Charity Commissioners must not make any order to appoint, discharge or remove a charity trustee or trustee for a charity, other than the official custodian, unless not less than one month previously there has been given the like public notice as is required by ibid s 18(1) (see para 503 post) for an order establishing a scheme: s 20(2). However, this does not apply in the case of an order appointing an additional trustee or trustees to protect a charity under s 18(1)(ii), or when discharging or removing a trustee if they consider it unnecessary and not in his interest to give publicity to the proposal to discharge or remove him: s 20(2)(a), (b). Before making an order removing a trustee or other person without his consent, the Commissioners must give notice to the person to be removed, inviting representations to be made to them: see s 20(3); and para 508 post. A person removed from any office or employment by an order of the Commissioners may appeal against the order to the High Court unless he is removed with the concurrence of the charity trustees or with the approval of the special visitor, if any: see s 16(12); and para 190 ante. Except where the removal is under s 18, following an inquiry, the certificate of the Commissioners or the leave of the court is required: see ss 16(13), 18(9); and para 190 ante.

6  See ibid s 18; and para 190 et seq post.

### (iii) Discharge and Retirement

**271. Discharge by order of Charity Commissioners.** The Charity Commissioners[1] may exercise their jurisdiction to discharge a charity trustee[2] or trustee for a charity[3] on his own application[4].

1   As to the Charity Commissioners see paras 486–512 post.
2   For the meaning of 'charity trustees' see para 1 note 10 ante.
3   For the meaning of 'charity' see para 1 ante.
4   Charities Act 1993 s 16(8). They must give notice to the other trustees: see s 16(9); and para 180 ante.

**272. Retirement without a new appointment.** Under the Trustee Act 1925, a trustee may retire from the trust by deed, provided that after his discharge there will be a trust corporation or at least two individuals to act as trustees, and provided that his co-trustees and any person entitled to appoint new trustees consent by deed to his retirement[1]. There may also be express provision in the trust instrument for the possibility of retirement without a new appointment.

1   See the Trustee Act 1925 s 39; and TRUSTS vol 48 (2000 Reissue) para 785 et seq.

## (6) THE OFFICIAL CUSTODIAN FOR CHARITIES

**273. Status and capacity.** The official custodian for charities is the successor for all purposes both of the Official Trustee of Charity Lands and of the Official Trustees of Charitable Funds[1]. He is a corporation sole having perpetual succession and using an official seal, which is officially and judicially noticed[2]. His function is to act as trustee for charities in the cases provided for by the Charities Act 1993[3]. In relation to property vested in him in trust for a charity, he may not exercise any powers of management, and is in the position of a corporate custodian trustee[4] save that he may not charge fees[5].

1   Charities Act 1960 s 48(6). This provision also vested in the official custodian property previously vested in the official trustee or official trustees, and provides that any Act, scheme, deed or other document referring to or relating to the official trustee or official trustees is, so far as the context permits, to have effect as if the official custodian had been mentioned instead: s 48(6)(a), (b). Documents under the seal of the Official Trustees of Charitable Funds may be proved as if the Charities Act 1960 had not been passed: s 48(4).
2   Charities Act 1993 s 2(1). The office is held by an officer of the Charity Commissioners designated by them from time to time: s 2(2). Where any instrument issued by the official custodian in connection with a disposal of any property under the Charities Act 1992 s 29 (as amended) (see paras 275–277 post) contains a printed reproduction of his official seal, that instrument has effect as if it were duly sealed with his official seal: s 30(5). As to the Charity Commissioners see paras 486–512 post.
3   Charities Act 1993 s 2(1). These cases are discussed in the ensuing paragraphs. He may also act as trustee for shared church buildings under the Sharing of Church Buildings Act 1969 s 2, and the ownership of an existing or proposed church building which is subject to a sharing agreement and which is, or will be, owned by all or some of the sharing churches may be vested in him: see s 2(2); and ECCLESIASTICAL LAW vol 14 (Reissue) para 1188. The vesting of ownership in the official custodian is by order under the Charities Act 1993: see the Sharing of Church Buildings Act 1969 s 2(4) (amended by the Charities Act 1993 s 98(1), Sch 6 para 11(1), (2)). As to vesting property in the official custodian see para 275 post.

The purposes of a sharing agreement must be limited to purposes which are exclusively charitable according to the law of England and Wales: Sharing of Church Buildings Act 1969 s 2(5). See generally ECCLESIASTICAL LAW vol 14 para 1186 et seq.

4    Ie a corporation appointed under the Public Trustee Act 1906 s 4: see TRUSTS vol 48 (2000 Reissue) para 687.

5    See the Charities Act 1993 s 22(1); and para 279 post.


**274. Performance of functions; accounts.** The official custodian for charities[1] must perform his duties in accordance with directions, general or special, given by the Charity Commissioners[2]; his expenses, so far as they are not reimbursed to or recovered by him as trustee for any charity[3], must be defrayed by the Commissioners[4]. Anything which is required to or may be done by, to or before the official custodian may be done by, to or before any officer of the Commissioners generally or specially authorised by them to act for him during a vacancy in his office or otherwise[5]. He must keep accounts and records relating to them as directed by the Treasury in such form, in such manner and at such times as may be so directed[6]. The accounts so prepared must be examined and certified by the Comptroller and Auditor General[7], and the report to be made by the Commissioners to the Secretary of State[8] for any year must include a copy of the accounts so prepared for any period ending in or with the year and of the certificate and report of the Comptroller and Auditor General with respect to those accounts[9].

1    As to the official custodian for charities see para 273 et seq ante.
2    As to the Charity Commissioners see paras 486–512 post.
3    For the meaning of 'charity' see para 1 ante.
4    Charities Act 1993 s 2(3). As to service of directions see s 91; and para 493 post.
5    Ibid s 2(4).
6    Ibid s 2(6).
7    As to the Comptroller and Auditor General see CONSTITUTIONAL LAW AND HUMAN RIGHTS vol 8(2) (Reissue) paras 724–726.
8    As to the Secretary of State see para 513 post. As to the duty of the Charity Commissioners to report to the Secretary of State see para 490 post.
9    Charities Act 1993 s 2(7).


**275. Vesting property in official custodian.** Prior to 1 September 1992[1], the court could by order vest any property held by or in trust for a charity in the official custodian for charities[2], or authorise or require persons in whom such property was vested to transfer it to him, or appoint any person to transfer such property to him[3]. The Charity Commissioners had the same powers in this respect[4]. Personal property[5] held by or in trust for a charity or comprised in a testamentary gift to a charity could be transferred to the official custodian with his agreement[6].

Under the Charities Act 1992 the provision relating to personal property[7] was repealed[8], and the official custodian is required to divest himself of all the property he holds in that capacity, except any land[9] and any property other than land vested in him by virtue of an order of the Charity Commissioners acting under their power[10] to act for the protection of charities[11]. Further, the power of the court is now limited to land or an interest in land[12].

When the Commissioners are satisfied that the official custodian has divested himself of all the property (subject to the exceptions mentioned above[13]) held by him in trust for particular charities, all remaining funds held by him are to be paid into the Consolidated Fund[14].

Any funds vested in the Accountant General[15] and held by him in trust for any charity or ecclesiastical corporation[16] in the Church of England may be transferred to the official custodian or the Church Commissioners[17] if, on an application made to him by the Charity Commissioners or the Church Commissioners, the Accountant General thinks fit so to direct[18]. Any funds so transferred vest in and are held by the official custodian or the Church Commissioners respectively in trust for the charity or ecclesiastical corporation upon the trusts on which the funds were held before the transfer[19].

1   Ie date on which the Charities Act 1992 s 29 came into force. Section 29 not repealed by the Charities Act 1993.
2   As to the official custodian for charities see para 273 ante.
3   Charities Act 1960 s 16(1) (repealed: see now the Charities Act 1993 s 21(1); and the text and note 12 infra).
4   See the Charities Act 1960 s 18(1)(c) (repealed). This was subject to the conditions contained in s 18(4), (5) (repealed) as to exercise of the jurisdiction. These provisions have been repealed and re-enacted in the Charities Act 1993 s 16(1)(c), (4), (5): see para 180 ante. As to the Charity Commissioners see paras 486–512 post.
5   In this provision 'personal property' extended to any real security but did not include any interest in land other than by way of security: Charities Act 1960 s 16(2) (repealed) (see the text and note 7 infra).
6   Ibid s 16(2) (repealed) (see the text and note 7 infra). In the case of a testamentary gift to a charity, the official custodian's receipt was a complete discharge of the personal representative: s 16(2) (repealed).
7   Ie ibid s 16(2).
8   See the Charities Act 1992 ss 47, 78(2), Sch 3 para 4, Sch 7 (s 47, Sch 3 repealed). Any provision of the trusts of a charity, or of any directions given by an order of the Commissioners made in connection with a transaction requiring the sanction of an order under the Charities Act 1960 s 29(1) (repealed), ceases to have effect if and to the extent that it requires or authorises personal property (including any mortgage or other real security, but excluding any interest in land other than such an interest by way of mortgage or other security) of the charity to be transferred to or held by the official custodian: Charities Act 1992 s 30(2). Section 30(2) does not apply to: (1) any provision of an order made under the Charities Act 1960 s 20 (repealed) or the Charities Act 1993 s 18 (see paras 503, 507–508 post); or (2) any provision of any other order, or of any scheme, of the Commissioners if the provision requires trustees of a charity to make payments into an account maintained by the official custodian with a view to the accumulation of a sum as capital of the charity, whether or not by way of recoupment of a sum expended out of a charity's permanent endowment: s 30(3) (amended by the Charities Act 1993 s 98(1), Sch 6 para 29(1), (4)). Such a provision under head (2) supra has effect as if, instead of requiring the trustees to make such payments into an account maintained by the official custodian, it required the trustees to make such payments into an account maintained by them or by any other person (apart from the official custodian) who is either a trustee for the charity or a person nominated by them to hold such payments in trust for the charity: Charities Act 1992 s 30(3).
9   For these purposes, 'land' does not include any interest in land by way of mortgage or other security: ibid s 29(13).
10  Ie under the Charities Act 1960 s 20 (repealed) or the Charities Act 1993 s 18 (see para 503 post).
11  Charities Act 1992 s 29(1), (2) (amended by the Charities Act 1993 Sch 6 para 29(2)). The disposal of any property by the official custodian in accordance with the Charities Act 1992 s 29 (as amended) operates to discharge him from his trusteeship of that property: s 30(4).
12  See the Charities Act 1993 s 21(1). The court may by order vest in the official custodian any land held by or in trust for a charity, authorise or require the persons in whom any such land is vested to transfer it to him or appoint any person to transfer any such land to him, but this does not apply to any interest in land by way of mortgage or other security: s 21(1). As to the concurrent jurisdiction of the Commissioners see para 180 ante.
13  Nothing in ibid s 29(11) applies in relation to any property held by the official custodian which falls into s 29(2) (see the text and notes 8–11 supra): s 29(12).
14  Ibid s 29(11). As to the Consolidated Fund see CONSTITUTIONAL LAW AND HUMAN RIGHTS vol 8(2) (Reissue) para 711 et seq; PARLIAMENT vol 34 (Reissue) paras 952–955.
15  As to the Accountant General see COURTS.
16  'Ecclesiastical corporation' means a capitular body within the meaning of the Cathedrals Measure 1963 (see ECCLESIASTICAL LAW vol 14 paras 610, 636) or the incumbent of a benefice (see ECCLESIASTICAL

LAW vol 14 para 541): Administration of Justice Act 1982 s 41(3). As from the relevant date, any reference in the Administration of Justice Act 1982 s 41(3) to a capitular body is to be construed as a reference to the corporate body of the cathedral: see the Cathedrals Measure 1999 ss 36(2), 38(2), (3); and ECCLESIASTICAL LAW. 'Relevant date', in relation to any cathedral existing at the passing of the Cathedrals Measure 1999, means the date appointed by the Archbishops of Canterbury and York under s 38(2): see s 35(1). See further ECCLESIASTICAL LAW.

17   As to the Church Commissioners see ECCLESIASTICAL LAW vol 14 para 363 et seq.
18   Administration of Justice Act 1982 s 41(1).
19   Ibid s 41(2).


**276. Divestment of charity property held by official custodian.**   Where any relevant property[1] is held by the official custodian for charities[2] in trust for particular charities, he must divest himself of such property as the Charity Commissioners may direct[3]. Such directions may make different provision in relation to different property held by the official custodian or in relation to different classes or descriptions of property held by him[4], including in particular: (1) provision designed to secure that the divestment required[5] is effected in stages or by means of transfers or other disposals taking place at different times[6]; (2) provision requiring the official custodian to transfer any specified investments, or any specified class or description of investments, held by him in trust for a charity to the charity trustees or any trustee for the charity, or to a person nominated by the charity trustees to hold any such investments in trust for the charity[7]; (3) provision requiring the official custodian to sell or call in any specified investments, or any specified class or description of investments, so held by him and to pay any proceeds of sale or other money accruing from it to the charity trustees or any trustee for the charity, or into any bank account kept in its name[8].

The charity trustees of a charity may nominate a person to hold in trust for the charity any property so directed to be transferred by the official custodian, but the person nominated must, if an individual, reside in England or Wales, and, if a body corporate, have its place of business there[9]. In the case of common investment funds vested in the official custodian[10], the directions given by the Commissioners must provide for the property so vested to be transferred to the trustees appointed to manage the common investment fund concerned, or to any person nominated by those trustees who is authorised by or under the common investment scheme concerned to hold that fund or any part of it[11].

The disposal of any property by the official custodian under these provisions[12] operates to discharge him from his trusteeship of it[13].


1   As to the relevant property see para 275 text and notes 8–11 ante.
2   As to the official custodian for charities see para 273 et seq ante.
3   Charities Act 1992 s 29(3). As to the Charity Commissioners see paras 486–512 post. Any directions have effect notwithstanding anything in the trusts of a charity, or in the Charities Act 1960 s 17(1) (repealed) or the Charities Act 1993 s 22(1) (see para 279 post): Charities Act 1992 s 30(1) (amended by the Charities Act 1993 s 98(1), Sch 6 para 29). See also the Charities Act 1992 s 30(5); and para 273 note 2 ante.
4   Ibid s 29(4).
5   Ie by ibid s 29(1): see para 275 text and notes 1–8 ante.
6   Ibid s 29(4)(a).
7   Ibid s 29(4)(b).
8   Ibid s 29(4)(c).
9   Ibid s 29(5).
10   Under the Charities Act 1960 s 22(6) (repealed).

11   Charities Act 1992 s 29(6).
12   Ie any of the provisions of ibid s 29 (as amended): see the text and notes 1–11 supra.
13   Ibid s 30(4). As to his official seal see para 274 ante.

**277. Divestment in the case of dormant charities.** Where the official custodian for charities[1] holds any relevant property[2] in trust for a charity but after making reasonable inquiries is unable to locate the charity ('the dormant charity') or any of its trustees, he must sell it (so far as it does not consist of money) and hold the proceeds of sale and any money pending receipt of a direction[3] from the Charity Commissioners[4]. The Commissioners may direct the official custodian to pay such amount as is so held by him to such other charity as is specified in the direction, or to pay to each of two or more other charities so specified in the direction such part of that amount as is there specified in relation to that charity[5]. The Commissioners may specify in a direction such charity or charities as they consider appropriate, being in each case a charity whose purposes are, in the opinion of the Commissioners, as similar in character to those of the dormant charity as is reasonably practicable, but they must not specify any charity unless they have received from the charity trustees written confirmation that they are willing to accept the amount proposed to be paid to the charity[6]. Any amount received by a charity under these provisions is received on terms that it will be held and applied by the charity for its purposes but will, as property of the charity, nevertheless be subject to any restrictions on expenditure to which it, or (as the case may be) the property which it represents, was subject as property of the dormant charity[7].

The disposal of any property by the official custodian under these provisions operates to discharge him from his trusteeship of it[8].

1    As to the official custodian for charities see para 273 et seq ante.
2    For these purposes, 'relevant property' means property to which the Charities Act 1992 s 29(1) applies (see para 275 text and notes 8–11 ante) or any proceeds of sale or other money accruing to the official custodian in consequence of a direction under s 29(3) (see para 276 text to notes 1–3 ante): s 29(7).
3    Ie under s 29(9): see the text and note 6 infra.
4    Charities Act 1992 s 29(7). As to the Charity Commissioners see paras 486–512 post.
5    Ibid s 29(8). Any directions take effect notwithstanding anything in the trusts of a charity, or in the Charities Act 1960 s 17(1) (repealed) or the Charities Act 1993 s 22(1) (see para 279 post): Charities Act 1992 s 30(1) (amended by the Charities Act 1993 Sch 6 para 29).
6    Charities Act 1992 s 29(9).
7    Ibid s 29(10).
8    Ibid s 30(4). As to his official seal see para 274 ante.

**278. Divestment in the case of land subject to the Reverter of Sites Act 1987.** Where any land is vested in the official custodian for charities[1] in trust for a charity and it appears to the Charity Commissioners[2] that the provisions of the Reverter of Sites Act 1987[3] which replace a right of reverter by trust will, or are likely to, operate in relation to the land at a particular time or in particular circumstances, the concurrent jurisdiction[4] of the Commissioners in relation to the discharge of a trustee for a charity[5] may, at any time before those provisions of that Act operate, be exercised by them of their own motion for the purpose of making an order discharging the official custodian from his trusteeship of the land, and making consequential vesting orders and giving consequential directions[6]. Where (1) the provisions of the Reverter of Sites Act 1987[7] have already operated in relation to any land which, immediately before the time when that provision operated, was vested in the official custodian in trust for a charity[8]; and (2) it remains vested in him but on the trust arising under that Act[9], the court[10] or the Commissioners (of their own motion) may make an order discharging the official custodian from his trusteeship of the land, and make such vesting orders and give such directions as appear to it or them to be necessary or expedient in consequence[11]. Where, in certain circumstances[12], an order is made discharging the official custodian from his trusteeship of any land, the persons in whom the land is to be vested on the discharge of the official custodian are the relevant charity trustees[13] unless the court (or as the case may be) the Commissioners is or are satisfied that it would be appropriate for it to be vested in some other persons[14].

1   As to the official custodian for charities see para 273 et seq ante.
2   As to the Charity Commissioners see paras 486–512 post.
3   Ie the Reverter of Sites Act 1987 s 1 (as amended): see para 63 ante.
4   Under the Charities Act 1993 s 16: see paras 180, 182–183, 271 ante, 509 post.
5   For the meaning of 'charity' see para 1 ante.
6   Charities Act 1993 s 23(1) (amended by the Trusts of Land and Appointment of Trustees Act 1996 Sch 3 para 26). The vesting or transfer of any property in accordance with such an order does not operate as a breach of any covenant or condition against alienation or give rise to a forfeiture: see para 180 note 6 ante.
7   See note 3 supra. Any reference to the Reverter of Sites Act 1987 s 1 (as amended) (see para 63 ante) operating in relation to any land is a reference to a trust arising in relation to the land under that provision: Charities Act 1993 s 23(9) (amended by the Trusts of Land and Appointment of Trustees Act 1996 Sch 3 para 26).
8   Charities Act 1993 s 23(2)(a).
9   Ibid s 23(2)(b).
10  For the meaning of 'the court' see para 168 note 12 ante.
11  Charities Act 1993 s 23(2). Where the Reverter of Sites Act 1987 s 1 (as amended) (see para 63 ante) has operated in relation to any such land as is mentioned in the Charities Act 1993 s 23(2)(a) (see the text to note 8 supra) and the land remains vested in the official custodian as mentioned in s 23(2)(b) (see the text to note 9 supra), then, all the powers, duties and liabilities that would, apart from s 23 (as amended), be those of the official custodian as trustee of the land are instead those of the charity trustees of the charity concerned; and those trustees have power in his name and on his behalf to execute and do all assurances and things which they could properly execute or do in their own name and on their own behalf if the land were vested in them: s 23(5) (amended by the Trusts of Land and Appointment of Trustees Act 1996 Sch 3 para 26). The Charities Act 1993 s 23(5) is not to be taken to require or authorise those trustees to sell the land at a time when it remains vested in the official custodian: s 23(6).
12  Ie where an order: (1) is made by the court under ibid s 21(2) (see para 280 post) by the Commissioners under s 16 (see paras 180, 182–183, 271 ante, 509 post), on the grounds that the Reverter of Sites Act 1987 s 1 (as amended) (see para 63 ante) will, or is likely to, operate in relation to the land; or (2) is made by the court or the Commissioners under the Charities Act 1993 s 23(2) (see the text and notes 7–11 supra): s 23(3)(a), (b).
13  For these purposes, 'the relevant charity trustees' means: (1) in relation to an orders made under ibid s 21(2) (see para 280 post) by the Commissioners under s 16 (see paras 180, 182–183, 271 ante, 509 post), on the grounds that the Reverter of Sites Act 1987 s 1 (as amended) (see para 63 ante) will, or is likely to, operate in relation to the land, the charity trustees of the charity in trust for which the land is vested in the official custodian immediately before the time when the order takes effect; or (2) in relation to an order made by the court or the Commissioners under the Charities Act 1993 s 23(2) (see the text and notes 7–11 supra), the charity trustees of the charity in trust for which the land was vested in the official custodian immediately before the time when the Reverter of Sites Act 1987 s 1 (as amended) operated in relation to the land: Charities Act 1993 s 23(3), (4). For the meaning of 'charity trustees' generally see para 1 note 10 ante.
14  Ibid s 23(3). Where the official custodian has been discharged from his trusteeship of any land by an order under s 23(2) (see the text and notes 7–11 supra), and the land has been vested in the charity trustees or other persons in accordance with s 23(3) (see the text and notes 12–13 supra), the land is to be held by those trustees, or as the case may be by those persons, as trustees on the terms of the trust arising under the Reverter of Sites Act 1987 s 1 (as amended) (see para 63 ante): Charities Act 1993 s 23(7) (amended

by the Trusts of Land and Appointment of Trustees Act 1996 Sch 3 para 26). The official custodian is not liable to any person in respect of any loss or misapplication of any land vested in him in accordance with that provision (semble, the Reverter of Sites Act 1987 s 1 (as amended)) unless it is occasioned by or through any wilful neglect or default of his or of any person acting for him; but the Consolidated Fund is liable to make good to any person any sums for which the official custodian may be liable by reason of any such neglect or default: Charities Act 1993 s 23(8). As to the Consolidated Fund see CONSTITUTIONAL LAW AND HUMAN RIGHTS vol 8(2) (Reissue) para 711 et seq; PARLIAMENT vol 34 (Reissue) paras 952–955.

**279. Management of property vested in official custodian.** As regards land vested in the official custodian for charities[1] in trust for a charity, the charity trustees[2] have the power in his name and on his behalf to execute and do all assurances and things which they could properly execute or do in their own name and on their own behalf if the land were vested in them[3]. However, if any land is so vested in the official custodian by virtue of an order under the Charity Commissioners' powers to act for the protection of charities[4], the power conferred on the charity trustees[5] is not exercisable by them in relation to any transaction affecting that land, unless the transaction is authorised by order of the court[6] or the Charity Commissioners[7]. Where any land is vested in the official custodian in trust for a charity[8], the charity trustees have the same power to make obligations entered into by them binding on the land as if it were vested in them, and any covenant, agreement or condition which is enforceable by or against the official custodian by reason of the land being vested in him is enforceable by or against the charity trustees as if the land were vested in them[9]. These provisions do not authorise any charity trustees or charity to impose any personal liability on the official custodian[10].

Where property is vested in the official custodian in trust for a charity, he must not exercise any powers of management, but, as trustee of any property, he has all the same powers, duties and liabilities, and is entitled to the same rights and immunities, and is subject to the control and orders of the court, as a corporation appointed custodian trustee[11], except that he has no power to charge fees[12]. However, where the official custodian is entitled as trustee for a charity to the custody of securities or documents of title relating to the trust property, he may permit them to be in the possession or under the control of the charity trustees without thereby incurring any liability[13].

1   As to the official custodian for charities see para 273 et seq ante.
2   For the meaning of 'charity trustees' see 1 note 10 ante. In the case of a corporate charity, references in the Charities Act 1993 s 22(2), (3), (4) to 'charity trustees' should be read as references to 'the charity': s 22(5).
3   Ibid s 22(2). Charity trustees are not required to obtain the official custodian's permission or to join him in proceedings claiming possession of charitable property: *Muman v Nagasena* [1999] 4 All ER 178, [2000] 1 WLR 299, CA.
4   Ie an order under the Charities Act 1993 s 18: see para 503 post. As to the Charity Commissioners see paras 486–512 post.
5   Ie by ibid s 22(2): see the text and notes 1–3 supra.
6   For the meaning of 'the court' see para 168 note 12 ante.
7   Charities Act 1993 s 22(3).
8   For the meaning of 'charity' see para 1 ante.
9   Charities Act 1993 s 22(4).
10  Ibid s 22(6).
11  Ie under the Public Trustee Act 1906 s 4: see TRUSTS vol 48 (2000 Reissue) para 687.
12  Charities Act 1993 s 22(1).
13  Ibid s 22(7).

**280. Discharge and termination of trusts; effect of orders.** The court[1] may by order discharge the official custodian for charities[2] from his trusteeship as regards all or any property vested in him in trust for a charity[3]. Where the official custodian is discharged from his trusteeship of any property, or the trusts on which he holds any property come to an end, the court may make such vesting orders and give such directions as may seem to the court to be necessary or expedient in consequence[4]. No person is liable for any loss occasioned by his acting in conformity with such an order or any order vesting property in the official custodian[5], or by his giving effect to anything done in pursuance of such orders, and no person is excused from so doing by reason of the order having been in any respect improperly obtained[6].

1   For the meaning of 'the court' see para 168 note 12 ante. This power may also be exercised by the Charity Commissioners: see the Charities Act 1993 s 16(1)(b), (c); and para 180 ante. As to the Commissioners' powers see para 275 ante. As to the Charity Commissioners see paras 486–512 post.
2   As to the official custodian for charities see para 273 et seq ante.
3   Charities Act 1993 s 21(2).
4   Ibid s 21(3). The vesting or transfer of any property in accordance with such an order does not operate as a breach of any covenant or condition against alienation or give rise to a forfeiture: see para 180 note 6 ante.
5   Ie under ibid s 21(1): see para 275 ante.
6   Ibid s 21(4).

**281. Liability of official custodian.** The official custodian for charities[1] is not liable as trustee for any charity in respect of any loss or of the misapplication of any property, unless it is occasioned by or through the wilful neglect or default of the custodian[2] or any person acting for him[3]. The Consolidated Fund is liable to make good to any charity any sums for which the official custodian is liable by reason of such neglect or default[4].

1   As to the official custodian for charities see para 273 et seq ante.
2   'Wilful default' has been considered judicially in other contexts (eg *Re Vickery, Vickery v Stephens* [1931] 1 Ch 572; *Re Lucking's Will Trusts, Renwick v Lucking* [1967] 3 All ER 726, [1968] 1 WLR 866; *Re City Equitable Fire Insurance Co Ltd* [1925] Ch 407, CA), but it is doubtful whether those decisions are useful in relation to the official custodian's liability.
3   Charities Act 1993 s 2(5). As to the power to delegate his functions see s 2(4); and para 274 ante.
4   Ibid s 2(5). As to the Consolidated Fund see CONSTITUTIONAL LAW AND HUMAN RIGHTS vol 8(2) (Reissue) para 711 et seq; PARLIAMENT vol 34 (Reissue) paras 952–955.

## 7. REGISTRATION OF CHARITIES; LOCAL AUTHORITIES' INDEXES AND FUNCTIONS

## (1) REGISTRATION OF CHARITIES

### (i) Obligation to Register

**282. The register.** It is the duty of the Charity Commissioners to continue to keep a register of charities[1], in which every charity, apart from some which are specifically excepted[2], must be entered[3]. Those which are excepted, other than exempt charities[4], may be entered in the register at their own request, but may at any time be removed, and must be removed at their own request[5]. The register must contain the name of every registered charity and such other particulars of, and such other information relating to, them as the Commissioners think fit[6]. An institution which no longer appears to the Commissioners to be a charity must be removed from the register; if the removal is due to a change in its purposes or trusts, the removal has effect from the date of the change[7]. A charity which ceases to exist or does not operate must also be removed[8].

The register, including entries cancelled on removal of an institution, must be kept open to public inspection at all reasonable times, and copies or particulars of the trusts of a registered charity, as supplied to the Commissioners, must be kept by them so long as it remains registered and be open to public inspection except in so far as regulations made by the Secretary of State otherwise provide[9]. Where any information contained in the register is not in documentary form, it must be made available for public inspection in legible form at all reasonable times[10].

The Commissioners must, on request, furnish any person with copies of, or extracts from, any document in their possession which is for the time being open to inspection[11].

---

1  Charities Act 1993 s 3(1). The Commissioners must keep the register in such manner as they think fit: s 3(1). As to the Charity Commissioners see paras 486–512 post.
2  As to such charities see para 283 post.
3  Charities Act 1993 s 3(2).
4  As to exempt charities see paras 283, 293 post. Prior to the coming into force of the Charities Act 1992 s 2 on 1 September 1992, exempt charities could be registered voluntarily. The registration of any such charity ceased to have effect at that time: s 2(8) (repealed).
5  Charities Act 1993 s 3(2).
6  Ibid s 3(3).
7  Ibid s 3(4).
8  Ibid s 3(4).
9  Ibid s 3(8). If the Commissioners so determine, s 3(8) will not apply to any particular information contained in the register and specified in their determination: s 3(10). However, a person is not required to supply the Commissioners with copies of schemes for the administration of a charity made otherwise than by the court, or to notify the Commissioners of any change made with respect to a registered charity by such a scheme, or require a person, if he refers the Commissioners to a document or copy already in the possession of the Commissioners, to supply a further copy of the document; but where a copy of any document need not thus be supplied to the Commissioners, a copy of it, if it relates to a registered charity, must be open to inspection under s 3(8) as if supplied to the Commissioners: s 3(11).

10  Ibid s 3(9).

11  Ibid s 84. For the meaning of 'document' see para 236 note 2 post. As to the fees payable see s 85; the Charity Commissioners' Fees (Copies and Extracts) Regulations 1992, SI 1992/2986; and para 495 post.

**283. Charities not obliged to be registered.** The categories of charities which are not required to be registered are:

(1)   exempt charities[1];

(2)   any charity which is excepted by order or regulations[2]; and

(3)   any charity having neither any permanent endowment[3] nor the use and occupation of any land, and whose income from all sources[4] does not in aggregate amount to more than £1,000 a year[5].

No charity is required to be registered in respect of any registered place of worship[6].

1   Charities Act 1993 s 3(5)(a). Head (1) in the text is to be read as referring also to: (1) any higher education corporation within the meaning of the Education Reform Act 1988; and (2) any further education corporation within the meaning of the Further and Higher Education Act 1992 (see EDUCATION): Charities Act 1993 s 3(5A) (added by the Teaching and Higher Education Act 1998 s 44(1), Sch 3 para 9). Head (1) in the text is to be read as also referring to: (a) any body to which the School Standards and Framework Act 1998 s 23(1)(a) or (b) applies; and (b) any Education Action Forum established by virtue of s 10(1) (see EDUCATION): Charities Act 1993 s 3(5B)(a) (added by the School Standards and Framework Act 1998 s 140(1), Sch 30 para 48).
    As to exempt charities see para 293 post.

2   Charities Act 1993 s 3(5)(b). 'Charity excepted by order or regulations' means a charity for the time being permanently or temporarily excepted by order of the Charity Commissioners, or which is of a description permanently or temporarily excepted by regulations, and which complies with any conditions of the exception: s 3(13). As to the Charity Commissioners see paras 486–512 post.
    As to the making of regulations generally see s 86 (as amended); and para 517 post. Note that these charities are not necessarily excepted from other obligations under the Charities Act 1993. Statutory instruments have been made excepting certain charities or types of charity from registration: see the Charities (Exception of Voluntary Schools from Registration) Regulations 1960, SI 1960/2366; Charities (Exception of Certain Charities for Boy Scouts and Girl Guides from Registration) Regulations 1961, SI 1961/1044; Charities (Exception from Registration and Accounts) Regulations 1965, SI 1965/1056; Charities (Exception of Universities from Registration) Regulations 1966, SI 1966/965; and the Charities (Exception from Registration) Regulations 1996, SI 1996/180 (amended by SI 2001/260) (which give exception from registration to charities for the advancement of religion where the application of income is conditional upon the upkeep of graves and the income does not exceed a specified amount). In other cases charities have been excepted individually by order: see eg the *Report of the Charity Commissioners for England and Wales for 1963* (HC Paper (1963–64) no 298) p 10 (Roman Catholic Church and Church of Wales charities).
    Head (2) in the text is to be read as referring also to any foundation to which the School Standards and Framework Act 1998 s 23(3) applies (see EDUCATION): Charities Act 1993 s 3(5B)(b) (as added: see note 1 supra). However, an order of the Charity Commissioners, or regulations made by the Secretary of State, may provide that the School Standards and Framework Act 1998 s 23(3) ceases to apply to any such foundation as is mentioned in that provision or to any such foundation of a description specified in the order or regulations: Charities Act 1993 s 3(5B) (as so added).

3   A charity is deemed to have a permanent endowment unless all property held for the purposes of the charity may be expended for those purposes without distinction between capital and income, and 'permanent endowment' means, in relation to any charity, property held subject to a restriction on its being expended for the purposes of the charity: ibid s 96(3).

4   As to how this is determined see ibid s 96(4); and para 180 note 8 ante.

5   Ibid s 3(5)(c). The Secretary of State may by order alter the specified amount in consequence of changes in the value of money or with a view to extending the scope of the exception: s 3(12).

6   Ibid s 3(5). For these purposes, 'registered place of worship' means any land or building falling within the Places of Worship Registration Act 1855 s 9 (as amended) (ie the land and buildings which if the Charities Act 1960 had not been passed, would by virtue of that section as amended by subsequent

enactments be partially exempted from the operation of the Charitable Trusts Act 1853): Charities Act 1993 s 3(14). For these purposes, 'building' includes part of a building: s 3(14). As to the registration of places of worship see ECCLESIASTICAL LAW.


**284. Duty to apply for registration.** It is the duty of the charity trustees[1] of any charity[2] which is not registered nor excepted from registration[3] to apply for it to be registered[4]. They must supply to the Charity Commissioners copies or particulars of its trusts[5] and such other documents or information as may be prescribed[6] or as the Commissioners may require for the purposes of the application[7]. Any person not fulfilling these duties may be required by order of the Commissioners to make good the default[8].

1   For the meaning of 'charity trustees' see para 1 note 10 ante.
2   For the meaning of 'charity' see para 1 ante.
3   As to exception from registration see para 283 ante.
4   Charities Act 1993 s 3(7)(a).
5   For the meaning of 'trusts' see para 210 note 5 ante. As to the Charity Commissioners see paras 486–512 post.
6   Ie prescribed by regulations made by the Secretary of State: see Charities Act 1993 s 86(1), (3); and para 517 post. As to the Secretary of State see para 513 post. As to the making of regulations generally see s 86 (as amended); and para 517 ante.
7   Ibid s 3(6), (7)(a). They need not, however, supply copies of schemes made otherwise than by the court, or copies of documents already in the Commissioners' possession: see s 3(11); and para 282 ante. For the meaning of 'document' see para 236 note 2 ante.
8   See ibid s 87; and para 494 post. Disobedience to such an order attracts the same sanctions as a contempt of court: see s 88; and para 494 post.


**285. Continuing duty to supply information.** The charity trustees[1], or the last charity trustees, of any institution[2] for the time being registered, must notify the Charity Commissioners[3] if it ceases to exist, or if there is any change in its trusts[4] or in the particulars entered in the register, and must supply particulars of any such change and copies of any new or altered trusts[5]. Any person failing to do so may be required by order to make good the default[6].

1   For the meaning of 'charity trustees' see para 1 note 10 ante.
2   For the meaning of 'institution' see para 1 ante.
3   As to the Charity Commissioners see paras 486–512 post.
4   For the meaning of 'trusts' see para 210 note 5 ante.
5   Charities Act 1993 s 3(7)(b). They need not, however, supply copies of schemes made otherwise than by the court, or copies of documents already in the Commissioners' possession: see s 3(11); and para 282 ante.
        It is submitted that duty is not applicable in a case where the trusts have been modified under s 74 (see para 210–211 ante), for the Commissioners will then have all the relevant information. Section 74, however, unlike the provision which it replaced (the Charities Act 1985 s 2 (repealed)) does not contain a provision corresponding to the Charities Act 1985 s 2(12), which specifically excluded the Charities Act 1960 s 4(6)(b) (repealed: see now the Charities Act 1993 s 3(7)(b)). If, however, the resolution of the trustees under the Charities Act 1993 s 74 can be construed as a 'scheme for the administration of a charity' the duty would be excluded by s 3(11).
6   See ibid s 87; and para 494 post.

**286. Publication of registered charity's status.** Where a charity[1] is a registered charity whose gross income[2] in its last financial year[3] exceeded £10,000[4], the fact that it is a registered charity must be stated in legible characters[5]:

(1) in all notices, advertisements and other documents issued by or on behalf of the charity and soliciting money or other property for the benefit of the charity[6];

(2) in all bills of exchange, promissory notes, endorsements, cheques and orders for money or goods purporting to be signed on behalf of the charity[7]; and

(3) in all bills rendered by the charity and in all its invoices, receipts and letters of credit[8].

If any person[9] issues or authorises the issue of any document falling within head (1) or (3) above or signs any document falling within head (2) above, and in either case the fact that the charity is a registered charity is not stated[10], he is guilty of an offence[11]. However, no proceedings for such an offence may be instituted except by or with the consent of the Director of Public Prosecutions[12].

1 For the meaning of 'charity' see para 1 ante.
2 For the meaning of 'gross income' see para 210 note 2 ante.
3 For the meaning of 'financial year' see para 210 note 3 ante.
4 Charities Act 1993 s 5(1) (amended by the Charities (Substitution of Sums) Order 1995, SI 1995/2696, arts 1, 2). The Secretary of State may by order substitute a different sum for the sum for the time being specified: Charities Act 1993 s 5(6). As to the making of orders see s 86(1), (3); and para 517 post.
5 Ibid s 5(2) (amended by the Welsh Language Act 1993 ss 32(2), 35, Sch 2). The statement must be in English, except that, in the case of a document which is otherwise wholly in Welsh, the statement may be in Welsh if it consists of or includes the words 'elusen cofrestredig' (the Welsh equivalent of 'registered charity'): Charities Act 1993 s 5(2A) (added by the Welsh Language Act 1993 s 32(3)).
6 Charities Act 1993 s 5(2)(a). This provision has effect whether the solicitation is express or implied, and whether the money or other property is to be given for any consideration or not: s 5(3).
7 Ibid s 5(2)(b).
8 Ibid s 5(2)(c). See also s 68(1); and para 226 ante.
9 'Person' includes a body of persons corporate or unincorporate: Interpretation Act 1978 s 5, Sch 1. As to offences by corporate bodies see the Charities Act 1993 s 95; and para 515 post.
10 Ie the statement as required by ibid s 5(2): see the text and notes 5–8 supra.
11 Ibid s 5(4), (5) (amended by the Welsh Language Act 1993 s 32(4), (5)). A person guilty of such an offence is liable on summary conviction to a fine not exceeding level 3 on the standard scale: Charities Act 1993 s 5(4), (5).
'Standard scale' means the standard scale of maximum fines for summary offences as set out in the Criminal Justice Act 1982 s 37 (as amended): see the Interpretation Act 1978 s 5, Sch 1 (definition added by the Criminal Justice Act 1988 s 170(1), Sch 15 para 58); and CRIMINAL LAW, EVIDENCE AND PROCEDURE vol 11(2) (Reissue) para 808; MAGISTRATES. At the date at which this volume states the law, the standard scale is as follows: level 1, £200; level 2, £500; level 3, £1,000; level 4, £2,500; level 5, £5,000: Criminal Justice Act 1982 s 37(2) (substituted by the Criminal Justice Act 1991 s 17(1)). As to the determination of the amount of the fine actually imposed, as distinct from the level on the standard scale which it may not exceed, see the Powers of Criminal Courts (Sentencing) Act 2000 s 128; and MAGISTRATES.
12 Charities Act 1993 s 94(1), (2)(a).

**287. Direction for change of name of charity.** In certain specified circumstances the Charity Commissioners[1] may give a direction to the charity trustees[2] requiring the name of the charity to be changed to such other name as the charity trustees may determine with the approval of the Commissioners[3]. The circumstances specified are if[4]:

(1) it is a registered charity and its name ('the registered name') (a) is the same as, or (b) is in the opinion of the Commissioners too like, the name, at the time when

the registered name was entered in the register in respect of the charity, of any other charity (whether registered or not)[5];

(2) the name[6] of the charity is in the opinion of the Commissioners likely to mislead the public as to the true nature of (a) the purposes of the charity as set out in its trusts, or (b) the activities which the charity carries on under its trusts in pursuit of those purposes[7];

(3) the name[8] of the charity includes any word or expression for the time being specified in regulations made by the Secretary of State[9] and the inclusion in its name of that word or expression is in the opinion of the Commissioners likely to mislead the public in any respect as to the status of the charity[10];

(4) the name[11] of the charity is in the opinion of the Commissioners likely to give the impression that the charity is connected in some way with Her Majesty's government or any local authority, or with any other body of persons or any individual, when it is not so connected[12]; or

(5) the name of the charity is in the opinion of the Commissioners offensive[13].

A change of name by a charity under these provisions does not affect any rights or obligations of the charity; and any legal proceedings that might have been continued or commenced by or against it in its former name may be continued or commenced by or against it in its new name[14].

These provisions do not apply to an exempt charity[15].

1    As to the Charity Commissioners see paras 486–512 post.
2    For these purposes, any reference to charity trustees in relation to a charity which is a company, is to be read as a reference to the directors of the company: Charities Act 1993 s 6(8). For the meaning of 'charity trustees' generally see para 1 note 10 ante.
      On receiving such a direction the charity trustees must give effect to it notwithstanding anything in the trusts of the charity, and, having done so, must forthwith notify the Commissioners of the charity's new name and of the date on which the change occurred: s 6(4), (5).
3    Ibid s 6(1).
4    Ibid s 6(2).
5    Ibid s 6(2)(a). Any direction on this ground must be given within 12 months of the time when the registered name was entered in the register in respect of the charity: s 6(3). For the purposes of this provision minor variations in names are to be disregarded. The Companies Act 1985 s 26(3) (as amended) (minor variations in names to be disregarded: see COMPANIES vol 7(1) (1996 Reissue) para 156) applies for the purposes of the Charities Act 1993 s 6 as if the reference to the Companies Act 1985 s 26(1)(c) were a reference to the Charities Act 1993 s 6(2)(a): s 6(7).
6    Ie in relation to a registered charity the name by which it is registered: ibid s 6(2).
7    Ibid s 6(2)(b).
8    See note 6 supra.
9    See the Charities (Misleading Names) Regulations 1992, SI 1992/1901. As to the making of regulations see the Charities Act 1993 s 86(1), (3); and para 517 post. As to the Secretary of State see para 513 post.
10   Ibid s 6(2)(c).
11   See note 6 supra.
12   Charities Act 1993 s 6(2)(d).
13   Ibid s 6(2)(e).
14   Ibid s 6(6).
15   Ibid s 6(9). As to exempt charities see para 293 post.

**288. Direction to change name of a charity which is a company.** Where a direction[1] requiring a charity's[2] name to be changed is given with respect to a charity which is a company, the direction must require the name of the charity to be changed by resolution of the directors of the company[3]. Where the name of such a charity is changed accordingly, the registrar of companies must[4] enter the new name on the register of companies in place of the former name[5] and issue a certificate of incorporation altered to meet the circumstances of the case[6].

1    Ie a direction under the Charities Act 1993 s 6: see para 287 ante.
2    For the meaning of 'charity' see para 1 ante.
3    Charities Act 1993 s 7(1). The Companies Act 1985 s 380 (as amended) (registration etc of resolutions and agreements: see COMPANIES vol 7(1) (1996 Reissue) paras 691–692) applies to such a resolution: Charities Act 1993 s 7(2).
4    Ie subject to the Companies Act 1985 s 26 (as amended) (see COMPANIES vol 7(1) (1996 Reissue) para 156): Charities Act 1993 s 7(3)(a).
5    Ibid s 7(3)(a).
6    Ibid s 7(3)(b). The change of name has effect from the date on which the altered certificate is issued: s 7(3).

## (ii)  Effect of, and Claims for and Objections to, Registration

**289.  Effect of registration.** For all purposes other than rectification of the register of charities[1], any institution[2] must be conclusively presumed to have been a charity[3] at any time when it is or was on the register[4]. It has been held that the same presumption applies where a body which is not registered at a material date later becomes registered without any intervening alteration in its constitution or purposes[5].

Refusal of registration does not, however, conclusively establish that the body is not charitable[6].

1    As to the register see para 282 et seq ante.
2    For the meaning of 'institution' see para 1 ante.
3    For the meaning of 'charity' see para 1 ante.
4    Charities Act 1993 s 4(1). For examples of the application of this presumption see *Wynn v Skegness UDC* [1966] 3 All ER 336, [1967] 1 WLR 52; *Finch v Poplar Borough Council* (1967) 66 LGR 324.
5    *Re Murawski's Will Trusts, Lloyds Bank Ltd v Royal Society for the Prevention of Cruelty to Animals* [1971] 2 All ER 328, [1971] 1 WLR 707.
6    *Over Seventies Housing Association v Westminster City Council* [1974] RA 247, where refusal of registration did not prevent the body from arguing that it was a charity and therefore entitled to rating relief, though the argument in fact failed.

**290.  Objections to registration and claims for removal.** Any person who is or may be affected by the registration of an institution[1] as a charity[2] may object, on the ground that it is not a charity, to its being entered by the Charity Commissioners[3] in the register of charities, and if the institution is already registered any such person may apply to the Commissioners for it to be removed from the register on that ground[4]. Provision may be made by regulations made by the Secretary of State[5] as to the manner in which any such objection or application is to be made, prosecuted or dealt with[6].

Questions affecting the registration of or the removal from the register of an institution may be considered afresh by the Commissioners, notwithstanding that they may have been determined on an appeal to the court relating to registration[7], if it appears to the Commissioners that there has been a change of circumstances or that the decision is inconsistent with a later judicial decision, whether given on such an appeal or not[8].

1    For the meaning of 'institution' see para 1 ante.
2    For the meaning of 'charity' see para 1 ante.
3    As to the Charity Commissioners see paras 486–512 post.
4    Charities Act 1993 s 4(2).
5    As to the making of regulations generally see s 86 (as amended); and para 517 post. As to the Secretary of State see para 513 post.
6    Charities Act 1993 s 4(2). At the date at which this volume states the law, no such regulations had been made. The informal procedure adopted is described in the *Report of the Charity Commissioners for England and Wales for 1964* (HC Paper (1965–66) no 8) p 12.
7    Ie under the Charities Act 1993 s 4(3): see para 292 post.
8    Ibid s 4(5).

**291. Disclosure of information to and by the Charity Commissioners.** With the exception of the Commissioners of Customs and Excise and the Commissioners of Inland Revenue[1], and subject to any express restriction imposed by or under any enactment[2], any government department[3], any local authority[4], any constable[5], and any other body or person discharging functions of a public nature[6] may disclose to the Charity Commissioners[7] any information received by that body or person under or for the purposes of any enactment, where the disclosure is made by the body or person for the purpose of enabling or assisting the Commissioners to discharge any of their functions[8].

Either of the two excepted bodies of commissioners referred to above (the relevant body) may disclose to the Charity Commissioners the name and address of any institution[9] which has for any purpose been treated by the relevant body as established for charitable purposes[10]; information as to the purposes of an institution and the trusts under which it is established or regulated, where the disclosure is made by the relevant body in order to give or obtain assistance in determining whether the institution ought for any purpose to be treated as established for charitable purposes[11]; and information with respect to an institution which has for any purpose been treated as so established but which appears to the relevant body to be, or to have been, carrying on activities which are not charitable, or to be, or to have been, applying any of its funds for purposes which are not charitable[12].

The Charity Commissioners may disclose to any body or person falling within any of the above provisions any information received by them under or for the purposes of any enactment, where the disclosure is made by the Commissioners for any purpose connected with the discharge of their functions, and for the purpose of enabling or assisting that body or person to discharge any of its or his functions[13]. The Commissioners are, however, bound by any express restriction on the disclosure of information that was imposed when the information was disclosed to them[14].

The provisions described above do not affect any other power of disclosure that may be exercisable[15].

1    See the Charities Act 1993 s 10(2); and the text and notes 9–12 infra. As to the Commissioners of Customs and Excise see further CUSTOMS AND EXCISE vol 12(2) (Reissue) para 905 et seq. As to the Commissioners of Inland Revenue see INCOME TAXATION.
2    For these purposes, 'enactment' includes an enactment comprised in subordinate legislation: ibid s 10(9).
3    Ibid s 10(6)(a). This includes a Northern Ireland department: s 10(6)(a).

4	Ibid s 10(6)(b).

5	Ibid s 10(6)(c).

6	Ibid s 10(6)(d). This includes a body or person discharging regulatory functions in relation to any description of activities: s 10(6)(d). See also note 13 infra.

7	As to the Charity Commissioners see paras 486–512 post.

8	Charities Act 1993 s 10(1).

9	In relation to the Commissioners of Inland Revenue, references in ibid s 10(2) to an institution are to be construed as references to an institution in England and Wales: s 10(3).

10	Ibid s 10(2)(a).

11	Ibid s 10(2)(b).

12	Ibid s 10(2)(c).

13	Ibid s 10(4). The reference to any body or person discharging functions of a public nature (including a body or person discharging regulatory functions in relation to any description or activities) in s 10(6)(d) (see the text to note 6 supra), is to be construed, in relation to a disclosure by the Charity Commissioners under s 10(4), as including a reference to any such body or person in a country or territory outside the United Kingdom: s 10(7).

14	See ibid s 10(5).

15	Ibid s 10(8). For example, the restrictions contained in the Financial Services Act 1986 s 179 (as amended) and the Companies Act 1985 s 449 (as amended) (see COMPANIES vol 7(2) (1996 Reissue) para 1387) on the disclosure of certain restricted information by certain persons do not preclude the disclosure of such information for the purpose of enabling or assisting the Charity Commissioners to discharge any of their functions specified in the Financial Services (Disclosure of Information) (Designated Authorities) (No 5) Order 1989, SI 1989/940. See also the Financial Services Act 1986 (Miscellaneous Exemptions) Order 1988, SI 1988/350 (amended by SI 1994/1517), the Financial Services Act 1986 (Miscellaneous Exemptions) (No 2) Order 1988, SI 1988/723; and the Financial Services Act 1986 (Miscellaneous Exemptions) Order 1989, SI 1989/431. As to restrictions on disclosure of information generally see CONFIDENCE AND DATA PROTECTION.

**292. Appeals relating to registration.** An appeal against any decision of the Charity Commissioners[1] to enter or not to enter an institution[2] in the register of charities[3], or to remove or not to remove an institution from the register, lies to the High Court at the instance of the Attorney General or of the persons who are or claim to be the charity trustees[4] of the institution or of any person whose objection to registration or application for removal[5] has been disallowed[6].

If the Commissioners decide to enter an institution in the register or not to remove one from the register and there is an appeal to the High Court against that decision, then until it is known whether the decision is to stand or not, the entry in the register must be maintained, but must be in suspense and marked as such[7]. While the entry is in suspense, the institution is deemed not to be on the register for the purposes of the conclusive presumption as to charitable status[8] which arises from the fact of registration[9].

1	As to the Charity Commissioners see paras 486–512 post.

2	For the meaning of 'institution' see para 1 ante.

3	As to the register see para 282 et seq ante.

4	For the meaning of 'charity trustees' see para 1 note 10 ante. Strictly speaking, where the institution is a corporate body it cannot itself appeal, but this point was not taken in the first two appeals to be heard: *Incorporated Council of Law Reporting for England and Wales v A-G* [1972] Ch 73, [1971] 3 All ER 1029, CA; *Construction Industry Training Board v A-G* [1973] Ch 173, [1972] 2 All ER 1339, CA (decided under earlier legislation).

5	Ie under the Charities Act 1993 s 4(2): see para 290 ante.

6	Ibid s 4(3). As to the procedure on appeals see para 549 post.

7	Ibid s 4(4).

8	As to this presumption see ibid s 4(1); and para 289 ante.

9    Ibid s 4(4). By analogy with *Re Murawski's Will Trusts, Lloyds Bank Ltd v Royal Society for the Prevention of Cruelty to Animals* [1971] 2 All ER 328, [1971] 1 WLR 707, the statutory presumption would probably be applied retrospectively if it was ultimately determined that the decision was to stand.

## (iii) Exempt Charities

**293. Exempt charities.** Certain charities[1] are largely exempt from the Charity Commissioners' jurisdiction[2]. They are known as exempt charities[3] for the purposes of the Charities Act 1993, and are not required to be entered in the register of charities[4].

1    These include certain institutions exempted under earlier Acts (specifically, any institution which, if the Charities Act 1960 had not been passed, would be exempted from the powers and jurisdiction, under the Charitable Trusts Acts 1853 to 1939 (repealed), of the Commissioners or Minister of Education (apart from any power of the Commissioners or Minister to apply those Acts in whole or in part to charities otherwise exempt) by the terms of any enactment not contained in those Acts other than the Places of Worship Registration Act 1855 s 9 (as amended: see ECCLESIASTICAL LAW); the universities of Oxford, Cambridge, London, Durham and Newcastle; the colleges and halls in the universities of Oxford, Cambridge, Durham and Newcastle; Queen Mary and Westfield College in the University of London; the colleges of Winchester and Eton; any university, university college or institution connected with it declared by Order in Council to be an exempt charity (see infra for a list of Orders in Council made under, or having effect as if made under, this provision); the Qualifications and Curriculum Authority; the Qualifications and Curriculum Authority for Wales; a successor company to a higher education corporation; the Boards of Trustees of the Victoria and Albert Museum, the Science Museum, the Armouries, the Royal Botanic Gardens, Kew, the National Museums and Galleries on Merseyside, the National Gallery, the Tate Gallery, the National Portrait Gallery and the Wallace Collection; the trustees of the British Museum, the trustees of the Natural History Museum, the trustees of the Imperial War Museum and the trustees of the National Maritime Museum; any institution administered by or on behalf of an institution included above for the general purposes of, or for any special purpose of or in connection with, the last-mentioned institution; the Church Commissioners and any institution administered by them; registered industrial and provident societies; societies or branches registered under the Friendly Societies Act 1974; the Board of Governors of the Museum of London; the British Library Board; and the National Lottery Charities Board: Charities Act 1993 ss 3(5)(a), 96(1), Sch 2 (amended by the Education Act 1993 s 307(1), Sch 19 para 175 (repealed); the National Lottery etc Act 1993 s 37(2), Sch 5 para 12; the Education Act 1996 s 582(2), Sch 38 Pt I; the Education Act 1997 s 57(1), Sch 7 para 7; School Standards and Framework Act 1998 s 140(3), Sch 31; and the Teaching and Higher Education Act 1998 s 44(2), Sch 4).
      The following Orders in Council have been made under the Charities Act 1960 Sch 2 para (c) (repealed) or under the Charities Act 1993 Sch 3 para (c) and designate numerous universities and institutions as exempt charities: see the Exempt Charities Orders 1962, SI 1962/1343; SI 1965/1715; SI 1966/1460; SI 1967/821; SI 1969/1496; SI 1978/453; SI 1982/1661; SI 1983/1516; SI 1984/1976; SI 1987/1823; SI 1989/2394; SI 1993/2359; SI 1994/1905; SI 1994/2956; SI 1995/2998; SI 1996/1637; SI 1996/1932; SI 1996/1933; SI 1999/3139; SI 2000/1826.
2    As to the Charity Commissioners see paras 486–512 post.
3    See the Charities Act 1993 s 96(1). In addition, certain common investment funds are exempt charities under s 24(8): see para 367 post.
4    See ibid s 3(5)(a); and para 283 ante.

## (iv) Other Registration Requirements

**294. Registration in connection with lotteries.** There are registration requirements where a lottery is promoted on behalf of a charity. These are considered elsewhere in this work[1].

1   See the Lotteries and Amusements Act 1976; the Lotteries Regulations 1993, SI 1993/3223 (as amended); Lotteries (Variation of Monetary Limits) Order 1989 SI 1989/1218; and BETTING, GAMING AND LOTTERIES vol 4(1) (Reissue) para 148 et seq.

# (2) LOCAL AUTHORITIES' FUNCTIONS

## (i) Local Indexes

**295. Power to maintain a local index.** A council[1] has power to maintain an index of local charities[2] or of any class of local charities in its area, and to publish information contained in the index or summaries or extracts from it[3]. Where any of a council's functions are carried out by a joint board, the board has the same powers as the council as respects local charities in the area which are established for purposes similar or complementary to those of the board[4]. A council may employ a voluntary organisation[5] as its agent for these purposes, on such terms and within such limits or in such cases as they may agree[6].

1   The council referred to in the Charities Act 1993 ss 76, 77 (as amended) is a county, or county borough, or district or London borough council, or the Common Council of the City of London: ss 76(1), 77(1) (both amended by the Local Government (Wales) Act 1994 s 66(6), Sch 16 para 101). As to such councils see further LOCAL GOVERNMENT. The references to 'council' in the Charities Act 1993 ss 76–78 (as amended) have effect as if the references to a council for any area included references to a national park authority and as if the relevant park were the authority's area: Environment Act 1995 s 70, Sch 9 para 15. As to national park authorities see OPEN SPACES AND ANCIENT MONUMENTS vol 34 (Reissue) para 157 et seq.
2   For the meaning of 'local charity' see para 180 note 10 ante.
3   Charities Act 1993 s 76(1).
4   Ibid s 76(5).
5   'Voluntary organisation' means any body whose activities are carried on otherwise than for profit, not being a public or local authority: ibid s 76(4).
6   Ibid s 76(4).

**296. The index and its contents.** The Charity Commissioners[1] must, on request, supply free of charge to a council[2] proposing to establish or maintaining an index of local charities, copies of any entries in the central register of charities relevant to the index, and particulars of any changes in entries of which copies have already been supplied; they may also arrange to supply particulars of such changes without further request[3].

An index maintained under these powers is required to be open to public inspection at all reasonable times[4].

1   As to the Charity Commissioners see paras 486–512 post.
2   For the meaning of 'council' see para 295 note 1 ante.
3   Charities Act 1993 s 76(2).
4   Ibid s 76(3).

## (ii) Review of Local Charities

**297. Power to carry out reviews.** A council[1] has power to initiate and carry out, in co-operation with the charity trustees[2], a review of the working of any group of local charities with the same or similar purposes in the council's area[3]. It may make to the Charity Commissioners[4] such report on the review and recommendations arising from it as the council, after consultation with the charity trustees, thinks fit[5]. It may also co-operate with other persons in a review of the working of local charities in its area, with or without other charities, or join with other persons in initiating and carrying out such a review[6]. The ancillary powers and provisions which exist in relation to the maintaining of local indexes[7] apply also to local reviews[8].

1   For the meaning of 'council' see para 295 note 1 ante.
2   For the meaning of 'charity trustees' see para 1 note 10 ante.
3   Charities Act 1993 s 77(1).
4   As to the Charity Commissioners see paras 486–512 post.
5   Charities Act 1993 s 77(1).
6   Ibid s 77(2).
7   Ie as to the employment of voluntary organisations (ie ibid s 76(4): see para 295 ante) and the powers of joint boards (ie s 76(5): see para 295 ante).
8   Ibid s 77(5).


**298. Scope of reviews.** Reviews of local charities initiated under the Charities Act 1993[1] may not extend to any ecclesiastical charity[2], and may not extend to any charity without the consent of the charity trustees[3]. Reviews initiated by a district council may not extend to the working in any county of a local charity established for purposes similar or complementary to any services provided by county councils, unless the county council consents to the review's being so extended[4].

1   Ie under the Charities Act 1993 s 77 (as amended): see para 297 ante.
2   For the meaning of 'ecclesiastical charity' see para 240 note 4 ante.
3   Charities Act 1993 s 77(3). For the meaning of 'charity trustees' see para 1 note 10 ante.
4   Ibid s 77(4), which does not apply to Wales: s 77(4A) (added by the Local Government (Wales) Act 1994 s 66(6), Sch 16 para 101).


### (iii)  Co-operation with and between Charities


**299. Local authorities' powers.** Any local council[1] or joint board discharging the functions of such a council may make arrangements with any charity established for purposes similar or complementary to services provided by the council or board for co-ordinating the activities of the council or board with those of the charity in the interests of persons who may benefit from those services or from the charity[2]. Whether or not such arrangements have been made with such a charity, it may also disclose to the charity, in the interests of those persons, information obtained in connection with the services provided by the council or board[3].

1   In this context, 'local council' means, in relation to England, the council of a county, district, London borough, parish, and includes also the Common Council of the City of London and the Council of the Isles of Scilly, and in relation to Wales means the council of a county, county borough or community: Charities Act 1993 s 78(1) (amended by the Local Government (Wales) Act 1994 s 66(6), Sch 16 para 101). As to such councils see generally LOCAL GOVERNMENT.
2   Charities Act 1993 s 78(1)(a).
3   Ibid s 78(1)(b).

**300. Charity trustees' powers.** Notwithstanding anything in the trusts[1] of a charity, where it appears to charity trustees[2] likely to promote or make more effective the work of the charity, they may co-operate in any review[3] of the working of charities or any class of charities[4], or make arrangements with a local authority[5] or with another charity for co-ordinating their activities with those of the authority or of the other charity[6], or publish information of other charities with a view to bringing them to the notice of those for whose benefit they are intended[7]. They may also defray the expense of doing any of those things out of any income or money applicable as income of the charity[8].

1 For the meaning of 'trusts' see para 210 note 5 ante.
2 For the meaning of 'charity trustees' see para 1 note 10 ante.
3 Ie whether or not initiated under the Charities Act 1993 s 77 (as amended): see paras 297–298 ante.
4 Ibid s 78(2)(a).
5 Ie acting under ibid s 78(1) (as amended): see para 299 ante.
6 Ibid s 78(2)(b).
7 Ibid s 78(2)(c).
8 Ibid s 78(2).

# 8. CONDUCT AND ADMINISTRATION OF CHARITABLE TRUSTS

## (1) DUTIES OF CHARITY TRUSTEES

### (i) In general

**301. Observance of the trust.** The duties of trustees of charitable trusts do not differ in principle from those of non-charitable trustees[1]. Their primary duty is to execute the trust in accordance with its terms, whether contained in a will, a deed, a scheme or any other instrument, and with the general law, in the interests of the intended beneficiaries[2].

It is a breach of trust for trustees to divert a charitable fund given for one object to another not contemplated by the donor[3], or for a trustee of more than one charity to mix the funds and apply them indiscriminately for the charities[4], or for trustees to vary the specific mode of application directed by the founder[5], or for the trustees of one charity to subscribe its funds to the funds of another charity unless the recipient charity is expressly or by implication a purpose or object of the donor charity[6]. If capital has been applied for income purposes, it should if possible be replaced out of future income[7].

It is a breach of trust to extend the benefits of a charity intended exclusively for members of one religion or sect to persons holding different religious beliefs[8]. If, but only if, an intention to that effect is expressed, this rule applies equally in the case of charities not established for purely religious purposes[9].

Chapels established for particular forms of worship or doctrinal teaching must not be converted by the trustees to other forms[10], even with the consent of the congregation[11]. However, congregations of the same sect may differ upon non-fundamental[12] doctrines, and yet remain proper objects of the same charity[13].

Although it is a breach of trust to alter or depart from the trusts of the foundation, it is competent for a congregation, or the majority if power is given to it, to make new regulations in matters not involving a contravention of the trusts, or to alter those in existence[14].

However, a charitable trust will be construed liberally, and an expenditure may be allowed which is not within a narrow reading of the words declaring the trust[15]. Thus, where a charity was established for the benefit of a guild and its poor brethren, the trustees committed no breach of trust by subscribing out of the trust fund towards the erection of a school in return for a right to have a number of boys educated there gratuitously[16].

Where a trustee of charity property inadvertently pays more than the income of the property to the charity, he has no claim against the charity for reimbursement[17].

Charities, other than exempt charities[18], are not permitted to spend money applicable for the purposes of the charity in promoting or preparing a Bill in Parliament, without the consent of the court or of the Charity Commissioners[19].

Charity trustees have statutory power to do various things to promote the work of the charity, notwithstanding the terms of the trusts of the charity[20], but a charity has no power to give a gratuitous guarantee in respect of the liability of a third party with whom it has no legal tie[21].

1   These include, eg, the duty not to deviate from the terms of the trust, not to profit from the trust, not to delegate the trust, to act impartially between the beneficiaries, to distribute the trust property only to those properly entitled, and to invest prudently: see TRUSTS vol 48 (2000 Reissue) para 840 et seq. As to the duty to act gratuitously and the position regarding the remuneration of charity trustees see para 305 post.

2   See *Andrews v M'Guffog* (1886) 11 App Cas 313 at 329, HL, per Lord Herschell LC. Trustees are also subject to a statutory duty of care: see the Trustee Act 2000 ss 1, 2, Sch 1; para 306 post; and TRUSTS vol 48 (2000 Reissue) paras 848–849.

3   *A-G v Brandreth* (1842) 1 Y & C Ch Cas 200 (where a gift for the poor of one parish was wrongfully applied in aid of the poor of another parish); *Re St John the Evangelist, D'Aungre's Charity* (1888) 59 LT 617 (where funds given for the repair of one church were applied for another). See also *Wivelescom Case* (1629) Duke 94; *A-G v Vivian* (1826) 1 Russ 226; *A-G v Goldsmith's Co* (1833) Coop Pr Cas 292 at 309 per Leach MR; *Re Church Estate Charity, Wandsworth* (1871) 6 Ch App 296. As to the effect of a union of benefices upon charities connected with one of the united parishes or churches see para 242 ante. A church in the City of London which becomes a guild church retains the benefit of a charity enjoyed by the church: see the City of London (Guild Churches) Act 1952 s 28.

4   *A-G v Newbury Corpn* (1838) Coop Pr Cas 72 at 77 per Lord Brougham LC; *Andrews v M'Guffog* (1886) 11 App Cas 313, HL. The rule is different where one fund is given for several charities: *A-G v Geary* (1817) 3 Mer 513.

5   Eg a gift for the benefit of decayed householders cannot be applied for the poor of the parish generally: *Ex p Fowlser* (1819) 1 Jac & W 70. Nor can a fund to provide a preacher be applied in aid of the poor (Duke on Charitable Uses 116), or property devised to discharge a tax be diverted to the use of certain poor persons (*A-G v Bushby* (1857) 24 Beav 299), or a grammar school, founded for classical teaching, be used for instruction in English, writing and arithmetic, or its surplus revenue be applied for enlarging the school chapel for the town use (*A-G v Earl of Mansfield* (1827) 2 Russ 501).

6   *Baldry v Feintuck* [1972] 2 All ER 81, [1972] 1 WLR 552.

7   *Andrews v M'Guffog* (1886) 11 App Cas 313 at 329, HL, per Lord Herschell LC.

8   *Shore v Wilson* (1842) 9 Cl & Fin 355, HL; *A-G v Calvert* (1857) 23 Beav 248 (charity restricted to members of Church of England). See also *Baker v Lee* (1860) 8 HL Cas 495 (non-eligibility of dissenters as trustees of Church of England charity); *A-G v Murdoch* (1852) 1 De GM & G 86; *A-G v Anderson* (1888) 57 LJCh 543 at 550 per Kekewich J (charities confined to Protestant dissenters and Presbyterians); *Drummond v A-G for Ireland* (1849) 2 HL Cas 837 (Unitarians excluded).

9   *A-G v Calvert* (1857) 26 LJCh 682 at 686 per Romilly MR; *Re Perry Almshouses, Re Ross' Charity* [1899] 1 Ch 21, CA.

10  *Craigdallie v Aikman* (1813) 1 Dow 1; *A-G v Pearson* (1817) 3 Mer 353 at 400, 418–419 per Lord Eldon LC; *Foley v Wontner* (1820) 2 Jac & W 245 at 247 per Lord Eldon LC; *Dill v Watson* (1836) 2 Jo Ex Ir 48; *Milligan v Mitchell* (1837) 3 My & Cr 72; *A-G v Munro* (1848) 2 De G & Sm 122; *A-G v Wilson* (1848) 16 Sim 210; *General Assembly of the Free Church of Scotland v Lord Overtoun, Macalister v Young* [1904] AC 515 at 613 et seq, HL, per Earl of Halsbury LC. But see *Westwood v McKie* (1869) 21 LT 165.

11  *Broom v Summers* (1840) 11 Sim 353; *A-G v Welsh* (1844) 4 Hare 572; *A-G v Murdoch* (1852) 1 De GM & G 86; *A-G v Rochester Corpn* (1854) 5 De GM & G 797; *Ward v Hipwell* (1862) 3 Giff 547; *A-G v Aust* (1865) 13 LT 235; and see *A-G v Anderson* (1888) 57 LJCh 543. As to the effect of acquiescence in a change of doctrine see *Cairncross v Lorimer* (1860) 3 Macq 827, HL.

12  It is for the court, not for the trustees, to decide what doctrines are fundamental and must be held by congregations to entitle them to participate in a charity: *Newsome v Flowers* (1861) 30 Beav 461.

13  *A-G v Gould* (1860) 28 Beav 485; *A-G v Etheridge* (1862) 32 LJCh 161 (cases relating to the doctrines of strict or free communion, both being admissible among the sect of Particular Baptists).

14  *Milligan v Mitchell* (1837) 3 My & Cr 72; *A-G v Murdoch* (1852) 1 De GM & G 86; *A-G v Gould* (1860) 28 Beav 485; *A-G v Anderson* (1888) 57 LJCh 543 at 549 per Kekewich J.

15  *A-G v Stamford Corpn* (1747) 2 Swan 591; *Wilkinson v Malin* (1832) 2 Tyr 544 at 570 per Lord Lyndhurst CB; *A-G v Foyster* (1794) 1 Anst 116 at 122 per Eyre CB.

16  *Anderson v Wrights of Glasgow* (1865) 12 LT 805, HL.

17  *A-G v Gibbs* (1847) 1 De G & Sm 156 at 160 per Knight Bruce V-C; affd 2 Ph 327.

18  As to exempt charities see para 293 ante.

19  Charities Act 1993 s 17(7). For an example of the application of what is now s 17(7) see the *Report of the Charity Commissioners for England and Wales for 1986* (HC Paper (1986–87) no 306) App D. As to the Charity Commissioners see paras 486–512 post.

20  See the Charities Act 1993 s 78(2); and para 300 ante.

21  *Rosemary Simmons Memorial Housing Association Ltd v United Dominions Trust Ltd (Bates & Partners (a firm), third party)* [1987] 1 All ER 281, [1986] 1 WLR 1440.

**302. Duty towards the trust property.** It is the duty of charity trustees to protect the trust property[1], but they are not bound to look with more prudence to the affairs of the charity than to their own[2].

The deliberate destruction of charity property by trustees is a gross breach of trust[3].

---

1    See TRUSTS vol 48 (2000 Reissue) para 842 et seq. Thus, for example, it would be a breach of trust for trustees to alienate trust property improperly (*A-G v East Retford Corpn* (1833) 2 My & K 35; revsd (1838) 3 My & Cr 484), or negligently to permit others to appropriate it (*A-G v Leicester Corpn* (1844) 7 Beav 176). In particular they must reduce the property into possession and invest it properly in authorised investments: see para 363 et seq post; and TRUSTS vol 48 (2000 Reissue) para 862 et seq.

2    *A-G v Dixie, ex p Bosworth School* (1805) 13 Ves 519 at 534 per Lord Eldon LC; *Learoyd v Whiteley* (1887) 12 App Cas 727 at 733, HL, per Lord Halsbury LC. But see *A-G v Kerr* (1840) 2 Beav 420 at 428 per Lord Langdale MR.

3    *Ex p Greenhouse* (1815) 1 Madd 92 at 108 per Plumer V-C, where the trustees of a chapel pulled it down.

**303. Duty towards beneficiaries.** It is improper for a trustee holding property subject to charitable trusts to retain the fund without taking any steps to apply the property for charity[1].

Where there is a temporary or permanent failure of the particular object of the charitable trust, the trustee may not merely retain the property for himself[2].

---

1    *A-G v Alford* (1855) 4 De GM & G 843 at 852 per Lord Cranworth LC.

2    *Aylet v Dodd* (1741) 2 Atk 238; *Incorporated Society v Price* (1844) 1 Jo & Lat 498 at 500 per Lord Sugden LC (trust to pay schoolmasters' salaries and maintain schools; schools discontinued): *A-G v Cambridge Corpn* (1836) 5 LJCh 357; *A-G v Bolton* (1796) 3 Anst 820; *A-G v West* (1858) 27 LJCh 789.

**304. Duty to apply for scheme.** If there is a failure of the objects of the trust, or if for any other reason the statutory conditions for a cy-près application are satisfied, the trustees are under a duty to secure the effective use of the charity property by taking steps to enable it to be applied cy-près[1]. Similarly, if there is some difficulty of administration, the trustees should apply to the Charity Commissioners[2] or to the court for directions.

---

1    See the Charities Act 1993 s 13(5); and para 204 ante. The usual procedure is to apply to the Charity Commissioners for a scheme under s 16 or s 17: see para 180 et seq ante. As to cy-près schemes see para 201 et seq ante. In rare cases it may be proper to apply to the court, but the leave of the Commissioners is required: see para 521 post. Trustees may not apply the trust property cy-près on their own initiative: see para 204 ante. As to the Charity Commissioners see paras 486–512 post.

2    As to the direction of schemes see para 170 et seq ante.

**305. Remuneration.** The equitable rule precluding private trustees from drawing remuneration for their services[1] may be overridden by express provision allowing remuneration[2]. Such an express provision will be strictly construed[3]. The same principle applies in the case of charitable trusts, though the policy of the Charity Commissioners in relation to remuneration clauses in charitable trusts varies according to the circumstances[4].

Provision is made to deal with the remuneration of professional trustees where there is an express provision in the trust instrument entitling him to receive payment out of the trust funds in respect of services provided by him to or on behalf of the trust[5] and where there is no such express provision[6]. However trustees of, and trustee corporations acting as trustees for, charitable trusts are excluded from the ambit of these general rules[7]. The Secretary of State[8] may by regulations[9] make provision for the remuneration of trustees of charitable trusts[10] who are trust corporations[11] or act in a professional capacity[12]. This power includes power to make provision for the remuneration of a trustee who has been authorised[13] to exercise functions[14] as an agent of the trustees or to act as a nominee or custodian[15].

1   See *Brocksopp v Barnes* (1820) 5 Madd 90; *Barrett v Hartley* (1866) LR 2 Eq 789; and TRUSTS vol 48 (2000 Reissue) para 822.
2   See *Willis v Kibble* (1839) 1 Beav 559; and TRUSTS vol 48 (2000 Reissue) para 822.
3   *Re Gee (decd), Wood v Staples* [1948] Ch 284, [1948] 1 All ER 498.
4   See *Remuneration of Trustees (1993)* Decisions of the Charity Commissioners (1994) vol 2 p 14; and Picarda *Law and Practice Relating to Charities* (3rd Edn, 1999) pp 487–491. As to the Charity Commissioners see paras 486–512 post.
5   See the Trustee Act 2000 s 28; and TRUSTS vol 48 (2000 Reissue) para 825.
6   See ibid s 29; and TRUSTS vol 48 (2000 Reissue) para 826.
7   See ibid s 30; and TRUSTS vol 48 (2000 Reissue) para 827.
8   As to the Secretary of State see para 513 post.
9   Regulations made under the Trustee Act 2000 s 30 may make different provision for different cases, and may contain such supplemental, incidental, consequential and transitional provisions as the Secretary of State considers appropriate: s 30(3). The power to make regulations under s 30 is exercisable by statutory instrument, but no such instrument is to be made unless a draft of it has been laid before Parliament and approved by a resolution of each House of Parliament: s 30(4). At the date at which this volume states the law no such regulations had been made.
10  'Charitable trust' means a trust under which property is held for charitable purposes: ibid s 39(1). For the meaning of 'charitable purposes' see para 1 ante; definition applied by s 39(1).
11  'Trust corporation' has the same meaning as in the Trustee Act 1925 (see TRUSTS vol 48 (2000 Reissue) para 693): Trustee Act 2000 s 39(1).
12  Ibid s 30(1). For these purposes, a trustee acts in a professional capacity if he acts in the course of a profession or business which consists of or includes the provision of services in connection with: (1) the management or administration of trusts generally or a particular kind of trust; or (2) any particular aspect of the management or administration of trusts generally or a particular kind of trust, and the services he provides to or on behalf of the trust fall within that description: ss 28(5), 39(2).
13  Ie under a power conferred by ibid Pt IV (ss 11–27) (see TRUSTS vol 48 (2000 Reissue) para 882 et seq) or any other enactment or any provision of subordinate legislation, or by the trust instrument.
14  'Functions' includes powers and duties: ibid s 39(2).
15  Ibid s 30(2). A person is a custodian in relation to assets if he undertakes the safe custody of the assets or of any documents or records concerning the assets: ss 17(2), 39(2). As to the remuneration of agents nominees and custodians see TRUSTS vol 48 (2000 Reissue) para 828.

**306. Statutory duty of care under the Trustee Act 2000.** Trustees are subject to a statutory duty of care[1] in the certain circumstances[2] in relation to: (1) investment[3]; (2) the acquisition of land[4]; (3) agents, nominees and custodians[5]; (4) the compounding of liabilities[6]; (5) insurance[7]; (6) reversionary interests, valuations and audit[8]. The duty of care does not apply if or in so far as it appears from the trust instrument that the duty is not meant to apply[9].

The duty of care required of a trustee is to exercise such care and skill as is reasonable in the circumstances having regard in particular to any special knowledge or experience that he has or holds himself out as having and, if he acts as trustee in the course of a business or profession, to any special knowledge or experience that it is reasonable to expect of a person acting in the course of that kind of business or profession[10].

1   See the Trustee Act 2000 ss 1(1), (2), 39(2); and TRUSTS vol 48 (2000 Reissue) para 848. The new duty does not, however, alter the principles relating to the exercise of discretionary powers by trustees. As to the exercise of discretionary powers see TRUSTS vol 48 (2000 Reissue) para 868.
2   See ibid s 2, Sch 1; and TRUSTS vol 48 (2000 Reissue) para 849.
3   See ibid Sch 1 para 1. As to the power to invest see para 363 et seq post; and TRUSTS vol 48 (2000 Reissue) para 895 et seq.
4   See ibid Sch 1 para 2; and TRUSTS vol 48 (2000 Reissue) para 849.
5   See ibid Sch 1 para 3. As to the power to delegate and employ agents see TRUSTS vol 48 (2000 Reissue) para 875 et seq.
6   See ibid Sch 1 para 4.
7   See ibid Sch 1 para 5. As to the power to insure see TRUSTS vol 48 (2000 Reissue) para 927 et seq.
8   See ibid Sch 1 para 6.
9   See ibid Sch 1 para 7.
10  See ibid ss 1(1), (2), 39(2); and TRUSTS vol 48 (2000 Reissue) para 848.

## (ii)   Accounts

### A.   ACCOUNTING RECORDS

**307.   Duty to keep accounting records.** The charity trustees[1] of a charity[2], other than an exempt charity[3] and a charity which is a company[4], must ensure that accounting records are kept which are sufficient to show and explain all the charity's transactions, and which are such as to[5]: (1) disclose at any time, with reasonable accuracy, the financial position of the charity at that time[6]; and (2) enable the trustees to ensure that where any annual statements of account are prepared by them[7], those statements comply with the statutory requirements[8]. In particular they must contain entries showing from day to day all sums of money received and expended by the charity and the matters in respect of which the receipt and expenditure takes place, and a record of the assets and liabilities of the charity[9]. The charity trustees of a charity must preserve any accounting records made for these purposes for at least six years from the end of the financial year[10] of the charity in which they are made[11].

1   For the meaning of 'charity trustees' see para 1 note 10 ante.
2   For the meaning of 'charity' see para 1 ante.
3   Charities Act 1993 s 46(1). As to exempt charities see para 293 ante. As to the duty of charity trustees of an exempt charity see para 324 post.
4   Ibid s 41(5). For the meaning of 'company' see para 216 ante.
5   Ibid s 41(1).
6   Ibid s 41(1)(a).
7   Ie under ibid s 42(1): see para 308 post.
8   Ibid s 41(1)(b). As to the statutory requirements see s 42(1) and the regulations made under it: see para 308 post. Cf the Companies Act 1985 ss 221, 222 (both as substituted): see COMPANIES vol 7(2) (1996 Reissue) paras 801–802.
9   Charities Act 1993 s 41(2).
10  For the meaning of 'financial year' see para 210 note 3 ante; and para 309 note 4 post.
11  Charities Act 1993 s 41(3). Where a charity ceases to exist within the six year period, the obligation to preserve the records continues to be discharged by the last charity trustees of the charity, unless the Charity Commissioners consent in writing to the records being destroyed or otherwise disposed of: s 41(4). As to the Charity Commissioners see paras 486–512 post.

B. ANNUAL STATEMENTS OF ACCOUNT

**308. Annual statement of accounts.** The charity trustees[1] of a charity[2], other than an exempt charity[3] and a charity which is a company[4], must prepare in respect of each financial year[5] of the charity a statement of accounts complying with such requirements as to its form and contents as may be prescribed by the regulations[6] made by the Secretary of State[7]. However, instead of such a statement of accounts, where a charity's gross income[8] in any financial year does not exceed £100,000[9], the charity trustees may in respect of that year elect to prepare a receipts and payments account, and a statement of assets and liabilities[10]. The charity trustees of a charity must preserve any statement of accounts[11], or any account and statement[12] for at least six years from the end of the financial year to which any such statement relates or, as the case may be, to which any such account and statement relate[13].

1 For the meaning of 'charity trustees' see para 1 note 10 ante.
2 For the meaning of 'charity' see para 1 ante.
3 Charities Act 1993 s 46(1). As to exempt charities see para 293 ante. As to the duty of charity trustees of an exempt charity see para 324 post.
4 Ibid s 42(7). For the meaning of 'company' see para 216 ante.
5 For the meaning of 'financial year' see para 210 note 3 ante; and para 309 note 4 post.
6 In the exercise of the power conferred under the Charities Act 1993 s 42, the Charities (Accounts and Reports) Regulations 1995, SI 1995/2724 (amended and modified in relation to financial years beginning on or after 1 January 2001); and the Charities (Accounts and Reports) Regulations 2000, SI 2000/2868, have been made. See para 309 et seq post.
     The Charities (Accounts and Reports) Regulations 2000, SI 2000/2868, replace the Charities (Accounts and Reports) Regulations 1995, SI 1995/2724, with respect to the form and content of the accounts of charities and the annual reports of charity trustees for financial years beginning on or after 1 January 2001. The Charities (Accounts and Reports) Regulations 1995, SI 1995/2724, continue to apply for earlier financial years unless the trustees opt to prepare accounts and reports in accordance with the Charities (Accounts and Reports) Regulations 2000, SI 2000/2868. As to the form and content of statements of account see para 309 et seq post.
     In relation to the audit and examination of charity accounts after 1 January 2001, the Charities (Accounts and Reports) Regulations 1995, SI 1995/2724, apply as modified by the Charities (Accounts and Reports) Regulations 2000, SI 2000/2868. The Charities (Accounts and Reports) Regulations 1995, SI 1995/2724, (as amended) continue to apply for earlier financial years.
7 Charities Act 1993 s 42(1). Before making any regulations under s 42 the Secretary of State must consult such persons or bodies or persons as he considers appropriate: s 86(4). As to the making or regulations generally see s 86 (as amended); and para 517 post. See also para 290 note 6 ante. The regulations may make provision for the statement to be prepared in accordance with such methods and principles as are specified or referred to in the regulations, and as to any information to be provided by way of notes to the accounts: s 42(2). The regulations may also make provision for determining the financial years of a charity for the purposes of the Charities Act 1993 and any regulations made under it: s 42(2). As to the Secretary of State see para 513 post.
8 For the meaning of 'gross income' see para 210 note 2 ante.
9 The Secretary of State may by order amend the specified sum: Charities Act 1993 s 42(6). In the exercise of this power, the Charities Act 1993 (Substitution of Sums) Order 1995, SI 1995/2696, has been made. See also note 7 supra.
10 Charities Act 1993 s 42(3) (amended by the Charities Act 1993 (Substitution of Sums) Order 1995, SI 1995/2696, art 2).
11 Ie prepared by them under the Charities Act 1993 s 42(1): see the text and notes 5–7 supra.
12 Ie prepared by them under ibid s 42(3): see the text and notes 8–10 supra.
13 Ibid s 42(4). Where a charity ceases to exist within the six year period, the obligation to preserve the statement of accounts (or account and statement) continues to be discharged by the last charity trustees of the charity, unless the Charity Commissioners consent in writing to their being destroyed or otherwise disposed of: ss 41(4), 42(5).

C. FORM AND CONTENT OF STATEMENTS GENERALLY

**309. Application of requirements as to form and statements of accounts.**
There are statutory requirements[1] as to the form and content of a statement of accounts
prepared by the charity trustees[2] of a charity[3] in respect of a financial year[4]: (1) which
begins on or after 1 January 2001[5]; or (2) which begins before that date if the charity
trustees determine that these provisions[6] apply to the statement of accounts[7] and the
charity trustees have not, before 15 November 2000[8], either approved the accounts of
the charity in respect of that financial year, or authorised the signature of an annual
report[9] in respect of that financial year[10].

1　The statutory requirements as to form and content of statements of account are set out in para 310 et seq
　　post.
2　For the meaning of 'charity trustees' see para 1 note 10 ante.
3　Ie in accordance with the Charities Act 1993 s 42(1): see para 308 ante. For the meaning of 'charity' see
　　para 1 ante.
4　Charities (Accounts and Reports) Regulations 2000, SI 2000/2868, reg 3(1), (3). As to the financial years
　　to which these provisions apply see para 308 note 6 ante.
　　　　The financial year of a charity is, for the purposes of the Charities Act 1993 and regulations made under
　　it, determined in accordance with the Charities (Accounts and Reports) Regulations 1995,
　　SI 1995/2724, reg 5(2)–(4) (see infra): regs 2(1), 5(1); Charities (Accounts and Reports) Regulations
　　2000, SI 2000/2868, reg 2(1). The first financial year of a charity is:
　　(1)　in the case of a charity which is established before 1 March 1996 (ie the date on which the
　　　　　Charities (Accounts and Reports) Regulations 1995, SI 1995/2724, came into force), the period
　　　　　beginning with the day immediately following the end of the period in respect of which a
　　　　　statement of accounts was required to be prepared under any statutory provision contained in or
　　　　　having effect under an Act of Parliament applicable to that charity before 1 March 1996 (ie the
　　　　　coming into force of the Charities Act 1993 s 42) and ending with the accounting reference date
　　　　　of the charity or such other date, not more than seven days before or after the accounting
　　　　　reference date, as the charity trustees may determine (Charities (Accounts and Reports)
　　　　　Regulations 1995, SI 1995/2724, reg 5(2)(a));
　　(2)　in the case of a charity which is established on or after 1 March 1996, the period beginning with
　　　　　the day on which the charity is established and ending with the accounting reference date of the
　　　　　charity or such other date, not more than seven days before or after the accounting reference date,
　　　　　as the charity trustees may determine (reg 5(2)(b)).
　　Subsequent financial years of a charity begin with the day immediately following the end of the
　　charity's previous financial year and end with its accounting reference date or such other date, not more
　　than seven days before or after the accounting reference date, as the charity trustees may determine:
　　reg 5(3). For these purposes, the accounting reference date of a charity:
　　(a)　in the first financial year of a charity which is established before 1 March 1996, such date, not less
　　　　　than 6 months nor more than 18 months after the date on which that financial year began, as the
　　　　　charity trustees may determine (reg 5(4)(a));
　　(b)　in the first financial year of a charity which is established on or after 1 March 1996, such date, not
　　　　　less than 6 months nor more than 18 months after the date on which the charity was established,
　　　　　as the charity trustees may determine (reg 5(4)(b));
　　(c)　in any subsequent financial year of a charity, the date 12 months after the previous accounting
　　　　　reference date of the charity or such other date, not less than 6 months nor more than 18 months
　　　　　after the previous accounting reference date of the charity as the trustees may determine
　　　　　(reg 5(4)(c)).
　　This is provided that (i) the charity trustees do not exercise their powers under head (c) supra so as to
　　determine an accounting reference date in respect of any financial year which is consecutive, or follows
　　immediately after a financial year which is consecutive, to a previous financial year in respect of which
　　that power was exercised (reg 5(4) proviso (i)); and (ii) the charity trustees exercise their powers under
　　head (a) or (c) supra so as to determine a date earlier or later than 12 months from the beginning of the
　　financial year only where satisfied that there are exceptional reasons to do so (which reasons must, in the
　　case of a charity subject to the requirements of reg 3(4) or reg 4(4), be disclosed in a note to the accounts)
　　(reg 5(4) proviso (ii)). For the purposes of the Charities (Accounts and Reports) Regulations 2000,

SI 2000/2868, the reference in head (ii) supra to the Charities (Accounts and Reports) Regulations 1995, SI 1995/2724, reg 3(4) is to be read as a reference to Charities (Accounts and Reports) Regulations 2000, SI 2000/2868, reg 3(10): reg 3(10).
5   Ibid reg 3(1)(a).
6   Ie the provisions of ibid reg 3, rather than the Charities (Accounts and Reports) Regulations 1995, SI 1995/2724, reg 3.
7   If the charity trustees make such a determination, they must also make a determination under Charities (Accounts and Reports) Regulations 2000, SI 2000/2868, reg 7(1)(b) (see para 322 text to note 11 post) if they are required to prepare an annual report in respect of the financial year in question: reg 3(2).
8   Ie the date when the Charities (Accounts and Reports) Regulations 2000, SI 2000/2868, came into force.
9   Ie in accordance with Charities (Accounts and Reports) Regulations 1995, SI 1995/2724, reg 10(1)(c).
10  Charities (Accounts and Reports) Regulations 2000, SI 2000/2868, reg 3(1)(b).


**310. Prescribed form and content of statements of accounts.** The requirements as to form and content of statements of accounts[1] are as follows[2]. The statement must consist of a statement of financial activities which must show the total incoming resources and application of the resources, together with any other movements in the total resources, of the charity during the financial year[3] in respect of which the statement is prepared[4]. The statement must also consist of a balance sheet which shows the state of affairs of the charity as at the end of the financial year in respect of which the statement is prepared[5].

The statement must be prepared in accordance with the following principles.

(1)   The statement of financial activities must give a true and fair view of the incoming resources and application of the resources of the charity in the financial year in respect of which the statement is prepared[6].

(2)   The balance sheet must give a true and fair view of the state of affairs of the charity at the end of that year[7].

(3)   Where compliance with certain requirements[8] would not be sufficient to give a true and fair view, the necessary additional information must be given in the statement of accounts or in notes to the accounts[9].

(4)   If in special circumstances compliance with any of those requirements would be inconsistent with giving a true and fair view, the charity trustees may depart from the requirement to the extent necessary to give a true and fair view[10].

The statement must be prepared in accordance with the methods and principles set out in the *Statement of Recommended Practice for Accounting and Reporting by Charities* (the 'SORP')[11]. With respect to any amount required to be shown in the statement of financial activities or in the balance sheet, the statement must also show the corresponding amount[12] for the financial year immediately preceding that to which the statement or balance sheet relates[13]. Where a charity has more than one fund[14], only amounts corresponding to the entries in the statement of financial activities relating to the totals of both or all of the funds of the charity need be shown[15].

1   Ie the requirements as to the form and content of a statement of accounts to which Charities (Accounts and Reports) Regulations 2000, SI 2000/2868, reg 3 applies: see para 309 ante.
2   Ibid reg 3(3). These provisions apply to financial years beginning on or after 1 January 2001: see para 308 note 6 ante.
3   For the meaning of 'financial year' see para 309 note 4 ante.
4   Charities (Accounts and Reports) Regulations 2000, SI 2000/2868, reg 3(4)(a).

5    Ibid reg 3(4)(b). The balance sheet must be signed by one or more of the charity trustees of the charity, each of whom has been authorised to do so, and must specify the date on which the statement of accounts of which the balance sheet forms part was approved by the charity trustees: reg 3(11).

6    Ibid reg 3(5)(a).

7    Ibid reg 3(5)(b).

8    Ie the requirements of ibid reg 3(6)–(11): see the text and notes 11–15 infra; and para 311 post.

9    Ibid reg 3(5)(c).

10   Ibid reg 3(5)(d).

11   Ibid reg 3(6)(a). The SORP was issued in 1995 by the Charity Commissioners, and revised and reissued on 17 October 2000. The references in the Charities (Accounts and Reports) Regulations 2000, SI 2000/2868, are to the version of the SORP revised and issued in 2000.
     Where in the financial year to which the statement of accounts relates the effect of the Charities (Accounts and Reports) Regulations 2000, SI 2000/2868, reg 3(5), (6)(a) (see the text and notes 6–10 supra) is that there is nothing required to be shown in respect of a particular item, but an amount was required to be shown in respect of that item in the statement of accounts for the immediately preceding financial year, those provisions have effect as if such an amount were required to be shown in the statement of accounts in the financial year to which the statement relates, and that amount were nil: reg 3(8).

12   Where that corresponding amount is not comparable with the amount to be shown for the item in question in respect of the financial year to which the statement of financial activities or balance sheet relates, the former amount is to be adjusted: ibid reg 3(7).

13   Ibid reg 3(6)(b). This provision is expressed to be subject to regs 3(7)–(9) (see the text and notes 11–12 supra, 14–15 infra): see reg 3(6)(b).

14   'Fund' means particular assets of a charity held on trusts which, as respects the purposes for which those assets are held, or as respects the powers of the charity trustees to use or apply those assets, are not identical with those on which other assets of the charity are held: ibid reg 2(1).

15   Ibid reg 3(9).

**311. Information provided in notes to the accounts.** Specified information[1] must be provided by way of notes to the accounts the information[2]. Such information, in so far as not provided in the statement of financial activities or in the balance sheet, is as follows[3]:

(1)   particulars of any material adjustment[4];

(2)   a description of the accounting policies of, and assumptions made for the purposes of preparing the statement of accounts by, the charity trustees[5], including any material change in these, the reason for such change and its effect, if material, on the accounts, in accordance with the methods and principles set out in the *Statement of Recommended Practice for Accounting and Reporting by Charities* (the 'SORP')[6];

(3)   a description of the nature and purpose of all material funds[7] of the charity in accordance with the methods and principles set out in the SORP[8];

(4)   such particulars of the related party transactions of the charity, or of any institution or body corporate connected with the charity[9], as may be required by the SORP to be disclosed[10];

(5)   such particulars of the cost to the charity of employing staff as may be required by the SORP to be disclosed[11];

(6)   such particulars of the emoluments of staff employed by the charity as may be required by the SORP to be disclosed[12];

(7)   particulars of the cost to the charity of (a) any policies of insurance against loss arising from the neglect or default of any of the charity trustees or trustees for the

charity; or (b) indemnifying the charity trustees, or trustees for the charity, or any of them, in respect of the consequences of any such loss[13];

(8) a description of any incoming resources which represent capital, according to whether or not that capital is permanent endowment[14];

(9) an itemised analysis of any material movement between any of the restricted funds of the charity, or between a restricted and an unrestricted fund[15] of the charity, together with an explanation of the nature and purpose of each of those funds[16];

(10) the name of any institution or body corporate connected with the charity, together with a description of the nature of the charity's relationship with that institution or body corporate and of its activities, including, where material, its turnover and net profit or loss for the corresponding financial year[17] of the institution or body corporate and any qualification expressed in an auditor's report on its accounts[18];

(11) particulars of any guarantee given by the charity, where any potential liability under the guarantee is outstanding at the date of the balance sheet[19];

(12) particulars of any loan outstanding at the date of the balance sheet (a) which was made to the charity, and which is secured by an express charge on any of the assets of the charity; or (b) which was made by the charity to any institution or body corporate connected with the charity[20];

(13) particulars of any fund of the charity which is in deficit at the date of the balance sheet[21];

(14) particulars of any remuneration paid to an auditor or independent examiner in respect of auditing or examining the accounts of the charity and particulars of any remuneration paid to him in respect of any other services rendered to the charity[22];

(15) such particulars of any grant made by the charity as may be required by the SORP to be disclosed[23];

(16) particulars of any ex gratia payment[24] made by the charity[25];

(17) an analysis of any entry in the balance sheet relating to fixed assets[26], debtors and creditors, according to the categories set out in the SORP[27];

(18) an analysis of all material changes during the financial year in question in the values of fixed assets, in accordance with the methods and principles set out in the SORP[28];

(19) the following particulars of any contingent liability existing at the date of the balance sheet, that is to say, its amount or estimated amount, its legal nature and whether any valuable security has been provided by the charity in connection with that liability and, if so, what[29];

(20) particulars of any other financial commitments which are outstanding at the date of the balance sheet, and which have not been provided for and are relevant to assessment of the state of affairs of the charity[30];

(21) if the market value (as at the date of the balance sheet) of any land forming part of the property of the charity differs substantially from the amount at which that land is included in the balance sheet, and the difference is, in the opinion of the

charity trustees, of such significance as to require that attention be drawn to it, particulars of that difference[31];

(22) in the case of any amount required by any of heads (1) to (21) above (other than heads (9), (15) or (18) to be disclosed)[32], the corresponding amount for the financial year immediately preceding that to which the accounts relate[33];

(23) a statement as to whether or not the accounts have been prepared in accordance with any applicable accounting standards and statements of recommended practice and particulars of any material departure from those standards and statements of practice and the reasons for such departure[34];

(24) where the charity trustees have exercised their powers[35] so as to determine an accounting reference date earlier or later than 12 months from the beginning of the financial year, a statement of their reasons for doing so[36];

(25) if the charity trustees have departed[37] from any requirements of the provisions relating to the form and content of statements of account[38], particulars of any such departure, the reasons for it, and its effect[39]; and

(26) any additional information: (a) which is required to ensure that the statement of accounts complies with the requirements of the provisions relating to the form and content of statements of account[40]; or (b) which may reasonably assist the user to understand the statement of accounts[41].

---

1    Ie information specified in Charities (Accounts and Reports) Regulations 2000, SI 2000/2868, reg 3(10), Schedule: see the text and notes 3–41 infra.
2    Ibid reg 3(10). These provisions apply to financial years beginning on or after 1 January 2001: see para 308 note 6 ante.
3    Ibid Schedule para 1.
4    Ibid Schedule para 1(a). The material adjustment referred to in the text is the adjustment made pursuant to reg 3(7) (see para 310 note 12 ante): Schedule para 1(a).
5    For the meaning of 'charity trustees' see para 1 note 10 ante.
6    Charities (Accounts and Reports) Regulations 2000, SI 2000/2868, Schedule para 1(b). As to the SORP see para 310 note 11 ante.
7    For the meaning of 'fund' see para 310 note 14 ante.
8    Charities (Accounts and Reports) Regulations 2000, SI 2000/2868, Schedule para 1(c).
9    'Institution or body corporate connected with the charity', in relation to a charity, means an institution or body corporate which: (1) in the case of an institution, is controlled by; (2) in the case of a body corporate, in which a substantial interest is held by, the charity or any one or more of the charity trustees acting in his or their capacity as such: Charities (Accounts and Reports) Regulations 1995, SI 1995/2724, reg 2(1); Charities (Accounts and Reports) Regulations 2000, SI 2000/2868, reg 2(1).
10   Ibid Schedule para 1(d).
11   Ibid Schedule para 1(e).
12   Ibid Schedule para 1(f).
13   Ibid Schedule para 1(g). This provision does not apply in the case of any financial year of a charity in which the gross income of the charity does not exceed £250,000: Schedule para 2.
14   Ibid Schedule para 1(h).
15   'Unrestricted fund' means a fund which is to be used or applied in any way determined by the charity trustees for the furtherance of the objects of a charity, and 'restricted fund' means any other fund of a charity: ibid reg 2(1).
16   Ibid Schedule para 1(i).
17   For the meaning of 'financial year' see para 309 note 4 ante.
18   Charities (Accounts and Reports) Regulations 2000, SI 2000/2868, Schedule para 1(j).
19   Ibid Schedule para 1(k).
20   Ibid Schedule para 1(l).
21   Ibid Schedule para 1(m).
22   Ibid Schedule para 1(n).

23 Ibid Schedule para 1(o).

24 'Ex gratia payment' means any such application of the property of a charity, or any such waiver by a charity of any entitlement to receive any property, as may be authorised under the Charities Act 1993 s 27(1) (see para 370 post): Charities (Accounts and Reports) Regulations 2000, SI 2000/2868, reg 2(1).

25 Ibid Schedule para 1(p).

26 'Fixed assets' means the assets of a charity which are intended for use or investment on a continuing basis: ibid reg 2(1).

27 Ibid Schedule para 1(q).

28 Ibid Schedule para 1(r).

29 Ibid Schedule para 1(s).

30 Ibid Schedule para 1(t).

31 Ibid Schedule para 1(u).

32 Ie other than amounts required by ibid Schedule para 1(i), (o), (r) to be disclosed: see heads (9), (15), (18) in the text.

33 Ibid Schedule para 1(v).

34 Ibid Schedule para 1(w). This provision does not apply in the case of any financial year of a charity in which the gross income of the charity does not exceed £250,000: Schedule para 2.

35 Ie under the Charities (Accounts and Reports) Regulations 1995, SI 1995/2724, reg 5(4)(a) or (c): see para 309 note 4 ante.

36 Charities (Accounts and Reports) Regulations 2000, SI 2000/2868, Schedule para 1(x).

37 Ie under ibid reg 3(5)(d): see para 310 text to note 10 ante.

38 Ie the provisions of ibid reg 3: see para 310 ante.

39 Ibid Schedule para 1(y).

40 See note 38 supra.

41 Charities (Accounts and Reports) Regulations 2000, SI 2000/2868, Schedule para 1(z).


D. FORM AND CONTENT OF STATEMENTS: SPECIAL CASES


**312. Prescribed form and content of statements of accounts in special cases.**
There are statutory requirements[1] as to the form and content of a statement of accounts prepared by the charity trustees of a special case charity[2] in respect of a financial year[3] which begins on or after 1 January 2001[4].

The requirements as to form and content of such statement of accounts are as follows[5]. The statement must consist of an income and expenditure account and a balance sheet as at the end of the financial year in respect of which the statement of accounts is prepared[6]. It must also be prepared in accordance with the following principles:

(1) The income and expenditure account must give a true and fair view of the income and expenditure of the charity for the financial year in respect of which the statement of accounts is prepared[7].

(2) The balance sheet must give a true and fair view of the state of affairs of the charity at the end of that year[8].


1 Ie the requirements contained in the Charities (Accounts and Reports) Regulations 2000, SI 2000/2868, reg 5: see the text and notes 4–8 infra. As to the financial years to which these provisions apply see para 308 note 6 ante.

2 Ie under the Charities Act 1993 s 42(1): see para 208 ante. 'Special case charity' means a charity which is either (1) a registered social landlord within the meaning of the Housing Act 1996 and whose registration has been recorded under s 3(3) (as amended) (see HOUSING vol 22 (Reissue) para 61 et seq); or (2) has during the financial year in question (a) conducted an institution in relation to which a designation made, or having effect as if made, under the Education Reform Act 1988 s 129 (as amended) or the Further and Higher Education Act 1992 s 28 (as amended) (see EDUCATION) has effect;

(b) received financial support from funds administered by a higher education funding council or further education funding council within the meaning of the Further and Higher Education Act 1992 in respect of expenditure incurred or to be incurred by the charity in connection with that institution; and (c) incurred no expenditure for charitable purposes other than the purposes of that institution or any other such institution: Charities (Accounts and Reports) Regulations 2000, SI 2000/2868, reg 2(1). For the meaning of 'charity trustees' see para 1 note 10 ante.

3    For the meaning of 'financial year' see para 309 note 4 ante.
4    Charities (Accounts and Reports) Regulations 2000, SI 2000/2868, reg 5(1).
5    Ibid reg 5(2).
6    Ibid reg 5(3).
7    Ibid reg 5(4)(a).
8    Ibid reg 5(4)(b).

E.  ANNUAL AUDITS OR INDEPENDENT EXAMINATIONS

**313. Annual audit or examination of charity accounts.**    If a charity's gross income[1] or total expenditure for a financial year[2] ('the relevant year') or either of the two preceding financial years (if any) exceeds the specified figure (presently £250,000)[3], the accounts of the charity for that year must be audited by a person who is: (1) eligible[4] for appointment as a company auditor[5]; or (2) a member of a body for the time being specified in regulations[6] and is under the rules of that body eligible for appointment as auditor of the charity[7]. If neither the gross income nor the total expenditure for a financial year or either of the two preceding financial years (if any) exceeds the specified figure, and its gross income or total expenditure in that year exceeds £10,000, the accounts of the charity for that year may, at the election of the charity trustees[8], either be examined by an independent examiner[9], or be audited by such person mentioned in head (1) or (2) above[10].

Where it appears to the Charity Commissioners that: (a) the requirement for an audit or, as the case may be, examination[11] has not been complied with in relation to a financial year of a charity within 10 months from the end of that year[12]; or that (b) although it is not a case in which an audit is required[13], it would nevertheless be desirable for the accounts for that year to be audited by such a person mentioned in head (1) or (2) above[14], the Commissioners may by order require the accounts of the charity for that year to be audited by such a person[15]. Unless the circumstances are those set out in head (b) above, and the charity trustees themselves appoint an auditor in accordance with the order of the Commissioners, the auditor will be appointed by the Commissioners[16]. The expenses of any audit carried out by an auditor so appointed by the Commissioners are recoverable by them from the charity trustees of the charity concerned, who are personally liable, jointly and severally for those expenses[17]. To the extent that the expenses are not practically recoverable from the charity trustees they are recoverable from the charity funds[18].

The above provisions do not apply to an exempt charity[19], certain charities with an annual income not exceeding £1,000 which are not required to be registered[20], and are not registered[21], or a charity which is a company[22].

1    For the meaning of 'gross income' see para 210 note 2 ante. For the meaning of 'charity' see para 1 ante.
2    For the meaning of 'financial year' see paras 210 note 3, 309 note 4 ante.
3    See the Charities Act 1993 s 43(1) (amended by the Charities Act 1993 (Substitution of Sums) Order 1995, SI 1995/2696, art 2). The Secretary of State may by order amend the Charities Act 1993 s 43(1)

(as amended) or (3) (as amended) by substituting a different sum for the sum for the time being specified there: s 43(8) (amended by the Deregulation and Contracting Out Act 1994 s 28). In the exercise of this power, the Charities Act 1993 (Substitution of Sums) Order 1995, SI 1995/2696, has been made. As to the making of orders generally see the Charities Act 1993 s 86 (as amended); and para 517 post. As to the Secretary of State see para 513 post.

4    Ie in accordance with the Companies Act 1989 s 25: see COMPANIES vol 7(2) (1996 Reissue) para 956.
5    Charities Act 1993 s 43(2)(a).
6    Ie under ibid s 44: see para 314 post.
7    Ibid s 43(2)(b).
8    For the meaning of 'charity trustees' see para 1 note 10 ante.
9    The independent examiner is an independent person who is reasonably believed by the trustees to have the requisite ability and practical experience to carry out a competent examination of the accounts: Charities Act 1993 ss 43(3)(a), 97(1). The Charity Commissioners may give guidance to charity trustees in connection with the selection of a person for appointment as an independent examiner, and give such directions as they think appropriate with respect to the carrying out of an examination under s 43(3)(a): s 43(7)(a), (b). Any such guidance or directions may either be of general application or apply to a particular charity only: s 43(7). As to the Charity Commissioners see paras 486–512 post.
10   Ibid s 43(3) (amended by the Deregulation and Contracting Out Act 1994 s 28).
11   Ie under the Charities Act 1993 s 43(2) or (3): see the text and notes 5–10 supra.
12   Ibid s 43(4)(a).
13   Ie under ibid s 43(2): see the text and notes 5–7 supra.
14   Ibid s 43(4)(b).
15   Ibid s 43(4).
16   Ibid s 43(5).
17   Ibid s 43(6)(a).
18   Ibid s 43(6)(b).
19   Ibid s 46(1). As to exempt charities see para 293 ante.
20   Ie under ibid s 3(5)(c): see para 283 ante.
21   See ibid s 46(3); and para 324 post.
22   Ibid s 43(9). For the meaning of 'company' see para 216 ante.

**314. Regulations and supplementary provisions relating to audits and examinations.**
The Secretary of State[1] may by regulations make provision[2]:

(1)    specifying bodies whose members may be eligible[3] for appointment as auditor of a charity[4];

(2)    with respect to the duties of an auditor[5], including provision with respect to the making by him of a report on the statement of accounts[6], or the account and statement[7], as the case may be[8];

(3)    with respect to the making by an independent examiner[9] of a report in respect of an examination[10] carried out by him[11];

(4)    conferring on such an auditor or on an independent examiner a right of access with respect to books, documents[12] and other records which relate to the charity concerned[13];

(5)    entitling such an auditor or an independent examiner to require information and explanations from past or present charity trustees or trustees for the charity, or from past or present officers or employees of the charity[14];

(6)    enabling the Charity Commissioners[15], in circumstances specified in the regulations, to dispense with the requirements for an audit or examination[16] in the case of a particular charity or in the case of any particular financial year of a charity[17].

If any person fails to afford to an auditor or an independent examiner any facility to which he is entitled in respect of head (4) or (5) above, the Commissioners may give him or the charity trustees for the time being of the charity concerned, such directions as the Commissioners think appropriate for securing that the default is made good[18]. The power of the court to grant relief to a person employed as auditor of a company[19] is applied in relation to an auditor or independent examiner appointed[20] by a charity[21].

The above provisions do not apply to an exempt charity[22] or certain charities with an annual income not exceeding £1,000 which are not required to be registered[23], and are not registered[24].

1    As to the Secretary of State see para 513 post.
2    Charities Act 1993 s 44(1). In the exercise of the power conferred by s 44, the Charities (Accounts and Reports) Regulations 1995, SI 1995/2724 (amended and modified in relation to financial years beginning on or after 1 January 2001), and the Charities (Accounts and Reports) Regulations 2000, SI 2000/2868, have been made. The Charities (Accounts and Reports) Regulations 2000, SI 2000/2868, apply to financial years beginning on or after 1 January 2001: see para 308 note 6 ante. Before making any regulations under the Charities Act 1993 s 44 the Secretary of State must consult such persons or bodies or persons as he considers appropriate: s 86(4). As to the making of regulations generally see s 86 (as amended); and para 517 post. See also para 290 note 6 ante.
3    Ie for the purposes of ibid s 43(2)(b): see para 313 head (2) ante.
4    Ibid s 44(1)(a).
5    Ie the duties of an auditor carrying our the duties under ibid s 43 (as amended): see para 313 ante.
6    Ie that for the financial year in question under ibid s 42(1): see para 308 ante. For the meaning of 'financial year' see paras 210 note 3, 309 note 4 ante.
7    Ie that for the financial year in question under ibid s 42(3): see para 308 ante.
8    Ibid s 44(1)(b).
9    For the meaning of 'independent examiner' see para 313 note 9 ante.
10   Ie an examination under the Charities Act 1993 s 43 (as amended): see para 313 ante.
11   Ibid s 44(1)(c).
12   For the meaning of 'document' see para 236 note 2 ante.
13   Charities Act 1993 s 44(1)(d).
14   Ibid s 44(1)(e).
15   As to the Charity Commissioners see paras 486–512 post.
16   Ie under the Charities Act 1993 s 43(2), (3) (as amended): see para 313 ante.
17   Ibid s 44(1)(f).
18   Ibid s 44(2). A person guilty of disobedience to an order of the Commissioners made under s 44(2) may on the application of the Commissioners to the High Court be dealt with as for disobedience to an order of the High Court: s 88; and see para 494 post.
19   Ie under the Companies Act 1985 s 727: see COMPANIES vol 7(1) (1996 Reissue) para 624.
20   Ie in pursuance of the Charities Act 1993 s 43: see para 313 ante.
21   Ibid s 44(3).
22   Ibid s 46(1). As to exempt charities see para 293 ante.
23   Ie under ibid s 3(5)(c): see para 283 ante.
24   See ibid s 46(3); and para 324 post.

**315. Auditor's report on statement of accounts.** Where a statement of accounts has been prepared[1] for the financial year[2] in question, the duties of an auditor carrying out an audit of the accounts of a charity[3] include the duty to make a report on that statement to the charity trustees[4].

The report must (1) state the name and address of the auditor and the name of the charity concerned[5]; (2) be signed by him, or where the office of auditor is held by a body corporate or partnership, in its name by a person authorised to sign on its behalf, and state that the auditor falls within certain statutory requirements[6]; (3) be dated and specify the financial year in respect of which the accounts to which it relates have been prepared[7];

and (4) specify that it is a report in respect of an audit carried out under the statutory provisions[8] relating to annual audits or examinations of charity accounts[9]. The report must also state whether in the auditor's opinion the statement of accounts complies with the relevant statutory requirements[10].

Where the auditor has formed the opinion:

(a)   that accounting records have not been kept in respect of the charity in accordance with the statutory duty[11]; or

(b)   that the statement of accounts does not accord with those records[12]; or

(c)   that any information contained in the statement of accounts is inconsistent in any material respect with any report of the charity trustees prepared in accordance with the statutory provisions[13] in respect of the financial year in question[14]; or

(d)   that any information or explanation to which he is entitled[15] has not been afforded to him[16],

the auditor's report must contain a statement of the opinion he has formed and of his grounds for forming it[17].

The auditor may, in preparing such a report for these purposes[18], carry out such investigations as will enable him to form an opinion as to certain specified matters[19].

1   Ie under the Charities Act 1993 s 42(1).
2   For the meaning of 'financial year' see para 309 note 4 ante.
3   Ie under the Charities Act 1993 s 43 (as amended): see para 313 ante. For the meaning of 'charity' see para 1 ante.
4   Charities (Accounts and Reports) Regulations 1995, SI 1995/2724, reg 6(1), (2). For the meaning of 'charity trustees' see para 1 note 10 ante. These provisions apply to financial years beginning on or after 1 January 2001: see para 308 note 6 ante.
      In the case of an auditor appointed by the Charity Commissioners, the report required by reg 6(2) must be made to the Commissioners instead of to the charity trustees: reg 6(7). As to the Charity Commissioners see paras 486–512 post.
5   Ibid reg 6(2)(a).
6   Ibid reg 6(2)(b). The statutory requirements referred to in the text are the requirements of the Charities Act 1993 s 43(2)(a), or as the case may be, s 43(2)(b): see para 313 heads (1), (2) ante.
7   Charities (Accounts and Reports) Regulations 1995, SI 1995/2724, reg 6(2)(c).
8   Ie under the Charities Act 1993 s 43 (as amended) (see para 313 ante) and in accordance with regulations made under s 44 (see para 314 ante).
9   Charities (Accounts and Reports) Regulations 1995, SI 1995/2724, reg 6(2)(d).
10  Ibid reg 6(2)(e). As to the statutory requirements see reg 6(2)(e) (modified by the Charities (Accounts and Reports) Regulations 2000, SI 2000/2868, regs 4(a), 6(a)).
11  Charities (Accounts and Reports) Regulations 1995, SI 1995/2724, reg 6(f)(i). The statutory duty referred to in the text is the duty in accordance with the Charities Act 1993 s 41 (see para 307 ante): Charities (Accounts and Reports) Regulations 1995, SI 1995/2724, reg 6(f)(i).
12  Ibid reg 6(2)(f)(ii).
13  Ie under the Charities Act 1993 s 45 (as amended): see para 321 post.
14  Charities (Accounts and Reports) Regulations 1995, SI 1995/2724, reg 6(2)(f)(iii).
15  Ie under ibid reg 8: see para 319 post.
16  Ibid reg 6(2)(f)(iv).
17  Ibid reg 6(2)(f).
18  Ie for the purposes of ibid reg 6(2): see the text and notes 1–17 supra.
19  Ibid reg 6(4). The matters specified are those in reg 6(2)(e) (see the text and note 10 supra), and reg 6(2)(f) (see the text and notes 11–17 supra).

**316. Auditor's report on annual accounts on the receipts and payments basis.**
Where a receipts and payments account and statement of assets and liabilities have been prepared[1] for the financial year[2] in question, the auditor must make a report on that account and statement to the charity trustees[3].

The report must: (1) state the name and address of the auditor and the name of the charity concerned[4]; (2) be signed by him or, where the office of auditor is held by a body corporate or partnership, in its name by a person authorised to sign on its behalf, and state that the auditor falls within certain statutory requirements[5]; (3) be dated and specify the financial year in respect of which the accounts to which it relates have been prepared[6]; (4) specifies that it is a report in respect of an audit carried out under the statutory provisions[7] relating to annual audits or examinations of charity accounts[8].

The report must also state whether in the auditor's opinion the amount and statement properly present the receipts and payments of the charity for the financial year in question and its assets and liabilities as at the end of that year and whether in his opinion the account and statement adequately distinguish any material special trust or other restricted fund[9] of the charity[10].

Where the auditor has formed the opinion:

(a)    that accounting records have not been kept in respect of the charity in accordance with the statutory[11] duty[12]; or

(b)    that the account and statement do not accord with those records[13]; or

(c)    that any information or explanation to which he is entitled[14] has not been afforded to him[15],

the report must contain a statement of that opinion and of his grounds for forming it[16].

The auditor may, in preparing such a report for these purposes[17], carry out such investigations as will enable him to form an opinion as to certain specified matters[18].

1    Ie under the Charities Act 1993 s 42(3) (as amended): see para 308 ante.
2    For the meaning of 'financial year' see paras 210 note 3, 309 note 4 ante.
3    Charities (Accounts and Reports) Regulations 1995, SI 1995/2724, reg 6(3). These provisions apply to financial years beginning on or after 1 January 2001: see para 308 note 6 ante. For the meaning of 'charity trustees' see para 1 note 10 ante.
        In the case of an auditor appointed by the Charity Commissioners, the report required by reg 6(3) must be made to the Commissioners instead of to the charity trustees: reg 6(7). As to the Charity Commissioners see paras 486–512 post.
4    Ibid reg 6(3)(a).
5    Ibid reg 6(3)(b). The statutory requirements referred to in the text are the requirements of the Charities Act 1993 s 43(2)(a), or as the case may be, s 43(2)(b): see para 313 heads (1), (2) ante.
6    Charities (Accounts and Reports) Regulations 1995, SI 1995/2724, reg 6(3)(c).
7    Ie under the Charities Act 1993 s 43 (as amended) (see para 313 ante) and in accordance with regulations made under s 44 (see para 314 ante).
8    Charities (Accounts and Reports) Regulations 1995, SI 1995/2724, reg 6(3)(d).
9    This term is not defined for these purposes. For the meaning of 'restricted fund' for the purposes of the Charities (Accounts and Reports) Regulations 2000, SI 2000/2868, see para 311 note 15 ante.
10   Charities (Accounts and Reports) Regulations 1995, SI 1995/2724, reg 6(3)(e).
11   Ie under Charities Act 1993 s 41: see para 307 ante.
12   Charities (Accounts and Reports) Regulations 1995, SI 1995/2724, reg 6(3)(f)(i).
13   Ibid reg 6(3)(f)(ii).
14   Ie under ibid reg 8: see para 319 post.
15   Ibid reg 6(3)(f)(iii).
16   Ibid reg 6(3)(f).

17  Ie for the purposes of ibid reg 6(3): see the text and notes 1–16 supra.
18  Ibid reg 6(4). The matters specified are those in reg 6(3)(e) (see the text and notes 9–10 supra), and reg 6(3)(f) (see the text and notes 11–16 supra).

**317. Communications with Charity Commissioners and with charity trustees.** The auditor must communicate to the Charity Commissioners[1], in writing, any matter of which he becomes aware in his capacity as auditor which relates to the activities or affairs of the charity or of an institution or body corporate connected with the charity[2] and which the auditor has reasonable cause to believe is, or is likely to be, of material significance for the exercise, in relation to the charity of the Commissioners' functions in relation to the general power to institute inquiries[3] or the power[4] to act for the protection of charities[5].

Where an auditor appointed by charity trustees[6] ceases for any reason to hold office he must send a statement to the charity trustees[7]. The statement must set out any circumstances connected with his ceasing to hold office which he considers ought be brought to their attention or, if he considers that there are no circumstances, a statement that there are none[8]. Where the auditor sends a statement containing circumstances to be brought to the attention of the charity trustees, he must also send a copy to the Commissioners[9].

1  As to the Charity Commissioners see paras 486–512 post.
2  For the meaning of 'charity' see para 1 ante.
3  Ie under the Charities Act 1993 s 8: see paras 497–498 post.
4  Ie under ibid s 18: see para 503 et seq post.
5  Charities (Accounts and Reports) Regulations 1995, SI 1995/2724, reg 6(5). These provisions apply to financial years beginning on or after 1 January 2001: see para 308 note 6 ante.
6  For the meaning of 'charity trustees' see para 1 note 10 ante.
7  Charities (Accounts and Reports) Regulations 1995, SI 1995/2724, reg 6(6).
8  Ibid reg 6(6).
9  Ibid reg 6(6).

**318. Reports to charity trustees by an independent examiner.** An independent examiner[1] who has carried out an examination of the accounts of a charity[2] under the statutory provisions providing for independent examination[3] must make a report to the charity trustees[4].

The report must: (1) state the independent examiner's name and address and the name of the charity concerned[5]; (2) be signed by him and specify any relevant professional qualifications or professional body of which he is a member[6]; (3) be dated and specify the financial year[7] in respect of which the accounts to which it relates have been prepared[8]; (4) specify that it is a report in respect of an examination carried out under the statutory provisions[9] relating to annual audits or examinations of charity accounts and in accordance with any directions given by the Charity Commissioners[10] which are applicable[11].

The report must also state whether or not any matter has come to the examiner's attention in connection with the examination which gives him reasonable cause to believe that in any material respect[12]: (a) accounting records have not been kept in respect of the charity in accordance with the statutory duty[13]; (b) the accounts do not accord with those records[14]; and (c) in the case of an examination of accounts, the statement of accounts[15] does not comply with any of the relevant statutory requirements[16].

The report must state whether or not any matter has come to the examiner's attention in connection with the examination to which, in his opinion, attention should be drawn in the report in order to enable a proper understanding of the accounts to be reached[17]. Further, where certain matters become apparent to the examiner during the course of an examination, the report must contain a statement to that effect[18]. The relevant matters are that: (i) there has been any material expenditure or action which appears not to be in accordance with the trusts of the charity[19]; or (ii) any information or explanation to which he is entitled[20] has not been afforded to him[21]; or (iii) in the case of an examination of accounts a statement of which has been prepared[22], any information contained in the statement of accounts is inconsistent in any material respect with any report of the charity trustees prepared under the statutory provisions relating to annual reports[23] in respect of the financial year in question[24].

1    For the meaning of 'independent examiner' see para 313 note 9 ante.
2    For the meaning of 'charity' see para 1 ante.
3    Ie under the Charities Act 1993 s 43 (as amended): see para 313 ante.
4    Charities (Accounts and Reports) Regulations 1995, SI 1995/2724, reg 7. These provisions apply to financial years beginning on or after 1 January 2001: see para 308 note 6 ante. For the meaning of 'charity trustees' see para 1 note 10 ante.
5    Ibid reg 7(a).
6    Ibid reg 7(b).
7    For the meaning of 'financial year' see paras 210 note 3, 309 note 4 ante.
8    Charities (Accounts and Reports) Regulations 1995, SI 1995/2724, reg 7(c).
9    See note 3 supra.
10   Ie under Charities Act 1993 s 43(7)(b): see para 313 ante. From time to time, the Charity Commissioners publish guidance relating to independent examinations, see eg *The Carrying Out of an Independent Examination: Directions and Guidance Notes* (March 1996). As to the Charity Commissioners see paras 486–512 post.
11   Charities (Accounts and Reports) Regulations 1995, SI 1995/2724, reg 7(d).
12   Ibid reg 7(e)
13   Ibid reg 7(e)(i). The statutory duty referred to in the text is a statutory duty under the Charities Act 1993 s 41 (see para 307 ante): see Charities (Accounts and Reports) Regulations 1995, SI 1995/2724, reg 7(e)(i).
14   Ibid reg 7(e)(ii).
15   Ie as prepared under the Charities Act 1993 s 42(1): see para 308 ante.
16   Charities (Accounts and Reports) Regulations 1995, SI 1995/2724, reg 7(e)(iii). As to the relevant statutory requirements see reg 7(e)(iii) (modified by Charities (Accounts and Reports) Regulations 2000, SI 2000/2868, regs 4(b), 6(b)).
17   Charities (Accounts and Reports) Regulations 1995, SI 1995/2724, reg 7(f).
18   Ibid reg 7(g).
19   Ibid reg 7(g)(i).
20   Ie under ibid reg 8: see para 319 post.
21   Ibid reg 7(g)(ii).
22   Ie under the Charities Act 1993 s 42(1): see para 308 ante.
23   Ie under ibid s 45 (as amended): see para 321 post.
24   Charities (Accounts and Reports) Regulations 1995, SI 1995/2724, reg 7(g)(iii).

**319. Access to books, documents and records, and obtaining information and explanations.** An auditor or independent examiner[1] carrying out an audit or examination of the accounts[2] has a right of access to any books, documents[3] and other records (however kept) which relate to the charity[4] concerned and which the auditor or examiner in question considers it necessary to inspect for the purposes of carrying out the audit or, as the case may be, examination[5].

Such an auditor or independent examiner is also entitled to require, in the case of the charity concerned, such information and explanations from past or present charity trustees[6] or trustees for the charity, or from past or present officers or employees of the charity, as he considers necessary to obtain for the purposes of carrying out the audit or, as the case may be, examination[7].

1   For the meaning of 'independent examiner' see para 313 note 9 ante.
2   Ie under the Charities Act 1993 s 43 (as amended): see para 313 ante.
3   For the meaning of 'document' see para 236 note 2 ante.
4   For the meaning of 'charity' see para 1 ante.
5   Charities (Accounts and Reports) Regulations 1995, SI 1995/2724, reg 8(1). These provisions apply to financial years beginning on or after 1 January 2001: see para 308 note 6 ante.
6   For the meaning of 'charity trustees' see para 1 note 10 ante.
7   Charities (Accounts and Reports) Regulations 1995, SI 1995/2724, reg 8(2).

**320. Dispensation from audit or examination requirements.** The Charity Commissioners[1] may, in certain circumstances[2], dispense with the statutory requirements for the audit or independent examination of charity accounts[3] in the case of a particular charity[4] or in respect of a particular financial[5] year of a charity[6].

Such circumstances are where the Commissioners:

(1)   are satisfied that the accounts of the charity concerned are required to be audited in accordance with any statutory provision contained in or having effect under an Act of Parliament which, in the opinion of the Commissioners, imposes requirements which are sufficiently similar to the requirements for the audit of charity accounts under the Charities Act 1993[7] for those requirements to be dispensed with[8];

(2)   are satisfied that the accounts of the charity concerned have been audited by the Comptroller and Auditor General or by the Auditor General for Wales[9];

(3)   are satisfied that the accounts of the charity concerned for the financial year in question have been or will be audited or, as the case may be, examined in accordance with requirements or arrangements which, in the opinion of the Commissioners, are sufficiently similar to the statutory requirements for the audit or independent examination of charity accounts[10] applicable to that financial year of that charity for those requirements to be dispensed with[11];

(4)   are satisfied that there has, in the financial year in question, been no transaction on the part of the charity concerned which would be required to be shown and explained in the accounting records kept in pursuance of the duty[12] to keep such records[13];

(5)   consider that, although the financial year in question of the charity concerned is one to which the statutory requirements for the audit of charity accounts apply[14], there are exceptional circumstances which justify the examination of the accounts by an independent examiner instead of their audit in accordance with those requirements, and the accounts have been so examined[15],

and where the charity trustees[16] of the charity concerned have supplied to the Commissioners any report made to them with respect to the accounts of that charity for the financial year in question which the Commissioners have requested[17].

1   As to the Charity Commissioners see paras 486–512 post.
2   Ie in the circumstances referred to in the Charities (Accounts and Reports) Regulations 1995, SI 1995/2724, reg 9(2): see the text and notes 7–17 infra.
3   Ie the requirements of the Charities Act 1993 s 43(2), (3) (as amended): see para 313 ante.
4   For the meaning of 'charity' see para 1 ante.
5   For the meaning of 'financial year' see para 210 note 3, 309 note 4 ante.
6   Charities (Accounts and Reports) Regulations 1995, SI 1995/2724, reg 9(1). These provisions apply to financial years beginning on or after 1 January 2001: see para 308 note 6 ante.
7   Ie under the Charities Act 1993 s 43(2): see para 313 ante.
8   Charities (Accounts and Reports) Regulations 1995, SI 1995/2724, reg 9(2)(a).
9   Ibid reg 9(2)(b) (amended by the Charities (Accounts and Reports) Regulations 2000, SI 2000/2868, reg 8(3)). As to the Comptroller and Auditor General see CONSTITUTIONAL LAW AND HUMAN RIGHTS vol 8(2) (Reissue) paras 724–726. As to the Auditor General for Wales see CONSTITUTIONAL LAW AND HUMAN RIGHTS.
10  Ie under the Charities Act 1993 s 43: see para 313 ante.
11  Charities (Accounts and Reports) Regulations 1995, SI 1995/2724, reg 9(2)(c) (amended by the Charities (Accounts and Reports) Regulations 2000, SI 2000/2868, reg 8(3)).
12  Ie under the Charities Act 1993 s 41: see para 307 ante.
13  Charities (Accounts and Reports) Regulations 1995, SI 1995/2724, reg 9(2)(d).
14  See note 7 supra.
15  Charities (Accounts and Reports) Regulations 1995, SI 1995/2724, reg 9(2)(e).
16  For the meaning of 'charity trustees' see para 1 note 10 ante.
17  Charities (Accounts and Reports) Regulations 1995, SI 1995/2724, reg 9(2).

F.   ANNUAL REPORTS AND ANNUAL RETURNS

**321. Annual reports.** The charity trustees[1] of a charity[2] (other than an exempt charity[3], and certain charities with an annual income not exceeding £1,000 excepted from the requirement of registration[4] and not registered[5]) must prepare an annual report in respect of each financial year[6] of the charity[7]. The report must contain such a report by the trustees on the activities of the charity during that year[8], and such other information relating to the charity or to its trustees or officers[9], as is prescribed by regulations[10] made by the Secretary of State[11].

Where in any financial year of a charity its gross income[12] or total expenditure exceeds £10,000, the annual report required to be so prepared in respect of that year must be transmitted to the Charity Commissioners by the charity trustees within ten months from the end of that year, or within such longer period as the Commissioners may for any special reason allow in the case of that report[13]. Where in any financial year of a charity neither its gross income nor its total expenditure exceeds £10,000, the annual report required to be so prepared in respect of that year may, if the Commissioners so request, be transmitted to them by the charity trustees: (1) in the case of a request made before the end of seven months from the end of the financial year to which the report relates, within ten months from the end of that year[14]; and (2) in the case of a request not so made, within three months from the date of the request[15]; or (3) in either case, within such longer period as the Commissioners may for any special reason allow in the case of that report[16].

Any annual report transmitted to the Commissioners under these provisions must have attached to it the statement of accounts prepared for the financial year in question[17] or, as the case may be, the account and statement so prepared[18] together with[19]: (a) where the accounts of the charity for that year have been audited[20], a copy of the report made by the auditor on that statement of accounts or, as the case may be, on that account and statement[21]; (b) where the accounts of the charity for that year have been examined[22], a copy of the report made by the independent examiner[23] in respect of the examination so carried out by him[24]. However, this requirement does not apply to a charity which is a company[25], and any annual report transmitted by the charity trustees of such a charity under these provisions must instead have attached to it a copy of the charity's annual accounts prepared for the financial year in question under the provisions of the Companies Act 1985 which relate to accounts and audits[26], together with a copy of any auditors' report or report in respect of the company's individual accounts on that year made to the company's members[27] on those accounts[28].

1 For the meaning of 'charity trustees' see para 1 note 10 ante.
2 For the meaning of 'charity' see para 1 ante.
3 Charities Act 1993 s 46(1). As to exempt charities see para 293 ante.
4 Ie under ibid s 3(5)(c): see para 283 ante.
5 See ibid s 46(3); and para 324 post.
6 For the meaning of 'financial year' see paras 210 note 3, 309 note 4 ante.
7 Charities Act 1993 s 45(1). The charity trustees of a charity must preserve, for at least six years from the end of the financial year to which it relates, any annual report prepared by them under s 45(1) which they have not been required to transmit to the Charity Commissioners: s 45(7) (s 45(7), (8) added by the Deregulation and Contracting Out Act 1994 s 29). Where a charity ceases to exist within the six year period, the obligation to preserve the records continues to be discharged by the last charity trustees of the charity, unless the Commissioners consent in writing to the records being destroyed or otherwise disposed of: Charities Act 1993 ss 41(4), 45(8) (s 45(8) as so added). As to the Charity Commissioners see paras 486–512 post. See also R Vincent and A Francis *Charity Accounting and Taxation* (2nd Edn, 1997) pp 58–60, paras 5.21–5.25.
8 Charities Act 1993 s 45(1)(a).
9 Ibid s 45(1)(b).
10 In the exercise of the power conferred under ibid s 45 (as amended), the Charities (Accounts and Reports) Regulations 1995, SI 1995/2724 (amended and modified in relation to financial years beginning on or after 1 January 2001) and the Charities (Accounts and Reports) Regulations 2000, SI 2000/2868, have been made. As to the financial years to which these provisions apply see para 308 note 6 ante.
11 Charities Act 1993 s 45(1). Before making any regulations he must consult such persons or bodies of persons as he considers appropriate: s 86(4). As to the making of regulations generally see s 86 (as amended); and para 517 post. See also para 290 note 6 ante. As to the contents, application of requirements as to annual reports see para 322 et seq ante. Without prejudice to the generality of s 45(1), such regulations may make provision: (1) for any such report under s 45(1)(a) (see the text to note 8 supra) to be prepared in accordance with such principles as are specified or referred to in the regulations; (2) enabling the Charity Commissioners to dispense with the requirement prescribed by virtue of s 45(1)(b) (see the text to note 9 supra) in the case of a particular charity or a particular class of charities, or in the case of a particular financial year of a charity or of any class of charities: s 45(2). As to the Secretary of State see para 513 post.
12 For the meaning of 'gross income' see para 210 note 2 ante.
13 Charities Act 1993 s 45(3) (amended by the Deregulation and Contracting Out Act 1994 s 29). The Secretary of State may by order amend the Charities Act 1993 s 45(3) (as amended) or s 45(3A) (as added) by substituting a different sum for the sum for the time being specified there: s 45(9) (added by the Deregulation and Contracting Out Act 1994 s 29). As to the making of orders generally see the Charities Act 1993 s 86 (as amended); and para 517 post.
Any person who, without reasonable excuse, is persistently in default in relation to any requirement imposed by s 45(3) (as amended) or s 45(3A) (as added) (see the text and notes 14–16 infra) (taken with s 45(4) (as amended) or s 45(5) (as amended) (see the text and notes 17–28 infra), as the case may require) is guilty of an offence and liable on summary conviction to a fine not exceeding level 4 on the standard scale: s 49 (amended by the Deregulation and Contracting Out Act 1994 s 29). As to the standard scale see para 286 note 11 ante. However, proceedings may only be instituted by or with the consent of the Director of Public Prosecutions: Charities Act 1993 s 94(1), (2)(d). As to offences by bodies corporate see s 95; and para 515 post. As to the Director of Public Prosecutions see CRIMINAL LAW, EVIDENCE AND PROCEDURE vol 11(1) (Reissue) para 637 et seq.

Any annual report transmitted to the Commissioners under the Charities Act 1993 s 45 (as amended), together with the documents attached to it, must be kept by the Commissioners for such period as they think fit: s 45(6) (amended by the Deregulation and Contracting Out Act 1994 s 29). For the meaning of 'document' see para 236 note 2 ante.

14   Charities Act 1993 s 45(3A)(a) (s 45(3A) added by the Deregulation and Contracting Out Act 1994 s 29).
15   Charities Act 1993 s 45(3A)(b) (as added: see note 14 supra).
16   Ibid s 45(3A) (as added: see note 14 supra). A persistent default of s 45(3A) (as added) is an offence: see note 13 supra.
17   Ie under ibid s 42(1): see para 308 ante.
18   Ie under ibid s 42(3): see para 308 ante.
19   Ibid s 45(4) (amended by the Deregulation and Contracting Out Act 1994 s 29).
20   Ie under the Charities Act 1993 s 43 (as amended): see para 313 ante.
21   Ibid s 45(4)(a).
22   See note 20 supra.
23   For the meaning of 'independent examiner' see para 310 note 9 ante.
24   Charities Act 1993 s 45(4)(b).
25   For the meaning of 'company' see para 216 ante.
26   Ie the Companies Act 1985 Pt VII (ss 221–262A) (as amended): see COMPANIES.
27   Ie made for the purposes of ibid s 249A(2) (as added and amended): see COMPANIES vol 7(1) (1996 Reissue) para 1054.
28   Charities Act 1993 s 45(5) (amended by the Deregulation and Contracting Out Act 1994 s 29; and the Companies Act 1985 (Audit Exemption) Regulations 1994, SI 1994/1935, reg 4, Sch 1 para 6).

**322. Contents and application of requirements as to annual reports.**     There are statutory requirements[1] as to annual reports prepared[2] by the charity trustees[3] of a charity[4] in respect of a financial year[5]: (1) which begins on or after 1 January 2001[6]; or (2) which begins before that date if the charity trustees determine that these provisions[7] apply to the annual report, and the charity trustees have not, before 15 November 2000[8], either authorised the signature of an annual report in respect of that financial year[9] or approved a statement of accounts which has been prepared[10] for the charity in respect of that financial year[11].

The report on the activities of a charity during the year which is required to be contained in the annual report[12] in respect of each financial year of the charity must specify the financial year to which it relates and must[13]:

(a)   in the case of any financial year of a charity in which its gross income[14] does not exceed £250,000, be a brief summary of the main activities and achievements of the charity during the year in relation to its objects[15];

(b)   in the case of any financial year of a charity in which its gross income exceeds £250,000[16]:

(i)    be a review of all activities, including: (A) material transactions, significant developments and achievements of the charity during the year in relation to its objects; (B) any significant changes in those activities during the year; (C) any important events affecting those activities which have occurred since the end of the year and any likely future developments in those activities; and (D) where any fund of the charity was in deficit at the beginning of the financial year, the steps taken by the charity trustees to eliminate that deficit[17]; and

(ii)   contain a statement as to whether the charity trustees have given consideration to the major risks to which the charity is exposed and systems designed to mitigate those risks[18]; and

(c)   in either case, be dated and be signed by one or more of the charity trustees, each of whom has been authorised to do so[19].

1   The statutory requirements as to annual reports are set out in the text and notes 2–9 infra; and para 323 post.

2   Ie in accordance with the Charities Act 1993 s 45(1): see para 321 ante.

3   For the meaning of 'charity trustees' see para 1 note 10 ante.

4   This applies to any charity other than a charity specified in Charities (Accounts and Reports) Regulations 1995, SI 1995/2724, reg 10(4) (ie a common investment fund or common deposit fund which is deemed to be a charity by virtue of the Charities Act 1993 ss 24(8), 25(2) (see paras 366–367 post): Charities (Accounts and Reports) Regulations 2000, SI 2000/2868, reg 7(1). For the meaning of 'charity' see para 1 ante.

5   Ibid reg 7(1). For the meaning of 'financial year' see paras 210 note 3, 309 note 4 ante.

6   Ibid reg 7(1)(a). As to the financial years to which these provisions apply see para 308 note 6 ante.

7   Ie the provisions of ibid reg 7 (see the text and notes supra and infra; and para 323 post) rather than Charities (Accounts and Reports) Regulations 1995, SI 1995/2724, reg 10.

8   Ie the date on which the Charities (Accounts and Reports) Regulations 2000, SI 2000/2868, came into force.

9   Ie in accordance with the Charities (Accounts and Reports) Regulations 1995, SI 1995/2724, reg 10(1)(c).

10  Ie under ibid reg 3.

11  Charities (Accounts and Reports) Regulations 2000, SI 2000/2868, reg 7(1)(b). If the charity trustees make a determination under reg 7(1)(b), they must also make a determination under reg 3(1)(b) (see para 309 ante), if they prepare a statement of accounts under the Charities Act 1993 s 42(1) (see para 308 ante) in respect of the financial year in question and the charity is one to which Charities (Accounts and Reports) Regulations 2000, SI 2000/2868, reg 3 may apply: reg 7(2).

12  Ie prepared under the Charities Act 1993 s 45 (as amended): see para 321 ante.

13  Charities (Accounts and Reports) Regulations 2000, SI 2000/2868, reg 7(3).

14  For the meaning of 'gross income' see para 210 note 2 ante.

15  Charities (Accounts and Reports) Regulations 2000, SI 2000/2868, reg 7(3)(a).

16  Ibid reg 7(3)(b).

17  Ibid reg 7(3)(b)(i).

18  Ibid reg 7(3)(b)(ii).

19  Ibid reg 7(3)(c).

**323. Information required in annual reports.** The following information relating to a charity[1] and to its trustees and officers is required to be contained in the annual report[2]:

(1)   the name of the charity as it appears in the register of charities and any other name by which it makes itself known[3];

(2)   the number assigned to it in the register and, in the case of a charitable company, the number with which it is registered as a company[4];

(3)   the principal address of the charity and, in the case of a charitable company, the address of its registered office[5];

(4)   particulars, including the date if known, of any deed or other document[6] containing provisions which regulate the purposes and administration of the charity[7];

(5)   a description of the objects of the charity[8];

(6)   the name of any person or body of persons entitled by the trusts of the charity to appoint one or more new charity trustees, and a description of the method provided by those trusts for such appointment[9];

(7)   the name of any person who is a charity trustee of the charity on the date when the authority to sign and date the annual report[10] is given, and, where any charity

trustee on that date is a body corporate, the name of any person who is a director[11] of the body corporate on that date[12];

(8)   the name of any other person who has, at any time during the financial year[13] in question, been a charity trustee of the charity[14];

(9)   the name of any person who is a trustee for the charity on the date referred to in head (7) above[15];

(10)   the name of any other person who has, at any time during the financial year in question, been a trustee for the charity[16];

(11)   a description of the policies (if any) which have been adopted by the charity trustees: (a) for the purpose of determining the level of income reserves[17] which it is appropriate for the charity to maintain in order to meet effectively the needs designated by its trusts; (b) for the selection of investments for the charity; and (c) for the selection of individuals and institutions who are to receive grants out of the assets of the charity[18];

(12)   a statement regarding the performance during the financial year of the investments belonging to the charity (if any)[19];

(13)   a description of the organisational structure of the charity[20]; and

(14)   a description of any assets held by the charity or by any charity trustee of, or trustee for, the charity, on behalf of another charity, and particulars of any special arrangements made with respect to the safe custody of such assets and their segregation from assets of the charity not so held and a description of the objects of the charity on whose behalf the assets are held[21].

1    For the meaning of 'charity' see para 1 ante.
2    Charities (Accounts and Reports) Regulations 2000, SI 2000/2868, reg 7(4). This provision is expressed to be subject to reg 7(5)–(8) (see the text and notes 5–17 infra): see reg 7(4). As to annual reports see paras 321–322 ante. These provisions apply to financial years beginning on or after 1 January 2001: see para 308 note 6 ante.
3    Ibid reg 7(4)(a). In the case of a report prepared under the Charities Act 1993 s 46(5) (see para 324 post) (excepted charities which are not registered), the Charities (Accounts and Reports) Regulations 2000, SI 2000/2868, reg 7(4)(a) is modified so that the information required to be contained in the annual report under reg 7(4)(a) is the name of the charity: reg 7(4)(a), (7)(a). As to the register of charities see para 282 et seq ante.
4    Ibid reg 7(4)(b). For the meaning of 'company' see para 216 ante.
     In the case of a report prepared under the Charities Act 1993 s 46(5) (see para 324 post) (excepted charities which are not registered), the Charities (Accounts and Reports) Regulations 2000, SI 2000/2868, reg 7(4)(b) is modified so that the information required to be contained in the annual report under reg 7(4)(b) is, in the case of a charitable company, the number with which it is registered as a company: reg 7(4)(a), (7)(b).
5    Ibid reg 7(4)(c). Where they are satisfied that, in the case of a particular charity or class of charities, or in the case of a particular financial year of a charity or class of charities, the disclosure of the principal address of the charity in accordance with reg 7(4)(c) could lead to any such person being placed in any personal danger, the Charity Commissioners may dispense with the requirement so far as it applies to the principal address of the charity, as the case may require: reg 7(5). As to the Charity Commissioners see paras 486–512 post.
6    For the meaning of 'document' 236 note 2 ante.
7    Charities (Accounts and Reports) Regulations 2000, SI 2000/2868, reg 7(4)(d).
8    Ibid reg 7(4)(e).
9    Ibid reg 7(4)(f). For the meaning of 'charity trustees' see para 1 note 10 ante. Where they are satisfied that, in the case of a particular charity or class of charities, or in the case of a particular financial year of a charity or class of charities, the disclosure of the name of any person whose name is required by any of the provisions contained in heads (6)–(10) in the text (ie reg 7(4)(f)–(j)) to be contained in the annual

report of a charity could lead to that person being placed in any personal danger, the Commissioners may dispense with the requirement so far as it applies to the name of any such person as the case may require: reg 7(5).

10  Ie the authority referred to in ibid reg 7(3)(c): see para 322 head (c) ante.

11  'Director' includes any person occupying the position of a director, by whatever name called, and in relation to a body corporate whose affairs are managed by its members means a member of the body corporate: ibid reg 2(1).

12  Ibid reg 7(4)(g). See also note 9 supra. In the case of a charity having more than 50 charity trustees on the date referred to in the text, reg 7(4)(g) is modified so that the information required to be contained in the annual report is the names of not less than 50 of the charity trustees of the charity, including any charity trustee who is also an officer of the charity on the date when the authority to sign and date the annual report referred to in reg 7(3)(c) (see para 322 ante) is given, and, where any charity trustee on that date is a body corporate, the name of any person who is a director of the body corporate on that date: reg 7(4)(g), (6)(a).

13  For the meaning of 'financial year' see paras 210 note 3, 309 note 4 ante.

14  Charities (Accounts and Reports) Regulations 2000, SI 2000/2868, reg 7(4)(h). See also note 9 supra. In the case of a charity having more than 50 charity trustees on the date referred to in head (7) in the text, reg 7(4)(h) is modified so that the information required to be contained in the annual report is the name of any other person who has, at any time during the financial year in question, been a charity trustee of the charity other than the name of any charity trustee whose name has been excluded from the report in pursuance of reg 7(4)(g) (see head (7) in the text): reg 7(4)(h), (6)(b).

15  Ibid reg 7(4)(i). See also note 9 supra.

16  Ibid reg 7(4)(j). See also note 9 supra.

17  'Income reserves' means those assets in the unrestricted fund of a charity which the charity trustees have, or can make, available to apply for all or any of its purposes, once they have provided for the commitments of the charity and its other planned expenditure: ibid reg 2(1). For the meaning of 'unrestricted fund' see para 311 note 15 ante.

18  Ibid reg 7(4)(k).

19  Ibid reg 7(4)(l). In the case of a report in respect of a financial year of a charity in which its gross income does not exceed £250,000, reg 7(4)(l)–(n) (see heads (12)–(14) in the text) does not apply: reg 7(8).

20  Ibid reg 7(4)(m). See also note 18 supra.

21  Ibid reg 7(4)(n). See also note 18 supra.

**324. Special provision as respects accounts and annual reports of exempt and other excepted charities.** None of the provisions in the Charities Act 1993 relating to accounts, audits and annual reports[1] applies to an exempt charity[2]. The charity trustees[3], however, must keep proper books of account with respect to the affairs of the charity and, if not required by or under the authority of any other Act to prepare periodical statements of account, must prepare consecutive statements of account consisting on each occasion of an income and expenditure account relating to a period of not more than 15 months and a balance sheet relating to the end of that period[4]. The books of accounts and statements of account relating to an exempt charity must be preserved for a period of six years at least unless the charity ceases to exist and the Charity Commissioners[5] consent in writing to their being destroyed or otherwise disposed of[6].

The provisions of the Charities Act 1993 relating to annual reports and annual audits or examination of charity accounts[7] do not apply to any charity which has neither any permanent endowment[8], nor the use and occupation of any land, and whose income from all sources does not in aggregate amount to more than £1,000 a year[9], in the case where the charity thus excepted from the requirement of registration is not registered[10].

A charity which does not fall within either of the exceptions referred to above[11] is nevertheless absolved from the obligation to prepare annual reports[12] if it is excepted by the statutory provisions which state which charities are not required to be registered[13], and is not registered[14]. However, in this case, if requested to do so by the Charity Commissioners, the charity trustees must prepare an annual report in respect of such financial year[15] as is specified in the Commissioners' request[16]. Any report so prepared must contain such a report by the charity trustees on the activities of the charity during the year in question, and such other information relating to the charity or to its trustees or officers, as may be prescribed by regulations[17] made in relation to annual reports[18].

1   Ie the Charities Act 1993 ss 41–45 (as amended): see para 307 et seq ante.
2   Ibid s 46(1). As to exempt charities see para 293 ante. For the meaning of 'charity' see para 1 ante.
3   For the meaning of 'charity trustees' see para 1 note 10 ante.
4   Charities Act 1993 s 46(1).
5   As to the Charity Commissioners see paras 486–512 post.
6   Charities Act 1993 s 46(2).
7   Ie ibid s 43 (as amended) (see para 313 ante), s 44 (see para 314 ante), s 45 (as amended) (see para 321 ante).
8   For the meaning of 'permanent endowment' see para 283 note 3 ante.
9   Ie any charity excepted from the requirement of registration by the Charities Act 1993 s 3(5)(c) (whether or not it is also excepted from registration by s 3(5)(b)): s 46(8). See para 284 ante.
10  Ibid s 46(3).
11  Ie is not an exempt charity or a charity which falls within ibid s 3(5)(c): see para 283 ante.
12  Ie those contained in ibid s 45 (as amended): see para 321 ante.
13  Ie ibid s 3(5): see paras 283–285 ante.
14  See ibid s 46(4).
15  For the meaning of 'financial year' see paras 210 note 3, 309 note 4 ante.
16  Charities Act 1993 s 46(5). In relation to any report required to be prepared under s 46(5), the provisions of s 45(3)–(6) (as originally enacted) apply as if it were an annual report required to be prepared under s 45(1) (para 321 ante): s 46(7).
17  Ie by regulations under ibid s 45 (as amended) (see para 321 ante): see para 323 ante.
18  Ibid s 46(6).


**325. Public inspection of annual reports and other documents.** Any annual report or other document kept by the Charity Commissioners[1] is open to public inspection at all reasonable times during the period for which it is so kept, or if the Commissioners so determine, during such lesser period as they may specify[2]. On request the Commissioners must furnish any person with copies of, or extracts from, any document in their possession which is for the time being open to public inspection[3].

Where any person requests the charity trustees[4] of a charity[5] in writing to provide him with a copy of the charity's most recent accounts[6], and pays them such reasonable fee, if any, as they may require in respect of the costs of complying with the request, those trustees must comply with the request within the period of two months beginning with the date on which it is made[7].

1   Ie in pursuance of the Charities Act 1993 s 45(6): see para 321 ante. As to the Charity Commissioners see paras 486–512 post.
2   Ibid s 47(1).
3   Ibid s 84.
4   For the meaning of 'charity trustees' see para 1 note 10 ante.
5   For the meaning of 'charity' see para 1 ante.
6   The reference to a charity's most recent accounts means:
    (1)  in the case of a charity other than one falling within head (2) or (3) infra, a reference to the statement of accounts or account and statement prepared in pursuance of the Charities Act 1993 s 42(1) or (3) (as amended) (see para 308 ante) in respect of the last financial year of the charity in respect of which a statement of accounts or account and statement has or have been so prepared (s 47(3)(b) (amended by the Deregulation and Contracting Out Act 1994 s 39, Sch 11 para 12));
    (2)  in the case of a charity which is a company, a reference to the most recent annual accounts of the company prepared under the Companies Act 1985 Pt VII (ss 221–262A) (as amended) (see

COMPANIES) in relation to which any of the following conditions is satisfied: (a) they have been audited; (b) a report required for the purposes of s 249A(2) (as added and amended) (see COMPANIES vol 7(1) (1996 Reissue) para 1054) has been made in respect of them; or (c) they relate to a year in respect of which the company is exempt from audit by virtue of s 249A(1) (as added) (Charities Act 1993 s 47(3)(c) (substituted by the Companies Act 1985 (Audit Exemption) Regulations 1994, SI 1994/1935, reg 4, Sch 1 para 7)); and

(3)  in the case of an exempt charity, a reference to the accounts of the charity most recently audited in pursuance of any statutory or other requirement or, if its accounts are not required to be audited, the accounts most recently prepared in respect of the charity (Charities Act 1993 s 47(3)(d)).

For the meaning of 'financial year' see paras 210 note 3, 309 note 4 ante. For the meaning of 'company' see para 216 ante.

7   Ibid s 47(2). Any person who, without reasonable excuse, is persistently in default in relation to any requirement imposed by s 47(2) is guilty of an offence and liable on summary conviction to a fine not exceeding level 4 on the standard scale: s 49. As to the standard scale see para 286 note 11 ante. However, proceedings may only be instituted by or with the consent of the Director of Public Prosecutions: s 94(1), (2),(d). As to the Director of Public Prosecutions see CRIMINAL LAW, EVIDENCE AND PROCEDURE vol 11(1) Reissue para 637 et seq. As to offences by bodies corporate see s 95; and para 515 post.

**326. Annual returns by registered charities.** Every registered charity[1] must prepare in respect of each of its financial years[2] an annual return in such form, and containing such information, as may be prescribed by regulations[3] made by the Charity Commissioners[4]. However, this does not apply in relation to any financial year of a charity in which neither the gross income[5] nor the total expenditure of the charity exceeds £10,000[6].

Any such return under these provisions must be transmitted to the Commissioners by the date by which the charity trustees[7] are required[8] to transmit to them the annual report required to be prepared in respect of the financial year in question[9].

The Commissioners may dispense with these requirements[10] in the case of a particular charity or a particular class of charities, or in the case of a particular financial year of a charity or of any class of charities[11].

1   Ie registered under the Charities Act 1993 s 3 (as amended) (see paras 282–285 ante): s 97(1). For the meaning of 'charity' see para 1 ante.
2   For the meaning of 'financial year' see paras 210 note 3, 309 note 4 ante.
3   Such regulations are made and published annually by the Charity Commission.
4   Charities Act 1993 s 48(1) (amended by the Deregulation and Contracting Out Act 1994 s 30(2)). As to the Charity Commissioners see paras 486–512 post.
5   For the meaning of 'gross income' see para 210 note 2 ante.
6   Charities Act 1993 s 48(1A) (added by the Deregulation and Contracting Out Act 1994 s 30(3)). The Secretary of State may by order amend the Charities Act 1993 s 48(1A) (as added) by substituting a different sum for the sum for the time being specified there: s 48(4) (added by the Deregulation and Contracting Out Act 1994 s 30(4)). At the date at which this volume states the law no such order had been made. As to the making of orders generally see the Charities Act 1993 s 86 (as amended); and para 517 post. As to the Secretary of State see para 513 post.
7   For the meaning of 'charity trustees' see para 1 note 10 ante.
8   Ie by virtue of the Charities Act 1993 s 45(3) (as amended): see para 321 ante.
9   Ibid s 48(2). Any person who, without reasonable excuse, is persistently in default in relation to any requirement imposed by s 48(2) is guilty of an offence and liable on summary conviction to a fine not exceeding level 4 on the standard scale: s 49. As to the standard scale see para 286 note 11 ante. However, proceedings may only be instituted by or with the consent of the Director of Public Prosecutions: Charities Act 1993 s 94(1), (2),(d). As to the Director of Public Prosecutions see CRIMINAL LAW, EVIDENCE AND PROCEDURE vol 11(1) Reissue para 637 et seq. As to offences by bodies corporate see s 95; and para 515 post.
10  Ie the requirements of ibid s 48(1) (as amended): see the text and notes 1–4 supra.
11  Ibid s 48(3).

## (2) POWERS OF CHARITY TRUSTEES

### (i)  Exercise of Powers generally

**327.  Exercise of discretionary powers.** Trustees invested with discretionary powers must exercise them honestly and with a fair consideration of the subject[1]. They need not give reasons for their actions[2]. Where they state reasons which do not justify their conclusions[3], or where they have acted corruptly or improperly[4], the court will interfere; but the court is generally reluctant to interfere with the discretion of trustees by means of schemes[5], although in order to retain some control over the trustees it may refuse to dismiss an action seeking the interference of the court[6], or may refuse to order payment out to trustees of a fund in court without an affidavit by them stating how they propose to apply the money[7].

1   *Re Beloved Wilkes' Charity* (1851) 20 LJCh 588 at 597 per Lord Truro LC. The exercise by trustees of discretionary powers was discussed in *McPhail v Doulton* [1971] AC 424 at 449, [1970] 2 All ER 228 at 240, HL, per Lord Wilberforce.
2   *Re Beloved Wilkes' Charity* (1851) 20 LJCh 588.
3   *Re Beloved Wilkes' Charity* (1851) 20 LJCh 588. See, however, *A-G v Mosely* (1848) 17 LJCh 446, where it was said that a discretionary consent might be withheld for an insufficient reason or none.
4   *A-G v Glegg* (1738) Amb 584; *A-G v Governors of Harrow School* (1754) 2 Ves Sen 551; *Waldo v Caley* (1809) 16 Ves 206 at 212 per Lord Eldon LC; *Ex p Berkhampstead Free School* (1813) 2 Ves & B 134 at 138 per Lord Eldon LC; *Re Bedford Charity* (1833) 5 Sim 578; *A-G v Boucherett* (1858) 25 Beav 116. See also *A-G v Governors etc of Sherborne Grammar School* (1854) 18 Beav 256 (discretion of visitor).
5   *Powerscourt v Powerscourt* (1824) 1 Mol 616 (trust of a temporary nature); *A-G v Gaskell* (1831) 9 LJOS Ch 188; *Re Lea, Lea v Cooke* (1887) 34 ChD 528 (where no permanent charity was intended). In *Re Hurley, Nichols v Pargiter* (1900) 17 TLR 115 a scheme was ordered by the court, although the trustees were given a discretionary power.
6   *A-G v Governors of Harrow School* (1754) 2 Ves Sen 551.
7   *Re Devlin's Estate, Hagan v Duff* (1889) 23 LR Ir 516.

**328.  Who may exercise discretionary powers.** Where a power to prescribe the mode of applying a charitable gift is contained in the trust instrument, it is a question of construction to determine who is capable of exercising the power[1]. Powers given to trustees, and even to a testator's 'said trustees' (being named earlier in the will) are prima facie regarded as annexed to the office and therefore exercisable by the trustees for the time being[2].

A power given to executors only is exercisable by continuing[3] or surviving[4] executors, but not by one who renounces[5], or by persons subsequently appointed trustees[6]. The question whether it is exercisable by a substituted personal representative appointed by the court under the Administration of Justice Act 1985 has not yet come before the court[7].

A power given to a person who is not a trustee of the property cannot be exercised by any other person[8]; if the named person does not or cannot exercise the power, the court must exercise the discretion[9].

The permissible manner of exercise of a power and its scope also depend upon the construction of the trust instrument[10].

1   *Re Mainwaring, Crawford v Forshaw* [1891] 2 Ch 261 at 267–268, CA, per Bowen LJ; and see the non-charity cases of *Re Smith, Eastick v Smith* [1904] 1 Ch 139; *Re Hayes' Will Trusts, Pattinson v Hayes* [1971] 2 All ER 341, [1971] 1 WLR 758.

2   *Re Smith, Eastick v Smith* [1904] 1 Ch 139. See also *Re Taylor's Charity, ex p Blackburne* (1820) 1 Jac & W 297 (where the selection of objects was left with the persons nominated by the testator as trustees, although new trustees were appointed); *Re Hampton, Public Trustee v Hampton* (1918) 88 LJCh 103. See also the Trustee Act 1925 ss 18, 36(7), 43; the Law of Property Act 1925 s 156; and TRUSTS.

3   *Re Mainwaring, Crawford v Forshaw* [1891] 2 Ch 261, CA.

4   *A-G v Glegg* (1738) Amb 584.

5   *A-G v Fletcher* (1835) 5 LJCh 75; cf the Administration of Estates Act 1925 s 8; and see EXECUTORS AND ADMINISTRATORS vol 17(2) (Reissue) para 25.

6   *Hibbard v Lamb* (1756) Amb 309.

7   See the Administration of Justice Act 1985 s 50; and EXECUTORS AND ADMINISTRATORS vol 17(2) (Reissue) para 706.

8   *Re M'Auliffe's Goods* [1895] P 290; cf *Re Lalor's Goods* (1901) 85 LT 643.

9   *Moggridge v Thackwell* (1792) 1 Ves 464 at 475 per Lord Thurlow LC; on rehearing (1803) 7 Ves 36 at 86 per Lord Eldon LC; affd (1807) 13 Ves 416, HL; cf *Doyley v A-G* (1735) 4 Vin Abr 485 pl 16 (a trustee who refused to act). See also para 116 ante.

10  See para 116 ante; and POWERS; TRUSTS.

**329. Powers of majority of trustees or quorum.** Apart from powers exercisable under statutory provisions by a majority of trustees, the general rule is that a majority of the trustees of a trust of a public or charitable nature acting within the limits of the instrument of foundation[1] bind the minority[2].

Schemes for the administration of a charity may contain a provision that a certain number of trustees shall constitute a quorum[3].

1   *Ward v Hipwell* (1862) 3 Giff 547.

2   *Re Whiteley, Bishop of London v Whiteley* [1910] 1 Ch 600; *Doe d Read v Godwin* (1822) 1 Dow & Ry KB 259 (conveyance by majority); but see *Re Ebsworth and Tidy's Contract* (1889) 42 ChD 23, CA (where it was held that without statutory authority a majority of trustees could not pass the legal estate if vested in all); *Re Congregational Church, Smethwick* [1866] WN 196; *A-G v Shearman* (1839) 2 Beav 104 (lease); *Doe d Dupleix v Roe* (1794) 1 Anst 86 (action of ejectment); *Withnell v Gartham* (1795) 6 Term Rep 388; *Wilkinson v Malin* (1832) 2 Cr & J 636; *A-G v Scott* (1750) 1 Ves Sen 413 at 416 per Lord Hardwicke LC; *A-G v Cuming* (1843) 2 Y & C Ch Cas 139 (election of minister of Established Church by advowson trustees); *Davis v Jenkins* (1814) 3 Ves & B 151 at 159 per Lord Eldon LC; *Perry v Shipway* (1859) 4 De G & J 353; *A-G v Lawson* (1866) 36 LJCh 130 (appointment and dismissal of minister of dissenting chapel).

3   Cf *Re Beverley Grammar School* (1839) 9 LJCh 91.

### (ii) Authorisation of Dealings by the Charity Commissioners

**330. General power.** If it appears to the Charity Commissioners[1] that an action which is proposed or contemplated in the administration of a charity[2] is expedient in the interests of the charity, they may by order[3] sanction that action, whether or not if would otherwise be within the powers exercisable by the charity trustees[4] in the administration of the charity[5]. Anything done under the authority of such an order is deemed to be properly done in the exercise of those powers[6].

Such an order may be made to authorise a particular transaction, compromise[7] or the like, or a particular application of property, or so as to confer a more general authority[8], and in particular may authorise[9] a charity to use common premises or employ a common staff or otherwise combine for any administrative purpose with another charity[10].

1    As to the Charity Commissioners see paras 486–512 post.
2    For the meaning of 'charity' see para 1 ante.
3    It has been held that the order should be made formally under seal: see *BIU Estates Ltd v Chichester Diocesan Fund and Board of Finance Inc* (1963) 186 Estates Gazette 261 (decided under earlier legislation).
4    For the meaning of 'charity trustees' see para 1 note 10 ante.
5    Charities Act 1993 s 26(1). This provision is expressed to be subject to s 26(2)–(7) (see the text to note 10 infra; and para 333 post): see s 26(1).
6    Ibid s 26(1).
7    See eg *Report of the Charity Commissioners for England and Wales for 1978* (HC Paper (1979–80) no 94) paras 146–149; *Report of the Charity Commissioners for England and Wales for 1982* (HC Paper (1982–83) no 370) paras 90–96.
8    Eg a general authority to invest in land: see *Report of the Charity Commissioners for England and Wales for 1988* (HC Paper (1988–89) no 319) paras 73–75.
9    Ie without prejudice to the generality of the Charities Act 1993 s 26(1).
10    Ibid s 26(2).

**331. Directions as to expenditure.** An order of the Charity Commissioners[1] authorising action in the administration of a charity[2] may give directions as to the manner in which any expenditure is to be borne and as to other matters connected with or arising out of the action thereby authorised[3]. Where anything is done under the authority of such an order, the directions are binding on the charity trustees[4] for the time being as if contained in the trusts[5] of the charity[6]. Any such directions may, on the application of the charity, be modified or superseded by a further order[7]. In particular, such directions include directions for meeting any expenditure out of a specified fund, for charging any expenditure to capital or to income, for requiring expenditure charged to capital to be recouped out of income within a specified period, for restricting the costs to be incurred at the expense of the charity, or for the investment of moneys arising from any transaction[8].

1    As to the Charity Commissioners see paras 486–512 post.
2    Ie under the Charities Act 1993 s 26(1): see para 330 ante. For the meaning of 'charity' see para 1 ante.
3    Ibid s 26(3).
4    For the meaning of 'charity trustees' see para 1 note 10 ante.
5    For the meaning of 'trusts' see para 210 note 5 ante.
6    Charities Act 1993 s 26(3).
7    Ibid s 26(3).
8    Ibid s 26(4).

**332. Transactions affected by the disabling Acts or requiring a court order.** An order of the Charity Commissioners[1] authorising action in the administration of a charity[2] may also authorise any act notwithstanding that it is prohibited by disabling Act[3], and notwithstanding that the trusts[4] of the charity provide for the act to be done by or under the authority of the court[5].

1    As to the Charity Commissioners see paras 486–512 post.
2    For the meaning of 'charity' see para 1 ante.

3    The Acts referred to as the disabling Acts are the Ecclesiastical Leases Act 1571 (repealed), the Ecclesiastical Leases Act 1572 (repealed), the Ecclesiastical Leases Act 1575 (repealed), and the Ecclesiastical Leases Act 1836 (see ECCLESIASTICAL LAW vol 14 para 1153 et seq): Charities Act 1993 s 26(6).

4    For the meaning of 'trusts' see para 210 note 5 ante.

5    Charities Act 1993 s 26(5). For the meaning of 'the court' see para 168 note 12 ante.

**333. Acts which may not be authorised.** No order of the Charity Commissioners[1] authorising action in the administration of a charity[2] may authorise the doing of any act expressly prohibited by an Act of Parliament other than the disabling Acts[3] or by the trusts[4] of the charity, or extend or alter the purposes of the charity[5]; not may it confer any authority in relation to a building which has been consecrated and the use or disposal of which is regulated, and can be further regulated, by a scheme under the Pastoral Measure 1983[6]. The power of the Commissioners to authorise dealings with trust property[7] is not, however, affected by the Redundant Churches and Other Religious Buildings Act 1969[8].

Any provision in the trusts of an almshouse[9] charity[10] which relates to the payment by persons resident in the charity's almshouses of contributions towards the cost of maintaining those almshouses and essential services in them has no effect if and to the extent that it provides for the amount, or the maximum amount, of such contributions to be a sum specified, approved or authorised by the Commissioners[11].

1    As to the Charity Commissioners see paras 486–512 post.

2    For the meaning of 'charity' see para 1 ante. See para 330 ante.

3    As to the disabling Acts see para 332 note 3 ante.

4    For the meaning of 'trusts' see para 210 note 5 ante.

5    Charities Act 1993 s 26(5).

6    Ibid s 26(7). The reference to a building is taken to include part of a building and any land which under such a scheme is to be used or disposed of with a building to which the scheme applies: s 26(7). Reference is also made in s 26(7) to schemes having effect under the Union of Benefices Measures 1923 to 1952, the Reorganisation Areas Measures 1944 and 1954, or the Pastoral Measure 1968 (all of which have been repealed).

7    Ie under the Charities Act 1993 s 26: see para 330 et seq ante.

8    See the Redundant Churches and Other Religious Buildings Act 1969 s 7(2); and ECCLESIASTICAL LAW vol 14 para 1134.

9    'Almshouse' means any premises maintained as an almshouse, whether they are called an almshouse or not: Charities Act 1992 s 50(2).

10    'Almshouse charity' means a charity which is authorised under its trusts to maintain almshouses: ibid s 50(2).

11    Ibid s 50(1).

**334. Charge for agricultural improvements.** The powers conferred by the Agricultural Holdings Act 1986 on landlords as regards charging land with the amount paid or expended as compensation for improvements[1] are not exercisable by trustees for charitable purposes except with the approval in writing of the Charity Commissioners[2].

1    See the Agricultural Holdings Act 1986 s 86(1)–(3); and AGRICULTURE vol 1(2) (Reissue) paras 480, 491.

2    Ibid s 86(4). As to the Charity Commissioners see paras 486–512 post.

## (iii) Advice by the Charity Commissioners

**335. Power to give advice.** On the written application of any charity trustee[1], the Charity Commissioners[2] may give him their opinion or advice on any matter affecting the performance of his duties as charity trustee[3]. The accuracy of the Commissioners' opinion or advice may be challenged under the procedure set up under the Charities Act 1993[4], but a common law action in negligence cannot be brought on the ground that the opinion or advice is not only wrong but was given negligently[5].

1   For the meaning of 'charity trustees' see para 1 note 10 ante.
2   As to the Charity Commissioners see paras 486–512 post.
3   Charities Act 1993 s 29(1).
4   See ibid s 33; and para 519 et seq post.
5   *Mills v Winchester Diocesan Board of Finance* [1989] Ch 428, [1989] 2 All ER 317.

**336. Consequences of acting on advice.** If the Charity Commissioners[1] give their opinion or advice on the application of a charity trustee[2] with respect to a charity, then a charity trustee or trustee for the charity[3] acting in accordance with the opinion or advice is deemed to have acted in accordance with his trust, as regards his responsibility for so acting, unless, when he does so act, either he knows or has reasonable cause to suspect that the opinion or advice was given in ignorance of material facts, or the decision of the court[4] has been obtained on the matter or proceedings are pending to obtain one[5].

1   As to the Charity Commissioners see paras 486–512 post.
2   Ie under the Charities Act 1993 s 29(1): see para 335 ante. For the meaning of 'charity trustees' see para 1 note 10 ante.
3   For the meaning of 'charity' see para 1 ante.
4   For the meaning of 'the court' see para 168 note 12 ante.
5   Charities Act 1993 s 29(2).

## (iv) Execution of Documents

**337. Power to delegate.** Subject to the trusts[1] of the charity, charity trustees[2] may confer on any of their body, not being less than two of number, a general or authority limited in such manner as the trustees think fit, to execute in the names and on behalf of the trustees assurances or other deeds or instruments for giving effect to transactions to which the trustees are a party[3].

1   For the meaning of 'trusts' see para 210 note 5 ante.
2   For the meaning of 'charity trustees' see para 1 note 10 ante.
3   Charities Act 1993 s 82(1). Any deed or instrument executed in pursuance of an authority so given is of the same effect as if executed by the whole body: s 82(1). This power is in addition to and not in derogation of any other power (eg the general power to act by a majority (see para 329 ante)): s 82(5).

**338. Manner of delegating authority.** An authority to execute any deed or instrument[1] is sufficient if given in writing or by resolution of a meeting of the trustees, notwithstanding the want of any formality which would otherwise be required[2]. It may be given so that the powers conferred are exercisable by any of the trustees or may be restricted to named persons or in any other way[3].

1  Ie under the Charities Act 1993 s 82(1): see para 337 ante.
2  Ibid s 82(2)(a).
3  Ibid s 82(2)(b).

**339. Effect of authority.** An authority to execute instruments on behalf of charity trustees[1] has effect, subject to any restriction expressed in it and until it is revoked, as a continuing authority given by the charity trustees from time to time of the charity[2] and exercisable by such trustees, notwithstanding any change in the charity trustees[3]. A deed or instrument executed in pursuance of such an authority has the same effect as if executed by all the trustees[4]. Such an authority also includes an implied authority to execute deeds and instruments in the name and on behalf of the official custodian for charities[5], in cases where the charity trustees could do so[6].

Where a deed or instrument purports to be executed in pursuance of such an authority, then in favour of a person who, then or afterwards, in good faith acquires for money or money's worth an interest in or charge on property or the benefit of a covenant or agreement expressed to be entered into by the charity trustees, it is presumed conclusively to have been duly executed under proper authority[7].

1  Ie under the Charities Act 1993 s 82: see paras 337–338 ante. For the meaning of 'charity trustees' see para 1 note 10 ante.
2  For the meaning of 'charity' see para 1 ante.
3  Charities Act 1993 s 82(2)(c).
4  Ibid s 82(1).
5  As to the official custodian for charities see para 273 et seq ante.
6  Charities Act 1993 s 82(3). As to where the charity trustees can execute deeds and instruments on behalf of the official custodian for charities see para 279 ante.
7  Ibid s 82(4).

## (v) Preservation of Charity Documents

**340. Enrolment and deposit of documents.** The Charity Commissioners[1] may provide books in which any deed, will and other document[2] relating to a charity[3] may be enrolled[4]. They may also accept for safe keeping any document of or relating to a charity, and the charity trustees[5] or other persons having the custody of such documents, including documents relating to a charity which has ceased to exist, may, with the consent of the Commissioners, deposit them with the Commissioners for safe keeping, except in the case of documents required by some enactment other than the Charities Act 1993 to be kept elsewhere[6]. Regulations made by the Secretary of State[7] may make provision for such documents so deposited with the Commissioners as may be prescribed by the regulations to be destroyed or otherwise disposed of after such period or in such circumstances as may be so prescribed[8].

1    As to the Charity Commissioners see paras 486–512 post.
2    For the meaning of 'document' see para 236 note 2 ante.
3    For the meaning of 'charity' see para 1 ante.
4    Charities Act 1993 s 30(1).
5    For the meaning of 'charity trustees' see para 1 note 10 ante.
6    Charities Act 1993 s 30(2).
7    As to the Secretary of State see para 513 post.
8    Charities Act 1993 s 30(4). At the date at which this volume states the law, no such regulations had been made. As to the making of regulations generally see s 86 (as amended); and para 517 post. This power applies also to any document transmitted to the Commissioners under s 9 and kept by them under s 9(3) (see para 500 post) as if the document had been deposited with them for safe keeping under s 30: s 30(5). As to evidence of such documents see para 341 post.

**341. Evidence of documents.** Evidence of the contents of a document enrolled by or deposited with the Charity Commissioners[1] may be given by means of a copy certified by an officer of theirs generally or specially authorised by them to act for this purpose. A document[2] purporting to be such a copy must be received in evidence without proof of the official position, authority or handwriting of the person certifying it, or of the original document being enrolled or deposited[3].

1    Ie under the Charities Act 1993 s 30: see para 340 ante. As to the Charity Commissioners see paras 486–512 post.
2    For the meaning of 'document' see para 236 note 2 ante.
3    Charities Act 1993 s 30(3). This also applies to any document transmitted to the Commissioners under s 9 and kept by them under s 9(3) (see para 500 post) as if the document had been deposited with them for safe keeping under s 30: s 30(5).

## (vi)  Notices

**342. Service of notices.** All notices required or authorised by the trusts[1] of a charity[2] to be given to a charity trustee[3], member or subscriber may be sent by post, addressed to any address given as his in the list of charity trustees, members or subscribers for the time being in use at the principal office of the charity[4]. If the charity trustee, member or subscriber has no address in the United Kingdom on that list, no notice of an election or meeting need be given even though required by the trusts of the charity[5]. Where any such notice required is given by post, it is deemed to have been given at the time when the letter containing it would be delivered in the ordinary course of post[6].

1    For the meaning of 'trusts' see para 210 note 5 ante.
2    For the meaning of 'charity' see para 1 ante.
3    For the meaning of 'charity trustees' see para 1 note 10 ante.
4    Charities Act 1993 s 81(1).
5    Ibid s 81(3).
6    Ibid s 81(2).

## (3) MANAGEMENT OF TRUST PROPERTY

### (i) Disposal of Property

**343. Restrictions on dispositions of charity land.** The Charities Act 1992 made new provisions with respect to restrictions on the disposition of land held in trust for a charity and on the charging of charity property, which are consolidated in the Charities Act 1993[1]. The basic rule that no land held by or in trust for a charity may be sold, leased or otherwise disposed of without an order of the court or of the Charity Commissioners[2] is subject to important exceptions[3], as a result of which many transactions can take place without an order being obtained. The basic rule does not apply to a disposition of such land if the disposition is made to person who is not a connected person, or a trustee for, or nominee of, a connected person[4]. 'Connected person', in relation to a charity, means[5]: (1) a charity trustee or trustee for a charity[6]; (2) a person who is the donor of any land to the charity[7]; (3) a child[8], parent, grandchild, grandparent, brother or sister of any such trustee or donor[9]; (4) an officer, agent or employee of the charity[10]; (5) the spouse[11] of any person falling within any of heads (1) to (4) above[12]; (6) an institution which is controlled[13] by any person falling within any of heads (1) to (5) above, or by two or more such persons taken together[14]; or (7) a body corporate in which any connected person falling within any of heads (1) to (6) above has a substantial interest, or two or more such persons, taken together, have a substantial interest[15].

Where the disposition is made to a person other than a connected person or a trustee for, or nominee of a connected person, an order is not required where, before entering into the agreement for the sale, or as the case may be, for the lease or other disposition of the land[16], the charity trustees comply with the following requirements[17], namely, that they: (a) obtain and consider a written report on the proposed disposition from a qualified surveyor[18] instructed by the trustees and acting exclusively for the charity[19]; (b) advertise the proposed disposition for such period and in such manner as the surveyor has advised in his report[20]; and (c) decide that they are satisfied, having considered the surveyor's report, that the terms on which the disposition is proposed to be made are the best that can reasonably be obtained for the charity[21].

The requirements are modified where the proposed disposition is the granting of a lease for a term ending not more than seven years after it is granted, other than one granted wholly or partly in consideration of a fine[22]. In this case the above requirements[23] do not apply, but the charity trustees must, before entering into the agreement for the lease, obtain and consider the advice on the proposed disposition of a person who is reasonably believed by the trustees to have the requisite ability and practical experience to provide them with competent advice thereon[24]. The charity trustees must also decide that they are satisfied, having considered that person's advice, that the terms on which the disposition is proposed to be made are the best that can reasonably be obtained for the charity[25].

Where any land is held by or in trust for a charity and the trusts[26] on which it is held stipulate that it is to be used for the purposes, or for any particular purposes, of the charity, the land must not be sold, leased or otherwise disposed of unless the charity trustees have previously given public notice of the proposed disposition, inviting representations to be made to them[27], and taken into consideration any representations duly made to them about the proposed disposition[28]. This requirement does not, however, apply if the disposition is to be effected with a view to acquiring by way of replacement other property to be held on the same trusts[29]. Nor does it apply if the disposition is the granting of a lease for a term ending not more than two years after it is granted, other than one granted wholly or partly in consideration of a fine[30]. Moreover, the Charity Commissioners may direct that this requirement is not to apply to dispositions of land held by or in trust for a charity or class of charities[31], or that it is not to apply to a particular disposition of land held by or in trust for a charity[32]. Such a direction may be given if, on an application made to them in writing by or on behalf of the charity or charities in question, the Commissioners are satisfied that it would be in the interests of the charity or charities for them to do so[33].

All these restrictions on disposition apply notwithstanding anything in the trusts of a charity[34]. They do not apply, however, to: (i) any disposition for which general or special authority is expressly given[35] by any statutory provision contained in or having effect under an Act of Parliament or by any scheme legally established[36]; or (ii) to any disposition of land held by or in trust for a charity which is made to another charity otherwise than for the best price that can reasonably be obtained, and is authorised to be so made by the trusts of the first mentioned charity[37]; or (iii) to the granting, by or on behalf of a charity and in accordance with its trusts, of a lease to any beneficiary under those trusts, where the lease is granted otherwise than for the best rent that can reasonably be obtained and is intended to enable the demised premises to be occupied for the purposes, or any particular purposes, of the charity[38].

None of the above provisions applies to any disposition of land held by or in trust for an exempt charity[39], to any disposition of land by way of mortgage or other security, or to any disposition of an advowson[40].

1   See the Charities Act 1992 ss 32–36 (repealed, except for s 36): see now the Charities Act 1993 ss 36–39. Any provision establishing or regulating a particular charity and contained in, or having effect under, any Act of Parliament, or contained in the trusts of a charity, has ceased to have effect if and to the extent that it provides for dispositions of, or other dealings with, land in England and Wales held by or in trust for the charity to require the consent of the Charity Commissioners, whether signified by order or otherwise: Charities Act 1992 s 36(1), (3). Similarly, any provision of an order or scheme under the Education Acts 1944 (repealed: see now the Education Act 1996) or Education Act 1973 (see EDUCATION) relating to a charity has ceased to have effect if and to the extent that it requires in relation to any sale, lease or other disposition of land in England or Wales held by or in trust for the charity, approval by the Commissioners or the Secretary of State of the amount payable in respect of the sale, lease or disposition: Charities Act 1992 s 36(2), (3). As to the Charity Commissioners see paras 486–512 post. As to the Secretary of State see para 513 post.
2   Charities Act 1993 s 36(1). For these purposes, 'land' means land in England and Wales: s 36(11). For the meaning of 'the court' see para 168 note 12 ante.
3   Ie the exceptions contained in ibid ss 36(2)–(11), 40.
4   Ibid s 36(2)(a).
5   Ibid s 36(2), Sch 5 para 1.
6   Ibid Sch 5 para 1(a). For the meaning of 'charity trustees' see para 1 note 10 ante. For the meaning of 'charity' see para 1 ante.
7   Ibid Sch 5 para 1(b). This applies whether the gift was made on or after the establishment of the charity: Sch 5 para 1(b).
8   'Child' includes a stepchild and an illegitimate child: ibid Sch 5 para 2(1).
9   Ibid Sch 5 para 1(c).
10  Ibid Sch 5 para 1(d).
11  A person living with another as that person's husband or wife is treated as that person's spouse: ibid Sch 5 para 2(2).
12  Ibid Sch 5 para 1(e).

13 A person controls an institution if he is able to secure that the affairs of the institution are conducted in accordance with his wishes: ibid Sch 5 para 3.

14 Ibid Sch 5 para 1(f).

15 Ibid Sch 5 para 1(g). A connected person has a substantial interest in a body corporate if the person or institution in question: (1) is interested in shares comprised in the equity share capital of that body of a nominal value of more than one-fifth of that share capital; or (2) is entitled to exercise, or control the exercise of, more than one-fifth of the voting power at any general meeting of that body: Sch 5 para 4(1). The rules relating to the interpretation of 'connected person' set out in the Companies Act 1985 Sch 13 Pt I (as amended) apply for the purposes of the Charities Act 1993 Sch 5 para 4(1) as they apply for the purposes of the Companies Act 1985 s 346(4), and the terms 'equity share capital' and 'share' have the same meaning as in that Act: Charities Act 1993 Sch 5 para 4(2), (3). See COMPANIES vol 7(1) (1996 Reissue) paras 565, 568, 607.

16 This applies except where the proposed disposition is the granting of a lease for not more than seven years under ibid s 36(5) (see text and notes 22–25 infra): see s 36(3).

17 Ibid s 36(2), (3).

18 A person is a qualified surveyor if (1) he is a fellow or professional associate of the Royal Institution of Chartered Surveyors or of the Incorporated Society of Valuers and Auctioneers or satisfies such other requirement or requirements as may be prescribed by regulations made by the Secretary of State; and (2) he is reasonably believed by the charity trustees to have ability in, and experience of, the valuation of land of the particular kind, and in the particular area, in question: ibid s 36(4)(a), (b). Any report must contain such information, and deal with such matters, as may be prescribed by regulations: s 36(4). At the date at which this volume states the law no such regulations had been made under s 36(4) but, by virtue of the Interpretation Act s 17(2)(b), the Charities (Qualified Surveyors' Reports) Regulations 1992, SI 1992/2980, have effect as if made under it. As to the Charities (Qualified Surveyors' Reports) Regulations 1992, SI 1992/2980 see para 344 post. As to the making of regulations generally see the Charities Act 1993 s 86 (as amended); and para 517 post.

19 Ibid s 36(3)(a).

20 Ibid s 36(3)(b). This provision applies unless the surveyor has advised in his report that it would not be in the best interests of the charity to advertise the proposed disposition: s 36(3)(b).

21 Ibid s 36(3)(c).

22 Ibid s 36(5).

23 Ie those under ibid s 36(3): see the text and notes 17–21 supra.

24 Ibid s 36(5)(a).

25 Ibid s 36(5)(b).

26 For the meaning of 'trusts' see para 210 note 5 ante.

27 The notice must specify a time within which representations must be made, being not less than one month from the date of the notice: Charities Act 1993 s 36(6)(i).

28 Ibid s 36(6). This provision is expressed to be subject to s 36(7), (8) (see the text and notes 29–33 infra): see s 36(6).

29 Ibid s 36(7)(a).

30 Ibid s 36(7)(b).

31 Whether generally or only in the case of a specified class of dispositions or land, or otherwise as may be provided in the direction: ibid s 36(8)(a).

32 Ibid s 36(8)(a), (b).

33 Ibid s 36(8).

34 Ibid s 36(9).

35 Without the authority being made subject to the sanction of an order of the court: ibid s 36(9)(a).

36 Ibid s 36(9)(a). See also *Sales of land: Powers of sale and leasing conferred by scheme and the effect of sections 36(1) of the Charities Act 1992 and 36(9)(a) of the Charities Act 1993 (1994)* Decisions of the Charity Commissioners (1997) vol 5 p 21.

37 Charities Act 1993 s 36(9)(b).

38 Ibid s 36(9)(c).

39 As to exempt charities see para 293 ante.

40 Charities Act 1993 s 36(10). As to advowsons see ECCLESIASTICAL LAW vol 14 para 776.

**344. Information to be contained in, and matters to be dealt with ·by, qualified surveyors' reports.** A surveyor's report prepared for the purposes of enabling the disposal of land held by or in trust for a charity[1] (otherwise than with an order of the court or of the Charity Commissioners[2]) must contain such information and deal with such matters as are prescribed[3] together with such other information and such other matters as the surveyor[4] believes should be drawn to the attention of the charity trustees[5]. The report must contain a description of the relevant land[6] and its location, which includes the measurements of the relevant land, its current use, the number of buildings, if any, included in the relevant land, the measurements of any such buildings, and the number of rooms in any such buildings and the measurements of those rooms[7]. Where any such information required may be clearly given by means of a plan, it may be so given and any such plan need not be drawn to scale[8].

Further information required includes whether the relevant land, or any part of it, is leased by or from the charity trustees and, if it is, details of[9]:

(1)   the length of the lease and the period of it which is outstanding[10];

(2)   the rent payable under the lease[11];

(3)   any service charge which is so payable[12];

(4)   the provisions in the lease for any review of the rent payable under it or any service charge so payable[13];

(5)   the liability under the lease for repairs and dilapidations[14]; and

(6) · any other provision in the lease which, in the opinion of the surveyor, affects the value of the relevant land[15].

The report must further provide information on whether the relevant land is subject to the burden of, or enjoys the benefit of, any easement or restrictive covenant[16] or is subject to any annual or other periodic sum charged on, or issuing out of, the land except rent reserved by a lease or tenancy[17]. It must deal with whether any buildings included in the relevant land are in good repair and, if not, the surveyor's advice: (a) as to whether or not it would be in the best interests of the charity for repairs to be carried out prior to the proposed disposition; (b) as to what those repairs, if any, should be; and (c) as to the estimated cost of any repairs he advises[18]. The report must also include where, in the opinion of the surveyor, it would be in the best interests of the charity to alter any buildings included in the relevant land prior to disposition, because, for example, adaptations to the buildings for their current use are not such as to command the best market price on the proposed disposition, that opinion and an estimate of the outlay required for any alterations which he suggests[19].

The report must further contain advice as to the manner of disposing of the relevant land so that the terms on which it is disposed of are the best that can reasonably be obtained for the charity, including[20]:

(i)    where appropriate, a recommendation that the land should be divided for the purposes of the disposition[21];

(ii)   unless the surveyor's advice is that it would not be in the best interests of the charity to advertise the proposed disposition, the period for which and the manner in which the proposed disposition should be advertised[22];

(iii)  where the surveyor's advice is that it would not be in the best interests of the charity to advertise the proposed disposition, his reasons for that advice, for example, that the proposed disposition is the renewal of a lease to someone who enjoys statutory protection or that he believes someone with a special interest in acquiring the relevant land will pay considerably more than the market price for it[23]; and

(iv) any view the surveyor may have on the desirability or otherwise of delaying the proposed disposition and, if he believes such delay is desirable, what the period of that delay should be[24].

Where the surveyor feels able to give such advice and where such advice is relevant, the report must contain advice as to the chargeability or otherwise of value added tax on the proposed disposition and the effect of such advice on the valuations given under heads (A) to (E) below[25]. Where either the surveyor does not feel able to give such advice or such advice is not in his opinion relevant, a statement to that effect must be included in the report[26].

The report must also include the surveyor's opinion as to:

(A) the current value of the relevant land having regard to its current state of repair and current circumstances, such as the presence of a tenant who enjoys statutory protection, or, where the proposed disposition is a lease, the rent which could be obtained under it having regard to such matters[27];

(B) what the value of the relevant land or what the rent under the proposed disposition would be where he has given advice[28] if that advice is followed, or where he has expressed an opinion[29] if that opinion is acted upon, or if both that advice is followed and that opinion is acted upon[30];

(C) where he has made a recommendation under head (i) above, the increase in the value of the relevant land or rent in respect of it if the recommendation were followed[31];

(D) where his advice is that it would not be in the best interests of the charity to advertise the proposed disposition because he believes a higher price can be obtained by not doing so, the amount by which that price exceeds the price that could be obtained if the proposed disposition were advertised[32]; and

(E) where he has advised a delay in the proposed disposition under head (iv) above, the amount by which he believes the price which could be obtained consequent on such a delay exceeds the price that could be obtained without it[33].

Where the surveyor is of the opinion that the proposed disposition is not in the best interests of the charity because it is not a disposition that makes the best use of the relevant land, the report must include that opinion and the reasons for it, together with his advice as to the type of disposition which would constitute the best use of the land, including such advice as may be relevant as to the prospects of buying out any sitting tenant or of succeeding in an application for change of use of the land[34] under the laws relating to town and country planning[35].

1   Ie a report for the purposes of the Charities Act 1993 s 36(3) (see para 343 ante) or where the Charities Act 1993 s 36(5) (see para 343 ante) applies: Charities (Qualified Surveyors' Reports) Regulations 1992, SI 1992/2980, reg 2; Interpretation Act 1978 s 17(2)(b). For the meaning of 'charity' see para 1 ante.
2   As to the Charity Commissioners see paras 486–512 post.
3   Ie prescribed by the Charities (Qualified Surveyors' Reports) Regulations 1992, SI 1992/2980, reg 2, Schedule: see the text and notes 7–35 infra.
4   'The surveyor' means the qualified surveyor from whom such a report is being obtained: ibid reg 1(2).
5   Ibid reg 2. For the meaning of 'charity trustees' see para 1 note 10 ante.
6   'Relevant land' means the land in respect of which a report is being obtained for the purposes of the Charities Act 1993 s 36(3) (see para 343 ante): Charities (Qualified Surveyors' Reports) Regulations 1992, SI 1992/2980, reg 1(2); Interpretation Act 1978 s 17(2)(b).
7   Charities (Qualified Surveyors' Reports) Regulations 1992, SI 1992/2980, Schedule para 1(1).
8   Ibid Schedule para 1(2).

9    Ibid Schedule para 2.
10   Ibid Schedule para 2(a).
11   Ibid Schedule para 2(b).
12   Ibid Schedule para 2(c).
13   Ibid Schedule para 2(d).
14   Ibid Schedule para 2(e).
15   Ibid Schedule para 2(f).
16   As to easements and restrictive covenants see EASEMENTS AND PROFITS À PRENDRE.
17   Charities (Qualified Surveyors' Reports) Regulations 1992, SI 1992/2980, Schedule para 3.
18   Ibid Schedule para 4.
19   Ibid Schedule para 5.
20   Ibid Schedule para 6.
21   Ibid Schedule para 6(a).
22   Ibid Schedule para 6(b).
23   Ibid Schedule para 6(c).
24   Ibid Schedule para 6(d).
25   Ibid Schedule para 7(1).
26   Ibid Schedule para 7(2).
27   Ibid Schedule para 8(a).
28   Ie under ibid Schedule para 4: see the text to note 18 supra.
29   Ie under ibid Schedule para 5: see the text to note 19 supra.
30   Ibid Schedule para 8(b).
31   Ibid Schedule para 8(c).
32   Ibid Schedule para 8(d).
33   Ibid Schedule para 8(e).
34   As to a material change of use of the land see TOWN AND COUNTRY PLANNING vol 46 (Reissue) para 149.
35   Charities (Qualified Surveyors' Reports) Regulations 1992, SI 1992/2980, Schedule para 9. See generally TOWN AND COUNTRY PLANNING.

**345. Supplementary provisions relating to dispositions of charity land.**     Any contract for the sale, or for a lease or other disposition, of land[1] which is held by or in trust for a charity[2], and any conveyance, transfer, lease or other instrument effecting a disposition of such land[3], must state: (1) that the land is held by or in trust for a charity[4]; (2) whether the charity is an exempt charity[5] and whether the disposition is one excepted[6] from the statutory restrictions[7]; and (3) if it is not an exempt charity and the disposition is not one so excepted, that the land is land to which the statutory restrictions[8] apply[9].

Where any land held by or in trust for a charity is sold, leased or otherwise disposed of[10], the charity trustees[11] must certify in the instrument by which the disposition is effected: (a) in a case where an order of the court or of the Charity Commissioners is required[12], that the disposition has been sanctioned by an order of the court or of the Commissioners, as the case may be[13]; or (b) in a case where such an order is not required[14], that the charity trustees have power under the trusts of the charity to effect the disposition, and that they have complied with the statutory provisions so far as applicable to it[15]. In the case of a duly certified disposition it is conclusively presumed, in favour of a person who (whether under the disposition or afterwards) acquires an interest in the land for money or money's worth that the facts were as stated in the certificate[16].

Where a disposition is not duly certified[17], and any land held by or in trust for a charity is sold, leased or otherwise disposed of by a disposition to which these provisions apply[18], the disposition will nevertheless be valid in favour of a person who (whether under the disposition or afterwards) in good faith acquires an interest in the land for money or money's worth[19]. This is so whether or not the disposition has been sanctioned by an order of the court or of the Commissioners, or whether or not the charity trustees have power under the trusts of the charity to effect the disposition and have complied with the statutory provisions so far applicable to it[20].

Any contract for the sale, or for a lease or other disposition, of land which will, as a result of the disposition, be held by or in trust for a charity, and any conveyance, transfer, lease or other instrument effecting a disposition of such land[21] must state: (i) that the land will, as a result of the disposition, be held by or in trust for a charity[22]; (ii) whether the charity is an exempt charity[23]; and (iii) if it is not an exempt charity, that the statutory restrictions on disposition[24] will apply to the land[25].

There are additional provisions in relation to the Land Registration Act 1925. Where the conveyance, transfer, lease or other instrument[26] effecting a disposition of land[27] is a registered disposition[28], or where it will on taking effect be an instrument falling within statutory provisions relating to the compulsory registration of title[29], the statement required to be contained in the instrument[30] must be in the prescribed[31] form[32]. Where: (A) an application is duly made for registration of a disposition of registered land[33] or for the registration of a person's title under a disposition of unregistered land[34]; and (B) the instrument by which the disposition is effected contains the statutory[35] statement[36]; and (C) the charity by or in trust for which the land is held as a result of the disposition is not an exempt charity[37], the registrar must enter in the register a restriction in the prescribed form[38]. Where any such restriction is entered in the register in respect of any land, and the charity by or in trust for which the land is held becomes an exempt charity, the charity trustees must apply to the registrar for the restriction to be withdrawn[39]. On receiving any application duly made, the registrar must withdraw the restriction[40]. Conversely, where any registered land is held by or in trust for an exempt charity and the charity ceases to be an exempt charity, or where any registered land becomes, as a result of a declaration of trust by the registered proprietor[41], land held in trust for a charity (other than an exempt charity), the charity trustees must apply to the registrar for the entry of a restriction in the prescribed form and, on receiving an application duly made, the registrar must enter it accordingly[42].

Where there is a conveyance of land[43] held on charitable trusts, if neither of the mandatory provisions for inclusion in contracts and dispositive instruments[44] or mortgages[45] applies the conveyance must state the land is held on such trusts and if neither of these provisions has been complied with in relation to the conveyance and a purchaser has notice that the land is held on such trusts, he must see that any consents or orders necessary to authorise the transaction have been obtained[46].

---

1  For these purposes, references to a disposition of land do not include references to a disposition of land by way of mortgage or other security, any disposition of an advowson, or any release of a rentcharge falling within the Charities Act 1993 s 40(1) (see para 348 post): s 37(11)(a). 'Land' means land in England and Wales: s 37(11)(b). As to advowsons see ECCLESIASTICAL LAW vol 14 para 776.

2  For the meaning of 'charity' see para 1 ante.

3  Charities Act 1993 s 37(1)(a), (b).

4  Ibid s 37(1)(i).

5  As to exempt charities see para 293 ante.

6  Ie excepted by the Charities Act 1993 s 36(9)(a), (b) or (c): see para 343 text and notes 35–38 ante.

7  Ibid s 37(1)(ii). The statutory restrictions referred to in the text are the restrictions contained in s 36 (see para 343 ante): see s 37(1)(ii).

8  See note 7 supra.

9    Charities Act 1993 s 37(1)(iii). For the form of statement required by this provision see the Land Registration Rules 1925, SI 1925/1093, r 62 (as substituted); and LAND REGISTRATION vol 26 (Reissue) para 769.

10   Ie by a disposition falling within the Charities Act 1993 s 36(1) or (2): see para 343 ante.

11   For the meaning of 'charity trustees' see para 1 note 10 ante.

12   Ie where the case falls within the Charities Act 1993 s 36(1): see para 343 ante. As to the Charity Commissioners see paras 486–512 post. For the meaning of the 'the court' see para 168 note 12 ante.

13   Ibid s 37(2)(a).

14   Ie where the case falls within ibid s 36(2): see para 343 ante.

15   Ibid s 37(2).

16   See ibid s 37(3).

17   Ie under ibid s 37(2): see the text and notes 10–15 supra.

18   Ie under ibid s 36(1), (2): see para 343 ante.

19   Ibid s 37(4).

20   Ibid s 37(4).

21   Ibid s 37(5)(a), (b).

22   Ibid s 37(5)(i).

23   Ibid s 37(5)(ii).

24   Ie imposed by ibid s 36: see para 343 ante. The provisions of s 36, subject to s 36(9), apply to the land: s 37(5).

25   Ibid s 37(5). For the form of statement required see the Land Registration Rules 1925, SI 1925/1093, r 61 (as substituted and amended); and LAND REGISTRATION vol 26 (Reissue) para 769.

26   'Instrument' has the same meaning as in the Land Registration Act 1925 s 3: see LAND REGISTRATION.

27   Ie under the Charities Act 1993 s 37(1)(b) or (5)(b): see the text and notes 3, 21 supra.

28   'Registered disposition' has the same meaning as in the Land Registration Act 1925 s 3: see LAND REGISTRATION.

29   Ie under the Land Registration Act 1925 s 123A (as added): see LAND REGISTRATION.

30   Ie under the Charities Act 1993 s 37(1) or (5): see the text and notes 1–9, 21–25 supra.

31   'Prescribed' has the same meaning as in the Land Registration Act 1925 s 3: see LAND REGISTRATION.

32   Charities Act 1993 s 37(7) (amended by the Land Registration Act 1997 s 4(1), Sch 1 para 6(1)). The Charities Act 1993 s 37(7) (as amended) is to be construed as one with the Land Registration Act 1925: Charities Act 1993 s 37(11); and see LAND REGISTRATION.

33   'Registered land' has the same meaning as in the Land Registration Act 1925 s 3: see LAND REGISTRATION.

34   Charities Act 1993 s 37(8)(a).

35   Ie complying with ibid s 37(5), (7): see the text and notes 21–32 supra.

36   Ibid s 37(8)(b).

37   Ibid s 37(8)(c).

38   Ibid s 37(8). Section 37(8) is to be construed as one with the Land Registration Act 1925: Charities Act 1993 s 37(11); and see LAND REGISTRATION. As to the registrar see LAND REGISTRATION vol 26 (Reissue) para 1203 et seq

39   Ibid s 37(9).

40   Ibid s 37(9). Section 37(9) is to be construed as one with the Land Registration Act 1925: Charities Act 1993 s 37(11); and see LAND REGISTRATION.

41   'Proprietor' has the same meaning as in the Land Registration Act 1925 s 3: see LAND REGISTRATION.

42   Charities Act 1993 s 37(10). Section 37(10) is to be construed as one with the Land Registration Act 1925: Charities Act 1993 s 37(11); and see LAND REGISTRATION.

43   This applies to land other than land to which the Universities and College Estates Act 1925 applies (see EDUCATION): Trusts of Land and Appointment of Trustees Act 1996 s 2, Sch 1 para 4(1).

44   Ie the Charities Act 1993 s 37(1): see the text and notes 1–9 supra.

45   Ie ibid s 39(1): see para 347 post.

46   See the Trusts of Land and Appointment of Trustees Act 1996 Sch 1 para 4(1), (2); and SETTLEMENTS vol 42 (Reissue) para 677. Where any trustees or the majority of any set of trustees have power to transfer or create any legal estate in the land, the estate must be transferred or created by them in the names and on behalf of the persons in whom it is vested: Sch 1 para 4(3).

**346. Restrictions on mortgaging charity land.** The basic rule is that no mortgage[1] of land[2] held by or in trust for a charity[3] is to be granted without an order of the court[4]

or of the Charity Commissioners[5]. However, this does not apply to a mortgage of any such land by way of security for the repayment of a loan where the charity trustees[6] have, before executing the mortgage, obtained and considered proper advice, given to them in writing, on the following matters, namely[7]: (1) whether the proposed loan is necessary in order for the charity trustees to be able to pursue the particular course of action in connection with which the loan is sought by them[8]; (2) whether the terms of the proposed loan are reasonable having regard to the status of the charity as a prospective borrower[9]; and (3) the ability of the charity to repay on those terms the sum proposed to be borrowed[10].

For these purposes, proper advice is the advice of a person who is reasonably believed by the charity trustees to be qualified by his ability in and practical experience of financial matters, and who has no financial interest in the making of the loan in question[11]. Such advice may constitute proper advice notwithstanding that the person giving it does so in the course of his employment as an officer or employee of the charity or of the charity trustees[12].

These provisions apply notwithstanding anything in the trusts[13] of a charity, but they do not apply to a mortgage for which general or special authority is expressly given (without the authority being made subject to the sanction of an order of the court) by any statutory provision contained in or having effect under an Act of Parliament or by any scheme legally established[14].

1 'Mortgage' includes a charge: Charities Act 1993 s 38(6). As to mortgages generally see MORTGAGE.
2 For these purposes, 'land' means land in England and Wales: ibid s 38(6).
3 For the meaning of 'charity' see para 1 ante.
4 For the meaning of the 'the court' see para 168 note 12 ante.
5 Charities Act 1993 s 38(1). Nothing in s 38 applies to an exempt charity: s 38(7). As to exempt charities see para 293 ante. See also the Charities Act 1992 s 36, which removes certain requirements under statutory provisions for consent to dealings with charity land; and para 343 note 1 ante. As to the Charity Commissioners see paras 486–512 post.
6 For the meaning of 'charity trustees' see para 1 note 10 ante.
7 Charities Act 1993 s 38(2).
8 Ibid s 38(3)(a).
9 Ibid s 38(3)(b).
10 Ibid s 38(3)(c).
11 Ibid s 38(4).
12 Ibid s 38(4).
13 For the meaning of 'trusts' see para 210 note 5 ante.
14 Charities Act 1993 ss 36(9)(a), 38(5).

**347. Supplementary provisions relating to mortgaging of charity land.** Any mortgage[1] of land[2] held by or in trust for a charity[3] must state[4]: (1) that the land is held by or in trust for a charity[5]; (2) whether the charity is an exempt charity[6] and whether the mortgage is one for which general or special authority is expressly given[7] (without the authority being made subject to the sanction of an order of the court) by any statutory provision contained in or having effect under an Act of Parliament or by any scheme legally established[8]; and (3) if it is not an exempt charity and it does not fall within head (2) above, that the mortgage is one to which the statutory restrictions[9] apply[10].

Where any such mortgage will be one falling within the statutory provisions relating to the requirements of compulsory registration[11] the statement required[12] must be in such form as may be prescribed and, if the charity is not an exempt charity, the mortgage must also contain a statement, in such form as may be prescribed, that the restrictions on disposition[13] apply to the land[14]. Where an application is duly made for registration of a person's title to land in connection with such a mortgage falling within the statutory provisions relating to the requirements of compulsory registration[15], the mortgage contains statements complying with the above provisions[16], and the charity is not an exempt charity, the registrar must enter in the register, in respect of the land, a restriction in such form as may be prescribed[17].

Where the restrictions on mortgaging[18] apply to any mortgage of land held by or in trust for a charity, the charity trustees[19] must certify in the mortgage: (a) in the case where an order of the court[20] or the Charity Commissioners[21] is required[22], that the mortgage has been sanctioned by an order of the court or of the Commissioners[23]; or (b) in a case where such an order is not required[24], that the charity trustees have power under the trusts of the charity to grant the mortgage, and that they have obtained and considered proper advice[25]. In the case of a duly certified mortgage it is conclusively presumed, in favour of a person who (whether under the mortgage or afterwards) acquires an interest in the land in question for money or money's worth, that the facts were as stated in the certificate[26]. Where a disposition is not duly certified, and the restrictions on mortgaging[27] apply to any mortgage of land held by or in trust for a charity it will nevertheless be valid in favour of a person who (whether under the mortgage or afterwards) in good faith acquires an interest in the land for money or money's worth[28]. This is so whether or not the mortgage has been sanctioned by an order of the court or of the Commissioners, or whether or not the charity trustees have power under the trusts of the charity to grant the mortgage and have obtained and considered proper advice[29].

1   'Mortgage' includes a charge, and 'mortgagee's is to be construed accordingly: Charities Act 1993 s 39(6). As to mortgages generally see MORTGAGE.
2   For these purposes, 'land' means land in England and Wales: ibid s 39(6).
3   For the meaning of 'charity' see para 1 ante.
4   Charities Act 1993 s 39(1). Where the mortgage will be a registered disposition the statement must be in the prescribed form: s 39(1). 'Prescribed' and 'registered disposition' have the same meaning as in the Land Registration Act 1925 s 3: see LAND REGISTRATION. The Charities Act 1993 s 39(1) is to be construed as one with the Land Registration Act 1925: Charities Act 1993 s 39(6) (amended by the Land Registration Act 1997 s 4(1), Sch 1 para 6(3)); and see LAND REGISTRATION.
    As to a conveyance of land held on charitable trusts see the Trusts of Land and Appointment of Trustees Act 1996 s 2, Sch 1 para 4; and para 345 text and notes 44–46 ante.
5   Charities Act 1993 s 39(1)(a).
6   As to exempt charities see para 293 ante.
7   Ie a mortgage falling within the Charities Act 1993 s 38(5): see para 346 ante.
8   Ibid ss 36(9)(a), 39(1)(b).
9   Ie those imposed by ibid s 38: see para 346 ante.
10  Ibid s 39(1)(c).
11  Ie the Land Registration Act 1925 s 123(2) (as substituted): see LAND REGISTRATION vol 26 (Reissue) para 1196.
12  Ie under the Charities Act 1993 s 39(1): see the text and notes 2–10 supra.
13  Ie imposed under ibid s 36: see para 343 ante. The provisions of s 36, subject to s 36(9), apply to the land: s 39(1A) (added by the Land Registration Act 1997 s 4(1), Sch 1 para 6(2)).
14  Charities Act 1993 s 39(1A) (as added: see note 13 supra). Section 39(1A) (as added) is to be construed as one with the Land Registration Act 1925: Charities Act 1993 s 39(6) (amended by the Land Registration Act 1997 s 4(1), Sch 1 para 6(3)); and see LAND REGISTRATION.
15  See note 11 supra.
16  Ie the Charities Act 1993 s 39(1), (1A) (as added): see the text and notes 2–14 supra.
17  Ibid s 39(1B) (added by the Land Registration Act 1997 s 4(1), Sch 1 para 6(2)). The Charities Act 1993 s 37(9) (application by the trustees for restriction to be withdrawn) (see para 345 ante) applies in relation to any such restriction as it applies in relation to one entered in pursuance of s 37(8) (see para

345 ante): s 39(1B) (as added). Section 39(1B) (as added) is to be construed as one with the Land Registration Act 1925: Charities Act 1993 s 39(6) (amended by the Land Registration Act 1997 s 4(1), Sch 1 para 6(3)); and see LAND REGISTRATION. As to the registrar see LAND REGISTRATION vol 26 (Reissue) para 1203 et seq.

18  Ie the Charities Act 1993 s 38(1), (2): see para 346 ante.
19  For the meaning of 'charity trustees' see para 1 note 10 ante.
20  For the meaning of 'the court' see para 168 note 12 ante.
21  As to the Charity Commissioners see paras 486–512 post.
22  Ie where the Charities Act 1993 s 38(1) applies: see para 446 ante.
23  Ibid s 39(2)(a).
24  Ie where ibid s 38(2) applies: see para 446 ante.
25  Ibid s 39(2)(b). The reference to proper advice is a reference to the advice mentioned in s 38(2) (see para 446 text to notes 6–7 ante): see s 39(2).
26  Ibid s 39(3).
27  Ie under ibid s 38(1), (2): see para 446 ante.
28  Ibid s 39(4).
29  Ibid s 39(4). The reference to proper advice is a reference to the advice mentioned in s 38(2) (see para 446 text to notes 6–7 ante): see s 39(4).


**348. Release of charity rentcharges.** The restrictions on the disposition of charity land[1] do not apply to the release by a charity of a rentcharge which it is entitled to receive if the release is given in consideration of the payment of an amount which is not less than ten times the annual amount of the rentcharge[2], nor do they apply where a rentcharge which a charity is entitled to receive is redeemed under the provisions of the Rentcharges Act 1977[3]. Where a charity which is entitled to receive a rentcharge releases it in consideration of the payment of an amount not exceeding £500[4], any costs incurred by the charity in connection with proving its title are recoverable by the charity from the person or persons in whose favour the rentcharge is being released, but this provision does not apply where a rentcharge which a charity is entitled to receive is redeemed under the provisions of the Rentcharges Act 1977[5].

1  Ie those contained in the Charities Act 1993 s 36(1): see para 343 ante. For the meaning of 'charity' see para 1 ante.
2  Ibid s 40(1).
3  Ie the Rentcharges Act 1977 ss 8–10 (s 10 as amended): see RENTCHARGES AND ANNUITIES vol 39(2) (Reissue) paras 900–902.
4  The specified sum may be altered by the Secretary of State by order: Charities Act 1993 s 40(4). At the date at which this volume states the law no such order had been made. As to the making of orders generally see s 86 (as amended); and para 517 ante. As to the Secretary of State see para 513 post.
5  Ibid s 40(2), (3). The provisions of the Rentcharges Act 1977 referred to in the text are ss 8–10 (s 10 as amended) (see RENTCHARGES AND ANNUITIES vol 39(2) (Reissue) paras 900–902): Charities Act 1993 s 40(3).


**349. Powers to deal with charity land in relation to the Chequers Estate Act 1917 and the Chevening Estate Act 1959.** In relation to the deed of settlement set out in the Chequers Estate Act 1917[1] or the trust instrument set out in the Chevening Estate Act 1959[2], all land vested or to be vested in trustees on or for charitable, ecclesiastical or public trusts or purposes is deemed to be settled land[3], and in relation to that land the trustees have all the powers conferred by the Settled Land Act 1925 on a tenant for life and on the trustees of a settlement[4]. Where the land is vested in persons having no powers of management, the Settled Land Act powers are exercisable by the managing trustees or committee of management, and the persons in whom the land is vested are not liable for giving effect to directions given by the managing trustees or committee[5]. The Settled Land Act powers are exercisable subject to obtaining any consents or orders which would, apart from that Act, have been required for the exercise of an express power under the trust instrument[6]. These provisions of the Settled Land Act do not affect the jurisdiction of the court, Charity Commissioners, or other competent authority in regard to the administration of charitable and other trusts[7].

Any conveyance of land held on charitable, ecclesiastical or public trusts must state that the land is held on such trusts[8].

1   Ie in the Chequers Estate Act 1917 s 1, Schedule.
2   Ie in the Chevening Estate Act 1959 s 1, Schedule.
3   Ie for the purposes of the Settled Land Act 1925 s 29 (repealed) (see note 4 infra); see *Re Booth and Southend-on-Sea Estate Co's Contract* [1927] 1 Ch 579.
4   See the Settled Land Act 1925 s 29(1). Section 29 is repealed, except in relation to the deed of settlement set out in the Chequers Estate Act 1917 s 1, Schedule or the trust instrument set out in the Chevening Estate Act 1959 s 1, Schedule: Trusts of Land and Appointment of Trustees Act 1996 s 25(3). As to the powers under the Settled Land Act 1925 see paras 352–355 post. Section 29 (as amended) does not apply to consecrated land and buildings vested in an incumbent during his incumbency: *Re St Swithin's, Norwich* [1960] P 77, [1959] 3 All ER 301, Consistory Ct; and see ECCLESIASTICAL LAW vol 14 para 1074.
5   See the Settled Land Act 1925 s 29(2) (amended by the Charities Act 1960 s 48(2), Sch 7 Pt I). Where trustees, or a majority of them, have power to transfer or create any legal estate, it must be transferred or created by them in the names of the persons in whom the legal estate is vested: Settled Land Act 1925 s 29(5) (amended by the Charities Act 1960 s 48(2), Sch 7 Pt I (repealed)).
6   See the Settled Land Act 1925 s 29(2). Thus, an order of the court or of the Charity Commissioners is sometimes required before the Settled Land Act powers may be exercised: see the Charities Act 1993 s 36; and para 343 ante. Where a disposition or dealing is to be effected for less than full consideration in money, or where any interest in land is to be acquired, the same consent or order, if any, is required as if the intended transaction were a sale: Settled Land Act 1925 s 29(2) proviso. As to the Charity Commissioners see paras 486–512 post.
7   See ibid s 29(3).
8   Ibid s 29(1).

**350. Express powers.** Where a trust deed gives to the trustees powers of disposal wider than those under the Settled Land Act 1925, they are not cut down by that Act, nor need they be exercised in accordance with the provisions of that Act as if they were additional powers comprised in a settlement[1]. Nothing in that Act converts revenue into capital money[2]. The statutory restrictions on dispositions of charity land apply notwithstanding anything in the trusts of the charity[3].

Regulations made by the founders of old charities that rents should not be increased have been held ineffective in changed circumstances[4], but regulations fixing the maximum duration of leases were generally upheld[5].

1   *Re Booth and Southend-on-Sea Estate Co's Contract* [1927] 1 Ch 579 (power for a sole trustee to give a good receipt for purchase money).
2   *Re Booth and Southend-on-Sea Estate Co's Contract* [1927] 1 Ch 579 at 588 per Astbury J.
3   See the Charities Act 1993 s 36(9); and para 343 ante.
4   *Watson v Hinsworth Hospital* (1707) 2 Vern 596; *A-G v Catherine Hall, Cambridge* (1820) Jac 381.
5   *A-G v Griffith* (1807) 13 Ves 565; *Watson v Master, etc of Hemsworth Hospital* (1807) 14 Ves 324.

**351. Powers at common law.** Before the disposition of charity land was regulated by statute[1] it was held that charitable corporations and trustees had power to sell, lease or mortgage charity land, but that the transaction was liable to be set aside unless it was shown to be beneficial to the charity, the onus to establish that being on the purchaser[2]. It may be that transactions relating to property which could be dealt with as income were not vulnerable in this way[3].

It is not clear whether the statutory powers supersede the powers which existed at common law, but it is not safe for a purchaser to rely on the common law powers as authorising a transaction. In the absence of statutory power, special authority may be granted by the Charity Commissioners[4].

1   Ie before the Charitable Trusts Amendment Act 1855 (repealed).
2   See eg *A-G v Warren* (1818) 2 Swan 291; *President etc of St Mary Magdalen College, Oxford v A-G* (1857) 6 HL Cas 189; *A-G v South Sea Co* (1841) 4 Beav 453; *A-G v Brettingham* (1840) 3 Beav 91; *Re Clergy Orphan Corpn* [1894] 3 Ch 145, CA.
3   See *Re Clergy Orphan Corpn* [1894] 3 Ch 145 at 154, CA, obiter per Davey J.
4   Ie under the Charities Act 1993 s 26: see para 330 ante. As to the Charity Commissioners see paras 486–512 post.

**352. Statutory powers: sale and exchange.** The Settled Land Act powers enjoyed by charity trustees include power to sell the land, any part of it or any easement, right or privilege of any kind over or in relation to the land[1], and to make exchanges for other land or rights over or in relation to land, with or without the payment of money for equality of exchange[2]. Sales must be made for the best consideration in money that can reasonably be obtained[3], which may be in the form of a perpetual or terminable rent[4]. Exchanges must be made for the best consideration in land or in land and money that can reasonably be obtained[5].

1   See the Settled Land Act 1925 s 38(i); and SETTLEMENTS vol 42 (Reissue) para 827.
2   See ibid s 38(iii); and SETTLEMENTS vol 42 (Reissue) para 827.
3   See ibid s 39(1); and SETTLEMENTS vol 42 (Reissue) para 828. However, see also s 39(5) (fully paid shares as consideration on sale to company); and SETTLEMENTS vol 42 (Reissue) para 830.
4   See ibid s 39(2)–(4) (as amended); and SETTLEMENTS vol 42 (Reissue) paras 828–829.
5   See ibid s 40(1); and SETTLEMENTS vol 42 (Reissue) para 835.

**353. Statutory powers: leases.** The Settled Land Act powers include power to grant leases of the land, any part of it or right over or in relation to it, for any purpose for a term not exceeding 999 years in the case of a building or forestry lease, or 100 years in the case of a mining lease, or 50 years in the case of any other lease[1]. The lease must be made by deed, except in the case of a term of not more than three years, and must take effect in possession within one year or in reversion after a current term with seven years or less outstanding[2]. The best rent reasonably obtainable must be reserved, having regard to any fine taken[3] and to the circumstances generally[4], and there must be a covenant by the lessee to pay the rent and a condition of re-entry on non-payment[5]. A counterpart must be executed by the lessee and delivered to the trustees[6].

1   See the Settled Land Act 1925 s 41; and SETTLEMENTS vol 42 (Reissue) para 837. As to mining leases generally see MINES, MINERALS AND QUARRIES vol 31 (Reissue) para 322 et seq.

2    See ibid s 42(1)(i), (5)(ii); and SETTLEMENTS vol 42 (Reissue) para 839.
3    Any fine taken on a lease under the statutory powers is capital money: ibid s 42(4).
4    See ibid s 42(1)(ii); and SETTLEMENTS vol 42 (Reissue) para 839.
5    See ibid s 42(1)(iii); and SETTLEMENTS vol 42 (Reissue) para 839. In the case of a short lease in writing, there must be an agreement rather than a covenant: s 42(5)(ii).
6    See ibid s 42(2); and SETTLEMENTS vol 42 (Reissue) para 839.


**354. Statutory powers: mortgages.** The Settled Land Act 1925 only permits the legal estate in the land to be mortgaged for specified purposes, all of which relate to the well-being of the land, either by authorised improvements or by discharging incumbrances or other liabilities[1].

1    See the Settled Land Act 1925 s 71 (as amended); and SETTLEMENTS vol 42 (Reissue) paras 849–850. As to mortgages generally see MORTGAGES.


**355. Statutory powers: options.** The Settled Land Act powers include power to grant options over the land, any part of it or any right over or in relation to it, at a price which must be fixed at the time of granting the option[1] and must be the best reasonably obtainable in all the circumstances[2], to be exercisable within an agreed number of years not exceeding ten[3].

1    See the Settled Land Act 1925 s 51(1). See also SETTLEMENTS vol 42 (Reissue) para 871.
2    See ibid s 51(3).
3    See ibid s 51(2).


**356. Miscellaneous statutory powers.** Trustees holding land for charitable purposes may grant up to one acre of land for the purposes of the School Sites Act 1841[1]. They may also, with the consent of the Charity Commissioners[2], grant up to one acre of land as a site for a literary or scientific institution[3].

Where charity trustees, as landlords, are liable to pay compensation for improvements to their tenants, they are expressly empowered to grant a lease which relieves them from that liability[4].

1    See the School Sites Act 1841 ss 2 (as amended), 6 (as amended); and EDUCATION.
2    As to the Charity Commissioners see paras 486–512 post.
3    See the Literary and Scientific Institutions Act 1854 s 6 (as amended); and LIBRARIES AND OTHER SCIENTIFIC AND CULTURAL INSTITUTIONS vol 28 (Reissue) paras 486.
4    See the Landlord and Tenant Act 1927 s 14. For the circumstances in which such liability exists and the leases which may be granted see generally Pt I (ss 1–17) (as amended); and LANDLORD AND TENANT.


**357. Disposal by local authorities.** A principal council[1], parish and community councils[2], and the parish trustees of a parish acting with the consent of the parish meeting[3], may dispose of land held by them, including land held for charitable purposes, in any manner they wish[4]. However, this does not authorise local authorities to dispose of land in breach of any trust, covenant or agreement binding on them[5], or to dispose of charitable land without an order of the court or the Charity Commissioners, where such an order is required[6].

Capital money received by a parish or community council, or the parish trustees of a parish acting with the consent of the parish meeting in respect of a disposal of land held for charitable purposes must be applied in accordance with any directions given under the Charities Act 1993[7].

1 For the meaning of 'principal council' see the Local Government Act 1972 s 270(1); and LOCAL GOVERNMENT.
2 As to parish and community councils see LOCAL GOVERNMENT.
3 As to parish trustees and parish meeting see LOCAL GOVERNMENT.
4 See the Local Government Act 1972 ss 123(1), 127(1); and LOCAL GOVERNMENT. Unless the disposal is by way of short tenancy, the Secretary of State's consent is required if the disposal is for a consideration less than the best that could reasonably be expected: see ss 123(2), 127(2); and LOCAL GOVERNMENT.
5 See ibid s 131(1)(a); and LOCAL GOVERNMENT.
6 See the Charities Act 1993 s 36; the Local Government Act 1972 s 131(3) (as amended); para 343 ante; and LOCAL GOVERNMENT. In particular, the provisions of the Local Government Act 1972 ss 111–130 (as amended) are not to be treated as statutory authority under the Charities Act 1993 s 36(9)(a) enabling charitable property to be disposed of without an order: see the Local Government Act 1972 s 131(3) (as amended); and LOCAL GOVERNMENT. As to the Charity Commissioners see paras 486–512 post.
7 Ibid s 127(1), (4) (s 127(4) amended by the Charities Act 1993 Sch 6 para 12(3)). See also LOCAL GOVERNMENT. As to other local authorities see the Local Government and Housing Act 1989 Pt IV (ss 39–66) (as amended), especially ss 59(7), 60(1); and LOCAL GOVERNMENT. The Local Government Act 1972 s 123(6) (amended by the Charities Act 1993 Sch 6 para 12(3)), which made similar provision for principal councils, has been repealed for certain purposes (see the Local Government and Housing Act 1989 s 194, Sch 12 Pt I; and the Local Government and Housing Act 1989 (Commencement No 5 and Transitional Provisions) Order 1990, SI 1990/431, art 4, Sch 1 para 1).

**358. Compulsory purchase and tenant's right of first refusal.** Charity land is subject to compulsory purchase under statutory procedure[1], and charity trustees have express power to sell by agreement land which is subject to a compulsory purchase order[2]. If the purchase money on a compulsory purchase is paid into court[3], the acquiring authority is liable for the cost of investing the funds in court and may be ordered to pay the cost of reinvestment in land[4]. If the purchase is made by agreement, the acquiring authority may also have to bear the cost of reinvesting in land.

The collective right of first refusal given to qualifying tenants of flats to buy their landlord's interest if he proposes to dispose of it[5] does not apply to a disposal by way of gift to a charity, nor when the flats are the functional property of a charity which is being disposed of to another charity for functional purposes, nor where the landlord is a housing trust or a registered social landlord[6]. It does apply where flats held as investment property are to be disposed of[7].

1 For the procedure see the Compulsory Purchase Act 1965, which largely superseded the Lands Clauses Consolidation Act 1845; and COMPULSORY ACQUISITION OF LAND. Under the latter Act it was held that unless the statutory procedure was followed strictly owners of land under a disability, such as charity trustees, could not be forced to sell to the acquiring authority: *Wycombe Rly Co v Donnington Hospital* (1866) 1 Ch App 268; *Bridgend Gas and Water Co v Dunraven* (1885) 31 ChD 219.
2 See the Compulsory Purchase Act 1965 ss 2, 3 (as amended), Sch 1 para 2(2); and COMPULSORY ACQUISITION OF LAND vol 8(1) (Reissue) para 96. This power is probably superfluous in view of the other statutory powers of sale (see para 352 ante).
3 Ie under ibid ss 2, 3 (as amended), Sch 1 para 6(2): see COMPULSORY ACQUISITION OF LAND vol 8(1) (Reissue) para 156.
4 See ibid s 26(2); and COMPULSORY ACQUISITION OF LAND vol 8(1) (Reissue) para 148.

5   Ie under the Landlord and Tenant Act 1987: see generally LANDLORD AND TENANT.

6   See ibid ss 1(4), 4(1), (2)(f), 58(1)(f), (g) (s 58(1)(g) as substituted); and LANDLORD AND TENANT vol 27(2) (Reissue) para 1590 et seq.

7   Such a sale would not need the consent of the Commissioners under the Charities Act 1993 s 36 because it would be a transaction for which general or special authority had been given by Act of Parliament: see s 36(9)(a); para 343 ante; and *Report of the Charity Commissioners for England and Wales for 1987* (HC Paper (1987–88) no 427) App C(c).

## (ii) Investment

**359. Powers of investment.** The powers and duties of charity trustees in regard to the investment of funds belonging to the charity are, like those of private trustees in relation to private trusts, governed by any special provisions of the trust instrument extending or limiting their statutory powers. The investment clause contained in the trust instrument may, for example, be so drawn as not to permit investment in some securities authorised by law for the investment of trust funds[1]. On the other hand, if the trust instrument directs and requires trustees to make some specified investment, they are under a duty to do so even it is one of which they disapprove[2]. Subject to any express directions contained in that instrument[3], and to any conditions prescribed by it, the trustees may invest[4] the money in any manner authorised by it, provided that in making the selection they use proper care and caution, and avoids investments which are accompanied by risk[5].

Charity trustees should not allow their own personal opinions or moral judgements to affect their investment decisions[6]. If they consider that the charitable purposes for which the funds are held require that certain types of investment should be avoided or that an ethical investment policy is in the interests of the charity they may adopt such a policy but only in so far as this is compatible with obtaining the best possible financial return on capital[7].

1   See eg *Re Warren, Public Trustee v Fletcher* [1939] Ch 684, [1939] 2 All ER 599; *Re Rider's Will Trusts, Nelson v Rider* [1958] 3 All ER 135, [1958] 1 WLR 974.

2   *Beauclerk v Ashburnham* (1845) 8 Beav 322; *Cadogan v Earl of Essex* (1854) 2 Drew 227; *Re Hurst, Addison v Topp* (1890) 63 LT 665 (all private trust cases).

     As to the powers of investment under the Trustee Investments Act 1961 (repealed, except in so far as it is applied by another enactment) see para 363 post; and TRUSTS vol 48 (2000 Reissue) para 900 et seq. As to the statutory powers of investment under the Trustee Act 2000 see paras 360–362 post; and TRUSTS vol 48 (2000 Reissue) para 924 et seq.

3   *Beauclerk v Ashburnham* (1845) 8 Beav 322; *Cadogan v Earl of Essex* (1854) 2 Drew 227.

4   To 'invest' prima facie means to apply money in the purchase of some property from which interest or profit is expected and which property is purchased in order to be held for the sake of the income it will yield: *Re Wragg, Wragg v Palmer* [1919] 2 Ch 58 at 65 per Lawrence J; *Moss's Trustees v King* 1952 SC 523 at 527 per Lord President Cooper. The purchase of freehold land for some purpose other than the receipt of income is not an investment: *Re Power, Public Trustee v Hastings* [1947] Ch 572, [1947] 2 All ER 282. As to the mode of investment see TRUSTS vol 48 (2000 Reissue) para 895.

5   *Re Whiteley, Whiteley v Learoyd* (1886) 33 Ch D 347 at 353, CA, per Cotton LJ; affd sub nom *Learoyd v Whiteley* (1887) 12 App Cas 727 at 733, HL, per Lord Watson. As to consent and discretion in relation to investment see TRUSTS vol 48 (2000 Reissue) para 920.

6   *Cowan v Scargill* [1985] Ch 270 at 287–288, [1984] 2 All ER 750 per Megarry V-C.

7   *Harries v Church Comrs for England* [1993] 2 All ER 300, [1992] 1 WLR 1241.

**360. Statutory general power of investment.** The powers to make specified authorised investments given to trustees under the Trustee Investment Act 1961 have been largely repealed[1]. Under the Trustee Act 2000, a trustee may make any kind of investment that he could make if he were absolutely entitled to the assets of the trust[2]. This statutory power is called 'the general power of investment'[3]. The general power of investment does not permit a trustee to make investments in land other than in loans secured on land[4]. A person invests in a loan secured on land if he has rights under any contract under which one person provides another with credit[5] and the obligation of the borrower to repay is secured on land[6]. An investment for these purposes does not include an asset from which no profit or income is expected[7].

1 See para 363 post. As to the powers of investment under the Trustee Investments Act 1961 see para 363 et seq post; and TRUSTS vol 48 (2000 Reissue) para 900 et seq.
2 See the Trustee Act 2000 s 3(1); and TRUSTS vol 48 (2000 Reissue) para 924. As to statutory powers of investment under the Trustee Act 2000 see further TRUSTS vol 48 (2000 Reissue) para 924 et seq. Part II (ss 3–7), Pt III (ss 8–10) and Pt IV (ss 11–27) do not apply to (1) trustees of authorised unit trusts (s 37(1)); (2) trustees managing a fund under a common investment scheme made, or having effect as if made, under the Charities Act 1993 s 24 (see para 366 post), other than such a fund the trusts of which provide that property is not to be transferred to the fund except by or on behalf of a charity the trustees of which are the trustees appointed to manage the fund (Trustee Act 2000 s 38(a)); or (3) trustees managing a fund under a common deposit scheme made, or having effect as if made, under s 25 (see para 367 post) (s 38(b)): see TRUSTS vol 48 (2000 Reissue) para 924.
3 See ibid s 3(2); and TRUSTS vol 48 (2000 Reissue) para 924.
4 See ibid s 3(3); and TRUSTS vol 48 (2000 Reissue) para 924. As to the power to acquire freehold and leasehold land see s 8; and TRUSTS vol 48 (2000 Reissue) para 935.
5 'Credit' includes any cash loan or other financial accommodation: ibid s 3(5). 'Cash' includes money in any form: s 3(6).
6 See ibid s 3(4); and TRUSTS vol 48 (2000 Reissue) para 924.
7 See the cases cited in para 359 note 4 ante.

**361. Application of the general power of investment.** The general power of investment is in addition to powers conferred on trustees otherwise than by the Trustee Act 2000, but is subject to any restriction or exclusion imposed by the trust instrument or by any enactment or any provision of subordinate legislation[1].

The provisions relating to the general power of investment introduced by the Trustee Act 2000[2] apply in relation to trusts whether created before or after its commencement on 1 February 2001[3]. However, no provision relating to the powers of a trustee contained in an instrument made before 3 August 1961[4] is to be treated as restricting or excluding[5] the general power of investment[6]. A provision contained in a trust instrument made before 1 February 2001[7] which has effect under the Trustee Investment Act 1961[8] as a power to invest under that Act or confers power to invest under that Act is to be treated as conferring the general power of investment on a trustee[9].

Common investment funds for charities and common deposit funds[10] for charities fall outside the provisions dealing with the statutory general power of investment[11].

1 See the Trustee Act 2000 s 6(1); and TRUSTS vol 48 (2000 Reissue) para 924. For these purposes, an enactment or a provision of subordinate legislation is not to be regarded as being, or as being part of, a trust instrument: s 6(2). For the meaning of 'subordinate legislation' see s 6(3); and TRUSTS vol 48 (2000 Reissue) para 825.
2 Ie by ibid Pt II (ss 3–7): see TRUSTS vol 48 (2000 Reissue) para 924 et seq.
3 See ibid s 7(1); Trustee Act 2000 (Commencement) Order 2001, SI 2001/49 art 2; and TRUSTS vol 48 (2000 Reissue) para 924.

4   Ie the date of the commencement of the Trustee Investment Act 1961.
5   Ie under the Trustee Act 2000 s 6(1)(b): see TRUSTS vol 48 (2000 Reissue) para 924.
6   See ibid s 7(2); and TRUSTS vol 48 (2000 Reissue) para 924.
7   Ie the commencement of ibid Pt II: see note 4 supra.
8   Ie under the Trustee Investments Act 1961 s 3(2): see para 363 post; and TRUSTS vol 48 (2000 Reissue) para 901.
9   See the Trustee Act 2000 s 7(3); and TRUSTS vol 48 (2000 Reissue) para 924.
10  Ie under the Charities Act 1993 ss 24, 25: see paras 366–367 post.
11  See the Trustee Act 2000 s 38; para 360 note 2 ante; and TRUSTS vol 48 (2000 Reissue) para 924.

**362. Exercising skill and care in investment.** When exercising the general power of investment or any other power of investment, however conferred, and when carrying out duties relating to the exercise of a power of investment or to the review of investments[1], trustees are under a duty to exercise such skill and care as is reasonable in the circumstances[2].

Further, in exercising any power of investment, a trustee must have regard to the standard investment criteria[3]. The standard investment criteria, in relation to a trust, are:

(1)   the suitability to the trust of investments of the same kind as any particular investment proposed to be made or retained and of that particular investment as an investment of that kind[4]; and

(2)   the need for diversification of investments of the trust, in so far as is appropriate to the circumstances of the trust[5].

Before exercising any power of investment, the trustee must, unless the exception applies[6], seek proper advice[7] about the way in which, having regard to the standard investment criteria, the powers ought to be exercised[8].

A trustee must from time to time review the investments of the trust and consider whether, having regard to the standard investment criteria, they ought to be varied[9]. When reviewing the investments of the trust, a trustee must, unless the exception applies[10], obtain and consider proper advice about whether, having regard to the standard investment criteria, the investments ought to be varied[11].

1   Ie under the Trustee Act 2000 ss 4, 5: see TRUSTS vol 48 (2000 Reissue) paras 925–926.
2   See ibid s 1, Sch 1; and TRUSTS vol 48 (2000 Reissue) paras 848–849.
3   See ibid s 4(1); and TRUSTS vol 48 (2000 Reissue) para 925.
4   See ibid s 4(3)(a); and TRUSTS vol 48 (2000 Reissue) para 925.
5   See ibid s 4(3)(b); and TRUSTS vol 48 (2000 Reissue) para 925.
6   The exception is that a trustee need not obtain such advice if he reasonably concludes that in all the circumstances it is unnecessary or inappropriate to do so: ibid s 5(3).
7   As to proper advice for the purposes of ibid s 5 see s 5(4); and TRUSTS vol 48 (2000 Reissue) para 926.
8   See ibid s 5(1); and TRUSTS vol 48 (2000 Reissue) para 926.
9   See ibid s 4(2); and TRUSTS vol 48 (2000 Reissue) para 925.
10  See note 6 supra.
11  See the Trustee Act 2000 s 5(2); and TRUSTS vol 48 (2000 Reissue) para 926.

**363. General investment powers under the Trustee Investment Act 1961.** The powers to make specified authorised investments given to trustees under the Trustee Investment Act 1961 have been largely repealed[1], but certain provisions still have effect either in so far as they are applied by or under any other enactment or in so far as they relate to a trustee having a power of investment conferred on him under an enactment passed before the 3 August 1961[2] and which has not been amended[3] by the Trustee Act 2000[4].

Trustees of charitable trusts have the same powers of investment as private trustees. Except in so far as they may be limited by any statutory provision, whenever made, or by express provision in any other instrument made after 3 August 1961[5], their powers and duties are laid down and regulated by the Trustee Investment Act 1961, but those statutory powers are in addition to any other power of investment given to the trustees[6].

Where property is held by trustees as an investment, the trustees should normally seek to obtain therefrom the maximum return, whether by way of income or capital growth, which is consistent with commercial prudence. In most case the best interests of the charity require that the trustees' choice of investments should be made solely on the basis of well-established investment criteria, including the need for diversification[7]. Exceptionally, if trustees are satisfied that investing in a company engaged in a particular type of business would conflict with the very objects their charity is seeking to achieve, they should not so invest[8]. Another exceptional case might be where trustees' holdings of particular investments might hamper a charity's work either by making potential recipients of aid unwilling to be helped because of the source of the charity's money, or by alienating some of those who support the charity financially. If the trust deed so provides, trustees would be entitled, or even required, to take into account non-financial criteria[9].

1    Ie by the Trustee Act 2000 s 40(1), (3), Sch 2 Pt I para 1, Sch 4 Pt I. As to powers of investment under the Trustee Investments Act 1961 see further TRUSTS vol 48 (2000 Reissue) para 900 et seq. As to the statutory powers of investment under the Trustee Act 2000 see paras 360–362 ante TRUSTS vol 48 (2000 Reissue) para 924 et seq.
2    Ie the date on which the Trustee Investment Act 1961 was passed.
3    Ie by the Trustee Act 2000 Sch 2.
4    See ibid Sch 2 Pt I para 1(1), (2). The Trustee Investments Act 1961 ss 1, 2, 5, 6, 12, 13 and 15 cease to have effect, except in so far as they are applied by or under any other enactment: Trustee Act 2000 Sch 2 Pt I para 1(1). The Trustee Investments Act 1961 s 3 and Sch 2, 3 cease to have effect, except in so far as they relate to a trustee having a power of investment conferred on him under an enactment which was passed before the passing of the Trustee Investment Act 1961, and which is not amended by the Trustee Act 2000 Sch 2: Sch 2 Pt I para 1(2). As to the Trustee Investments Act 1961 see TRUSTS vol 48 (2000 Reissue) paras 900–923.
5    See the Trustee Investments Act 1961 s 1; and TRUSTS vol 48 (2000 Reissue) para 900.
6    See ibid s 3; and TRUSTS vol 48 (2000 Reissue) para 901. Guidance was given by the Charity Commissioners in the *Report of the Charity Commissioners for England and Wales for 1978* (HC Paper (1979–80) no 94) App G, and the *Report of the Charity Commissioners for England and Wales for 1985* (HC Paper (1985–86) no 391) paras 65–70.
       The court has jurisdiction to widen the powers of investment of charitable trustees either by way of an administrative scheme (*Re Royal Society's Charitable Trusts* [1956] Ch 87, [1955] 3 All ER 14; *Re Royal Naval and Royal Marine Children's Homes, Portsmouth, Lloyds Bank Ltd v A-G* [1959] 2 All ER 716n, [1959] 1 WLR 755) or under the Trustee Act 1925 (see the Trustee Act 1925 s 57; *Re Shipwrecked Fishermen and Mariners' Royal Benevolent Society* [1959] Ch 220, [1958] 3 All ER 465; *Mason v Farbrother* [1983] 2 All ER 1078; and TRUSTS vol 48 (2000 Reissue) para 957). Initially, the view of the courts was that the powers of investment given by the Trustee Investments Act 1961 should be taken to be prima facie sufficient, though there was power to act if a very special case was made out: *Re London University's Charitable Trusts* [1964] Ch 282, [1963] 3 All ER 859 (applying non-charity trust cases such as *Re Kolb's Will Trusts, Lloyds Bank Ltd v Ullman* [1962] Ch 531, [1961] 3 All ER 811; compromised on appeal 106 Sol Jo 669, CA); *Re Cooper's Settlement, Cooper v Cooper* [1962] Ch 826, [1961] 3 All ER 636. Subsequently it has been held that this principle is no longer applicable: *Trustees of the British Museum v A-G* [1984] 1 All ER 337, [1984] 1 WLR 418. Before the Charities Act 1960 the jurisdiction was sometimes used to permit the funds of several charitable trusts to be consolidated and managed together: *Re Royal Society's Charitable Trusts* [1956] Ch 87, [1955] 3 All ER 14.
7    Expert advice should be taken where appropriate. Due regard should be taken of the need to balance income against capital growth and the need to balance risk against return: *Harries v Church Comrs for*

*England* [1993] 2 All ER 300, [1992] 1 WLR 1241. Note also the observations of Lord Templeman in *Hazell v Hammersmith and Fulham London Borough Council* [1992] 2 AC 1, [1991] 1 All ER 545, HL.

8    Eg cancer research charities investing in tobacco shares. It is very unlikely that this would disable the trustees from choosing a properly diversified portfolio.

9    *Harries v Church Comrs for England* [1993] 2 All ER 300, [1992] 1 WLR 1241. See also *Cowan v Scargill* [1985] Ch 270, [1984] 2 All ER 750 (a non-charity case).

**364. Deposits in trustee savings banks.** Under the Trustee Savings Bank Act 1981[1] the treasurer of any charitable or provident institution or society, or charitable donation or bequest for the maintenance, education, or benefit of the poor, could, subject to the statutory provisions restricting the amount of deposits, invest the trust funds in the funds of a trustee savings bank. The receipt of the treasurer, trustee, or other officer of the charitable or provident institution or society apparently authorised to require payment discharged the savings bank[2]. These provisions were repealed by the Trustee Savings Bank Act 1985[3], which reorganised trustee savings banks into companies incorporated under the Companies Acts, with savings in relation to funds already invested in the funds of a trustee savings bank and in relation to receipts[4].

1    Trustee Savings Banks Act 1981 s 29(1), consolidating earlier legislation (now repealed: see the text and notes 3–4 infra).

2    Ibid s 29(2) (repealed).

3    See the Trustee Savings Banks Act 1985 s 7(3), Sch 4.

4    See ibid ss 4(3), (5), 7(3), Sch 4; Trustee Savings Banks Act 1985 (Appointed Day) (No 4) Order 1986, SI 1986/1223, arts 2(a), 8, 9, 12, Sch 1. See further BANKING vol 3(1) (Reissue) para 11.

**365. Investment in land.** The Trustee Investments Act 1961 did not itself permit investment in land[1]. In the absence of an express power, the purchase of land may be authorised out of capital money arising on the sale of settled land[2], or it may be specially authorised by the Charity Commissioners[3].

However, under the Trustee Act 2000, trustees may acquire freehold or leasehold land as an investment, for occupation by a beneficiary or for any other reason[4].

1    It did permit investment in certain mortgages: see the Trustee Investments Act 1961 s 1, Sch 1 Pt II para 13; and TRUSTS vol 48 (2000 Reissue) para 907. Section 1 was repealed, with savings, by the Trustee Act 2000: see para 363 ante. As to the Trustee Investments Act 1961 see para 363 ante; and TRUSTS vol 48 (2000 Reissue) para 900 et seq.

2    See the Settled Land Act 1925 s 73(1)(x); and SETTLEMENTS vol 42 (Reissue) para 808.

3    Ie under the Charities Act 1993 s 26: see para 333 ante. See the *Report of the Charity Commissioners for England and Wales for 1988* (HC Paper (1988–89) no 319) paras 73–75. As to the Charity Commissioners see paras 486–512 post.

4    See the Trustee Act 2000 ss 8–10; and TRUSTS vol 48 (2000 Reissue) para 935.

**366. Schemes to establish common investment funds.** Under the Charities Act 1993, the court[1] and the Charity Commissioners[2] may by order[3] make and bring into effect schemes ('common investment schemes') to establish common investment funds providing: (1) for property transferred to the fund by or on behalf of a charity[4] participating in the scheme to be invested under the control of the trustees managing the fund[5]; and (2) for the participating charities to be entitled, subject to the provisions of the scheme, to the capital and income of the fund in shares determined by reference to the amount or value of the property transferred to it by or on behalf of each of them and to the value of the fund at the time of the transfer[6].

Common investment schemes may be made on the application of any two or more charities[7]. Every charity has power to participate in common investment schemes as part of its investment powers, unless that power is excluded specifically by the trusts[8] of the charity[9]. Unless the scheme provides otherwise, the rights of a participating charity may not be assigned or charged[10].

Common investment schemes may be made in terms admitting any charity to participate, or may restrict the right to participate in any manner[11]. A common investment fund is deemed for all purposes to be a charity[12]; and if the scheme only admits exempt charities[13] the fund is treated as an exempt charity[14].

A common investment scheme may make provision for, and for all matters connected with, the establishment, investment, management and winding up of the common investment fund, and may in particular include provision[15]:

(a)  for remunerating persons appointed trustees to hold or manage the fund or any part of it, with or without provision authorising a person to receive the remuneration notwithstanding that he is also a charity trustee[16] of or trustee for a participating charity[17];

(b)  for restricting the size of the fund, and for regulating as to time, amount or otherwise the right to transfer property to or withdraw it from the fund, and for enabling sums to be advanced out of the fund by way of loan to a participating charity pending the withdrawal of property from the fund by the charity[18];

(c)  for enabling income to be withheld from distribution with a view to avoiding fluctuations in the amounts distributed, and generally for regulating distributions of income[19];

(d)  for enabling money to be borrowed temporarily for the purpose of meeting payments to be made out of the funds[20];

(e)  for enabling questions arising under the scheme as to the right of a charity to participate, or as to the rights of participating charities, or as to any other matter, to be conclusively determined by the decision of the trustees managing the fund or in any other manner[21];

(f)  for regulating the accounts and information to be supplied to participating charities[22].

1   For the meaning of 'the court' see para 168 note 12 ante.
2   As to the Charity Commissioners see paras 486–512 post.
3   By order of the Commissioners dated 4 December 1962 a scheme was made establishing the Charities Official Investment Fund. The original scheme is printed in full in the *Report of the Charity Commissioners for England and Wales for 1962* (HC Paper (1963–64) no 17) pp 34–49, App B, and in Tudor on Charities (6th Edn, 1967) pp 721–735. It has been amended subsequently. As to the unification of trusts by specified universities and colleges under the Universities and Colleges (Trusts) Act 1943 see EDUCATION; and *Re Freeston's Charity, Sylvester v Master and Fellows of University College, Oxford* [1979] 1 All ER 51, [1978] 1 WLR 741, CA. As to the making or orders generally see the Charities Act 1993 s 86 (as amended); and para 517 post.
4   For the meaning of 'charity' see para 1 ante.
5   Charities Act 1993 s 24(1)(a). As to the disapplication of the Trustee Act 2000 in relation to common investment schemes see para 360 note 2 ante.
6   Charities Act 1993 s 24(1)(b).

7    Ibid s 24(2). This means on the application of the trustees of two or more charitable trusts; the trustees
     may be the same: *Re London University's Charitable Trusts* [1964] Ch 282, [1963] 3 All ER 859 (decided
     under previous legislation).
8    For the meaning of 'trusts' see para 210 note 5 ante.
9    Charities Act 1993 s 24(7).
10   Ibid s 24(6). Trustees and persons concerned in the management of the fund are not required or entitled
     to take account of any trust or equity affecting participating charities or its property or rights: s 24(6).
11   Ibid s 24(3).
12   Ibid s 24(8).
13   As to exempt charities see para 293 ante.
14   Charities Act 1993 s 24(8). This applies not only to the common investment funds established under the
     powers of s 24 but also to similar funds established under statutory powers for the exclusive benefit of
     charities by or under any enactment relating to any particular charities or class of charities: s 24(9).
15   Ibid s 24(4). A common investment scheme, in addition to the provision for property to be transferred
     to the fund on the basis that the charity is entitled to a share in the capital and income of the fund, may
     include provision for enabling sums to be deposited by or on behalf of a charity on the basis that (subject
     to the provisions of the scheme) the charity is entitled to repayment of the sums deposited and to interest
     thereon at a rate determined by or under the scheme: s 24(5). Where a scheme makes any such provision
     it must also provide for excluding from the amount of capital and income to be shared between charities
     participating otherwise than by way of deposit such amounts (not exceeding the amounts properly
     attributable to the making of deposits) as are from time to time reasonably required in respect of the
     liabilities of the fund for the repayment of deposits and for the interest on deposits, including amounts
     required by way of reserve: s 24(5).
16   For the meaning of 'charity trustees' see para 1 note 10 ante.
17   Charities Act 1993 s 24(4)(a).
18   Ibid s 24(4)(b).
19   Ibid s 24(4)(c).
20   Ibid s 24(4)(d).
21   Ibid s 24(4)(e).
22   Ibid s 24(4)(f).

**367. Schemes to establish common deposit funds.** The court[1] or the Charity Commissioners[2] may by order make and bring into effect schemes ('common deposit schemes') for the establishment of common deposit funds under trusts which provide: (1) for sums to be deposited by or on behalf of a charity[3] participating in the scheme and invested under the control of trustees appointed to manage the fund[4]; and (2) for any such charity to be entitled to repayment of any sums so deposited and to interest thereon at a rate determined under the scheme[5].

Common deposit schemes may be made on the application of any two or more charities[6]. Every charity has power to participate in common deposit schemes as part of its investment powers, unless that power is excluded specifically by the trusts[7] of the charity[8]. Unless the scheme provides otherwise, the rights of a participating charity may not be assigned or charged[9].

Common deposit schemes may be made in terms admitting any charity to participate, or may restrict the right to participate in any manner[10]. A common deposit fund is deemed for all purposes to be a charity[11]; and if the scheme only admits exempt charities[12] the fund is treated as an exempt charity[13].

A common deposit scheme may make provision for, and for all matters connected with, the establishment, investment, management and winding up of the common deposit fund, and may in particular include provision[14]:

(a)    for remunerating persons appointed trustees to hold or manage the fund or any part of it, with or without provision authorising a person to receive the remuneration notwithstanding that he is also a charity trustee[15] of or trustee for a participating charity[16];

(b)   for regulating as to time, amount or otherwise the right to repayment of sums deposited in the fund[17];

(c)   for authorising a part of the income for any year to be credited to a reserve account maintained for the purpose of counteracting any losses accruing to the fund, and generally for regulating the manner in which the rate of interest on deposits is to be determined from time to time[18];

(d)   for enabling money to be borrowed temporarily for the purpose of meeting payments to be made out of the funds[19];

(e)   for enabling questions arising under the scheme as to the right of a charity to participate, or as to the rights of participating charities, or as to any other matter, to be conclusively determined by the decision of the trustees managing the fund or in any other manner[20];

(f)   for regulating the accounts and information to be supplied to participating charities[21].

1   For the meaning of 'the court' see para 168 note 12 ante.
2   As to the Charity Commissioners see paras 486–512 post.
3   For the meaning of 'charity' see para 1 ante.
4   Charities Act 1993 s 25(1)(a). As to the making of orders generally see s 86 (as amended); and para 517 post. As to the disapplication of the Trustee Act 2000 in relation to common deposit schemes see para 360 note 2 ante.
5   Charities Act 1993 s 25(1)(b).
6   Ibid ss 24(2), 25(2).
7   For the meaning of 'trusts' see para 210 note 5 ante.
8   Charities Act 1993 ss 24(7), 25(2).
9   Ibid ss 24(6), 25(2). Trustees and persons concerned in the management of the fund are not required or entitled to take account of any trust or equity affecting participating charities or its property or rights: ss 24(6), 25(2).
10  Ibid ss 24(3), 25(2).
11  Ibid ss 24(8), 25(2).
12  As to exempt charities see para 293 ante.
13  Charities Act 1993 ss 24(8), 25(2). This applies not only to the common deposit funds, but also to similar funds established under statutory powers for the exclusive benefit of charities by or under any enactment relating to any particular charities or class of charities: ss 24(9), 25(2).
14  Ibid ss 24(4), 25(2).
15  For the meaning of 'charity trustees' see para 1 note 10 ante.
16  Charities Act 1993 ss 24(4)(a), 25(2).
17  Ibid ss 24(4)(b), 25(2), (3).
18  Ibid ss 24(4)(c), 25(2), (3).
19  Ibid ss 24(4)(d), 25(2).
20  Ibid ss 24(4)(e), 25(2).
21  Ibid ss 24(4)(f), 25(2).

### (iii)   Ex Gratia Payments

**368. Circumstances in which payments may be made.**   Notwithstanding the rule that trust property may only be applied in accordance with the terms of the trust[1], there are cases in which trustees of property for charitable purposes may be authorised to make payments out of the trust property to persons with a moral but no legal claim to the property[2].

Just as trustees have power to compromise claims[3] and the court, acting on the advice of the Attorney General, may relieve charity trustees from the obligation to make good in full breaches of trust for which they are answerable[4], so, where by mistake or owing to some legal technicality a charity has received more than was apparently intended[5], the charity or the trustees may apply for authority to pay out some part of the fund to the persons who have a moral claim to it[6]. The charity or the trustees will not necessarily be authorised to pay out as much as they wish[7].

1  See para 302 ante.

2  *Re Snowden, Shackleton v Eddy, Re Henderson, Henderson v A-G* [1970] Ch 700, [1969] 3 All ER 208.

3  See the Trustee Act 1925 s 15(f); and TRUSTS vol 48 (2000 Reissue) para 947. For further protection, they may apply to the court to sanction the compromise. The court will take into account the moral merits of the claim in question: see *Re Snowden, Shackleton v Eddy, Re Henderson, Henderson v A-G* [1970] Ch 700 at 709, [1969] 3 All ER 208 at 213 per Cross J.

4  See *A-G v Brettingham* (1840) 3 Beav 91 at 95 per Lord Langdale MR; *A-G v Exeter Corpn* (1827) 2 Russ 362; *A-G v Pretyman* (1841) 4 Beav 462; *Re Snowden, Shackleton v Eddy, Re Henderson, Henderson v A-G* [1970] Ch 700 at 710, [1969] 3 All ER 208 at 213 per Cross J.

5  There might be other circumstances, as where a testator had broken a solemn but unenforceable promise to give the property to an individual: see eg *National Provincial Bank Ltd v Moore* (1967) 111 Sol Jo 357. As to this type of case see *Re Snowden, Shackleton v Eddy, Re Henderson, Henderson v A-G* [1970] Ch 700 at 710, [1969] 3 All ER 208 at 214 per Cross J.

6  *Re Snowden, Shackleton v Eddy, Re Henderson, Henderson v A-G* [1970] Ch 700, [1969] 3 All ER 208. The trustees cannot be made to apply.

7  See the order made in *Re Snowden, Shackleton v Eddy, Re Henderson, Henderson v A-G* [1970] Ch 700, [1969] 3 All ER 208.

**369. Procedure prior to the Charities Act 1992.** The procedure prior to the Charities Act 1992 was that if the property was that of a specific charity, application would be made in the first instance to the Charity Commissioners[1]; if it was held on trust for charitable purposes generally the application would first be made to the Treasury Solicitor[2]. After an investigation into the facts a report might be made to the Attorney General, who might decide himself or might apply ex parte to the court for guidance[3]. This procedure has not been abolished, but it is thought that application will now normally be made under the statutory provisions introduced by the Charities Act 1992 and re-enacted in the Charities Act 1993[4].

1  As to the Charity Commissioners see paras 486–512 post.

2  As to the Treasury Solicitor see CONSTITUTIONAL LAW AND HUMAN RIGHTS vol 8(2) (Reissue) para 541.

3  This procedure was indicated as appropriate in *Re Snowden, Shackleton v Eddy, Re Henderson, Henderson v A-G* [1970] Ch 700 at 711, [1969] 3 All ER 208 at 214 per Cross J. It has been followed since, though it may be modified in the light of experience. Reference may be made to the annual reports of the Charity Commissioners (eg *Report of the Charity Commissioners for England and Wales for 1970* (HC Paper (1970–71) no 409) p 30 and the *Report of the Charity Commissioners for England and Wales for 1976* (HC Paper (1976–77) no 389) paras 113–116 which contains an example of an ex gratia payment authorised by the Attorney General on a proposal by the Commissioners) for guidance on this matter.

4  See the Charities Act 1993 s 27 (see para 370 post), which re-enacts the Charities Act 1960 s 23A (added by the Charities Act 1992 s 17; but now repealed).

**370. Power of Charity Commissioners to authorise ex gratia payments.** The Charity Commissioners[1] may by order[2] exercise the same power as is exercisable by the Attorney General to authorise charity trustees[3] to make any application of property of the charity, or to waive to any extent, on behalf of the charity, its entitlement to receive any property[4]. This may be done where the charity trustees otherwise have no power to do so, but in all the circumstances regard themselves as under a moral obligation to do so[5].

The power is exercisable under the supervision of, and in accordance with any directions given by, the Attorney General, which may, in particular, require the Commissioners, in such circumstances as are specified in the directions, to refrain from exercising the power, or to consult the Attorney General before exercising it[6]. Where an application is made to the Commissioners for them to exercise that power in a case where they are not precluded from doing so by any such directions, but they consider that it would nevertheless be desirable for the application to be entertained by the Attorney General rather than by them, they may refer the application to the Attorney General[7]. Where, in the case of any such application, the Commissioners determine the application by refusing to authorise charity trustees to take any action under these provisions[8], that refusal does not preclude the Attorney General, on an application subsequently made to him by the trustees, from authorising the trustees to take that action[9].

1   As to the Charity Commissioners see paras 486–512 post.
2   As to the making or orders generally see the Charities Act 1993 s 86 (as amended); and para 517 post.
3   For the meaning of 'charity trustees' see para 1 note 10 ante.
4   Charities Act 1993 s 27(1).
5   Ibid s 27(1).
6   Ibid s 27(2).
7   Ibid s 27(3).
8   Ie under ibid s 27(1): see the text and notes 1–5 supra.
9   Ibid s 27(4).

## (iv) Rating

### A.  MANDATORY RELIEF FOR CHARITIES

#### (A)  In general

**371. Scope of relief in general.** Before new valuation lists came into force in 1956 there was a divergence between the law and practice with regard to the rating of charities. At law, it had long been established that charitable organisations were rateable in respect of the hereditaments they occupied[1], but in practice rating authorities frequently undervalued the hereditaments of charitable and kindred bodies, and by this means those bodies paid only reduced or nominal rates. When rating authorities[2] ceased to be responsible for preparing and amending valuation lists[3] this divergence of law and practice was ended, and in the valuation lists which came into force in 1956 the valuation officers of the Inland Revenue Commissioners[4] assessed such hereditaments at their full value[5].

The Local Government Finance Act 1988, which repealed the General Rate Act 1967, abolished domestic rates and replaced them with a system of community charges[6].

So far as non-domestic rates were concerned a new form of rating was set up, though it is broadly similar to the system it replaced.

Under the Local Government Finance Act 1988, in respect of two categories of hereditament[7], ratepayers that are charities[8] or trustees for a charity qualify for a reduction by 80 per cent of the amount the ratepayer would otherwise have to pay[9]. The relief applies to: (1) any occupied hereditament[10] where the ratepayer is a charity or trustees for a charity and the hereditament is wholly or mainly used for charitable purposes[11] (whether of that charity or of that and other charities)[12]; and (2) any unoccupied hereditament where the ratepayer is a charity or trustees for a charity and where it appears that when next in use the hereditament will be wholly or mainly used for charitable purposes (whether of that charity or of that and other charities)[13]. Certain hereditaments, namely places of religious worship and property used for the disabled, are wholly exempt from non-domestic rating[14].

 1  *Mersey Docks v Cameron, Jones v Mersey Docks* (1865) 11 HL Cas 443; *London Corpn v Stratton* (1875) LR 7 HL 477.
 2  Rating authorities have been replaced by billing authorities. As to billing authorities see RATING AND COUNCIL TAX vol 39(1) (Reissue) para 606.
 3  Ie by virtue of the Local Government Act 1948 s 33 (repealed). As to valuation lists see RATING AND COUNCIL TAX vol 39(1) (Reissue) para 711 et seq.
 4  As to the functions of the valuation officers of the Inland Revenue Commissioners see RATING AND COUNCIL TAX vol 39(1) (Reissue) para 607.
 5  As to the history of the rating legislation see RATING AND COUNCIL TAX vol 39(1) (Reissue) para 602.
 6  Domestic rates were abolished by the Local Government Finance Act 1988 and replaced by the community charge, itself replaced by the council tax in 1993: see the Local Government Finance Act 1992; and RATING AND COUNCIL TAX vol 39(1) (Reissue) para 602; LOCAL GOVERNMENT.
 7  For the meaning of 'hereditament' see RATING AND COUNCIL TAX vol 39(1) (Reissue) para 634 et seq.
 8  For the meaning of 'charity' see para 373 note 2 post.
 9  See the Local Government Finance Act 1988 ss 43(5), (6), 45(5), (6); and para 373 post.
10  As to rateable occupation see RATING AND COUNCIL TAX vol 39(1) (Reissue) para 613 et seq. As to occupation by a charity see para 374 post.
11  For the meaning of 'wholly or mainly used for charitable purposes' see para 375 post.
12  See the Local Government Finance Act 1988 s 43(5), (6); and para 373 post.
13  See ibid s 45(5), (6); and para 373 post.
14  See ibid s 51, Sch 5 paras 11 (as amended), 16; and RATING AND COUNCIL TAX vol 39(1) (Reissue) paras 642–643, 653.

**372. Establishment of right to relief.** Under the General Rate Act 1967 (now repealed)[1], the right to charity rating relief could be established by resisting proceedings in the magistrates court brought by the rating authority[2] for non-payment of rates[3] or by proceedings in the High Court for a declaration[4]. It would seem that both procedures are still available under the Local Government Finance Act 1988.

 1  As to the history of the rating legislation see RATING AND COUNCIL TAX vol 39(1) (Reissue) para 602.
 2  See eg *Meriden RDC v White* [1972] RA 530, DC; *Ealing London Borough Council v Ladyeholme Co Ltd* [1974] RA 399; *Royal Society for the Protection of Birds v Hornsea UDC* [1975] RA 26, DC.
 3  Then by means of an application for a distress warrant, now by means of an application for a liability order (as to which see RATING AND COUNCIL TAX vol 39(1) (Reissue) para 789).
 4  This was done in eg *Over Seventies Housing Association v Westminster City Council* [1974] RA 247; *Oxfam v Birmingham City District Council* [1976] AC 126, [1975] 2 All ER 289, HL; *Forces Help Society and Lord Roberts Workshops v Canterbury City Council* [1979] RA 68. As to declaratory orders see ADMINISTRATIVE LAW vol 1(1) (2001 Reissue) para 151 et seq.

*(B)   Occupied Hereditaments*

**373.   Calculating the amount payable for hereditaments in the local rating list occupied by charities.** Where on the day concerned the ratepayer[1] is a charity[2] or trustees for a charity and the occupied hereditament is wholly or mainly used for charitable purposes[3] (whether of that charity or of that and other charities)[4], the chargeable amount[5] for a chargeable day[6] is calculated by multiplying the rateable value[7] by the non-domestic rating multiplier[8] for the financial year, and dividing the product by five times the number of days in the financial year[9]. The result is a reduction by 80 per cent of the amount the ratepayer would have had to pay were he not entitled to the reduction[10].

1   Ie the person subject to the non-domestic rate of a hereditament in a local rating list: see the Local Government Finance Act 1988 s 43(1). For the meaning of 'hereditament' see RATING AND COUNCIL TAX vol 39(1) (Reissue) para 634 et seq. As to the liability to the non-domestic rate for occupied hereditaments in the local non-domestic rating lists see RATING AND COUNCIL TAX vol 39(1) (Reissue) para 660. As to rating lists see RATING AND COUNCIL TAX vol 39(1) (Reissue) para 711 et seq.
2   For these purposes, 'charity' means an institution or other organisation established for charitable purposes only or any persons administering a trust established for charitable purposes only: ibid s 67(10). For the general definition of a charity see para 1 ante. Registration under the charities legislation is conclusive that the organisation is a charity for the purposes of the relief from rates: see eg *Wynn v Skegness UDC* [1966] 3 All ER 336, [1967] 1 WLR 52, ChD; *Finch v Poplar Borough Council* (1967) 66 LGR 324, [1968] RA 208, ChD; *Meriden RDC v White* [1972] RA 530, 17 RRC 187.
      The cases cited in this paragraph which were decided prior to the coming into force of the Local Government Finance Act 1988 must now be considered in relation to the non-domestic rating provisions in Pt III (ss 41–67) (as amended) (see RATING AND COUNCIL TAX vol 39(1) (Reissue) para 603 et seq). As to the history of the rating legislation see RATING AND COUNCIL TAX vol 39(1) (Reissue) para 602.
3   Ibid s 43(5), (6). For the meaning of 'wholly or mainly used for charitable purposes' see para 375 post. As to occupation by a charity see para 374 post.
4   See ibid ss 43(6), 67(7).
5   The chargeable amount for occupied property is calculated by the formula in ibid s 43(5).
6   A 'chargeable day' is one which falls within the financial year and for which the ratepayer's name is shown in the list: ibid s 54(3). A 'financial year' is a period of 12 months beginning with 1 April: s 145(3).
7   The 'rateable value' is the value entered in the local non-domestic rating list: see ibid s 42(4) (amended by the Local Government and Housing Act 1989 s 139, Sch 5 paras 1, 20, 79(3)); Local Government Finance Act 1988 s 44(2) (amended by the Local Government and Housing Act 1989 s 194(4), Sch 5 paras 1, 21, 79(3), Sch 12 Pt II).
8   Local Government Finance Act 1988 s 44(4). Where the billing authority is a special authority, this figure is the authority's non-domestic rating multiplier for the financial year: s 44(5) (amended by the Local Government Finance Act 1992 s 117(1), Sch 13 para 61). The multiplier is a uniform amount applying to every billing authority area and is fixed annually by the Secretary of State using the method set out in the Local Government Finance Act 1988 s 56(2), Sch 7 (as amended): see RATING AND COUNCIL TAX vol 39(1) (Reissue) para 679. As to billing authorities see RATING AND COUNCIL TAX vol 39(1) (Reissue) para 606; and as to special authorities see RATING AND COUNCIL TAX vol 39(1) (Reissue) para 660.
9   Ibid s 44(6). The formula is set out in s 43(5).
10  As to the scope of relief in general see para 371 ante.

**374.   Occupation by a charity.** Charities registered under the Charities Act 1993[1] are conclusively presumed to be charities for the purposes of the rating legislation[2]. However, a body whose application to be registered as a charity has been rejected by the Charity Commissioners[3] may still contend that it is a charity for the purposes of the rating legislation[4]. For rating purposes a charity occupies a house in which one of its officers or servants resides if it is essential to the performance of his duties that he should reside in it or in one close by and it is the mutual understanding that he should do so; or, even though it is not essential that he reside in the house or in one close by, if he can by doing so better perform his duties to a material degree and there is an express term in the contract that he should reside there[5]. Charities which provided flats for the dependants of deceased officers of the armed services, and for ex-servicemen, have been held to be in occupation of the flats[6].

1    As to the registration of charities under the Charities Act 1993 see para 282 et seq ante.
2    See eg *Wynn v Skegness UDC* [1966] 3 All ER 336, [1967] 1 WLR 52, ChD; *Finch v Poplar Borough Council* (1967) 66 LGR 324, [1968] RA 208, ChD; *Meriden RDC v White* [1972] RA 530, 17 RRC 187.
      The cases cited in this paragraph which were decided prior to the coming into force of the Local Government Finance Act 1988 must now be considered in relation to the non-domestic rating provisions in Pt III (ss 41–67) (as amended) (see RATING AND COUNCIL TAX vol 39(1) (Reissue) para 603 et seq). As to the history of the rating legislation see RATING AND COUNCIL TAX vol 39(1) (Reissue) para 602.
3    As to the Charity Commissioners see paras 486–512 post.
4    See *Over Seventies Housing Association v Westminster City Council* [1974] RA 247.
5    *Glasgow Corpn v Johnstone* [1965] AC 609, [1965] 1 All ER 730, HL (house occupied by church officer); *Northern Ireland Comr of Valuation v Fermanagh Protestant Board of Education* [1969] 3 All ER 352, [1969] 1 WLR 1708, HL (teachers' houses); *Valuation Comr v Redemptorist Order Trustees* [1972] RA 145, NI CA (monastery where members of religious order lived and from where they carried out its charitable purposes); *Royal Society for the Protection of Birds v Hornsea UDC* [1975] RA 26, DC (house for warden at bird reserve); *Welsh National Water Development Authority (formerly Taf Fechan Water Board) v Mid-Glamorgan County Council (formerly Glamorgan County Council)* [1975] RA 106, CA (caretaker living on school premises).
6    *Soldiers', Sailors' and Airmen's Families Association v Merton Corpn* [1966] 3 All ER 780, [1967] 1 WLR 127, CA; *Forces Help Society and Lord Roberts Workshops v Canterbury City Council* [1979] RA 68; and see *Ealing London Borough Council v Ladyeholme Co Ltd* [1974] RA 399.

**375. Wholly or mainly used for charitable purposes.**   In deciding whether a hereditament[1] is wholly or mainly[2] used for charitable purposes, the use made of the hereditament by the occupier must be considered[3]. The use must be for purposes which directly facilitate the carrying out of the main charitable purposes of the charity[4], and use for the purpose of raising money to further the charitable objects does not qualify for relief[5]. However, a hereditament is to be treated as wholly or mainly used for charitable purposes at any time if at the time it is wholly or mainly used for the sale of goods donated to a charity and the proceeds of sale of the goods, after any deduction of expenses, are applied for the purposes of a charity[6].

1    For the meaning of 'hereditament' see RATING AND COUNCIL TAX vol 39(1) (Reissue) para 634 et seq.
2    It has been said in another context that 'mainly' probably means 'more than half ': *Fawcett Properties Ltd v Buckingham County Council* [1961] AC 636 at 669, [1960] 3 All ER 503 at 512, HL, per Lord Morton of Henryton.
3    See *Glasgow Corpn v Johnstone* [1965] AC 609, [1965] 1 All ER 730, HL, where the residence of a church officer was held to be occupied by the church authority and used for charitable purposes, because his residence there was of material assistance to the church authority in carrying out its main charitable activities.
      The cases cited in this paragraph which were decided prior to the coming into force of the Local Government Finance Act 1988 must now be considered in relation to the non-domestic rating provisions in Pt III (ss 41–67) (as amended) (see RATING AND COUNCIL TAX vol 39(1) (Reissue) para 603 et seq). As to the history of the rating legislation see RATING AND COUNCIL TAX vol 39(1) (Reissue) para 602.
4    *Glasgow Corpn v Johnstone* [1965] AC 609, [1965] 1 All ER 730, HL; *Oxfam v Birmingham City District Council* [1976] AC 126, [1975] 2 All ER 289, HL. See also *Polish Historical Institution Ltd v Hove Corpn* (1963) 61 LGR 438, DC; *Aldous v Southwark Corpn* [1968] 3 All ER 498, 15 RRC 269, CA. In *Wynn v*

*Skegness UDC* [1966] 3 All ER 336, [1967] 1 WLR 52, trustees of a holiday centre for miners in need of a change of air admitted to it persons other than beneficiaries if there was surplus accommodation at charges sufficient to cover their cost; the admission of such persons, not to raise money, but to assist in keeping the centre functioning, was held to facilitate wholly and directly the carrying out of the trustees' main purpose. See also *Meriden RDC v White* [1972] RA 530, DC (colliery sports and social club); *Royal British Legion Attendants Co (Belfast) Ltd v Valuation Comr* [1979] NI 138, NI Lands Tribunal (employment of ex-servicemen as car park attendants); *MacConnell v Northern Ireland Valuation Comr* [1989] RA 221, NI Lands Tribunal (garage used for servicing charity's buses not exempt because hereditament not used wholly or mainly for charitable purposes); *Re Hatschek's Patents, ex p Zerenner* [1909] 2 Ch 68; *Miller v Ottilie (Owners)* [1944] KB 188, [1944] 1 All ER 277, CA; *Franklin v Gramophone Co Ltd* [1948] 1 KB 542 at 555, [1948] 1 All ER 353 at 358, CA, per Somervell LJ; *Berthelemy v Neale* [1952] 1 All ER 437, CA. For the meaning of 'charity' see para 373 note 2 ante.

5   *Oxfam v Birmingham City District Council* [1976] AC 126, [1975] 2 All ER 289, HL, where shops occupied by a charity and used to sell goods, most of which were donated, in order to raise funds for spending on charitable purposes were held not to be mainly used for charitable purposes. It does not appear to provide relief to trading shops run by charities, ie shops wholly or mainly used to sell goods bought under normal trading conditions, or to ' fifty-fifty' shops in which goods are deposited for sale and the net proceeds of sale are divided between the donor and the charity. Nor did it cover the facts of *Royal Society for the Protection of Birds v Brighton Borough Council* [1982] RA 33. The actual decision in *Oxfam v Birmingham City District Council* supra, but not its reasoning, was reversed by what is now the Local Government Finance Act 1988 s 64(10) (which has its origins in the Rating (Charity Shops) Act 1976 s 1(1) (repealed)) (see the text to note 6 infra). However, the selling in a shop of goods manufactured by blind persons in order to facilitate the provision of employment for the blind has been held to be a use for charitable purposes: *Belfast Association for Employment of Industrious Blind v Northern Ireland Valuation Comr* [1968] NI 21; and see *Royal Society for the Protection of Birds v Brighton Borough Council* supra.

6   Local Government Finance Act 1988 s 64(10). This has the effect of reversing the decision in *Oxfam v Birmingham City District Council* [1976] AC 126, [1975] 2 All ER 289, HL (see note 5 supra). However, the reasoning of the decision in *Oxfam v Birmingham City District Council* supra is unaffected.

## *(C) Unoccupied Hereditaments*

**376. Liability for unoccupied hereditaments where the ratepayer is a charity.** Where on the day concerned the ratepayer[1] is a charity[2] or trustees for a charity and it appears that when next in use the hereditament[3] will be wholly or mainly used for charitable purposes[4] (whether of that charity or of that and other charities)[5], the chargeable amount for a chargeable day[6] is calculated by multiplying the rateable value[7] by the non-domestic rating multiplier[8] for the financial year[9], and dividing the product by ten times the number of days in the financial year[10].

1   Ie the person subject to the non-domestic rate: see the Local Government Finance Act 1988 s 45(1); and RATING AND COUNCIL TAX vol 39(1) (Reissue) para 662.
2   For the meaning of 'charity' see para 373 note 2 ante.
3   For the meaning of 'hereditament' see RATING AND COUNCIL TAX vol 39(1) (Reissue) para 634 et seq.
4   For the meaning of 'wholly or mainly used for charitable purposes' see para 375 ante.
5   See the Local Government Finance Act 1988 ss 45(6), 67(7).
6   For the meaning of a chargeable day see ibid s 45(3); and RATING AND COUNCIL TAX vol 39(1) (Reissue) para 662.
7   See ibid ss 45(5), 46(1), (2) (amended by the Local Government and Housing Act 1989 ss 139, 194, Sch 5 paras 24, 79(3), Sch 12 Pt II).
8   See the Local Government Finance Act 1988 ss 45(5), 46(1), (3).
9   For the meaning of 'financial year' see para 373 note 6 ante.
10  See the Local Government Finance Act 1988 ss 45(5), 46(5). The formula is set out in s 45(5).

B. DISCRETIONARY RELIEF FOR CHARITIES

**377. Scope of discretion.** Where (1) the first condition[1] and the second condition[2]; or (2) the rural settlement condition[3] and the second condition[4], are fulfilled for a day which is a chargeable day[5], the chargeable amount for the day is such as is determined by, or found in accordance with rules determined by, the billing authority[6] concerned[7]. Consequently, certain provisions[8] do not apply as regards the day.

The first condition is that one or more of the following applies on the chargeable day:

(a)    the ratepayer is a charity[9] or trustees for a charity, and the hereditament[10] is wholly or mainly used for charitable purposes[11] (whether of that charity or of that and other charities)[12];

(b)    the hereditament is not an excepted hereditament[13], and all or part of it is occupied[14] for the purposes of[15] one or more institutions or other organisations[16] none of which is established or conducted for profit[17] and each of whose main objects[18] are charitable or are otherwise philanthropic or religious[19] or concerned with[20] education[21], social welfare[22], science, literature or the fine arts[23];

(c)    the hereditament is not an excepted hereditament, it is wholly or mainly used for purposes of recreation[24], and all or part of it is occupied for the purposes of a club, society or other organisation not established or conducted for profit[25].

The second condition is that, during a period which consists of or includes the chargeable day, a decision of the billing authority concerned operates to the effect that these provisions[26] apply as regards the hereditament concerned[27].

The rural settlement condition is that on the chargeable day the hereditament is within a settlement identified in the billing authority's rural settlement list[28] for the chargeable financial year[29] in which that day falls[30], and that the rateable value of the hereditament shown in the local non-domestic rating list at the beginning of the chargeable financial year is not more than any amount prescribed by the Secretary of State by order[31].

1    Ie the condition mentioned in the Local Government Finance Act 1988 s 47(2) (see the text to notes 9–25 infra).

2    Ie the condition mentioned in ibid s 47(3) (as amended) (see the text to notes 26–27 infra).

3    Ie the condition mentioned in the local Government Finance Act 1988 s 47(3A) (s 47(3A), (3B) added by the Local Government and Rating Act 1997 s 1, Sch 1 para 3(b)) (see the text to notes 28–31 infra).

4    See note 2 supra.

5    Ie a chargeable day within the meaning of the Local Government Finance Act 1988 s 43 (as amended) or s 45 (as amended) as the case may be.

6    As to billing authorities see RATING AND COUNCIL TAX vol 39(1) (Reissue) para 606.

7    Local Government Finance Act 1988 s 47(1)(a) (s 47(1) amended by the Local Government and Housing Act 1989 s 139, Sch 5 paras 26, 79(3); the Local Government Finance Act 1992 s 117(1), Sch 13 para 65(1); and the Local Government and Rating Act 1997 Sch 1 para 3(a)). As to the grant of the relief see para 378 post.

8    Ie the Local Government Finance Act 1988 s 43(4)–(6B) (as amended) (see para 373 ante; and RATING AND COUNCIL TAX vol 39(1) (Reissue) paras 660, 668), s 44 (as amended) (see RATING AND COUNCIL TAX vol 39(1) (Reissue) para 660), s 45(4)–(6) (see para 376 ante; and RATING AND COUNCIL TAX vol 39(1) (Reissue) para 662), s 46 (as amended) (see RATING AND COUNCIL TAX vol 39(1) (Reissue) para 662), regulations under s 58 (as amended) (see RATING AND COUNCIL TAX vol 39(1) (Reissue) para 681) or any provision of or made under s 57, Sch 7A (as added and amended) (see para 680 post), as the case may be: s 47(1)(b) (as amended: see note 7 supra).

9    For the meaning of 'charity' see para 373 note 2 ante.

10  For the meaning of 'hereditament' see RATING AND COUNCIL TAX vol 39(1) (Reissue) para 634 et seq.

11  For the meaning of 'wholly or mainly used for charitable purposes' see para 375 ante. A hereditament not in use is to be treated as wholly or mainly used for charitable purposes if it appears that when next in use it will be wholly or mainly used for charitable purposes: Local Government Finance Act 1988 s 48(1), (2).

12  Ibid ss 47(2)(a), 67(7).

13  A hereditament is an excepted hereditament if all or part of it is occupied (otherwise than as trustee) by (1) a billing authority; or (2) a precepting authority, other than the Receiver for the Metropolitan Police District or charter trustees; or (3) a functional body, within the meaning of the Greater London Authority Act 1999: Local Government Finance Act 1988 s 47(9) (amended by the Local Government Finance Act 1992 Sch 13 para 65; and the Greater London Authority Act 1999 s 138). As from a day to be appointed the reference to the Receiver for the Metropolitan Police District in head (2) supra is repealed by the Greater London Authority Act 1999 s 423, Sch 34 Pt I. At the date at which this volume states the law no such day had been appointed. As to the Receiver for the Metropolitan Police District see POLICE vol 36(1) (Reissue) para 355. A hereditament which is wholly unoccupied is to be treated as an excepted hereditament if it appears that when any of it is next occupied the hereditament will be an excepted hereditament: Local Government Finance Act 1988 s 48(1), (4). As to precepting authorities see RATING AND COUNCIL TAX vol 39(1) (Reissue) para 601; LOCAL GOVERNMENT.

14  As to occupation see RATING AND COUNCIL TAX vol 39(1) (Reissue) para 613 et seq. If a hereditament is wholly unoccupied but it appears that it or any part of it when next occupied will be occupied for particular purposes, the hereditament or part concerned is to be treated as occupied for these purposes: ibid s 48(5). Note that this does not apply for the purposes of s 47(3B)(a) (as added) (see note 31 infra): see s 48(1).

15  The phrase 'occupied for the purposes of' is not to be read as 'occupied exclusively for the purposes of': *Royal London Mutual Insurance Society Ltd v Hendon Corpn* (1958) 3 RRC 76.

   The cases cited in this paragraph which were decided prior to the coming into force of the Local Government Finance Act 1988 must now be considered in relation to the non-domestic rating provisions in Pt III (ss 41–67) (as amended) (see RATING AND COUNCIL TAX vol 39(1) (Reissue) para 603 et seq). As to the history of the rating legislation see RATING AND COUNCIL TAX vol 39(1) (Reissue) para 602.

16  On similar wording in the Rating and Valuation (Miscellaneous Provisions) Act 1955 s 8 (repealed), it was held to be not always right to take the occupier and treat him as the organisation: *Skegness UDC v Derbyshire Miners' Welfare Committee* [1959] AC 807 at 827, [1959] 2 All ER 258 at 265, HL, per Lord Denning; *Isaacs v Market Bosworth RDC* [1960] 1 All ER 433, [1960] 1 WLR 277 (trustees of trade union memorial home; organisation for whose purposes hereditament occupied was the trade union; hereditament not entitled to relief); cf *National Children's Home and Orphanage Registered Trustees v Penarth UDC* (1960) 53 R & IT 166 (trustees of approved school not occupying for purposes of Home Secretary; school entitled to relief); *Trustees of the Benevolent and Orphan Fund, National and Local Government Officers' Association v Bournemouth Corpn* (1957) 1 RRC 363 (quarter sessions).

17  The same words in the Rating and Valuation (Miscellaneous Provisions) Act 1955 s 8 (repealed) were held to mean not established or conducted for the purpose of making profit; accordingly a direction to the trustees of a charity to make investments in order to produce revenue and increase capital does not make the organisation one which is established or conducted for profit: *Guinness Trust (London Fund) Founded 1890, Registered 1902 v West Ham Corpn* [1959] 1 All ER 482, [1959] 1 WLR 233, CA. The financial gains made by a friendly society from investments do not make the society one which is established or conducted for profit: *Trustees of National Deposit Friendly Society v Skegness UDC* [1959] AC 293, [1958] 2 All ER 601, HL. A zoo held to be an educational charity is not conducted for profit merely because it makes a financial surplus on its operations: *North of England Zoological Society v Chester RDC* [1959] 3 All ER 116, [1959] 1 WLR 773, CA. See also *Working Men's Club and Institute Union Ltd v Swansea Corpn* [1959] 3 All ER 769, [1959] 1 WLR 1197, CA, where a society registered under what is now the Industrial and Provident Societies Act 1965 was held not to be established or conducted for profit. See also *Ladbroke Park Golf Club Ltd v Stratford-on-Avon RDC* (1957) 1 RRC 202; *Reinshaw Park Golf Club v Chesterfield RDC* (1957) 1 RRC 281; *Mid-Kent Golf Club Ltd v Gravesend Borough Council* (1957) 50 R & IT 613, where golf clubs were held, at quarter sessions, not to be established or conducted for profit merely because of incidental financial gains.

18  On the same words in the Rating and Valuation (Miscellaneous Provisions) Act 1955 (repealed), it was held that the main objects must be sought in the written constitution, if there is one: *Berry v St Marylebone Borough Council* [1958] Ch 406, [1957] 3 All ER 677, CA; *General Nursing Council for England and Wales v St Marylebone Borough Council* [1959] AC 540 at 559, [1959] 1 All ER 325 at 332, HL, per Lord Keith of Avonholm; *Victory (Ex-Services) Association Ltd v Paddington Borough Council* [1960] 1 All ER 498, [1960] 1 WLR 106, DC; *Royal College of Nursing v St Marylebone Corpn* [1959] 3 All ER 663, [1959] 1 WLR 1077, CA. The activities of the organisation may be relevant in determining which of the objects

are the main objects (*Berry v St Marylebone Borough Council supra; Working Men's Club and Institute Union Ltd v Swansea Corpn* [1959] 3 All ER 769, [1959] 1 WLR 1197, CA; *Trustees of National Deposit Friendly Society v Skegness UDC* [1959] AC 293 at 320, [1958] 2 All ER 601 at 612, HL, per Lord Denning); or where there is ambiguity in the objects (*North of England Zoological Society v Chester RDC* [1959] 3 All ER 116, [1959] 1 WLR 773, CA; *Nottingham Mechanics Institution v City of Nottingham* (1958) 3 RRC 359; *English-Speaking Union v Westminster City Council* (1959) 4 RRC 97, DC).

19    The objects of theosophy were held not to be 'concerned with the advancement of religion' within the meaning of the Rating and Valuation (Miscellaneous Provisions) Act 1955 s 8 (repealed) (*Berry v St Marylebone Borough Council* [1958] Ch 406, [1957] 3 All ER 677, CA); and so were the objects of freemasonry (*United Grand Lodge of Ancient Free and Accepted Masons of England v Holborn Borough Council* [1957] 3 All ER 281, [1957] 1 WLR 1080, CA). See also *Trustees of National Deposit Friendly Society v Skegness UDC* [1959] AC 293 at 322, [1958] 2 All ER 601 at 614, HL, per Lord Denning.

20    On the words in the Rating and Valuation (Miscellaneous Provisions) Act 1955 s 8 (repealed) 'concerned with the advancement of religion, education or social welfare', it was held that the organisation must be substantially altruistic or benevolent in its purposes, although not necessarily in the limited sense applied to charities: *Trustees of National Deposit Friendly Society v Skegness UDC* [1959] AC 293, [1958] 2 All ER 601, HL; *Independent Order of Odd Fellows, Manchester Unity Friendly Society v Manchester Corpn* [1958] 3 All ER 378, [1958] 1 WLR 1171, CA; *Working Men's Club and Institute Union Ltd v Swansea Corpn* [1959] 3 All ER 769, [1959] 1 WLR 1197, CA. The crucial test was the purpose to which the money was devoted, not the motives of its donors: *Skegness UDC v Derbyshire Miners' Welfare Committee* [1959] AC 807 at 824, [1959] 2 All ER 258 at 263, HL, per Viscount Simonds; explained in *Waterson v Hendon Borough Council* [1959] 2 All ER 760, [1959] 1 WLR 985. The size of the class of persons to be benefited was irrelevant: *Skegness UDC v Derbyshire Miners' Welfare Committee supra*.

21    The main objects of the Chartered Insurance Institute are not the advancement of education but the benefit of the profession of insurance generally: *Chartered Insurance Institute v London Corpn* [1957] 2 All ER 638, [1957] 1 WLR 867, DC. The main objects of the English-Speaking Union are not concerned with the advancement of education (*English-Speaking Union v Westminster City Council* (1959) 4 RRC 97); nor are those of the Theosophical Society (*Berry v St Marylebone Borough Council* [1958] Ch 406, [1957] 3 All ER 677, CA). See *Trustees of National Deposit Friendly Society v Skegness UDC* [1959] AC 293 at 322, [1958] 2 All ER 601 at 613, HL, per Lord Denning. At quarter sessions, the Oxford Union Society (*Oxford Union Society v City of Oxford* (1957) 2 RRC 54) and two dramatic societies (*Newport Playgoers' Society v Newport County Borough Council* (1957) 1 RRC 279; *Trustees of Stoke-on-Trent Repertory Players v Stoke-on-Trent Corpn* (1957) 1 RRC 353) have been held to be concerned with the advancement of education.

22    It has been said that 'social welfare' is not the same as 'social well-being', but savours more of those needs of the community which, as a matter of social ethics, ought to be met in the attainment of some acceptable standard: *Trustees of National Deposit Friendly Society v Skegness UDC* [1959] AC 293 at 314, [1958] 2 All ER 601 at 609, HL, per Lord MacDermott. The needs which are met need not be financial: *Victory (Ex-Services) Association Ltd v Paddington Borough Council* [1960] 1 All ER 498, [1960] 1 WLR 106, DC, where it was held that to promote comradeship between and improve the conditions and welfare of all ranks past and present advanced social welfare. Public benefit alone is not the test of social welfare (*General Nursing Council for England and Wales v St Marylebone Borough Council* [1959] AC 540, [1959] 1 All ER 325, HL); and 'social welfare' is a narrower phrase than 'social improvement' (*Nottingham Mechanics Institution v City of Nottingham* (1958) 3 RRC 359). An organisation which provides benefits only for its members is not concerned with the advancement of social welfare: *Working Men's Club and Institute Union Ltd v Swansea Corpn* [1959] 3 All ER 769, [1959] 1 WLR 1197, CA; *Waterson v Hendon Borough Council* [1959] 2 All ER 760, [1959] 1 WLR 985. A holiday camp run by a miners' welfare committee has been held to be concerned with the advancement of 'social welfare': *Skegness UDC v Derbyshire Miners' Welfare Committee* [1959] AC 807, [1959] 2 All ER 258, HL. See also *Independent Order of Odd Fellows, Manchester Unity Friendly Society v Manchester Corpn* [1958] 3 All ER 378, [1958] 1 WLR 1171, CA; *Berry v St Marylebone Borough Council* [1958] Ch 406, [1957] 3 All ER 677, CA; and, at quarter sessions, *Trustees of West Ham Boys' and Amateur Boxing Club v West Ham County Borough Council* (1957) 2 RRC 44; *Trustees of Fegg Hayes Welfare Club and Institute v Stoke-on-Trent Corpn* (1957) 1 RRC 353; *Trustees of Wearmouth Colliery Welfare Fund v Sunderland County Borough Council* (1956) 1 RRC 272; *Wearmouth Colliery Cricket Club v Sunderland County Borough Council* (1956) 1 RRC 277.

23    Local Government Finance Act 1988 ss 47(2)(b), 67(7). Societies which were instituted for the purpose of science, literature or the fine arts exclusively were at one stage exempted from rates, provided that certain other conditions were fulfilled, by the Scientific Societies Act 1843 s 1 (repealed). Many decisions were made as to societies which were to be treated as exempt, and as to others which were so instituted but were not exempt because a condition of exemption was not satisfied; some societies were held not to be exclusively instituted for the requisite purposes but might now qualify for discretionary relief on

the ground that their main objects are concerned with science, literature or the fine arts. 'Science' has been held to include applied science: *R v Royal Medical and Chirurgical Society of London* (1857) 21 JP 789 at 791. The fine arts must be distinguished from the arts: *R v Institution of Civil Engineers* (1879) 5 QBD 48 at 52, DC. Music is one of the fine arts (*Royal College of Music v Westminster Vestry* [1898] 1 QB 809, CA), and drama and acting may be (*Nonentities Society v Linley (Valuation Officer) and Kidderminster Borough Council* (1954) 47 R & IT 426, CA), but folk dancing is not (*O'Sullivan (Valuation Officer) v English Folk Dance and Song Society* [1955] 2 All ER 845, [1955] 1 WLR 907, CA).

24  A hereditament not in use is to be treated as wholly or mainly used for the purposes of recreation if it appears that when next in use it will be wholly or mainly used for such purposes: Local Government Finance Act 1988 s 48(1), (3).

25  Ibid ss 47(2)(c), 67(7).

26  Ie ibid s 47 (as amended).

27  Ibid s 47(3) (amended by the Local Government Finance Act 1992 Sch 13 para 65). As to the grant of the relief see para 378 post.

28  As to the rural settlement lists see RATING AND COUNCIL TAX vol 39(1) (Reissue) para 717.

29  Chargeable financial years are financial years beginning in 1990 and subsequent years: Local Government Finance Act 1988 s 145(1).

30  Ibid s 47(3A)(a) (as added: see note 3 supra).

31  Ibid s 47(3A)(b) (as added: see note 3 supra). See the Non-Domestic Rating (Rural Settlements) (England) Order 1997, SI 1997/2792 (amended by SI 2000/521); and the Non-Domestic Rating (Rural Settlements) (Wales) Order 1997, SI 1997/2885 (amended by SI 1998/390). As to subordinate legislation see RATING AND COUNCIL TAX vol 39(1) (Reissue) para 604.

Where the Local Government Finance Act 1988 s 43(6B)(c) (as added) (see RATING AND COUNCIL TAX vol 39(1) (Reissue) para 668) does not apply, the billing authority must not, by virtue of s 47(3A) (as added), make such a decision as is referred to in s 47(3) (see the second condition in the text) unless it is satisfied that: (1) the hereditament is used for purposes which are of benefit to the local community; and (2) it would be reasonable for the billing authority to make such a decision, having regard to the interests of persons liable to pay council tax set by it: s 47(3B)(a), (b) (as added: see note 3 supra). As to council tax see RATING AND COUNCIL TAX vol 39(1) (Reissue) para 817 et seq.

**378. Grant of the relief.** The relief is not available on any day unless a decision of the billing authority[1] concerned operates to the effect that the provisions for discretionary relief[2] apply as regards the hereditament[3] concerned[4]. Such a decision is invalid if made more than six months after the end of the financial year[5] in which the day falls[6]; and such a decision may be revoked by a further decision of the authority[7]. The quantum of the relief given may either be determined by the billing authority or be determined in accordance with rules set by it[8]. The determination must be such that the chargeable amount for the day is less than would otherwise be chargeable[9] and may be nil[10]. It may be varied by a further determination of the authority[11].

The Secretary of State[12] may make regulations containing provision (1) requiring notice to be given of any determination or decision; (2) limiting the power to revoke a decision or vary a determination; (3) as to other incidental matters[13]. In exercise of this power, he has made the following provisions. The billing authority making a decision or making or varying a determination must give notice in writing to the ratepayer or ratepayers concerned stating (a) in the case of the making of a decision, the first day with respect to which the decision operates and (if the decision is expressed to operate by reference to a particular period) the last day with respect to which it operates; (b) in the case of the making or variation of a determination, the chargeable amount or the rules in accordance with which that amount is to be found, as the case may be, as so made or varied[14]. The billing authority revoking a decision must give notice in writing to the ratepayer or ratepayers concerned stating the day on which the revocation has effect[15]. Notice of the making of a decision or determination, or of the variation of a determination which is not a relevant variation, is to be given as soon as practicable after the decision or determination is made or varied[16].

1   As to billing authorities see RATING AND COUNCIL TAX vol 39(1) (Reissue) para 606.
2   Ie the Local Government Finance Act 1988 s 47 (as amended): see para 377 ante.
3   For the meaning of 'hereditament' see RATING AND COUNCIL TAX vol 39(1) (Reissue) para 634 et seq.
4   See the Local Government Finance Act 1988 s 47(3) (as amended); and para 377 ante.
5   For the meaning of 'financial year' see para 373 note 6 ante.
6   Local Government Finance Act 1988 s 47(7) (amended by the Local Government and Rating Act 1997 s 33(1), Sch 3 para 23).
7   Local Government Finance Act 1988 s 47(6).
8   See ibid s 47(1) (as amended); and para 377 ante.
9   Ibid s 47(4)(a). In deciding what the chargeable amount for the day would be apart from s 47 (as amended) the effect of any regulations under s 58 (as amended) and of any provision of or made under s 57, Sch 7A (as added and amended) must be taken into account but anything which has been done or could be done under s 49 (as amended) (see RATING AND COUNCIL TAX vol 39(1) (Reissue) para 678) must be ignored: s 47(5) (amended by the Local Government and Housing Act 1989 s 139, Sch 5 paras 26, 79(3)).
10  Local Government Finance Act 1988 s 47(4)(b).
11  Ibid s 47(4)(c). A variation can only be made so that it takes effect at the expiry of a financial year: see the Non-Domestic Rating (Discretionary Relief) Regulations 1989, SI 1989/1059, reg 2(3).
12  As to the Secretary of State see RATING AND COUNCIL TAX vol 39(1) (Reissue) para 605.
13  Local Government Finance Act 1988 s 47(8). See the Non-Domestic Rating (Discretionary Relief) Regulations 1989, SI 1989/1059 (as amended); and the text to notes 14–16 infra.
14  Non-Domestic Rating (Discretionary Relief) Regulations 1989, SI 1989/1059, reg 2(1) (amended by SI 1993/616).
15  Non-Domestic Rating (Discretionary Relief) Regulations 1989, SI 1989/1059 reg 2(2) (amended by SI 1993/616).
16  Non-Domestic Rating (Discretionary Relief) Regulations 1989, SI 1989/1059 reg 2(4). A variation of a determination is a relevant variation for these purposes if it increases the chargeable amount for any day: reg 2(5).

## (v)  Taxes

**379. Income taxation.** Charities enjoy a number of exemptions from the incidence of income tax[1], in particular from tax under Schedules A and D in respect of the rents and profits of land vested in trustees for charitable purposes, so far as they are applied for charitable purposes only[2], from tax under certain Cases of Schedule D[3] and under Schedule F in respect of distributions, in each case so far as it is applied to charitable purposes only[4]. In respect of the profits of a trade carried on by a charity, exemption from tax under Schedule D is allowed if the profits are applied solely for the purposes of the charity, and either the trade is exercised in the course of the actual carrying out of a primary purpose of the charity or the work in connection with the trade is mainly carried on by beneficiaries of the charity[5].

Any payment which (1) is received by a charity from another charity; (2) is not made for full consideration in money or money's worth; (3) is not otherwise chargeable to tax; and (4) is not otherwise of a description which (on a claim) would be eligible[6] for relief from tax, is chargeable to tax under Case III of Schedule D but is eligible for relief from tax[7] as if it were an annual payment[8].

If in any chargeable period of a charity (a) its relevant income and gains[9] are not less than £10,000[10]; and (b) its relevant income and gains exceed the amount of its qualifying expenditure[11]; and (c) the charity incurs or is treated as incurring non-qualifying expenditure[12], relief is not available[13] for so much of the excess as does not exceed the non-qualifying expenditure incurred in that period[14].

In general, income tax principles apply to the computation of income for the purposes of corporation tax, and the provisions of the Income Tax Acts[15] which confer an exemption from income tax, except as otherwise provided, have the like effect for the purposes of corporation tax[16].

Tax relief is given, under the Gift Aid scheme, for donations to charity by individuals if the donation is a qualifying one[17]. The donor must give an appropriate declaration in relation to the donation to the charity[18]. Qualifying donations to charity by companies may also be given tax relief under the Gift Aid scheme, and are, subject to certain conditions, deductible in computing their profits[19]. Relief is also given for donations under a payroll deduction scheme[20].

1   See the Income and Corporation Taxes Act 1988 s 505 (as amended); and INCOME TAXATION. For these purposes, 'charity' means any body of persons or trust established for charitable purposes only (s 506(1)), and it was held in *Camille and Henry Dreyfus Foundation Inc v IRC* [1956] AC 39, [1955] 3 All ER 97, HL, that it is limited to a body of persons or trust established in the United Kingdom and excludes a body or trust established elsewhere. As to the determination of what charitable purposes are by reference to the activities of the organisation see *IRC v Oldham Training and Enterprise Council* [1996] STC 1218, 69 TC 231; *Southwood v A-G* [1998] 40 LS Gaz R 37, Times, 26 October; affd [2000] NLJR 1017, Times, 18 July, CA; and Picarda *Law and Practice Relating to Charities* (3rd Edn, 1999) pp 32–34.

    As to exemptions from tax in relation to the National Heritage Memorial Fund, the Historic Buildings and Monuments Commission for England, the British Museum and the Natural History Museum see the Income and Corporation Taxes Act 1988 s 507 (as amended); and INCOME TAXATION. As to exemptions from tax in relation to scientific research organisations see the Income and Corporation Taxes Act 1988 s 508; and INCOME TAXATION.

2   See ibid s 505(1)(a) (as substituted); and INCOME TAXATION. As to Schedules A, D and F see INCOME TAXATION.

3   Exemption is granted: (1) from tax under Cases III of Schedule D; (2) from tax under Case IV or V of Schedule D in respect of income equivalent to income chargeable under Case III of that Schedule but arising from securities or other possessions outside the United Kingdom; and (3) from tax under Case V of Schedule D in respect of income consisting in any such dividend or other distribution of a company not resident in the United Kingdom as would be chargeable to tax under Schedule F if the company were so resident: see s 505(1)(c)(ii), (iia), (iib) (s 505(1)(c)(ii) as substituted; s 505(1)(c)(iia), (iib) as added); and INCOME TAXATION.

4   See ibid s 505(1)(c) (as amended); and INCOME TAXATION. The importance of the requirement that the income be applied for charitable purposes only is illustrated by *IRC v Educational Grants Association Ltd* [1967] Ch 993, [1967] 2 All ER 893, CA; and see also *George Drexler Ofrex Foundation Trustees v IRC* [1966] Ch 675, [1965] 3 All ER 529; *Sheppard (Trustees of the Woodland Trust) v IRC (No 2)* [1993] STC 240. It was held in *IRC v Helen Slater Charitable Trust Ltd* [1982] Ch 49, [1981] 3 All ER 98, CA, that income had been so applied where a charitable corporation, acting intra vires, made an outright transfer of money applicable to charitable purposes to another charity so as to pass to that other charity full title to the money. See also *Report of the Charity Commissioners for England and Wales for 1988* (HC Paper (1988–89) no 319) paras 41–44. As to problems in relation to annual payments to charities see *IRC v National Book League* [1957] Ch 488, [1957] 2 All ER 644, CA; *Campbell v IRC* [1970] AC 77, [1968] 3 All ER 588, HL.

5   See the Income and Corporation Taxes Act 1988 s 505(1)(e); and INCOME TAXATION.

6   Ie by virtue of ibid s 505(1) (as amended): see INCOME TAXATION.

7   Under ibid s 505(1)(c) (as amended): see INCOME TAXATION.

8   See ibid s 505(2); and INCOME TAXATION. This provision effectively reverses the decision in *IRC v Helen Slater Charitable Trust Ltd* [1982] Ch 49, [1981] 3 All ER 98, CA (see note 4 supra), and is designed to ensure that tax can be charged on the receipt of money by the transferee charity if it is not applied by it for charitable purposes only.

9   Ie (1) income which apart from the Income and Corporation Taxes Act 1988 s 505(1) (as amended) (see INCOME TAXATION) would not be exempt from tax, together with any income which is taxable notwithstanding that provision; and (2) gains which apart from the Taxation of Chargeable Gains Act

1992 s 256 (see CAPITAL GAINS TAXATION vol 5(1) (Reissue) para 228) would be chargeable gains, together with any gains which are chargeable gains notwithstanding that provision: Income and Corporation Taxes Act 1988 s 505(5) (amended by the Taxation of Chargeable Gains Act 1992 s 290(1), Sch 10 para 14(1), (31)).

10  Income and Corporation Taxes Act 1988 s 505(3)(a).

11  Ibid s 505(3)(b). 'Qualifying expenditure', in relation to a chargeable period of a charity, means, subject to the Income and Corporation Taxes Act 1988 s 506(3), expenditure incurred in that period for charitable purposes only: s 506(1).

12  Ibid s 505(3)(b). 'Non-qualifying expenditure' means expenditure which is not qualifying expenditure: s 506(1).

13  Ie under either ibid s 505(1) (as amended) or the Taxation of Chargeable Gains Act 1992 s 256 (see CAPITAL GAINS TAXATION vol 5(1) (Reissue) para 228).

14  See the Income and Corporation Taxes Act 1988 s 505(3) (amended by the Taxation of Chargeable Gains Act 1992 Sch 10 para 14(1), (31)); and INCOME TAXATION. In relation to a chargeable period of less than 12 months, the Income and Corporation Taxes Act 1988 s 505(3) (as amended) has effect as if the amount specified in head (a) in the text were proportionately reduced: s 505(4). In relation to covenanted payments made by companies on or after 1 April 2000, or by individuals on or after 6 April 2000, where by virtue of s 505(3) (as amended) there is an amount of the charity's relevant income and gains for which relief under s 505(1) (as amended) and the Taxation of Chargeable Gains Act 1992 s 256 is not available, the charity may, by notice to the Commissioners of Inland Revenue ('the Board'), specify which items of its relevant income and gains are in whole or in part to be attributed to that amount and if, within 30 days of its being required to do so by the Board, a charity does not give notice under this provision, the items of its relevant income and gains which are to be attributed to the amount in question are to be such as the Board may determine: Income and Corporation Taxes Act 1988 ss 505(6), 832(1); Finance Act 2000 s 41(9). Where it appears to the Board that two or more charities acting in concert are engaged in transactions of which the main purpose or one of the main purposes is the avoidance of tax (whether by the charities or by any other person), the Board may by notice given to the charities provide that, for such chargeable periods as may be specified, the Income and Corporation Taxes Act 1988 s 505(3) (as amended) is to have effect in relation to them with the omission of s 505(3)(a) (see the text to note 10 supra): s 505(7). See further INCOME TAXATION.

15  'The Income Tax Acts' means the enactments relating to income tax, including any provisions of the Corporation Tax Acts which relate to income tax: Income and Corporation Taxes Act 1988 s 831(1). 'The Corporation Tax Acts' means the enactments relating to the taxation of the income and chargeable gains of companies and of company distributions (including provisions relating also to income tax): Income and Corporation Taxes Act 1988 s 831(1).

16  See ibid s 9(1)–(4); and INCOME TAXATION.

17  See the Finance Act 1990 s 25 (as amended); the Finance Act 2000 s 39; and INCOME TAXATION.

18  See the Finance Act 1990 s 25(1) (as amended); and INCOME TAXATION.

19  See the Income and Corporation Taxes Act 1988 ss 338, 339 (as amended); the Finance Act 2000 s 40; and INCOME TAXATION.

20  See the Income and Corporation Taxes Act 1988 s 202 (as amended); the Finance Act 2000 s 38; and INCOME TAXATION.

**380. Capital gains tax and inheritance tax.** A capital gain which accrues to a charity[1] and is applicable and applied for charitable purposes is not chargeable to capital gains tax[2]. However, if property held on charitable trusts ceases to be subject to those trusts, the property is deemed to have been disposed of and immediately re-acquired by the trustees at current market value, and capital gains tax is charged on any notional gain resulting[3]. Capital gains tax is not chargeable on gifts to charities[4].

Transfers of value are exempt from inheritance tax to the extent that the values transferred by them are attributable to property which is given to charities so as to become the property of charities or held on trust for charitable purposes only[5]. The exemption does not apply to a disposition which: (1) takes effect on the termination after the transfer of value of any interest or period; or (2) depends upon a condition which is not satisfied within 12 months after the transfer; or (3) is defeasible[6]. Nor does it apply in relation to property which is an interest in other property if that interest is less than the donor's, or the property is given for a limited period[7], nor where property is given subject to the reservation of an interest[8].

1    This requirement is not satisfied if the asset is comprised in a deceased person's estate and the estate is still being administered, even though the residue, once ascertained, will be held on exclusively charitable trusts: *Prest (Inspector of Taxes) v Bettinson* [1980] STC 607, 53 TC 437.

2    See the Taxation of Chargeable Gains Act 1992 s 256(1); and CAPITAL GAINS TAXATION vol 5(1) (Reissue) para 228.

3    See ibid s 256(2); and CAPITAL GAINS TAXATION vol 5(1) (Reissue) para 228.

4    See ibid s 257; and CAPITAL GAINS TAXATION vol 5(1) (Reissue) para 229.

5    See the Inheritance Tax Act 1984 s 23(1), (6); and INHERITANCE TAXATION vol 24 (Reissue) para 520. As to gifts for national purposes see s 25, Sch 3; and INHERITANCE TAXATION vol 24 (Reissue) para 523. The Inheritance Tax Act 1984 consolidated provisions of the Finance Act 1975 Pt III and other enactments relating to capital transfer tax, renamed by the Finance Act 1986 s 100 as inheritance tax, which replaced estate duty. See generally INHERITANCE TAXATION.

6    See the Inheritance Tax Act 1984 s 23(2); and INHERITANCE TAXATION vol 24 (Reissue) para 520.

7    See ibid s 23(3); and INHERITANCE TAXATION vol 24 (Reissue) para 520.

8    See ibid s 23(4); and INHERITANCE TAXATION vol 24 (Reissue) para 520.

**381. Stamp duty.** The appointment of a new trustee is no longer liable to stamp duty[1]. A conveyance, transfer or lease made or agreed to be made to a charity[2] is now[3] exempt from stamp duty[4], provided it has been adjudicated and duly stamped[5].

1    See the Finance Act 1985 ss 85, 98(6), Sch 24, Sch 27 Pt IX (2) which repealed the relevant part of the Stamp Act 1891 Sch 1.

2    Including the Trustees of the National Heritage Memorial Fund or to the National Endowment for Science, Technology and the Arts: see the Finance Act 1982 s 129(1) (as amended); and STAMP DUTIES AND STAMP DUTY RESERVE TAX vol 44(1) (Reissue) para 1093.

3    Ie in relation to instruments executed on or after 22 March 1982: see ibid s 129(3); and STAMP DUTIES AND STAMP DUTY RESERVE TAX vol 44(1) (Reissue) para 1093.

4    Ie stamp duty under the Finance Act 1999 s 112(3), Sch 13 paras 1–16 (as amended): see STAMP DUTIES AND STAMP DUTY RESERVE TAX.

5    See the Finance Act 1982 s 129(1), (2) (as amended); and STAMP DUTIES AND STAMP DUTY RESERVE TAX vol 44(1) (Reissue) para 1093. See also the Stamp Act 1891 s 62, Sch 1 (repealed with savings in relation to transfers or other instruments relating to units under a unit trust scheme); the Stamp Duty (Exempt Instruments) Regulations 1987, SI 1987/516 (as amended); and STAMP DUTIES AND STAMP DUTY RESERVE TAX.

**382. Value added tax.** Value added tax is only chargeable on the supply of goods and services by a charity when the supply is in the course of a business carried on by the charity[1]. Apart from tax paid on goods or services supplied to a charity for the purposes of any such business, a charity cannot recover by deduction or otherwise the input tax on goods or services supplied to it[2]. In relation to a charity, the supply of certain goods or services are zero-rated supplies, including the supply by a charity of any goods donated to it for sale, the sale of donated goods by a taxable person who has agreed in writing to give all the profits of the sale to such a charity, and the export of any goods by a charity[3].

1    See the Value Added Tax Act 1994 s 4(1); and VALUE ADDED TAX vol 49(1) (Reissue) para 12. It is not, therefore, chargeable on the supply of goods or services to objects of the charity, even if some payment is made for the goods or services. As to value added tax generally see VALUE ADDED TAX. See also *Yoga for Health Foundation v Customs and Excise Comrs* [1985] 1 CMLR 340, [1984] STC 360.

2   As to input tax see the Value Added Tax Act 1994 ss 24–26 (as amended); and VALUE ADDED TAX vol
    49(1) (Reissue) para 201 et seq. See *Customs and Excise Comrs v British Railways Board* [1976] 3 All ER
    100, [1976] 1 WLR 1036, CA; *British Institute of Management v Customs and Excise Comrs* [1978] VATTR
    101 (institute supplied part of its services through a company limited by guarantee and the other part of
    its services as the sole trustee of the foundation it had set up: no justification for separate registration in
    respect of its activities as such charitable trustee); *Whitechapel Art Gallery v Customs and Excise Comrs*
    [1986] STC 156; *Customs and Excise Comrs v Bell Concord Educational Trust Ltd* [1990] 1 QB 1040, [1989]
    2 All ER 217, CA.
3   See the Value Added Tax Act 1994 s 30 (as amended), Sch 8, Pt II, Group 15 (as amended); and VALUE
    ADDED TAX vol 49(1) (Reissue) para 173. See *Lancer UK Ltd v Customs and Excise Comrs* [1986] VATTR
    112 (washing machines designed primarily to clean medical and surgical equipment not 'relevant goods'
    within the Value Added Tax Act 1994 Sch 8 Pt II Group 15 note (3a)).

# (4) RECOVERY OF TRUST PROPERTY

## (i) In general

**383. Payment of legacies to charity.** Trustees of charities or charitable institutions
who   are   entitled   absolutely   to   legacies   may   demand   immediate   payment,
notwithstanding any direction for accumulation[1]. In the case of a charitable bequest
which remained unapplied and accumulated for 30 years, the accumulations were held
to pass with the original bequest[2]. It is a different matter where there is an indefinite gift
of income. It is a well-established proposition that such a gift to an individual carries the
right to corpus, but that principle does not apply to a bequest to a charity, as a charity
continues in perpetuity and effect can be given to a perpetual trust of income for its
purposes[3].

Interest is allowed on a charitable legacy as from the end of a year after the testator's
death[4].

1   *Harbin v Masterman* [1894] 2 Ch 184, CA (affd sub nom *Wharton v Masterman* [1895] AC 186, HL,
    overruling a previous doubt upon this point expressed in *Harbin v Masterman* (1871) LR 12 Eq 559);
    *Re Knapp, Spreckley v A-G* [1929] 1 Ch 341, where a direction to accumulate was held not to be binding,
    but to be a directory provision which the trustees ought prima facie to bear in mind and carry out.
2   *Forbes v Forbes* (1854) 18 Beav 552.
3   *Re Levy, Barclays Bank Ltd v Board of Guardians and Trustees for the Relief of the Jewish Poor* [1960] Ch 346,
    [1960] 1 All ER 42, CA; *Re Beesty's Will Trusts, Farrar v Royal Alfred Merchant Seamen's Society* [1966] Ch
    223, [1964] 3 All ER 82. See paras 80, 123, 133 ante.
4   *Fisher v Brierley (No 3)* (1861) 30 Beav 268.

**384. Remedies for recovery of trust property.** In addition to their right of action
against the trustees for breach of trust[1], beneficiaries who have suffered from an improper
alienation of the trust estate may in many instances follow the trust estate into the hands
of the alienee[2], or attach the property into which the trust estate has been improperly
converted[3]. They are entitled to take whichever remedy appears more beneficial[4]. To
this extent, they have an equitable right to recover money paid to charitable institutions
by executors under a mistake[5], and that money may be traced, provided that it can be
identified or disentangled where it has been mixed with other assets of the recipient
institution[6].

Unless the purchaser is protected by reason of the statutes of limitation[7] or on the ground that he is a purchaser for value without notice, a conveyance to him of charity property which constitutes a breach of trust may be set aside[8]. The same rule applies in the case of a lease in breach of trust[9]. In the absence of collusion or fraud, the court, on setting aside a sale[10] or a lease[11], may direct that an allowance should be made in respect of buildings or other permanent improvements erected or made on the land.

1   See paras 394–295 post; and TRUSTS vol 48 (2000 Reissue) para 980 et seq.
2   *A-G v Kell* (1840) 2 Beav 575; *A-G v Compton* (1842) 1 Y & C Ch Cas 417.
3   *A-G v Newcastle Corpn* (1842) 5 Beav 307; affd sub nom *Newcastle-upon-Tyne Corpn v A-G* (1845) 12 Cl & Fin 402, HL.
4   *A-G v Newcastle Corpn* (1842) 5 Beav 307 at 314 per Lord Langdale MR.
5   *Ministry of Health v Simpson* [1951] AC 251, [1950] 2 All ER 1137, HL. See further EXECUTORS AND ADMINISTRATORS vol 17(2) (Reissue) paras 514–524.
6   *Re Diplock, Diplock v Wintle* [1948] Ch 465, [1948] 2 All ER 318, CA; affd, without reference to tracing of money, sub nom *Ministry of Health v Simpson* [1951] AC 251, [1950] 2 All ER 1137, HL. See further EQUITY vol 16 (Reissue) para 911 et seq.
7   For the statutory provisions governing the limitation of actions see generally the Limitation Act 1980; and LIMITATION OF ACTIONS.
8   *A-G v Christ's Hospital* (1834) 3 My & K 344; *A-G v Brettingham* (1840) 3 Beav 91; *A-G v Kerr* (1840) 2 Beav 420; *A-G v Bishop of Manchester* (1867) LR 3 Eq 436. See also TRUSTS.
9   *Re Lawford Charity, ex p Skinner* (1817) 2 Mer 453 at 457 per Lord Eldon LC.
10  *A-G v Magdalen College, Oxford* (1854) 18 Beav 223.
11  *A-G v Kerr* (1840) 2 Beav 420.

**385. Purchaser with notice of trust.** A purchaser for value with notice that the property purchased is subject to charitable trusts takes subject to those trusts[1], and apart from the Statutes of Limitation[2], no length of possession will protect him[3]. Notice given at any time prior to the execution of the conveyance binds the purchaser[4].

A person acquiring a charity estate for no valuable consideration is not entitled to protection, whether he had notice of the trusts or not[5].

Where a person who purchased land with notice of an equitable right sells to another for value without notice, the latter is protected, even where the right is vested in a charity[6].

After getting notice of the trust a purchaser for value without notice of a trust cannot subsequently protect himself by taking a conveyance of the legal estate from the trustee, for by taking such a conveyance he becomes a trustee himself[7].

1   *Harding v Edge* (1682) 2 Cas in Ch 94; *A-G v Christ's Hospital* (1834) 3 My & K 344; *A-G v Flint* (1844) 4 Hare 147; *A-G v Hall* (1853) 16 Beav 388 at 392 per Romilly MR.
2   See *Incorporated Society in Dublin v Richards* (1841) 1 Dr & War 258; *A-G v Payne* (1859) 27 Beav 168; *A-G v Davey* (1859) 4 De G & J 136; and paras 391–392 post. As to the Limitation Act 1980 (which consolidated previous legislation relating to limitation of actions) generally see LIMITATION OF ACTIONS.
3   *A-G v Christ's Hospital* (1834) 3 My & K 344; and see *Churcher v Martin* (1889) 42 ChD 312.
4   *Woodford Inhabitants v Parkhurst* (1639) Duke 70; and see *Roots v Williamson* (1888) 38 ChD 485 at 497–498 per Stirling J.
5   *Mansell v Mansell* (1732) 2 P Wms 678 at 681 per Lord King LC.
6   *Re Alms Corn Charity, Charity Comrs v Bode* [1901] 2 Ch 750, where, however, the early cases to the contrary, namely *East-Greensted's Case* (1633) Duke 64, and *Sutton Colefield Case* (1635) Duke 68, were not quoted. See also *Charitable Donations and Bequests Comrs v Wybrants* (1845) 2 Jo & Lat 182 at 194 per Lord Sugden LC; *A-G v Lord Gower* (1736) 2 Eq Cas Abr 195; Dart's Vendor and Purchaser (8th Edn, 1929) p 712; and EQUITY vol 16 (Reissue) para 911.
7   *Mumford v Stohwasser* (1874) LR 18 Eq 556 at 563 per Jessel MR, approving *Saunders v Dehew* (1692) 2 Vern 271.

**386. Boundaries of charity land.** A tenant of charity land is under an obligation to the charity to keep that land distinct from his own property during the tenancy[1]. If the charity land has become intermixed with other land, the boundaries of the charity land must be ascertained by inquiry at chambers[2], and if they cannot be pointed out, then the value of the land formerly belonging to the charity must be ascertained[3].

1    *A-G v Fullerton* (1813) 2 Ves & B 263; *Spike v Harding* (1878) 7 ChD 871, where it was said that the obligation rests on the tenant not merely at the end of the term when he comes to deliver up the property, but during the subsistence of the term also.
2    *Spike v Harding* (1878) 7 ChD 871. Formerly the procedure used was to issue a commission to inquire: see *A-G v Fullerton* (1813) 2 Ves & B 263 at 266 per Lord Eldon LC; *Reresby v Farrer* (1700) 2 Vern 414; *A-G v Bowyer* (1800) 5 Ves 300; *Solicitor-General v Bath Corpn* (1849) 18 LJCh 275; *A-G v Stephens* (1855) 6 De GM & G 111. In *Spike v Harding* supra this practice was said to have fallen into disuse in 1852.
3    *A-G v Fullerton* (1813) 2 Ves & B 263.

## (ii)  Rentcharges

**387. Purchase of land subject to charitable rentcharge.** A purchaser for value of land subject to a legal or equitable rentcharge in favour of a charity will take subject to that rentcharge unless (1) the rentcharge is registrable as a land charge and is void against him for want of registration[1]; or (2) the sale is made in exercise of powers under the Settled Land Act 1925, and the rentcharge is capable of being overreached on such a sale[2]; or (3) in the case of an equitable rentcharge, the purchaser had no notice of it[3].

1    See the Land Charges Act 1972 s 2 (as amended), s 4 (as amended); the Law of Property Act 1969 s 24; the Law of Property Act 1925 s 2(1)(i); and LAND CHARGES vol 26 (Reissue) paras 516, 522 et seq; REAL PROPERTY vol 39(2) (Reissue) para 248. As to rentcharges generally see RENTCHARGES AND ANNUITIES.
2    See the Settled Land Act 1925 s 72; the Law of Property Act 1925 s 2(1)(i); and SETTLEMENTS vol 42 (Reissue) para 674; REAL PROPERTY vol 39(2) (Reissue) para 248.
3    *Re Alms Corn Charity, Charity Comrs v Bode* [1901] 2 Ch 750 at 760 per Stirling LJ. In the case of a legal rentcharge not within head (1) or (2) in the text, a purchaser for value takes subject to the charge whether or not he has notice: *East-Greensted's Case* (1633) Duke 64; *Peacock v Thewer* (1638) Duke 82; *Wharton v Charles* (1673) Cas *temp* Finch 81; Sugden's Law of Vendors and Purchasers (14th Edn, 1862) p 722. See *Ind Coope & Co v Emmerson* (1887) 12 App Cas 300 at 306–307, HL, per Earl of Selborne; and cf *A-G v Wilkins* (1853) 17 Beav 285, discussed in Sugden's Law of Vendors and Purchasers (14th Edn, 1862) p 794 et seq.

**388. Remedies: in general.** Rentcharges created for charitable purposes and rentcharges created out of land belonging to charity are both subject to the same incidents and recoverable by the same remedies as other rentcharges[1].

Actions to recover rentcharges which appear to belong to charities may be brought by the Attorney General[2], or by the Charity Commissioners[3]. Charity trustees may also institute such proceedings[4]; and the county court has jurisdiction[5].

If in any such proceedings it is shown that the rentcharge or other payment has at any time been paid for 12 consecutive years to or for the benefit of the charity, that is prima facie evidence of perpetual liability to the payment, and no proof of its origin is necessary[6].

The repeal[7] of the provisions in the Charities Act 1960[8] relating to the redemption of rentcharges does not affect any notice to treat given prior to 1 January 1993[9].

1    See RENTCHARGES AND ANNUITIES vol 39(2) (Reissue) para 831 et seq.
2    See *A-G v Bolton* (1796) 3 Anst 820; *A-G v Jackson* (1805) 11 Ves 365; *A-G v Gascoigne* (1833) 2 My & K 647; *A-G v Naylor* (1863) 1 Hem & M 809.
3    Under the Charities Act 1993 s 32: see para 496 post. As to the Charity Commissioners see paras 486–512 post.
4    Such proceedings do not require the consent of the Commissioners under the Charities Act 1993 s 33 (see para 521 post), nor did they under the old law (see *Bassano v Bradley* [1896] 1 QB 645, DC).
5    See *Bassano v Bradley* [1896] 1 QB 645, DC; the County Courts Act 1984 s 21(2) (as amended); and COUNTY COURTS.
6    See the Charities Act 1993 s 93(1).
7    Ie by the Charities Act 1992 ss 37(5), 78(2), Sch 7.
8    Ie the Charities Act 1960 s 27(2)–(8).
9    See the Charities Act 1992 (Commencement No 1 and Transitional Provisions) Order 1992, SI 1992/1900, art 4(3).

**389. Uncertainty as to land charged.** Where there is a confusion of boundaries, or it is not known out of what land the rentcharge issues[1], or the legal title is not clear or is defective[2], a legal rentcharge may be enforced in equity in favour of a charity where the right could not be enforced at law[3].

1    *A-G v Wilkins* (1853) 22 LJCh 830 at 832 per Romilly MR. See also RENTCHARGES AND ANNUITIES.
2    *Re Herbage Rents, Greenwich, Charity Comrs v Green* [1896] 2 Ch 811 at 825 per Stirling J; *Foley's Charity Trustees v Dudley Corpn* [1910] 1 KB 317, CA.
3    The law here enunciated is in accordance with the well-established principle that equity will aid defective assurances in favour of charity: see Shelford's Law of Mortmain (1836) 514.

**390. Time for recovery.** A defence founded on the Limitation Act 1980[1] may be a complete bar to an action to recover a charitable rentcharge[2], but time does not run where, by reason of the circumstances, no beneficiary is in a position to make a claim[3].

1    The Limitation Act 1980 consolidated previous legislation relating to the limitation of actions. See generally LIMITATION OF ACTIONS.
2    *A-G v Wilkins* (1853) 17 Beav 285 at 293 per Romilly MR; *A-G v Stephens* (1855) 6 De GM & G 111 at 146 per Lord Cranworth LC; *President etc of St Mary Magdalen College, Oxford v A-G* (1857) 6 HL Cas 189.
3    *A-G v Persse* (1842) 2 Dr & War 67, where a rentcharge was given as a salary for a schoolmaster to be appointed by a certain person; no appointment was made for 27 years, but nevertheless the rentcharge was not barred. See also *Incorporated Society in Dublin v Richards* (1841) 1 Dr & War 258 at 288 per Lord Sugden LC.

### (iii) Limitation of Actions

**391. Limitation periods.** In proceedings against trustees[1], whether express or constructive, the general rule is that, except in cases of fraud, retention of the trust property, or conversion by the trustee to his own use[2], the right of a beneficiary to recover trust property, whether real or personal, or to sue in respect of any breach of trust, is barred after the expiration of six years[3]. Time runs from the date on which the right of action accrued[4] or the date of the breach of trust[5]. It is very doubtful, however, whether these provisions have any application to a charitable trust because in most, if not all, charitable trusts there are no individual beneficiaries[6]. Certainly it has no application to an action by the Attorney General to enforce public charitable trusts[7].

Claims by charities to land or rent are barred after the expiration of 12 years[8], and claims by charities to an interest in the estate of a deceased person are also barred after the expiration of 12 years, and claims to arrears of interest of a legacy after the expiration of six years[9].

1 'Trustee' has the same meaning as in the Trustee Act 1925 (see TRUSTS vol 48 (2000 Reissue) para 501): Limitation Act 1980 s 38(1).
2 See ibid s 21(1); and LIMITATION OF ACTIONS vol 28 (Reissue) para 1037 et seq. See also s 21(2); and LIMITATION OF ACTIONS vol 28 (Reissue) para 1037.
3 See ibid s 21(3); and LIMITATION OF ACTIONS vol 28 (Reissue) para 1040.
4 See ibid s 21(3); and LIMITATION OF ACTIONS vol 28 (Reissue) para 1041. As to what is the date of accrual of the right of action to recover land see s 15(6), (7), Sch 1 (as amended); and LIMITATION OF ACTIONS vol 28 (Reissue) para 933 et seq.
5 *Thorne v Heard and Marsh* [1895] AC 495, HL.
6 *A-G v Cocke* [1988] Ch 414, [1988] 2 All ER 391, citing *Thomson v Trustees of the Honourable Society of the Inner Temple* (30 May 1967, unreported).
7 *A-G v Cocke* [1988] Ch 414 at 421, [1988] 2 All ER 391 at 395 per Harman J where it was also held that an action for an account was not 'an action … to recover trust property or in respect of any breach of trust' within the wording of the Limitation Act 1980 s 21(3).
8 See ibid s 15; and LIMITATION OF ACTIONS vol 28 (Reissue) para 928 et seq.
9 See ibid s 22; and LIMITATION OF ACTIONS vol 28 (Reissue) para 1058. Cf *Cadbury v Smith* (1869) LR 9 Eq 37.

**392. Possession of land under void lease or conveyance.** Charity trustees may acquire a valid title to land by possession under a void lease[1]. If no rent is paid, no tenancy is created, and the period of limitation runs from the date on which possession is acquired[2]. The payment of rent, however small, establishes the relation of landlord and tenant; and where there is a tenancy at will the period of limitation runs from the actual termination of the tenancy[3], but where there is a tenancy from year to year or other period without a lease in writing, it runs from the end of the first year or other period[4] or from the last payment of rent[5].

1 *President and Governors of Magdalen Hospital v Knotts* (1879) 4 App Cas 324, HL (disabling Acts); *Bunting v Sargent* (1879) 13 ChD 330; *Webster v Southey* (1887) 36 ChD 9 at 19 per Kay J (mortmain); cf *Bishop of Bangor v Parry* [1891] 2 QB 277 (lack of consent of Charity Commissioners). It was held in *Churcher v Martin* (1889) 42 ChD 312 that under the Statutes of Limitation charity trustees might also acquire a valid title to land of which they had enjoyed possession under a conveyance rendered void for not complying with the Mortmain and Charitable Uses Act 1888 (repealed: see para 76 ante).
2 *President and Governors of Magdalen Hospital v Knotts* (1879) 4 App Cas 324 at 334, HL, per Earl Cairns LC.
3 See LIMITATION OF ACTIONS vol 28 (Reissue) paras 956, 967. The Limitation Act 1939 s 9, which provided that a tenancy of will was deemed to be determined at the expiration of one year from its commencement, unless determined earlier, has been repealed: see LIMITATION OF ACTIONS vol 28 (Reissue) para 967.
4 See the Limitation Act 1980 s 15(6), Sch 1 para 5(1); and LIMITATION OF ACTIONS vol 28 (Reissue) paras 957, 1056.

5    See ibid Sch 1 para 5(2); and LIMITATION OF ACTIONS vol 28 (Reissue) paras 957, 1056. See also
     *Bunting v Sargent* (1879) 13 ChD 330; *Webster v Southey* (1887) 36 ChD 9; *President and Governors of*
     *Magdalen Hospital v Knotts* (1879) 4 App Cas 324 at 335, HL, per Lord Selborne.


**393. Claims adverse to charity barred.** The right to claim the benefit of a gift over
of land from one charity to another, or of a reverter to the grantor, may be barred by
effluxion of time[1]. The charity trustees remain in possession under the original trusts, and
not for their own benefit[2].

Time does not run in favour of a person who has obtained possession of charity land
by fraud so long as the fraud is concealed, but it begins to run from the date of discovery
or the date when with reasonable diligence it could have been discovered[3].


1    See *Re Orchard Street Schools Trustees* [1878] WN 211; *Christ's Hospital v Grainger* (1849) 1 Mac & G 460;
     *Re Ingleton Charity, Croft v A-G* [1956] Ch 585, [1956] 2 All ER 881.
2    *Re Ingleton Charity, Croft v A-G* [1956] Ch 585, [1956] 2 All ER 881.
3    See the Limitation Act 1980 s 32 (as amended); and LIMITATION OF ACTIONS vol 28 (Reissue) para 1119
     et seq. See also *Hovenden v Lord Annesley* (1806) 2 Sch & Lef 607 at 634 per Lord Redesdale LC; *Charitable*
     *Donations and Bequests Comrs v Wybrants* (1845) 2 Jo & Lat 182.


# (5) LIABILITY OF TRUSTEES


**394. Misapplication of trust property.** In the absence of evidence to the contrary,
it is presumed that trustees have faithfully discharged their duty[1].

Charity trustees, whether a corporate body or individuals, using trust money for their
own purposes[2], for purposes not in accordance with the trusts[3], occasioning the
destruction of the trust property[4], improperly alienating it[5], or negligently allowing
others to misappropriate it[6], are strictly liable to make good any deficiency or loss[7]. A
threatened application of charity property for non-charitable purposes will be restrained
by injunction[8].

Parish officials are not liable for breaches of trust committed by their predecessors in
office[9].

Although the court is severe with trustees who wilfully, corruptly or negligently
misapply the trust property, it acts leniently where the administration of the funds has
been honest but mistaken[10], as, for example, where a wrong construction has been put
on an ambiguous instrument of trust[11]. Where a corporation is trustee, the court tends
to leniency more than in the case of individual trustees[12].

If it appears to the court that a trustee is or may be personally liable for any breach of
trust but has acted honestly and reasonably and ought fairly to be excused for the breach
and for omitting to obtain the court's directions in the matter in which he committed
the breach, the court may relieve him wholly or partly from that personal liability[13]. In
such a case the onus is upon the trustee to prove that he acted both honestly and
reasonably[14]: this is a question of fact depending on the circumstances of each case[15].


1    *A-G v Earl of Stamford* (1843) 1 Ph 737 at 747 per Lord Cottenham LC. As to the liabilities of trustees
     generally see TRUSTS vol 48 (2000 Reissue) para 980 et seq.
2    *Kennington Hastings Case* (1612) Duke 71 (retainer by trustee of increase of rent on reletting of charity
     lands); *A-G v Bedford Corpn* (1754) 2 Ves Sen 505 (retainer by schoolmaster of charity school of usher's

salary); *A-G v Bolton* (1796) 3 Anst 820 (retainer by vicar of charity annuity payable to preacher); *A-G v Dixie, ex p Bosworth School* (1805) 13 Ves 519.
3    *A-G v Brewers' Co* (1816) 1 Mer 495; *A-G v Cambridge Corpn* (1836) 5 LJCh 357.
4    *Ex p Greenhouse* (1815) 1 Madd 92 at 109 per Plumer V-C (chapel pulled down by trustees).
5    *A-G v East Retford Corpn* (1838) 3 My & Cr 484; *A-G v Wisbeach Corpn* (1842) 11 LJCh 412 (innocent but improper sale of charity lands in redemption of land tax on other lands belonging to the trustees); and see *A-G v Newark-upon-Trent Corpn* (1842) 1 Hare 395.
6    *A-G v Leicester Corpn* (1844) 7 Beav 176.
7    Charity trustees may obtain complete protection by seeking the advice of the Charity Commissioners under the Charities Act 1993 s 29 (see paras 335–336 ante), or their authorisation for transactions under s 26 (see paras 330–333 ante). They may also pay trust money into court under the Trustee Act 1925 s 63 (as amended) (see para 537 post). As to funding of indemnity insurance by charities for trustees, particularly in relation to recklessness and wrongful trading, see *Trustees' Indemnity Insurance (1993)* Decisions of the Charity Commissioners (1994) vol 2 p 24.
8    *Baldry v Feintuck* [1972] 2 All ER 81, [1972] 1 WLR 552.
9    *Ex p Fowlser* (1819) 1 Jac & W 70; *French v Dear* (1800) 5 Ves 547.
10   *A-G v Exeter Corpn* (1826) 2 Russ 45 at 54 per Lord Eldon LC ('to act on any other principles would be to deter all prudent persons from becoming trustees of charities); *A-G v Dean and Canons of Christ Church* (1826) 2 Russ 321; *A-G v Pretyman* (1841) 4 Beav 462 at 464; *Andrews v M'Guffog* (1886) 11 App Cas 313 at 324, HL, per Lord Watson. See also *A-G v Bowyer* (1798) 3 Ves 714 at 729 per Lord Thurlow LC.
11   *A-G v Master, Wardens etc of the Wax Chandlers' Co* (1873) LR 6 HL 1. See, however, *Ministry of Health v Simpson* [1951] AC 251, [1950] 2 All ER 1137, HL; affg *Re Diplock, Diplock v Wintle* [1948] Ch 465, [1948] 2 All ER 318, CA.
12   *A-G v Baliol College, Oxford* (1744) 9 Mod Rep 407 at 409–410 per Lord Hardwicke LC; *A-G v East Retford Corpn* (1833) 2 My & K 35 at 37–38 per Leach MR; *A-G v Newbury Corpn* (1834) 3 My & K 647 at 651 per Lord Brougham LC; *A-G v Caius College* (1837) 2 Keen 150 at 169 per Lord Langdale MR; *Edinburgh Corpn v Lord Advocate* (1879) 4 App Cas 823, HL.
13   See the Trustee Act 1925 s 61; and TRUSTS vol 48 (2000 Reissue) para 1019. As to the court's jurisdiction under this provision see *Re Allsop, Whittaker v Bamford* [1914] 1 Ch 1, CA (decided under earlier legislation); *Re Pauling's Settlement Trusts, Younghusband v Coutts & Co* [1964] Ch 303, [1963] 3 All ER 1, CA. As to when relief will be granted see TRUSTS vol 48 (2000 Reissue) para 1019.
14   *National Trustees Co of Australasia v General Finance Co of Australasia* [1905] AC 373, PC; *Re Stuart, Smith v Stuart* [1897] 2 Ch 583.
15   *Re Turner, Barker v Ivimey* [1897] 1 Ch 536.

## 395. Accounts against defaulting trustees.

The general rule is that, in the absence of special circumstances[1], accounts are to be taken against the trustees from the date at which the misapplication commenced[2]. Each case is, however, decided on its merits at the court's discretion, and therefore the dates to which accounts against charity trustees are carried back differ widely[3]. The court may decline to direct an account where the litigation would be expensive and the benefit to the charity problematical or trifling[4].

Where the misapplication has been innocent, accounts are usually directed from the commencement of the action[5]; but they may also be ordered from the date at which notice was given to the trustees questioning the propriety of the application[6], from the date of the decree declaring the application improper[7], or from the date of the last appointment of a new trustee[8]. An account is not, it seems, directed against innocent trustees where their co-trustees are entirely responsible for the breach of trust[9].

In dealing with charitable corporations which have acted mistakenly but honestly the court likewise has a considerable measure of discretion[10].

1    Eg innocent misapplication: see the text and notes 5–9 infra.
2    *A-G v Cashel Corpn* (1842) 3 Dr & War 294; *A-G v Davey* (1854) 19 Beav 521 at 527 per Romilly MR, where accounts were ordered from the dates when improper leases were granted. See also *A-G v Newbury Corpn* (1834) 3 My & K 647 at 653 per Lord Brougham LC, where the question of directing an account from the date of the foundation of the charity was discussed.

3    *A-G v Davey* (1854) 19 Beav 521 at 527 per Romilly MR. In *A-G v Pretyman* (1841) 4 Beav 462 at 467 per Lord Langdale MR, the question was referred by the court to the consideration of the Attorney General. As to the Attorney General's power to sanction compromises in such cases see *A-G v Exeter Corpn* (1822) Jac 443 at 448 per Plumer MR; *A-G v Exeter Corpn* (1827) 2 Russ 362; *A-G v Brettingham* (1840) 3 Beav 91; and cf *A-G v Carlisle Corpn* (1831) 4 Sim 275.

4    *A-G v Dixie, ex p Bosworth School* (1805) 13 Ves 519; *A-G v Cullum* (1836) 1 Keen 104; *A-G v Shearman* (1839) 2 Beav 104.

5    *A-G v Joliffe* (1822) 1 LJOS Ch 43; *A-G v Winchester Corpn* (1824) 3 LJOS Ch 64; *A-G v Stationers' Co* (1831) 9 LJOS Ch 229; *A-G v Caius College* (1837) 2 Keen 150 at 166 per Lord Langdale MR; *A-G v Harper, A-G v Nash* (1838) 8 LJCh 12; *A-G v Drapers' Co, Kendrick's Charity* (1841) 4 Beav 67; *A-G v Drapers' Co, Kendrick's Charity* (1847) 10 Beav 558; *A-G v Christ's Hospital* (1841) 4 Beav 73; *A-G v Hall* (1853) 16 Beav 388 at 395 per Romilly MR; *A-G v Davey* (1854) 19 Beav 521; *A-G v Master, Wardens etc of the Wax Chandlers' Co* (1873) LR 6 HL 1 at 15 per Lord Chelmsford.

6    *A-G v Berwick-upon-Tweed Corpn* (1829) Taml 239; *A-G v East Retford Corpn* (1833) 2 My & K 35 at 37 per Leach MR; *A-G v Cambridge Corpn* (1836) 5 LJCh 357.

7    *A-G v Tufnell* (1849) 12 Beav 35.

8    *A-G v Newbury Corpn* (1834) 3 My & K 647.

9    *A-G v Joliffe* (1822) 1 LJOS Ch 43; *A-G v Holland* (1837) 2 Y & C Ex 683, where co-trustees of a charity under a will were directed to act annually in rotation.

10   *Re Freeston's Charity, Sylvester v Master and Fellows of University College, Oxford* [1978] 1 All ER 481, [1978] 1 WLR 120; affd [1979] 1 All ER 51, [1978] 1 WLR 741, CA.


**396. Liability for interest or profits.** It has been held that, where a charity trustee uses the trust funds for trading purposes, he is accountable to the charity for any profit made, or for interest at the rate of 5 per cent if the latter is the larger amount[1]; but in general a defaulting trustee is charged with interest at 4 per cent[2]. However, these rates have been thought to be unrealistic in modern conditions[3], and in some relatively recent non-charity cases it has been held that the proper rate of interest is 1 per cent above bank rate[4], while in others it has been said that it should be that allowed from time to time on the court's short term investment account[5]. Whether the interest is simple or compound is in the discretion of the court[6].

1    *A-G v Solly* (1829) 2 Sim 518, where a charity trustee who used the trust property for trading purposes was charged 5%, but not compound interest; *A-G v Cambridge Corpn* (1836) 5 LJCh 357; *Re Davis, Davis v Davis* [1902] 2 Ch 314, applied in the non-charity case of *Gordon v Gonda* [1955] 2 All ER 762, [1955] 1 WLR 885, CA.

2    *Jones v Foxall* (1852) 15 Beav 388 at 392 per Romilly MR; *A-G v Alford* (1855) 4 De GM & G 843 at 851 per Lord Cranworth LC; *Re Emmet's Estate, Emmet v Emmet* (1881) 17 ChD 142. In *A-G v Cambridge Corpn* (1836) 5 LJCh 357, the interest was 5%. As to trustees' liability to pay interest see TRUSTS vol 48 (2000 Reissue) paras 1002–1004.

3    See *Bartlett v Barclays Bank Trust Co Ltd (No 2)* [1980] Ch 515 at 547, [1980] 2 All ER 92 at 98 per Brightman LJ.

4    See *Belmont Finance Corpn Ltd v Williams Furniture Ltd (No 2)* [1980] 1 All ER 393, CA; *O'Sullivan v Management Agency and Music Ltd* [1985] QB 428, [1985] 3 All ER 351, CA.

5    See *Bartlett v Barclays Bank Trust Co Ltd (No 2)* [1980] Ch 515, [1980] 2 All ER 92. As to the court's short term investment account see the Administration of Justice Act 1965 s 6(1) (repealed: see now the Administration of Justice Act 1982 Pt VI (ss 38–48) (as amended)).

6    See the cases cited in notes 1–5 supra; *Incorporated Society in Dublin v Richards* (1841) 1 Dr & War 258 (where a trustee who set up a title adverse to the charity was charged compound interest); *A-G v Alford* (1855) 4 De GM & G 843 at 851 per Lord Cranworth LC. In other cases relating to private trusts (*Heighington v Grant* (1840) 5 My & Cr 258; *Jones v Foxall* (1852) 15 Beav 388) compound interest has been charged where trust funds had been employed in trade. See also the non-charity cases of *Burdick v Garrick* (1870) 5 Ch App 233; *Re Davis, Davis v Davis* [1902] 2 Ch 314; and TRUSTS.

**397. Liability of trustee's agent.** Where a trustee administers a charity by means of a mere agent, the latter is usually accountable in case of default only to his principal and not to the charity, as the ordinary law of agency is applicable to charity cases[1]; but if the agent, knowing that a breach of trust is being committed, interferes and assists in the breach, or if a stranger intermeddles with the affairs and administration of a charity, each makes himself a quasi-trustee and as such personally answerable[2].

1    *A-G v Earl of Chesterfield* (1854) 18 Beav 596. Note that in that case it was not alleged that the agent himself was in any sense a trustee. As to the relationship between principal and agent see further AGENCY.
2    *A-G v Earl of Chesterfield* (1854) 18 Beav 596 at 599 per Romilly MR. See also *A-G v Leicester Corpn* (1844) 7 Beav 176 (where a town clerk who retained trust funds with the consent of a municipal corporation, the actual trustee of the charity, was held jointly liable with the corporation for the breach of trust); *A-G v Wilson* (1840) Cr & Ph 1 (where a corporation was trustee of a charity and the members of the governing body were held liable for injury to the charity occasioned by their default); *Charitable Corpn v Sutton* (1742) 2 Atk 400 at 405 per Lord Hardwicke LC. See also TRUSTS vol 48 (2000 Reissue) paras 597, 985.

**398. Remedy against trustee corporation.** When a corporation is declared liable to make good a loss caused by a breach of trust, the court does not charge the loss upon the general property of the corporation. The remedy is enforceable by process of sequestration[1].

1    *A-G v East Retford Corpn* (1838) 3 My & Cr 484.

**399. Liability of trust property.** Charity property cannot be taken to indemnify a person injured by a breach of trust committed by the trustees of the charity[1].

1    *Heriot's Hospital (Feoffees) v Ross* (1846) 12 Cl & Fin 507, HL (a Scottish case).

# (6)  EDUCATIONAL CHARITIES

## (i)  In general

**400. Endowments for maintenance of voluntary schools.** Where the trust deed[1] of a voluntary school requires that the income of any endowment is to be applied towards the maintenance of a school which a local education authority is required to maintain as a voluntary school, any such income must not be paid to the local education authority but must be applied by the governors of the school towards the discharge of their obligations, if any[2], with respect to the maintenance of the school, or in such other manner, if any, as may be determined by a scheme[3] for the administration of the endowment[4].

1    'Trust deed' means, in relation to any voluntary school, any instrument, other than an instrument of government, regulating the constitution of the school's governing body or the maintenance, management or conduct of the school: Education Act 1996 s 579(1) (definition added by the School

Standards and Framework Act 1998 s 140(1), Sch 30 para 183(a)(iv)); School Standards and Framework Act 1998 s 183. As to voluntary schools see EDUCATION.

2    In the case of a controlled school, the governors have no obligations with respect to the maintenance of the school. The governors of aided and special agreement schools are responsible for the expenses referred to in the School Standards and Framework Act 1998 s 22, Sch 3 para 3: see EDUCATION. As to controlled schools and aided and special agreement schools see EDUCATION.

3    Ie a scheme made by the Charity Commissioners. As to the Charity Commissioners see paras 486–512 post.

4    School Standards and Framework Act 1998 Sch 3 para 11.

**401. Power of local education authorities to accept gifts for educational purposes.** A local education authority is empowered to accept, hold and administer any property on trust for purposes connected with education[1]. Any intention on the part of the authority that a school, other than a nursery school[2] or a special school[3], should be vested in the authority as trustees is treated[4] as an intention to establish a new community school[5]. Accordingly proposals for that purpose must be published and submitted to the Secretary of State[6].

1    Education Act 1996 s 529(1). As to the application of an endowment of an existing school transferred to the local education authority see *Re Poplar and Blackwall Free School* (1878) 8 ChD 543.

2    As to nursery schools see EDUCATION.

3    As to special schools see EDUCATION.

4    Ie treated for the purposes of the School Standards and Framework Act 1998 s 28: see EDUCATION.

5    Education Act 1996 s 529(2). As to community schools see EDUCATION.

6    Ibid s 529(2). Such proposals are published in accordance with s 28 and submitted to the Secretary of State in accordance with that provision: s 529(2) (amended by the School Standards and Framework Act 1998 s 140(1), Sch 30 para 145(a)). Any school which, in accordance with the Education Act 1996 s 529(2) (as amended), is vested in a local education authority as trustees, is a community school: s 529(3) (amended by the School Standards and Framework Act 1998 Sch 30 para 145(b)).

**402. Extent of local authority's powers relating to charitable purposes.** It is the duty of the local education authority to contribute towards the spiritual, moral, mental and physical development of the community by securing that efficient primary education, secondary education and further education is available to meet the needs of the population of its area, so far as its powers extend[1]. This duty does not extend to matters in respect of which the higher education funding councils[2] or the further education funding councils[3] have a duty[4]. A local education authority has no locus standi to institute legal proceedings for the construction of a will purporting to create a charitable trust[5]. However, a local authority which is not a local education authority may help with education matters by establishing a trust fund to provide free or assisted places at independent schools[6].

1    Education Act 1996 s 13(1). As from a day to be appointed the reference to further education in s 13(1) is repealed by the Learning Skills Act 2000 s 149, Sch 9 paras 1, 52(1), (2). At the date at which this volume states the law no such day had been appointed.

2    Ie established under the Further and Higher Education Act 1992 s 62 (as amended): see EDUCATION.

3    Ie established under ibid s 1 (prospectively repealed): see EDUCATION.

4    Education Act 1996 s 13(2). As from a day to be appointed the reference to the further education funding councils is repealed and replaced by a reference to the Learning and Skills Council for England or the National Council for Education and Training for Wales by the Learning and Skills Act 2000 Sch 9 paras 1, 52(1), (3). At the date at which this volume states the law no such day had been appointed. As to the

Learning and Skills Council for England and the National Council for Education and Training for Wales see EDUCATION.

5    *Re Belling, Enfield London Borough Council v Public Trustee* [1967] Ch 425, [1967] 1 All ER 105

6    *Manchester City Council v Greater Manchester Metropolitan County Council* (1980) 78 LGR 560, HL. As to independent schools see EDUCATION.


## (ii)  Trusts


**403. Secretary of State's powers as to educational trusts.** The Secretary of State[1] may by order make such modifications of any trust deed[2] or other instrument relating to[3]: (1) a school which is or is to become a foundation, voluntary or foundation special school[4]; or (2) property held on trust for the purposes of such a school[5]. Such an order may be made so as to have permanent effect or to have effect for such period as is specified in the order[6]. However, before making such an order the Secretary of State must consult: (a) the governing body of the school in question; (b) any trustees holding property on trust for the purposes of the school; (c) in the case of a Church of England, Church in Wales or Roman Catholic Church school, the appropriate diocesan authority[7]; and (d) such other persons as he considers appropriate[8].

The Secretary of State may by order make such modifications of any trust deed or other instrument relating to or regulating any institution that provides or is concerned in the provision of educational services, or is concerned in educational research, as, after consultation with the persons responsible for the management of the institution, appear to him to be requisite to enable them to fulfil any condition or meet any requirement imposed by regulations[9]. Any modification made by such an order may be made to have permanent effect or to have effect for such period as may be specified in the order[10].

1    Ie the Secretary of State for Education and Employment: see CONSTITUTIONAL LAW AND HUMAN RIGHTS vol 8(2) (Reissue) paras 448–451. In relation to Wales, the functions of the Secretary of State under the School Standards and Framework Act 1998 and the Education Act 1996 are carried out by the National Assembly for Wales: see the National Assembly for Wales (Transfer of Functions) Order 1999, SI 1999/672, art 2, Sch 1. As to the National Assembly for Wales see CONSTITUTIONAL LAW AND HUMAN RIGHTS.

2    For the meaning of 'trust deed' see para 400 note 1 ante.

3    School Standards and Framework Act 1998 s 82(1).

4    Ibid s 82(1)(a). As to foundation, voluntary and foundation special schools see EDUCATION.

5    Ibid s 82(1)(b).

6    Ibid s 82(3).

7    As to the appropriate diocesan authority for a Church of England, Church in Wales or Roman Catholic Church school see EDUCATION.

8    School Standards and Framework Act 1998 s 82(2). Where any scheme for the regulation of endowed charities includes any provision for the benefit of children who are or have been scholars in a county or voluntary school, an army school is deemed to be a county or voluntary school within the meaning of those provisions: Army Schools Act 1891 s 1(1) (modified by the Education Act 1944 s 120(1)(a)). An army school is a school established for the purpose of affording education to children of non-commissioned officers and men of Her Majesty's regular land forces and conducted under the authority of a Secretary of State: Army Schools Act 1891 s 1(2). As to voluntary schools see EDUCATION.

9    Education Act 1996 s 489(3). As to the regulations made under s 485 (grants in aid of educational services or research) see EDUCATION.

10   Ibid s 489(4).

**404. Secretary of State's powers as to trusts for religious education.** Where in relation to any time before 1 Septembet 1999[1], the premises of a voluntary or grant-maintained school[2] have ceased to be used for such a school[3], or in relation to any time on or after 1 September 1999[4]: (1) the premises of a foundation or voluntary school[5] have ceased to be used for such a school[6]; or (2) in the opinion of the Secretary of State[7] it is likely such premises will cease to be so used[8], he may by order[9] made by statutory instrument make new provision as to the use of any endowment[10] if it is shown[11] either[12]: (a) that the endowment is or has been held wholly or partly for or in connection with the provision at the school of religious education in accordance with the tenets of a particular religion or religious denomination[13]; or (b) that the endowment is or has been used wholly or partly for or in connection with the provision at the school of such religious education and that the following requirements are fulfilled[14], namely (i) that the school was or has been maintained as a voluntary or grant-maintained school[15] or as a foundation or voluntary school[16] since 1 April 1945[17]; and (ii) that religious education in accordance with the tenets of the religion or denomination concerned is, and from that date has been, provided at the school or, where the premises have ceased to be used for the purposes of the school, was provided at the school from that date until immediately before the premises ceased to be so used[18].

Such an order by the Secretary of State may require or authorise the disposal by sale or otherwise of any land or other property forming part of an endowment affected by the order, including the premises of the school and any teacher's dwelling-house, and may also consolidate any endowments to be dealt with by the scheme[19]. Subject to this and to any statutory provisions affecting the endowments, the order must establish and give effect, with a view to enabling the denomination concerned to participate more effectively in the administration of the statutory system of public education, to a scheme or schemes[20] for the endowments dealt with by the order to be used[21] for appropriate educational purposes[22]. The order may include any necessary or expedient incidental or supplementary provisions[23].

1 School Standards and Framework Act 1998 s 20(7); School Standards and Framework Act 1998 (Appointed Day) Order 1998, SI 1998/2083, art 2.
2 As to voluntary schools and grant-maintained schools see EDUCATION.
3 Education Act 1996 s 554(1)(a) (s 554(1) substituted by the School Standards and Framework Act 1998 s 140(1), Sch 30 para 168(2)).
4 Education Act 1996 s 554(1)(b) (as substituted: see note 3 supra).
5 Ie within the meaning of the School Standards and Framework Act 1998: see EDUCATION. As to foundation schools see EDUCATION.
6 Education Act 1996 s 554(1)(b)(i) (as substituted: see note 3 supra).
7 Ie the Secretary of State for Education and Employment: see CONSTITUTIONAL LAW AND HUMAN RIGHTS vol 8(2) (Reissue) paras 448–451. In relation to Wales, the functions of the Secretary of State under the Education Act 1996 are carried out by the National Assembly for Wales: National Assembly for Wales (Transfer of Functions) Order 1999, SI 1999/672, art 2, Sch 1. As to the National Assembly for Wales see CONSTITUTIONAL LAW AND HUMAN RIGHTS.
8 Education Act 1996 s 554(1)(b)(ii) (as substituted: see note 3 supra).
9 The order may be made only on the application of the persons appearing to the Secretary of State to be the appropriate authority of the denomination concerned: ibid s 555(1). The Secretary of State must, not less than one month before making the order give notice of the proposed order and of the right of persons interested to make representations on it: s 555(2). The order must take into account any representations that may be made to the Secretary of State by any person interested in it before the order is made: s 555(4). The notice must be given: (1) by giving to any persons appearing to the Secretary of State to be trustees of an endowment affected by the proposed order a notice of the proposal to make it, together with a draft or summary of the provisions proposed to be included; and (2) by publishing, in such manner as the Secretary of State thinks sufficient for informing any other persons interested, a notice of the

proposal to make the order and of the place where any person interested may, during a period of not less than a month, inspect such a draft or summary, and by keeping a draft or summary available for inspection in accordance with the notice: s 555(3).

10   'Endowment' includes property not subject to any restriction on the expenditure of capital: ibid s 554(5). As to the extension to army schools of certain provisions relating to endowments see EDUCATION.

11   'Shown' means shown to the satisfaction of the Secretary of State: ibid s 554(5).

12   Ibid s 554(2), which is expressed to be subject to s 555 (see note 9 supra), s 556(1), (2) (as amended) (see the text and notes 19–22 infra).

13   Ibid s 554(2)(a).

14   Ibid s 554(2)(b), which is expressed to be subject to s 554(4) (see the text and note 18 infra).

15   Ie within the meaning of the Education Act 1996: see EDUCATION.

16   Ie within the meaning of the School Standards and Framework Act 1998: see EDUCATION.

17   Education Act 1996 s 554(3)(a) (substituted by the School Standards and Framework Act 1998 Sch 30 para 168(3)(a)). The text refers to the date on which the Education Act 1944 Pt II (ss 6–69) (now repealed) came into force.

18   Education Act 1996 s 554(3)(b). 'Used' in this context means used in pursuance of ss 377, 378, 380, 381 (all repealed) (or any corresponding earlier enactment), or the School Standards and Framework Act 1998 Sch 19 paras 3 or 4 (see EDUCATION): Education Act 1996 s 554(3)(b) (amended by the School Standards and Framework Act 1998 Sch 30 para 168(3)(b)). Where religious education in accordance with such tenets is shown to have been given to any pupils at: (1) a controlled school (within the meaning of the Education Act 1996); (2) a grant-maintained school (within the meaning of the Education Act 1996) which was a controlled school immediately before it became a grant-maintained school; or (3) a foundation or voluntary controlled school with a religious character (within the meaning of the School Standards and Framework Act 1998 Pt II (ss 22–83) (as amended)), the religious education is taken to have been given to them at the request of their parents, unless the contrary is shown: Education Act 1996 s 554(4)(b) (substituted by the School Standards and Framework Act 1998 Sch 30 para 168(4)). As to controlled schools see EDUCATION.

As to the adoption of uniform statutory trusts as the trusts on which endowments regulated by an order under the Education Act 1996 s 554 (as amended) are to be held see s 557 (as amended), Sch 36; and EDUCATION.

19   Ibid s 556(1).

20   Such a scheme may provide for the retention of the capital of any endowment and the application of the accruing income, or may authorise the application or expenditure of capital to such extent and on such conditions as may be determined under the scheme: see ibid s 556(4).

21   Ie either in connection with schools which are foundation schools or voluntary schools or partly in connection with such schools (or either description of such schools) and partly in other ways related to the locality served by the school at the premises referred to in ibid s 554(1) (as substituted) (see the text and notes 1–8 supra): s 556(2) (amended by the School Standards and Framework Act 1998 Sch 30 para 169(a), (b)).

22   Education Act 1996 s 556(2). 'Use for appropriate educational purposes' means use for educational purposes in connection with the provision of religious education in accordance with the tenets of the religion or denomination concerned (including use for any purpose specified in Sch 36 (uniform statutory trusts for educational endowments): see EDUCATION): s 556(3).

23   Ibid s 556(6). Thus it may provide for the appointment and powers of trustees and for vesting property in trustees: see s 556(6).

**405. Sex discrimination: application by trustees to remove or modify restriction.** Where a trust deed or other instrument concerns property available for or in connection with the provision of education in certain establishments[1] and in any way restricts the benefits available under the instrument to persons of one sex[2], the trustees or the responsible body[3] may apply to the Secretary of State[4] for the removal or modification of the restriction[5]. If, on such an application, the Secretary of State is satisfied that the removal or modification of the restriction would conduce to the advancement of education without sex discrimination, he may by order make such modifications of the instrument as appear to him expedient for removing or modifying the restriction, and for any supplemental or incidental purposes[6]. If the trust was created by gift or bequest, no such order may be made until 25 years after the date on which the gift or bequest took effect, unless the donor or his personal representatives, or the personal representatives of the testator, have consented in writing to the making of the application for the order[7].

The Secretary of State must require the applicant to publish a notice containing particulars of the proposed order and stating that representations may be made to the Secretary of State within a period specified in the notice[8]. That period must be not less than one month from the date of the notice[9]. The applicant must publish the notice in such manner as may be specified by the Secretary of State, and the cost of any publication of the notice may be defrayed out of the property of the trust[10]. Before making the order the Secretary of State must take into account any representations duly made in accordance with the notice[11].

1 Sex Discrimination Act 1975 s 78(1)(a). The establishments mentioned in the text are any of the following establishments: (1) an educational establishment maintained by a local education authority; (2) an independent school not being a special school; (3) a special school not maintained by a local education authority; (4) an institution within the further education sector (within the meaning of the Further and Higher Education Act 1992 s 91(3)); (5) a university; (6) an institution, other than a university, within the higher education sector (within the meaning of the Further and Higher Education Act 1992 s 91(5)); (7) an establishment (not falling within heads (1)–(6) supra) providing full-time or part-time education, being an establishment designated under the Sex Discrimination Act 1975 s 24(1): ss 78(1)(a), 22 Table (amended by the Education Act 1980 s 1(3), Sch 1 para 27; the Further and Higher Education Act 1992 s 93(1), Sch 8 Pt II paras 75, 76; and the School Standards and Framework Act 1998 s 140(3), Sch 31). See further EDUCATION.
2 Sex Discrimination Act 1975 s 78(1)(b).
3 The 'responsible body' in respect of the establishments specified in note 1 supra is, respectively: (1) the local education authority or governors, according to which of them has the function in question; (2) the proprietor; (3) the proprietor; (4) the governing body; (5) the governing body; (6) the governing body; (7) the governing body: ibid s 22 Table (as amended: see note 1 supra).
4 Ie the Secretary of State for Education and Employment: see CONSTITUTIONAL LAW AND HUMAN RIGHTS vol 8(2) (Reissue) paras 448–451. In relation to Wales, the functions of the Secretary of State under the Sex Discrimination Act 1975 are carried out by the National Assembly for Wales: see the National Assembly for Wales (Transfer of Functions) Order 1999, SI 1999/672, art 2, Sch 1. As to the National Assembly for Wales see CONSTITUTIONAL LAW AND HUMAN RIGHTS.
5 Sex Discrimination Act 1975 s 78(2)
6 Ibid s 78(2).
7 Ibid s 78(3).
8 Ibid s 78(4).
9 Ibid s 78(5).
10 Ibid s 78(6).
11 Ibid s 78(7).

# 9. CONTROL OF CHARITABLE FUND RAISING

## (1) INTRODUCTION

**406. Statutory control of charitable fund raising.** Fund raising for charities is subject to various statutory controls. The House to House Collections Act 1939, which provides for the regulation of house to house collection for charitable purposes, is prospectively repealed[1]. The regime introduced by the Charities Act 1992 deals with control of fund raising for charitable institutions[2], and public charitable collections[3]. The provisions dealing with public charitable collections, however, which are concerned with charitable appeals made in any public place or by means of visits from house to house[4], are not yet in force[5].

1    The House to House Collections Act 1939 is repealed by the Charities Act 1992 s 78(2), Sch 7 as from a day to be appointed under s 79(2). At the date at which this volume states the law no such day had been appointed. As to the House to House Collections Act 1939 see paras 407–417 post.
2    See the Charities Act 1992 Pt II (ss 58–64) (as amended); and paras 419–433 post.
3    See ibid Pt III (ss 65–74) (as amended) (not yet in force); and paras 434–441 post.
4    See ibid s 65(1)(a); and para 434 post.
5    Ibid Pt III is to be brought into force by order made by the Secretary of State under s 79(2) as from a day to be appointed. At the date this volume state the law no such day had been appointed.

## (2) HOUSE TO HOUSE COLLECTIONS, WAR CHARITIES AND CHARITIES FOR THE DISABLED

**407. Promoter must be licensed.** It is generally necessary to have a licence[1] to promote[2] a house to house collection for any charitable purpose[3]. If a person promotes a collection for a charitable purpose, and a collection for that purpose is made in any locality pursuant to his promotion, then, unless there is in force, throughout the period during which the collection is made in that locality, a licence authorising him, or authorising another under whose authority he acts, to promote a collection in that locality for that purpose, he is guilty of an offence[4]. A collector who acts in any locality for the purpose of a collection for a charitable purpose without there being in force, at all times when he so acts, a licence authorising a promoter under whose authority he acts, or authorising the collector himself, to promote a collection in that locality for that purpose is guilty of an offence[5].

1    'Licence' means a licence under the House to House Collections Act 1939: s 11(1) (prospectively repealed: see para 406 ante).
2    'Promoter' means, in relation to a collection, a person who causes others to act, whether for remuneration or otherwise, as collectors for the purposes of the collection; and 'promote' and 'promotion' have corresponding meanings: ibid s 11(1) (prospectively repealed: see para 406 ante). 'Collection' means an appeal to the public, made by means of visits from house to house, to give, whether for consideration or not, money or other property; and 'collector' means, in relation to a collection, a person who makes the appeal in the course of such visits as aforesaid: s 11(1) (prospectively

repealed: see para 406 ante). See also *Carasu Ltd v Smith* [1968] 2 QB 383, [1968] 2 All ER 529, DC ('collection' included a case where a person is induced to purchase an article on the representation that part of the proceeds will go to charity); followed in *Cooper v Coles* [1987] QB 230, [1987] 1 All ER 91, DC, where the view of Forbes J in *Murphy v Duke* [1985] QB 905, [1985] 2 All ER 274 that the earlier decision was made per incuriam was said to be wrong.

'House' includes place of business: House to House Collections Act 1939 s 11(1). The House to House Collections Act 1939 is prospectively repealed: see para 406 ante. A public house has been held to be a place of business within the House to House Collections Act 1939: see *Report of the Charity Commissioners for England and Wales for 1986* (HC Paper (1986–87) no 306) para 66.

3    See the House to House Collections Act 1939 s 1(1) (prospectively repealed: see para 406 ante). 'Charitable purpose' means any charitable, benevolent or philanthropic purpose, whether or not charitable within the meaning of any rule of law: s 11(1) (prospectively repealed: see para 406 ante). A collection is deemed to be made for a particular purpose where the appeal is made in association with a representation that the money or other property appealed for, or part of it, will be applied for that purpose: s 11(2) (prospectively repealed: see para 406 ante). The Act did not apply to house to house collections made by a registered pool promoter who held a licence under the Pool Competitions Act 1971 permitting house to house collection of entry money etc: s 3(5). However, the Pool Competitions Act 1971 expired on 26 July 1987 (the date to which it was continued in force by the Pool Competitions Act 1971 (Continuance) Order 1986, SI 1986/1234 (spent)). At the date at which this volume states the law no subsequent order has been made continuing it in force.

4    House to House Collections Act 1939 s 1(2) (prospectively repealed: see para 406 ante). See also *Carasu Ltd v Smith* [1968] 2 QB 383, [1968] 2 All ER 529, DC. Any promoter guilty of such an offence is liable on summary conviction to a penalty not exceeding six months' imprisonment or a fine not exceeding level 3 on the standard scale or both such imprisonment and such fine: House to House Collections Act 1939 s 8(1) (amended by virtue of the Criminal Justice Act 1982 ss 38, 46). The House to House Collections Act 1939 is prospectively repealed: see para 406 ante. As to the standard scale see para 286 note 11 ante.

5    House to House Collections Act 1939 s 1(3) (prospectively repealed: see para 406 ante). See also *Carasu Ltd v Smith* [1968] 2 QB 383, [1968] 2 All ER 529, DC. Any collector guilty of such an offence is liable, on summary conviction, to a fine not exceeding level 2 on the standard scale or to imprisonment for a term not exceeding three months, or to both such imprisonment and such fine: House to House Collections Act 1939 s 8(2) (amended by virtue of the Criminal Justice Act 1982 ss 35, 46). The House to House Collections Act 1939 is prospectively repealed: see para 406 ante. It must be proved that the person charged went from house to house or was about to do so when found collecting in one house: *Hankinson v Dowland* [1974] 3 All ER 655, [1974] 1 WLR 1327.

**408. Local exemption certificate.** If the chief officer of police for the police area[1] comprising a locality in which a collection[2] for a charitable purpose[3] is being or is proposed to be made is satisfied that the purpose is local in character and that the collection is likely to be completed within a short period of time, he may grant to the person appearing to be principally concerned in the promotion[4] a certificate in the prescribed[5] form exempting the grantee, or any person authorised by him to act as promoter[6] or collector[7] in relation to that collection, from the provisions of the House to House Collections Act 1939 (other than those relating to the unauthorised use of badges[8] and the requirement of collectors' names[9]), within the locality and for the period specified in the certificate[10], and from the provisions of regulations made under the Act within the same locality and period[11].

1    As to chief officers of police see POLICE vol 36(1) (Reissue) para 341 et seq. As to police areas see POLICE vol 36(1) (Reissue) para 313 et seq. The functions conferred on a chief officer of police by the House to House Collections Act 1939 or any regulations made under it may be delegated by him to any officer not below the rank of inspector: s 7(2) (prospectively repealed: see para 406 ante). The functions which may be so delegated do not include any functions conferred on the Metropolitan Police Commissioner by virtue of his being a licensing authority within the meaning of s 2 (see para 410 post): s 9(2) (amended by the Local Government Act 1972 s 251(2), Sch 29 para 23(5)). The House to House Collections Act

1939 is prospectively repealed: see para 406 ante. As to the Metropolitan Police Commissioner see POLICE vol 36(1) (Reissue) para 342.
2  For the meaning of 'collection' see para 407 note 2 ante.
3  For the meaning of 'charitable purposes' see para 407 note 3 ante.
4  As to the meaning of 'promotion' see para 407 note 3 ante.
5  'Prescribed' means prescribed by regulations made under the House to House Collections Act 1939: s 11(1) (prospectively repealed: see para 406 ante). For the form of the certificate see the House to House Collections Regulations 1947, SR & O 1947/2662, reg 3(1), Sch 1.
6  For the meaning of 'promoter' see para 407 note 2 ante.
7  For the meaning of 'collector' see para 407 note 2 ante.
8  Ie the House to House Collections Act 1939 ss 5, 8(4) (prospectively repealed): see para 412 post.
9  Ie ibid ss 6, 8(5) (prospectively repealed): see para 413 post.
10  Ibid s 1(4) (prospectively repealed: see para 406 ante).
11  See the House to House Collections Regulations 1947, SR & O 1947/2662, reg 3(2).


**409. Exemption of collections over wide areas.** Where the Secretary of State[1] is satisfied that a person pursues a charitable purpose[2] throughout the whole or a substantial part of England and is desirous of promoting collections[3] for that purpose, he may by order[4], direct that that person is exempt from the necessity of having a licence[5] as respects all collections for that purpose in the localities described in the order[6]. Whilst the order is in force as respects collections in any locality, the House to House Collections Act 1939 has effect in relation to the person exempted, to a promoter[7] of a collection in that locality for that purpose acting under the authority of the person exempted, and to a person who so acts as a collector[8] for the purposes of any such collection, as if a licence authorising the exempted person to promote[9] a collection in that locality for that purpose were in force[10].

1  As to the Secretary of State see para 513 post.
2  For the meaning of 'charitable purposes' see para 407 note 3 ante.
3  For the meaning of 'collection' see para 407 note 2 ante.
4  At the date at which this volume states the law no such orders had been made. Any order made under the House to House Collections Act 1939 s 3 (prospectively repealed) may be revoked or varied by a subsequent order made by the Secretary of State: s 3(2) (prospectively repealed: see para 406 ante).
5  For the meaning of 'licence' see para 407 note 1 ante.
6  House to House Collections Act 1939 s 3(1) (prospectively repealed: see para 406 ante). An application for an order must be made not later than the first day of the month preceding that in which it is proposed to commence the collection, but the licensing authority or, as the case may be, the Secretary of State may grant an application made out of time if satisfied that there are special reasons for doing so: House to House Collections Regulations 1947, SR & O 1947/2662, reg 4(2) (modified SI 1974/595).
7  For the meaning of 'promoter' see para 407 note 2 ante.
8  For the meaning of 'collector' see para 407 note 2 ante.
9  As to the meaning of 'promote' see para 407 note 2 ante.
10  House to House Collections Act 1939 s 3(1) (prospectively repealed: see para 406 ante).


**410. Grant or refusal of licences.** If a person promoting or proposing to promote[1] a collection[2] in any locality for a charitable purpose[3] makes to the licensing authority[4] for the area comprising that locality an application in the prescribed manner[5] specifying the purpose of the collection and the locality, whether being the whole of the area of the authority or a part of it, within which the collection is to be made, and furnishes it with the prescribed information, the authority must, subject to the provisions following, grant him a licence[6] to promote a collection within that locality for that purpose[7]. The licence is generally granted for such period, not being longer than 12 months, as is specified in the application, and remains in force for that period unless revoked[8], provided that, if it appears to a licensing authority to be expedient to provide for the simultaneous expiration of licences to be granted by it in respect of collections which in its opinion are likely to be proposed to be made annually or continuously over a long period, it may, on the grant of such a licence, grant it for a period shorter or longer than that specified in the application, or for a period longer than 12 months (but not exceeding 18 months), as may be requisite for that purpose[9].

The licensing authority may refuse or revoke the grant of a licence if it appears to it that[10]:

(1) the total amount likely to be applied for charitable purposes as a result of the collection, including any amount already so applied, is inadequate in proportion to the value of the proceeds[11] likely to be or already received[12];

(2) remuneration which is excessive in relation to that total amount is likely to be, or has been, retained out of the proceeds of the collection by any person[13];

(3) the grant of a licence would be likely to facilitate the commission of an offence of begging[14], or that such an offence has been committed in connection with the collection[15];

(4) the applicant or licensee is not a fit and proper person to hold a licence by reason of conviction in the United Kingdom of certain offences[16], or conviction in any part of the Queen's dominions of any offence conviction for which necessarily involved a finding that he acted fraudulently or dishonestly, or of an offence of a kind the commission of which would be likely to be facilitated by the grant of a licence[17];

(5) the applicant or licensee has failed, in promoting a licensed collection, to exercise due diligence to secure that persons authorised by him to act as collectors[18] were fit and proper persons, to secure the compliance of persons so authorised with regulations under the House to House Collections Act 1939, or to prevent prescribed badges or certificates of authority[19] being obtained by unauthorised persons[20]; or

(6) the applicant or licensee has refused or neglected to furnish the authority with such information as it has reasonably required for informing itself as to matters specified in heads (1) to (5) above[21].

If the authority refuses or revokes a licence, it must forthwith give written notice to the applicant or licensee stating the ground or grounds on which the licence has been refused or revoked and informing him of the right of appeal, and he may, within 14 days of the notice, appeal to the Secretary of State, whose decision is final[22]. If the appeal is allowed, the authority must forthwith issue a licence or cancel the revocation, as the case may be[23].

1   As to the meaning of 'promote' see para 407 note 2 ante.
2   For the meaning of 'collection' see para 407 note 2 ante.
3   For the meaning of 'charitable purposes' see para 407 note 3 ante.
4   The 'licensing authority' means (1) in relation to the City of London, the Common Council of the City of London; (2) in relation to the metropolitan police district the Metropolitan Police Commissioner; and (3) in relation to a district exclusive of any part of it within the metropolitan police district, the district council: House to House Collections Act 1939 s 2(1A) (added by the Local Government Act 1972 s 251(2), Sch 29 para 23(2)). The House to House Collections Act 1939 is prospectively repealed: see para 406 ante. As to the delegation of functions of the Metropolitan Police Commissioner see para 408

note 1 ante. As to the Common Council of the City of London see LONDON GOVERNMENT. As to the metropolitan police district see POLICE vol 36(1) (Reissue) para 314 post. As to the Metropolitan Police Commissioner see POLICE vol 36(1) (Reissue) para 342. As to district councils see LOCAL GOVERNMENT.

5    Ie prescribed by regulations made under the House to House Collections Act 1939 (prospectively repealed: see para 406 ante). An application for a licence must be in the form specified in the House to House Collections Regulations 1947, SR & O 1947/2662, reg 4(1), Sch 2, and must be made not later than the first day of the month preceding that in which it is proposed to commence the collection, but the licensing authority or, as the case may be, the Secretary of State may grant an application made out of time if satisfied that there are special reasons for doing so: reg 4(2) (modified by SI 1974/595). As to the Secretary of State see para 513 post.

6    For the meaning of 'licence' see para 407 note 1 ante.

7    House to House Collections Act 1939 s 2(1) (amended by the Local Government Act 1972 s 272, Sch 29 para 23(1), Sch 30). The House to House Collections Act 1939 is prospectively repealed: see para 406 ante.

8    House to House Collections Act 1939 s 2(2) (prospectively repealed: see para 406 ante).

9    Ibid s 2(2) proviso (amended by the Local Government Act 1972 Sch 29 para 23(3)). The House to House Collections Act 1939 is prospectively repealed: see para 406 ante.

10    House to House Collections Act 1939 s 2(3) (amended by the Local Government Act 1972 Sch 29 para 23(3)). The House to House Collections Act 1939 is prospectively repealed: see para 406 ante.

11    'Proceeds' means, in relation to a collection, all money and other property given, whether for consideration or not, in response to the appeal: ibid s 11(1) (prospectively repealed: see para 406 ante).

12    Ibid s 2(3)(a) (prospectively repealed: see para 406 ante).

13    Ibid s 2(3)(b) (prospectively repealed: see para 406 ante).

14    Ie an offence under the Vagrancy Act 1824 s 3 (as amended): see CRIMINAL LAW, EVIDENCE AND PROCEDURE vol 11(1) (Reissue) para 417.

15    House to House Collections Act 1939 s 2(3)(c) (prospectively repealed: see para 406 ante).

16    The offences are: (1) offences under the Offences Against the Person Act 1861 ss 47–56 (s 47 as amended, ss 48–56 repealed) (assault occasioning bodily harm); (2) robbery, burglary and blackmail; (3) offences under the Police, Factories, etc (Miscellaneous Provisions) Act 1916 s 5 (as amended; prospectively repealed, except in relation to Northern Ireland) (regulation of street collections): House to House Collections Act 1939 s 2(3)(d), Schedule (amended by the Theft Act 1968 s 33(2), Sch 2 Pt III). The House to House Collections Act 1939 is prospectively repealed: see para 406 ante. See further CRIMINAL LAW, EVIDENCE AND PROCEDURE; POLICE.

17    House to House Collections Act 1939 s 2(3)(d) (prospectively repealed: see para 406 ante).

18    For the meaning of 'collector' see para 407 note 2 ante.

19    As to badges and certificates of authority see para 412 post.

20    House to House Collections Act 1939 s 2(3)(e) (prospectively repealed: see para 406 ante).

21    Ibid s 2(3)(f) (prospectively repealed: see para 406 ante).

22    Ibid s 2(4), (5) (s 2(4) amended by the Local Government Act 1972 Sch 29 para 23(3)). The House to House Collections Act 1939 is prospectively repealed: see para 406 ante.

23    Ibid s 2(6) (amended by the Local Government Act 1972 Sch 29 para 23(3)). The House to House Collections Act 1939 is prospectively repealed: see para 406 ante.

**411. Conduct of collections; offences against regulations.** The Secretary of State[1] may make regulations[2] for prescribing anything which by the House to House Collections Act 1939 is required to be prescribed[3], and for regulating the manner in which collections[4], in respect of which licences[5] have been granted or orders have been made[6], may be carried out and the conduct of promoters[7] and collectors[8] in relation to such collections[9].

Such regulations may make provision for all or any of the following matters:

(1)    for requiring and regulating the use by collectors, of prescribed badges and prescribed certificates of authority[10], and the issue, custody, production and return thereof, and, in particular, for requiring collectors on demand by a police constable or by any occupant of a house visited to produce their certificates of authority[11];

(2) in the case of collections in respect of which licences have been granted, for requiring that the prescribed certificates of authority of the collectors must be authenticated in a manner approved by the chief officer of police[12] for the area in respect of which the licence was granted, and that their prescribed badges must have inserted therein or annexed thereto in a manner and form so approved a general indication of the purpose of the collection[13];

(3) for prohibiting persons below a prescribed age from acting, and others from causing them to act, as collectors[14];

(4) for preventing annoyance to the occupants of houses visited by collectors[15];

(5) for requiring the prescribed information with respect to the expenses, proceeds[16] and application of the proceeds of collections to be furnished, in the case of collections in respect of which licences have been granted, by the person to whom the licence was granted to the authority by whom it was granted, and, in the case of collections in respect of which an order has been made, by the person thereby exempted[17] to the Secretary of State, and for requiring the information furnished to be vouched and authenticated in such manner as may be prescribed[18].

Any person who contravenes or fails to comply with the provisions of a regulation made under the House to House Collections Act 1939 is guilty of an offence[19].

Street collections for charities, as distinct from house to house collections, are governed by other statutory provisions and regulations[20].

1   As to the Secretary of State see para 513 post.
2   In the exercise of this power, the Secretary of State has made the House to House Collections Regulations 1947, SR & O 1947/2662 (amended by SI 1963/684; SI 1974/595).
3   Ie prescribed by regulations made under the House to House Collections Act 1939 (prospectively repealed: see para 406 ante).
4   For the meaning of 'collection' see para 407 note 2 ante.
5   For the meaning of 'licence' see para 407 note 1 ante.
6   Ie under the House to House Collections Act 1939 s 3 (prospectively repealed): see para 409 ante.
7   For the meaning of 'promoter' see para 407 note 2 ante.
8   For the meaning of 'collector' see para 407 note 2 ante.
9   House to House Collections Act 1939 s 4(1) (prospectively repealed: see para 406 ante). Any regulations so made must be laid before Parliament as soon as may be after they are made, and if either House of Parliament, within the period of 40 days beginning with the date on which the regulations are laid before it, resolves that the regulations be annulled, the regulations thereupon become void, without prejudice, however, to anything previously done thereunder or to the making of new regulations: s 4(4) (prospectively repealed: see para 406 ante). In reckoning any such period of 40 days, no account is to be taken of any time during which Parliament is dissolved or prorogued or during which both Houses are adjourned for more than four days: s 4(4) (prospectively repealed: see para 406 ante).
10  As to badges and certificates of authority see para 412 post.
11  House to House Collections Act 1939 s 4(2)(a) (prospectively repealed: see para 406 ante). See para 412 post.
12  As to chief officers of police see POLICE vol 36(1) (Reissue) para 341 et seq.
13  House to House Collections Act 1939 s 4(2)(b) (prospectively repealed: see para 406 ante). See para 412 post.
14  Ibid s 4(2)(c) (prospectively repealed: see para 406 ante). See para 413 post.
15  Ibid s 4(2)(d) (prospectively repealed: see para 406 ante). See para 413 post.
16  For the meaning of 'proceeds' see para 410 note 11 ante.
17  Ie exempted from the provisions of the House to House Collections Act 1939 s 1(2) (prospectively repealed): see para 407 ante.
18  Ibid s 4(2)(e) (prospectively repealed: see para 406 ante). See para 414 post.

19  Ibid s 4(3) (prospectively repealed: see para 406 ante). Any person guilty of such an offence is liable, on summary conviction, to a fine not exceeding level 1 on the standard scale: s 8(3) (amended by virtue of the Criminal Justice Act 1982 ss 38, 46). The House to House Collections Act 1939 is prospectively repealed: see para 406 ante. As to the standard scale see para 286 note 11 ante.

20  See the Police, Factories, etc (Miscellaneous Provisions) Act 1916 s 5 (as amended; prospectively repealed, except in relation to Northern Ireland) (see POLICE vol 36(1) (Reissue) para 333; CRIMINAL LAW, EVIDENCE AND PROCEDURE); the Local Government (Miscellaneous Provisions) Act 1982 s 3, Sch 4 (as amended and prospectively further amended); the London Local Authorities Act 1990 Pt III (ss 21–41) (as amended); and regulations made thereunder. It was held in *Meaden v Wood* [1985] Crim LR 678, DC, that the Home Secretary had acted within his powers under the Police, Factories, etc (Miscellaneous Provisions) Act 1916 s 5 (now amended and prospectively repealed) in setting up the system contained in the Street Collections (Metropolitan Police District) Regulations 1979, SI 1979/1230 (subsequently amended) (see CRIMINAL LAW, EVIDENCE AND PROCEDURE), by which the Metropolitan Police Commissioner was empowered to regulate persons wishing to make street collections. As to the Metropolitan Police Commissioner see POLICE vol 36(1) (Reissue) para 342.

## 412. Badges and certificates of authority.

A promoter[1] of a house to house collection[2] must provide a collector[3] with a prescribed certificate of authority[4] and a prescribed badge[5] and, if money is to be collected, a collecting box or receipt book[6]. He must also exercise all due diligence to secure that all certificates of authority and prescribed badges obtained for the purposes of a collection are destroyed when no longer required[7].

A person who, in connection with any appeal[8] made by him to the public in association with a representation that the appeal is for a charitable purpose[9], displays or uses (1) a prescribed badge or prescribed certificate of authority not being a badge or certificate for the time being held by him[10] for the purposes of the appeal; or (2) any badge or device, or any certificate or other document so nearly resembling a prescribed badge or, as the case may be, a prescribed certificate of authority as to be calculated to deceive[11], is guilty of an offence[12].

1  For the meaning of 'promoter' see para 407 note 2 ante.

2  For the meaning of 'collection' see para 407 note 2 ante.

3  For the meaning of 'collector' see para 407 note 2 ante.

4  'Prescribed certificate of authority' means a certificate in the form set out in the House to House Collections Regulations 1947, SR & O 1947/2662, regs 2(1), 6, Sch 3: see reg 2(1). The House to House Collections Regulations 1947, SR & O 1947/2662, are made under the House to House Collections Act 1939 which is prospectively repealed: see para 406 ante.

5  'Prescribed badge' means a badge in the form set out in the House to House Collections Regulations 1947, SR & O 1947/2662, Sch 4: see reg 2(1).

6  See ibid reg 6(1). 'Collecting box' means a box or other receptacle for monetary contributions, securely closed and sealed in such a way that it cannot be opened without breaking the seal: reg 2(1). 'Receipt book' means a book of detachable forms of receipt consecutively numbered with counterfoils or duplicates correspondingly numbered: reg 2(1).

7  See ibid reg 17.

8  An appeal is not limited to an appeal by way of house to house collections: *R v Davison* [1972] 3 All ER 1121, [1972] 1 WLR 1540, CA.

9  For the meaning of 'charitable purposes' see para 407 note 3 ante.

10  Ie pursuant to the House to House Collections Regulations 1947, SR & O 1947/2662 (as amended).

11  'Calculated to deceive' means likely to deceive: *R v Davison* [1972] 3 All ER 1121, [1972] 1 WLR 1540, CA. See also that case for the proper direction to be given to the jury.

12  House to House Collections Act 1939 s 5 (prospectively repealed: see para 406 ante). Any person guilty of such an offence is liable, on summary conviction, to imprisonment for a term not exceeding six months or to a fine not exceeding level 3 on the standard scale, or to both such imprisonment and such fine: s 8(4) (amended by virtue of the Criminal Justice Act 1982 ss 38, 46). The House to House

Collections Act 1939 is prospectively repealed: see para 406 ante. As to the standard scale see para 286 note 11 ante.

There is no power to grant exemptions from s 5 (prospectively repealed) under s 1(4) (prospectively repealed): see para 408 ante.


**413. Collectors.** Promoters[1] must exercise due diligence to ensure that collectors[2] are fit and proper persons to act as such and to secure their compliance with the provisions of the regulations governing house to house collections[3]. No collector may importune any person to his annoyance, or remain in or at the door of any house if requested by the occupant to leave[4]. No person under the age of 16 years may act or be authorised to act as a collector of money[5].

Collectors must sign the prescribed certificate of authority[6] and prescribed badge[7], produce the certificate on demand, wear the badge during collecting, and return both to the promoter when the collection is completed or on demand of the promoter[8]. A police constable may require any person whom he believes to be acting as a collector for the purpose of a collection[9] for a charitable purpose[10] to declare to him immediately his name and address and to sign his name[11]. If any person fails to comply with such a requirement he is guilty of an offence[12].

A collector collecting money by a means of a collecting box[13] may receive it only by permitting the person from whom it is received to place it in the box, and when he is collecting money by other means he must give a signed receipt[14]. Collectors are trustees of the funds they collect[15]. Collecting boxes, with seals unbroken, and receipt books[16], together with the total sum of money which is entered in them, must be returned to the promoter when the collection is completed, upon the demand of the promoter, when the collector does not desire to act as a collector or upon completion of the collection[17].

1   For the meaning of 'promoter' see para 407 note 2 ante.
2   For the meaning of 'collector' see para 407 note 2 ante.
3   See the House to House Collections Regulations 1947, SR & O 1947/2662, reg 5. The House to House Collections Regulations 1947, SR & O 1947/2662, which govern house to house collections, are made under the House to House Collections Act 1939 which is prospectively repealed: see para 406 ante.
4   See the House to House Collections Regulations 1947, SR & O 1947/2662, reg 9.
5   Ibid reg 8 (substituted by SI 1963/684).
6   For the meaning of 'prescribed certificate of authority' see para 412 note 4 ante.
7   For the meaning of 'prescribed badge' see para 412 note 5 ante.
8   See the House to House Collections Regulations 1947, SR & O 1947/2662, reg 7. As to badges and certificates see para 412 ante.
9   For the meaning of 'collection' see para 407 note 2 ante.
10  For the meaning of 'charitable purposes' see para 407 note 3 ante.
11  House to House Collections Act 1939 s 6 (prospectively repealed: see para 406 ante).
12  Ibid s 6 (prospectively repealed: see para 406 ante). Any person guilty of such an offence is liable, on summary conviction, to a fine not exceeding level 1 on the standard scale: s 8(5) (amended by virtue of the Criminal Justice Act 1982 ss 38, 46). The House to House Collections Act 1939 is prospectively repealed see para 406 ante. As to the standard scale see para 286 note 11 ante.

     There is no power to grant exemptions from s 6 (prospectively repealed) under s 1(4) (prospectively repealed): see para 408 ante.
13  For the meaning of 'collecting box' see para 412 note 6 ante.
14  See the House to House Collections Regulations 1947, SR & O 1947/2662, reg 10. Where a promoter has been granted an order of exemption (see para 409 ante) he may, with the Secretary of State's permission, arrange an envelope collection: see reg 13. As to the Secretary of State see para 513 post.
15  *Jones v A-G* (1976) unreported, discussed in *Unreported Legal Decisions Affecting Charities: Jones v Attorney General (1976)* Decisions of the Charity Commissioners (1994) vol 2 p 33.
16  For the meaning of 'receipt book' see para 412 note 6 ante.

17  See House to House Collections Regulations 1947, SR & O 1947/2662, reg 11. Collecting boxes must
    be opened in the presence of the promoter and another responsible person, or by an official of a bank:
    reg 12(1), (2). Receipt books and sums received with them must be examined by the promoter and
    another responsible person: reg 12(4). In each case the amount collected must be listed with the
    distinguishing number of the box or book: reg 12(3), (4).

**414.  Accounts.** An account of the collections[1] for which a licence[2] has been granted
must be furnished by the chief promoter[3] to the authority[4] granting the licence within
one month of the expiry of the licence[5], and where an order of exemption[6] has been
made an account must be made annually to the Secretary of State[7]. The time for
furnishing the account may in either case be extended[8]. In appropriate cases the account
for the house to house collections may be combined with that required[9] for street
collections[10]. The account must be in the prescribed form, duly certified and vouched[11].

1   For the meaning of 'collection' see para 407 note 2 ante.
2   For the meaning of 'licence' see para 407 note 1 ante.
3   'Chief promoter', in relation to a collection, means a person to whom a licence has been granted
    authorising him to promote that collection or in respect of whom an order has been made directing that
    he is exempt from the provisions of the House to House Collections Act 1939 s 1(2) (prospectively
    repealed: see para 406 ante) as respects that collection: House to House Collections Regulations 1947,
    SR & O 1947/2662, reg 2(1). For the meaning of 'promoter' see para 407 note 2 ante. The House to
    House Collections Regulations 1947, SR & O 1947/2662, are made under the House to House
    Collections Act 1939 which is prospectively repealed: see para 406 ante.
4   As to licensing authorities see para 410 note 4 ante.
5   As to the duration of a licence see para 410 ante.
6   Ie under the House to House Collections Act 1939 s 3 (prospectively repealed: see para 406 ante): see
    para 409 ante.
7   See the House to House Collections Regulations 1947, SR & O 1947/2662, reg 14(1), (2) (amended by
    SI 1974/595). As to the Secretary of State see para 513 post.
8   See the House to House Collections Regulations 1947, SR & O 1947/2662, reg 14(3) (amended by
    SI 1974/595).
9   Ie under the Police, Factories, etc (Miscellaneous Provisions) Act 1916: see para 411 note 20 ante.
10  See the House to House Collections Regulations 1947, SR & O 1947/2662, reg 14(4) (amended by
    SI 1974/595).
11  See the House to House Collections Regulations 1947, SR & O 1947/2662, regs 15, 16, Schs 5–7.

**415.  False statements.** A person who, in furnishing any information for the purposes
of the House to House Collections Act 1939, knowingly or recklessly makes a statement
false in a material particular is guilty of an offence[1].

1   House to House Collections Act 1939 s 8(6) (prospectively repealed: see para 406 ante). Any person
    guilty of such an offence is liable, on summary conviction, to imprisonment for a term not exceeding six
    months or to a fine not exceeding level 3 on the standard scale, or to both such imprisonment and such
    fine: s 8(6) (amended by virtue of the Criminal Justice Act 1982 ss 38, 46). The House to House
    Collections Act 1939 is prospectively repealed: see para 406 ante. As to the standard scale see para 286
    note 11 ante.

**416.  Offences by corporations.** Where an offence under the House to House
Collections Act 1939 committed by a corporation is proved to have been committed
with the consent and connivance of, or to be attributable to any culpable neglect of duty

on the part of, any director, manager, secretary or other officer of the corporation, he, as well as the corporation, is deemed to be guilty of an offence and is liable to be proceeded against and punished accordingly[1].

1    House to House Collections Act 1939 s 8(7) (prospectively repealed: see para 406 ante).

**417. War charities and charities for the disabled.** The War Charities Act 1940, which had been extended to cover the disabled[1], was repealed by the Charities Act 1992[2], which contains new and different provisions designed to deal with the same problems and is considered elsewhere in this title[3].

1    Ie by the National Assistance Act 1948 s 41 (repealed).
2    Ie by the Charities Act 1992 s 78(2), Sch 7.
3    As to the control of charitable fund raising under the Charities Act 1992 Pt II (ss 58–64) see paras 419–433 post. As to public charitable collections under the Charities Act 1992 III (ss 65–74) (as amended) see paras 434–441 post. Part III is to be brought into force by order made by the Secretary of State under s 79(2) as from a day to be appointed. At the date this volume state the law no such day had been appointed. As to the Secretary of State see para 513 post.
    As to the statutory regulation of street collections and street trading see the Police, Factories, etc (Miscellaneous Provisions) Act 1916 s 5 (as amended; prospectively repealed, except in relation to Northern Ireland) (see POLICE vol 36(1) (Reissue) para 333; CRIMINAL LAW, EVIDENCE AND PROCEDURE); the Local Government (Miscellaneous Provisions) Act 1982 s 3, Sch 4 (amended and prospectively further amended); and the London Local Authorities Act 1990 Pt III (ss 21–41) (as amended).

# (3)  TRADING REPRESENTATIONS RELATING TO BLIND OR DISABLED PERSONS

**418. Trading representations relating to blind or disabled persons.** The Trading Representations (Disabled Persons) Act 1958 makes it an offence when selling or soliciting orders for goods in the course of a business to represent, in the course of visits from house to house or by post or by telephone, that blind or disabled persons are employed in producing, preparing or packing the goods, or benefit from the sale[1]. These provisions do not, however, apply: (1) where the business is being carried on (a) by a local authority[2]; (b) by a company, association or body providing facilities under the Disabled Persons (Employment) Act 1944[3]; (c) by any body of persons carrying on business without profit to its members and exempted by the Secretary of State for Education and Employment[4]; or (2) where the person carrying on the business is substantially disabled and all the goods in respect of which the representation is made were produced by his own labour[5]. A charity is not exempt from the provisions of the Trading Representations (Disabled Persons) Act 1958 unless it falls within one of these cases[6].

1    See the Trading Representations (Disabled Persons) Act 1958 s 1(1) (as amended); and SALE OF GOODS AND SUPPLY OF SERVICES vol 41 (Reissue) para 824. A person who contravenes s 1(1) is guilty of an offence and liable on summary conviction to a fine not exceeding the prescribed sum, and on conviction on indictment to a fine or imprisonment for a term not exceeding two years, or both: see s 1(1) (as amended); and SALE OF GOODS AND SUPPLY OF SERVICES vol 41 (Reissue) para 824. As to the prescribed

sum see para 226 note 5 ante. As to offences by a body corporate s 1(4); and SALE OF GOODS AND SUPPLY OF SERVICES vol 41 (Reissue) para 824.

2    See ibid s 1(2)(a); and SALE OF GOODS AND SUPPLY OF SERVICES vol 41 (Reissue) para 824. For the meaning of 'local authority' see SALE OF GOODS AND SUPPLY OF SERVICES vol 41 (Reissue) para 824.

3    See ibid s 1(2)(c); and SALE OF GOODS AND SUPPLY OF SERVICES vol 41 (Reissue) para 824. As to a company, association or body providing facilities under the Disabled Persons (Employment) Act 1944 see EMPLOYMENT vol 16 (2000 Reissue) para 380.

4    See ibid s 1(2)(d); Transfer of Functions (Education and Employment) Order 1995, SI 1995/2986; and SALE OF GOODS AND SUPPLY OF SERVICES vol 41 (Reissue) para 824. As to the Secretary of State for Education and Employment see CONSTITUTIONAL LAW AND HUMAN RIGHTS vol 8(2) (Reissue) para 448 et seq.

5    See ibid s 1(2) (as amended); and SALE OF GOODS AND SUPPLY OF SERVICES vol 41 (Reissue) para 824.

6    Prior to the commencement of the relevant provisions of the Charities Act 1992 on 1 September 1992, the Trading Representations (Disabled Persons) Act 1958 did not apply to a war charity or charity for disabled persons which was duly registered or exempted from registration: s 1(2)(b); but that provision has been repealed by the Charities Act 1992 s 78 (2), Sch 7.

# (4) CONTROLS UNDER THE CHARITIES ACT 1992

## (i)  Control of Fund Raising for Charitable Institutions

**419.  Charitable institutions; professional fund raisers; commercial participators.** The provisions of the Charities Act 1992 which deal with the control of fund raising extend beyond charities within the meaning of the Charities Act 1993[1]. They apply to any 'charitable institution', which is defined as a charity or an institution[2], other than a charity, which is established for charitable, benevolent or philanthropic purposes[3]. The main controls are on professional fund raisers and commercial participators.

A professional fund raiser is: (1) any person, apart from a charitable institution or a company[4] connected with such an institution[5], who carries on a fund raising business[6]; or (2) any other person who for reward solicits[7] money or other property for the benefit of a charitable institution, if he does so otherwise than in the course of any fund raising venture undertaken by a person falling within head (1) above[8]. There are important exceptions to this definition. Head (2) above does not apply to any of the following:

(a)    any charitable institution or any company connected with any such institution[9];

(b)    any officer or employee of any such institution or company, or any trustee of any such institution, acting (in each case) in his capacity as such[10];

(c)    any person acting as a collector[11] in respect of a public charitable collection[12];

(d)    any person who in the course of a relevant programme, that is to say a radio or television programme in the course of which a fund raising venture is undertaken by a charitable institution, or a company connected with such an institution, makes any solicitation at the instance of that institution or company[13]; or

(e)    any commercial participator[14].

Nor does head (2) apply to a person if he does not receive: (i) more than £5 per day, or £500 per year, by way of remuneration in connection with soliciting money or other property for the benefit of the charitable institution[15]; or (ii) more than £500 by way of remuneration in connection with any fund raising venture in the course of which he solicits money or other property for the benefit of that institution[16].

'Commercial participator', in relation to any charitable institution, means any person (apart from a company connected with the institution) who carries on for gain a business other than a fund raising business, but in the course of that business, engages in any promotional venture[17] in the course of which it is represented that charitable contributions[18] are to be given to or applied for the benefit of the institution[19].

1   See the Charities Act 1992 s 58(1) (as amended) (see notes 2–8 infra); and para 1 ante. As to fund raising for charitable purposes otherwise than by professional fund raisers or commercial participators see the Charities Act 1992 s 64(2)(e); and the Charitable Institutions (Fund Raising) Regulations 1994, SI 1994/3024, regs 7, 8; and paras 431, 433 post.

2   'Institution' includes any trust or undertaking: Charities Act 1992 s 58(1). For the meaning of 'charity' see para 1 ante; definition applied by the Charities Act 1992 s 58(1) (definition amended by the Charities Act 1993 s 98(1), Sch 6 para 29(1), (5)). 'Charitable purposes', where the term occurs in the context of a reference to charitable, benevolent or philanthropic purposes, is a reference to charitable purposes whether or not they are charitable within the meaning of any rule of law: Charities Act 1992 s 58(4).

3   Ibid s 58(1).

4   For the meaning of 'company' see para 216 ante; definition applied by ibid s 58(1) (definition amended by the Charities Act 1993 s 98(1), Sch 6 para 29(5)).

5   A company is connected with a charitable institution if the institution, or the institution and one or more other charitable institutions taken together, is or are entitled (whether directly or through one or more nominees) to exercise, or control the exercise of, the whole of the voting power at any general meeting of the company: Charities Act 1992 s 58(5).

6   Ibid s 58(1)(a) (definition amended by Deregulation and Contracting Out Act 1994 s 25). The definition of 'professional fund raiser' applies to any person apart from a person excluded by virtue of the Charities Act 1992 s 58(2), (3): see the text and notes 9–16 infra. 'Fund raising business' means any business carried on for gain and wholly or primarily engaged in soliciting or otherwise procuring money or other property for charitable, benevolent or philanthropic purposes: s 58(1).

7   'Represent' and 'solicit' mean respectively represent and solicit in any manner whatever, whether expressly or impliedly and whether done by speaking directly to the person or persons to whom the representation or solicitation is addressed (whether when in his or their presence or not), or by means of a statement published in any newspaper, film or radio or television programme, or otherwise and references to a representation or solicitation must be construed accordingly: ibid s 58(6)(a). Any reference to soliciting or otherwise procuring money or other property is a reference to soliciting or otherwise procuring money or other property whether any consideration is, or is to be, given in return for the money or other property or not: s 58(6)(b). Where any solicitation of money or other property for the benefit of a charitable institution is made in accordance with arrangements between any person and that institution, and under those arrangements that person will be responsible for receiving on behalf of the institution money or other property given in response to the solicitation, then that person is to be regarded as soliciting money or other property for the benefit of the institution: s 58(7). Where any fund raising venture is undertaken by a professional fund raiser in the course of a radio or television programme, any solicitation which is made by a person in the course of the programme at the instance of the fund raiser is to be regarded as made by the fund raiser and not by that person, whether or not the solicitation is made by that person for any reward: s 58(8). 'Radio or television programme' includes any item included in a programme service within the meaning of the Broadcasting Act 1990 s 201 (as amended) (see TELECOMMUNICATIONS AND BROADCASTING vol 45(1) (Reissue) para 253): Charities Act 1992 s 58(1).

8   Ibid s 58(1)(b). The definition of 'professional fund raiser' applies to any person apart from a person excluded by virtue of s 58(2), (3): see the text and notes 9–16 infra.

9   Ibid s 58(2)(a).

10  Ibid s 58(2)(b).

11  For the meaning of 'collector' see para 434 note 6 post; definition applied by ibid s 58(2).

12  Ibid s 58(2)(c). This provision applies to any person acting as a collector in respect of a public charitable collection apart from a person who is to be treated as a promoter of such a collection by virtue of s 65(3) (see para 434 post): see s 58(2)(c). For the meaning of 'public charitable collection' see para 434 post; definition applied by s 58(2).

13  Ibid s 58(2)(d).

14  Ibid s 58(2)(e).
15  Ibid s 58(3)(a). The Secretary of State may by order amend s 58(3) by substituting a different sum for any specified sum for the time being specified there: s 58(10). At the date at which this volume states the law no such order had been made. As to the making of orders generally see s 77 (as amended); and para 517 post. As to the Secretary of State see para 513 post.
16  Ibid s 58(3)(b). See note 15 supra.
17  'Promotional venture' means any advertising or sales campaign or any other venture undertaken for promotional purposes: ibid s 58(1).
18  'Charitable contributions', in relation to any representation made by any commercial participator or other person, means:
    (1)  the whole or part of the consideration given for goods or services sold or supplied by him, or of any proceeds (other than such consideration) of a promotional venture undertaken by him (ibid s 58(1)(a)); or
    (2)  sums given by him by way of donation in connection with the sale or supply of any such goods or services (whether the amount of such sums is determined by reference to the value of any such goods or services or otherwise) (s 58(1)(b)).
    'Services' includes facilities, and in particular access to any premises or event, membership of any organisation, the provision of advertising space, and the provision of any financial facilities, and references to the supply of services must be construed accordingly: s 58(9).
19  Ibid s 58(1) (amended by the Deregulation and Contracting Out Act 1994 s 25).


**420. Prescribed agreement with charitable institution.**  It is unlawful for a professional fund raiser[1] to solicit[2] money or other property for the benefit of a charitable institution[3], or for a commercial participator[4] to represent[5] that charitable contributions[6] are to be given or applied for the benefit of a charitable institution unless, in either case, he does so in accordance with an agreement with the institution satisfying the prescribed requirements[7]. Where on the application of a charitable institution the court[8] is satisfied that any person has contravened or is contravening these provisions in relation to the institution, and that, unless restrained, any such contravention is likely to continue or be repeated, the court may grant an injunction restraining the contravention, but no other remedy is available[9].

Where (1) a charitable institution makes any agreement with a professional fund raiser or a commercial participator by virtue of which the professional fund raiser is authorised to solicit money or other property for the benefit of the institution or the commercial participator is authorised to represent that charitable contributions are to be given to or applied for the benefit of the institution, as the case may be[10]; but (2) the agreement does not satisfy the prescribed requirements in any respect[11], the agreement is not enforceable against the institution except to such extent, if any, as may be provided by an order of the court[12]. A professional fund raiser or commercial participator who is a party to any such agreement is not entitled to receive any amount by way of remuneration or expenses in respect of anything done by him in pursuance of the agreement unless[13]: (a) he is so entitled under any provision of the agreement[14]; and (b) either the agreement satisfies the prescribed requirements or any such provision has effect[15] by virtue of an order of the court[16].

1  For the meaning of 'professional fund raiser' see para 419 ante.
2  For the meaning of 'solicit' see para 419 note 7 ante.
3  For the meaning of 'solicit' see para 419 note 7 ante.
4  For the meaning of 'commercial participator' see para 419 ante.
5  For the meaning of 'represent' see para 419 note 7 ante.
6  For the meaning of 'charitable contributions' see para 419 note 18 ante. As to references to soliciting money or other property for the benefit of the institution see para 419 note 7 ante. For the meaning of 'institution' see para 419 note 2 ante.

7　Charities Act 1992 s 59(1), (2). 'Prescribed requirements' means such requirements as are prescribed by regulations made by virtue of s 64(2)(a) (see the Charitable Institutions (Fund Raising) Regulations 1994, SI 1994/3024 (as amended); and para 426 et seq post): Charities Act 1992 s 59(6).
8　'The court' means the High Court or a county court: ibid s 58(1).
9　Ibid s 59(3).
10　Ibid s 59(4)(a).
11　Ibid s 59(4)(b).
12　Ibid s 59(4).
13　Ibid s 59(5).
14　Ibid s 59(5)(a).
15　Ie under ibid s 59(4): see the text and notes 10–12 supra.
16　Ibid s 59(5)(b).

**421. Requirement to indicate institutions benefiting and arrangements for remuneration.** Where a professional fund raiser[1] solicits[2] money or other property for the benefit of one or more particular charitable institutions[3], the solicitation must be accompanied by a statement clearly indicating the name or names of the institution or institutions concerned and, if more than one, the proportions in which they are respectively to benefit; and, in general terms, the method by which the fund raiser's remuneration in connection with the appeal[4] is to be determined[5]. Where a professional fund raiser solicits money or other property for charitable, benevolent or philanthropic purposes[6] of any description, rather than the benefit of one or more particular charitable institutions, the solicitation must be accompanied by a statement clearly indicating[7]: (1) the fact that he is soliciting money or other property for those purposes and not for the benefit of any particular charitable institution or institutions[8]; (2) the method by which it is to be determined how the proceeds of the appeal are to be distributed between different charitable institutions[9]; and (3) in general terms, the method by which his remuneration in connection with the appeal is to be determined[10].

Where any representation[11] is made by a commercial participator[12] to the effect that charitable contributions[13] are to be given to or applied for the benefit of one or more particular charitable institutions, the representation must be accompanied by a statement clearly indicating[14]: (a) the name or names of the institution or institutions concerned[15]; and (b) if there is more than one institution concerned, the proportions in which they are respectively to benefit[16]; and (c) in general terms, the method by which it is to be determined what proportion of the consideration given for goods or services[17] sold or supplied by him, or of any other proceeds of a promotional venture[18] undertaken by him, is to be given to or applied for the benefit of the institution or institutions concerned, or what sums by way of donations by him in connection with the sale or supply of any such goods or services are to be so given or applied, as the case may require[19].

If any such solicitation or representation as is referred to above is made in the course of a radio or television programme[20], and in association with an announcement to the effect that payment may be made by means of a credit or debit card[21], the statement required must include full details of the right to have refunded[22] any payment of £50 or more which is so made[23].

If any such solicitation or representation as is referred to above is made orally, but is not made by speaking directly to the particular person or persons to whom it is addressed and in his or their presence, or in the course of any radio or television programme, the professional fund raiser or commercial participator concerned must within seven days of any payment of £50 or more being made to him in response to the solicitation or representation, give the person making the payment[24] a written statement of the matters which are required to be contained in the statements[25], and full details of the right to cancel an agreement made in response to his solicitation or representation[26] and the right to a refund[27] of the payment made in response[28].

Where any requirement of the provisions described above[29] is not complied with in relation to any solicitation or representation, the professional fund raiser or commercial participator concerned is guilty of an offence[30]. It is a defence for such a person to prove that he took all reasonable precautions and exercised all due diligence to avoid the commission of the offence[31].

1   For the meaning of 'professional fund raiser' see para 419 ante.
2   For the meaning of 'solicit' see para 419 note 7 ante. As to the meaning of 'solicitation' see para 419 note 7 ante.
3   For the meaning of 'charitable institution' see para 419 ante. As to references to soliciting money or other property for the benefit of an institution: see para 419 note 7 ante.
4   In relation to any solicitation by a professional fund raiser 'the appeal' means the campaign or other fund raising venture in the course of which the solicitation is made: Charities Act 1992 s 60(10).
5   Ibid s 60(1). Regulations may specify the manner in which money or other property acquired by professional fund raisers or commercial participators for the benefit of, or otherwise falling to be given to or applied by such persons for the benefit of, charitable institutions is to be transmitted to such institutions: see s 64; and para 426 post. Regulations may also provide for s 60 to apply, with any specified modifications, in relation to solicitations or representations made in the course of radio or television programmes by charitable institutions or by companies connected with such institutions: see s 64; and para 426 post.
6   For the meaning of 'charitable purposes' see para 419 note 2 ante.
7   Charities Act 1992 s 60(2).
8   Ibid s 60(2)(a).
9   Ibid s 60(2)(b).
10  Ibid s 60(2)(c).
11  As to the meaning of 'representation' see para 419 note 7 ante.
12  For the meaning of 'commercial participator' see para 419 ante.
13  For the meaning of 'charitable contributions' see para 419 note 18 ante.
14  Charities Act 1992 s 60(3).
15  Ibid s 60(3)(a).
16  Ibid s 60(3)(b).
17  As to the meaning of 'services' see para 419 note 18 ante.
18  For the meaning of 'promotional venture' see para 491 note 17 ante.
19  Charities Act 1992 s 60(3)(c).
20  For the meaning of 'radio or television programme' see para 419 note 7 ante.
21  'Credit card' means a card which is a credit-token within the meaning of the Consumer Credit Act 1974 (see CONSUMER CREDIT vol 9(1) (Reissue) para 88): Charities Act 1992 s 58(1). 'Debit card' means a card the use of which by its holder to make a payment results in a current account of his at a bank, or at any other institution providing banking services, being debited with the payment: s 58(1).
22  Ie under ibid s 61(1): see para 422 post. The Secretary of State may by order amend s 61(1) by substituting a different sum for the sum for the time being specified there and make such consequential amendments in s 60 as he considers appropriate: see s 61(8); and para 422 post. At the date at which this volume states the law no such order had been made. As to the Secretary of State see para 513 post. As to the making of orders generally see s 77 (as amended); and para 517 post.
23  Ibid s 60(4). Regulations may provide for s 60(4) to apply, with any specified modifications, in relation to solicitations or representations made in the course of radio or television programmes by charitable institutions or by companies connected with such institutions: see s 64(2)(d); and para 426 post.
24  The reference to the making of a payment is a reference to the making of a payment of whatever nature and by whatever means, including a payment made by means of a credit card or a debit card, and for these purposes: (1) where the person making any such payment makes it in person, it is regarded as made at the time when it is so made; (2) where the person making any such payment sends it by post, it is regarded as made at the time when it is posted; and (3) where the person making any such payment makes it by giving, by telephone or by means of any other telecommunication apparatus, authority for an account to be debited with the payment, it is regarded as made at the time when any such authority is

given: ibid s 60(6). For these purposes, 'telecommunication apparatus' has the same meaning as in the Telecommunications Act 1984 (see TELECOMMUNICATIONS AND BROADCASTING vol 45(1) (Reissue) para 1): see the Charities Act 1992 s 60(10).

25  Ie those required by ibid s 60(1), (2) or (3): see the text and notes 1–19 supra.

26  Ie under ibid s 61(2): see para 422 post.

27  Ie under ibid s 61(2), (3): see para 422 post.

28  Ibid s 60(5).

29  Ie those contained in ibid s 60(1)–(5): see the text and notes 1–28 supra.

30  Ibid s 60(7). A person guilty of such an offence is liable on summary conviction to a fine not exceeding level 5 on the standard scale: s 60(7). As to the standard scale see para 286 note 11 ante. Where the commission by any person of an offence under s 60(7) is due to the act or default of some other person, that other person is also guilty of the offence and may be charged and convicted whether or not proceedings are taken against the first named person: s 60(9). As to offences by a body corporate see s 75; and para 515 post.

31  Ibid s 60(8).


**422. Cancellation of payments and agreements made in response to appeals.**
Where: (1) a person (the 'donor') in response to solicitation[1] by a professional fund raiser[2] or a representation[3] by a commercial participator[4] which is made in the course of a radio or television programme[5], makes any payment[6] of £50[7] or more to the relevant fund raiser[8] by means of a credit card or a debit card[9]; but (2) before the end of a period of seven days beginning with the date of the solicitation or representation, the donor serves on the relevant fund raiser a notice in writing which, however expressed, indicates the donor's intention to cancel the payment[10], the donor is entitled[11] to have the payment refunded to him forthwith by the relevant fund raiser[12].

Certain agreements entered into by a donor in response to any solicitation or representation made orally but not made by speaking directly to the particular person or persons to whom it is addressed and in his or their presence, or in the course of any radio or television programme[13] may be cancelled[14]. This can be done in the case of an agreement with the relevant fund raiser under which the donor is, or may be, liable to make any payment or payments[15] to the relevant fund raiser, and the amount or the aggregate amount which the donor is, or may be, liable to pay to him under the agreement is £50 or more[16]. If, before the end of the period of seven days beginning with the date when he is given the required written statement[17], the donor serves on the relevant fund raiser a notice in writing which, however expressed, indicates the donor's intention to cancel the agreement, the notice operates, as from the time when it is served, to cancel the agreement and any liability of any person other than the donor in connection with the making of any such payment or payments[18]. The donor is further entitled[19] to have any payment of £50 or more[20] made by him under the agreement refunded to him forthwith by the relevant fund raiser[21]. Where no such agreement has been entered into but, in response to such solicitation or representation as is referred to above[22], the donor has made any payment of £50[23] or more to the relevant fund raiser, the donor may before the end of the period of seven days beginning with the date when the donor is given any such written statement as is required[24] serve on the relevant fund raiser a notice in writing indicating his intention to cancel the payment[25]. However the notice is expressed, it entitles the donor to have the payment refunded to him forthwith by the relevant fund raiser[26].

Further, none of the above provisions[27] has effect in relation to any payment made or to be made in respect of services[28] which have been supplied at the time when the relevant notice is served[29]. In any of the cases mentioned above the right of any person to have a payment refunded to him[30]: (a) is a right to have refunded to him the amount of the payment less any administrative expenses reasonably incurred by the relevant fund raiser in connection with the making of the refund or, as the case may require[31], in dealing with the notice of cancellation served upon him[32]; and (b) is, in the case of a payment for goods already received, conditional upon the restitution being made of the goods in question[33].

1   For the meaning of 'solicitation' see para 419 note 7 ante.
2   Ie under the Charities Act 1992 s 60(1), (2): see para 421 ante. For the meaning of 'professional fund raiser' see para 419 ante.
3   For the meaning of 'representation' see para 419 note 7 ante.
4   Ie under the Charities Act 1992 s 60(3): see para 421 ante. For the meaning of 'commercial participator' see para 419 ante.
5   For the meaning of 'radio or television programme' see para 419 note 7 ante.
6   For these purposes, any reference to the making of a payment is a reference to the making of a payment of whatever nature and, in the case of the Charities Act 1992 s 61(2) or (3) (see the text and notes 7–21 infra), a payment made by whatever means, including a payment made by means of a credit card or a debit card: s 61(6). As to when a payment is to be regarded as having been made see s 60(6), applied by s 61(6); and para 421 note 24 ante. For the meaning of 'credit card' and 'debit card' para 421 note 20 ante.
7   The Secretary of State may by order amend any provision of ibid s 61 by substituting a different sum for the sum for the time being specified there and make such consequential amendments in s 60 (see para 421 ante) as he considers appropriate: s 61(8). At the date at which this volume states the law no such orders had been made. As to the making of orders generally see s 77 (as amended); and para 517 post. As to the Secretary of State see para 513 post.
8   'Relevant fund raiser', in relation to any solicitation or representation, means the professional fund raiser or commercial participator by whom it is made: ibid s 61(7).
9   Ibid s 61(1)(a). For the meaning of 'credit card' and 'debit card' para 421 note 21 ante.
10   Ibid s 61(1)(b).
11   Ie subject to ibid s 61(4): see the text and notes 31–33 infra.
12   Ibid s 61(1). Regulations may provide for s 61 to apply, with any specified modifications, in relation to solicitations or representations made in the course of radio or television programmes by charitable institutions or by companies connected with such institutions: see s 64; and para 426 post.
13   Ie one falling within ibid s 60(5): see para 421 text and notes 25–28 ante. For the meaning of 'radio or television programme' see para 419 note 7 ante.
14   See ibid s 61(2).
15   See note 6 supra.
16   See the Charities Act 1992 s 61(2). See also note 7 supra.
17   Ie the statement required under ibid s 60(5)(a): see para 421 ante.
18   See ibid s 61(2).
19   See note 11 supra.
20   See note 7 supra.
21   Charities Act 1992 s 61(2).
22   See note 13 supra.
23   See note 7 supra.
24   See note 17 supra.
25   Charities Act 1992 s 61(3).
26   Ibid s 61(3).
27   Ie under ibid s 61(1)–(3): see the text and notes 1–26 supra.
28   As to the meaning of 'services' see para 419 note 18 ante.
29   Charities Act 1992 s 61(5).
30   See note 27 supra.
31   Ie under the Charities Act 1992 s 61(2): see the text and notes 13–14 supra.
32   Ibid s 61(4)(a).
33   Ibid s 61(4)(b).

**423. Right of charitable institutions to prevent unauthorised fund raising.**
Where on the application of any charitable institution[1]:

(1) the court[2] is satisfied that any person has done or is doing either of the following, namely: (a) soliciting money or other property for the benefit of the institution[3]; or (b) representing that charitable contributions[4] are to be given to or applied for the benefit of the institution, and that, unless restrained, he is likely to do further acts of that nature[5]; and

(2) the court is also satisfied as to one or more of the following: (a) that the person in question is using methods of fund raising to which the institution objects; (b) that that person is not a fit and proper person to raise funds for the institution; and (c) where the conduct complained of is the making of such representations as are mentioned in head (1)(b) above, that the institution does not wish to be associated with the particular promotional or other fund raising venture in which that person is engaged[6],

then the court may grant an injunction restraining the doing of any such acts[7]. However, the power to grant an injunction is not exercisable on the application of a charitable institution unless the institution has, not less than 28 days before making the application, served on the person in question a notice in writing[8]:

(i) requesting him to cease forthwith soliciting money or other property for the benefit of the institution or representing that charitable contributions are to be given to or applied for the benefit of the institution, as the case may be[9]; and

(ii) stating that, if he does not comply with the notice, the institution will make an application under these provisions for an injunction[10].

Where (A) a charitable institution has served on any person such a notice and that person has complied with the notice[11]; but (B) that person has subsequently begun to carry on activities which are the same, or substantially the same, as those in respect of which the relevant notice was served[12], the institution is not, in connection with an application made by it under these provisions in respect of the activities carried on by that person, required to serve a further notice on him, if the application is made not more than 12 months after the date of service of the relevant notice[13].

1 For the meaning of 'charitable institution' see para 419 ante.
2 For the meaning of 'the court' see para 420 note 8 ante.
3 As to references to soliciting money or other property for the benefit of an institution: see para 419 note 7 ante. For the meaning of 'solicit' see para 419 note 7 ante.
4 For the meaning of 'charitable contributions' see para 419 note 18 ante. For the meaning of 'represent' see para 419 note 7 ante.
5 Charities Act 1992 s 62(1)(a).
6 Ibid ss 62(1)(b), 62(2). For the meaning of 'promotional venture' see para 491 note 17 ante.
7 Ibid s 62(1). Section 62 does not have the effect of authorising a charitable institution to make an application in respect of anything done by a professional fund raiser or commercial participator in relation to the institution: s 62(5). For the meaning of 'professional fund raiser' and 'commercial participator' see para 419 ante. As to injunctions see generally INJUNCTIONS.
8 Ibid s 62(3). Such a notice served must also specify the circumstances which gave rise to the serving of the notice and the grounds on which an application for an injunction is to be made: see the Charitable Institutions (Fund Raising) Regulations 1994, SI 1994/3024, reg 4.
9 Charities Act 1992 s 62(3)(a).
10 Ibid s 62(3)(b).
11 Ibid s 62(4)(a).
12 Ibid s 62(4)(b).
13 Ibid s 62(4).

**424. False statements relating to institutions which are not registered charities.** Where a person solicits money or other property for the benefit of an institution[1] in association with a representation[2] that the institution is a registered charity[3] and the institution is not such a charity, he is guilty of an offence[4]. However, in any proceedings for such an offence, it is a defence for the accused to prove that he believed, on reasonable grounds, that the institution was a registered charity[5].

1 As to references to soliciting money or other property for the benefit of an institution: see para 419 note 7 ante. For the meaning of 'solicit' see para 419 note 7 ante. For the meaning of 'institution' see para 419 note 2 ante.

2 As to the meaning of 'representation' see para 419 note 7 ante.

3 For these purposes, 'registered charity' means a charity which is for the time being registered in the register of charities kept under the Charities Act 1993 s 3 (as amended) (see para 283 ante): Charities Act 1992 s 63(2) (amended by the Charities Act 1993 s 98(1), Sch 6 para 29(1), (6); and the Deregulation and Contracting Out Act 1994 s 26(3)).

4 Charities Act 1992 s 63(1). A person guilty of such an offence is liable on summary conviction to a fine not exceeding level 5 on the standard scale: s 63(1). As to the standard scale see para 286 note 11 ante.

5 Ibid s 63(1A) (added by the Deregulation and Contracting Out Act 1994 s 26(2)).


**425. Service of notices and other documents.** Any notice or other document required or authorised to be given or served in connection with the control of fund raising for charitable institutions[1] or any notice required to be served in relation to public charitable collections[2] may be served or given to a person (other than a body corporate) by delivering it to that person, by leaving it at his last known address in the United Kingdom[3], or by sending it by post to him at that address[4]. In the case of a body corporate, such notice or document may be served or given by delivering it or sending it by post to the registered or principal office of the body in the United Kingdom, or, if it has no such office in the United Kingdom, to any place in the United Kingdom where it carries on business or conducts its activities, as the case may be[5]. Any such document may also be served on or given to a person (including a body corporate) by sending it by post to that person at an address notified by that person for these purposes to the person or persons by whom it is required or authorised to be served or given[6].

1 Ie under the Charities Act 1992 Pt II (ss 58–64) (as amended): see paras 419–433 ante.

2 Ie under ibid Pt III (ss 65–74) (as amended): see paras 434–441 post. At the date at which this volume states the law the provisions of the Charities Act 1992 Pt III (as amended) are not yet in force: see para 406 ante.

3 For the meaning of 'United Kingdom' see para 180 note 16 ante.

4 Charities Act 1992 s 76(1)(b), (c), (2).

5 Ibid s 76(3).

6 Ibid s 76(4).


**426. Secretary of State's power to make regulations about fund raising.** The Secretary of State[1] may make such regulations[2] as appear to him to be necessary or desirable for any purposes connected with the provisions of the Charities Act 1992[3] relating to the control of charitable fund raising[4].

Any such regulations may[5]:

(1) prescribe the form and content of agreements made in relation to raising funds for charitable institutions[6], and notices served[7] in relation to injunctions granted by the court preventing unauthorised fund raising[8];

(2) require professional fund raisers[9] or commercial participators[10] who are parties to such agreements with charitable institutions[11] to make available to the institutions books, documents or other records (however kept) which relate to the institutions[12];

(3) specify the manner in which money or other property acquired by professional fund raisers or commercial participators for the benefit of, or otherwise falling to be given to or applied by such persons for the benefit of, charitable institutions is to be transmitted to such institutions[13];

(4) provide for: (a) the provisions relating to the requirement to indicate institutions benefiting and arrangements for remuneration[14]; and (b) the provisions relating to the cancellation of payments and agreements made in response to appeals[15], which have effect in relation to solicitations or representations made in the course of radio or television programmes[16] to have effect, subject to any modifications specified in the regulations, in relation to solicitations or representations made in the course of such programmes by charitable institutions, or by companies connected with such institutions[17], and, in that connection, provide for any other provisions of Part II of the Charities Act 1992 to have effect for the purposes of the regulations subject to any modifications so specified[18];

(5) make other provision regulating the raising of funds for charitable, benevolent or philanthropic purposes[19], whether by professional fund raisers or commercial participators or otherwise[20].

Regulations under these provisions may provide that any failure to comply with a specified provision of the regulations is an offence[21].

1   As to the Secretary of State see para 513 post.

2   In the exercise of this power, the Charitable Institutions (Fund Raising) Regulations 1994, SI 1994/3024, have been made. As to the making of regulations generally see the Charities Act 1992 s 77 (as amended); and para 517 post.

3   Ie ibid Pt II (ss 58–64) (as amended): see paras 419–433 ante.

4   Ibid s 64(1).

5   Ibid s 64(2). This provision is expressed to be without prejudice to s 64(1) (see the text and notes 1–4 supra): s 64(2).

6   Ie agreements under ibid s 59: see para 420 ante.

7   Ie under ibid s 62(3): see para 423 ante.

8   Ibid s 64(2)(a). As to regulations in relation to agreements between charitable institutions and professional fund raisers see the Charitable Institutions (Fund Raising) Regulations 1994, SI 1994/3024, reg 2; and para 427 post. As to regulations in relation to agreements between charitable institutions and commercial participators see reg 3; and para 428 post. As to regulations in relation to notices prior to injunction to prevent unauthorised fund raising see reg 4; and para 429 post.

9   For the meaning of 'professional fund raiser' see para 419 ante.

10   For the meaning of 'commercial participator' see para 419 ante.

11   For the meaning of 'charitable institution' see para 419 ante.

12   Charities Act 1992 s 64(2)(b). As to regulations in relation to the availability of books, documents or other records see the Charitable Institutions (Fund Raising) Regulations 1994, SI 1994/3024, reg 5; and para 432 post.

13  Charities Act 1992 s 64(2)(c). For these purposes, reference to such money or other property mentioned in s 64(2)(c) includes a reference to money or other property which, in the case of a professional fund raiser or commercial participator (1) has been acquired by him otherwise than in accordance with an agreement with a charitable institution; but (2) by reason of any solicitation or representation in consequence of which it has been acquired, is held by him on trust for such an institution: s 64(3). As to the meaning of 'solicitations' and 'representations' see para 419 note 7 ante.

    As to regulations in relation to the transmission of money and other property to charitable institutions see the Charitable Institutions (Fund Raising) Regulations 1994, SI 1994/3024, reg 6; and para 430 post.

14  Ie Charities Act 1992 s 60: see para 421 ante.

15  Ie ibid s 61: see para 422 ante.

16  For the meaning of 'radio or television programmes' see para 419 note 7 ante.

17  As to references to a company connected with charitable institutions see para 419 note 5 ante. For the meaning of 'company' see para 216 ante; definition applied by the Charities Act 1992 s 58(1).

18  Ibid s 64(2)(d).

19  For the meaning of 'charitable purposes' see para 419 note 2 ante.

20  Charities Act 1992 s 64(2)(e). As to regulations in relation to fund raising for charitable, benevolent or philanthropic purposes otherwise than by professional fund raisers or commercial participators see the Charitable Institutions (Fund Raising) Regulations 1994, SI 1994/3024, reg 7; and para 431 post.

21  Charities Act 1992 s 64(4). Such regulations may also provide that any such offence is punishable on summary conviction by a fine not exceeding the level 2 on the standard scale: s 64(4). As to the standard scale see para 286 not 11 ante.

    As to regulations in relation to offences and penalties for failure to comply with specified provisions see the Charitable Institutions (Fund Raising) Regulations 1994, SI 1994/3024, reg 8; and para 433 post.

**427. Agreements between charitable institutions and professional fund raisers.** An agreement between a professional fund raiser and a charitable institution enabling the fund raiser to solicit money or other property for the benefit of the charitable institution[1] must fulfil the following requirements as to form and content[2]. Such an agreement must be in writing and be signed by or on behalf of the charitable institution and the professional fund raiser[3]. It must specify:

(1)   the name and address of each of the parties to the agreement[4];

(2)   the date on which the agreement was signed by or on behalf of each of those parties[5];

(3)   the period for which the agreement is to subsist[6];

(4)   any terms relating to the termination of the agreement prior to the date on which that period expires[7]; and

(5)   any terms relating to the variation of the agreement during that period[8].

The agreement must also contain: (a) a statement of its principal objectives and the methods to be used in pursuit of those objectives[9]; (b) if there is more than one charitable institution party to the agreement, provision as to the manner in which the proportion in which the institutions are respectively to benefit under the agreement is to be determined[10]; and (c) provision as to the amount by way of remuneration or expenses which the professional fund raiser is entitled to receive in respect of things done by him in pursuance of the agreement and the manner in which that amount is to be determined[11].

1  Ie under the Charities Act 1992 s 59(1): see para 420 ante. For these purposes any reference, in relation to an agreement made for the purposes of s 59 (see para 420 ante), to a charitable institution, commercial participator or professional fund raiser, is, unless the contrary intention appears, to be construed as a reference to any charitable institution, commercial participator or professional fund raiser, respectively,

which is or who is a party to the agreement: Charitable Institutions (Fund Raising) Regulations 1994, SI 1994/3024, reg 1(3). For the meanings of 'professional fund raiser', 'charitable institution' and 'commercial participator' see para 419 ante.

2   Ibid reg 2(1).
3   Ibid reg 2(2).
4   Ibid reg 2(3)(a).
5   Ibid reg 2(3)(b).
6   Ibid reg 2(3)(c).
7   Ibid reg 2(3)(d).
8   Ibid reg 2(3)(e).
9   Ibid reg 2(4)(a).
10  Ibid reg 2(4)(b).
11  Ibid reg 2(4)(c).

**428. Agreements between charitable institutions and commercial participators.** An agreement between a commercial participator[1] and a charitable institution[2] enabling the commercial participator to represent that charitable contributions are to be given to or applied for the benefit of the charitable institution[3] must fulfill the following requirements as to form and content[4]. Such an agreement must be in writing and be signed by or on behalf of the charitable institution and the commercial participator[5]. It must specify:

(1)   the name and address of each of the parties to the agreement[6];

(2)   the date on which the agreement was signed by or on behalf of each of those parties[7];

(3)   the period for which the agreement is to subsist[8];

(4)   any terms relating to the termination of the agreement prior to the date on which that period expires[9]; and

(5)   any terms relating to the variation of the agreement during that period[10].

The agreement must also contain a statement of its principal objectives and the methods to be used in pursuit of those objectives[11]. Additionally it must contain provision as to the manner in which are to be determined:

(a)   if there is more than one charitable institution party to the agreement, the proportion in which the institutions which are so party are respectively to benefit under the agreement[12]; and

(b)   the proportion of the consideration given for goods or services sold or supplied by the commercial participator, or of any other proceeds of a promotional venture undertaken by him, which is to be given to or applied for the benefit of the charitable institution[13]; or

(c)   the sums by way of donations by the commercial participator in connection with the sale or supply of any goods or services sold or supplied by him which are to be so given or applied[14],

as the case may require[15]. The agreement must also contain provision as to any amount by way of remuneration or expenses which the commercial participator is to be entitled to receive in respect of things done by him in pursuance of the agreement and the manner in which any such amount is to be determined[16].

1    For the meaning of 'commercial participator' see para 419 ante. A reference to a commercial participator
     is to be construed as a reference to any commercial participator who is a party to the agreement: see the
     Charitable Institutions (Fund Raising) Regulations 1994, SI 1994/3024, reg 1(3); and para 427 note 1 ante.
2    For the meaning of 'charitable institution' see para 419 ante. A reference to a charitable institution is to
     be construed as a reference to any charitable institution who is a party to the agreement: see ibid reg 1(3)
     para 427 note 1 ante.
3    Ie under the Charities Act 1992 s 59(2): see para 420 ante.
4    Charitable Institutions (Fund Raising) Regulations 1994, SI 1994/3024, reg 3(1).
5    Ibid reg 3(2).
6    Ibid reg 3(3)(a).
7    Ibid reg 3(3)(b).
8    Ibid reg 3(3)(c).
9    Ibid reg 3(3)(d).
10   Ibid reg 3(3)(e).
11   Ibid reg 3(4)(a). The statement of methods must include, in relation to each method specified, a
     description of the type of charitable contributions which are to be given to, or applied for the benefit of,
     the charitable institution and of the circumstances in which they are to be so given or applied: reg 3(5).
     For the meaning of 'charitable contributions' see para 419 note 18 ante.
12   Ibid reg 3(4)(b)(i).
13   Ibid reg 3(4)(b)(ii).
14   Ibid reg 3(4)(b)(iii). As to the supply of services see para 419 note 18 ante.
15   Ibid reg 3(4)(b).
16   Ibid reg 3(4)(c).


**429. Notice prior to injunction to prevent unauthorised fund raising.** A notice
served by a charitable institution[1] to prevent unauthorised fund raising[2] must[3] specify the
circumstances which gave rise to the serving of the notice and the grounds on which an
application to prevent unauthorised fundraising[4] is to be made[5].

1    For the meaning of 'charitable institution' see para 419 ante.
2    Ie under the Charities Act 1992 s 62(3): see para 423 ante.
3    Ie in addition to satisfying the requirements of ibid s 62(3): see para 423 ante.
4    Ie under ibid s 62: see para 423 ante.
5    Charitable Institutions (Fund Raising) Regulations 1994, SI 1994/3024, reg 4.


**430. Transmission of money and other property to charitable institutions.**
Any money or other property[1] acquired by a professional fund raiser[2] or commercial
participator[3] for the benefit of, or otherwise falling to be given to or applied by such a
person for the benefit of, a charitable institution[4] must, notwithstanding any inconsistent
term in the agreement[5] with the charitable institution, be transmitted to that institution
in accordance with the following provisions[6].

A professional fund raiser or commercial participator holding any such money or
property must, unless he has a reasonable excuse[7]:

(1)   in the case of any money, and any negotiable instrument which is payable to or
      to the account of the charitable institution, as soon as is reasonably practicable
      after its receipt and in any event not later than the expiration of 28 days after that
      receipt or such other period as may be agreed with the institution[8]: (a) pay it to
      the person or persons having the general control and management of the
      administration of the institution[9]; or (b) pay it into an account held by a bank[10]
      or building society[11] in the name of or on behalf of the institution which is under
      the control of the person, or any of the persons, specified in head (a) above[12]; and

(2)    in the case of any other property, deal with it in accordance with any instructions given for that purpose, either generally or in a particular case, by the charitable institution provided that[13]: (a) any property in the possession of the professional fund raiser or commercial participator either pending the obtaining of such instructions as are referred to above or in accordance with such instructions must be securely held by him[14]; (b) the proceeds of the sale or other disposal of any property are, from the time of their receipt by the professional fund raiser or commercial participator, subject to the requirements of head (1) above[15].

Failure to comply with these provisions is an offence punishable on summary conviction by a fine[16].

1    Including such money or other property referred to in the Charities Act 1992 s 64(3): see para 426 ante.
2    For the meaning of 'professional fund raiser' see para 419 ante. A reference to a professional fund raiser is to be construed as a reference to any professional fund raiser who is a party to the agreement: see the Charitable Institutions (Fund Raising) Regulations 1994, SI 1994/3024, reg 1(3); and para 427 note 1 ante.
3    For the meaning of 'commercial participator' see para 419 ante. A reference to a commercial participator is to be construed as a reference to any commercial participator who is a party to the agreement: see ibid reg 1(3); and para 427 note 1 ante.
4    For the meaning of 'charitable institution' see para 419 ante. A reference to a charitable institution is to be construed as a reference to any charitable institution which is a party to the agreement: see ibid reg 1(3); and para 427 note 1 ante.
5    Ie an agreement made for the purposes of the Charities Act 1992 s 59: see para 420 ante.
6    Charitable Institutions (Fund Raising) Regulations 1994, SI 1994/3024, reg 6(1).
7    Ibid reg 6(2).
8    Ibid reg 6(2)(a).
9    Ibid reg 6(2)(a)(i).
10   'Bank' means the Bank of England or an institution which is authorised to operate a deposit taking business under the Banking Act 1987 Pt I (ss 1–49) (as amended): Charitable Institutions (Fund Raising) Regulations 1994, SI 1994/3024, reg 1(2) (definition amended by SI 1998/1129).
11   'Building society' means a building society which is authorised by the Building Societies Commission under the Building Societies Act 1986 s 9 (as amended; prospectively repealed) (see BUILDING SOCIETIES vol 4(2) (Reissue) para 939) to raise money from its members: Charitable Institutions (Fund Raising) Regulations 1994, SI 1994/3024, reg 1(2). As to the Building Societies Commission see BUILDING SOCIETIES vol 4(2) (Reissue) paras 707–709.
12   Ibid reg 6(2)(a)(ii).
13   Ibid reg 6(2)(b).
14   Ibid reg 6(2)(b)(i).
15   Ibid reg 6(2)(b)(ii).
16   Ibid reg 8(1), (2)(b). The fine must not exceed level 2 on the standard scale: reg 8(1). As to the standard scale see para 286 note 11 ante.

**431. Fund raising for charitable etc purposes otherwise than by professional fund raisers or commercial participators.** The following requirements apply to any person who carries on for gain a business other than a fund raising business[1] but, in the course of that business, engages in any promotional venture in the course of which it is represented that charitable contributions[2] are to be applied for charitable, benevolent or philanthropic purposes[3] of any description, rather than for the benefit of one or more particular charitable institutions[4].

Where such a person makes a representation to the effect that charitable contributions are to be applied for such charitable, benevolent or philanthropic purposes he must, unless he has a reasonable excuse, ensure that the representation is accompanied by a statement clearly indicating[5]:

(1)    the fact that the charitable contributions referred to in the representation are to be applied for those purposes and not for the benefit of any particular charitable institution or institutions[6];

(2)    in general terms, the method by which it is to be determined: (a) what proportion of the consideration given for goods or services sold or supplied by him, or of any other proceeds of a promotional venture undertaken by him, is to be applied for those purposes[7]; or (b) what sums by way of donations by him in connection with the sale or supply of any such goods or services are to be so applied[8]; and

(3)    the method by which it is to be determined how the charitable contributions referred to in the representation are to be distributed between different charitable institutions[9].

Failure to comply with these provisions is an offence punishable on summary conviction by a fine[10].

1    For the meaning of 'fund raising business' see para 419 note 6 ante.
2    For the meaning of 'charitable contributions' see para 419 note 18 ante.
3    As to references to charitable, benevolent or philanthropic purposes see para 419 note 2 ante.
4    Charitable Institutions (Fund Raising) Regulations 1994, SI 1994/3024, reg 7(1). For the meaning of 'charitable institution' see para 419 ante.
5    Ibid reg 7(2).
6    Ibid reg 7(2)(a).
7    Ibid reg 7(2)(b)(i).
8    Ibid reg 7(2)(b)(ii).
9    Ibid reg 7(2)(c).
10   Ibid reg 8(1), (2)(c). The fine must not exceed level 2 on the standard scale: reg 8(1). As to the standard scale see para 286 note 11 ante.

**432. Availability of books, documents or other records.** A professional fund raiser[1] or commercial participator[2] who is a party to an agreement[3] with a charitable institution[4] must, on request and at all reasonable times, make available[5] to any charitable institution which is a party to that agreement any books, documents or other records, however kept, which relate to that institution and are kept for the purposes of the agreement[6]. Failure to comply with these provisions is an offence punishable on summary conviction by a fine[7].

1    For the meaning of professional fund raiser see para 419 ante. A reference to a professional fund raiser is to be construed as a reference to any professional fund raiser who is a party to the agreement: see the Charitable Institutions (Fund Raising) Regulations 1994, SI 1994/3024, reg 1(3); and para 427 note 1 ante.
2    For the meaning of 'commercial participator' see para 419 ante. A reference to a commercial participator is to be construed as a reference to any commercial participator who is a party to the agreement: see ibid reg 1(3); and para 427 note 1 ante.
3    Ie an agreement made for the purposes of the Charities Act 1992 s 59: see para 420 ante.
4    For the meaning of 'charitable institution' see para 419 ante. A reference to a charitable institution is to be construed as a reference to any charitable institution which is a party to the agreement: see para 427 note 1 ante.
5    In the case of any record which is kept otherwise than in legible form, the reference in the text to making that record available is construed as a reference to making it available in legible form: Charitable Institutions (Fund Raising) Regulations 1994, SI 1994/3024, reg 5(2).
6    Ibid reg 5(1).
7    Ibid reg 8(1), (2)(a). The fine must not exceed level 2 on the standard scale: reg 8(1). As to the standard scale see para 286 note 11 ante.

**433. Offences and penalties.** Failure to comply with any of the provisions relating to: (1) the availability of books, documents or other records[1]; (2) a professional fund raiser[2] or commercial participator[3] holding money or property[4]; and (3) the statement accompanying a representation to the effect that charitable contributions[5] are to be applied for charitable, benevolent or philanthropic purposes[6] of any description[7], is an offence punishable on summary conviction by a fine[8].

1   Ie under the Charitable Institutions (Fund Raising) Regulations 1994, SI 1994/3024, reg 5(1): see para 432 ante.
2   For the meaning of 'professional fund raiser' see para 419 ante.
3   For the meaning of 'commercial participator' see para 419 ante.
4   Ie under Charitable Institutions (Fund Raising) Regulations 1994, SI 1994/3024, reg 6(2): see para 430 ante.
5   For the meaning of 'charitable contributions' see para 419 note 18 ante.
6   As to references to charitable, benevolent or philanthropic purposes see para 419 note 2 ante.
7   Ie under the Charitable Institutions (Fund Raising) Regulations 1994, SI 1994/3024, reg 7(2): see para 431 ante.
8   Ibid reg 8(1), (2). The fine must not exceed level 2 on the standard scale: reg 8(1). As to the standard scale see para 286 note 11 ante.

## (ii)  Public Charitable Collections

**434. Prohibition on conducting public charitable collections without authorisation.** As from a day to be appointed, the following provisions have effect[1]. No public charitable collection may be conducted in the area of the local authority[2] except in accordance with a permit issued by the authority[3] or an order[4] made by the Charity Commissioners[5]. Where a public charitable collection is conducted in contravention of these provisions, any promoter[6] of that collection is guilty of an offence[7].

A 'public charitable collection' means a charitable appeal which is made in any public place[8], or by means of visits from house to house[9]. 'Charitable appeal' is itself defined as an appeal to members of the public to give money or other property, whether for consideration or not, which is made in association with a representation that the whole or any part of the proceeds[10] is to be applied for charitable[11], benevolent or philanthropic purposes[12]. The definition of 'public charitable collection' does not, however, apply to a charitable appeal which: (1) is made in the course of a public meeting[13]; or (2) is made on enclosed land within a churchyard or burial ground contiguous or adjacent to a place of public worship, or on other enclosed land occupied for the purposes of a place of public worship and contiguous or adjacent to it, being in each case, land which is enclosed or substantially enclosed, whether by any wall or building or otherwise[14]; or (3) is an appeal to members of the public to give money or other property by placing it in an unattended receptacle[15].

1   The Charities Act 1992 Pt III (ss 65–74) (as amended) is to be brought into force by order made by the Secretary of State under s 79(2) as from a day to be appointed. At the date at which this volume states the law no such day had been appointed. See para 406 ante.
2   'Local authority' means the council of a Welsh county or county borough, of a district or of a London borough, the Common Council of the City of London, or the Council of the Isles of Scilly: Charities Act 1992 s 65(4) (amended by the Local Government (Wales) Act 1994 s 66(6), Sch 16 para 99). The

functions exercisable by a local authority are exercisable as respects the Inner Temple, by its Sub-Treasurer, and as respects the Middle Temple, by its Under Treasurer and references to a local authority or to the area of a local authority are to be construed accordingly: Charities Act 1992 s 65(6).

3    Ie under ibid s 68 (not yet in force): see para 435 post.

4    Ie under ibid s 72 (as amended) (not yet in force): see para 439 post.

5    Ibid s 66(1) (not yet in force). As to the Charity Commissioners see paras 486–512 post.

6    'Promoter' means a person who, whether alone or with others and whether for remuneration or otherwise, organises or controls the conduct of the charitable appeal in question, as associated expressions are to be construed accordingly, but where no person acts in this way in respect of a public charitable collection, any person who acts as a collector in respect of it is treated as a promoter of it as well: ibid s 65(3) (not yet in force). 'Collector' means any person by whom that appeal is made, whether made by him alone or with others and whether made by him for remuneration or otherwise: s 65(3) (not yet in force).

7    Ibid s 66(2) (not yet in force). Any promoter guilty of such an offence is liable on summary conviction to a fine not exceeding level 4 on the standard scale: s 66(2) (not yet in force). As to the standard scale see para 286 note 11 ante. As to offences by a body corporate see para 515 post.

8    'Public place', in relation to a charitable appeal, means any highway, and any other place to which, at any time when the appeal is made, members of the public have or are permitted access and which either is not within a building, or, if it is, is a public area within a station, airport or shopping precinct or similar public area: ibid s 65(8) (not yet in force). The definition excludes, however, any place to which members of the public are permitted to have access only if any payment or ticket required as a condition of access has been made or purchased, and any place to which members of the public are permitted to have access only by virtue of permission given for the purposes of the appeal: s 65(9) (not yet in force).

9    Ibid s 65(1)(a) (not yet in force). See *Carasu Ltd v Smith* [1968] 2 QB 383, [1968] 2 All ER 529, DC, and *Cooper v Coles* [1987] QB 230, [1987] 1 All ER 91, DC (decisions holding that for the purposes of the House to House Collections Act 1939 (prospectively repealed: see para 406 ante) 'collection' included an inducement to purchase an article on the representation that part of the proceeds would go to a charity); and para 407 et seq ante. 'House' includes any part of a building constituting a separate dwelling: Charities Act 1992 s 65(8) (not yet in force). It was held that in order to convict a person under the House to House Collections Act 1939 s 1(3) (prospectively repealed: see para 407 ante) it had to be proved that the person charged went from house to house or was about to do so when found collecting in one house: *Hankinson v Dowland* [1974] 3 All ER 655, [1974] 1 WLR 1327. Unlike the House to House Collections Act 1939, the Charities Act 1992 does not define 'house' as including a place of business.

As to street collections under the Police, Factories, etc (Miscellaneous Provisions) Act 1916 s 5 (as amended; prospectively repealed, except in relation to Northern Ireland) see para 411 text and note 20 ante; POLICE vol 36(1) (Reissue) para 333; CRIMINAL LAW, EVIDENCE AND PROCEDURE.

10   'Proceeds', in relation to a public charitable collection, means all money or other property given, whether for consideration or not, in response to the charitable appeal in question: Charities Act 1992 s 65(4) (not yet in force).

11   References to charitable purposes, where occurring in the context of a reference to charitable, benevolent or philanthropic purposes, is a reference to charitable purposes whether or not they are charitable within the meaning of any rule of law: ibid s 65(5) (not yet in force).

12   Ibid s 65(1)(b) (not yet in force). Without prejudice to the generality of s 65(1)(b), it is expressly provided that an appeal to members of the public, other than one falling within s 65(2) (not yet in force) is a public charitable collection if it consists in or includes the making of an offer to sell goods or to supply services, or the exposing of goods for sale, to members of the public, and it is made as mentioned in s 65(1)(a) (not yet in force) (see the text and notes 8–9 supra) and in association with a representation that the whole or any part of its proceeds is to be applied for charitable, benevolent or philanthropic purposes: s 65(7) (not yet in force).

13   Ibid s 65(2)(a) (not yet in force).

14   Ibid s 65(2)(b) (not yet in force).

15   Ibid s 65(2)(c) (not yet in force). A receptacle is unattended if it is not in the possession or custody of a person acting as collector: s 65(2)(c) (not yet in force).

## 435. Determination of applications and issue of permits to conduct public charitable collections.

As from a day to be appointed, the following provisions have effect[1]. An application for a permit to conduct a public charitable collection[2] in the area of a local authority[3] must be made to the authority by the person or persons proposing to promote that collection[4]. Any such application must specify the period for which it is desired that the permit should have effect, being a period not exceeding 12 months, and contain the prescribed[5] information[6]. Any person who, for the purposes of an application, knowingly or recklessly furnishes any information which is false in a material particular is guilty of an offence[7]. The application must be made at least one month before the day on which the collection is to be conducted or where it is to be conducted on more than one day, the first of those days, or before such later date as the local authority may in the case of that application allow[8]. Before determining an application, the local authority must consult the chief officer of police[9] for the police area[10] which comprises or includes its area and may make such other inquiries as it thinks fit[11].

Where an application for a permit is duly made to the local authority, the authority must either issue a permit in respect of the collection, or refuse the application on one or more of the specified[12] grounds[13]. A local authority may, at the time of issuing such a permit, attach to it such conditions as it thinks fit, having regard to the local circumstances of the collection[14]. In particular, the conditions may specify the day of the week, date, time or frequency of the collection and the locality or localities within the authority's area in which the collection may be conducted, and may regulate the manner in which the collection is to be conducted[15]. Where the local authority refuses to issue a permit or attach any such condition, it must serve written notice of the decision to do so, and of the reasons for its decision; and the notice must inform him of his right of appeal[16] and the time within which an appeal must be brought[17].

A person is guilty of an offence if, in connection with any charitable appeal[18], he displays or uses a prescribed badge or a prescribed certificate of authority[19] which is not for the time being held by him for the purposes of the appeal pursuant to regulations[20], or displays or uses any badge or article, or any certificate or other document, so nearly resembling a prescribed badge or, as the case may be, a prescribed certificate of authority as to be likely to deceive a member of the public[21].

---

1    The Charities Act 1992 Pt III (ss 65–74) (as amended) is to be brought into force by order made by the Secretary of State under s 79(2) as from a day to be appointed. At the date at which this volume states the law no such day had been appointed. See para 406 ante.

2    For the meaning of 'public charitable collection' see para 434 ante.

3    For the meaning of 'local authority' see para 434 note 2 ante.

4    Charities Act 1992 s 67(1). The Secretary of State may make regulations prescribing the information which is to be contained in applications under s 67 (as amended): see s 73(1)(a) (not yet in force); and para 441 post. At the date at which this volume states the law no such regulations had been made. As to the Secretary of State see para 513 post.

5    Ie prescribed by regulations made under ibid s 73 (not yet in force): see para 441 post.

6    Ibid s 67(2) (not yet in force).

7    Ibid s 74(3) (not yet in force). A person guilty of such an offence is liable on summary conviction to a fine not exceeding level 4 on the standard scale: s 74(3) (not yet in force). As to the standard scale see para 286 note 11 ante.

8    Ibid s 67(3) (amended by the Deregulation and Contracting Out Act 1994 ss 27, 81, Sch 17). The Charities Act 1992 s 67(3) is not yet in force.

9    As to chief officers of police see POLICE vol 36(1) (Reissue) para 341 et seq.

10   As to police areas see POLICE vol 36(1) (Reissue) para 313 et seq.

11   Charities Act 1992 s 67(4) (not yet in force).

12   Ie specified under ibid s 69 (not yet in force): see para 436 post.

13   Ibid s 68(1) (not yet in force). As to the specified grounds see para 436 post. Where the authority issues the permit, it has effect, subject to s 70 (not yet in force) (see para 437 post) for the period specified in the application in accordance with s 67(2) (not yet in force): s 68(1) (not yet in force).

The Secretary of State may make regulations for the purpose of regulating the conduct of public charitable collections authorised under permits issued under s 68 (not yet in force): see s 73(1)(b)(i) (not yet in force); and para 441 post. At the date at which this volume states the law no such regulations had been made.

14  Ibid s 68(2) (not yet in force). The terms of any such conditions must be consistent with the provisions of any regulations under s 73 (not yet in force) (see para 441 post): s 68(2) (not yet in force).
15  Ibid s 68(3) (not yet in force).
16  Ie under ibid s 71(2) (not yet in force): see para 438 post.
17  Ibid s 68(4) (not yet in force).
18  For the meaning of 'charitable appeal' see para 434 ante.
19  'Prescribed badge' and 'prescribed certificate of authority' mean respectively a badge and a certificate of authority in such form as may be prescribed by regulations under the Charities Act 1992 s 73 (see para 441 post) (not yet in force): s 74(4) (not yet in force).
20  Ie under ibid s 73 (not yet in force): see para 441 post.
21  Ibid s 74(1) (not yet in force). A person guilty of such an offence is liable on summary conviction to a fine not exceeding level 4 on the standard scale: s 74(2) (not yet in force).

**436. Refusal of permits.** As from a day to be appointed, the following provisions have effect[1]. A local authority[2] may refuse to issue a permit to conduct a public charitable collection[3] on any of the following grounds[4]:

(1)  that it appears to it that the collection would cause undue inconvenience to members of the public by reason of the day of the week or date on which, the time at which, the frequency with which, or the locality or localities in which, it is proposed to be conducted[5];

(2)  that the collection is proposed to be conducted on a day on which another public charitable collection is already authorised[6] to be conducted in the authority's area or on the day falling immediately before, or immediately after any such day[7];

(3)  that it appears to the authority that the amount likely to be applied for charitable, benevolent or philanthropic purposes[8] in consequence of the collection would be inadequate, having regard to the likely amount of the proceeds[9] of the collection[10];

(4)  that it appears to it that the applicant[11] or any other person would be likely to receive an excessive amount by way of remuneration in connection with the collection[12];

(5)  that the applicant has been convicted of one of certain specified offences[13], or of any offence involving dishonesty or of a kind the commission of which would in the authority's opinion be likely to be facilitated by the issuing to him of a permit[14] to conduct a public charitable collection[15];

(6)  where the applicant is a person other than a charitable, benevolent or philanthropic institution for whose benefit the collection is proposed to be conducted, that the authority is not satisfied that the applicant is authorised, whether by any such institution or by any person acting on behalf of any such institution, to promote the collection[16];

(7)  that it appears to it that the applicant, in promoting any other collection[17], failed to exercise due diligence[18]: (a) to secure that persons authorised by him to act as collectors were fit and proper persons[19]; (b) to secure that such persons complied with the provisions of regulations[20]; or (c) to prevent badges or certificates of authority[21] being obtained by persons other than those he had so authorised[22].

1   The Charities Act 1992 Pt III (ss 65–74) (as amended) is to be brought into force by order made by the Secretary of State under s 79(2) as from a day to be appointed. At the date at which this volume states the law no such day had been appointed. See para 406 ante.

2   For the meaning of 'local authority' see para 434 note 2 ante.

3   For the meaning of 'public charitable collection' see para 434 ante.

4   Charities Act 1992 s 69(1) (not yet in force).

5   Ibid s 69(1)(a) (not yet in force).

6   Ie under ibid s 68 (not yet in force) (see para 435 ante) or otherwise.

7   Ibid s 69(1)(b) (not yet in force). A local authority may not, however, refuse to issue such a permit on the ground in s 69(1)(b) (not yet in force) if it appears to it that the collection would be conducted only in one location, which is on land to which members of the public would have access only by virtue of the express or implied permission of the occupier of the land, and that the occupier of the land consents to the collection being conducted there: s 69(2) (not yet in force). For these purposes, the 'occupier', in relation to unoccupied land, means the person entitled to occupy it: s 69(2) (not yet in force).

8   As to the meaning of 'charitable purposes' see para 434 note 11 ante.

9   For the meaning of 'proceeds' see para 434 note 10 ante.

10   Charities Act 1992 s 69(1)(c) (not yet in force).

11   For the purposes of ibid s 69(1) (not yet in force), in the case of a collection in relation to which there is more than one applicant, any reference to the applicant is to be construed as a reference to any of the applicants: s 69(3)(a) (not yet in force).

12   Ibid s 69(1)(d) (not yet in force).

13   Ie offences under the Police, Factories, etc (Miscellaneous Provisions) Act 1916 s 5 (as amended; prospectively repealed, except in relation to Northern Ireland) (regulation of street collections) (see POLICE vol 36(1) (Reissue) para 333; CRIMINAL LAW, EVIDENCE AND PROCEDURE), under the House to House Collections Act 1939 (prospectively repealed: see para 406 ante) (see paras 407–417 ante), under the Civic Government (Scotland) Act 1982 s 119 or regulations made under it, or under the Charities Act 1992 Pt III (ss 65–74) (as amended) or regulations made under s 73: s 69(1)(e)(i), (5) (not yet in force).

14   Ie under ibid s 68 (not yet in force): see para 435 ante.

15   Ibid s 69(1)(e) (not yet in force).

16   Ibid s 69(1)(f) (not yet in force).

17   Ie one authorised under the Charities Act 1992 Pt III (as amended) (not yet in force) (see paras 434–435 ante, 437–441 post) or under the Civic Government (Scotland) Act 1982 s 119: see the Charities Act 1992 s 65(1)(g) (not yet in force).

18   Ibid s 65(1)(g) (not yet in force). Section 65(1)(g) (not yet in force) applies to the conduct of the applicant, or any of the applicants, in relation to any public charitable collection authorised under regulations made under the Police, Factories, etc (Miscellaneous Provisions) Act 1916 s 5 (as amended; prospectively repealed, except in relation to Northern Ireland) (see POLICE vol 36(1) (Reissue) para 333; CRIMINAL LAW, EVIDENCE AND PROCEDURE) (collection of money or sale of articles in a street or other public place), or authorised under the House to House Collections Act 1939 (prospectively repealed: see para 406 ante) (collection of money or other property by means of visits from house to house), as it applies to his conduct in relation to a collection authorised under the Charities Act 1992 Pt III (not yet in force), subject to the following modifications (s 69(4) (not yet in force)):

   (1)   in the case of a collection authorised under regulations made under the Police, Factories, etc (Miscellaneous Provisions) Act 1916:
      (a)   the reference in head (7)(b) in the text to regulations under the Charities Act 1992 s 73 (not yet in force) (see para 435 ante) is to be construed as a reference to the regulations under which the collection in question was authorised (s 69(4)(a)(i) (not yet in force)); and
      (b)   the reference in head (7)(c) in the text to badges or certificates of authority is to be construed as a reference to any written authority provided to a collector pursuant to those regulations (s 69(4)(a)(ii) (not yet in force)); and

   (2)   in the case of a collection authorised under the House to House Collections Act 1939 (prospectively repealed):
      (a)   the reference in head (7)(b) in the text to regulations under the Charities Act 1992 s 73 (not yet in force) is to be construed as a reference to regulations under the House to House Collections Act 1939 s 4 (prospectively repealed: see para 406 ante) (see para 411 ante) (Charities Act 1992 s 69(4)(b)(i) (not yet in force)); and
      (b)   the reference in head (7)(c) in the text to badges or certificates of authority is to be construed as a reference to badges or certificates of authority in a form prescribed by such regulations (s 69(4)(b)(i) (not yet in force)).

19   Ibid s 65(1)(g)(i) (not yet in force). For the meaning of 'collector' see para 434 note 6 ante.

20  Ibid s 65(1)(g)(ii) (not yet in force). The regulations referred to in the text are the regulations made under s 73 (not yet in force) (see para 435 ante) or as the case may be, made under the Civic Government (Scotland) Act 1982 s 119: see the Charities Act 1992 s 65(1)(g)(ii) (not yet in force).

21  Subject to ibid s 69(4) (not yet in force) (see note 18 supra), the reference to badges or certificates of authority is a reference to badges or certificates of authority in a form prescribed by regulations under s 73 (not yet in force) (see para 435 ante) or, as the case may be, the Civic Government (Scotland) Act 1982 s 119: Charities Act 1992 s 69(3)(b) (not yet in force).

22  Ibid s 69(1)(g)(iii) (not yet in force).

**437. Withdrawal of, and attachment of conditions to, a permit.** As from a day to be appointed, the following provisions have effect[1]. Where a local authority[2] who has issued a permit in respect of a public charitable collection[3]:

(1)  has reason to believe that there has been a change in the circumstances which prevailed at the time when it issued a permit, and is of the opinion that, if the application for the permit had been made in the new circumstances of the case, it would not have issued the permit[4]; or

(2)  has reason to believe that any information furnished to it by the promoter[5], or, in the case of a collection in relation to which there is more than one promoter, by any of them, for the purposes of the application was false in a material particular[6],

it may withdraw the permit, attach any condition[7] to it, or vary any existing condition of the permit[8]. It may also withdraw a permit where it has reason to believe that there has been or is likely to be a breach of any its conditions, or that a breach of such condition is continuing[9]. Where a local authority so withdraws, attaches any condition to, or varies an existing condition of, a permit, it must serve on the promoter written notice of its decision to do so and of the reasons for it[10]. The notice must inform the promoter of his right of appeal[11] and the time within which an appeal may be brought[12].

Where a local authority so withdraws, attaches any condition to, or varies an existing condition of, a permit, the permit nevertheless continues to have effect as if it had not been withdrawn or, as the case may be, as if the condition had not been attached or the variation had not been made until the time for bringing an appeal[13] has expired, or if such an appeal is duly brought, until the determination or abandonment of the appeal[14].

1  The Charities Act 1992 Pt III (ss 65–74) (as amended) is to be brought into force by order made by the Secretary of State under s 79(2) as from a day to be appointed. At the date at which this volume states the law no such day had been appointed. See para 406 ante.

2  For the meaning of 'local authority' see para 434 note 2 ante.

3  Ie a permit under the Charities Act 1992 s 68 (not yet in force): see para 435 ante.

4  Ibid s 70(1)(a) (not yet in force).

5  For the meaning of 'promoter' see para 434 note 6 ante.

6  Charities Act 1992 s 70(1)(b) (not yet in force).

7  Any condition so imposed by the local authority, whether by attaching a new condition to the permit or by varying an existing condition, must be one that could have been attached to the permit under ibid s 68(2) (not yet in force) (see para 435 ante) at the time when it was issued, assuming for these purposes that the new circumstances of the case had prevailed at that time, or, in the case of false information, (see head (2) in the text) that the authority had been aware of the true circumstances of the case at that time: s 70(2) (not yet in force).

8  Ibid s 70(1) (not yet in force).

9  Ibid s 70(3) (not yet in force).

10  Ibid s 70(4) (not yet in force).
11  Ie under ibid s 71(2) (not yet in force): see para 438 post.
12  Ibid s 70(4) (not yet in force).
13  See note 11 supra.
14  Charities Act 1992 s 70(5) (not yet in force).

**438. Appeal against refusal or withdrawal of permit and attachment or variation of conditions.** As from a day to be appointed, the following provisions have effect[1]. A person who has duly applied to a local authority[2] for a permit to conduct a public charitable collection[3] in the authority's area may appeal by way of complaint for an order to a magistrates' court[4] against a decision of the authority to refuse to issue a permit to him[5].

A person to whom a permit has been issued[6] may appeal by way of complaint for an order to a magistrates' court against a decision of the local authority[7] to attach any condition to the permit or a decision of the local authority[8] to vary any condition so attached or to withdraw the permit[9].

Any such appeal must be brought within 14 days of the date of service on the person in question of the relevant[10] notice[11]. An appeal against the decision of a magistrates' court may be brought to the Crown Court[12]. On an appeal to a magistrates' court or the Crown Court under these provisions, the court may confirm, vary or reverse the local authority's decision and generally give such directions as it thinks fit[13]. It is the duty of the local authority to comply with any directions so given by the court, but the authority need not comply with any directions given by a magistrates' court until the time for bringing an appeal to the Crown Court[14] has expired, or if such an appeal is duly brought, until the determination or abandonment of the appeal[15].

1  The Charities Act 1992 Pt III (ss 65–74) (as amended) is to be brought into force by order made by the Secretary of State under s 79(2) as from a day to be appointed. At the date at which this volume states the law no such day had been appointed. See para 406 ante.
2  For the meaning of 'local authority' see para 434 note 2 ante.
3  Ie under the Charities Act 1992 s 67 (not yet in force): see para 435 ante.
4  References in ibid s 71 (not yet in force) to a magistrates' court are to a magistrates' court acting for the petty sessions area in which is situated the office or principal office of the local authority against whose decision the appeal is brought: s 71(3) (not yet in force). The Magistrates' Courts Act 1980 (see MAGISTRATES) applies to the proceedings: see the Charities Act 1992 s 71(3) (not yet in force).
5  Ibid s 71(1), (3) (not yet in force).
6  Ie under ibid s 68 (not yet in force): see para 435 ante.
7  Ie under ibid ss 68, 70 (not yet in force): see paras 435, 437 ante.
8  Ie under ibid s 70 (not yet in force): see para 437 ante.
9  Ibid s 71(2), (3) (not yet in force). As to withdrawal and attachment of conditions see para 437 ante.
10  Ie under ibid s 68(4) (not yet in force) or s 70(4) (not yet in force), as the case may be: see paras 435, 437 ante.
11  Ibid s 71(4) (not yet in force). An appeal is brought when the complaint is made: s 71(4) (not yet in force).
12  Ibid s 71(5) (not yet in force).
13  Ibid s 71(6) (not yet in force). The court must have regard to the provisions of Pt III (ss 65–74) (as amended) (not yet in force) and of regulations made under s 73 (not yet in force) (see para 435 ante): s 71(6) (not yet in force).
14  Ie under ibid s 71(5) (not yet in force): see the text and note 12 supra.
15  Ibid s 71(7) (not yet in force).

**439. Orders made by the Charity Commissioners.** As from a day to be appointed, the following provisions have effect[1]. Where the Charity Commissioners[2] are satisfied, on the application of any charity, that that charity[3] proposes to promote[4] public charitable collections[5] throughout England and Wales, or a substantial part thereof, in connection with any charitable purposes[6] pursued by the charity, or to authorise other persons to promote such public charitable collections, the Commissioners may make an order in respect of the charity[7].

Such an order has the effect of authorising public charitable collections which: (1) are promoted by the charity in respect of which the order is made, or by persons authorised by the charity[8]; and (2) are so promoted in connection with the charitable purposes pursued by the charity[9], to be conducted in such area or areas as may be specified in the order[10]. The order may: (a) include such conditions as the Commissioners think fit[11]; (b) be expressed to have effect without limit of time, or for a specified period only[12]; and (c) be revoked or varied by a further order of the Commissioners[13]. Where the Commissioners make a further order revoking or varying the order they have made, they must serve on the charity written notice of their reasons for making the further order, unless it appears to them that the interests of the charity would not be prejudiced by the further order[14].

Any person who knowingly or recklessly provides the Commissioners with information which is false or misleading in a material particular is guilty of an offence if the information is provided in circumstances in which he intends, or could reasonably be expected to know, that it would be used by them for the purpose of discharging their functions[15] to authorise public charitable collections[16].

1   The Charities Act 1992 Pt III (ss 65–74) (as amended) is to be brought into force by order made by the Secretary of State under s 79(2) as from a day to be appointed. At the date at which this volume states the law no such day had been appointed. See para 406 ante.
2   As to the Charity Commissioners see paras 486–512 post.
3   For the meaning of 'charity' see para 1 ante; definition applied by the Charities Act 1992 s 72(6) (added by the Charities Act 1993 s 98(1), Sch 6 para 29(1), (7)).
4   For the meaning of 'promote' see para 434 note 6 ante.
5   For the meaning of 'public charitable collections' see para 434 ante.
6   For the meaning of 'charitable purposes' see para 1 ante; definition applied by the Charities Act 1992 s 72(6) (as added: see note 3 supra) (not yet in force).
7   Ibid s 72(1) (not yet in force). The Secretary of State may make regulations for the purpose of regulating the conduct of public charitable collections authorised under orders made by the Commissioners under s 72 (not yet in force): see s 73(1)(b)(ii) (not yet in force); and para 441 post. At the date at which this volume states the law no such regulations had been made. As to the Secretary of State see para 513 post.
8   Ibid s 72(2)(a) (not yet in force).
9   Ibid s 72(2)(b) (not yet in force).
10  Ibid s 72(2) (not yet in force).
11  Ibid s 72(3)(a) (not yet in force).
12  Ibid s 72(3)(b) (not yet in force). This provision is expressed to be without prejudice to s 72(3)(c) (see the text and note 13 infra): see s 72(3)(b) (not yet in force).
13  Ibid s 72(3)(c) (not yet in force). The provisions of the Charities Act 1993 s 89(1), (2) and (4) (provisions as to orders made by the Commissioners) (see para 492 post) apply to an order made by them under the Charities Act 1992 s 72 as they apply to an order made by them under the Charities Act 1993: Charities Act 1992 s 72(5) (substituted by the Charities Act 1993 Sch 6 para 29(7)). The Charities Act 1992 s 72 is not yet in force.
14  Charities Act 1992 s 72(4) (not yet in force).
15  Ie under ibid s 72 (not yet in force): see the text and notes 1–14 supra.

16  Ibid s 74(3A) (s 74(3A), (3B) added by the Charities Act 1993 Sch 6 para 29(8)). The Charities Act 1992
    s 74 is not yet in force. A person guilty of such offence is liable, on summary conviction, to a fine not
    exceeding the statutory maximum, and, on conviction on indictment, to imprisonment for a term not
    exceeding two years or a fine or both: s 74(3B) (as so added) (not yet in force). As to the statutory
    maximum see para 226 note 5 ante.

**440. Service of notices.** Any notice required to be served in relation to a public
charitable collection[1] may be served in the same way as a notice in relation to the control
of fund raising for charitable institutions[2].

1   Ie under the Charities Act 1992 Pt III (ss 65–74) (as amended): see paras 434–439 ante, 441 post. The
    Charities Act 1992 Pt III (ss 65–74) (as amended) is to be brought into force by order made by the
    Secretary of State under s 79(2) as from a day to be appointed. At the date at which this volume states
    the law no such day had been appointed. See para 406 ante.
2   See ibid s 76; and para 425 ante.

**441. Power to make regulations in relation to public charitable collections.**
As from a day to be appointed, the following provisions have effect[1]. The Secretary of
State[2] may make regulations: (1) prescribing the information which is to be contained in
applications for permits[3] to conduct public charitable collections[4]; (2) for the purpose of
regulating the conduct of public charitable collections authorised under permits issued
by a local authority[5] or orders made by the Charity Commissioners[6]. Such regulations
may provide that any failure to comply with a specified provision of the regulations is an
offence[7].

Regulations made for the purposes in head (2) above may, without prejudice to the
generality of that provision, make provision:

(a)  about the keeping and publication of accounts[8];

(b)  for the prevention of annoyance to members of the public[9];

(c)  with respect to the use by collectors[10] of badges and certificates of authority, or
     badges incorporating such certificates, and to other matters relating to such
     badges and certificates, including, in particular, provision[11]:
     (i)   prescribing the form of such badges and certificates[12];
     (ii)  requiring a collector, on request, to permit his badge, or any certificate of
           authority held by him for the purposes of the collection, to be inspected by
           a constable or a duly authorised officer of a local authority, or by an occupier
           of any premises visited by him in the course of the collection[13];

(d)  for prohibiting persons under a prescribed age from acting as collectors, and
     prohibiting others from causing them so to act[14].

1   The Charities Act 1992 Pt III (ss 65–74) (as amended) is to be brought into force by order made by the
    Secretary of State under s 79(2) as from a day to be appointed. At the date at which this volume states
    the law no such day had been appointed. See para 406 ante.
2   As to the Secretary of State see para 513 post.
3   Ie under the Charities Act 1992 s 67 (not yet in force): see para 435 ante. For the meaning of 'public
    charitable collection' see para 434 ante.
4   Ibid s 73(1)(a) (not yet in force).
5   Ie under ibid s 68 (not yet in force): see para 435 ante. For the meaning of 'local authority' see para 434
    note 2 ante.

6    Ibid s 73(1)(b) (not yet in force). The reference in the text to orders made by the Charity Commissioners is a reference to orders made under s 72 (not yet in force) (see para 439 ante): s 73(1)(b). As to the Charity Commissioners see paras 486–512 post.

     At the date at which this volume states the law, no such regulations had been made under s 73 (not yet in force). As to the making of regulations generally see s 77 (as amended); and para 517 post.

7    Ibid s 73(3) (not yet in force). Regulations may provide that such an offence is punishable on summary conviction by a fine not exceeding the level 2 on the standard scale: s 73(3) (not yet in force). As to the standard scale see para 286 note 11 ante.

8    Ibid s 73(2)(a) (not yet in force).

9    Ibid s 73(2)(b) (not yet in force).

10    For the meaning of 'collector' see para 434 note 6 ante.

11    Charities Act 1992 s 73(2)(c) (not yet in force).

12    Ibid s 73(2)(c)(i) (not yet in force).

13    Ibid s 73(2)(c)(ii) (not yet in force).

14    Ibid s 73(2)(d) (not yet in force).

# (5) THE NATIONAL LOTTERY AS A PROVIDER FOR CHARITIES

## (i) In general

**442. National Lottery etc Act 1993 and National Lottery Act 1998.**    The National Lottery etc Act 1993 constituted the machinery necessary to set up and administer a National Lottery to be run for the benefit of, among other good causes, charity and charitability[1].

The National Lottery etc Act 1993 created an office the holder of which was to be appointed by the Secretary of State[2] and known as the Director General of the National Lottery[3], who had the power to grant a single licence to a body corporate to run the National Lottery[4]. The National Lottery distribution fund was established for apportionment, after the deduction of certain expenses, of the proceeds of the National Lottery among a variety of specified distributing bodies for expenditure on good causes[5]. The National Lottery Act 1998 replaced, with effect from 1 April 1999[6], the office of Director General of the National Lottery with the National Lottery Commission[7], and constituted the New Opportunities Fund which may make grants or enter into arrangements which are designed to give effect to such initiatives concerned or connected with health, education or the environment[8]. The National Lottery Act 1998 also altered the apportionment of money in, and the allocation for expenditure held by, the National Lottery distribution fund[9].

1    The National Lottery was based on *A National Lottery Raising Money for Good Causes* (Cm 1861) (1992) (white paper). As to the National Lottery generally see BETTING, GAMING AND LOTTERIES; LIBRARIES AND OTHER SCIENTIFIC AND CULTURAL INSTITUTIONS vol 28 (Reissue) paras 608–612.

2    As to the Secretary of State see para 513 post.

3    See the National Lottery etc Act 1993 s 3 (repealed).

4    See ibid s 5 (as originally enacted).

5    See ibid s 21(2) (as amended), s 22(2), (3) (as amended), s 24, s 31 (as amended); and BETTING, GAMING AND LOTTERIES; LIBRARIES AND OTHER SCIENTIFIC AND CULTURAL INSTITUTIONS vol 28 (Reissue) paras 608–612. As to the constitution of the National Lottery distribution fund see para 444 post; and BETTING, GAMING AND LOTTERIES; LIBRARIES AND OTHER SCIENTIFIC AND CULTURAL INSTITUTIONS. As to distribution of the net proceeds of the National Lottery see Pt II (ss 21–44) (as

amended); and BETTING, GAMING AND LOTTERIES; LIBRARIES AND OTHER SCIENTIFIC AND CULTURAL INSTITUTIONS vol 28 (Reissue) paras 608–612.

6   See the National Lottery Act 1998 (Commencement) Order 1999, SI 1999/650, art 2.

7   See the National Lottery Act etc 1993 s 3A (as added); the National Lottery Act 1998 s 1; para 443 post; and BETTING, GAMING AND LOTTERIES.

8   See the National Lottery etc Act 1993 s 43B(1) (as added); and BETTING, GAMING AND LOTTERIES; LIBRARIES AND OTHER SCIENTIFIC AND CULTURAL INSTITUTIONS. As to the New Opportunities Fund see s 43A (as added), s 43B (as added and amended), s 43C (as added), s 43CC (as added), s 43D (as added and amended), Sch 6A (as added); and para 445 post; BETTING, GAMING AND LOTTERIES; LIBRARIES AND OTHER SCIENTIFIC AND CULTURAL INSTITUTIONS.

9   See ibid ss 22, 23 (as amended); and BETTING, GAMING AND LOTTERIES; LIBRARIES AND OTHER SCIENTIFIC AND CULTURAL INSTITUTIONS vol 28 (Reissue) para 608.

**443. Function of National Lottery Commission.** The National Lottery Commission[1] consists of five members appointed by the Secretary of State[2], for no longer than five years, subject to reappointment[3]. The National Lottery Commission is now empowered to grant a licence authorising a body corporate to run the National Lottery, and only one body may be licensed for these purposes at any one time[4]. The National Lottery Commission also has power to grant licences authorising a body corporate to promote lotteries as part of the National Lottery[5].

1   As to the National Lottery generally see BETTING, GAMING AND LOTTERIES; LIBRARIES AND OTHER SCIENTIFIC AND CULTURAL INSTITUTIONS. As to the National Lottery Commission see the National Lottery etc Act 1993 s 3A, Sch 2A (s 3A added by the National Lottery Act 1998 s 1(3), the National Lottery etc Act Sch 2A added by the National Lottery Act 1998 s 1(5), Sch 1 para 7); and BETTING, GAMING AND LOTTERIES.

2   As to the Secretary of State see para 513 post.

3   See the National Lottery etc Act 1993 s 3A, Sch 2A paras 2, 3 (s 3A added by the National Lottery Act 1998 s 1(3), the National Lottery etc Act Sch 2A added by the National Lottery Act 1998 s 1(5), Sch 1 para 7). The functions previously conferred or imposed on the Director General of the National Lottery were transferred to the National Lottery Commission: see the National Lottery Act 1998 s 1(4); and para 442 ante; BETTING, GAMING AND LOTTERIES.

4   See the National Lottery Act etc 1993 s 5(1), 5(2) (s 5(1) as amended); and BETTING, GAMING AND LOTTERIES.

5   See ibid s 6 (as amended); and BETTING, GAMING AND LOTTERIES.

**444. Constitution of National Lottery distribution fund.** The net proceeds of the National Lottery[1] are paid to the Secretary of State[2] who must pay any sums so received into the National Lottery distribution fund[3]. After the payment of certain expenses[4] the balance in the fund is apportioned among distributing bodies for expenditure on the arts, sport, national heritage, charitable expenditure, projects to mark the year 2000 and the beginning of the third millennium, and expenditure on or connected with health, education or the environment[5].

It is particularly to be noted that 'charitable expenditure' means expenditure by charities or by institutions other than charities that are established for charitable purposes (whether or not those purposes are charitable within the meaning of any rule of law), benevolent purposes or philanthropic purposes[6]. Therefore, an institution established for purposes charitable in law would of course be a charity, but an institution for a purpose that is charitable in the popular sense even if not in the legal sense will be a qualifying institution, as will be one established for benevolent or philanthropic purposes[7].

1    As to the National Lottery generally see BETTING, GAMING AND LOTTERIES; LIBRARIES AND OTHER
     SCIENTIFIC AND CULTURAL INSTITUTIONS.
2    Ie under the National Lottery etc Act 1993 s 5(6): see BETTING, GAMING AND LOTTERIES. As to the
     Secretary of State see para 513 post.
3    See ibid s 21(2) (as amended); and BETTING, GAMING AND LOTTERIES; LIBRARIES AND OTHER
     SCIENTIFIC AND CULTURAL INSTITUTIONS. As to distribution of the net proceeds of the National
     Lottery see Pt II (ss 21–44) (as amended); and LIBRARIES AND OTHER SCIENTIFIC AND CULTURAL
     INSTITUTIONS vol 28 (Reissue) paras 608–612.
4    See ibid ss 22(2), 31 (as amended); and BETTING, GAMING AND LOTTERIES.
5    See ibid s 22(3) (as amended), s 24; and BETTING, GAMING AND LOTTERIES; LIBRARIES AND OTHER
     SCIENTIFIC AND CULTURAL INSTITUTIONS vol 28 (Reissue) paras 608–612. As to the distributing bodies
     see LIBRARIES AND OTHER SCIENTIFIC AND CULTURAL INSTITUTIONS vol 28 (Reissue) para 609.
         The provision for expenditure on or connected with health, education or the environment was added
     to the original list of good causes contained in the National Lottery etc Act 1993 by the National Lottery
     Act 1998 and its introduction required adjustments in the allocation to the existing five good causes: see
     ss 22, 23 (both as amended); and BETTING, GAMING AND LOTTERIES; LIBRARIES AND OTHER
     SCIENTIFIC AND CULTURAL INSTITUTIONS vol 28 (Reissue) para 608 et seq. 'Education' includes
     training and the provision of activities for children; and 'the environment' includes the living and social
     environment: see the National Lottery etc Act 1993 s 44(1) (definitions added by the National Lottery
     Act 1998 s 6(8)); and BETTING, GAMING AND LOTTERIES. The New Opportunities Fund may make
     grants or enter into arrangements designed to give effect to initiatives concerned or connected with
     health, education or the environment as may from time to time be specified in an order made by the
     Secretary of State: see the National Lottery etc Act 1993 s 43(B)(1) (as added); para 445 post; and
     BETTING, GAMING AND LOTTERIES; LIBRARIES AND OTHER SCIENTIFIC AND CULTURAL
     INSTITUTIONS.
6    Ibid s 44(1). As to charitable purposes generally see *Income Tax Special Purposes Comrs v Pemsel* [1891] AC
     531 at 580, 583, HL; and para 16 et seq ante. As to benevolent and philanthropic purposes see *Re Macduff*
     [1896] 2 Ch 451, CA; *Chichester Diocesan Fund and Board of Finance Inc v Simpson* [1944] AC 341, [1944]
     2 All ER 60, HL; *Campbell College Belfast (Governors) v Comr of Valuation for Northern Ireland* [1964] 2 All
     ER 705, [1964] 1 WLR 912, HL (public purposes).
7    See note 6 supra.

**445. New Opportunities Fund.** The New Opportunities Fund[1] is a distributor of
funds derived from the National Lottery[2]. It may make grants out of any money it
receives to fund or assist in the funding of projects, or may make or enter into
arrangements which are designed to give effect to such initiatives concerned or
connected with health, education or the environment as may from time to time be
specified in an order[3] made by the Secretary of State[4]. The currently specified initiatives
include:

(1)    an initiative to provide facilities, services and advice to promote healthy living[5];

(2)    an initiative to train teachers, staff in school libraries and staff working in public
       library services to use information and communications technology in order to
       assist learning; and to make materials of an educational nature available in a digital
       form or such technology[6];

(3)    an initiative to provide activities outside school hours for children who attend
       school[7];

(4)    an initiative to promote access to education[8] for persons aged 16 or over,
       particularly through the development of facilities[9] for providing such access by
       means of information and communications technology[10];

(5)    an initiative to improve: (a) the prevention, detection, diagnosis and treatment
       of cancer, including by promoting awareness of, and access to, facilities for
       preventing, detecting, diagnosing and treating cancer[11]; (b) an initiative to

improve the provision of palliative care for persons suffering from cancer[12]; (c) an initiative to improve the provision to such persons, or to their families or others caring for them, of support and information services associated with such palliative care[13];

(6)    an initiative to help communities to understand, improve and care for their environment (including the living and social environment), which may involve the acquisition of land, the promotion and management of access to the countryside or to other land which is (or is to be) open to the public, and the promotion of the use of land for the benefit of the community[14];

1    As to the constitution of the New Opportunities Fund see the National Lottery etc Act 1993 s 43A, Sch 6A (s 43A added by the National Lottery Act 1998 s 7(2); and the National Lottery etc Act 1993 Sch 6A added by the National Lottery Act 1998 s 7(3), Sch 2); and BETTING, GAMING AND LOTTERIES; LIBRARIES AND OTHER SCIENTIFIC AND CULTURAL INSTITUTIONS. As to the New Opportunities Fund generally see the National Lottery etc Act 1993 ss 43A, 43B (as amended), 43C, 43CC, 43D (as amended), Sch 6A (ss 43A, 43B, 43C, 43D added by the National Lottery Act 1998 s 7(2); the National Lottery etc Act 1993 s 43CC added by the Scotland Act 1998 (Modification of Functions) Order 1999, SI 1999/1756, art 2, Schedule para 15(10); and the National Lottery etc Act 1993 Sch 6A added by the National Lottery Act 1998 s 7(3), Sch 2); and BETTING, GAMING AND LOTTERIES; LIBRARIES AND OTHER SCIENTIFIC AND CULTURAL INSTITUTIONS.
2    As to the National Lottery generally see BETTING, GAMING AND LOTTERIES; LIBRARIES AND OTHER SCIENTIFIC AND CULTURAL INSTITUTIONS.
3    In exercise of this power, the New Opportunities Fund (Specification of Initiatives) Order 1998, SI 1998/1598, and the New Opportunities Fund (Specification of Initiatives) Order 1999, SI 1999/966, have been made: see BETTING, GAMING AND LOTTERIES; LIBRARIES AND OTHER SCIENTIFIC AND CULTURAL INSTITUTIONS.
4    See the National Lottery etc Act 1993 s 43B(1) (as added); and BETTING, GAMING AND LOTTERIES; LIBRARIES AND OTHER SCIENTIFIC AND CULTURAL INSTITUTIONS. As to the Secretary of State see para 513 post.
5    See the New Opportunities Fund (Specification of Initiatives) Order 1998, SI 1998/1598, art 3(1).
6    Ibid art 3(2).
7    Ibid art 3(3). A child is to be regarded as attending school notwithstanding that he is excluded permanently or temporarily from school: art 4. As to exclusion from school see EDUCATION.
8    The reference to access to education includes a reference to access to information to be used for the purposes of education: New Opportunities Fund (Specification of Initiatives) Order 1999, SI 1999/966, art 4(b).
9    The reference to the development of facilities includes a reference to the training of persons ('users') in the use of facilities, and to the training of persons to assist or train users: ibid art 4(a).
10    Ibid art 3(3).
11    Ibid art 3(1)(a).
12    Ibid art 3(1)(b).
13    Ibid art 3(1)(c).
14    Ibid art 3(2).

**446. Distribution of National Lottery proceeds.** So much of any sum paid into the National Lottery distribution fund[1] as is allocated for expenditure on good causes[2] is held in the fund in varying percentages for distribution by the distributing bodies, which are the Arts Councils[3], the Sports Councils[4], the trustees of the National Heritage Memorial Fund[5], the National Lottery Charities Board[6], the Millennium Commission[7] and the New Opportunities Fund[8]. The exact proportion to be distributed to each distributing body is specified by the National Lottery etc Act 1993[9].

Provision is made as to the manner in which the distributing bodies should apply the money from the National Lottery distribution fund. They are under a duty both to distribute the money they receive from the distribution fund[10] according to the statutorily specified[11] proportions and to distribute it only for the expenditure so specified[12]. The distributing bodies are also authorised to defray out of any money paid to them[13] the expenses they incur meeting their obligations[14].

1    As to the National Lottery distribution fund see para 444 ante; and BETTING, GAMING AND LOTTERIES; LIBRARIES AND OTHER SCIENTIFIC AND CULTURAL INSTITUTIONS vol 28 (Reissue) para 608. As to distribution of the net proceeds of the National Lottery see the National Lottery etc Act 1993 Pt II (ss 21–44) (as amended); and BETTING, GAMING AND LOTTERIES; LIBRARIES AND OTHER SCIENTIFIC AND CULTURAL INSTITUTIONS vol 28 (Reissue) paras 608–612.

2    As to the apportionment of money in the distribution fund see ibid s 22 (as amended); and BETTING, GAMING AND LOTTERIES; LIBRARIES AND OTHER SCIENTIFIC AND CULTURAL INSTITUTIONS vol 28 (Reissue) para 608.

3    Ie the Arts Council of England, the Scottish Arts Council, the Arts Council of Wales, the Arts Council of Northern Ireland, the Film Council and Scottish Council: see s 23(1) (as amended); and BETTING, GAMING AND LOTTERIES; LIBRARIES AND OTHER SCIENTIFIC AND CULTURAL INSTITUTIONS vol 28 (Reissue) para 609. As to the Arts Council of England, the Arts Council of Wales and the Arts Council of Northern Ireland see LIBRARIES AND OTHER SCIENTIFIC AND CULTURAL INSTITUTIONS vol 28 (Reissue) paras 584–586.

4    Ie the English Sports Council, the Scottish Sports Council, the Sports Council for Wales, the Sports Council for Northern Ireland and the United Kingdom Sports Council: see ibid s 23(2) (as amended); and BETTING, GAMING AND LOTTERIES; LIBRARIES AND OTHER SCIENTIFIC AND CULTURAL INSTITUTIONS vol 28 (Reissue) para 609. As to the English Sports Council and the Sports Council for Wales see LIBRARIES AND OTHER SCIENTIFIC AND CULTURAL INSTITUTIONS vol 28 (Reissue) para 589.

5    See ibid s 23(3); and BETTING, GAMING AND LOTTERIES; LIBRARIES AND OTHER SCIENTIFIC AND CULTURAL INSTITUTIONS vol 28 (Reissue) para 609. As to the National Heritage Memorial Fund see LIBRARIES AND OTHER SCIENTIFIC AND CULTURAL INSTITUTIONS vol 28 (Reissue) paras 596–598.

6    See ibid s 23(4); and BETTING, GAMING AND LOTTERIES; LIBRARIES AND OTHER SCIENTIFIC AND CULTURAL INSTITUTIONS vol 28 (Reissue) para 609. As to the National Lotteries Charities Board see para 448 et seq post.

7    See ibid s 23(5); and BETTING, GAMING AND LOTTERIES; LIBRARIES AND OTHER SCIENTIFIC AND CULTURAL INSTITUTIONS vol 28 (Reissue) para 609. As to the Millennium Commission see LIBRARIES AND OTHER SCIENTIFIC AND CULTURAL INSTITUTIONS vol 28 (Reissue) para 599.

8    See ibid s 23(6) (as added); and BETTING, GAMING AND LOTTERIES; LIBRARIES AND OTHER SCIENTIFIC AND CULTURAL INSTITUTIONS vol 28 (Reissue) para 609. As to the New Opportunities Fund see para 445 ante; and BETTING, GAMING AND LOTTERIES; LIBRARIES AND OTHER SCIENTIFIC AND CULTURAL INSTITUTIONS.

9    See ibid s 23 (as amended); and BETTING, GAMING AND LOTTERIES; LIBRARIES AND OTHER SCIENTIFIC AND CULTURAL INSTITUTIONS vol 28 (Reissue) para 609.

10   Ie under ibid s 24: see BETTING, GAMING AND LOTTERIES; LIBRARIES AND OTHER SCIENTIFIC AND CULTURAL INSTITUTIONS vol 28 (Reissue) para 609.

11   Ie under ibid s 22(3) (as amended): see BETTING, GAMING AND LOTTERIES; LIBRARIES AND OTHER SCIENTIFIC AND CULTURAL INSTITUTIONS

12   See ibid s 25(1), (2); and BETTING, GAMING AND LOTTERIES; LIBRARIES AND OTHER SCIENTIFIC AND CULTURAL INSTITUTIONS vol 28 (Reissue) para 609.

13   See note 11 supra.

14   See the National Lottery etc Act 1993 s 25(3); and BETTING, GAMING AND LOTTERIES; LIBRARIES AND OTHER SCIENTIFIC AND CULTURAL INSTITUTIONS vol 28 (Reissue) para 609.

**447. Control by the Secretary of State.** The Secretary of State[1] is empowered to give directions as to the matters to be taken into account in determining the persons to whom, the purposes for which and the conditions subject to which, money from the National Lottery is distributed by the distributing bodies[2]. In the context of charities, therefore, the Secretary of State may give directions both to the National Lottery Charities Board[3] and to the National Heritage Memorial Fund[4]. The body in question must comply with the directions[5]. A distributing body must comply also with any directions which the Secretary of State may consider it appropriate to give the body for securing the proper management and control of the money paid[6] to the body[7]. For this purpose the Secretary of State may require a distributing body to provide him with such information as he requires[8] and to obtain his consent before it does anything in accordance with a direction[9]. The Secretary of State is required to consult the distributing bodies before giving any directions to it under these provisions[10].

In addition, the Secretary of State has power, by order, to prohibit the distribution of money by the distributing bodies to a person specified in the order[11] where:

(1)    at the time the order is made: (a) the person specified is a company[12] of which the body or wholly-owned subsidiary[13] of the body is a member; or (b) the Secretary of State considers that the body is able, whether directly or indirectly, to control or materially to influence the policy of the person specified in carrying on any undertaking or performing any functions[14]; or

(2)    if at the time the directions are given the Secretary of State considers that a proscribed organisation for the purposes of the Northern Ireland (Emergency Provisions) Act 1991[15], or any other organisation that appears to him to be concerned in terrorism in Northern Ireland or in promoting or encouraging it, might directly or indirectly derive benefit from the distribution of money to the person specified[16].

1    As to the Secretary of State see para 513 post.
2    See the National Lottery etc Act 1993 s 26(1); and BETTING, GAMING AND LOTTERIES; LIBRARIES AND OTHER SCIENTIFIC AND CULTURAL INSTITUTIONS vol 28 (Reissue) para 610. As to the distributing bodies see para 446 ante; and BETTING, GAMING AND LOTTERIES; LIBRARIES AND OTHER SCIENTIFIC AND CULTURAL INSTITUTIONS vol 28 (Reissue) para 609. Any directions under the National Lottery etc Act 1993 must be given in writing and may be varied or revoked by subsequent directions: s 61.
3    As to the National Lotteries Charities Board see para 448 et seq post.
4    See the National Lottery etc Act 1993 ss 23(3), (4), 25(1), 26(1); para 446 ante; and BETTING, GAMING AND LOTTERIES; LIBRARIES AND OTHER SCIENTIFIC AND CULTURAL INSTITUTIONS vol 28 (Reissue) paras 609–610. As to the National Heritage Memorial Fund see LIBRARIES AND OTHER SCIENTIFIC AND CULTURAL INSTITUTIONS vol 28 (Reissue) paras 596–598.
        The trustees of the National Heritage Memorial Fund must comply with any directions given to them as to the matters to be taken into account in determining the purposes for which and the conditions subject to which the trustees apply money paid to them from the distribution fund: see s 25(4) (as amended), s 26(2); and BETTING, GAMING AND LOTTERIES; LIBRARIES AND OTHER SCIENTIFIC AND CULTURAL INSTITUTIONS vol 28 (Reissue) paras 609–610. As to the National Lottery distribution fund see para 444 ante; and BETTING, GAMING AND LOTTERIES; LIBRARIES AND OTHER SCIENTIFIC AND CULTURAL INSTITUTIONS vol 28 (Reissue) para 608.
5    See ibid s 26(1); and BETTING, GAMING AND LOTTERIES; LIBRARIES AND OTHER SCIENTIFIC AND CULTURAL INSTITUTIONS vol 28 (Reissue) para 610.
6    Ie under ibid s 24: see BETTING, GAMING AND LOTTERIES; LIBRARIES AND OTHER SCIENTIFIC AND CULTURAL INSTITUTIONS vol 28 (Reissue) para 609.
7    See ibid s 26(3); and BETTING, GAMING AND LOTTERIES; LIBRARIES AND OTHER SCIENTIFIC AND CULTURAL INSTITUTIONS vol 28 (Reissue) para 610.
8    See ibid s 26(4)(b); and BETTING, GAMING AND LOTTERIES; LIBRARIES AND OTHER SCIENTIFIC AND CULTURAL INSTITUTIONS vol 28 (Reissue) para 610.
9    See ibid s 26(4)(a); and BETTING, GAMING AND LOTTERIES; LIBRARIES AND OTHER SCIENTIFIC AND CULTURAL INSTITUTIONS vol 28 (Reissue) para 610.
10   See ibid s 26(5); BETTING, GAMING AND LOTTERIES; LIBRARIES AND OTHER SCIENTIFIC AND CULTURAL INSTITUTIONS vol 28 (Reissue) para 610.
11   Ibid s 27(1); and BETTING, GAMING AND LOTTERIES; LIBRARIES AND OTHER SCIENTIFIC AND CULTURAL INSTITUTIONS vol 28 (Reissue) para 610.

12  'Company' means a company formed and registered under the Companies Act 1985 (see COMPANIES vol 7(1) (1996 Reissue) para 60 et seq) or the Companies (Northern Ireland) Order 1986, SI 1986/1032, or a company to which the provisions of that Act or Order apply as they apply to a company so formed and registered: see the National Lottery etc Act 1993 s 27(3)(a); and BETTING, GAMING AND LOTTERIES; LIBRARIES AND OTHER SCIENTIFIC AND CULTURAL INSTITUTIONS vol 28 (Reissue) para 610.

13  'Wholly-owned subsidiary' has the meaning given by the Companies Act 1985 s 736 (as substituted) (see COMPANIES vol 7(2) (1996 Reissue) para 827) or the Companies (Northern Ireland) Order 1986, SI 1986/1032, art 4: National Lottery etc Act 1993 s 27(3)(a); and BETTING, GAMING AND LOTTERIES; LIBRARIES AND OTHER SCIENTIFIC AND CULTURAL INSTITUTIONS vol 28 (Reissue) para 610.

14  See ibid s 27(2); and BETTING, GAMING AND LOTTERIES; LIBRARIES AND OTHER SCIENTIFIC AND CULTURAL INSTITUTIONS vol 28 (Reissue) para 610.

15  The Northern Ireland (Emergency Provisions) Act 1991 was repealed and replaced by the Northern Ireland (Emergency Provisions) Act 1996: see CONSTITUTIONAL LAW AND HUMAN RIGHTS vol 8(2) (Reissue) para 81.

16  See the National Lottery etc Act 1993 s 27(4), (5); and BETTING, GAMING AND LOTTERIES; LIBRARIES AND OTHER SCIENTIFIC AND CULTURAL INSTITUTIONS vol 28 (Reissue) para 610.


### (ii)  National Lotteries Charities Board


**448.  Membership, committees and status.** The National Lottery etc Act 1993 established a body corporate known as the National Lotteries Charities Board[1], which consists of a chairman and 21 other members[2], all of whom are appointed by the Secretary of State[3].

The Board established four committees for the purpose of exercising its functions in relation to applications by charities[4] for grants in respect of appropriate activities[5] in England, Scotland, Wales and Northern Ireland respectively[6]. Any function of the Board may be exercised by any of its committees authorised by it, whether generally or specially, for that purpose[7]. Any such committee of the Board must consist of or include one or more members, or one or more employees, of the body establishing the committee, but may include persons who are neither members nor employees of that body[8].

The Board may regulate its own procedure and that of any of its committees, and in particular may specify a quorum for meetings[9]. The quorum for meetings of any committee of the Board is not less than three[10]. The validity of any proceedings of the Board is not affected by any vacancy among its members, or by any defect in the appointment of any person as chairman or a member[11].

The Board is not to be regarded as the servant or agent of the Crown or as enjoying any status, immunity or privilege of the Crown[12].


1  National Lottery etc Act 1993 s 37(1). See further BETTING, GAMING AND LOTTERIES. On 9 April 2001 the National Lottery Charities Board changed its name to the Community Fund: see the Community Fund Press Release (9 April 2001).

2  The Secretary of State may by order increase the number of members: ibid Sch 5 para 1(2). In exercise of this power the Secretary of State has made the National Lottery Charities Board (Increase in Membership) Order 1995, SI 1995/1645 (revoked by SI 1999/1878). As to the Secretary of State see para 513 post.

3  National Lottery etc Act 1993 Sch 5 para 1(1) (amended by the National Lottery Charities Board (Increase in Membership) Order 1995, SI 1995/1645, art 2).

4  'Charities' includes institutions other than charities, that are established for charitable purposes (whether or not those purposes are charitable within the meaning of any rule of law), benevolent purposes or philanthropic purposes: National Lottery etc Act 1993 s 44(1), Sch 5 para 2(2).

5   'Appropriate activities' means activities in relation to which the Board considers it appropriate to delegate
    its functions to a committee established under ibid Sch 5 para 2(1) (see the text and note 6 infra): Sch 5
    para 2(2).
6   Ibid Sch 5 para 2(1).
7   Ibid Sch 5 para 2(3).
8   Ibid Sch 5 para 2(7) (added by the National Lottery Act 1998 s 11(5)); National Lottery Act 1998 s 11(1).
9   National Lottery etc Act 1993 Sch 5 para 6(1), which is expressed to be subject to the provisions of Sch
    5 (see paras 449–453 post): Sch 5 para 6(1).
10  Ibid Sch 5 para 6(2).
11  Ibid Sch 5 para 6(3).
12  Ibid Sch 5 para 10.

**449. Tenure of office.** A person holds and vacates office as chairman or other
member of the National Lotteries Charities Board[1] in accordance with the terms of his
appointment[2]. The Secretary of State[3] may not appoint a person to hold office as a
member of the Board for a term of more than five years[4], and a chairman or member of
the Board may at any time resign his office by notice in writing addressed to the Secretary
of State[5]. A member of the Board may be removed from office by the Secretary of State
on the ground that[6]:

(1)   he has been absent for a period longer than three consecutive months from
      meetings of the Board without the Board's consent, or from meetings of a
      committee of the Board without the committee's consent[7];

(2)   a bankruptcy order has been made against him or his estate has been sequestrated
      or he has made a composition or arrangement with, or granted a trust deed for,
      his creditors[8]; or

(3)   he is unable or unfit to discharge the functions of his office[9].

If a chairman of the Board ceases to be a member of the Board he also ceases to be
chairman[10]. A person who ceases, otherwise than by virtue of heads (1), (2) or (3) above,
to be a member or chairman of the Board is eligible for re-appointment[11].

1   The National Lottery Charities Board has changed its name to the Community Fund: see para 448 note
    1 ante.
2   National Lottery etc Act 1993 s 37(2), Sch 5 para 3(1) (amended by the National Lottery Act 1998 s 26,
    Sch 5 Pt II), which is expressed to be subject to the National Lottery etc Act 1993 Sch 5 para 3(2)–(6)
    (see the text and notes 3–11 infra): Sch 5 para 3(1). See further BETTING, GAMING AND LOTTERIES.
3   As to the Secretary of State see para 513 post.
4   National Lottery etc Act 1993 Sch 5 para 3(2) (amended by the National Lottery Act 1998 s 26, Sch 5
    Pt II).
5   National Lottery etc Act 1993 Sch 5 para 3(3) (amended by the National Lottery Act 1998 s 26, Sch 5
    Pt II).
6   National Lottery etc Act 1993 Sch 5 para 3(4) (amended by the National Lottery Act 1998 s 26, Sch 5
    Pt II).
7   National Lottery etc Act 1993 Sch 5 para 3(4)(a) (amended by the National Lottery Act 1998 s 11(6)).
8   National Lottery etc Act 1993 Sch 5 para 3(4)(b).
9   Ibid Sch 5 para 3(4)(c).
10  Ibid Sch 5 para 3(5) (amended by the National Lottery Act 1998 s 26, Sch 5 Pt II).
11  National Lottery etc Act 1993 Sch 5 para 3(6) (amended by the National Lottery Act 1998 s 26, Sch 5
    Pt II).

**450. Remuneration and allowances.** The National Lotteries Charities Board[1] may pay such remuneration to its chairman and any other member of the Board, and such travelling and other allowances to its chairman and any other member of the Board or any of its committees as the Secretary of State[2] may determine[3]. Where the Secretary of State so determines in the case of a holder of the office of chairman of the Board, or in the case of any other member of the Board, the Board must pay to or in respect of him such pension, allowances or gratuities, or make such payments towards the provision of a pension, allowances or gratuities to or in respect of him, as the Secretary of State may determine[4]. If the Secretary of State determines that there are special circumstances that make it right for a person ceasing to hold office as chairman, or ceasing to be a member of the Board, to receive compensation, the Board may pay to him such compensation as the Secretary of State may determine[5].

1   The National Lottery Charities Board has changed its name to the Community Fund: see para 448 note 1 ante.
2   As to the Secretary of State see para 513 post.
3   National Lottery etc Act 1993 s 37(2), Sch 5 para 4(1) (amended by the National Lottery Act 1998 s 14(3)). See further BETTING, GAMING AND LOTTERIES.
4   National Lottery etc Act 1993 Sch 5 para 4(2) (amended by the National Lotteries Act 1998 s 14(4)).
5   National Lottery etc Act 1993 Sch 5 para 4(3) (amended by the National Lotteries Act 1998 s 14(5)).

**451. Staff.** The National Lotteries Charities Board[1] may appoint such staff on such terms and conditions of service as it thinks fit[2]. It may also[3]:

(1)   pay such pensions, allowances or gratuities to or in respect of any persons who have been or are members of its staff as it may determine[4];

(2)   make such payments as it may determine towards the provision of pensions, allowances or gratuities to or in respect of any such persons[5];

(3)   provide and maintain such schemes as it may determine, whether contributory or not, for the payment of pensions, allowances or gratuities to or in respect of any such persons[6].

Any reference in heads (1) to (3) above to pensions, allowances or gratuities to or in respect of any such persons as are mentioned in those heads includes pensions, allowances or gratuities by way of compensation to or in respect of any members of the Board's staff who suffer loss of office or employment[7].

1   The National Lottery Charities Board has changed its name to the Community Fund: see para 448 note 1 ante.
2   National Lottery etc Act 1993 s 37(2), Sch 5 para 5(1) (substituted by the National Lotteries Act 1998 s 14(8)), which is expressed to be subject to any directions under the National Lottery etc Act 1993 s 26(3) (directions for securing the proper management and control of money paid to the distributing body): National Lottery etc Act 1993 Sch 5 para 5(1). See further BETTING, GAMING AND LOTTERIES.
3   Ibid Sch 5 para 5(2) (amended by the National Lottery Act 1998 ss 14(9)(a), (b), 26, Sch 5 Pt II), which is expressed to be subject to any directions under the National Lottery etc Act 1993 s 26(3) (directions for securing the proper management and control of money paid to the distributing body): National Lottery etc Act 1993 Sch 5 para 5(2).
4   Ibid Sch 5 para 5(2)(a).
5   Ibid Sch 5 para 5(2)(b).
6   Ibid Sch 5 para 5(2)(c).
7   Ibid Sch 5 para 5(3).

**452. Application of seal and evidence.** The application of the seal of the National Lotteries Charities Board[1] must be authenticated by the signature of any member of the Board, or of any other person who has been authorised by the Board, whether generally or specially, for that purpose[2].

A document purporting to be duly executed under the seal of the Board or to be signed on its behalf must be received in evidence and, unless the contrary is proved, taken to be so executed or signed[3].

1    The National Lottery Charities Board has changed its name to the Community Fund: see para 448 note 1 ante.
2    National Lottery etc Act 1993 s 37(2), Sch 5 para 7. See further BETTING, GAMING AND LOTTERIES.
3    Ibid Sch 5 para 8; and see BETTING, GAMING AND LOTTERIES.

**453. Finance.** Until such time as the Secretary of State[1] considers that the sums paid to the National Lotteries Charities Board[2] by the distribution fund[3] are sufficient to enable it to meet[4] the expenses it incurred in exercising its functions[5], he must pay to the Board such sums as are necessary to defray those expenses[6].

1    As to the Secretary of State see para 513 post.
2    The National Lottery Charities Board has changed its name to the Community Fund: see para 448 note 1 ante.
3    Ie under the National Lottery etc Act 1993 s 24: see BETTING, GAMING AND LOTTERIES.
4    Ie under ibid s 25(3). See further BETTING, GAMING AND LOTTERIES.
5    Ie in exercising its functions under the National Lottery etc Act 1993: see para 443 ante.
6    Ibid s 37(2), Sch 5 para 9.

**454. Grants to charities.** The National Lotteries Charities Board[1] may make grants for meeting the expenditure of charities or of institutions, other than charities, that are established for charitable (whether or not those purposes are charitable within the meaning of any rule of law), benevolent or philanthropic purposes[2] out of any money it receives[3]. In making such a grant, the Board may impose such conditions as it thinks fit, including conditions requiring the amount of a grant to be repaid forthwith on the breach of any condition[4].

The Board may, for the purpose of enabling it to exercise its functions, acquire and dispose of land[5].

1    The National Lottery Charities Board has changed its name to the Community Fund: see para 448 note 1 ante.
2    Ie institutions such as are mentioned in the definition of 'charitable expenditure' in the National Lottery etc Act 1993 s 44(1)(b): see BETTING, GAMING AND LOTTERIES.
3    Ibid s 38(1). See further BETTING, GAMING AND LOTTERIES.
4    Ibid s 38(2).
5    Ibid s 38(3) (added by the National Lottery Act 1998 s 14(1)).

**455. Accounts.** The National Lotteries Charities Board[1] must keep proper accounts, and proper records in relation to the accounts, and prepare a statement of accounts in respect of each financial year[2]. The statement must comply with any directions that may be given by the Secretary of State[3] as to the information to be contained in such a statement, the manner in which such information is to be presented or the methods and principles according to which such a statement is to be prepared[4]. Copies of the statement must be sent to the Secretary of State and the Comptroller and Auditor General[5] within such period after the end of the financial year to which the statement relates as the Secretary of State may direct[6]. The Comptroller and Auditor General must examine, certify and report on the statement and must lay copies of it and of his report before Parliament[7].

The Secretary of State must not give any such direction[8] without the Treasury's[9] approval[10].

1    The National Lottery Charities Board has changed its name to the Community Fund: see para 448 note 1 ante.
2    National Lottery etc Act 1993 s 39(1). See further BETTING, GAMING AND LOTTERIES. 'Financial year', in relation to a body, means the period beginning with the date on which the body is established and ending with the next 31 March, and each successive period of 12 months ending with 31 March: s 44(1).
3    As to the Secretary of State see para 513 post.
4    National Lottery etc Act 1993 s 39(2).
5    As to the Comptroller and Auditor General see CONSTITUTIONAL LAW AND HUMAN RIGHTS vol 8(2) (Reissue) paras 724–726.
6    National Lottery etc Act 1993 s 39(3). Such functions which were exercisable by the Secretary of State under s 39(3) are, in so far as they are exercisable in or as regards Scotland, exercisable by the Scottish Ministers acting concurrently with the Secretary of State: see s 39(6) (added by the Scotland Act 1998 (Modification of Functions) Order 1999, SI 1999/1756, art 2, Schedule para 15(8)); Scotland Act 1998 (Transfer of Functions to the Scottish Ministers etc) Order 1999, SI 1999/1750, art 3, Sch 2.
7    National Lottery etc Act 1993 s 39(4); and see BETTING, GAMING AND LOTTERIES.
8    Ie any direction under ibid s 39 (as amended).
9    As to the Treasury see CONSTITUTIONAL LAW AND HUMAN RIGHTS vol 8(2) (Reissue) paras 512–517.
10   National Lottery etc Act 1993 s 39(5).

# 10. JURISDICTION OVER CHARITIES

## (1) THE CROWN

**456. The Crown as protector of charitable trusts.** The Crown as parens patriae is the constitutional protector of all property subject to charitable trusts, such trusts being essentially matters of public concern[1]. The Attorney General, who represents the Crown for all forensic purposes, is accordingly the proper person to take proceedings on behalf of and to protect charities[2].

The Crown also, acting through the Lord Chancellor or such other person as the Crown may nominate[3], exercises a visitatorial jurisdiction over certain charitable corporations[4].

1  *A-G v Brown* (1818) 1 Swan 265 at 291 per Lord Eldon LC; *A-G v Compton* (1842) 1 Y & C Ch Cas 417 at 427 per Knight Bruce V-C. As to the Crown as parens patriae see CONSTITUTIONAL LAW AND HUMAN RIGHTS vol 8(2) (Reissue) para 309.

2  *Eyre v Countess of Shaftsbury* (1724) 2 P Wms 103 at 118 per Lord Macclesfield; *Wellbeloved v Jones* (1822) 1 Sim & St 40 at 43 per Leach V-C; *A-G v Magdalen College, Oxford* (1854) 18 Beav 223 at 241 per Romilly MR; *A-G v Dean and Canons of Windsor* (1860) 8 HL Cas 369; *Wallis v Solicitor General for New Zealand* [1903] AC 173 at 182, PC; *Strickland v Weldon* (1885) 28 ChD 426; *Re Belling, Enfield London Borough Council v Public Trustee* [1967] Ch 425, [1967] 1 All ER 105; and see para 531 et seq post.

3  In *R v HM the Queen in Council, ex p Vijayatunga* [1990] 2 QB 444, sub nom *R v University of London Visitor, ex p Vijayatunga* [1989] 2 All ER 843, CA, the Crown had nominated a committee of the Privy Council.

4  See paras 461, 470–471 post.

**457. Gift of charity generally, without trust.** When no trust is created and property is given to charity generally, that is to say, where no trustees are nominated and the charitable objects are not defined, the duty of disposing of the property devolves on the Crown, as constitutional trustee[1]. Thus, in the case of an assurance, devise or bequest to charity[2], or to the poor[3], simpliciter, or where the testator intended but failed to name the objects of his bounty[4], the disposition of the property is made by the Crown in its character of parens patriae, not by means of a scheme settled by the court. So also, a legacy in exoneration of the National Debt[5], or to 'my country England'[6], or a legacy to an institution dissolved after the testator's death but before payment[7], or to a non-existent institution[8], is disposable by the Crown. The result is the same as when a charitable purpose is carried out by the court, though the procedure differs[9].

The power of the Crown to dispose of charitable gifts under the royal sign manual has been delegated to the Attorney General[10].

1  *Moggridge v Thackwell* (1803) 7 Ves 36 at 83 per Lord Eldon LC; *Cary v Abbot* (1802) 7 Ves 490; *Morice v Bishop of Durham* (1805) 10 Ves 522 at 541 per Lord Eldon LC; *Paice v Archbishop of Canterbury* (1807) 14 Ves 364; *Ommanney v Butcher* (1823) Turn & R 260 at 271 per Plumer MR; *Re Davis, Hannen v Hillyer* [1902] 1 Ch 876 at 888 per Buckley J; *Re Pyne, Lilley v A-G* [1903] 1 Ch 83; *Re Bennett, Sucker v A-G* [1960] Ch 18, [1959] 3 All ER 295. Formerly (ie before the series of relieving Acts: see para 56 ante), the Crown was also called upon to exercise its prerogative in the case of gifts to superstitious uses which were also charitable: see Boyle on Charities (1837) pp 242–280; *A-G v Bowyer* (1798) 3 Ves 714 at 729 per Lord Thurlow LC.

2    *Clifford v Francis* (1679) Freem Ch 330; *A-G v Syderfen* (1683) 1 Vern 224; *Jones' Case* (1690) cited in
     [1893] 2 Ch 49n, HL; *A-G v Herrick* (1772) Amb 712; *A-G v Bowyer* (1798) 3 Ves 714 at 729 per Lord
     Thurlow LC; *Legge v Asgill* (1818) Turn & R 265n; *Kane v Cosgrave* (1873) IR 10 Eq 211.
3    *A-G v Peacock* (1676) Cas *temp* Finch 245; *Ware v A-G* (1824) 3 Hare 194n.
4    *A-G v Syderfen* (1683) 1 Vern 224; *Moggridge v Thackwell* (1803) 7 Ves 36 at 75 per Lord Eldon LC. Cf
     the cases relating to the jurisdiction of the court: paras 477–478 post.
5    *Newland v A-G* (1809) 3 Mer 684.
6    *Re Smith, Public Trustee v Smith* [1932] 1 Ch 153, CA.
7    *Re Slevin, Slevin v Hepburn* [1891] 2 Ch 236, CA.
8    *Re Bennett, Sucker v A-G* [1960] Ch 18, [1959] 3 All ER 295.
9    *A-G v Peacock* (1676) Cas *temp* Finch 245; *Moggridge v Thackwell* (1803) 7 Ves 36 at 87 per Lord Eldon
     LC; Boyle on Charities (1837) pp 239–240.
10   *Report of the Charity Commissioners for England and Wales for 1989* (HC Paper (1989–90) no 343) para 38.
     See also *De Costa v De Paz* (1754) 2 Swan 487n; *A-G v Herrick* (1772) Amb 712; *Kane v Cosgrave* (1873)
     IR 10 Eq 211; and see para 533 post. As to the royal sign manual see CONSTITUTIONAL LAW AND
     HUMAN RIGHTS vol 8(2) (Reissue) paras 908, 912.

## (2) THE VISITOR

### (i)  Nature of Visitatorial Power

**458. Settlement of disputes and correction of abuses.**   A visitatorial power
attaches as a necessary incident to all eleemosynary corporations[1], and may be exercisable
in respect of all corporations[2]. It enables the person exercising it, who is called the visitor,
to settle disputes between the members of the corporation, to inspect and regulate their
actions and behaviour, and generally to correct all abuses and irregularities in the
administration of the charity[3].

The tribunal of the visitor is forum domesticum, in other words, the court of the
founder[4], its jurisdiction being derived from the founder's right to determine concerning
his own creation[5].

A visitor's decision on matters within his jurisdiction is exclusive[6] and final, and not
subject to review by the High Court[7]. Even the visitor himself cannot relieve against his
own sentence[8]; but an action for damages will lie against him for exceeding his
jurisdiction[9].

The extent of the power varies according to the terms of the foundation. If the power
given to the visitor is unlimited and universal he has, in respect of the foundation and
property moving from the founder, no rule but his sound discretion. If there are
particular statutes they are the rule by which he is bound, and if he acts contrary to or
exceeds them, he acts without jurisdiction, and consequently his act is a nullity[10].

1    *Appleford's Case* (1672) 1 Mod Rep 82 at 85 per Hale CJ; *Philips v Bury* (1694) Skin 447 at 483–484, HL.
     As to the meaning of 'eleemosynary corporation' see para 213 ante.
2    See Tudor on Charities (7th Edn, 1984) p 312; cf Tudor on Charities (8th Edn, 1995) p 369.
3    1 Bl Com 467; *Philips v Bury* (1694) Skin 447 at 484, HL. As to the visitor's power to settle questions
     see para 468 post.
4    *Green v Rutherforth* (1750) 1 Ves Sen 462 at 472 per Lord Hardwicke LC; *St John's College, Cambridge v
     Todington* (1757) 1 Burr 158 at 200 per Lord Mansfield; *Spencer v All Souls College* (1762) Wilm 163;
     *Philips v Bury* (1694) Skin 447, HL.

5    *Green v Rutherforth* (1750) 1 Ves Sen 462 at 472 per Lord Hardwicke LC; *R v Lord President of the Privy Council* [1993] AC 682, sub nom *Page v Hull University Visitor* [1993] 1 All ER 97, HL. Cf the maxim *cuius est dare, eius est disponere*: he who gives something may also direct how it is to be used.

6    *Thomas v University of Bradford* [1987] AC 795, [1987] 1 All ER 834, HL; *Philips v Bury* (1694) Skin 447, HL; *A-G v Talbot* (1748) 3 Atk 662; *St John's College, Cambridge v Todington* (1757) 1 Burr 158; *R v Dean and Chapter of Chester* (1850) 15 QB 513; *R v Hertford College* (1878) 3 QBD 693, CA; *Thomson v University of London* (1864) 10 Jur NS 669; *Patel v University of Bradford Senate* [1978] 3 All ER 841, [1978] 1 WLR 1488 (affd [1979] 2 All ER 582, [1979] 1 WLR 1006, CA); *Re Wislang's Application* [1984] NI 63; *Hines v Birkbeck College* [1986] Ch 524, [1985] 3 All ER 156 (appeal dismissed [1987] Ch 457n, [1987] 3 All ER 1040n, CA). See also *Herring v Templeman* [1973] 2 All ER 581; affd on grounds not material to the present point [1973] 3 All ER 569, CA. As to the limits on jurisdiction see para 466 post.

7    See paras 472–473 post.

8    *Philips v Bury* (1694) as reported in Show Parl Cas 35 at 52.

9    *Green v Rutherforth* (1750) 1 Ves Sen 462 at 470 per Lord Hardwicke LC.

10   Shelford's Law of Mortmain 360; *Philips v Bury* (1694) as reported in 1 Ld Raym 5, HL. As to the extensive and arbitrary nature of the visitatorial power see also *A-G v Archbishop of York* (1831) 2 Russ & M 461 at 468 per Lord Brougham. As to the court's control over the visitor see paras 472–476 post.

**459. Visitors to the Inns of Court.** In general visitatorial powers only exist in relation to corporations. An Inn of Court is not a corporation: it does not have statutes, nor does it have a founder who nominated a visitor to hear and determine internal disputes. The Inns of Court are not eleemosynary corporations[1]: they are voluntary societies, some of whose activities, such as education, are charitable, but some of which are not, including call to the Bar and disciplining of barristers[2]. Nevertheless it is well established that there is an appeal from decisions of the benchers of the Inns of Court and the disciplinary tribunals of the Inns of Court to the judges as visitors, exercising a normal visitatorial jurisdiction[3]. Thus they may hear appeals against decisions on property matters such as the letting of chambers within the Inn and dues payable to the Inn by members; they may also hear appeals against disciplinary decisions, such as disbarment for professional misconduct[4]. The limited judicial review jurisdiction available in respect of visitors generally[5] is equally applicable to visitors to the Inns of Court[6].

1    As to eleemosynary corporations see para 213 ante.

2    See BARRISTERS vol 3(1) (Reissue) para 363 et seq.

3    *R v Visitors to the Inns of Court, ex p Calder, ex p Persaud* [1994] QB 1, [1993] 2 All ER 876, CA; *R v Gray's Inn* (1780) 1 Doug KB 353; *Manisty v Kenealy* (1876) 24 WR 918; *Lincoln v Daniels* [1962] 1 QB 237, [1961] 3 All ER 740, CA; *Re s (A Barrister)* [1981] QB 683, [1981] 2 All ER 952. See generally BARRISTERS.

4    *R v Visitors to the Inns of Court, ex p Calder, ex p Persaud* [1994] QB 1, [1993] 2 All ER 876, CA.

5    See para 472 et seq post.

6    *R v Visitors to the Inns of Court, ex p Calder, ex p Persaud* [1994] QB 1, [1993] 2 All ER 876, CA. The visitors sit as an appeal tribunal. In *R v Visitors to the Inns of Court, ex p Calder, ex p Persaud* supra the visitors apparently thought that they were sitting as a reviewing tribunal; this was a serious misapprehension of their function. On judicial review the Court of Appeal allowed the appeal on this ground and quashed the decision of the visitors.

**460. Quasi-visitatorial powers.** The Charity Commissioners[1] may reserve to themselves a quasi-visitatorial power to determine disputes in schemes settled by them under the Charities Act 1993[2]. However, true visitatorial powers can only exist in relation to corporations[3].

1    As to the Charity Commissioners see paras 486–512 post.
2    See *Re Hodgson's School* (1878) 3 App Cas 857, PC; *R v Wilson* [1888] WN 12. It is not, apparently, the
     modern practice to seek to oust the court's jurisdiction completely in this way. As to schemes under the
     Charities Act 1993 see para 180 et seq ante.
3    Formerly there was a statutory exception to this principle under the Grammar Schools Act 1840 s 15,
     but this was repealed by the Charities Act 1960.


### (ii)  Constitution of Visitor


**461.  The visitor.**  Where no visitor has been appointed by the founder, the rule is that
the Monarch and her successors are visitors of all lay charitable corporations founded by
the Crown alone[1], or by the Crown jointly with a private person, and of all royal
foundations endowed by a private person[2]. Where a university is incorporated by royal
charter which provides for the appointment of a visitor by the Crown, but no such
appointment has been made, the Crown is the visitor[3].

Where a private person alone was founder, the law before 1926 was that he and his
heirs were visitors[4], unless the heirs' jurisdiction was expressly excluded[5]. If the heirs of
the founder failed[6], were not discoverable[7], or were lunatic[8], and there was no
appointment by the founder, the visitatorial power devolved upon the Crown. Descent
to the heir has been abolished, but the effect of this upon visitatorial rights does not
appear clear.

The visitor of an ecclesiastical charitable corporation is the Ordinary[9].


1    *A-G v Dedham School* (1857) 23 Beav 350 at 356 per Romilly MR; *Eden v Foster* (1726) 2 P Wms 325;
     and see *Re Christ Church* (1866) 1 Ch App 526. See also para 471 post.
2    Shelford's Law of Mortmain (1836) 332, 339–340.
3    *Patel v University of Bradford Senate* [1978] 3 All ER 841, [1978] 1 WLR 1488 (affd [1979] 2 All ER 582,
     [1979] 1 WLR 1066, CA); *Thomas v University of Bradford* [1987] AC 795 at 811, [1987] 1 All ER 834
     at 839, HL, per Lord Griffiths. It is thought to have been wrongly conceded in *R v Aston University
     Senate, ex p Roffey* [1969] 2 QB 538, sub nom *R v Senate of University of Aston, ex p Roffey* [1969] 2 All
     ER 964, DC, that the university had no visitor. It should be noted that those new universities which
     have acquired that title under the Further and Higher Education Act 1992 s 77 (as amended) (see
     EDUCATION) were not created by Royal Charter and there is no provision for them to have a visitor.
4    *Eden v Foster* (1726) 2 P Wms 325; *Philips v Bury* (1694) Skin 447 at 483, HL.
5    *St John's College, Cambridge v Todington* (1757) 1 Burr 158 at 200 per Lord Mansfield.
6    *Anon* (1698) 12 Mod Rep 232; *R v Master and Fellows of St Catherine's Hall* (1791) 4 Term Rep 233;
     *Ex p Wrangham* (1795) 2 Ves 609; *A-G v Earl of Clarendon* (1810) 17 Ves 491 at 498 per Grant MR;
     *A-G v Ewelme Hospital* (1853) 17 Beav 366 at 381 per Romilly MR.
7    *A-G v Black* (1805) 11 Ves 191.
8    *A-G v Dixie, ex p Bosworth School* (1805) 13 Ves 519 at 533 per Lord Eldon LC.
9    *Philips v Bury* (1694) Skin 447, HL; *A-G v Archbishop of York* (1831) 2 Russ & M 461 at 466 per Lord
     Brougham LC. See also the Cathedrals Measure 1963 s 6 (repealed, with savings in relation to cathedrals
     existing on 30 June 1999); and ECCLESIASTICAL LAW vol 14 para 617. As to the Ordinary see
     ECCLESIASTICAL LAW vol 14 para 458. Some of the colleges of Oxford are visitable by the Bishop of
     Lincoln, in whose diocese Oxford originally was included; the colleges were formerly deemed
     ecclesiastical foundations, hence the bishop's jurisdiction: see 1 Bl Com 470.


**462.  Appointment of general and special visitors by founder.**  The founder
may delegate the visitatorial power wholly or partially to any other person and his heirs[1],
thereby appointing them general or special visitors.

A person appointed in general terms is a general visitor, having the same jurisdiction as the founder[2] unless his powers are expressly restricted[3]. Special visitors are those who are appointed for particular purposes, and their jurisdiction is limited accordingly[4]. A general visitor may also have jurisdiction as a special visitor and may proceed in either character in appropriate circumstances[5]. In addition to a general visitor there may also be a special visitor for a particular purpose, in which case that purpose will be excluded from the powers of the general visitor[6]. The visitatorial power may be divided among a number of special visitors, each appointed for special purposes[7]. In the absence of clear words to the contrary which remove his jurisdiction, it is normally inherent in the visitor that he has all the general powers of visitation and determination of disputes arising under the foundation's statutes. The mere fact that, in certain respects, his powers may be limited in the manner in which they can be exercised does not cut down his status from that of a general visitor to that of a special visitor[8].

1   *Eden v Foster* (1726) 2 P Wms 325; *A-G v Lock* (1744) 3 Atk 164; *A-G v Talbot* (1748) 1 Ves Sen 78; *St John's College, Cambridge v Todington* (1757) 1 Burr 158. Before the abolition of descent to the heir, the power of appointing and removing visitors might be vested in the heirs of a named person: *A-G v Middleton* (1751) 2 Ves Sen 327. See also *A-G v Talbot* supra; *St John's College, Cambridge v Todington* supra.
2   *A-G v Talbot* (1748) 1 Ves Sen 78; *St John's College, Cambridge v Todington* (1757) 1 Burr 158.
3   *R v Bishop of Worcester* (1815) 4 M & s 415 at 420 per Lord Ellenborough CJ.
4   *St John's College, Cambridge v Todington* (1757) 1 Burr 158 at 200 per Lord Mansfield. See also Shelford's Law of Mortmain (1836) 343 et seq; *Bishop of Ely v Bentley* (1732) 2 Bro Parl Cas 220, HL; *R v Bishop of Ely* (1788) 2 Term Rep 290 at 336 per Ashurst J; *R v Bishop of Worcester* (1815) 4 M & s 415 at 420 per Lord Ellenborough CJ.
5   *Bishop of Ely v Bentley* (1732) 2 Bro Parl Cas 220, HL.
6   *St John's College, Cambridge v Todington* (1757) 1 Burr 158.
7   *A-G v Middleton* (1751) 2 Ves Sen 327 at 329 per Lord Hardwicke LC.
8   *Oakes v Sidney Sussex College, Cambridge* [1988] 1 All ER 1004, [1988] 1 WLR 431.

**463. Appointment of visitor expressly and by implication.** No technical words are necessary for the appointment of a visitor; it is sufficient if the intention to appoint is manifested[1]. The question is invariably one of construction[2].

Moreover, a visitor may be appointed by implication[3], but the fact that the person has the power of construing statutes does not of itself constitute him a visitor if other visitatorial functions are exercisable by other persons[4]. The express exclusion of the jurisdiction of the founder's heirs implies an intention to appoint another as visitor[5].

By being appointed governors persons do not ipso facto become visitors[6], unless an appointment as visitors is implied or expressed[7]; but the appointment as governors may constitute them visitors as well, if they are not concerned in the management of the charity property, and if there is a manifested intention that they should visit[8]. However, the receipt and application of the charity revenues excludes governors from exercising visitatorial jurisdiction[9], although the bare possession of the legal estate does not do so[10].

If the charity property is not vested in the persons who are to partake, but in trustees for their benefit, there can be no visitor by implication, but the trustees have the powers of a visitor[11].

A beneficial interest in a charity prevents a person from becoming visitor of that charity[12].

1   *A-G v Talbot* (1748) 1 Ves Sen 78; *A-G v Middleton* (1751) 2 Ves Sen 327; *St John's College, Cambridge v Todington* (1757) 1 Burr 158.

2   *St John's College, Cambridge v Todington* (1757) 1 Burr 158; *Bishop of Ely v Bentley* (1732) 2 Bro Parl Cas 220 at 232, HL (where the words 'visitator Episcopus Eliensis sit', no Christian name being mentioned, were held to confer the visitatorial power on the Bishop of Ely and his successors); and see *Ex p Kirkby Ravensworth Hospital* (1808) 15 Ves 305 at 315 per Lord Eldon LC.

3   Eg by conferring powers of correction, removal or of construing statutes upon a person: *A-G v Lock* (1744) 3 Atk 164; *A-G v Talbot* (1748) 1 Ves Sen 78; *St John's College, Cambridge v Todington* (1757) 1 Burr 158.

4   *Ex p Kirkby Ravensworth Hospital* (1808) 15 Ves 305.

5   *St John's College, Cambrige v Todington* (1757) 1 Burr 158. See also paras 461–462 ante.

6   *Eden v Foster* (1726) 2 P Wms 325; *A-G v Governors of Harrow School* (1754) 2 Ves Sen 551.

7   *Sutton's Hospital Case* (1612) 10 Co Rep 1a at 23a, 31a, Ex Ch; *A-G v Lock* (1744) 3 Atk 164.

8   *Eden v Foster* (1726) 2 P Wms 325.

9   *Eden v Foster* (1726) 2 P Wms 325. In these circumstances they are simply trustees: *A-G v Lubbock* (1837) Coop Pr Cas 15.

10  *A-G v Middleton* (1751) 2 Ves Sen 327 at 329 per Lord Hardwicke LC.

11  *Green v Rutherforth* (1750) 1 Ves Sen 462 at 472 per Lord Hardwicke LC.

12  *R v Bishop of Chester* (1728) 2 Stra 797; *R v Dean and Chapter of Rochester* (1851) 17 QB 1. This is on the principle that a man cannot visit himself.

**464. Suspension of visitatorial powers.** If the visitatorial power is at any time suspended, the jurisdiction vests in the court[1]. Such powers may cease and revive in appropriate circumstances[2].

1   *R v Bishop of Chester* (1728) 2 Stra 797 (where the visitor was appointed warden of the college and therefore could not visit himself); and see *R v Bishop of Ely* (1788) 2 Term Rep 290; *Green v Rutherforth* (1750) 1 Ves Sen 462 at 471 per Lord Hardwicke LC.

2   *R v Bishop of Chester* (1728) 2 Stra 797; Shelford's Law of Mortmain (1836) 368.

**465. Substitution of bishops by Charity Commissioners.** The Charity Commissioners' powers[1] to substitute the bishop of one diocese for the bishop of another as trustee of charitable trusts[2] do not extend to or affect trusts of a visitatorial nature exercised in or over the colleges, halls or schools of the universities of Oxford or Cambridge, or the schools of Eton, Winchester or Westminster[3].

1   As to the Charity Commissioners see paras 486–512 post.

2   Ie under the Bishops Trust Substitution Act 1858: see para 243 ante.

3   See ibid s 4.

### (iii) Visitor's Powers and Duties

**466. Limits of jurisdiction.** The general jurisdiction[1] of a visitor is limited by the statutes regulating the charity[2], although under express powers he may be authorised to dispense with or alter those statutes[3]. The powers of a special visitor are confined within the limits imposed by the founder[4].

Where a dispute between a university and a member of its academic staff over his contract of employment concerns questions of the domestic laws of the university, the visitor has exclusive jurisdiction[5]. However, the exclusivity of the jurisdiction of the visitor may be modified by statute[6]. In particular, the jurisdiction of the visitor in relation to universities has been eroded by the Education Reform Act 1988. This Act provides that the University Commissioners[7] are to exercise their powers[8] with a view to securing that the statutes[9] of each qualifying institution[10] include provisions enabling members of the academic staff[11] to be dismissed[12] by an appropriate[13] body, or any delegate of such body, by reason of redundancy[14], or by an appropriate officer, or any delegate of such an officer, for good cause[15], establishing disciplinary procedures for dealing with complaints made against any members of the academic staff relating to his appointment or employment[16], establishing procedures for hearing and determining appeals by any members of the academic staff who are dismissed or under notice of dismissal or who are otherwise disciplined[17], and establishing procedures for affording to any member of the academic staff opportunities for seeking redress for any grievances relating to his appointment or employment[18]. It is further provided that the visitor of a qualifying institution is not to have jurisdiction in respect of any dispute relating to a member of the academic staff which concerns his appointment or employment or the termination of his appointment or employment[19]. This does not, however, prevent any person who is the visitor from hearing or determining appeals, or from hearing or redressing grievances, in accordance with the established[20] procedures[21].

1 See para 458 ante. As to the procedure of visitors see para 471 post.
2 *Green v Rutherforth* (1750) 1 Ves Sen 462 at 472 per Lord Hardwicke LC; *Philips v Bury* (1694) Skin 447 at 490, HL.
3 *St John's College, Cambridge v Todington* (1757) 1 Burr 158 at 201 per Lord Mansfield ('It must be collected from the whole purview of the statutes considered together what power the founder meant to give the visitor').
4 *Philips v Bury* (1694) Skin 447 at 478, HL.
5 See *Thomas v University of Bradford* [1987] AC 795, [1987] 1 All ER 834, HL; *R v Lord President of the Privy Council, ex p Page* [1993] AC 682, sub nom *Page v Hull University Visitor* [1993] 1 All ER 97, HL; and the cases cited in para 458 note 6 ante.
6 See *Thomas v University of Bradford* [1987] AC 795, [1987] 1 All ER 834, HL, where Lord Griffiths said at 824, 849, that, if in proceedings under the Employment Protection (Consolidation) Act 1978 (now repealed) a question arises concerning the interpretation or application of the internal laws of a university, the proceedings will not be adjourned and the question will have to be resolved for the purpose of the case by the tribunal hearing the application.
7 As to the University Commissioners see the Education Reform Act 1988 s 202, Sch 11; and EDUCATION.
8 Ie conferred by ibid s 204: see EDUCATION.
9 For the meaning of 'statutes' for these purposes, see ibid s 203(8); and EDUCATION.
10 Ie (1) any university or other institution to which, during the period of three years beginning 1 August 1987, grants in aid are or have been made by the Universities Funding Council, or by the Secretary of State acting on the advice of the University Grants Committee; (2) any constituent college, school or hall or other institution of a university falling within head (1) supra; and (3) any institution not falling within head (1) supra which is authorised by charter to grant degrees and to which, during the period of three years beginning 1 August 1987, grants are or have been made by the Secretary of State: ibid s 202(3); and see EDUCATION. As to the Universities Funding Council see EDUCATION.
11 Reference to academic staff includes a reference to persons whose terms of appointment or contracts of employment are, in the opinion of the University Commissioners, so similar to those of academic staff as to justify their being treated as academic staff for the purposes of this section: ibid s 203(4).
12 This includes removal from office, and, in relation to employment under a contract, is to be construed in accordance with the Employment Rights Act 1996 Pt X (ss 94–134A) (as amended): see the Education Reform Act 1988 s 203(7); and EMPLOYMENT vol 16 (2000 Reissue) para 471 et seq.
13 'Appropriate', in relation to a body or officer of a qualifying institution, means appearing to the University Commissioners to be appropriate having regard to the nature and circumstances of the institution: ibid s 203(7).
14 See ibid s 203(1)(a); and EDUCATION. For these purposes, the dismissal of a member of staff is taken to be a dismissal by reason of redundancy if it is attributable wholly or mainly to: (1) the fact that the institution has ceased, or intends to cease, to carry on the activity for the purposes of which he was

appointed or employed by the institution, or has ceased, or intends to cease, to carry on that activity in the place in which he carried out his work; or (2) the fact that the requirements of that activity for members of staff to carry out work of a particular kind, or for members of staff to carry out work of a particular kind in that place, have ceased or diminished or are expected to cease or diminish: s 203(5).

15  See ibid s 203(1)(b); and EDUCATION. For these purposes, 'good cause', in relation to a member of the academic staff of a qualifying institution, means a reason which is related to his conduct or to his capability or qualifications for performing work of the kind which he was appointed or employed to do: s 203(6). 'Capability', in relation to such a member, means capability assessed by reference to skill, aptitude, health or any other physical or mental quality: s 203(6)(a). 'Qualifications', in relation to such a member, means any degree, diploma or other academic, technical or professional qualification relevant to the office or position held by him: s 203(6)(b).

16  See ibid s 203(1)(c); and EDUCATION.

17  See ibid s 203(1)(d); and EDUCATION.

18  See ibid s 203(1)(e); and EDUCATION.

19  See ibid s 206(1); and EDUCATION. This provision only applies in relation to certain disputes: see s 206(2), (4). See *Pearce v University of Aston in Birmingham* [1991] 2 All ER 461, CA, where Dillon LJ gave a powerful dissenting judgment, and *Pearce v University of Aston in Birmingham (No 2)* [1991] 2 All ER 469, Visitor. See also *Hines v Birkbeck College (No 2)* [1992] Ch 33, [1991] 4 All ER 450, CA, where it was held that the reference to the visitor may be made either by the member of the academic staff or by the university.

20  Ie those established in pursuance of the Education Reform Act 1988 s 203(1)(d), (e): see the text and notes 17–18 supra.

21  See ibid s 206(3); and EDUCATION.

**467. Time of visitations.** As a rule the statutes of a charitable corporation provide for general visitations being made at fixed intervals of time, or upon the special request of the corporators. If made otherwise the proceedings are void[1]. General visitations have been said to be at least obsolescent[2]. A visitor may at all times hear complaints and appeals of individual members of the corporation and decree an appropriate remedy[3] which may be the award of damages[4].

1  *Philips v Bury* (1694) Skin 447 at 478, HL.

2  *Patel v University of Bradford Senate* [1978] 3 All ER 841 at 846, [1978] 1 WLR 1488 at 1493 per Megarry V-C; affd [1979] 2 All ER 582, [1979] 1 WLR 1066, CA.

3  *Philips v Bury* (1694) Skin 447 at 478, HL; *A-G v Price* (1744) 3 Atk 108.

4  *Thomas v University of Bradford* [1987] AC 795 at 823–824, [1987] 1 All ER 834 at 848–849, HL, per Lord Griffiths, disapproving dictum of Lord Hailsham of St Marylebone LC in *Casson v University of Aston in Birmingham* [1983] 1 All ER 88 at 91, Visitor.

**468. Power to settle questions.** The jurisdiction of the visitor is sometimes referred to as a domestic jurisdiction. It includes not only the interpretation and enforcement of the internal laws of the foundation but also those internal powers and discretions that derive from the internal laws, such as the discretion necessarily bestowed on those in authority in the exercise of their disciplinary functions over members of the foundation[1]. It extends beyond members of the foundation to other persons claiming to enforce rights which they enjoy under its internal laws[2]. The visitor's duties include the settling of questions arising as to the interpretation of the statutes relating to the foundation[3], and the internal management of a charitable corporation, such as abuses in the internal regulation[4], the increase of a professor's stipend out of unappropriated revenue[5], the refusal of the chairman of a university convocation to summon a meeting to consider certain matters[6], the conduct of examinations by a university[7], or the election of fellows of a college[8]; the residence of the master of a hospital in the master's house[9] or the performance of Divine Service by him[10], or his election[11]; or the election or removal of members of a corporation such as governors[12] or schoolmasters[13]. A visitor has power also to determine whether a person is entitled to become a member of the corporation[14], and whether a person has been properly removed from membership[15].

A member of a corporation refusing to recognise the authority of the visitor may be removed, whether or not the statutes expressly authorise this[16].

If the Charity Commissioners[17] make an order[18] removing a charity trustee[19] or an officer or servant of a charity[20] with the approval of the special visitor, the person remove cannot appeal to the court against the order[21].

1 'A visitor is … a Judge, not for the single purpose of interpreting laws, but also for the application of laws, that are perfectly clear: requiring no interpretation; and, farther, for the interpretations of questions of fact, involving no interpretation of laws': *Ex p Kirkby Ravensworth Hospital* (1808) 15 Ves 305 at 311 per Sir Samuel Romilly, cited as authoritative by Lord Griffiths in *Thomas v University of Bradford* [1987] AC 795 at 815, [1987] 1 All ER 834 at 846, HL.

2 *Oakes v Sidney Sussex College, Cambridge* [1988] 1 All ER 1004, [1988] 1 WLR 431.

3 *A-G v Stephens* (1737) 1 Atk 358 at 360 per Lord Hardwicke LC; *Ex p Berkhampstead Free School* (1813) 2 Ves & B 134; *A-G v Smythies* (1836) 2 My & Cr 135 (where the question was whether a fellow of a college might let his rooms).

4 *A-G v Dulwich College* (1841) 4 Beav 255; *A-G v Magdalen College, Oxford* (1847) 10 Beav 402. See *Thomas v University of Bradford* [1987] AC 795, [1987] 1 All ER 834, HL (the question whether the university council had correctly followed its disciplinary procedures in dismissing a lecturer was a matter exclusively within the jurisdiction of the visitor), approving *Hines v Birkbeck College* [1986] Ch 524, [1985] 3 All ER 156 (appeal dismissed [1987] Ch 457n [1987] 3 All ER 1040n, CA); *Casson v University of Aston in Birmingham* [1983] 1 All ER 88, Visitor (visitor's jurisdiction to hear petition alleging breach of contract by corporation).

5 *Re Christ Church* (1866) 1 Ch App 526.

6 *R v Dunsheath, ex p Meredith* [1951] 1 KB 127, [1950] 2 All ER 741.

7 *Thomson v London University* (1864) 10 Jur NS 669; *Thorn v University of London* [1966] 2 QB 237, [1966] 2 All ER 338, CA; cf *Herring v Templeman* [1973] 2 All ER 581 (affd on other grounds [1973] 3 All ER 569, CA) (dismissal of student at teacher-training college). See also *R v HM The Queen in Council, ex p Vijayatunga* [1990] 2 QB 444, sub nom *R v University of London Visitor, ex p Vijayatunga* [1989] 2 All ER 843, CA (claim that examiners not qualified to assess thesis: visitor properly refused to intervene).

8 *A-G v Talbot* (1748) 3 Atk 662 at 675 per Lord Hardwicke LC; *Ex p Wrangham* (1795) 2 Ves 609; *Re Catharine Hall, ex p Inge* (1831) 2 Russ & M 590.

9 *Re St Mary Magdalen Hospital, Colchester* (1843) 12 LJCh 375; *Ex p Berkhampstead Free School* (1813) 2 Ves & B 134; *A-G v Smythies* (1836) 2 My & Cr 135 at 142 per Lord Cottenham LC.

10 *A-G v Crook* (1836) 1 Keen 121.

11 *A-G v Archbishop of York* (1831) 2 Russ & M 461 at 468 per Lord Brougham LC.

12 *A-G v Dixie, ex p Bosworth School* (1805) 13 Ves 519; *A-G v Earl of Clarendon* (1810) 17 Ves 491 at 498 per Grant MR.

13 *Whiston v Dean and Chapter of Rochester* (1849) 7 Hare 532.

14 Eg in cases of claims of rejected candidates for fellowships and scholarships: *R v Warden of All Souls College, Oxford* (1681) T Jo 174; *St John's College, Cambridge v Todington* (1757) 1 Burr 158; *R v Master and Fellows of St Catharine's Hall* (1791) 4 Term Rep 233; *Ex p Wrangham* (1795) 2 Ves 609; *R v Hertford College* (1878) 3 QBD 693, CA.

15 *Re Wislang's Application* [1984] NI 63; *Thomas v University of Bradford* [1987] AC 795, [1987] 1 All ER 834, HL. It 'extends to all questions of disputed membership': *Patel v University of Bradford Senate* [1979] 2 All ER 582 at 584, [1979] 1 WLR 1066 at 1069, CA, per Orr LJ.

16 *Philips v Bury* (1694) Skin 447 at 477–478, HL.

17 As to the Charity Commissioners see paras 486–512 post.

18 Ie under the Charities Act 1993 s 16(1): see para 180 ante.

19 For the meaning of 'charity trustees' see para 1 note 10 ante.

20 For the meaning of 'charity' see para 1 ante.

21 See the Charities Act 1993 s 16(12); and para 190 ante.

**469. Restrictions on visitor's power.** A visitor is not entitled to interfere with the proceedings of corporators in matters over which they have discretion[1], unless their discretion has been exercised improperly[2]; nor may he insist upon a corporation performing some act which according to the statutes regulating the corporation may be performed by another if the corporation fails to do it[3], or interfere with the internal management of the charitable corporation unless the trusts of the foundation are disregarded[4], or appoint a master of a free school on the ground that the appointments previously made by the proper electors were invalid[5].

As the visitor's jurisdiction extends only over the members of the corporation[6], he has no power to compel specific performance of an agreement between the corporators and other parties[7], or to reverse a decision of a corporation concerning strangers to the foundation[8].

Except under an express power, a visitor cannot be judge in his own cause[9], nor can he alter the general constitution of the trust[10].

1   *Ex p Wrangham* (1795) 2 Ves 609 at 625 per Lord Thurlow LC (election of fellows).
2   *Re Catharine Hall, ex p Inge* (1831) 2 Russ & M 590 at 601 per Lord Brougham LC; *R v Hertford College* (1878) 3 QBD 693 at 701, CA, per Lord Coleridge CJ.
3   *Ex p Wrangham* (1795) 2 Ves 609 at 621 per Lord Thurlow LC, where the statutes provided that if a college failed to elect fellows, the right should be exercised by the master.
4   *A-G v Earl of Clarendon* (1810) 17 Ves 491 at 507 per Grant MR.
5   *A-G v Black* (1805) 11 Ves 191.
6   See *Herring v Templeman* [1973] 3 All ER 569, CA, in relation to a student at a teacher-training college. See also *Casson v University of Aston in Birmingham* [1983] 1 All ER 88, Visitor (no jurisdiction to hear petition alleging breach of pre-admission contract by corporation); *Oakes v Sidney Sussex College, Cambridge* [1988] 1 All ER 1004, [1988] 1 WLR 431 (visitor's jurisdiction dependent on whether claim arose under domestic law of college, not on nature of claimant's college membership).
7   *R v Windham* (1776) 1 Cowp 377.
8   *Ex p Davison* (1772) cited in 1 Cowp 319 (expulsion of commoners by a college). See also *R v Grundon* (1775) 1 Cowp 315.
9   This is upon the principle that the same person cannot be visitor and visited: *R v Bishop of Ely* (1788) 2 Term Rep 290; *A-G v Middleton* (1751) 2 Ves Sen 327 at 329 per Lord Hardwicke LC; and see *R v Hertford College* (1878) 3 QBD 693 at 703, CA, per Lord Coleridge CJ.
10  *Ex p Bolton School* (1789) 2 Bro CC 662.

**470. Accession to the foundation.** In the case of an accession of a new to an old foundation the visitor of the old foundation has no jurisdiction over the new foundation unless the visitatorial power is especially given to him by the subsequent founder, or his appointment as visitor is to be implied[1].

Where new property is annexed to an old foundation without a special trust being declared or a new visitor being appointed, the necessary implication is that the new property is intended to be subject to the existing visitatorial jurisdiction[2]. However, the visitor of the old foundation has no jurisdiction over an annexed estate concerning which a special trust has been declared[3]. If the Queen is visitor of an old foundation, which accepts an accession, it seems that she becomes visitor of the new foundation, even if the founder declares there shall be no visitor[4].

A lay corporation composed of an indefinite number of members may incorporate additional members, who will thereupon become subject to the jurisdiction of the visitor[5].

1   *Green v Rutherforth* (1750) 1 Ves Sen 462 at 472 per Lord Hardwicke LC.
2   *Green v Rutherforth* (1750) 1 Ves Sen 462 at 473 per Lord Hardwicke LC; *A-G v Talbot* (1748) 3 Atk 662
    (accession of fellowship to college foundation); *A-G v Flood* (1816) Hayes & Jo App xxi at p xxv. See
    also *Re Catharine Hall, ex p Inge* (1831) 2 Russ & M 590 at 596 per Lord Brougham LC.
3   *Green v Rutherforth* (1750) 1 Ves Sen 462 at 468–469, 473 per Lord Hardwicke LC.
4   *A-G v Catherine Hall, Cambridge* (1820) Jac 381 at 400 per Lord Eldon LC. It was doubted whether a
    college of which the King was visitor could accept an accession without his consent.
5   *A-G v Talbot* (1748) 3 Atk 662 at 675 per Lord Hardwicke LC.


**471. Procedure and duties of visitor.** Whether a visitor is exercising his jurisdiction
upon a general visitation or upon a special appeal[1], he need not proceed according to the
rules of common law[2] so long as he pays regard to the positive forms prescribed by the
statutes regulating the foundation[3], and subject to this condition, and provided he acts
judicially, the actual manner of hearing is within his discretion[4]. He must hear all appeals
not of a frivolous nature[5].

A visitor should cite the interested parties to appear before him[6], and no proceedings
ought to be taken against an absent party until he has been cited[7]. The visitor may decide
questions upon written or oral evidence[8], on oath or otherwise[9]; but he cannot give his
decision without hearing the parties concerned or, at least, affording them an
opportunity of being heard[10].

The visitatorial jurisdiction of the Crown is exercised by the Lord Chancellor[11], or
such other person as he may advise Her Majesty to nominate, on behalf of the Crown[12],
upon application by petition[13]. Like a private visitor, he is not bound by any particular
forms of procedure[14]. Unless the petitioner can prove that the Crown is in fact visitor,
the Lord Chancellor has no authority to hear the petition[15].


1   As to the jurisdiction of general or special visitors see para 462 ante.
2   *R v Bishop of Ely* (1788) 2 Term Rep 290 at 338 per Buller J. See, however, the text and note 10 infra.
3   Com Dig Visitor, C.
4   *A-G v Governors of Atherstone Free School* (1834) 3 My & K 544 at 550 per Lord Brougham LC; *R v HM
    The Queen in Council, ex p Vijayatunga* [1990] 2 QB 444, sub nom *R v University of London Visitor, ex p
    Vijayatunga* [1989] 2 All ER 843, CA (in some cases he should exercise a merely supervisory jurisdiction,
    and in others an appellate jurisdiction). In *Thomas v University of Bradford (No 2)* [1992] 1 All ER 964, the
    jurisdiction was said to be similar to that which the High Court exercises by way of judicial review. See
    also *Re Dean of York* (1841) 2 QB 1.
5   Shelford's Law of Mortmain (1836) 379.
6   *R v Cambridge University* (1723) 8 Mod Rep 148 at 163 per Pratt CJ. See also *Watson and Freemantle v
    Warden etc of All Souls College, Oxford* (1864) 11 LT 166.
7   Com Dig Visitor, C.
8   *R v Bishop of Ely* (1794) 5 Term Rep 475.
9   Shelford's Law of Mortmain (1836) 379. However, see *Green v Rutherforth* (1750) 1 Ves Sen 462 at 473
    per Lord Hardwicke LC.
10  *R v Bishop of Ely* (1788) 2 Term Rep 290 at 336 per Ashurst J; *R v Cambridge University* (1723) 8 Mod
    Rep 148; see also *R v Gaskin* (1799) 8 Term Rep 209; *Doe d Earl of Thanet v Gartham* (1823) 8 Moore
    CP 368 at 371 per Park J.
11  Co Litt 96a; Shelford's Law of Mortmain (1836) 333; *R v Master and Fellows of St Catherine's Hall* (1791) 4
    Term Rep 233 at 244 per Lord Kenyon CJ; *A-G v Dixie, ex p Bosworth School* (1805) 13 Ves 519; *A-G v
    Earl of Clarendon* (1810) 17 Ves 491 at 498 per Grant MR; *Re Christ Church* (1866) 1 Ch App 526. See
    paras 458, 461 ante. As to costs in hearings before the Lord Chancellor as visitor see *Queen's College,
    Cambridge, Case* (1821) Jac 1 at 47 per Lord Eldon LC; *A-G v Master and Fellows of Catherine Hall, Cambridge*
    (1820) Jac 381 at 401–402 per Lord Eldon LC.
12  *Thomas v University of Bradford* [1987] AC 795 at 811, [1987] 1 All ER 834 at 839, HL, per Lord Griffiths.
    In *R v HM The Queen in Council, ex p Vijayatunga* [1990] 2 QB 444, sub nom *R v University of London
    Visitor, ex p Vijayatunga* [1989] 2 All ER 843, CA, the Crown nominated a committee of the Judicial

Committee of the Privy Council, in *R v Lord President of the Privy Council, ex p Page* [1993] AC 682, sub nom *Page v Hull University Visitor* [1993] 1 All ER 97, HL, the Lord President of the Privy Council, and in *Thomas v University of Bradford (No 2)* [1992] 1 All ER 964, Lord Browne-Wilkinson, a Lord of Appeal in Ordinary. As to the Judicial Committee of the Privy Council see CONSTITUTIONAL LAW AND HUMAN RIGHTS vol 8(2) (Reissue) para 311; COURTS. As to Lords of Appeal in Ordinary see COURTS.

13  *Ex p Wrangham* (1795) 2 Ves 609; *A-G v Black* (1805) 11 Ves 191; *Re Catharine Hall, ex p Inge* (1831) 2 Russ & M 590; *Re Queen's College, Cambridge* (1828) 5 Russ 64; *Re University College, Oxford* (1848) 2 Ph 521; *Re Christ Church* (1866) 1 Ch App 526.

14  *Queen's College, Cambridge, Case* (1821) Jac 1 at 19 per Lord Eldon LC.

15  *Re Garstang Church Town School, ex p Pedder* (1829) 7 LJOS Ch 169 at 172 per Lord Lyndhurst LC. As to the costs of petitions to the Lord Chancellor see *Ex p Dann* (1804) 9 Ves 547; *Re Masters, Governors and Trustees of Bedford Charity* (1819) 2 Swan 470 at 532 per Lord Eldon LC; and note 11 supra.

## (iv)  Court's Control over Visitors

**472.  Discretionary powers of visitors.** The court's jurisdiction does not extend to matters within the properly exercised discretion of the visitor[1], or the trustee[2], governors[3] or other authority[4], but the court controls the visitor's discretionary powers if exercised corruptly or dishonestly[5].

1  *A-G v Harrow School Governors* (1754) 2 Ves Sen 551; *A-G v Dulwich College* (1841) 4 Beav 255; *A-G v Magdalen College, Oxford* (1847) 10 Beav 402; *Thomson v London University* (1864) 33 LJCh 625 at 634; *Thorne v University of London* [1966] 2 QB 237, [1966] 2 All ER 338, CA; *Herring v Templeman* [1973] 2 All ER 581; affd on other grounds [1973] 3 All ER 569, CA. As to what matters are within the visitor's discretion see para 458 et seq ante.

2  *A-G v Harrow School Governors* (1754) 2 Ves Sen 551.

3  *Eden v Foster* (1726) 2 P Wms 325. Cf *R v Governors of Christ's Hospital, ex p Dunn* [1917] 1 KB 19, a case where the matter was not within the governors' discretion.

4  *A-G v Bedford Corpn* (1754) 2 Ves Sen 505; *Costabadie v Costabadie* (1847) 6 Hare 410; *Hayman v Governors of Rugby School* (1874) LR 18 Eq 28.

5  *Ex p Kirkby Ravensworth Hospital* (1808) 15 Ves 305 at 314 per Lord Eldon LC; and see *A-G v Harrow School Governors* (1754) 2 Ves Sen 551.

**473.  Visitors acting in excess of authority.** The court will grant a prohibition[1] if a visitor exceeds the limits of his visitatorial authority[2], or proceeds contrary to his citation, or inflicts different penalties from those which the statutes prescribe[3]; or where a person purports to act as visitor when he has no jurisdiction[4]. Mere irregularity in the proceedings or informality in the acts of a visitor will not render him liable to a prohibition[5]. Where he has no jurisdiction, appearance or answer does not give him jurisdiction. If there is a want of jurisdiction it may be called in question at any time, even after sentence[6]. An order may also be granted to quash a decision of the visitor which amounts to an abuse of his powers, or if he has acted in breach of the rules of natural justice[7]. Judicial review does not, however, lie to impeach the decisions of a visitor taken within his jurisdiction (in the narrow sense[8]) on questions of either law or fact[9]. This is because the applicable law is not the common law of England but a peculiar or domestic law of which the visitor is the sole judge[10].

1  An application for prohibition must be made by an application for judicial review: see the Supreme Court Act 1981 s 31(1); and ADMINISTRATIVE LAW vol 1(1) (2001 Reissue) para 121.

2  *Bishop of Chichester v Harvard and Webber* (1787) 1 Term Rep 650.

3    *Bishop of Ely v Bentley* (1732) 2 Bro Parl Cas 220, HL.
4    *R v Bishop of Chester* (1748) 1 Wm Bl 22 at 25; *Whiston v Dean and Chapter of Rochester* (1849) 7 Hare
     532 at 558 per Shadwell V–C.
5    *Bishop of Ely v Bentley* (1732) 2 Bro Parl Cas 220, HL.
6    *Green v Rutherforth* (1750) 1 Ves Sen 462 at 471 per Lord Hardwicke LC.
7    *R v Lord President of the Privy Council, ex p Page* [1993] AC 682, sub nom *Page v Hull University Visitor*
     [1993] 1 All ER 97, HL; *Thomas v University of Bradford* [1987] AC 795 at 825, [1987] 1 All ER 834 at
     850, HL, per Lord Griffiths; *R v Committee of the Lords of the Judicial Committee of the Privy Council acting
     for the Visitor of the University of London, ex p Vijayatunga* [1988] QB 322, sub nom *R v University of London
     Visitor, ex p Vijayatunga* [1987] 3 All ER 204; affd sub nom *R v HM The Queen in Council, ex p
     Vijayatunga* [1990] 2 QB 444, sub nom *R v University of London Visitor, ex p Vijayatunga* [1989] 2 All ER
     843, CA. As to quashing orders see ADMINISTRATIVE LAW vol 1(1) (2001 Reissue) para 123 et seq;
     PRACTICE AND PROCEDURE.
8    Ie where he has power under the regulating documents to enter into the adjudication of the dispute.
9    Apart from the anomalous and unique case of the visitor, any error of law made by an administrative
     tribunal or inferior court may be a ground for quashing the decision on judicial review: *Anisminic Ltd v
     Foreign Compensation Commission* [1969] 2 AC 147, [1969] 1 All ER 208, HL; *O'Reilly v Mackman* [1983]
     2 AC 237, [1982] 3 All ER 1124, HL; *R v Lord President of the Privy Council, ex p Page* [1993] AC 682,
     sub nom *Page v Hull University Visitor* [1993] 1 All ER 97, HL. As to judicial review see ADMINISTRATIVE
     LAW vol 1(1) (2001 Reissue) para 59 et seq.
10   *R v Lord President of the Privy Council, ex p Page* [1993] AC 682, sub nom *Page v Hull University Visitor*
     [1993] 1 All ER 97, HL; *Appleford's Case* (1672) 1 Mod Rep 82; *R v Bishop of Chester* (1747) 1 WM Bl
     22; *R v Bishop of Ely* (1794) 5 Term Rep 475; *Ex p Buller* (1855) 1 Jur NS 709. See also *A-G v Lock*
     (1744) 3 Atk 164 at 165 per Lord Hardwicke LC; *A-G v Talbot* (1748) 3 Atk 622 at 674 per Lord
     Hardwicke LC; *A-G v Catherine Hall, Cambridge* (1820) Jac 381 at 392 per Lord Eldon LC; *A-G v
     Dedham School* (1857) 23 Beav 350.

**474. Where Charity Commissioners are visitors.** Where visitatorial jurisdiction is
reserved by a scheme to the Charity Commissioners[1], the court will not interfere in
matters coming within that jurisdiction which have already been determined
conclusively within the meaning of the scheme, before any application is made to the
court[2].

1    See the Charity Commissioners' powers under the Endowed Schools Act 1869 s 23 (repealed), and the
     decision thereunder in *Re Hodgson's School* (1878) 3 App Cas 857, PC. As to the Charity Commissioners
     see paras 486–512 post.
2    *R v Wilson* [1888] WN 12, DC (where the court refused to consider a question regarding the validity of
     the election of a governor which had already been determined conclusively by the Commissioners under
     the scheme). See also para 460 ante.

**475. Mandatory order to put visitatorial power in motion.** The object and
effect of a mandatory order is no more than to put the visitatorial power in motion,
whereupon the visitor is at liberty to pursue his own course without review by the
court[1].

The court may make a mandatory order to compel a visitor to exercise his visitatorial
power where he has not acted, declines to act, or acts improperly[2]; or to compel him to
receive and hear an appeal, although the court cannot force him to decide on the merits
if he considers the appeal is brought too late[3]; so, too, the court may make a mandatory
order against the head of a college and the fellows where the laws of the land have been
disobeyed by the fellows, even though there is a visitor[4].

A mandatory order will lie against the governors of a charity to compel them to appoint a person duly recommended to an office where, by the constitution of the charity, the governors are bound to act on the recommendation[5].

The court refuses, however, to make such an order where it is doubtful whether the visitatorial power is in the persons required to exercise it[6], or to compel an inferior officer of a college to execute the visitor's sentence in accordance with the statutes[7], or to restore a fellow or member of a college[8], or a chaplain[9] or a sister of a hospital[10].

1   *A-G v Archbishop of York* (1831) 2 Russ & M 461 at 468 per Lord Brougham LC. A mandatory order was formerly known as an order of mandamus, but was renamed by the Civil Procedure Rules: see CPR 51.1(2)(b). As to mandatory orders see further ADMINISTRATIVE LAW vol 1(1) (2001 Reissue) para 133 et seq. An application for a mandatory order must be made by an application for judicial review: see Supreme Court Act 1981 s 31(1); and ADMINISTRATIVE LAW vol 1(1) (2001 Reissue) para 121.

2   *R v Bishop of Ely* (1788) 2 Term Rep 290; *R v Cambridge University* (1723) 8 Mod Rep 148; *R v Bishop of Worcester* (1815) 4 M & s 415; *Whiston v Dean and Chapter of Rochester* (1849) 7 Hare 532 at 558 per Shadwell V-C. See also *Gunston v Dare* (1738) West *temp* Hard 573 at 576 per Lord Hardwicke LC.

3   *R v Bishop of Ely* (1794) 5 Term Rep 475. See also *R v Bishop of Lincoln* (1785) 2 Term Rep 338n; *Ferguson v Kinnoul* (1842) 4 State Tr NS 785 at 820, HL, per Lord Brougham.

4   *R v St John's College, Cambridge* (1693) 4 Mod Rep 233; but see *R v Gower* (1694) 3 Salk 230.

5   *R v Governors of Christ's Hospital, ex p Dunn* [1917] 1 KB 19.

6   *R v Bishop of Ely* (1750) 1 Wm Bl 52; *Brideoak's Case* (1714) cited in 1 Wm Bl 58.

7   *A-G v Aspinall* (1837) 2 My & Cr 613 at 627 per Lord Cottenham LC; *Stevens v Chown* [1901] 1 Ch 894 at 905 per Farwell J; *A-G v De Winton* [1906] 2 Ch 106 at 115 per Farwell J.

8   *Dr Widdrington's Case* (1662) 1 Lev 23; *Appleford's Case* (1672) 1 Mod Rep 82; *Parkinson's Case* (1689) 3 Mod Rep 265; *R v Warden of All Souls College, Oxford* (1681) T Jo 174; *A-G v Governors of Atherstone Free School* (1834) 3 My & K 544 at 550 per Lord Brougham LC; *R v Hertford College* (1878) 3 QBD 693, CA.

9   *Prohurst's Case* (1691) Carth 168.

10  *R v Wheeler* (1674) 3 Keb 360.

**476. Remedies against visitor.** The remedy, if any, of a person deprived or removed by a visitor has been said[1] to lie in an action of ejectment, long since replaced by an action to recover possession of land[2], or, if the visitor has acted contrary to or exceeded his jurisdiction, in a claim against him on that ground[3]. The appropriate modern procedure is by way of an application for judicial review[4].

1   In *R v Bishop of Chester* (1748) 1 Wils 206 at 209 per Lee CJ.

2   See *Gledhill v Hunter* (1880) 14 ChD 492.

3   See *Green v Rutherforth* (1750) 1 Ves Sen 462 at 472 per Lord Hardwicke LC.

4   See paras 473, 475 ante. As to judicial review see ADMINISTRATIVE LAW vol 1(1) (2001 Reissue) para 59 et seq.

# (3)  THE COURTS

**477. Jurisdiction to enforce trusts.** As a general rule the High Court has jurisdiction to enforce the observance or redress breaches of all trusts, charitable as well as private[1]. The court cannot exercise its charitable jurisdiction if no trust is ascertained[2]. The jurisdiction in the case of charities is more extensive than in the case of private trusts[3]; where the trust is charitable, the court has jurisdiction not only to enforce it and to redress all breaches[4], but also, in certain circumstances, to make schemes for the administration of the charity[5] and to alter or modify the trust to a greater or less degree by virtue of the cy-près doctrine[6].

The court equally enforces the execution of trusts where corporations eleemosynary[7], ecclesiastical[8], or civil[9] are trustees for charitable or public purposes.

1    *Dick v Audsley* [1908] AC 347 at 351, HL, per Lord Loreburn LC. This jurisdiction, formerly exercised by the Court of Chancery, is now vested in the High Court of Justice and exercised by the Chancery Division: see Supreme Court Act 1981 ss 5(4), (5), 19, 61(1), 64, 65, Sch 1 (as amended). The jurisdiction has been exercised by the court from the earliest times: see *Wakeryng v Bayle* (circa 1422–70) 1 Calendar of Proceedings in Chancery lvii; *Lyon v Hewe* (circa 1465–83) 2 Calendar of Proceedings in Chancery xliv; *Payne's Case* (temp Eliz) Duke ed Bridgman, 154. For an account of the early history of charitable trusts and uses, see Gareth Jones *History of the Law of Charity*.

2    *Ommanney v Butcher* (1823) Turn & R 260 at 270 per Plumer MR; *A-G v St John's Hospital, Bedford* (1865) 2 De GJ & Sm 621 at 635 per Turner LJ; but see also *Re Bennett, Sucker v A-G* [1960] Ch 18 at 26, [1959] 3 All ER 295 at 296 per Vaisey J. In this context the word 'trust' may have to be understood in a sense wider than usual, as companies and other corporate bodies are clearly subject to the court's charity jurisdiction where they are established for charitable purposes, although they may not necessarily be trustees of their property in a conventional sense. See also *Construction Industry Training Board v A-G* [1973] Ch 173, [1972] 2 All ER 1339, CA; and para 224 ante.

3    *A-G v Governors etc of Sherborne Grammar School* (1854) 18 Beav 256 at 280 per Romilly MR; *Clephane v Edinburgh Corpn* (1869) LR 1 Sc & Div 417 at 421, HL, per Lord Westbury; *Andrews v M'Guffog* (1886) 11 App Cas 313 at 316, HL, per Lord Watson. The courts are, perhaps, even more reluctant to sanction the remuneration of trustees in the case of a charity than in the case of a private trust: see *Report of the Charity Commissioners for England and Wales for 1990* (HC Paper (1990–91) no 362) App D (c); and TRUSTS vol 48 (2000 Reissue) para 822 et seq. See also the *Report of the Charity Commissioners for England and Wales for 1981* (HC Paper (1981–82) no 363) para 64; and the *Report of the Charity Commissioners for England and Wales for 1988* (HC Paper (1988–89) no 319) para 38.

4    *A-G v Governors etc of Sherborne Grammar School* (1854) 18 Beav 256. See also *Incorporated Society in Dublin v Richards* (1841) 1 Con & Law 58; *A-G v Dublin Corpn* (1827) 1 Bli NS 312 at 347, HL per Lord Redesdale; *A-G v St John's Hospital, Bedford* (1865) 2 De GJ & Sm 621.

5    See *Re Royal Society's Charitable Trusts* [1956] Ch 87, [1955] 3 All ER 14. As to schemes see para 170 et seq ante.

6    As to the doctrine of cy-près see para 201 et seq ante.

7    As to the court's jurisdiction over corporations see para 224 ante; and *A-G v Magdalen College, Oxford* (1847) 10 Beav 402 at 409 per Lord Langdale MR (where a college was trustee of a grammar school); *Whiston v Dean and Chapter of Rochester* (1849) 7 Hare 532 at 560 per Shadwell V-C (dean and chapter trustees); *Daugars v Rivaz* (1860) 28 Beav 233. The duty of appointing and removing schoolmasters may be (*Willis v Childe* (1851) 13 Beav 117), but is not necessarily, in the nature of a trust (*A-G v Magdalen College, Oxford* supra at 409 per Lord Langdale MR; *Whiston v Dean and Chapter of Rochester* supra). If it is a trust, an improper removal is restrained by injunction. If it is not a trust but only a duty imposed on trustees, any breach must be redressed by the visitor and not by the court: *A-G v Magdalen College, Oxford* supra. As to eleemosynary corporations see para 213 ante.

8    *A-G v St John's Hospital, Bedford* (1865) 2 De GJ & Sm 621 at 635 per Turner LJ. See also *A-G v Brereton* (1752) 2 Ves Sen 425.

9    *Coventry Corpn v A-G* (1720) 7 Bro Parl Cas 235, HL; *A-G v Shrewsbury Town* (1726) Bunb 215; *A-G v Governors of Foundling Hospital* (1793) 2 Ves 42 at 46 per Lord Commissioner Eyre; *Viscount Gort v A-G* (1817) 6 Dow 136, HL; *A-G v Brewers' Co* (1816) 1 Mer 495; *A-G v Stafford Corpn* (1826) 1 Russ 547; *A-G v Exeter Corpn* (1827) 2 Russ 362; *A-G v Dublin Corpn* (1827) 1 Bli NS 312, HL; *A-G v Carlisle Corpn* (1828) 2 Sim 437 at 449 per Shadwell V-C; *A-G v Liverpool Corpn* (1835) 1 My & Cr 171 at 201 per Pepys MR; and see *A-G v Plymouth Corpn* (1845) 9 Beav 67.

**478.  Extent of jurisdiction.** After some conflict of judicial opinion[1] the rule is now established that, when there is a gift to charity and the donor either created or intended to create a trust, whether the objects are specified or indefinite, the court has jurisdiction to enforce the execution of the trust, and, if necessary, to apply the gift to charitable purposes by means of a scheme[2].

1   *A-G v Berryman* (1755) Dick 168; *A-G v Herrick* (1772) Amb 712; *A-G v Marchioness of Londonderry* (1825) 3 Hare 195n; *A-G v Fletcher* (1835) 5 LJCh 75; *Felan v Russell* (1842) 4 I Eq R 701 (in the last-mentioned cases, though a trust was created, the disposition of the property was held to devolve on the Crown and not on the court).

2   *Cook v Duckenfield* (1743) 2 Atk 562 at 567, 569 per Lord Hardwicke LC; *Moggridge v Thackwell* (1803) 7 Ves 36 (affd (1807) 13 Ves 416, HL); *Mills v Farmer* (1815) 1 Mer 55; *Paice v Archbishop of Canterbury* (1807) 14 Ves 364; *Ommanney v Butcher* (1823) Turn & R 260 at 271 per Plumer MR; *Hayter v Trego* (1830) 5 Russ 113; *A-G v Ironmongers' Co* (1834) 2 My & K 576; *Reeve v A-G* (1843) 3 Hare 191 at 197 per Wigram V-C; *Re Davis, Hannen v Hillyer* [1902] 1 Ch 876 at 888 per Buckley J; *Re Pyne, Lilley v A-G* [1903] 1 Ch 83; *Re Bennett, Sucker v A-G* [1960] Ch 18, [1959] 3 All ER 295. As to the exercise of the court's jurisdiction to make schemes see para 192 et seq ante.

**479. Limits of jurisdiction.** It is not within the court's jurisdiction to determine whether ecclesiastical duties enjoined under a charitable foundation are properly performed[1]. The court cannot give a charity a larger interest in property than that intended by the testator[2], and it is extremely reluctant to prevent a gift over of property from one charity to another in circumstances expressly contemplated by the donor[3].

1   *A-G v Smithies* (1836) 1 Keen 289; cf *A-G v Dean and Chapter of Ripon Cathedral* [1945] Ch 239, [1945] 1 All ER 479.

2   *Re Randell, Randell v Dixon* (1888) 38 ChD 213 at 216 per North J; *Re Blunt's Trusts, Wigan v Clinch* [1904] 2 Ch 767.

3   In *Re Hanbey's Will Trusts, Cutlers' Co v President and Governors of Christ's Hospital, London* [1956] Ch 264, [1955] 3 All ER 874, Danckwerts J held that there was jurisdiction to make such a scheme, but did not exercise it. See also *Christ's Hospital v Grainger* (1849) 1 Mac & G 460 at 465 per Lord Cottenham LC; *Re Tyler, Tyler v Tyler* [1891] 3 Ch 252, CA. Quaere whether the court has jurisdiction even to defeat a resulting trust in this way: see para 174 note 7 ante.

**480. No charitable gift.** The court cannot exercise its charitable jurisdiction where the gift is not charitable in the legal sense, as in the case of a private charity[1], or where a gift fails entirely owing to the charitable intention not taking effect[2], or where the gift was never subject to a charitable trust[3], as in the case of a gift to charity subject to the fulfilment of a condition which was never satisfied[4], or in the case of voluntary subscriptions or funds impressed with no charitable trust[5].

1   *Ommanney v Butcher* (1823) Turn & R 260 at 273 per Plumer MR. As to private charities see para 52 ante.

2   *A-G v Boultbee* (1794) 2 Ves 380 at 387 per Arden MR (charitable object to build a church in parish of A, which the parish did not permit); *Biscoe v Jackson* (1887) 35 ChD 460 at 463, CA, per Kay J; *Re Wilson, Twentyman v Simpson* [1913] 1 Ch 314.

3   *De Themmines v De Bonneval* (1828) 5 Russ 288.

4   *Chamberlayne v Brockett* (1872) 8 Ch App 206 at 211 per Lord Selborne LC. See also *Re Gyde, Ward v Little* (1898) 79 LT 261, CA; *Re University of London Medical Sciences Institute Fund, Fowler v A-G* [1909] 2 Ch 1, CA.

5   *Anon* (1745) 3 Atk 277; *Leslie v Birnie* (1826) 2 Russ 114 at 119 per Lord Eldon LC.

**481. Charity founded by royal charter.** On the principle that the authority of the Crown is higher than that of the court[1], the court has generally no jurisdiction to refound or re-establish charities founded by royal charter[2], but it does have jurisdiction to regulate or control the charity by way of scheme[3], especially on financial grounds and in altered circumstances[4], and to see that the provisions of the charter are observed[5] where improper conduct is alleged[6].

The court has power under the Charities Act 1993 to make schemes in relation to chartered charities, including cy-près schemes[7], which necessitate altering the charter, but the schemes are not to come into operation until the charter has been amended[8], which may be done by Order in Council[9].

1   *A-G v Smart* (1748) 1 Ves Sen 72; *A-G v Middleton* (1751) 2 Ves Sen 327; *A-G v Bedford Corpn* (1754) 2 Ves Sen 505; *A-G v Governors of Foundling Hospital* (1793) 2 Ves 42 at 47 per Lord Commissioner Eyre; *A-G v Earl of Clarendon* (1810) 17 Ves 491; *A-G v Dedham School* (1857) 23 Beav 350 at 356 per Romilly MR; *A-G v Governors of Christ's Hospital* [1896] 1 Ch 879 at 888 per Chitty J. See also *Re Chertsey Market, ex p Walthew* (1819) 6 Price 261; *Re Browne's Hospital v Stamford* (1889) 60 LT 288.

2   Ie except where the charter is subsequent to the original foundation: *A-G v Dedham School* (1857) 23 Beav 350 at 356 per Romilly MR. See also *A-G v St Olave's Grammar School, Southwark* (1837) Coop Pr Cas 267.

3   *Re Whitworth Art Gallery Trusts, Manchester Whitworth Institute v Victoria University of Manchester* [1958] Ch 461, [1958] 1 All ER 176; *A-G v Hicks* (1810) 3 Bro CC 166n; *Re Yarm Free Grammar School* (1853) 10 Hare App I, V; *Re Berkhampsted Grammar School* [1908] 2 Ch 25; *Manchester School Case* (1867) 2 Ch App 497; and see *Berkhampstead School Case* (1865) LR 1 Eq 102.

4   *Re Whitworth Art Gallery Trusts, Manchester Whitworth Institute v Victoria University of Manchester* [1958] Ch 461, [1958] 1 All ER 176; *Clephane v Edinburgh Corpn* (1869) LR 1 Sc & Div 417, HL.

5   *Green v Rutherforth* (1750) 1 Ves Sen 462 at 468 per Lord Hardwicke LC; *A-G v Governors of Foundling Hospital* (1793) 2 Ves 42; *A-G v Earl of Mansfield* (1827) 2 Russ 501; *A-G v Smythies* (1833) 2 Russ & M 717 at 749 per Lord Brougham LC; *A-G v Wyggeston Hospital* (1849) 12 Beav 113 at 123 per Lord Langdale MR; and see *A-G v St John's Hospital, Bedford* (1865) 2 De GJ & Sm 621.

6   *A-G v Bedford Corpn* (1754) 2 Ves Sen 505.

7   As to cy-près schemes see para 201 et seq ante.

8   See the Charities Act 1993 s 15(1); and para 175 ante.

9   See ibid s 15(2); and para 175 ante.

**482. Charity regulated by statute.** If there were an institution established and regulated in every respect by statute, the court would have no jurisdiction to interfere in its administration, notwithstanding that its purposes were charitable[1], unless the statute gave the court such jurisdiction[2]. However, the court may make a scheme in respect of matters not provided for by the statute[3] or in aid of and supplemental to the provisions of the statute[4], and may enforce the observance of those provisions[5].

Certain statutes are declared not to exclude or restrict the court's jurisdiction with respect to charities, so that the court can make schemes superseding the statutory provisions[6].

The Charity Commissioners, but not the court, may make schemes (which are put into effect by statutory instrument) amending statutory provisions[7].

1   Cf *Re Shrewsbury Grammar School* (1849) 1 Mac & G 324. See also *London Parochial Charities Trustees v A-G* [1955] 1 All ER 1, [1955] 1 WLR 42; *Construction Industry Training Board v A-G* [1973] Ch 173, [1972] 2 All ER 1339, CA.

2   *Re Shrewsbury Grammar School* (1849) 1 Mac & G 324 at 331 per Lord Cottenham LC; *Ex p Bolton* (1789) 2 Bro CC 662; *Re Bedford Charity* (1833) 5 Sim 578. In *London Parochial Charities Trustees v A-G* [1955] 1 All ER 1, [1955] 1 WLR 42, the regulating scheme, which had statutory force, gave the Charity Commissioners power to make modifying schemes. Such provisions are not uncommon. As to the Charity Commissioners see paras 486–512 post.

3   *Re Shrewsbury Grammar School* (1849) 1 Mac & G 324.

4   *Re Shipwrecked Fishermen and Mariners' Royal Benevolent Society* [1959] Ch 220, [1958] 3 All ER 465.

5   *A-G v Wyggeston Hospital* (1849) 12 Beav 113. For the distinction between charities established by gifts,
    but with no regulations as to their exercise, in which cases the court has a general jurisdiction, and
    charities established and regulated by charter or Act of Parliament, in which cases the court only has
    jurisdiction in case of abuse: see Chitty's Prerogatives of the Crown (1820) 161; 3 Bl Com (14th Edn)
    426–427.

6   See the Charities Act 1993 s 15(3), Sch 4 (as amended); and para 176 ante.

7   See ibid s 17; and paras 184–185 ante.


**483. When the court will interfere.** The court does not interfere with the
execution of a charitable trust unless it appears that its interference will benefit the
charity[1]. However, the court has a general controlling power over all charitable
institutions[2]. Thus it can always enforce the performance of trusts and redress breaches
of trust, whether the trustee is an individual or an eleemosynary corporation[3], and
whether or not the corporation is subject to the control of a visitor[4]. On this ground it
exercises jurisdiction with respect to the dealings and conduct of governors who receive
and apply the revenues of charity property or manage charity estates[5].

Accordingly, the court may set aside a lease of charity property to one of the
governors, though there is no suggestion that the transaction was fraudulent[6], and
interfere when a school chapel is turned into a chapel of ease[7], and where the master of
a school is collusively appointed and takes his salary without fulfilling the duties of his
post[8]. On rare occasions it may be appropriate to appoint a receiver or receiver and
manager of a charity[9].

1   *A-G v Bosanquet* (1841) 11 LJCh 43.

2   See *A-G v Governors of Foundling Hospital* (1793) 2 Ves 42 at 49.

3   *Green v Rutherforth* (1750) 1 Ves Sen 462 at 475 per Lord Hardwicke LC; *Re Chertsey Market, ex p
    Walthew* (1819) 6 Price 261; *A-G v Earl of Clarendon* (1810) 17 Ves 491; *A-G v Earl of Mansfield* (1827)
    2 Russ 501; *A-G v Lubbock* (1837) Coop Pr Cas 15; *A-G v Dedham School* (1857) 23 Beav 350; *A-G v St
    Cross Hospital* (1853) 17 Beav 435; *Willis v Childe* (1851) 13 Beav 117; and see also *A-G v Bedford Corpn*
    (1754) 2 Ves Sen 505. As to eleemosynary corporations see para 213 ante.

4   *Daugars v Rivaz* (1860) 28 Beav 233; see also the cases cited in note 3 supra.

5   *Eden v Foster* (1726) 2 P Wms 325; *A-G v Lock* (1744) 3 Atk 164 at 165 per Lord Hardwicke LC; *A-G v
    Governors of Foundling Hospital* (1793) 2 Ves 42; *A-G v Middleton* (1751) 2 Ves Sen 327; *Ex p Kirkby
    Ravensworth Hospital* (1808) 15 Ves 305 at 314 per Lord Eldon LC; and note *Hynshaw v Morpeth Corpn*
    (1629) Duke 69; and *Sutton Colefield Case* (1635) Duke 68.

6   *A-G v Earl of Clarendon* (1810) 17 Ves 491.

7   *A-G v Earl of Mansfield* (1827) 2 Russ 501.

8   *A-G v Bedford Corpn* (1754) 2 Ves Sen 505.

9   *A-G v Schonfeld* [1980] 3 All ER 1, [1980] 1 WLR 1182. As to the statutory power of the Charity
    Commissioners to appoint a receiver and manager see para 504 post. As to the Charity Commissioners
    see paras 486–512 post. As to receivers generally see RECEIVERS.


**484. Jurisdiction not excluded by special remedies.** The fact that special remedies
are given by a statute to another authority or under a special procedure for the
infringement of a right does not exclude the ordinary jurisdiction of the court, unless that
jurisdiction is expressly excluded by the statute[1].

1   *R v Bishop of Ely* (1738) Andr 176; *Dr Walker's Case* (1736) Lee *temp* Hard 212 at 218 per Lord
    Hardwicke LC. See also para 217 note 2 ante.

**485. County court jurisdiction.** The county court has jurisdiction in proceedings for the execution of a charitable trust, or for a declaration that a charitable trust subsists, where the fund subject to the trust does not exceed the county court limit[1]. It is doubtful whether it will ever be called upon to exercise this jurisdiction.

1 See the County Courts Act 1984 s 23(b); and COUNTY COURTS. 'The county court limit' for the purposes of s 23 is £30,000: see s 147(1) (definition amended by the High Court and County Courts Jurisdiction Order 1991, SI 1991/724, art 2(8), Schedule); the County Courts Jurisdiction Order 1981, SI 1981/1123, art 2, Table (amended by SI 1991/724); and the Interpretation Act 1978 s 17(2)(b). Subject to the financial limit, the county court is included within the definition of 'the court' in the Charities Act 1993 s 97(1): see para 168 note 12 ante. It also has jurisdiction under the Open Spaces Act 1906 s 4 (as amended) to sanction the transfer of an open space within its district by charity trustees to the local authority: see OPEN SPACES AND ANCIENT MONUMENTS vol 34 (Reissue) para 305.

# (4) THE CHARITY COMMISSIONERS

## (i) Constitution and Functions

**486. Functions in general.** The Charity Commissioners for England and Wales are a statutory body regulated by the Charities Act 1993, with functions under that and other Acts[1]. The Commissioners have, without prejudice to their specific powers and duties under other enactments, the general function to promote the effective use of charitable resources by encouraging the development of better methods of administration, by giving charity trustees[2] information and advice on any matter affecting the charity[3] and by investigating and checking abuses[4]. It is their general object so to act in the case of any charity, unless it is a matter of altering its purposes, as best to promote and make effective the work of the charity in meeting the needs designated by its trusts[5]; but they do not themselves have power to act in the administration of a charity[6].

The Charity Commissioners have power to mediate informally in charity disputes, but not to arbitrate or to adjudicate[7].

1 Charities Act 1993 ss 1(1), 97(1). The Commissioners were first set up by the Charitable Trusts Act 1853 (repealed), and many of their powers under the Charities Act 1993 are similar to powers which they possessed under the Charitable Trusts Acts 1853 to 1939, which were repealed by the Charities Act 1960 s 48(2), Sch 7 (repealed). For transitional provisions arising out of the repeal see s 48(3), (4). As to the Commissioners' powers under other Acts see para 511 post.
2 For the meaning of 'charity trustees' see para 1 note 10 ante.
3 For the meaning of 'charity' see para 1 ante.
4 Charities Act 1993 s 1(3).
5 For the meaning of 'trusts' see para 210 note 5 ante.
6 Charities Act 1993 s 1(4).
7 See the *Report of the Charity Commissioners for England and Wales 1996* (HC Paper (1997–98) no 11) paras 151–152.

**487. Publications issued by the Charity Commission.** The Charity Commission produces publications, audio-cassettes and videos which provide information on a wide range of issues which affect charities, including the Commission's role, the duties of charity trustees and charity law. Such materials are available from the Commission[1]. The publications include leaflets which give information and guidance in relation to, for example, charity trustees[2], charity accounts[3], registration[4], investment[5] and fund raising[6]. The Commission also publishes the technical publications the *Statement of Recommended Practice for Accounting and Reporting by Charities* (the 'SORP')[7] and *SORP 2000: Examples Reports and Accounts* which set out the recommended best practice and guidance for charities in relation to the preparation of financial reports and accounts.

On behalf of the Charity Commission, The Stationery Office publishes: (1) the annual report the Charity Commissioners are under a duty to make to the Secretary of State[8] on the Commission's operations during the year[9]; and (2) the Decisions of the Charity Commissioners, which include decisions on points of law and individual cases, and guidance on matters of practice or policy in areas where there is no leaflet available on the subject.

1    For a list of the range of publications available from the Charity Commission see the Charity Commission website at www.charity-commission.gov.uk.
2    As to trustees see para 301 et seq ante.
3    As to the duties of charity trustees in relation to accounts see para 313 et seq ante.
4    As to the registration of charities see para 282 et seq ante.
5    As to the duties of charity trustees in relation to investment see para 359 et seq ante.
6    As to the control of charitable fund raising see para 406 et seq ante.
7    The SORP was issued in 1995 by the Charity Commissioners, and revised and reissued on 17 October 2000.
8    As to the Secretary of State see para 513 post.
9    The reports are published as House of Commons Parliamentary Papers, under the title *Report of the Charity Commissioners for England and Wales* for the appropriate year. See para 490 post.

**488. Constitution.** There must be a Chief Charity Commissioner and at least two other Commissioners[1], and two of them at least must be persons who have a seven year general qualification[2]. They are appointed by the Secretary of State and are deemed for all purposes to be employed in the civil service of the Crown[3]. There may be paid to each of the Commissioners such salary and allowances as the Secretary of State may, with the approval of the Treasury, determine[4].

The Chief Charity Commissioner may, with the approval of the Treasury as to number and conditions of service, appoint assistant Commissioners and other officers and such employees as he thinks necessary for the proper discharge of the functions of the Commissioners and of the official custodian[5]. There may be paid to officers and employees so appointed such salaries or remuneration as are determined by the Treasury[6].

The Commissioners may use an official seal for the authentication of documents, and their seal is to be officially and judicially noticed[7]. They have power to regulate their own procedure and, subject to any such regulations and to any directions of the Chief Commissioner, any one Commissioner or any assistant Commissioner may act for and in the name of the Commissioners[8]. When the Commissioners act as a board, the quorum is two if not more than four Commissioners hold office for the time being, and three if five Commissioners so hold office[9]. In the case of equality of votes, the Chief Commissioner, or in his absence, the Commissioner presiding, has a second or casting vote[10]. They may act notwithstanding any vacancy in their number[11].

Legal proceedings may be instituted by or against the Commissioners by the name of the Charity Commissioners for England and Wales[12]. Such proceedings do not abate and nor are they affected by any change in the persons who are the Commissioners[13].

1   Charities Act 1993 s 1(2), Sch 1 para 1(1). If at any time it appears to the Secretary of State that there should be more than three Commissioners, he may, with the approval of the Treasury, appoint not more than two additional Commissioners: Sch 1 para 1(5). At present there are five Commissioners. As to the Secretary of State see para 513 post. As to the Treasury see CONSTITUTIONAL LAW AND HUMAN RIGHTS vol 8(2) (Reissue) paras 512–517.

2   Ibid Sch 1 para 1(2). The seven year general qualification is a qualification within the meaning of the Courts and Legal Services Act 1990 s 71 (as amended) (see COURTS; SOLICITORS vol 44(1) (Reissue) para 91): Charities Act 1993 Sch 1 para 1(2). A person has a general qualification if he has a right of audience in relation to any class of proceedings in any part of the Supreme Court, or all proceedings in county courts or magistrates' courts: Courts and Legal Services Act 1990 s 71(3)(c).

3   Charities Act 1993 Sch 1 para 1(3). Their specific statutory functions (see para 486 ante) distinguish them from ordinary civil servants, but it follows from their deemed status that, for example, they may not be Members of Parliament: see the House of Commons Disqualification Act 1975 s 1(1)(b); and PARLIAMENT vol 34 (Reissue) para 608.

4   Charities Act 1993 Sch 1 para 1(4).

5   Ibid Sch 1 para 2(1). As to the official custodian for charities see para 273 et seq ante.

6   Ibid Sch 1 para 2(2).

7   Ibid Sch 1 para 3(1). Their orders and regulations may be proved in legal proceedings by means of purportedly certified copies without proof of the handwriting or official position of the certifying officer: see the Documentary Evidence Act 1868 s 2 (as amended), Schedule (as amended); Charities Act 1993 Sch 1 para 3(2); and EVIDENCE. As to evidence of orders, certificates and other documents issued by the Commissioners see s 93(3); and para 528 post.

8   Ibid Sch 1 para 3(3). In particular, a Commissioner or assistant Commissioner may act for and in the name of the Commissioners in relation to functions of the Commissioners under s 8 (see paras 497–498 post), s 18 (see para 496 et seq post), s 19 (see para 504 post), s 63 (see para 223 an e), including functions under ss 8, 18, 19 as applied by s 80(1): Sch 1 para 3(6). The Commissioners will very rarely hear counsel on the settling of a scheme by them: *Benthall v Earl of Kilmorey* (1884) Tudor on Charities (5th Edn, 1929) p 582; but see *Re Hackney Charities, ex p Nicholls* (1864) 34 LJCh 169 at 175 per Romilly MR; on appeal (1865) 4 De GJ & Sm 588.

9   Charities Act 1993 Sch 1 para 3(4). In either case, at least one of the Commissioners must be a person having such a seven year general qualification mentioned in Sch 1 para 1(2) (see the text and note 2 supra): Sch 1 para 3(4)(a), (b).

10  Ibid Sch 1 para 3(4).

11  Ibid Sch 1 para 3(5).

12  Ibid Sch 1 para 4.

13  Ibid Sch 1 para 4.

**489. Jurisdiction.** Any institution which is a charity within the statutory definition[1] is subject to the jurisdiction of the Charity Commissioners, but many of the specific powers given to the Commissioners are not exercisable in relation to exempt charities[2]. They may direct that institutions[3] established for special charitable purposes[4] of or in connection with a charity be treated for all or any of the purposes of the Charities Act 1993 as part of that charity or as forming a distinct charity[5]. They may also direct that for all or any of the purposes of the Charities Act 1993 two or more charities having the same charity trustees[6] are to be treated as a single charity[7].

1   See the Charities Act 1993 s 96(1), (2) (s 96(2) as amended); and paras 1, 187 ante. As to territorial limitations on the operation of the Charities Act 1993 (which does not generally extend to Scotland or Northern Ireland) see s 100(2)–(5); and cf *Re Duncan, Re Taylor's Trusts* (1867) 2 Ch App 356; *Construction Industry Training Board v A-G* [1973] Ch 173, [1972] 2 All ER 1339, CA.

2   See eg the Charities Act 1993 s 3(5)(a) (see para 284 ante), s 8(1) (see para 497 post), s 9(4) (see para 500 post), s 33(2) (see para 521 post), s 38(7) (see para 346 ante). As to exempt charities see para 293 ante.
3   For the meaning of 'institution' see para 1 ante.
4   For the meaning of 'charitable purposes' see para 1 ante.
5   Charities Act 1993 s 96(5).
6   For the meaning of 'charity trustees' see para 1 note 10 ante.
7   Charities Act 1993 s 96(6) (added by Charities (Amendment) Act 1995 s 1).

**490. Duty to report.** The Charity Commissioners are required, as soon as possible after the end of every year, to report on their operations during the year to the Secretary of State[1], who must lay a copy of the report before each House of Parliament[2]. The Charity Commission is subject to investigation by the Parliamentary Commissioner for Administration[3].

1   As to the Secretary of State see para 513 post.
2   Charities Act 1993 s 1(5). The reports are published as House of Commons Parliamentary Papers, under the titles *Report of the Charity Commissioners for England and Wales* for the appropriate year.
3   See the Parliamentary Commissioner Act 1967 s 4(1), Sch 2 (as substituted and amended); and ADMINISTRATIVE LAW vol 1(1) (2001 Reissue) paras 41, 43.

**491. Specific functions under the Charities Act 1993.** The Charity Commissioners have a number of specific functions and powers under the Charities Act 1993, which are dealt with elsewhere in this title:

(1)   the duty to maintain the central register of charities and duties in relation to registration[1];

(2)   the power to exchange information with regard to institutions treated as charitable[2];

(3)   the jurisdiction to make schemes, to appoint and remove trustees and officers and to make vesting orders in relation to charities[3];

(4)   the power to make common investment schemes or common deposit funds[4];

(5)   the power to authorise beneficial transactions[5];

(6)   the power to give advice to charity trustees[6];

(7)   the power to provide for the enrolment and preservation of documents belonging to charities[7];

(8)   the power to order the taxation of a solicitor's bill of costs for work done for a charity[8];

(9)   powers to take legal proceedings and compromise claims[9];

(10)   the requirement of their consent to the taking of charity proceedings[10];

(11)   the requirement of their consent to the expenditure of charity money on promoting legislation in Parliament[11];

(12)   the requirement of their consent to certain dispositions of charity property[12].

They also have various powers to act for the protection of charities by inquiry, audit and calling for documents, and by making orders in consequence of their investigations[13].

1   See the Charities Act 1993 s 3 (as amended); and para 283 ante.
2   See ibid s 10; and para 291 ante.
3   See ibid s 16; and paras 180, 182–183, 271 ante.
4   See ibid ss 24, 25; and paras 366–367 ante.
5   See ibid s 26; and paras 330–333 ante.
6   See ibid s 29; and paras 335–336 ante.
7   See ibid s 30; and paras 340–341 ante.
8   See ibid s 31; and para 575 post.
9   See ibid s 32; and para 496 post.
10  See ibid s 33; and para 521 post.
11  See ibid s 17(7); and para 301 ante.
12  See ibid s 36; and para 343 ante.
13  See ibid ss 8, 9, 18, 69; and paras 496–509 post. As to the exclusion of actions in negligence see *Mills v Winchester Diocesan Board of Finance* [1989] Ch 428, [1989] 2 All ER 317; and para 335 ante.

**492. Ancillary provisions as to Charity Commissioners' orders.** The Charities Act 1993 contains various ancillary provisions in relation to any order made under that Act and certain orders under the Charities Act 1992[1] by the Charity Commissioners[2]. Thus, an order made by the Commissioners may include such incidental or supplementary provisions as the Commissioners think expedient for carrying into effect the objects of the order, and where the Commissioners exercise any jurisdiction to make such an order on an application or reference to them, they may insert any such provisions in the order notwithstanding that the application or reference does not propose their insertion[3]. Where the Commissioners make an order under the Charities Act 1993, then they may themselves give such public notice as they think fit of the making or contents of the order, or may require it to be given by any person on whose application the order is made or by any charity[4] affected by the order[5].

Except for the purposes of discharging the order[6], or for the purposes of an appeal under the relevant Act, an order made by the Commissioners under the Charities Act 1993 is deemed to have been duly and formally made and is not to be called in question on the ground only of irregularity or informality, and, subject to any further order, has effect according to its tenor[7].

Any direction[8] given by the Commissioners[9] under any provision contained in the Charities Act 1993 must be given in writing, and may be varied or revoked by a further direction given under that provision[10].

At any time within 12 months of making an order under the Charities Act 1993, the Commissioners, if they are satisfied that the order was made by mistake or on misrepresentation or otherwise than in conformity with Charities Act 1993, may with or without any application or reference to them discharge the order in whole or in part, and subject or not to any savings or other transitional provisions[11].

1   Ie those under the Charities Act 1992 s 72: see s 72(5) (as substituted); and para 439 ante. The provisions of the Charities Act 1993 s 89(1), (2), (4) (see the text and notes 3–7 infra) apply to an order made by the Charity Commissioners under the Charities Act 1992 as they apply to an order made by them under the Charities Act 1993: see the Charities Act 1992 s 72(5) (as substituted); and para 439 ante.
2   The provisions of the Charities Act 1993 s 89 (see the text and notes 3–7 infra) also apply to orders under:
    (1) the Places of Worship Registration Act 1855 s 9(1)(b) (see s 9(2) (as added); and ECCLESIASTICAL LAW vol 14 para 1410);
    (2) the Open Spaces Act 1906 s 4 (see s 4(4) (as added); and OPEN SPACES AND ANCIENT MONUMENTS vol 34 (Reissue) para 305); and
    (3) the New Parishes Measure 1943 s 14(1)(b) (see s 14(4) (as added); and ECCLESIASTICAL LAW vol 14 para 1410)).

3    Charities Act 1993 s 89(1).
4    For the meaning of 'charity' see para 1 ante.
5    Charities Act 1993 s 89(2). This is without prejudice to the requirements of the Charities Act 1993 in a
     case where the order is subject to appeal: s 89(2). For such cases of appeal see s 16(11)–(14) (see para 190
     ante), s 18(8)–(10) (see para 509 post), and s 20(5) (see para 181 ante).
6    Ie under ibid s 89(3): see the text and note 11 infra.
7    Ibid s 89(4).
8    Except a direction contained in an order made by the Commissioners under ibid s 87(1) (see para 494
     post): s 90(4).
9    For these purposes, the reference to the Commissioners includes, in relation to a direction under ibid
     s 8(3) (see para 497 post), a reference to a person conducting an inquiry under that provision: s 90(3).
10   Ibid s 90(1). Section 88 (see para 494 post) (enforcement of orders of the Commissioners) and s 89(1),
     (2) and (4) (see the text and notes 3–7 supra) apply to any such directions as they apply to an order of
     the Commissioners: s 90(2).
11   Ibid s 89(3). This does not apply to an order under s 61 (see para 238 ante): see s 89(3).

**493.  Service of orders and directions.** Any order or direction made or given by the
Charity Commissioners[1] under the Charities Act 1993 may be served on a person (other
than a body corporate) either by delivering it to that person, or by leaving it at his last
known address in the United Kingdom[2], or by sending it by post to him at that address[3].
In the case of a body corporate it may be served by delivering it or sending it by post
either to the registered or principal office of the body in the United Kingdom, or, if it
has no such office in the United Kingdom, to any place in the United Kingdom where
it carries on business or conducts its activities[4]. Any such order or direction may also be
served on a person, including a body corporate, by sending it by post to that person at
an address notified by that person to the Commissioners for that purpose[5].

1    For these purposes, the reference to the Commissioners includes, in relation to a direction under the
     Charities Act 1993 s 8(3) (see para 497 post), a reference to a person conducting an inquiry under that
     provision: s 91(5).
2    For the meaning of 'United Kingdom' see para 180 note 16 ante.
3    Charities Act 1993 s 91(1), (2). There are corresponding provisions in relation to any order or direction
     made or given by the Commissioners under the Charities Act 1992 Pt II (ss 58–64) (as amended) or any
     notice required to be served under Pt III (ss 65–74) (as amended) (not yet in force): see s 76(1)–(4) (as
     amended); and para 425 ante.
4    Charities Act 1993 s 91(3).
5    Ibid s 91(4).

**494.  Enforcement of Charity Commissioners' orders.** A person guilty of
disobedience to orders of the Charity Commissioners calling for information or
documents[1], or in connection with the dissolution of an incorporated body[2], or relating
to a person acting as a charity trustee or trustee for a charity while disqualified[3], or for
the protection of certain Scottish charities[4], or orders requiring payment or transfer of
property or payment to be called for or made[5], or orders requiring a default to be made
good[6], may be dealt with on the application of the Commissioners to the High Court as
for disobedience to an order of the High Court[7].
    If a person fails to comply with any requirement imposed by or under the Charities
Act 1993, the Commissioners may by order give him such directions as they consider
appropriate for securing that the default is made good[8], and disobedience to such an order
likewise renders him liable to be dealt with as for disobedience to an order of the High
Court[9]. These provisions[10] do not apply, however, to any such requirement imposed by

or under the Charities Act 1993 if (1) the requirement is one imposed by an order of the Commissioners falling within any of the above provisions[11], or is imposed by a direction of the Commissioners to which those provisions apply[12]; or (2) if a person who fails to comply with, or is persistently in default in relation to, the requirement is liable to any criminal penalty[13].

1 Ie under the Charities Act 1993 s 9(1) (see para 500 post) or s 44(2) (see para 314 ante).
2 Ie under ibid s 61: see para 238 ante.
3 Ie under ibid s 73: see para 250 ante. For the meaning of 'charity trustees' see para 1 note 10 ante. For the meaning of 'charity' see para 1 ante.
4 Ie under ibid s 80 (as amended).
5 Ie under ibid s 16 or s 18: see paras 266 ante, 507–508 post.
6 See, eg, ibid s 69(4); and para 502 post.
7 Ibid s 88. The application is made to a single judge of the Chancery Division: see CPR Sch 1 RSC Ord 52 r 1(4); CPR Sch 1 RSC Ord 108 r 4. As to the enforcement of High Court orders see generally JUDGMENTS AND ORDERS. As to the CPR see para 522 post.
8 Charities Act 1993 s 87(1).
9 See ibid s 88(c).
10 Ie ibid s 87(1): see the text and note 8 supra.
11 Ie ibid s 88: see the text and notes 1–7 supra.
12 Ie under ibid s 90(2): see para 492 ante.
13 Ibid s 87(2).

**495. Fees and other amounts payable to Charity Commissioners.** The Secretary of State[1] may by regulations[2] require the payment to the Charity Commissioners of such fees as may be prescribed by the regulations in respect of the discharge by the Commissioners of such functions under the enactments relating to charities as may be so prescribed, and the inspection of the register of charities[3] or of other material kept by them under those enactments, or the furnishing of copies of or extracts from documents[4] so kept[5]. Such regulations may confer, or provide for the conferring of, exemptions from liability to pay a prescribed fee, or provide for the remission or refunding of a prescribed fee in prescribed circumstances[6]. The Commissioners may also impose charges of such amounts as they consider reasonable in respect of the supply of any publications produced by them[7].

Any fees and other payments received by the Commissioners under the above provisions must be paid into the Consolidated Fund[8].

1 As to the Secretary of State see para 513 post.
2 At the date at which this volume states the law no such regulations had been made under the Charities Act 1993 s 85 but, by virtue of the Interpretation Act 1978 s 17(2)(b), the Charity Commissioners' Fees (Copies and Extracts) Regulations 1992, SI 1992/2986, have effect as if made under it. Any regulations under the Charities Act 1993 s 85 which require the payment of a fee in respect of any matter for which no fee was previously payable must not be made unless a draft of the regulations has been laid before and approved by a resolution of each House of Parliament: s 85(3). Such regulations must be made by statutory instrument: s 86(1)(a). Regulations to which s 85(3) applies are not subject to annulment in pursuance of a resolution of either House of Parliament: see s 86(1)(b), (2)(c); and para 517 post. As to the making of regulations generally see s 86 (as amended); and para 517 post.
3 As to the register of charities see para 282 ante.
4 For the meaning of 'document' see para 236 note 2 ante.
5 Charities Act 1993 s 85(1).
6 Ibid s 85(2).
7 Ibid s 85(4). As to publications issued by the Charity Commission see para 487 ante.

8    Ibid s 85(5). As to the Consolidated Fund see CONSTITUTIONAL LAW AND HUMAN RIGHTS vol 8(2) (Reissue) para 711 et seq; PARLIAMENT vol 34 (Reissue) paras 952–955.

### (ii) Power to act for Protection of Charities

**496. Power of Charity Commissioners to bring proceedings with respect to charities.** Except that they cannot present a petition for the winding up of a charitable company[1], the Charity Commissioners may exercise the same powers with respect to the taking of legal proceedings with reference to charities[2] or the property or affairs of charities, or the compromise of claims with a view to avoiding or ending such proceedings, as are exercisable by the Attorney General acting ex officio[3]. The practice and procedure to be followed in relation to any such proceedings are in all respects, and in particular as regards costs, the same as if they were proceedings taken by the Attorney General acting ex officio[4]. No rule of law or practice is to be taken to require the Attorney General to be a party to any such proceedings[5]. Although these powers are exercisable by the Commissioners of their own motion, they are exercisable only with the agreement of the Attorney General on each occasion[6].

1    Ie under the Charities Act 1993 s 63(1): see para 223 ante.
2    For the meaning of 'charity' see para 1 ante.
3    Charities Act 1993 s 32(1), (2). As to the role of the Attorney General in legal proceedings see paras 516, 523, 531 et seq post.
4    Ibid s 32(3).
5    Ibid s 32(4).
6    Ibid s 32(5).

**497. Power to institute inquiries.** The Charity Commissioners may from time to time institute inquiries with regard to charities[1] or a particular charity or class of charities, either generally or for particular purposes[2], although no such inquiry may extend to any exempt charity[3].

For the purposes of any such inquiry the Commissioners, or a person appointed by them to conduct it, may direct any person[4]:

(1)    to furnish accounts and statements in writing with respect to any matter in question at the inquiry, being a matter on which he has or can reasonably obtain information, or to return answers in writing to any questions or inquiries addressed to him on any such matter, and to verify any such accounts, statements or answers by statutory declaration[5];

(2)    to furnish copies of documents[6] in his custody or under his control which relate to any matter in question at the inquiry, and to verify the same by statutory declaration[7]; and

(3)    also to attend and give evidence or produce any such documents[8].

Where an inquiry has been held under these provisions, the Commissioners may either cause the report of the person conducting the inquiry or such other statement of the results of the inquiry as they think fit to be printed and published, or publish any such report or statement in some other way which is calculated in their opinion to bring it to the attention of persons who might wish to make representations about the action to be taken[9].

1 For the meaning of 'charity' see para 1 ante.
2 As to determining the matters in respect of which the power conferred by the Charities Act 1993 s 8 may be exercised see s 28(9); and para 510 post.

    The Commissioners may either conduct such an inquiry themselves or appoint a person to conduct it and make a report to them: s 8(2). This power and the related powers under s 69 (see para 502 post) and s 18 (see para 503 post) have been used in a few cases: see *Report of the Charity Commissioners for England and Wales for 1964* (HC Paper (1965–66) no 8) paras 53–61; *Report of the Charity Commissioners for England and Wales for 1970* (HC Paper (1970–71) no 409) paras 50–52; *Report of the Charity Commissioners for England and Wales for 1971* (HC Paper (1971–72) no 269) paras 90–96; *Report of the Charity Commissioners for England and Wales for 1972* (HC Paper (1972–73) no 259) para 80; *Report of the Charity Commissioners for England and Wales for 1979* (HC Paper (1979–80) no 608) paras 24–36; and *Report of the Charity Commissioners for England and Wales for 1980* (HC Paper (1980–81) no 332) para 31.
3 Charities Act 1993 s 8(1). As to exempt charities see para 293 ante. For the purposes of any such inquiry evidence may be taken on oath, and the person conducting the inquiry may for that purpose administer oaths, or may instead of administering an oath require the person examined to make and subscribe a declaration of the truth of the matters about which he is examined: s 8(4). See generally EVIDENCE.
4 Ibid s 8(3). As to directions of the Commissioners generally see s 90; and para 492 ante. As to the service of directions see s 91; and para 493 ante.
5 Ibid s 8(3)(a).
6 For the meaning of 'document' see para 236 note 2 ante.
7 Charities Act 1993 s 8(3)(b).
8 Ibid s 8(3)(c). A person may not be required in obedience to a direction under s 8(3)(c) to go more than ten miles from his place of residence unless the expenses of his attendance are paid to him: see s 8(5); and para 498 post.
9 Ibid s 8(6).

## 498. Expenses in relation to inquiries.

The Charity Commissioners may pay to any person the necessary expenses of his attendance to give evidence or produce documents for the purpose of an inquiry[1]. No person may be required, in obedience to a direction to attend and give evidence or produce documents[2], to travel more than ten miles from his residence unless those expenses are paid or tendered to him[3].

    The council of a county or district, the Common Council of the City of London[4] and the council of a London borough[5] may contribute to the expenses of the Commissioners in connection with inquiries into local charities[6] in the council's area[7].

1 Charities Act 1993 s 8(5). As to inquiries see para 497 ante.
2 Ie in obedience to a direction under ibid s 8(3)(c): see para 497 ante.
3 Ibid s 8(5).
4 As to the Common Council of the City of London see LONDON GOVERNMENT.
5 As to areas and authorities see LOCAL GOVERNMENT.
6 For the meaning of 'local charity' see para 180 note 10 ante.
7 Charities Act 1993 s 8(7).

## 499. Offences in connection with inquiries.

Persons wilfully giving false evidence on oath before an inquiry[1] are guilty of perjury[2].

    Any person who knowingly or recklessly provides the Charity Commissioners[3] with information which is false or misleading in a material particular is guilty of an offence[4] if the information was provided in purported compliance with a requirement imposed by or under the Charities Act 1993, or in other circumstances in which the person providing the information intended, or could reasonably be expected to have known, that it would be used by the Commissioners for the purpose of discharging their functions under that Act[5]. Any person who wilfully alters, suppresses, conceals or destroys any document which he is or is liable to be required, by or under the Charities Act 1993, to produce to the Commissioners is likewise guilty of an offence[6]. No proceedings may be instituted for either of the above offences except by or with the consent of the Director of Public Prosecutions[7].

Persons who disobey orders calling for information or documents[8] may be dealt with as for disobedience to an order of the High Court[9].

1   As to inquiries see para 497 ante.
2   See the Perjury Act 1911 s 1 (as amended); and CRIMINAL LAW, EVIDENCE AND PROCEDURE vol 11(1) (Reissue) para 299 et seq; EVIDENCE.
3   For these purposes, references to the Commissioners include references to a person conducting an inquiry under the Charities Act 1993 s 8 (see para 497 ante): s 11(4).
4   Any person guilty of an offence under ibid s 11 is liable on summary conviction to a fine not exceeding the statutory maximum, and on conviction on indictment to a term of imprisonment not exceeding two years or to a fine, or both: s 11(3). As to the statutory maximum see para 226 note 5 ante. As to offences by bodies corporate see s 95; and para 515 post.
5   Ibid s 11(1).
6   Ibid s 11(2). The offender is liable to the punishment set out in note 4 supra.
7   Ibid s 94(1), (2)(b). As to the Director of Public Prosecutions see CRIMINAL LAW, EVIDENCE AND PROCEDURE vol 11(1) Reissue para 637 et seq.
8   Ie under ibid s 9(1): see para 500 post.
9   See ibid s 88; and para 494 ante.

**500.  Power to call for documents.** The Charity Commissioners may by order[1]:

(1)   require any person to furnish them with any information in his possession which relates to any charity[2] and is relevant to the discharge of their functions or of the functions of the official custodian for charities[3];

(2)   require any person who has in his custody or under his control any document[4] which relates to any charity and is relevant to the discharge of their functions or of the functions of the official custodian for charities: (a) to furnish them with a copy of, or extract from, the document; or (b) unless the document forms port of the records or other documents of a court or of a public or local authority, to transmit the document itself to them for their inspection[5].

The Commissioners may without payment keep any such copies or extracts[6]. Where an original document transmitted to them for inspection relates only to one or more charities and is not held by a person entitled as trustee or otherwise to the custody of it, they may keep it or deliver it to charity trustees[7] or other persons who are so entitled[8].

No person properly having the custody of documents relating only to an exempt charity[9] may be required to transmit to the Commissioners any of those documents or to furnish any copy of, or extracts from, any of them[10].

1   Charities Act 1993 s 9(1). A person guilty of disobedience to an order of the Commissioners under s 9(1) may on the application of the Commissioners to the High Court be dealt with as for disobedience to an order of the High Court: s 88(a).
2   For the meaning of 'charity' see para 1 ante.
3   Charities Act 1993 s 9(1)(a). As to the official custodian for charities see para 273 et seq ante.
4   For the meaning of 'document' see para 236 note 2 ante.

5   Charities Act 1993 s 9(1)(b). As to the power to inspect records see para 501 post. As to determining the
    matters in respect of which the power conferred by the Charities Act 1993 s 9 may be exercised see
    s 28(9); and para 510 post.
6   Ibid s 9(3).
7   For the meaning of 'charity trustees' see para 1 note 10 ante.
8   Charities Act 1993 s 9(3).
9   As to exempt charities see para 293 ante.
10  Charities Act 1993 s 9(4).

**501. Power to inspect records.** Any officer of the Charity Commissioners, if so
authorised by them, is entitled without payment to inspect and take copies of or extracts
from the records or other documents[1] of any court, public registry or office of records,
for any purpose connected with the discharge of the functions of the Commissioners or
of the official custodian for charities[2]. These rights, in relation to information recorded
otherwise than in legible form, include the right to require the information to be made
available in legible form for inspection or for a copy or extract to be made of or from it[3].

1   For the meaning of 'document' see para 236 note 2 ante.
2   Charities Act 1993 s 9(2). As to the official custodian for charities see para 273 et seq ante.
3   Ibid s 9(5).

**502. Investigation and audit of charity accounts.** In the case of a charity[1] which
is a company[2] the Charity Commissioners may by order require that the condition and
accounts of the charity for such period as they think fit be investigated and audited by an
auditor appointed by them[3]. The Commissioners must pay the expenses of the audit,
including the remuneration of the auditor[4].

The auditor has a right of access to all books, accounts and documents[5] relating to the
charity which are in the possession or control of the charity trustees[6] or to which they
have access[7]. The auditor is entitled to require from any past or present charity trustee,
and from any past or present officer or employee of the charity, such information and
explanation as he thinks necessary for the performance of his duties[8]. If a person fails to
afford to the auditor any such facilities, the Commissioners may by order give to that
person or to charity trustees for the time being directions as the Commissioners think
appropriate for securing that the default is made good[9].

At the conclusion or during the progress of the audit, the auditor must make such
reports to the Commissioners about the audit or the charity's accounts or affairs as he
thinks the case requires, and must send a copy of any such report to the charity trustees[10].

1   For the meaning of 'charity' see para 1 ante.
2   For the meaning of 'company' see para 216 ante.
3   Charities Act 1993 s 69(1). The auditor must be a person eligible for appointment as a company auditor
    under the Companies Act 1989 s 25 (see COMPANIES vol 7(2) (1996 Reissue) para 956): Charities Act
    1993 s 69(1). As to the use made of this power see para 497 note 2 ante.
4   Ibid s 69(3).
5   For the meaning of 'document' see para 236 note 2 ante.
6   For the meaning of 'charity trustees' see para 1 note 10 ante.
7   Charities Act 1993 s 69(2)(a).
8   Ibid s 69(2)(b).
9   Ibid s 69(4). As to the enforcement of such an order see para 497 ante.
10  Ibid s 69(2)(c).

**503. Power to protect charities from mismanagement.** Where, at any time after they have instituted an inquiry[1], the Charity Commissioners are satisfied:

(1)    that there is or has been any misconduct or mismanagement[2] in the administration of the charity[3]; or

(2)    that it is necessary or desirable to act for the purpose of protecting the property of the charity or securing a proper application for the purposes of the charity of that property or of property coming to the charity[4];

they may, except in the case of an exempt charity[5], of their own motion do one or more of the following things, namely[6]:

(a)    by order suspend any trustee, charity trustee, officer, agent or employee of the charity from the exercise of his office or employment pending consideration being given to his removal, whether under these provisions or otherwise[7];

(b)    by order appoint such number of additional charity trustees as they consider necessary for the proper administration of the charity[8];

(c)    by order vest any property held by or in trust for the charity in the official custodian for charities, or require the persons in whom any such property is vested to transfer it to him, or appoint any person to transfer any such property to him[9];

(d)    order any person who holds any property on behalf of the charity, or of any trustee for it, not to part with the property without the approval of the Commissioners[10];

(e)    order any debtor of the charity not to make any payment in or towards the discharge of his liability to the charity without the approval of the Commissioners[11];

(f)    by order restrict, notwithstanding anything in the trusts of the charity, the transactions which may be entered into, or the nature or amount of the payments which may be made, in the administration of the charity without the approval of the Commissioners[12];

(g)    by order appoint a receiver and manager in respect of the property and affairs of the charity[13].

The Commissioners must, at such intervals as they think fit, review any order made by them under these provisions, other than one appointing additional charity trustees[14], and if it appears to them that it would be appropriate to discharge the order in whole or in part, they must so discharge it, whether subject to any savings or other transitional provisions or not[15].

Further, if both heads (1) and (2) above are satisfied, the Commissioners may, except in the case of an exempt charity[16], of their own motion do either or both of the following things[17]:

(i)    by order remove any trustee, charity trustee, officer, agent or employee of the charity who has been responsible for or privy to the misconduct or mismanagement or has by his conduct contributed to it or facilitated it[18];

(ii)    by order establish a scheme for the administration of the charity[19].

For these purposes, misconduct or mismanagement extends, notwithstanding anything in the trusts[20] of the charity, to the employment for the remuneration or reward of persons acting in the affairs of the charity, or for other administrative purposes, of sums which are excessive in relation to the property which is likely to be applied or applicable for the purposes of the charity[21].

1   Ie under the Charities Act 1993 s 8: see para 497–498 ante.

2   For the meaning of 'misconduct or mismanagement' see the text to notes 20–21 infra.

3   Charities Act 1993 s 18(1)(a). For the meaning of 'charity' see para 1 ante.

4   Ibid s 18(1)(b).

5   The Charities Act 1993 s 18 does not apply to an exempt charity: s 18(16). As to exempt charities see para 293 ante.

6   Ibid s 18(1). A person guilty of disobedience to an order of the Commissioners under the Charities Act 1993 s 18 requiring a transfer of property or payment to be called for or made, may on the application of the Commissioners to the High Court be dealt with as for disobedience to an order of the High Court: see s 88; and para 494 post.

    The powers of the Commissioners under s 18 to remove or appoint charity trustees of their own motion includes power to make any such order with respect to the vesting in or transfer to the charity trustees of any property as the Commissioners could make on the removal or appointment of a charity trustee by them under s 16 (see paras 180, 182–183, 271 ante, 509 post): s 18(6). For the meaning of 'charity trustees' see para 1 note 10 ante.

7   Ibid s 18(1)(i). See *Jones v A-G* [1974] Ch 148, [1973] 3 All ER 518, CA; further proceedings (1976) Times, 10 November. The power of the Commissioners to make an order under the Charities Act 1993 s 18(1)(i) is not exercisable so as to suspend any person from the exercise of his office or employment for a period of more than 12 months: s 18(11). However, without prejudice to the generality of s 89(1) (see para 492 ante), any such order made in the case of any person may make provision as respects the period of his suspension for matters arising out of it, and in particular for enabling any person to execute any instrument in his name or otherwise act for him and, in the case of a charity trustee, for adjusting any rules governing the proceedings of the charity trustees to take account of the reduction in the number capable of acting: s 18(11).

8   Ibid s 18(1)(ii).

9   Ibid s 18(1)(iii). As to the official custodian for charities see para 273 et seq ante.

10   Ibid s 18(1)(iv). Contravention of an order under s 18(1)(iv), (v) or (vi) (see the text and notes 11–12 infra) is an offence punishable on summary conviction with a fine not exceeding level 5 on the standard scale: s 18(14). As to the standard scale see para 286 note 11 ante. However, proceedings for such an offence may only be instituted by or with the consent of the Director of Public Prosecutions: s 94(1), (2)(c). As to the Director of Public Prosecutions see CRIMINAL LAW, EVIDENCE AND PROCEDURE vol 11(1) (Reissue) para 637 et seq. Section 18(14) is not to be taken to preclude the bringing of proceedings for breach of trust against any charity trustee or trustee for a charity in respect of any such contravention of an order under s 18(1)(iv) or (vi), whether the proceedings in respect of the contravention are brought against him under s 18(14) or not: s 18(15). The amendments made by the Charities Act 1992 s 8(9) to the Charities Act 1960 s 20 (both repealed; now incorporated in the Charities Act 1993 s 18) have no effect for the purposes of any offence alleged to have been committed before 1 November 1992: see the Charities Act 1992 (Commencement No 1 and Transitional Provisions) Order 1992, SI 1992/1900, art 3(2). As to offences by bodies corporate see para 515 post.

11   Charities Act 1993 s 18(1)(v). Contravention of such an order is an offence: see s 18(14); and note 10 supra.

12   Ibid s 18(1)(vi). Contravention of such an order is an offence: see s 18(14); and note 10 supra.

13   Ibid s 18(1)(vii). The appointment must be made in accordance with s 19 (see para 504 post): see s 18(1)(vii).

14   Ie under ibid s 18(1)(ii): see the text and note 8 supra.

15   Ibid s 18(13).

16   See note 5 supra.

17   Charities Act 1993 s 18(2).

18   Ibid s 18(2)(i). See *Scargill v Charity Commissioners* (4 September 1998, unreported), ChD, noted in (1998) 12 TLI 254.

19   Ibid s 18(2)(ii).

20   For the meaning of 'trusts' see para 210 note 5 ante.

21   Charities Act 1993 s 18(3).

**504. Power to appoint a receiver and manager for a charity.**  The Charity Commissioners may appoint[1] to be receiver and manager in respect of the property and affairs of a charity[2] such person, other than an officer or employee of theirs, as they think fit[3]. The order appointing him may make provision with respect to the functions to be discharged by the receiver and manager appointed by the order, and those functions are to be discharged by him under the supervision of the Commissioners[4]. In connection with the discharge of those functions any such order may provide for the receiver and manager appointed by the order to have such powers and duties of the charity trustees[5] of the charity concerned, whether arising under the Charities Act 1993 or otherwise, as are specified in the order, and for such powers or duties to be performed by the receiver and manager to the exclusion of the charity trustees[6]. The Commissioners have the same power to advise a receiver and manager as they have to advise charity trustees[7], and they may apply to the High Court for directions in relation to any particular matter arising in connection with the functions of the receiver and manager[8]. The High Court may on such an application give such directions, or make such orders declaring the rights of any persons, whether before the court or not, as it thinks just, and the costs of any such application must be paid by the charity concerned[9].

Regulations made by the Secretary of State[10] may make provision with respect to the appointment and removal of persons appointed in accordance with these provisions, the remuneration of such persons out of the income of the charities concerned and the making of reports to the Commissioners by such persons[11]. Such regulations may, in particular, authorise the Commissioners to require security for the due discharge of his functions to be given by a person so appointed, to determine the amount of such a person's remuneration and to disallow any amount of remuneration in such circumstances as are prescribed by the regulations[12].

1   Ie under the Charities Act 1993 s 18(1)(vii): see para 503 ante.
2   For the meaning of 'charity' see para 1 ante.
3   Charities Act 1993 s 19(1).
4   Ibid s 19(2). This provision is expressed to be subject to s 89(1) (inclusion of incidental or supplemental provisions in the Commissioners' orders) (see para 492 ante): see s 19(2).
5   For the meaning of 'charity trustees' see para 1 note 10 ante.
6   Charities Act 1993 s 19(3).
7   Ie under ibid s 29: see paras 335–336 ante.
8   Ibid s 19(4).
9   Ibid s 19(5).
10  As to the Secretary of State see para 513 post.
11  Charities Act 1993 s 19(6). At the date at which this volume states the law no such regulations had been made under s 19, but by virtue of the Interpretation Act 1978 s 17(2)(b), the Charities (Receiver and Manager) Regulations 1992, SI 1992/2355, have effect as if made under it: see paras 505–506 post. As to the making of regulations generally see the Charities Act 1993 s 86 (as amended); and para 517 post.
12  Ibid s 19(7); and see paras 505–506 post.

**505. Appointment, remuneration and removal of the receiver and manager.** The Charity Commissioners[1] are authorised to require the person appointed by order to be receiver and manager in respect of the property and affairs of the charity (the 'appointed person')[2] to give security to them for the due discharge of his functions within such time and in such form as they may specify[3]. They are also authorised to determine the amount of an appointed person's remuneration[4], which is payable out of the income of the relevant charity[5].

Where it appears to the Charity Commissioners that an appointed person has failed: (1) to give security within such time or in such form as they have specified[6]; or (2) satisfactorily to discharge any function imposed on him by or by virtue of the relevant order[7] or in relation to the report made by him to the Charity Commissioners[8], and they wish to consider exercising their powers to disallow any amount of remuneration[9] or remove the appointed person[10], they must give him, whether in person or by post, a written notice complying with the following requirements[11]. Such a notice must inform him of:

(a) any such failure in respect of which the notice is issued[12];

(b) the Charity Commissioners' power to authorise the disallowance of any amount of remuneration if satisfied as to any such failure[13];

(c) their power to remove him if satisfied as to any such failure[14]; and

(d) his right to make representations to them in respect of any such alleged failure within such reasonable time as is specified in the notice[15].

The Charity Commissioners are authorised to disallow any amount of remuneration of an appointed person where, on the expiry of the time specified in the notice[16] for making representations and after consideration of such representations, if any, as are duly made in response to such a notice, they are satisfied that he has failed to give security or satisfactorily discharge any of his functions in such manner as is set out in the notice[17]. In addition, on the expiry of the time specified in the notice and after consideration of such representations, if any, as are duly made in response to such a notice, the Charity Commissioners may remove an appointed person where they are satisfied that he has failed in such manner as is specified in the notice, whether or not they also exercise their power to disallow any amount of remuneration[18].

1   As to the Charity Commissioners see paras 486–504 ante, 506–512 post.
2   Ie the person appointed by order under the Charities Act 1993 s 18(1)(vii) (see para 503 ante)) to be receiver and manager in respect of the property and affairs of a charity: Charities (Receiver and Manager) Regulations 1992, SI 1992/2355, reg 1(2); Interpretation Act 1978 s 17(2)(b).
3   Charities (Receiver and Manager) Regulations 1992, SI 1992/2355, reg 2.
4   Ibid reg 3(1).
5   Ibid reg 3(2). 'The relevant charity' means the charity in respect of which that person was appointed: reg 1(2).
6   Ibid reg 4(1)(a).
7   'The relevant order' means the order by which that person was appointed: ibid reg 1(2)
8   Ie a report made under ibid reg 5: see para 506 post.
9   Ibid reg 4(1)(b). The text refers to the Charity Commissioners' powers under reg 3(3): see the text and notes 16–17 infra.
10  Ie their powers under ibid reg 4(3): see the text to note 18 infra.
11  Ibid reg 4(1).
12  Ibid reg 4(2)(a).
13  Ibid reg 4(2)(b). The text refers to the Charity Commissioners' power under reg 3(3): see the text and notes 16–17 infra.
14  Ibid reg 4(2)(c). The text refers to the Charity Commissioners' power under reg 4(3): see the text to note 18 infra.
15  Ibid reg 4(2)(d).
16  Ie the notice referred to in ibid reg 4(2): see the text and notes 12–15 infra.
17  Ibid reg 3(3). The text refers to the appointed person having failed in such manner as is set out in reg 4(1)(a) or (b): see the text to notes 6, 9 supra.
18  Ibid reg 4(3).

**506. Reports by the appointed receiver and manager.** Reports which are to be made to the Charity Commissioners[1] by the person appointed to be receiver and manager[2], in addition to the matters which are required to be included set out below, may also include particulars of any matter which, in the opinion of the appointed person, should be brought to the Charity Commissioners' attention[3]. An appointed person must make a report to the Charity Commissioners not later than three months after the date of his appointment setting out[4]:

(1)    an estimate by him of the total value of the property of the relevant charity[5] on, or shortly after, the date of his appointment[6];

(2)    such information about the property and affairs of the relevant charity immediately prior to his appointment as he believes should be included in the report, notwithstanding that it may also be eventually included in another report[7];

(3)    his strategy for discharging the functions conferred on him by or by virtue of the relevant order[8].

For as long as an appointed person holds office as such, he must make a report to the Charity Commissioners not later than one month after each anniversary of his appointment setting out[9]:

(a)    an estimate by him of the total value of the property of the relevant charity on that anniversary of his appointment in respect of which the report is required to be made[10];

(b)    a summary of the discharge by him of the functions conferred on him by or by virtue of the relevant order during the 12 months ending with that anniversary[11]; and

(c)    where there are changes to his strategy as last set out in a report[12] those changes[13].

An appointed person must make a report to the Charity Commissioners not later than three months after the date when he ceased to hold office as such setting out[14]: (i) an estimate by him of the total value of the property of the relevant charity on that date[15]; and (ii) a summary of the discharge by him of the functions conferred on him by or by virtue of the relevant order during the period ending with that date and beginning with either the date of his appointment, or if that date is more than 12 months before the date when he ceased to hold office as an appointed person, the day immediately after the last anniversary of his appointment[16].

1    As to the Charity Commissioners see paras 486–505 ante, 507–512 post.
2    See para 505 note 2 ante.
3    Charities (Receiver and Manager) Regulations 1992, SI 1992/2355, reg 5(1).
4    Ibid reg 5(2).
5    For the meaning of 'the relevant charity' see para 505 note 5 ante.
6    Charities (Receiver and Manager) Regulations 1992, SI 1992/2355, reg 5(2)(a).
7    Ibid reg 5(2)(b). The text refers to a report which may be made under the Charities Act 1993 s 8 (see paras 497–498 ante): Charities (Receiver and Manager) Regulations 1992, SI 1992/2355, reg 5(2)(b); Interpretation Act 1978 s 12(2)(b).
8    Charities (Receiver and Manager) Regulations 1992, SI 1992/2355, reg 5(2)(c). For the meaning of 'the relevant order' see para 505 note 7 ante.
9    Ibid reg 5(3).
10   Ibid reg 5(3)(a).
11   Ibid reg 5(3)(b).
12   Ie changes to his strategy as last set out in a report in accordance with ibid reg 5(2)(c) (see head (3) in the text) or reg 5(3)(c) (see head (c) in the text): see reg 5(3)(c).

13  Ibid reg 5(3)(c).
14  Ibid reg 5(4), which is expressed to be subject to reg 5(5): see note 16 infra.
15  Ibid reg 5(4)(a). See note 16 infra.
16  Ibid reg 5(4)(b). Regulation 5(4) does not apply where an appointed person ceased to hold office one month or less after an anniversary of his appointment and a report had been made to the Charity Commissioners in accordance with heads (a)–(c) in the text in respect of that anniversary: reg 5(5).

**507. Power to remove and appoint charity trustees.** Save in the case of an exempt charity[1], the Charity Commissioners have power to remove a charity trustee[2] by order made of their own motion[3]:

(1)  where, within the last five years, the trustee[4]:

    (a)  having previously been adjudged bankrupt or had his estate sequestrated, has been discharged[5]; or

    (b)  having previously made a composition or arrangement with, or granted a trust deed for, his creditors, has been discharged in respect of it[6];

(2)  where the trustee is a corporation in liquidation[7];

(3)  where the trustee is incapable of acting by reason of mental disorder within the meaning of the Mental Health Act 1983[8];

(4)  where the trustee has not acted and will not declare his willingness or unwillingness to act[9]; or

(5)  where the trustee is outside England and Wales or cannot be found or does not act, and his absence or failure to act impedes the proper administration of the charity[10].

The Commissioners may by order made of their own motion appoint a person to be a charity trustee of a charity other than an exempt charity[11]:

(i)  in place of a charity trustee removed by them under these provisions or otherwise[12];

(ii)  where there are no charity trustees, or where by reason of vacancies in their number or the absence or incapacity of any of their number the charity cannot apply for the appointment[13];

(iii)  where there is a single charity trustee, not being a corporation aggregate, and the Commissioners are of opinion that it is necessary for the proper administration of the charity to increase the number[14]; or

(iv)  where the Commissioners are of opinion that it is necessary for the proper administration of the charity to have an additional trustee because one of the existing charity trustees who ought nevertheless to remain a charity trustee either cannot be found or does not act or is outside England and Wales[15].

An order for the appointment or removal of a charity trustee or trustee for a charity, or for the vesting or transfer of property under these powers, has the same effect as a similar order[16] made on the application of the charity or of other persons[17].

1  The Charities Act 1993 s 18 does not apply to an exempt charity: s 18(16). As to exempt charities see para 293 ante. For the meaning of 'charity' see para 1 ante.
2  For the meaning of 'charity trustees' see para 1 note 10 ante.
3  Charities Act 1993 s 18(4). The powers of the Commissioners under s 18 to remove or appoint charity trustees of their own motion includes power to make any such order with respect to the vesting in or

transfer to the charity trustees of any property as the Commissioners could make on the removal or appointment of a charity trustee by them under s 16 (see paras 180, 182–183, 271 ante, 509 post): s 18(6). The vesting or transfer of any property in accordance with such an order does not operate as a breach of any covenant or condition against alienation or give rise to a forfeiture: see para 180 note 6 ante.

4    Ibid s 18(4)(a).
5    Ibid s 18(4)(a)(i). See generally BANKRUPTCY AND INSOLVENCY.
6    Ibid s 18(4)(a)(ii). See generally BANKRUPTCY AND INSOLVENCY.
7    Ibid s 18(4)(b). See COMPANIES.
8    Ibid s 18(4)(c). As to mental disorders within the meaning of the Mental Health Act 1983 see MENTAL HEALTH vol 30 (Reissue) para 1202.
9    Charities Act 1993 s 18(4)(d).
10   Ibid s 18(4)(e).
11   Ibid s 18(5). See note 1 supra.
12   Ibid s 18(5)(a).
13   Ibid s 18(5)(b).
14   Ibid s 18(5)(c).
15   Ibid s 18(5)(d).
16   Ie under ibid s 16: see paras 180, 182–183, 271 ante, 509 post.
17   Ibid s 18(7). See also note 3 supra.


**508. Notice of orders.** Before exercising any of the powers relating to the protection of charities[1], other than the emergency powers[2], the Charity Commissioners must give notice[3] to each of the charity trustees[4] of their intention to do so[5]. They must also normally give public notice of their intention to make orders appointing, discharging or removing a charity trustee or trustee for a charity[6].

Before making an order removing a charity trustee or trustee for a charity or officer, employee or agent of a charity, without his consent, the Commissioners must give him not less than one month's notice of their proposal inviting representations to be made to them within a time specified in the notice[7].

1    Ie the jurisdiction under the Charities Act 1993 s 18: see paras 503, 507 ante.
2    Ie under ibid s 18(1): see para 503 ante.
3    Notice may be given by post and, if so, may be addressed to the recipient's last known address in the United Kingdom: ibid s 18(12). For the meaning of 'United Kingdom' see para 180 note 16 ante.
4    However, notice need not be given to any that cannot be found or has no known address in the United Kingdom: ibid s 18(12). For the meaning of 'charity trustees' see para 1 note 10 ante.
5    Ibid s 18(12).
6    See ibid s 20(2); and para 270 ante.
7    Ibid s 20(3). However, he need not be given notice if he cannot be found or has no known address in the United Kingdom: s 20(3). See further s 20(4); and para 181 ante. As to the contents of the notice see s 20(7); and para 181 ante.
     Notice (other than public notice) may be given by post and, if given by post, be addressed to the recipient's last known address in the United Kingdom: s 20(8). Only in the case of certain orders is a period specified for the giving of notice: see s 20(1)–(3); and paras 181, 270 ante.


**509. Appeals.** An appeal may be brought against any order made under the Charity Commissioners' powers to act for the protection of a charity[1], in the High Court by the Attorney General or, within three months of the publication of the order, by the charity[2], by any of the charity trustees[3] or by any person removed from any office or employment by the order[4]. There is no provision in the Charities Act 1993 for the Commissioners to be joined on an appeal against any such order[5]. No appeal may be so brought except with a certificate of the Commissioners that it is a proper case for an appeal or with the leave of a judge of the Chancery Division[6], although this requirement does not apply to: (1) an appeal by a charity or any of the charity trustees against an order[7] appointing a receiver and manager in respect of the charity's property and affairs[8]; or (2) an appeal by a person against an order[9] removing him from his office or employment on the ground of misconduct or mismanagement, or bankruptcy[10].

Where the Commissioners have established a scheme[11] for the administration of a charity, any person interested in the charity has the like right of appeal[12] as a charity trustee, and in the case of a charity which is a local charity[13] in any area, so do any two or more inhabitants of the area and the parish council of any parish or, in Wales, any community comprising the area or any part of it[14].

1  Ie under the Charities Act 1993 s 18: see paras 503, 507 ante.
2  For the meaning of 'charity' see para 1 ante.
3  For the meaning of 'charity trustees' see para 1 note 10 ante.
4  Charities Act 1993 ss 16(11), (12), 18(8). A person removed with the concurrence of the charity trustees or the approval of the special visitor, if any, may not appeal: ss 16(12), 18(8); and see paras 190, 468 ante. As to the procedure on such an appeal see para 549 post.
5  *Weth v A-G* [1999] 1 WLR 686, CA.
6  Charities Act 1993 ss 16(13), 18(8).
7  Ie an order under ibid s 18(1)(vii): see para 503 ante.
8  Charities Act 1993 s 18(8), (9)(a).
9  Ie an order under ibid s 18(2)(i) or (4)(a): see paras 503, 507 ante.
10  Ibid s 18(8), (9)(b).
11  Ie under ibid s 18: see paras 503, 507 ante.
12  Ie under s 16(12): see the text and notes 1–4 supra.
13  For the meaning of 'local charity' see para 180 note 10 ante.
14  Charities Act 1993 s 16(14), 18(10). As to areas and authorities in England and Wales see LOCAL GOVERNMENT.

### (iii) Miscellaneous Statutory Powers

**510. Dormant bank accounts of charities.** Where the Charity Commissioners: (1) are informed by a relevant institution[1] that it holds one or more accounts in the name or on behalf of a particular charity[2] ('the relevant charity'), and that the account or, if it holds two or more accounts, each of the accounts is dormant[3]; and (2) they are unable, after making reasonable inquiries, to locate that charity or any of its trustees[4], they may give a direction[5] which:

(a)  requires the institution concerned to transfer the amount[6], or, as the case may be, the aggregate amount, standing to the credit of the relevant charity in the account or accounts in question to such other charity as is specified[7] in the direction[8]; or

(b)  requires the institution concerned to transfer such part of that amount or aggregate amount as is specified to each of two or more other specified charities[9].

In such a direction the Commissioners may specify such other charity or charities as they consider appropriate, having regard, in a case where the purposes of the relevant charity are known to them, to those purposes and to the purposes of the other charity or charities[10]. Any amount received by a charity under these provisions is received on the terms that it will be held and applied by the charity for the purposes of the charity, but will, as property of the charity, nevertheless be subject to any restrictions on expenditure to which it was subject as property of the relevant charity[11].

Where the Commissioners have been informed by any relevant institution under head (1) above, and before any transfer is made by the institution in pursuance of a direction, the institution has, by reason of any circumstances, cause to believe that the account, or, as the case may be, any of the accounts is or are no longer dormant, it must forthwith notify those circumstances in writing to the Commissioners[12]. If it appears to the Commissioners that the account or accounts in question is or are no longer dormant, they must revoke the direction which has previously been given by them to the institution with respect to the relevant charity[13]. No obligation as to secrecy or other restriction precludes a relevant institution from disclosing any information to the Commissioners for the purpose of enabling them to discharge the above functions[14].

These provisions do not apply to any account held in the name of or on behalf of an exempt charity[15].

1   A 'relevant institution' means: (1) the Bank of England; (2) an institution which is authorised by the Financial Services Authority to operate a deposit-taking business under the Banking Act 1987 Pt I (ss 1–49) (as amended); (3) a European deposit-taker as defined in the Banking Co-ordination (Second Council Directive) Regulations 1992, SI 1992/3218, reg 82(3); (4) a building society which is authorised by the Building Societies Commission under the Building Societies Act 1986 s 9 (as amended; prospectively repealed) to raise money from its members; or (5) such other institution mentioned in the Banking Act 1987 s 4(1), Sch 2 (as amended) as the Secretary of State may prescribe by regulations: Charities Act 1993 s 28(8)(b) (amended by the Bank of England Act 1998 s 23(1), Sch 5 para 42). At the date at which this volume states the law no such regulations had been made. See also BANKING; BUILDING SOCIETIES. As to the Secretary of State see para 513 post.
2   For the meaning of 'charity' see para 1 ante.
3   Charities Act 1993 s 28(1)(a). An account is dormant if no transaction other than: (1) a transaction consisting in a payment into the account; or (2) a transaction which the institution holding the account has itself caused to be effected, has been effected in relation to the account within the period of five years immediately preceding the date when the Commissioners were so informed under s 28(1)(a): s 28(8)(a).
4   Ibid s 28(1)(b).
5   Ibid s 28(1). For the purpose of determining the matters in respect of which any of the powers conferred by s 8 or s 9 (see para 497 et seq ante) may be exercised, it is to be assumed that the Commissioners have no functions under s 28 (as amended) in relation to accounts to which this provision applies, with the result that, for example, a relevant institution is not, in connection with the functions of the Commissioners under s 28 (as amended), required under s 8(3)(a) to furnish any statements, or answer any questions or inquiries, with respect to any such accounts held by the institution: s 28(9). Section 28(9) applies to accounts which are dormant accounts by virtue of s 28(8)(a) (see note 3 supra) but would not be such accounts if s 28(8)(a)(i) (see note 3 head (1) supra) were omitted: s 28(9).
6   Reference to the transfer of any amount to a charity are references to its transfer to the charity trustees, or to any trustee for the charity, as the charity trustees may determine, and any reference to any amount received by the charity is to be construed accordingly: ibid s 28(8)(c). For the meaning of 'charity trustees' see para 1 note 10 ante.
7   Ie in accordance with ibid s 28(3): see the text and note 10 infra.
8   Ibid s 28(2)(a).
9   Ibid s 28(2)(b).
10  Ibid s 28(3). The Commissioners, however, must not specify any charity unless they have received from the charity trustees written confirmation that those trustees are willing to accept the amount proposed to be transferred to the charity: s 28(3).
11  Ibid s 28(4). The receipt of any charity trustees or trustees for a charity in respect of any amount received from a relevant institution under these provisions is a complete discharge of the institution in respect of that amount: s 28(6).
12  Ibid s 28(5).
13  Ibid s 28(5).
14  Ibid s 28(7).
15  Ibid s 28(10). As to exempt charities see para 293 ante.

**511. Miscellaneous powers.** Apart from their powers under the Charities Acts 1992 and 1993, the Charity Commissioners have specific powers and functions under a variety of other Acts: the Bishops Trusts Substitution Act 1858[1], the Voluntary Hospitals (Paying Patients) Act 1936[2], the Reserve Forces Act 1980[3], the Pastoral Measure 1983[4] and the Redundant Churches and Other Religious Buildings Act 1969[5].

The Charity Commissioners also have the power, on application by any person interested, to make such provision for the apportionment and management of endowments held partly for ecclesiastical purposes and partly for other purposes as seems to them necessary or expedient for giving effect to the Local Government Act 1894[6].

Their offices are a place of deposit for records of theirs selected for permanent preservation[7].

1   See para 243 ante.
2   See para 512 post.
3   See para 189 ante.
4   See para 187 ante.
5   See para 188 ante.
6   See the Local Government Act 1894 s 75(2); para 240 note 4 ante; and LOCAL GOVERNMENT.
7   Ie by virtue of an appointment by the Lord Chancellor under the Public Records Act 1958 s 4(1) (see CONSTITUTIONAL LAW AND HUMAN RIGHTS vol 8(2) (Reissue) para 838): see the *Report of the Charity Commissioners for England and Wales for 1961* (HC Paper (1962–63) no 30) para 43.

**512. Paying patients in voluntary hospitals.** On the application of the committee of management of a voluntary hospital[1], the Charity Commissioners may, by order, authorise the provision of specified facilities for the accommodation and treatment of patients able and willing to pay for it by the committee for specified periods[2]. The committee may charge for accommodation and maintenance, including medical and surgical attendance and treatment given by the resident staff, in accordance with the scale specified in the Commissioners' order[3], which may include any consequential or incidental provisions appearing to the Commissioners to be necessary or desirable[4]. The order may authorise the committee to defray out of any fund applicable to the general purposes of the hospital the difference between the full expense of accommodation and maintenance and the sum charged to a paying patient[5], but except to this extent no order may be construed as authorising any application of funds[6].

On the application of the committee, the Commissioners may from time to time vary an order, and they may of their own motion vary or revoke an order if they consider that there has been a material change in the circumstances and they first give the committee and others concerned an opportunity of making representations[7].

Generally the Commissioners must not make an order authorising any use or application of property or funds which, apart from the order, would involve a breach of any trusts upon which the property or funds are held, or a contravention of any prohibition or restriction expressly relating to the hospital[8]. But they may make such an order:

(1)   in the case of an application to use land, if they are satisfied that, if the order were not made, the land would not come into use for the purposes for which the trusts were created or the prohibition or restriction was imposed until after the expiration of a substantial period from the date of the application[9];

(2)    in the case of an application to use existing buildings or part of such buildings, if satisfied either[10]:

    (a)    that such use for the purposes for which the trusts were created or the prohibition or restriction was imposed is impracticable, or is likely soon so to become, because the committee of management have not at their disposal, and will be unable to obtain, sufficient funds to enable the buildings or part to be, or to continue to be, so used[11]; or

    (b)    that use for those purposes is impracticable, or is likely soon so to become, because of a shortage of demand for accommodation on the part of the persons for whose benefit the trusts were created or the prohibition or restriction was imposed[12]; or

    (c)    that the committee has, or is likely soon to have, at its disposal premises which could be put to the use to which the application relates without breach of any trust upon which those premises are held or contravention of any such prohibition or restriction, and that the buildings or part will be used by way of exchange for those premises[13];

(3)    in any case, if satisfied that the authorisation will not diminish or restrict the accommodation for such persons for whose benefit the trusts were created or the prohibition or restriction imposed which is provided in the hospital at the date of the application and which the committee would be able to continue to provide if the order were not made[14].

---

1    'Committee of management' includes any body or persons having the management or control of a voluntary hospital: Voluntary Hospitals (Paying Patients) Act 1936 s 1. 'Voluntary hospital' means an institution, not being an institution carried on for profit or which is maintained wholly or mainly at the expense of the rates or which is vested in an NHS trust or a primary care trust or which is vested in the Secretary of State, which provides medical or surgical treatment for in-patients: s 1 (definition amended by the National Health Service Act 1946 s 76, Sch 10 Pt I (repealed with savings by the National Health Service Act 1977 s 129, Sch 14 paras 1–3, 13, Sch 16); the National Health Service and Community Care Act 1990 s 66(1), Sch 9 para 2; and the Health Act 1999 (Supplementary, Consequential etc Provisions) Order 2000, SI 2000/90, art 3(1), Sch 1 para 1(a)). The functions of the Secretary of State under the Voluntary Hospitals (Paying Patients) Act 1936 are exercised, in relation to England, by the Secretary of State for Health, and in relation to Wales, by the Secretary of State for Wales: see the Secretary of State for Social Services Order 1968, SI 1968/1699; Transfer of Functions (Wales) Order 1969, SI 1969/388; Transfer of Functions (Health and Social Security) Order 1988, SI 1988/1843.
    'NHS trust' means a National Health Service trust established under the National Health Service and Community Care Act 1990 Pt I (ss 1–26) (as amended) (see NATIONAL HEALTH SERVICE vol 33 (Reissue) para 94 et seq): Voluntary Hospitals (Paying Patients) Act 1936 s 1 (definition added by the National Health Service and Community Care Act 1990 s 66(1), Sch 9 para 2(b)).
    'Primary care trust' means a primary care trust established under the National Health Service Act 1977 s 16A (as added) (see NATIONAL HEALTH SERVICE): Voluntary Hospitals (Paying Patients) Act 1936 s 1 (definition added by the Health Act 1999 (Supplementary, Consequential etc Provisions) Order 2000, SI 2000/90, art 3(1), Sch 1 para 1(b)).

2    See the Voluntary Hospitals (Paying Patients) Act 1936 s 2(1). As to the power of the Charity Commissioners to make rules for these purposes see s 5. As to the rules relating to applications see the Rules made by the Charity Commissioners under section 5(1) of the Voluntary Hospitals (Paying Patients) Act 1936, SR & O 1936/1025. The Commissioners may require a sum to cover their costs and expenses to be provided out of hospital funds: see the Voluntary Hospitals (Paying Patients) Act 1936 s 5(3). The powers conferred on the Charity Commissioners by the Voluntary Hospitals (Paying Patients) Act 1936 are in addition to and not in derogation of any other powers exercisable by them: s 6(2).

3    See ibid s 2(2). Except where satisfied that it would be inappropriate to do so, the Commissioners must include, in the scale of charges, charges fixed with a view to meeting the needs of patients who, although able to make some payment, are unable to pay sufficient to meet the full expense to the hospital of their accommodation and maintenance: see s 3(1). The Commissioners must make it a condition that, in the use of a specified number of authorised beds, priority is to be given to such patients: see s 3(1).

4    See ibid s 2(3).
5    See ibid s 3(2).
6    See ibid s 6(3).
7    See ibid s 2(4).
8    See ibid s 4.
9    See ibid s 4(a).
10   See ibid s 4(b).
11   See ibid s 4(b)(i).
12   See ibid s 4(b)(ii).
13   See ibid s 4(b)(iii).
14   See ibid s 4(c).

# (5) THE SECRETARY OF STATE

**513. The role of the Secretary of State.** In law 'Secretary of State' means one of Her Majesty's Principal Secretaries of State[1]. Accordingly, many modern statutes refer simply to 'the Secretary of State' without reference to a particular department or ministry[2].

At one time, the Secretary of State for Education and Science[3] had functions concurrent with the Charity Commissioners[4], as did the Secretary of State for Wales in relation to primary and secondary education in Wales[5]. By the Education Act 1973[6] these functions were terminated, and the Charity Commissioners, who previously had concurrent jurisdiction over educational trusts, now have exclusive jurisdiction over them in exactly the same way as they have jurisdiction over other charitable trusts. However, the Secretary of State for Education and Employment[7] does have powers in relation to the modification of trusts deeds relating to certain schools[8] or relating to the provision of educational services or educational research[9]. He also has powers in relation to religious educational trusts[10].

1    See the Interpretation Act 1978 s 5, Sch 1.
2    As to the office of Secretary of State see CONSTITUTIONAL LAW AND HUMAN RIGHTS vol 8(2) (Reissue) para 355.
3    References to the Secretary of State were substituted for the original references to the Minister of Education by the Secretary of State for Education and Science Order 1964, SI 1964/490, art 2(1).
4    See the Charities Act 1960 s 2(1) (repealed). As to the Charity Commissioners see paras 486–512 ante.
5    See the Transfer of Functions (Wales) Order 1970, SI 1970/1536, art 2(2).
6    Education Act 1973 s 1(1)(a), Sch 1 para 1 (as amended), Sch 2 Pt III. The functions were transferred as from 1 February 1974: see s 1(5); Education Act 1973 (Commencement) Order 1973, SI 1973/1661.
7    As to the Secretary of State for Education and Employment see CONSTITUTIONAL LAW AND HUMAN RIGHTS vol 8(2) (Reissue) para 448 et seq.
8    See the School Standards and Framework Act 1998 s 82; and EDUCATION.
9    See the Education Act 1996 s 489(3), (4): see EDUCATION.
10   See the Education Act 1996 ss 554–556 (as amended); and EDUCATION.

# (6) THE DIRECTOR OF PUBLIC PROSECUTIONS

**514. Consent of Director of Public Prosecutions to instigation of certain proceedings.** Proceedings for certain specified offences relating to charities may only be instigated by or with the consent of the Director of Public Prosecutions[1]. The offences in question relate to omission of a registered charity's status on official publications[2]; supplying false or misleading information[3]; failure to comply with orders made by the Charity Commissioners[4]; failure to comply with requirements as to annual reports and annual returns[5]; and acting as a trustee while disqualified[6].

1   Charities Act 1993 s 94(1). As to the Director of Public Prosecutions see CRIMINAL LAW, EVIDENCE AND PROCEDURE vol 11(1) (Reissue) para 637 et seq.
2   Ie under ibid s 5 (as amended): see para 286 ante.
3   Ie under ibid s 11: see para 499 ante.
4   Ie under ibid s 18(14): see para 503 ante. As to the Charity Commissioners see paras 486–512 ante.
5   Ie under ibid s 49 (as amended): see paras 321, 325–326 ante.
6   See ibid s 94(2). The reference to the offence of acting as a trustee while disqualified is a reference to an offence under s 73(1) (see para 250 ante): see s 94(2).


**515. Offences by bodies corporate.** Where any offence under the Charities Act 1993, or any offence under the Charities Act 1992 or any regulations made under it, is committed by a body corporate and is proved to have been committed with the consent or connivance of, or to be attributable to any neglect on the part of, any director[1], manager, secretary or other similar officer of the body corporate, or any person who was purporting to act in any such capacity, he as well as the body corporate is guilty of that offence and is liable to be proceeded against and punished accordingly[2].

1   In relation to a body corporate the affairs of which are managed by its members, 'director' means a member of the body corporate: Charities Act 1992 s 75; Charities Act 1993 s 95.
2   Charities Act 1992 s 75 (amended by the Charities Act 1993 s 98(2), Sch 7); Charities Act 1993 s 95. In relation to the Charities Act 1993, s 95 is not limited to cases where the Director of Public Prosecutions is necessarily involved under s 94: see para 514 ante.


# (7) THE ATTORNEY GENERAL


**516. The role of the Attorney General.** The Attorney General[1] represents the beneficial interest, or 'objects', of the charity[2]. His duty is to protect the interests of charity generally, and in so doing he contributes to a framework of supervision and control over charities in which the Charity Commission plays a significant, statutory role[3]. However, his role is particularly important in relation to exempt charities, which are largely outside the Charity Commissioners' jurisdiction[4].

The Attorney General is generally a necessary party to all claims relating to charities[5], and he may appear either in person or by counsel[6]. Where the Attorney General is a proper party, the Solicitor General[7] is the proper person to take his place if the Attorney General's office is vacant or if he is ill or concerned in the action in another capacity[8].

1   As to the Attorney General see CONSTITUTIONAL LAW AND HUMAN RIGHTS vol 8(2) (Reissue) para 529 et seq.
2   See *A-G v Brodie* (1846) 6 Moo PCC 12; *A-G v Bishop of Worcester* (1851) 9 Hare 328 at 361 per Turner V-C; *Ware v Cumberlege* (1855) 20 Beav 503; *Re Sekeford's Charity* (1861) 5 LT 488. See also *Brooks v Richardson* [1986] 1 All ER 952, [1986] 1 WLR 385.
3   As to the Charity Commission see para 486 et seq ante.
4   As to exempt charities see para 293 ante. As to the Charity Commissioners see paras 486–512 ante.

5   As to the role of the Attorney General in charity proceedings see further paras 523, 531 et seq post. As
    to the costs of the Attorney General see paras 550–553 post. As to when the Attorney General is not a
    necessary party see para 535 post.
6   See para 541 post.
7   As to the Solicitor General see CONSTITUTIONAL LAW AND HUMAN RIGHTS vol 8(2) (Reissue) para 529.
8   See *R v Wilkes* (1770) 4 Burr 2527 at 2554, HL, per Lord Mansfield; *Ludlow Corpn v Greenhouse* (1827)
    1 Bli NS 17 at 51, HL, per Lord Redesdale; *A-G v Bristol Corpn* (1820) 2 Jac & W 294; *A-G v
    Ironmongers' Co* (1834) 2 My & K 576; *A-G v Dean and Canons of Windsor* (1860) 8 HL Cas 369; *Brookes v
    Richardson* [1986] 1 All ER 952, [1986] 1 WLR 385; and paras 521, 531 post.

# (8) REGULATIONS AND ORDERS

**517. Regulations and orders made under the Charities Acts 1992 and 1993.**
Any regulations or order of the Secretary of State[1] under the Charities Act 1992 or the
Charities Act 1993 must be made by statutory instrument[2], and are subject to annulment
in pursuance of a resolution of either House of Parliament[3]. Any regulations of the
Secretary of State or the Charity Commissioners[4] and any order of the Secretary of State
under the Charities Act 1993 may make different provision for different cases, and may
make such supplemental, incidental, consequential or transitional provision or savings as
the Secretary of State or, as the case may be, the Commissioners consider appropriate[5].
Before making certain regulations[6] the Secretary of State must consult such persons or
bodies of persons as he considers appropriate[7].

1   As to the Secretary of State see para 513 ante.
2   Charities Act 1992 s 77(1)(a); Charities Act 1993 s 86(1)(a).
3   Charities Act 1992 s 77(1)(b); Charities Act 1993 s 86(1)(b). In relation to the Charities Act 1992,
    s 77(1)(b) does not apply to an order under s 79(2): s 77(2)(d). In relation to the Charities Act 1993,
    s 86(1)(b) does not apply to: (1) an order under s 17(2) (see para 184 ante) or s 99(2); or (2) to any
    regulations to which s 85(3) (see para 495 ante) applies: s 86(2) (amended by the Trustee Act 2000
    s 40(1), (3), Sch 2 Pt I, para 2(2), (3), Sch 4 Pt I).
4   As to the Charity Commissioners see paras 486–512 ante.
5   Charities Act 1992 s 77(3); Charities Act 1993 s 86(3).
6   Ie regulations under the Charities Act 1992 s 64 or s 73 (see para 426 ante) or regulations under the
    Charities Act 1993 s 42 (as amended) (see para 308 ante), s 44 (see para 314 ante) or s 45 (as amended)
    (see para 321 ante).
7   Charities Act 1992 s 77(4) (amended by the Charities Act 1993 s 98(2), Sch 7); Charities Act 1993
    s 86(4).

# 11. COURT PROCEEDINGS

## (1) INTRODUCTION

**518. Litigation involving charities.** A charity or a charity trustee may be involved in various different kinds of civil proceedings. These include ordinary litigation involving charities relating to disputes about contracts[1], allegations of tortious conduct[2], property disputes[3], interpretation of wills[4] and other documents referring to charities or charitable purposes, applications under the Inheritance (Provision for Family and Dependants) Act 1975[5], appeals from certain decisions of the Charity Commission[6], applications for judicial review by or against the charity[7], and 'charity proceedings'[8]. The following paragraphs are concerned exclusively with 'charity proceedings'.

1 See generally CONTRACT.
2 See generally TORT.
3 See eg LANDLORD AND TENANT; REAL PROPERTY.
4 As to wills generally see WILLS.
5 See EXECUTORS AND ADMINISTRATORS vol 17(2) (Reissue) para 665 et seq.
6 As to the Charity Commissioners see paras 486–512 ante.
7 As to judicial review see ADMINISTRATIVE LAW vol 1(1) (2001 Reissue) para 59 et seq; PRACTICE AND PROCEDURE.
8 See para 519 et seq post.

## (2) RESTRICTIONS ON CHARITY PROCEEDINGS

**519. Meaning of 'charity proceedings'.** The Charities Act 1993 imposes restrictions on the taking of charity proceedings[1]. 'Charity proceedings' means proceedings in any court in England or Wales brought under the court's jurisdiction with respect to charities[2] or under the court's jurisdiction with respect to trusts in relation to the administration of a trust for charitable purposes[3]. The definition does not include proceedings to determine whether a valid charitable trust has been created[4]. The statutory provisions with regard to the taking of charity proceedings[5] are concerned with jurisdiction over the domestic aspects of an institution, not with issues lying between the institution and outsiders[6]. Charity proceedings relate to the constitution or administration of a charity, which are internal matters, as opposed to disputes over contract, tort or property rights between a charity and a third party[7], but they may involve as parties persons who are not trustees who have an interest in ensuring that the charity is properly administered[8].

1 See the Charities Act 1993 s 33; the text and notes 2–3 infra; and paras 520–521 post. The Charities Act 1960 s 28(9) (repealed) provided that the Charities Procedure Act 1812 and also the provisions of any local or private Act regulating the persons by whom or the manner or form in which charity proceedings may be brought should cease to have effect. The repeal did not, however, affect any proceedings begun before 1 January 1961 (ie the commencement of the Charities Act 1960): s 48(5). The Charities Procedure Act 1812 (repealed), otherwise known as Romilly's Act, provided a summary procedure on

petition for determining simple questions arising in the administration of a charitable trust.

2 This phrase has been considered in *Construction Industry Training Board v A-G* [1973] Ch 173, [1972] 2 All ER 1339, CA (affg [1971] 3 All ER 449, [1971] 1 WLR 1303) (decided under previous legislation): see para 559 post. In the Charities Act 1993 s 33, 'charity' does not include an institution established under the laws of another legal system: *Gaudiya Mission v Brahmachary* [1998] Ch 341, [1997] 4 All ER 957, CA. For the meaning of 'charity' in the Charities Act 1993 see para 1 ante. For the meaning of 'the court' see para 168 note 12 ante.

3 Ibid s 33(8). See also *Brooks v Richardson* [1986] 1 All ER 952, [1986] 1 WLR 385; *Scott v National Trust for Places of Historic Interest or Natural Beauty* [1998] 2 All ER 705. The same definition, limited to High Court proceedings, appears in CPR Sch 1 RSC Ord 108 r 1(1). As to the CPR see para 522 post.

4 See *Re Belling, Enfield London Borough Council v Public Trustee* [1967] Ch 425, [1967] 1 All ER 105; *Hauxwell v Barton-upon-Humber UDC* [1974] Ch 432, [1973] 2 All ER 1022; *Mills v Winchester Diocesan Board of Finance* [1989] Ch 428, [1989] 2 All ER 317 (all decided under previous legislation).

5 Ie the Charities Act 1993 s 33: see the text and notes 2–3 supra; and paras 520–521 post.

6 *Construction Industry Training Board v A-G* [1973] Ch 173, [1972] 2 All ER 1339, CA (decided under previous legislation). The Charitable Trusts Act 1853 s 17 proviso (repealed by the Charities Act 1960) contained a similar restriction, in different terms, as to which see *Re Shum's Trusts* (1904) 91 LT 192; *Bassano v Bradley* [1896] 1 QB 645, DC; *Holme v Guy* (1877) 5 ChD 901, CA; *Rendall v Blair* (1890) 45 ChD 139, CA; *Re St Giles' and St George's, Bloomsbury, Volunteer Corps* (1858) 25 Beav 313; *Re Poplar and Blackwall Free School* (1878) 8 ChD 543; *Re Lister's Hospital* (1855) 6 De GM & G 184; *Falconer v Steam* [1932] 1 Ch 509; *Braund v Earl of Devon* (1868) 3 Ch App 800; *Rooke v Dawson* [1895] 1 Ch 480.

7 See *Rendall v Blair* (1890) 45 Ch D 139, CA.

8 See, eg, *Gunning v Buckfast Abbey Trustees Registered* (1994) Times, 9 June. See also *Ex p Scott* [1998] 1 WLR 226, sub nom *R v The National Trust for Places of Historic Interest or Natural Beauty, ex p Scott* [1998] JPL 465, which indicated a wider meaning for charity proceedings, to include an application for judicial review of the decision of a charity's governing body where the charity is a public body susceptible to judicial review. Bringing charity proceedings in the Chancery Division is the procedure which must be followed in all but the most exceptional cases: *Scott v The National Trust for Places of Historic Interest or Natural Beauty* [1998] 2 All ER 705 at 716 per Robert Walker J.

**520. Claimants in charity proceedings.** Charity proceedings[1] may be taken with reference to a charity[2] by the charity, or by any of the charity trustees[3], or by any person interested in the charity[4], or, if it is a local charity[5], by any two or more inhabitants of the area, but not by any other person[6]. This, however, does not prevent the taking of proceedings by the Charity Commissioners[7] or by the Attorney General, with or without a relator[8].

1 For the meaning of 'charity proceedings' see para 519 ante.
2 For the meaning of 'charity' see para 1 ante.
3 For the meaning of 'charity trustees' see para 1 note 10 ante.
4 See *Re Hampton Fuel Allotment Charity* [1989] Ch 484, sub nom *Richmond upon Thames London Borough Council v Rogers* [1988] 2 All ER 761, CA (to qualify as a claimant in his own right a person needs to have an interest materially greater than or different from that possessed by ordinary members of the public). A contract with the trustees relating to property of the charity does not suffice: *Haslemere Estates Ltd v Baker* [1982] 3 All ER 525, [1982] 1 WLR 1109. Nor are the executors of the will of the founder of a charity persons interested in the charity: *Bradshaw v University College of Wales, Aberystwyth* [1987] 3 All ER 200, [1988] 1 WLR 190. See also *Scott v National Trust for Places of Historic Interest or Natural Beauty* [1998] 2 All ER 705.

See also *Gunning v Buckfast Abbey Trustees* (1994) Times, 9 June, where charity proceedings were properly brought by parents of children attending an independent school run by a charity, and although the parents had a contractual relationship with the school, they were not suing on their contracts but seeking the proper administration of the charity. They were persons interested in the charity because they had a moral and legal duty regarding the education of their children and thus had a concern that the charity should fulfil its functions properly which was greater than the concern of an ordinary member of the public.

5 For the meaning of 'local charity' see para 180 note 10 ante.

6   Charities Act 1993 s 33(1).
7   Ie under ibid s 32: see para 496 ante. As to the Charity Commissioners see paras 486–512 ante.
8   Ibid s 33(6). As to relators see further para 539 et seq post. Relator proceedings are now rare in practice.


**521. Authority or permission to bring charity proceedings.** Apart from proceedings by the Attorney General, those taken by the Charity Commissioners under the powers conferred by the Charities Act 1993[1], and proceedings relating to an exempt charity[2], no charity proceedings[3] relating to a charity[4] may be entertained or proceeded with in any court unless the Charity Commissioners have by order authorised the taking of the proceedings[5]. The Commissioners must not, without special reasons, authorise the taking of proceedings where in their opinion the case can be dealt with by them under the other powers[6] conferred by the Charities Act 1993[7].

If an order of the Commissioners has been applied for and refused, the proceedings may nevertheless be entertained or proceeded with if, after the refusal, permission to take the proceedings is obtained from one of the judges of the High Court attached to the Chancery Division[8].

These provisions do not make necessary an order for the taking of proceedings in a pending cause or matter, or for the bringing of any appeal[9].

Under the former legislation[10] it was held that where proceedings were commenced without the authority which ought to have been obtained, the proper course was to stay the proceedings to see if authority could be obtained[11].

1   Ie under the Charities Act 1993 s 32: see para 496 ante. As to the Charity Commissioners see paras 486–512 ante.
2   As to exempt charities see para 293 ante.
3   For the meaning of 'charity proceedings' see para 519 ante.
4   For the meaning of 'charity' see para 1 ante.
5   Charities Act 1993 s 33(2), (6). See also para 521 ante.
6   Ie powers other than those conferred by ibid s 32: see para 496 ante.
7   Ibid s 33(3).
8   Ibid s 33(5). The application is made without notice at first and must be made within 21 days of the refusal of the order. As to the application for permission to appeal or take charity proceedings see CPR Sch 1 RSC Ord 108 r 3; and para 548 post. Leave was not granted in a case concerning Dulwich College Picture Gallery: see the *Report of the Charity Commissioners for England and Wales for 1979* (HC Paper (1979–80) no 608) paras 56–58.
9   Charities Act 1993 s 33(4). The equivalent provision under the former legislation (ie the Charitable Trusts Act 1853 s 17 (repealed)) was held to mean pending at the date of the commencement of the proceedings in question: *Re Lister's Hospital* (1855) 6 De GM & G 184. The question is to be determined on the facts of each case: *Ford's Charity* (1855) 3 Drew 324; *Re Jarvis' Charity* (1859) 1 Drew & Sm 97.
10   See note 9 supra.
11   *Rendall v Blair* (1890) 45 ChD 139, CA.


**522. Procedure.** The Rules of the Supreme Court and the County Court Rules were replaced by the Civil Procedure Rules on 26 April 1999[1].

The provisions of the Rules of the Supreme Court relating to charity proceedings have been preserved by the Civil Procedure Rules[2]. Charity proceedings and proceedings brought in the High Court by virtue of the Charities Act 1993 are assigned to the Chancery Division[3], and must be begun by a claim form[4], except for applications for permission to appeal or to take charity proceedings[5] and applications for committal[6].

The power to make rules of civil procedure is to be exercised with a view to securing that the civil justice system is accessible, fair and efficient[7]. The Civil Procedure Rules have the overriding objective of enabling the court to deal with cases justly[8]. Dealing with a case justly includes, so far as is practicable:

(1)   ensuring that the parties are on an equal footing[9];

(2)   saving expense[10];

(3)   dealing with the case in ways which are proportionate[11]:

    (a)   to the amount of money involved[12];

    (b)   to the importance of the case[13];

    (c)   to the complexity of the issues[14]; and

    (d)   to the financial position of each party[15];

(4)   ensuring that it is dealt with expeditiously and fairly[16]; and

(5)   allotting to it an appropriate share of the court's resources, while taking into account the need to allot resources to other cases[17].

The court must seek to give effect to the overriding objective when it exercises any power given to it by the Rules, or interprets any rule[18]. The parties are required to help the court to further the overriding objective[19]. The court must also further the overriding objective by actively managing cases[20]. Active case management includes:

(i)   encouraging the parties to co-operate with each other in the conduct of the proceedings[21];

(ii)   identifying the issues at an early stage[22];

(iii)   deciding promptly which issues need full investigation and trial and accordingly disposing summarily of the others[23];

(iv)   deciding the order in which issues are to be resolved[24];

(v)   encouraging the parties to use an alternative dispute resolution procedure if the court considers that appropriate and facilitating the use of such procedure[25];

(vi)   helping the parties to settle the whole or part of the case[26];

(vii)   fixing timetables or otherwise controlling the progress of the case[27];

(viii) considering whether the likely benefits of taking a particular step justify the cost of taking it[28];

(ix)   dealing with as many aspects of the case as it can on the same occasion[29];

(x)   dealing with the case without the parties needing to attend at court[30];

(xi)   making use of technology[31]; and

(xii)   giving directions to ensure that the trial of a case proceeds quickly and efficiently[32].

The Civil Procedure Rule Committee must, when making the Rules, try to make rules which are both simple and simply expressed[33]. Consequently, in relation to proceedings to which the Civil Procedure Rules apply, certain changes of terminology are introduced. In particular, proceedings are now called 'claims' rather than actions, and, accordingly, a person instituting proceedings is now known as a 'claimant' rather than a plaintiff. A claimant generally commences proceedings by way of a 'claim form', which may include his particulars of claim. Pleadings are now known as 'statements of case', and that term embraces the claim form. Leave of the court is now referred to as 'permission of the court'. Discovery is now referred to as 'disclosure'. 'Requests for information' have superseded interrogatories and requests for further and better particulars. Taxation of costs is now known as 'detailed assessment of costs'. Where former terms appear in existing enactments which have not been amended in the light of the new regime, they should nonetheless be read in that light and have been so presented in this title.

The Civil Procedure Rules are stated to be a new procedural code[34]. The principle that in construing a code the proper course is, in the first instance, to examine its language and to ask what is its natural meaning, uninfluenced by any considerations derived from the previous state of the law therefore applies[35]. It has been held that, in the light of the overriding objective[36], the court, in deciding how a case ought to proceed, must apply principles under the Civil Procedure Rules and not under the previous regime of Rules of the Supreme Court or County Court Rules[37]. Earlier authorities on matters of civil procedure (even where the provisions in question in the Civil Procedure Rules are identically worded to those under the Rules of the Supreme Court or County Court Rules) are therefore not necessarily applicable in interpreting the new rules[38].

1   See the Civil Procedure Rules 1998, SI 1998/3132 ('CPR'), made under the Civil Procedure Act 1997; and PRACTICE AND PROCEDURE. Certain provisions of the RSC and CCR have been saved and continue to apply in a modified form: see CPR Sch 1 (saved provisions of RSC), CPR Sch 2 (saved provisions of CCR). The CPR apply to proceedings issued on or after 26 April 1999, and to new steps taken in existing proceedings, as prescribed: CPR Pt 51; *Practice Direction—Transitional Arrangements* (1999) PD 51. As to proceedings to which the CPR apply see CPR Pts 2, 49, 51.
2   See CPR Sch 1 RSC Ord 108; paras 548–549 post; and PRACTICE AND PROCEDURE. As to evidence see para 528 post. For the meaning of 'charity proceedings' see para 519 ante.
3   CPR Sch 1 RSC Ord 108 rr 1, 2. For the procedure in actions begun by claim forms see PRACTICE AND PROCEDURE.
4   See CPR 7.2. Unless there is a serious dispute of fact requiring particulars of claim, it is usual to commence charity proceedings by CPR Pt 8 (see PRACTICE AND PROCEDURE) supported by witness statement.
5   See CPR Sch 1 RSC Ord 108 r 3(3); and para 548 post. In the case of appeals, the appeal must be brought by an appellant's notice: see CPR Sch 1 RSC Ord 108 r 5(2); and para 549 post.
6   See CPR Sch 1 RSC Ord 52 r 1(4), Ord 108 r 4. See also para 494 ante.
7   Civil Procedure Act 1997 s 1(3).
8   CPR 1.1(1).
9   CPR 1.1(2)(a).
10  CPR 1.1(2)(b).
11  CPR 1.1(2)(c).
12  CPR 1.1(2)(c)(i).
13  CPR 1.1(2)(c)(ii).
14  CPR 1.1(2)(c)(iii).
15  CPR 1.1(2)(c)(iv).
16  CPR 1.1(2)(d).
17  CPR 1.1(2)(e).
18  CPR 1.2.
19  CPR 1.3.
20  CPR 1.4(1).
21  CPR 1.4(2)(a).
22  CPR 1.4(2)(b).
23  CPR 1.4(2)(c).
24  CPR 1.4(2)(d).
25  CPR 1.4(2)(e).
26  CPR 1.4(2)(f).
27  CPR 1.4(2)(g).
28  CPR 1.4(2)(h).
29  CPR 1.4(2)(i).

30 CPR 1.4(2)(j).
31 CPR 1.4(2)(k).
32 CPR 1.4(2)(l).
33 Civil Procedure Act 1997 s 2(7).
34 See CPR 1.1(1).
35 See *Bank of England v Vagliano Bros* [1891] AC 107 at 144–145, HL, per Lord Herschell (an appeal to earlier decisions can only be justified on some special ground); and STATUTES vol 44(1) (Reissue) para 1418.
36 See the text to note 8 supra.
37 See *Biguzzi v Rank Leisure plc* [1999] 4 All ER 934, [1999] 1 WLR 1926, CA.
38 See *Natwest Lombard Factors Ltd v Arbis* (1999) Times, 10 December. Accordingly, cases cited in this title as authority for the interpretation of the former rules or in amplification or explanation of the practice under them will be binding over proceedings conducted under those rules, but are unlikely to be regarded as authoritative in relation to proceedings conducted under the new regime and should therefore be viewed with caution.

# (3) CLAIMS AND OTHER PROCEEDINGS

## (i) In general

**523. Parties.** In the case of proceedings involving charities the general rules as to who are the proper parties[1] are subject to two qualifications. In the first place, as already stated, only specified persons may take charity proceedings[2]; in the second place, the Attorney General is generally a necessary party[3].

He may either act alone ex officio as the officer of the Crown and, as such, the protector of charities, or ex relatione at the request of a private individual, called a relator, who thinks that the charity is being or has been abused[4].

With the sanction of the Attorney General an ordinary action may be turned into a relator action, by amendment of the particulars of claim[5]. Otherwise claims of this kind, if instituted by parties other than the Attorney General or the Solicitor General[6], are dismissed[7], unless the Attorney General applies to be substituted[8] as claimant and the court gives permission for the substitution[9].

1 See generally PRACTICE AND PROCEDURE. Note in particular CPR Sch 1 RSC Ord 85 r 3, which requires executors, administrators or trustees, and some at any rate of the beneficiaries, to be parties to claims for the administration of a deceased person's estate or for the execution of a trust. Cf *Re HMF* [1976] Ch 33, [1975] 2 All ER 795. As to the CPR see para 522 ante. As to the weight to be given to be given to cases concerning matters of civil procedure decided before 26 April 1999 (ie the date on which the CPR came into force) see para 522 ante.
2 See the Charities Act 1993 s 33(1); and para 520 ante. For the meaning of 'charity proceedings' see para 519 ante.
3 Where the Attorney General is a proper party, the Solicitor General is the proper person to take his place if the Attorney General's office is vacant or if he is ill or concerned in the action in another capacity: *R v Wilkes* (1770) 4 Burr 2527 at 2554, HL, per Lord Mansfield; *Ludlow Corpn v Greenhouse* (1827) 1 Bli NS 17 at 51, HL, per Lord Redesdale; *A-G v Bristol Corpn* (1820) 2 Jac & W 294; *A-G v Ironmongers' Co* (1834) 2 My & K 576; *A-G v Dean and Canons of Windsor* (1860) 8 HL Cas 369; *Brookes v Richardson* [1986] 1 All ER 952, [1986] 1 WLR 385; and see paras 531, 538 post. As to when the Attorney General is not a necessary party see para 535 post. As to the Attorney General and the Solicitor General see CONSTITUTIONAL LAW AND HUMAN RIGHTS vol 8(2) (Reissue) para 529.

Before the creation of the High Court of Chancery, proceedings by the Attorney General ex officio or at the relation of plaintiffs were taken by information, it being a public privilege that the Crown should be entitled to intervene by its officer for the purpose of asserting a public right: *A-G v Compton* (1842) 1 Y & C Ch Cas 417 at 427 per Knight Bruce V-C. After 1873 these proceedings became actions commenced by writ: cf *A-G v Shrewsbury Bridge Co* (1880) 42 LT 79. These actions were not affected by the abolition of Latin and English informations by the Crown Proceedings Act 1947 s 13, Sch 1, but, except so far as they are excepted by s 23(3)(a) as being relator proceedings, they appear to be civil proceedings by the Crown within s 23(1)(b): see CROWN PROCEEDINGS AND CROWN PRACTICE vol 12(1) (Reissue) paras 107, 110, 116. See further paras 531, 538 post.

4    *A-G v Logan* [1891] 2 QB 100 at 103, DC, per Wills J; and see *A-G v Cockermouth Local Board* (1874) LR 18 Eq 172 at 176 per Jessel MR. Except for the purposes of costs there is no practical difference between proceedings ex officio and ex relatione. As to relators see further para 539 et seq post. Relator proceedings are now rare in practice.

5    *Caldwell v Pagham Harbour Reclamation Co* (1876) 2 ChD 221 (reclamation of land covered by sea); *Wallasey Local Board v Gracey* (1887) 36 ChD 593 at 599 per Stirling J (public nuisance). For earlier practice see *President etc of St Mary Magdalen College, Oxford v Sibthorp* (1826) 1 Russ 154; *A-G v Newcombe* (1807) 14 Ves 1 at 6 per Lord Eldon LC; *A-G v Vivian* (1826) 1 Russ 226; *A-G v East India Co* (1840) 11 Sim 380; *A-G v Cuming* (1843) 2 Y & C Ch Cas 139 at 149 per Knight Bruce V-C. If the claim is or becomes one within the statutory definition of 'charity proceedings' (see para 519 ante), it should be begun by a claim form (see CPR 7.2; and para 522 ante), but the court could, no doubt, permit it to proceed with particulars of claim (cf CPR 8.1(3); and see PRACTICE AND PROCEDURE). The claim should normally be a CPR Part 8 claim: see PRACTICE AND PROCEDURE.

6    See note 3 supra.

7    *A-G v Hewitt* (1804) 9 Ves 232; *A-G v Green* (1820) 1 Jac & W 303 at 305 per Lord Eldon LC; *Strickland v Weldon* (1885) 28 ChD 426; *A-G v Wyggeston Hospital* (1853) 16 Beav 313, where a petition presented in the name, but without the authority, of the Attorney General was dismissed.

8    Ie under CPR 19.2: see PRACTICE AND PROCEDURE.

9    Cf *Hauxwell v Barton-upon-Humber UDC* [1974] Ch 432, [1973] 2 All ER 1022.

**524. Control of proceedings the court.** The court has a duty to actively manage cases[1] and its general powers of management are set out in the Civil Procedure Rules[2].

1    See CPR 1.4; para 522 ante; and PRACTICE AND PROCEDURE.

2    See CPR Pt 3; and PRACTICE AND PROCEDURE. Formerly, it was the case that the Attorney General had entire control of the proceedings, whether they were ex officio or at the request of a relator: *Andrew v Master and Wardens of the Merchant Taylors' Co* (1800) 7 Ves 223, HL; *A-G v Hewitt* (1804) 9 Ves 232; *Ludlow Corpn v Greenhouse* (1827) 1 Bli NS 17 at 65, HL, per Lord Redesdale; *A-G v Ironmongers' Co* (1840) 2 Beav 313 at 328–329 per Lord Langdale MR; *A-G v Haberdashers' Co* (1852) 15 Beav 397. See also the non-charity case of *LCC v A-G* [1902] AC 165, HL. As to relators see further para 539 et seq post. Relator proceedings are now rare in practice.

The Attorney General had control even where he did not act personally: *A-G v Hewitt* (1804) 9 Ves 232. No amendment could be made (*A-G v Fellows* (1820) 1 Jac & W 254), or notice of motion given (*A-G v Wright* (1841) 3 Beav 447), without his consent. He could also, at any time, stay the proceedings: *A-G v Ironmongers' Co* (1840) 2 Beav 313 at 329 per Lord Langdale MR; *A-G v Newark-upon-Trent Corpn* (1842) 1 Hare 395. A reference to arbitration could only be made with his sanction: *A-G v Hewitt* (1804) 9 Ves 232; *A-G v Fea* (1819) 4 Madd 274; and see *Prior v Hembrow* (1841) 8 M & W 873. His consent was also necessary before an award could be acted upon: *A-G v Hewitt* (1804) 9 Ves 232; and see *A-G v Clements* (1823) Turn & R 58 at 61 per Lord Eldon LC.

**525. Duty of Attorney General and of court.** It has been held that it is not the duty of the Attorney General in all charity cases to contend for his strict legal rights when the result of enforcing them would be oppressive to individuals. If, however, he insists on his strict rights, the court will enforce them[1].

The court formerly exercised a quasi-custodial jurisdiction over a charity when an action was brought for its regulation or administration[2].

1 *A-G v Brettingham* (1840) 3 Beav 91 at 95 per Lord Langdale MR. See also *Re Snowden, Shackleton v Eddy, Re Henderson, Henderson v A-G* [1970] Ch 700, [1969] 3 All ER 208; and para 369 ante. As to the Attorney-General see para 516 ante.

2 See *A-G v Governors of Harrow School* (1754) 2 Ves Sen 551 at 552 per Lord Hardwicke LC: 'though I will make no decree at present, yet I will not dismiss the information, but still keep a hand over them'. The principal example of this attitude was that the wrong prayer was never fatal in a charity case where it appeared that some relief might be given; cf *A-G v Coopers' Co* (1812) 19 Ves 187 at 194 per Lord Eldon LC: 'the court is not only to attend to an actual complaint but to see whether there is any cause for complaint'. Actions were generally not dismissed for want of form, though care was taken not to injure the defendant. These principles may be regarded as obsolete for general relief may now be given (see the Supreme Court Act 1981 s 49; and PRACTICE AND PROCEDURE), and amendment to statements of case is more freely available (see CPR Pt 17; and PRACTICE AND PROCEDURE). As to the CPR see para 522 ante.

In addition, the Charity Commissioners have powers of supervision, guidance and inquiry in relation to charities: see para 486 et seq ante. As to the Charity Commissioners see paras 486–512 ante.

## 526. Information to Attorney General with a view to proceedings by him.

Where it appears to the Charity Commissioners[1] that it is desirable for legal proceedings to be taken with reference to any charity[2] (other than an exempt charity[3]) or its property or affairs, and for the proceedings to be taken by the Attorney General, they must so inform him and send him such statements and particulars as they think necessary to explain the matter[4].

1 As to the Charity Commissioners see paras 486–512 ante.
2 For the meaning of 'charity' see para 1 ante.
3 As to exempt charities see para 293 ante.
4 Charities Act 1993 s 33(7). This may arise out of an application for the Commissioners' authority under s 33 to take charity proceedings or otherwise: s 33(7). For the meaning of 'charity proceedings' see para 519 ante. The Charity Commissioners may, by their own motion, also bring legal proceedings with reference to charities or the property or affairs of charities, with the agreement of the Attorney General: see s 32(5); and para 496 ante.

## 527. Proceedings by trustees.

If the Attorney General declines to interfere in a dispute over the administration of a trust, and the trustees of the charity differ amongst themselves as to the proper mode of administration, a certain number may bring the matter before the court by a claim on behalf of themselves and others, making some of the dissentients and the Attorney General defendants[1].

1 *Lang v Purves* (1862) 8 Jur NS 523 at 525, PC. Such proceedings would require the consent of the Charity Commissioners or the permission of the court: see para 521 ante. As to one or more of numerous parties suing or defending on behalf of all see CPR 19.6; *A-G v Fowler* (1808) 15 Ves 85 at 87; *Milligan v Mitchell* (1837) 3 My & Cr 72; and PRACTICE AND PROCEDURE. As to the CPR see para 522 ante. As to the weight to be given to be given to cases concerning matters of civil procedure decided before 26 April 1999 (ie the date on which the CPR came into force) see para 522 ante.

It is now relatively uncommon for the Attorney General to commence charity proceedings. It is more usual for one or more of the trustees to do so, making any dissentient trustees, as well as the Attorney General, defendants: see *Varsani v Jesani* [1999] Ch 219, [1998] 3 All ER 273, CA.

## 528. Evidence.

In any proceedings, the printed copies of the reports of the Charity Commissioners[1] for inquiring concerning charities between 1818 and 1837[2] and of the printed copies of the reports which were made for various counties and county boroughs to the Charity Commissioners by their assistant Commissioners and presented to the House of Commons as returns to orders of various dates between 8 December 1890 and 9 September 1909, are admissible as evidence of the documents[3] and facts stated in them[4].

A certified copy of a document enrolled by or deposited with the Charity Commissioners is sufficient evidence of the contents and enrolment or deposit of the document[5]. Evidence of any order, certificate or other document issued by the Commissioners may be given by means of a copy retained by them, or taken from a copy so retained, and certified to be a true copy by any officer of the Commissioners generally or specially authorised by them to act for this purpose[6]. The official seal of the Commissioners is judicially noticed[7].

In any legal proceedings instituted[8] by the Charity Commissioners, or instituted by the Attorney General in respect of a charity[9], a copy of the report of the person conducting an inquiry[10] is admissible, if certified by the Commissioners to be a true copy, as evidence of any fact stated in the report, and as evidence of the opinion of that person as to any matter referred to in it[11].

1   As to the Charity Commissioners see paras 486–512 ante.
2   Ie who were appointed under the Act 58 Geo 3 c 91 (the Inquiry Concerning Charities Act 1838) (repealed).
3   For the meaning of 'document' see para 236 note 2 ante.
4   Charities Act 1993 s 93(2).
5   See ibid s 30(3); and para 341 ante.
6   Ibid s 93(3). A document purporting to be a copy so certified is receivable in evidence without proof of the officer's position, authority or handwriting: s 93(3). Most of the evidence in charity proceedings takes the form of a witness statement exhibiting the relevant documents.
7   See ibid s 2(1), Sch 1 para 3(1); and para 488 ante.
8   Ie under ibid Pt IV (ss 13–35) (as amended).
9   For the meaning of 'charity' see para 1 ante.
10  Ie under the Charities Act 1993 s 8: see paras 497–498 ante.
11  Ibid s 34(1), (2). A document purporting to be a certificate issued for the purposes of s 34(1) must be received in evidence and is deemed to be such a certificate, unless the contrary is proved: s 34(3).

**529. Court's discretion.** Modern practice of the courts has been to consider what is in the interests of the charity in determining the issues arising in the case, and if it considers that the proceedings themselves are against its interests it will make this very clear, and either encourage the parties to settle or refuse relief on grounds of expense[1]. By its wide discretion over costs the court can discourage parties taking useless proceedings even if the proceedings are sanctioned by the Attorney General[2].

The court has disapproved of charity proceedings being promoted by public meetings and supported by public subscriptions[3].

Actual or contemplated breaches of trust may be restrained by injunction[4]. When necessary a claim for an injunction may be brought by a trustee against his co-trustees[5].

1   See eg *The Governing Body of the Henrietta Barnett School v Hampstead Garden Suburb Institute* (1995) 93 LRG 470, sub nom *Re Hampstead Garden Suburb Institute* (1995) Times, 13 April; *Varsani v Jesani* [1999] Ch 219, [1998] 3 All ER 273, CA. However, there are many cases in which the sole question for the court is whether proposed proceedings are in the interests of the charity: see eg *Weth v A-G* (3 December 1997, unreported); affd [2001] EWCA Civ 263 (proposed appeal against appointment of receiver and manager for charity held not in the interests of the charity because of charity's limited financial resources).

2   _A-G (ex rel Everett and Bottomley) v Merchant Tailors' Co_ (1834) 5 LJCh 62; but see _A-G v Cullum_ (1836) 1 Keen 104; and para 395 ante.

Instead of acting according to the strict rules of law, the court had discretion to refer matters arising out of proceedings to the Attorney General, and to act on his certificate or report: _A-G v Exeter Corpn_ (1827) 2 Russ 362 (where the court referred the matter to the Attorney General to certify whether a charity might accept from its debtor a smaller sum than was actually due); _A-G v Green_ (1820) 1 Jac & W 303; _A-G v Carlisle Corpn_ (1831) 4 Sim 275; _A-G v Pretyman_ (1841) 4 Beav 462 at 467 per Lord Langdale MR; _A-G v Tufnell_ (1849) 12 Beav 35 at 41 per Lord Langdale MR; and see _A-G v Brettingham_ (1840) 3 Beav 91 (where, in a hard case, the decision was postponed in order that the Attorney General might come to some arrangement). However, questions arising on the construction of wills and other documents were not referred to the Attorney General: _A-G v Fea_ (1819) 4 Madd 274.

3   _A-G v Bishop of Worcester_ (1851) 21 LJCh 25 at 46 per Turner V-C.

4   _Rigall v Foster_ (1853) 18 Jur 39 (to restrain improper mortgage by charity trustees); _A-G v Welsh_ (1844) 4 Hare 572 (to prevent user of chapel for unauthorised form of worship); _A-G v Murdoch_ (1849) 7 Hare 445 (affd (1852) 1 De GM & G 86); _Cooper v Gordon_ (1869) LR 8 Eq 249 (to restrain ministers from officiating); _Milligan v Mitchell_ (1833) 1 My & K 446 (to prevent election of unlicensed minister). As to injunctions generally see INJUNCTIONS.

5   _Re Chertsey Market, ex p Walthew_ (1819) 6 Price 261 at 279; _Perry v Shipway_ (1859) 4 De G & J 353 (where an improper retainer of a chapel by the minority of the trustees was prevented by the majority).


**530. Compromise.** Questions relating to charities may be compromised and the terms of the compromise confirmed by the court[1].

Trustees for charities have power to compromise claims under the Trustee Act 1925[2]. In addition, a compromise may be approved by the Charity Commissioners[3] under the Charities Act 1993[4].

Where the Attorney General is a party to any legal proceedings affecting a charity, no compromise can be enforced without his sanction[5]. Where, in proceedings in which a charity is cited but does not appear, the Attorney General assents to a compromise on behalf of the absent charity, that charity is bound by the compromise[6].


1   This may happen, for example, in cases where it is doubtful whether a bequest or devise to charity is valid, and a compromise is arrived at by a division of the property between the charity and other claimants, such as the persons entitled on intestacy, and residuary legatees: _A-G v Landerfield_ (1743) 9 Mod Rep 286; _Re Simpson's Will_ (circa 1786) cited in 5 Ves 304; _A-G v Bishop of Oxford_ (1786) cited in 4 Ves 431; _Andrew v Master and Wardens of the Merchant Taylors' Co_ (1800) 7 Ves 223; _Andrew v Trinity Hall, Cambridge_ (1804) 9 Ves 525 at 532–533 per Grant MR. See also _A-G v Trevelyan_ (1847) 16 LJCh 521 and _Re Freeston's Charity, Sylvester v Master and Fellows of University College, Oxford_ [1978] 1 All ER 481 at 490, [1978] 1 WLR 120 at 130 per Fox J; affd [1979] 1 All ER 51, [1978] 1 WLR 741, CA, without discussing this point.

2   See the Trustee Act 1925 s 15 (as amended); and TRUSTS vol 48 (2000 Reissue) para 947.

3   As to the Charity Commissioners see paras 486–512 ante.

4   See the Charities Act 1993 s 26(2); and para 330 ante.

5   _Andrew v Master and Wardens of the Merchant Taylors' Co_ (1800) 7 Ves 223; _Andrew v Trinity Hall, Cambridge_ (1804) 9 Ves 525 at 532–533 per Grant MR; _A-G v Exeter Corpn_ (1827) 2 Russ 362; _A-G v Fishmongers' Co_ (1837) Coop Pr Cas 85; _A-G v Ludlow Corpn_ (1842) 6 Jur 1003; _A-G v Trevelyan_ (1847) 16 LJCh 521; _A-G v Boucherett_ (1858) 25 Beav 116.

6   _Re King, Jackson v A-G_ [1917] 2 Ch 420.


### (ii)   The Attorney General as a Party


**531. Attorney General a necessary party.** The Attorney General[1] is generally a necessary party to all claims relating to charities[2]. Thus where proceedings[3] are necessary to test the validity of an alleged charitable gift[4], even where the class to benefit is a foreign community[5], or to determine whether a claim to the benefit of a charity is properly founded[6], or to enforce the execution of a charitable purpose, or to remedy abuse or misapplication of charitable funds, or to administer a charity[7], the Attorney General is generally[8] a necessary party[9], and is normally the proper claimant[10]. He represents the beneficial interest, in other words the objects, of the charity[11]. Even if all the subscribers to a charitable fund are made claimants, a claim for the regulation of the charity is defective unless the Attorney General is also a party[12].

1    The Solicitor General may in some circumstances discharge the Attorney General's functions: see para 523 note 3 ante. As to the Attorney General see para 516 ante.

2    The Attorney General's right to file an information (which was the procedure prior to the creation of the High Court of Chancery: see para 523 note 3 ante), and consequently his right to take proceedings today, was founded on the Crown's prerogative as parens patriae (see CONSTITUTIONAL LAW AND HUMAN RIGHTS vol 8(2) (Reissue) para 309) to inform the court of and demand a remedy for an injustice perpetrated against a subject of the Crown (eg a charity) who was incompetent to enforce a claim in person: see Shelford's Law of Mortmain (1836) 399; *A-G v Brown* (1818) 1 Swan 265 at 291; *Wellbeloved v Jones* (1822) 1 Sim & St 40; *A-G v Compton* (1842) 1 Y & C Ch Cas 417 at 427 per Knight Bruce V-C; *A-G v Magdalen College, Oxford* (1854) 23 LJCh 844 at 852 per Romilly MR. See also *Re Weir Hospital* [1910] 2 Ch 124 at 130, CA; *Re Belling, Enfield London Borough Council v Public Trustee* [1967] Ch 425, [1967] 1 All ER 105; *Hauxwell v Barton-upon-Humber UDC* [1974] Ch 432, [1973] 2 All ER 1022. Moreover, the Attorney General is the protector of the interests of all charities beneficially entitled under charitable gifts, and all beneficiaries are bound if he is made a party: *Re Sekeford's Charity* (1861) 5 LT 488; *Ware v Cumberlege* (1855) 20 Beav 503.

3    See para 523 note 3 ante.

4    See eg *Kirkbank v Hudson* (1819) 7 Price 212.

5    See *Re Love, Naper v Barlow* [1932] WN 17 (gift for benefit of parishes in Republic of Ireland: Attorney General of the Republic held not to be a proper party and struck out; Attorney General directed to be added).

6    *Re Magdalen Land Charity, Hastings* (1852) 9 Hare 624, where the proceeds of the charity had for many years been applied for other purposes.

7    See para 532 post.

8    *Wellbeloved v Jones* (1822) 1 Sim & St 40; *Ware v Cumberlege* (1855) 20 Beav 503; *Boughey v Minor* [1893] P 181 (compromise). The cases distinguish between gifts for charity generally, which cannot be represented by anyone other than the Attorney General, and cases where there are specified individual charities, when the Attorney General's presence is not universally necessary. However, if there is a gift to charity trustees and the question is whether the trust is validly established, the persons named as trustees are the proper parties, and it may not be necessary for the Attorney General to be a party: *Practice Note* [1945] WN 38. See also *Re HMF* [1976] Ch 33, [1975] 2 All ER 795.

9    *Wellbeloved v Jones* (1822) 1 Sim & St 40; *Christ's Hospital Governors v A-G* (1846) 5 Hare 257 (Attorney General as defendant); *Philipps v A-G* [1932] WN 100 (dormant fund, raised by subscription; cy-près application; Attorney General as defendant).

10   *Strickland v Weldon* (1885) 28 ChD 426 at 430 per Pearson J; *Re Belling, Enfield London Borough Council v Public Trustee* [1967] Ch 425, [1967] 1 All ER 105; *Hauxwell v Barton-upon-Humber UDC* [1974] Ch 432, [1973] 2 All ER 1022; but see *Baldry v Feintuck* [1972] 2 All ER 81, [1972] 1 WLR 552, where the Attorney General was not a party. When appearing on behalf of a charity, the Attorney General is not like an ordinary claimant endeavouring to obtain redress for a private wrong. It is one of his duties to protect the defendant against any hardship which he might suffer at the hands of the relators, eg if they mislead him or withhold documents or other necessary information: *A-G v Clapham* (1853) 10 Hare App II, lxviii at lxx per Wood V-C. Although the Attorney General is a proper claimant, he is most often involved as the defendant: see para 534 post. As to relators see further para 539 et seq post. Relator proceedings are now rare in practice.

      In High Court proceedings for the construction of wills or other documents or by personal representatives for directions, the Attorney General, if a party where a charity is concerned, is usually made a defendant: see eg *Re Lawton, Gartside v A-G* [1936] 3 All ER 378 (question whether bequest should lapse or be applied cy-près).

11   *A-G v Brodie* (1846) 6 Moo PCC 12; *A-G v Bishop of Worcester* (1851) 9 Hare 328 at 361 per Turner V-C; *Ware v Cumberlege* (1855) 20 Beav 503; *Re Sekeford's Charity* (1861) 5 LT 488. See also *Brooks v Richardson* [1986] 1 All ER 952, [1986] 1 WLR 385.

12 *Stickland v Weldon* (1885) 28 ChD 426. See also *Minn v Stant* (1851) 15 Beav 49, where, for a special transaction, it was held that the subscribers were necessary parties; but see *Baldry v Feintuck* [1972] 2 All ER 81, [1972] 1 WLR 552.

**532. Administration proceedings.** In administration proceedings where a question arises as to the application of a gift for charitable purposes, the Attorney General is a necessary party to represent the interests of charity in general[1]. Where there are gifts to specified individual charities and the establishment of a scheme or rules is required for the regulation of the internal conduct of the charity, the presence of the Attorney General is necessary[2]. Similarly, he is generally a necessary party when the question is whether a particular bequest is charitable[3], or is applicable cy-près[4], or where there is a gift to an established charitable institution to be held upon trusts differing from those upon which the general funds of the institution are held[5].

The Attorney General is not a necessary party in administration proceedings where the legacy is to an established charitable institution as part of its general funds[6], or to named trustees and the question is the validity of the trusts of which they are trustees[7], or to an action for account in respect of a legacy given to a charity[8], or where annual sums are given to specified trustees to be distributed in charity[9], or where a capital sum is given for immediate distribution[10]. Where the question is whether a charity is entitled to a particular legacy or not, the Attorney General may be made a party as being in the nature of a trustee for the charity, but his presence is not necessary, and the court prefers that the charity should itself appear rather than that the Attorney General should represent it[11].

1 *Ware v Cumberlege* (1855) 20 Beav 503 at 511 per Romilly MR. See also *A-G v Bowyer* (1798) 3 Ves 714 at 726 per Lord Hardwicke LC; *Boughey v Minor* [1893] P 181; *Re Pyne, Lilley v A-G* [1903] 1 Ch 83; and *Practice Note* [1945] WN 38.
2 *Ware v Cumberlege* (1855) 20 Beav 503.
3 *Cook v Duckenfield* (1743) 2 Atk 562 at 564 per Lord Hardwicke LC; and see para 531 ante.
4 *Re Taylor, Martin v Freeman* (1888) 58 LT 538. A legacy may be ordered to be paid to a legatee on his undertaking to the Attorney General to apply the sum for charitable purposes: see *Re Reddish, Penton v Waters* [1934] WN 198. As to the doctrine of cy-près see para 201 et seq ante.
5 *Wellbeloved v Jones* (1822) 1 Sim & St 40; *Sons of the Clergy Corpn v Mose* (1839) 9 Sim 610; and see *A-G v Warren* (1818) 2 Swan 291.
6 *Wellbeloved v Jones* (1822) 1 Sim & St 40; *Re M'Auliffe's Goods* [1895] P 290.
7 See *Practice Note* [1945] WN 38: in such cases the position is that there is no universal rule that the Attorney General must be a party.
8 *Chitty v Parker* (1792) 4 Bro CC 38.
9 *Waldo v Caley* (1809) 16 Ves 206; *M'Coll v Atherton* (1848) 12 Jur 1042. See also *Horde v Earl of Suffolk* (1833) 2 My & K 59 (where the Attorney General was a party but appeared to claim the legacy on behalf of the Crown, alleging failure of the charitable bequest and of the next of kin).
10 *Re Barnett* (1860) 29 LJCh 871. But see *Re Lea, Lea v Cooke* (1887) 34 ChD 528 (where the Attorney General was a party, the question being whether a charitable legacy should be paid over without a scheme).
11 *Ware v Cumberlege* (1855) 20 Beav 503.

**533. Claims by Crown.** The Attorney General represents the Crown where the Crown is claiming beneficially[1]. Therefore, when the Crown's private rights conflict with its rights as protector of charities, one of the law officers appears on behalf of the Crown's private interests and the other represents the charitable interest[2].

The Attorney General had to be a party to legal proceedings where the question concerned the Crown's right to appoint under the sign manual, even before the right was delegated to him[3].

1   *A-G v Magdalen College, Oxford* (1854) 18 Beav 223 at 241 per Romilly MR.
2   *A-G v Bristol Corpn* (1820) 2 Jac & W 294 at 312 per Lord Eldon LC; *A-G v Ironmongers' Co* (1834) 2 My & K 576 at 578; *A-G v Dean and Canons of Windsor* (1860) 8 HL Cas 369.
3   *De Themmines v De Bonneval* (1828) 5 Russ 288. See para 457 ante.

**534. Attorney General as defendant.** The Attorney General may be made a defendant in a claim by charity trustees for an account of the charity property and a personal discharge[1]; or for the purpose of protecting the interests of a charity[2], as, for example, where a claim is brought by executors to determine the validity of a doubtful charitable bequest[3]; or to decide whether a testator's general charitable intention should be carried into effect by a court scheme or under the royal sign manual[4].

1   *Clum Hospital Warden and Brethren v Lord Powys* (1842) 6 Jur 252; *Christ's Hospital Governors v A-G* (1846) 5 Hare 257. In such claims the trustees must render such accounts as the Attorney General demands, and, if he desires it, the court may direct a scheme. As to proceedings by trustees see para 527 ante. As to the direction of schemes see para 170 et seq ante.
2   *Ludlow Corpn v Greenhouse* (1827) 1 Bli NS 17 at 66, HL, per Lord Redesdale.
3   See *Re Waring, Hayward v A-G* [1907] 1 Ch 166; *Re Pardoe, McLaughlin v A-G* [1906] 2 Ch 184; *Re Mann, Hardy v A-G* [1903] 1 Ch 232.
4   *Re Pyne, Lilley v A-G* [1903] 1 Ch 83; *Re Bennett, Sucker v A-G* [1960] Ch 18, [1959] 3 All ER 295.

**535. When Attorney General is not a necessary party.** The Attorney General is not a necessary party where the proceedings concern a private charity[1], or where the trust is not charitable[2], or where, whether the trust is charitable or not, the parties taking the proceedings do so under express statutory powers[3], or where third persons are taking proceedings against charity trustees for specific performance of an agreement[4].

1   *Anon* (1745) 3 Atk 277 (society for providing for necessities of its members and their widows, being in the nature of a private charity, the Attorney General on behalf of the Crown is not concerned to see to its proper application). A private charity (see para 52 ante) in this sense is one for the benefit of private individuals, and not of the public or a section of the public (see para 8 ante). Quaere whether this would now be followed. If it is right, it is on the basis that the institution is not charitable at all in the legal sense.
2   *A-G v Hewer* (1700) 2 Vern 387 (school not a charity school); *A-G v Whorwood* (1750) 1 Ves Sen 534 at 536 per Lord Hardwicke LC (where it was held, in the case of a devise to a college, that there were no grounds for an information (see para 523 note 3 ante) by the Attorney General); *A-G v Brereton* (1752) 2 Ves Sen 425 at 426 per Lord Hardwicke LC; *A-G v Newcombe* (1807) 14 Ves 1 at 7 per Lord Eldon LC; *Prestney v Colchester Corpn and A-G* (1882) 21 ChD 111.
    The cases deciding that advowsons held on trust for parishioners were not charity property and that therefore an information by the Attorney General was not maintainable with regard to such trusts (see *A-G v Parker* (1747) 1 Ves Sen 43; *A-G v Forster* (1804) 10 Ves 335; *A-G v Newcombe* supra; *A-G v Webster* (1875) LR 20 Eq 483 at 491 per Jessel MR) cannot be supported on that point since the cases of *Re St Stephen, Coleman Street, Re St Mary the Virgin, Aldermanbury* (1888) 39 ChD 492 and *Hunter v A-G* [1899] AC 309 at 315, HL, per Earl of Halsbury LC, which decided that such trusts are charitable. See para 34 ante. As to advowsons see ECCLESIASTICAL LAW vol 14 para 776.
3   *Prestney v Colchester Corpn and A-G* (1882) 21 ChD 111 at 119–120 per Hall V-C (action by some freemen of a borough, on behalf of all, to establish a right for the benefit of all the freemen, suing under

powers conferred by the Municipal Corporations Act 1835 s 2 (repealed)); cf *A-G v Meyrick* [1893] AC 1, HL (where the Act did not contain similar provisions and the Attorney General was a party).

4   *A-G v Warren* (1818) 2 Swan 291 at 311 per Plumer MR; *Neville Estates Ltd v Madden* [1962] Ch 832, [1961] 3 All ER 769. See also *Rendall v Blair* (1890) 45 Ch D 139, CA.


**536. Parties bound by proceedings.** All beneficiaries are bound by the result of proceedings to which the Attorney General is a party[1], but the Attorney General is not bound by any proceedings taken by beneficiaries to which he is not made a party[2].

1   *Vince v Walsh* (1854) 3 WR 7.
2   *A-G v Leage* (1881) Tudor on Charities (4th Edn, 1906) 1041 at 1044 per Kay J, discussing *Saunders v Howes* (1857) cited in Tudor on Charities (4th Edn, 1906) 1043.


**537. Payment into court by trustees.** When charitable funds are paid into court by trustees under the Trustee Act 1925[1], the trustees' affidavit to which the lodgment schedule is attached should state that the Attorney General as representing the public has an interest in the funds, and he should be served with notice[2]. The payment into court discharges the trustees, and all future applications in regard to the fund so paid in must be made by the Attorney General only[3].

1   See the Trustee Act 1925 s 63 (as amended); and TRUSTS vol 48 (2000 Reissue) para 809 et seq.
2   See CPR Sch 1 RSC Ord 92 r 2; and PRACTICE AND PROCEDURE. See also *Re Poplar and Blackwall Free School* (1878) 8 ChD 543 at 546 per Jessel MR. As to the CPR see para 522 ante. As to the weight to be given to be given to cases concerning matters of civil procedure decided before 26 April 1999 (ie the date on which the CPR came into force) see para 522 ante.
3   *Re Poplar and Blackwall Free School* (1878) 8 ChD 543.


**538. Appeal by Attorney General.** With the permission of the Court of Appeal, the Attorney General may appeal against a decision in proceedings to which he was not a party in the court of first instance[1]. However, after a decree which he did not oppose in proceedings to which he was a party he should not reopen the discussion by an appeal, although the court will not dismiss the appeal on that ground alone[2].

1   *Re Faraker, Faraker v Durell* [1912] 2 Ch 488, CA.
2   *Christ's Hospital v Grainger* (1849) 19 LJCh 33 at 36 per Lord Cottenham LC.


### (iii)   The Relator


**539. Introduction of relator.** The introduction of a relator in claims relating to charities is not essential[1]. The Attorney General may, if he pleases, take proceedings without a relator[2], or may require one to be introduced even in cases certified by the Charity Commissioners[3], the object being to have before the court a person who may be made liable for any costs which may be awarded against the Crown[4]. In connection with the award of costs, the Crown is not deemed to be a party to proceedings by reason only that the proceedings are brought by the Attorney General on the relation of some other person[5].

Relator proceedings are now rare in practice.

1  *Mucklow v A-G* (1816) 4 Dow 1 at 15 per Lord Redesdale; *Re Masters, Governors and Trustees of the Bedford Charity* (1819) 2 Swan 470 at 520 per Lord Eldon LC; *A-G v Dublin Corpn* (1827) 1 Bli NS 312 at 351, HL, per Lord Redesdale.

2  *A-G v Logan* [1891] 2 QB 100 at 107, DC, per Williams J; *A-G v Lewis* (1845) 8 Beav 179.

3  *A-G v Boucherett* (1858) 25 Beav 116. As to the Charity Commissioners see paras 486–512 ante.

4  Shelford's Law of Mortmain (1836) 424, 425; *A-G v Brown* (1818) 1 Swan 265 at 305 per Lord Eldon LC; *Re Masters, Governors and Trustees of the Bedford Charity* (1819) 2 Swan 470; *A-G v Dublin Corpn* (1827) 1 Bli NS 312 at 351–352, HL, per Lord Redesdale; *A-G v Boucherett* (1858) 25 Beav 116 at 120 per Romilly MR; *A-G v Logan* [1891] 2 QB 100 at 106 per Vaughan Williams J: the practice of making the relator directly responsible for the costs of the action had its origin not in the protection of the defendant but of the Crown. However, see *Ludlow Corpn v Greenhouse* (1827) 1 Bli NS 17 at 48, HL, where Lord Redesdale suggests that a relator was joined in the interests of the defendant. See para 550 post.

5  See the Administration of Justice (Miscellaneous Provisions) Act 1933 s 7(2). This provision is not affected by the Crown Proceedings Act 1947: see s 23(3)(a); and CROWN PROCEEDINGS AND CROWN PRACTICE vol 12(1) (Reissue) para 116. See further para 550 post.

**540. Who may be relators.** The following persons and bodies may act as relators[1]: any private individual who thinks that a charity has been abused[2], several individuals[3], the trustees of the charities concerned or any of them[4], corporations[5], companies[6], district councils[7], local education authorities[8], and ratepayers[9]. A relator need not have any interest in the charity, its administration, or the subject of the suit[10], but he must not be a person in indigent circumstances[11].

The restrictions on the bringing of charity proceedings[12] do not apply to the taking of such proceedings by the Attorney General with a relator[13].

1  Relator proceedings are now rare in practice.

2  Shelford's Law of Mortmain (1836) 424.

3  *A-G v Earl of Clarendon* (1810) 17 Ves 491 (several inhabitants).

4  *A-G v Griffith* (1807) 13 Ves 565 at 571, citing *A-G v Talbot* (circa 1800; unreported).

5  *A-G v Logan* [1891] 2 QB 100 at 104 per Wills J; *A-G v Ashborne Recreation Ground Co* [1903] 1 Ch 101. As to corporations generally see CORPORATIONS.

6  *A-G v Merthyr Tydfil Union* [1900] 1 Ch 516, CA. As to companies generally see COMPANIES.

7  *A-G v Wimbledon House Estate Co Ltd* [1904] 2 Ch 34. As to areas and authorities in England and Wales see LOCAL GOVERNMENT.

8  *A-G v Price* (1908) 72 JP 208.

9  *LCC v A-G* [1902] AC 165, HL.

10  *A-G v Bucknall* (1742) 2 Atk 328; *A-G v Green* (1789) 2 Bro CC 492 at 497; *A-G v Vivian* (1826) 1 Russ 226 at 236 per Lord Gifford MR. See also *Southmolton Corpn v A-G* (1854) 5 HL Cas 1 at 27 per Lord Cranworth LC (where the court appeared to look with disfavour upon a relator who was a complete stranger to the charity). A paragraph in the statement of claim indicating the relator's interest has been held not irrelevant: *A-G v Rickards* (1843) 6 Beav 444; affd (1844) 1 Ph 383; on appeal, sub nom *Rickards v A-G* (1845) 12 Cl & Fin 30, HL.

11  *Fellows v Barrett* (1836) 1 Keen 119 at 120 per Lord Langdale MR. This is because he is liable for costs: see para 554 post. A solicitor's certificate of the relator's fitness to act and ability to pay costs is necessary.

12  See para 519 et seq ante.

13  See the Charities Act 1993 s 33(6); and para 520 ante. The Attorney General may take such proceedings without a relator: s 33(6).

**541. Relator and Attorney General.** The introduction of a relator's name does not make him a claimant[1], except where he is personally interested in the relief sought[2], and then he may be a co-claimant in his personal capacity. The Crown, acting through the Attorney General, is the real claimant[3].

A relator's claim is the claim of the Attorney General, and therefore the relator cannot appear separately[4], or take an opposite view[5] from the Attorney General; nor, when a relator is claimant, can he be heard in person on behalf of the Attorney General[6].

Under the Rules of the Supreme Court, it was the practice that before a person's name was used as a relator he was required to give a written authorisation, which had to be filed[7]. Before the claim form is issued the Attorney General's fiat must be obtained, and for this purpose counsel must certify that the proceedings are proper to be begun by the Attorney General[8].

The Attorney General may appear either in person or by counsel[9], or he may authorise the relator to conduct the case and instruct counsel on his behalf. The Attorney General cannot then appear independently[10] except by the court's special permission[11].

1   *A-G v Logan* [1891] 2 QB 100 at 106 per Williams J. Relator proceedings are now rare in practice.
2   *A-G v Heelis* (1824) 2 Sim & St 67; *A-G v Vivian* (1826) 1 Russ 226 at 236 per Lord Gifford MR; *Lang v Purves* (1862) 15 Moo PCC 389. Under the old practice, where the relator joined as plaintiff, the proceeding was called 'a bill and information'.
3   *A-G v Logan* [1891] 2 QB 100.
4   *A-G v Ironmongers' Co* (1840) 2 Beav 313 at 328 per Lord Langdale MR.
5   *A-G v Governors etc of Sherborne Grammar School* (1854) 18 Beav 256. However, in *Shore v Wilson* (1842) 9 Cl & Fin 355 at 475, HL, the Attorney General appeared for the defendants in an action by the Attorney with a relator.
6   *A-G v Barker* (1838) 4 My & Cr 262.
7   See RSC Ord 15 r 11 (revoked).
8   As to costs see para 553 post. Cf *Gouriet v Union of Post Office Workers* [1978] AC 435, [1977] 3 All ER 70, HL.
9   *A-G v Green* (1820) 1 Jac & W 303 at 305 per Lord Eldon LC; *Ludlow Corpn v Greenhouse* (1827) 1 Bli NS 17 at 65, HL, per Lord Redesdale.
10   *A-G v Governors etc of Sherborne Grammar School* (1854) 18 Beav 256 at 264 per Romilly MR. See also *A-G v Dove* (1823) Turn & R 328; *A-G v Barker* (1838) 4 My & Cr 262; *A-G v Ironmongers' Co* (1840) 2 Beav 313.
11   *A-G v Dove* (1823) Turn & R 328; *A-G v Earl of Stamford* (1843) 10 LJCh 58 at 66 per Lord Cottenham LC. See also *Re Hanson's Trust* (1852) 9 Hare, App I, liv; Seton's Judgments and Orders (7th Edn, 1912) 1246. See also para 552 post.

**542. Death of relator.** Where there are several relators the death of one does not affect the proceedings, but if all die, or if the sole relator dies[1] or becomes mentally disordered[2], the court will stay the proceedings until a new relator is appointed, in order that some person may be made answerable for costs[3]. The Attorney General's consent is required before an order appointing a new relator can be obtained[4], or the Attorney General must make the application himself[5]. Where a relator who is also claimant dies, and his interest does not pass to a co-claimant, an order to continue the proceedings is required[6].

1   *A-G v Powel* (1763) 1 Dick 355; *A-G v Haberdashers' Co* (1852) 15 Beav 397 at 404 per Romilly MR. Relator proceedings are now rare in practice.
2   *A-G v Tyler* (1764) 2 Eden 230.
3   *A-G v Smart* (1748) 1 Ves Sen 72.
4   *Anon* (1726) Cas *temp* King 69.

5    *A-G v Plumptree* (1820) 5 Madd 452.
6    See CPR Sch 1 RSC Ord 15 r 7, which provides that where a party to a claim dies but the cause of
     action survives, the claim does not abate by reason of the death. As to the CPR see para 522 ante. As to
     the weight to be given to be given to cases concerning matters of civil procedure decided before 26 April
     1999 (ie the date on which the CPR came into force) see para 522 ante.

## (iv)  Other Persons as Parties

**543.  Persons interested and strangers.** Apart from the statutory restriction on the
persons who may take proceedings in relation to the administration of a charity[1], all
persons interested[2] in the subject of the claim ought, generally speaking, to be parties, if
they are within the jurisdiction of the court[3].

In a claim to establish a charity rentcharge it is not necessary for all the persons whose
estates may be liable to be joined as parties; the court will decide whether the rentcharge
in question is charged on the estate of the person actually before the court[4].

It depends upon the circumstances in each case whether persons who have a
contingent interest in a charitable fund should be made parties to any proceedings
concerning it[5].

Where the Attorney General appears on behalf of a charity the court may allow the
trustees to argue in support of the Attorney General[6], and it will hear the trustees when,
in good faith, they differ from the relators[7].

Strangers to a charitable trust who are not joined as relators[8] are not proper parties to
any legal proceedings relating to it[9]; as for example the original subscribers to a charitable
fund[10], or an agent employed by charity trustees to manage the affairs of the charity[11].

Persons showing an apparent right of intervention in legal proceedings to which they
are not parties may be allowed by the court to attend[12]. Again, if any necessary parties
are omitted or unnecessary parties are added, the court upon application will usually
allow the proper alterations to be made[13].

1    See the Charities Act 1993 s 33(1); and para 520 ante.
2    This does not include persons who merely conceive themselves to be interested in establishing the
     validity of the trust: *Practice Note* [1945] WN 38; cf *Re Belling, Enfield London Borough Council v Public
     Trustee* [1967] Ch 425, [1967] 1 All ER 105.
3    Persons who may be interested parties include: purchasers, where land subject to a charge in favour of
     charity was alleged to have been improperly sold (*Southmolton Corpn v A-G* (1854) 5 HL Cas 1);
     executors, where a legacy charged on land was given to a charity and an action to ascertain the profits of
     the lands was instituted (*A-G v Twisden* (1678) Cas *temp* Finch 336); one tenant in common of lands,
     where a charity was claiming against the other tenant in common (*A-G v Flint* (1844) 4 Hare 147); the
     heir-at-law, where the proceedings were to decide whether surplus funds belonged to him or to a charity
     (*A-G v Haberdashers' Co* (1792) 4 Bro CC 103 at 106; *Ludlow Corpn v Greenhouse* (1827) 1 Bli NS 17 at
     55, HL, per Lord Redesdale), or whether there was a resulting trust for his benefit (*A-G v Green* (1789)
     2 Bro CC 492), or where he was by implication visitor of a charity and an action was instituted for the
     execution of the trusts (*A-G v Gaunt* (1790) 3 Swan 148n); a schoolmaster, where the action was to have
     surplus charity funds applied for his benefit (*A-G v Smart* (1748) 1 Ves Sen 72); lessees, underlessees and
     assignees of charity lands in an action to set aside the lease (*A-G v Backhouse* (1810) 17 Ves 283 at 285;
     *Ludlow Corpn v Greenhouse* supra at 73 per Lord Redesdale; *A-G v Greenhill* (1863) 33 Beav 193. See also
     *A-G v Pretyman* (1845) 8 Beav 316, where a lessee, though not made a party, was given leave to attend).
     Where certain parishioners, on behalf of themselves and others, claiming to be interested in certain
     charities, applied to the court to be served with notice of all proceedings in the matter and for liberty to
     attend an inquiry, their application was refused on the ground that the public were already represented
     by the Attorney General: *Ironmongers' Co v Roberts* (1909) Times, 24 June.

4    *A-G v Jackson* (1805) 11 Ves 365 at 367, 372 per Lord Eldon LC; *A-G v Naylor* (1863) 1 Hem & M 809.
     It is otherwise where the rentcharge is not charitable: *A-G v Jackson* supra at 367 per Lord Eldon LC.
5    *A-G v St John's College* (1835) 7 Sim 241 (where the information was held defective for want of parties
     because the person who was entitled to appoint the master of a charity school if he was not appointed
     by other persons within a limited period was not joined as party); *A-G v Goddard* (1823) Turn & R 348
     (where trustees of a charity who had a contingent interest in a legacy given to another charity were held
     not to be necessary parties to a suit establishing the second charity).
6    *Solicitor-General v Bath Corpn* (1849) 18 LJCh 275 at 276 per Wigram V-C; *Whicker v Hume* (1851) 14
     Beav 509 at 528 per Romilly MR; affd (1858) 7 HL Cas 124.
7    *Solicitor-General v Bath Corpn* (1849) 18 LJCh 275 at 277 per Wigram V-C. As to relators see further para
     539 et seq ante. Relator proceedings are now rare in practice.
8    See paras 539–542 ante.
9    *Lang v Purves* (1862) 15 Moo PCC 389.
10   *A-G v Gardner* (1848) 2 De G & Sm 102; *A-G v Munro* (1848) 2 De G & Sm 122 at 161–162 per Shadwell
     V-C. However, see *Minn v Stant* (1851) 15 Beav 49, where the original subscribers were in special
     circumstances held still to have an interest, and were joined as parties.
11   *A-G v Earl of Chesterfield* (1854) 18 Beav 596. As regards actions by some agents against others see also
     *Strickland v Weldon* (1885) 28 ChD 426.
12   *A-G v Shore* (1836) 1 My & Cr 394; *A-G v Pretyman* (1845) 8 Beav 316; *Re Shrewsbury Grammar School*
     (1849) 1 Mac & G 324; and see para 546 post. See also *Royal Society for the Prevention of Cruelty to Animals
     v A-G* (2001) Times, 13 February.
13   See CPR 19.2; and PRACTICE AND PROCEDURE. See also *Re Church Patronage Trust, Laurie v A-G* [1904]
     1 Ch 41; affd on another point [1904] 2 Ch 643. CA. As to the CPR see para 522 ante. As to the weight
     to be given to be given to cases concerning matters of civil procedure decided before 26 April 1999
     (ie the date on which the CPR came into force) see para 522 ante.


**544. Proceedings against trustees.** Where proceedings are taken against charity trustees, all must be joined, and not only the acting trustees[1]; but in a claim to remedy a breach of trust it is not necessary to make every person participating in the breach party to the suit[2].

New trustees appointed during the course of proceedings who ought to be, but are not, parties to proceedings for the administration of a charity are not so bound by a decree made in such proceedings as to be absolutely precluded from making a case by way of defence to the suit[3].

1    *Re Chertsey Market, ex p Walthew* (1819) 6 Price 261.
2    *A-G v Leicester Corpn* (1844) 7 Beav 176. See the following cases of *McCheane v Gyles (No 2)* [1902]
     1 Ch 911, where a claim was brought by a beneficiary against one of two trustees liable for breach of
     trust, and *Ideal Films Ltd v Richards* [1927] 1 KB 374, CA, neither of which involved charities. See also
     CPR 19.6, which provides that where more than one person has the same interest in a claim, the claim
     may be begun or the court may order that the claim be continued, by or against one or more of the
     persons who have the same interest as representatives of any other persons who have that interest. As to
     the CPR see para 522 ante.
3    *A-G v Foster* (1842) 2 Hare 81.


# (4)  PROCEDURE RELATING TO SCHEMES


**545. Drafting and settling schemes.** In many non–contentious cases schemes are settled by the Charity Commissioners[1], either on an application to them for the purpose[2] or on a reference by the court[3]. Otherwise, where the court directs a scheme to be settled, the matter is generally referred to a master and settled in private before the judge[4];

the scheme settled by the judge is scheduled to the order approving it. In simple cases, where a slight modification of a trust is required[5] or where the fund is small[6], a reference to the master may be dispensed with and the scheme set out in the order[7]. Sometimes a reference to the master is directed to apportion a fund without settling a scheme[8].

When a scheme is directed to be settled, the draft may be prepared by the Attorney General[9], or by other applicants, who would usually be the trustees of the charity[10]. If the draft is not prepared by the Attorney General it must be submitted to the Treasury Solicitor[11] for the Attorney General's approval. The draft scheme is brought before the judge in private for approval[12]. If there are any points objected to, the summons may be adjourned into court[13].

The Attorney General, whose presence at the settlement of a scheme is generally[14], but not invariably[15], required, should be served with a summons to attend[16], and he may then raise any objections[17].

1   As to the Charity Commissioners see paras 486–512 ante.
2   Ie under the Charities Act 1993 s 16(1): see para 180 ante.
3   Ie under ibid s 16(2): see para 182 ante.
4   *Wellbeloved v Jones* (1822) 1 Sim & St 40; and see *Doyley v Doyley* (1735) 7 Ves 58n; *Baylis v A-G* (1741) 2 Atk 239 at 240n per Lord Hardwicke LC; *Paice v Archbishop of Canterbury* (1807) 14 Ves 364 at 372 per Lord Eldon LC; *Waldo v Caley* (1809) 16 Ves 206 at 211 per Grant MR; *Re Hanson's Trust* (1852) 9 Hare, App I, liv. In practice, it is only in some cases that the court directs the scheme be settled by the master: where the scheme is either very short or particularly contentious the judge may make the scheme.
5   *Re Richardson's Will* (1887) 58 LT 45.
6   *Re Lousada, Bacon v Bacon* (1887) 82 LT Jo 358.
7   *A-G v Brandreth* (1842) 1 Y & C Ch Cas 200; *Clum Hospital Warden and Brethren v Lord Powys* (1842) 6 Jur 252; *Re Delmar Charitable Trust* [1897] 2 Ch 163 at 168 per Stirling J. See also *Gillan v Gillan* (1878) 1 LR Ir 114; *A-G v Earl of Mansfield, ex p Wardens and Governors of Highgate Free Grammar School* (1845) 14 Sim 601.
8   *White v White* (1778) 1 Bro CC 12 at 15 per Lord Thurlow LC; *Re Hyde's Trusts* (1873) 22 WR 69.
9   *Smith v Kerr (No 2)* (1905) 74 LJCh 763 at 767 per Farwell J.
10  *A-G v Stepney* (1804) 10 Ves 22 at 29 per Lord Eldon LC; *Jemmit v Verril* (1826) Amb 585n; and cf *Re Lea, Lea v Cooke* (1887) 34 ChD 528 at 533 per North J.
11  As to the Treasury Solicitor see CONSTITUTIONAL LAW AND HUMAN RIGHTS vol 8(2) (Reissue) para 541.
12  *Re Wyersdale School* (1853) 10 Hare, App II, lxxiv.
13  *Re Wyersdale School* (1853) 10 Hare, App II, lxxiv.
14  *Re Hanson's Trust* (1852) 9 Hare, App I, liv; *A-G v Goldsmiths' Co* (1833) Coop Pr Cas 292 at 312 per Leach MR; *A-G v Earl of Stamford* (1843) 1 Ph 737 at 739; *A-G v St Cross Hospital* (1854) 18 Beav 475; *Re Clergy Society* (1856) 2 K & J 615; *Re Taylor, Martin v Freeman* (1888) 58 LT 538.
15  Eg where the fund is small: *A-G v Haberdashers' Co* (1835) 2 My & K 817 (fund of £1,100).
16  *Re Hanson's Trust* (1852) 9 Hare, App I, liv.
17  *Re Lea, Lea v Cooke* (1887) 34 ChD 528.

**546. Attendance on settlement of scheme.** As the Attorney General attends the settlement of a scheme to protect the interests of all concerned in the charity, the court may refuse to allow the attendance of interested persons, even at their own expense[1]. As a rule strangers to the suit are not allowed to intervene or to attend the settlement of a scheme[2], unless their intervention or attendance will clearly be beneficial to the charity[3], or it is necessary, for the purpose of deciding a particular point, that someone should be allowed to intervene for the purpose of arguing a particular contention[4]. Permission to attend may be given to persons who are not parties, on the understanding that only one set of costs will be allowed[5], or that they do so at their own expense[6]. However, the

Attorney General is always ready to listen to any suggestion made by persons who have any real interest in the matter[7].

1   *A-G v St Cross Hospital* (1854) 18 Beav 475; *A-G v Wimborne School* (1847) 10 Beav 209 (Ecclesiastical Commissioners refused leave to attend); *Re Shrewsbury Grammar School* (1849) 1 Mac & G 324 at 334–335 per Lord Cottenham LC; *Re Sekeford's Charity* (1861) 5 LT 488.
2   *A-G v Attwood* (1852) 1 WR 64 at 91; *Smith v Kerr (No 2)* (1905) 74 LJCh 763 at 767 per Farwell J. See also the cases cited in note 1 supra.
3   *Smith v Kerr (No 2)* (1905) 74 LJCh 763 at 767 per Farwell J.
4   *Re Hyde Park Place Charity* [1911] 1 Ch 678, CA.
5   *A-G v Shore* (1836) 1 My & Cr 394.
6   *Re Shrewsbury Grammar School* (1849) 1 Mac & G 324 at 335 per Lord Cottenham LC.
7   *Smith v Kerr (No 2)* (1905) 74 LJCh 763. See also *Royal Society for the Prevention of Cruelty to Animals v A-G* (2001) Times, 13 February.

**547. Opposition by new trustee.** On an application for an order approving a scheme for the administration of a charity estate, a newly appointed trustee who has not been served with the proceedings may oppose the application on grounds not appearing upon the report or brought before the master[1].

1   *Re Loppington Parish* (1850) 8 Hare 198.

# (5) PROCEDURE ON APPLICATIONS AND APPEALS

**548. Applications.** Where it is necessary to obtain the authority or certificate of the Charity Commissioners[1] to take charity proceedings[2] or to appeal to the High Court against an order of the Commissioners[3], and the authority or certificate is refused[4], the leave of one of the judges of the High Court attached to the Chancery Division may instead be obtained[5]. Application for permission to take charity proceedings[6] must be made within 21 days after the refusal by the Commissioners of an order authorising proceedings[7]. The application must be made by lodging in Chancery Chambers a statement showing:

(1)   the name, address and description of the applicant[8];

(2)   particulars of the order against which it is desired to appeal or of the proceedings which it is desired to take[9];

(3)   the date of the Commissioners' refusal to grant a certificate or an order authorising the taking of proceedings[10];

(4)   the grounds on which the applicant alleges that it is a proper case for an appeal or for taking proceedings[11].

The application may be made without notice in the first instance and if it is made with the consent of any other party to the proposed appeal or proposed proceedings that fact must be mentioned in the statement[12]. If the judge on considering the application so directs, the Commissioners must furnish him with a written statement of their reasons for refusing a certificate or, as the case may be, an order authorising the taking of proceedings, and a copy of any such statement must be sent from Chancery Chambers to the applicant[13].

Unless, after considering the applicant's statement and the statement, if any, of the Commissioners, the judge decides to give the permission applied for without a hearing, the application must be set down for hearing and the hearing may be in private if the judge so directs[14]. Where the application is determined without a hearing, a copy of the judge's order must be sent from Chancery Chambers to the applicant and the Commissioners[15]. Where the application is to be set down for hearing, notice of the day and time fixed for the hearing must be sent from that office to the applicant[16].

1   As to the Charity Commissioners see paras 486–512 ante.
2   As to what are charity proceedings, and when the Charity Commissioners' authority or the permission of a judge is required, see paras 519, 521 ante.
3   Ie under the Charities Act 1993 s 16(12): see para 190 ante. The certificate referred to is a certificate that it is a proper case for an appeal: see s 16(13); and para 190 ante. For the purposes of CPR Sch 1 RSC Ord 108, 'certificate' means a certificate that a case is a proper one for an appeal: CPR Sch 1 RSC Ord 108 r 1(1). As to the CPR see para 522 ante. As to appeals to the High Court see para 549 post.
4   The authority or certificate must first have been applied for and refused: see the Charities Act 1993 s 33(5); and para 521 ante. An application may not be made under s 16(13) for permission to appeal against an order of the Commissioners unless the applicant has requested the Commissioners to grant a certificate and they have refused to do so: CPR Sch 1 RSC Ord 108 r 3(1).
5   See the Charities Act 1993 ss 16(13), 33(5): and paras 190, 521 ante.
6   Ie under ibid s 33(5): see para 521 ante.
7   CPR Sch 1 RSC Ord 108 r 3(2).
8   CPR Sch 1 RSC Ord 108 r 3(3)(a).
9   CPR Sch 1 RSC Ord 108 r 3(3)(b).
10   CPR Sch 1 RSC Ord 108 r 3(3)(c).
11   CPR Sch 1 RSC Ord 108 r 3(3)(d).
12   CPR Sch 1 RSC Ord 108 r 3(4).
13   CPR Sch 1 RSC Ord 108 r 3(5).
14   CPR Sch 1 RSC Ord 108 r 3(6).
15   CPR Sch 1 RSC Ord 108 r 3(7).
16   CPR Sch 1 RSC Ord 108 r 3(7).

**549. Appeals.** An appeal lies to the High Court in a number of cases against orders or decisions of the Charity Commissioners[1]. Such appeals are heard and determined by a single judge[2] of the Chancery Division[3]. On any such appeal the Attorney General is entitled to appear and be heard, as well as other persons allowed by the rules or directed by the court[4]. Such an appeal must be brought by an appellant's notice to which the Attorney-General, unless he is the appellant, must be made a respondent in addition to any other person who is a proper respondent[5]. Such an appellant's notice must state the grounds of the appeal and, except with the permission of the judge hearing the appeal, the appellant is not entitled to rely on any ground not so stated[6].

On the hearing of the appeal it is for the appellant to show that the order appealed from had been wrongly made; in the case of an appeal arising from a report on an inquiry into the affairs of a charity the appellant may challenge the findings of fact made in the report, which has evidential value on the appeal[7].

Appeals from the High Court in charity matters are regulated by the ordinary rules of civil procedure[8].

1   See the Charities Act 1993 ss 4(3) (registration), 16(11)–(14), 18(8) (schemes and orders relating to the administration of a charity); and paras 190, 265, 270, 468, 509 ante. As to the Charity Commissioners see paras 486–512 ante.

2     CPR Sch 1 RSC Ord 108 r 5(1). As to the CPR see para 522 ante.
3     See CPR Sch 1 RSC Ord 108 r 2. CPR Sch 1 RSC Ord 108 contains the rules made to regulate appeals, pursuant to the Charities Act 1993 s 92(1).
4     Ibid s 92(2).
5     CPR Sch 1 RSC Ord 108 r 5(2). Who is a proper respondent will vary according to the case: see eg *Incorporated Council of Law Reporting for England and Wales v A-G* [1972] Ch 73, [1971] 3 All ER 1029, CA; *Construction Industry Training Board v A-G* [1973] Ch 173, [1972] 2 All ER 1339, CA. On an appeal against an order made under the Charities Act 1993 s 18 (see paras 503, 507–509 ante) the Charity Commissioners should not be joined in the first place; if the Attorney General, as defendant, does not wish to support their order, they may be joined by amendment: *Jones v Charity Comrs for England and Wales* [1972] 2 All ER 637, [1972] 1 WLR 784; revsd sub nom *Jones v A-G* [1974] Ch 148, [1973] 3 All ER 518, CA, without affecting this point (see also further proceedings *Jones v A-G* (1976) Times, 10 November); followed in *Weth v A-G* [1999] 1 WLR 686 at 692, CA, per Nourse J. As to the weight to be given to be given to cases concerning matters of civil procedure decided before 26 April 1999 (ie the date on which the CPR came into force) see para 522 ante.
6     CPR Sch 1 RSC Ord 108 r 5(3).
7     *Jones v A-G* [1974] Ch 148, [1973] 3 All ER 518, CA; and see note 5 supra.
8     See CPR Pt 52; and PRACTICE AND PROCEDURE.

# (6) COSTS

## (i) The Attorney General

**550. Discretion as to costs.** In any civil proceedings to which the Crown is a party the costs of the proceedings are in the discretion of the court. The court must exercise this discretion in the same manner and on the same principles as in cases between subjects, and may order the payment of costs by or to the Crown accordingly[1]. Where the Attorney General as such is required to be made a party, the court must have regard to the nature of the proceedings and the character and circumstances in which the Attorney General appears and, in the exercise of its discretion, may order any other party to pay the Attorney General's costs whatever the result of the proceedings may be[2]; but the Crown is not deemed to be a party by reason only that the proceedings are by the Attorney General on the relation of some other person[3].

The Attorney General, it was formerly said, never pays costs when he sues as an officer of the Crown in the performance of a public duty, for example on behalf of a charity, even when he loses his case[4]. It is not clear whether this rule has survived the statutory provisions described above[5].

Where the Attorney General brings a claim for an injunction on behalf of the Crown as parens patriae he will not normally be required to give the usual cross-undertaking[6]. However, if the Crown is asserting proprietary rights and seeking to recover property alleged to belong to or to be owed to the charity, the court may think it right to give the defendant the benefit of a cross-undertaking if possible[7].

The court has a very wide discretionary jurisdiction to determine allocation of costs[8].

1     See the Administration of Justice (Miscellaneous Provisions) Act 1933 s 7(1); and CROWN PROCEEDINGS AND CROWN PRACTICE vol 12(1) (Reissue) para 136.
2     See ibid s 7(1) proviso (a); and CROWN PROCEEDINGS AND CROWN PRACTICE vol 12(1) (Reissue) para 136.

3    See ibid s 7(2) (as amended); and CROWN PROCEEDINGS AND CROWN PRACTICE vol 12(1) (Reissue) para 136. It seems that the Act does not affect the practice as to costs in charity proceedings: cf *A-G v Dean and Canons of Windsor* (1860) 8 HL Cas 369 at 459.

4    Shelford's Law of Mortmain (1836) 474; *A-G v Earl of Ashburnham* (1823) 1 Sim & St 394 at 397 per Leach V-C; *A-G v Dublin Corpn* (1827) 1 Bli NS 312 at 351–352, HL, per Lord Redesdale; *Ludlow Corpn v Greenhouse* (1827) 1 Bli NS 17 at 48, HL, per Lord Redesdale; *A-G v Chester Corpn* (1851) 14 Beav 338; *Re Macduff, Macduff v Macduff* [1896] 2 Ch 451 at 475, CA, per Rigby LJ. As to the general principle said to apply in courts of common law that 'the Crown neither receives nor pays costs' see also *A-G v London Corpn* (1850) 2 Mac & G 247 at 271 per Lord Cottenham LC; *R v Archbishop of Canterbury* [1902] 2 KB 503 at 572 per Wright J; *Thomas v Pritchard* [1903] 1 KB 209 at 215 per Lord Alverstone CJ; *Sanderson v Blyth Theatre Co* [1903] 2 KB 533 at 542, CA, per Stirling LJ; *Re Cardwell, A-G v Day* [1912] 1 Ch 779. As to the payment of costs by the Crown generally see CONSTITUTIONAL LAW AND HUMAN RIGHTS vol 8(2) (Reissue) para 392; CROWN PROCEEDINGS AND CROWN PRACTICE vol 12(1) (Reissue) para 136.

5    Ie the Administration of Justice (Miscellaneous Provisions) Act 1933 s 7(1): see the text and notes 1–2 supra; and CROWN PROCEEDINGS AND CROWN PRACTICE vol 12(1) (Reissue) para 136. See Tudor on Charities (7th Edn, 1984) p 345; and Picarda *Law and Practice Relative to Charities* (3rd Edn, 1999) p 715.

6    *A-G v Wright* [1987] 3 All ER 579, [1988] 1 WLR 164; *F Hoffmann-La Roche & Co A-G v Secretary of State for Trade and Industry* [1975] AC 295, [1974] 2 All ER 1128, HL. See INJUNCTIONS vol 24 (Reissue) paras 982–986.

7    There may be a difficulty about requiring an undertaking from the Attorney General since he does not have any right ex officio to resort to the charity funds for reimbursement. In *A-G v Wright* [1987] 3 All ER 579, [1988] 1 WLR 164, where the matter arose, a receiver of the charity had been appointed who would have such a right and the injunction was granted to the Attorney General conditional on the giving of a cross-undertaking by the receiver limited, however, to what he could recover by way of indemnity from the charity.

8    See *Aiden Shipping Co Ltd v Interbulk Ltd, The Vimeira* [1986] AC 965, [1986] 2 All ER 409, HL.

**551. When Attorney General receives costs.** As a rule in charity cases the Attorney General is entitled to receive costs which would have been awarded to him as a private litigant; but he is not entitled to receive costs in proceedings brought by him where, if he had brought them as a private individual, he could have been called upon to pay them[1].

Where the court sanctions an application to Parliament to effect certain changes in the constitution of a charity, the Attorney General's costs are allowed out of the charity estate, even if the application fails[2]. Costs may also be given to him in interim applications made independently of the relator[3].

If a defendant who has been ordered to pay the Attorney General's costs becomes insolvent, the costs may be ordered to be paid out of the charity estate[4].

In administration actions where the Attorney General is joined as the guardian of a charitable, or supposed charitable, legacy, he is usually given his costs on the standard basis[5] out of the estate[6], even if the proceedings are unsuccessful so far as the charity is concerned[7].

When the Attorney General takes proceedings as a result of information given to him by the Charity Commissioners[8], he is entitled to be put in the same position as any other claimant with regard to costs, and to have his costs out of the fund[9].

1    *A-G v London Corpn* (1850) 2 Mac & G 247 at 269 per Lord Cottenham LC; but see *Re Cardwell, A-G v Day* [1912] 1 Ch 779. The court has a very wide discretionary jurisdiction to determine allocation of costs: see para 550 ante.

2    *Re Bedford Charity* (1857) 26 LJCh 613.

3    *A-G v Earl of Ashburnham* (1823) 1 Sim & St 394. As to relators see further para 539 et seq ante. Relator proceedings are now rare in practice.

4    *A-G v Lewis* (1845) 8 Beav 179.

5    Previously the common fund basis. As to the basis of assessment now see CPR 44.4. As to the CPR see para 522 ante.

6    See eg *Mills v Farmer* (1815) 19 Ves 483 at 490 per Lord Eldon LC; and *Re Preston's Estate, Raby v Port of Hull Society's Sailors' Orphans' Homes* [1951] Ch 878 at 881, [1951] 2 All ER 421 at 423 per Vaisey J; *Re Amory, Westminster Bank Ltd v British Sailors' Society Inc at Home and Abroad* [1951] 2 All ER 947n. See also *Hunter v A-G* [1899] AC 309 at 325, HL, per Earl of Halsbury LC, where the Attorney General attempted unsuccessfully to support a judgment of the Court of Appeal in his favour, and the court intimated that, if the estate had not been large, costs would not necessarily have been given to the Attorney General. See also *Construction Industry Training Board v A-G* [1973] Ch 173, [1972] 2 All ER 1339, CA (appeal by Attorney General dismissed with costs).

7    *Moggridge v Thackwell* (1803) 7 Ves 36 at 88 per Lord Eldon LC; *A-G v Earl of Ashburnham* (1823) 1 Sim & St 394 at 396 per Leach V-C.

8    Ie under the Charities Act 1993 s 33(7); see para 526 ante. As to the Charity Commissioners see paras 486–512 ante.

9    Cf *Re Cardwell, A-G v Day* [1912] 1 Ch 779.


**552. Costs allowed.** Where the Attorney General takes proceedings at the instance of relators[1], he is not allowed the costs of attending separately by his own solicitor[2]; but if there is a suspicion of collusion between the relators and the defendant, for example where the same solicitor appears for both, application ought to be made for permission of the court for the Attorney General to appear separately[3].

Even when the Attorney General does not appear personally at the hearing of proceedings instituted by him, the costs of his brief should be allowed upon detailed assessment, on the ground that the Attorney General's duty is distinct from the mere duty and responsibility of counsel attending at the hearing to argue the cause[4].

Costs of particular proceedings taken and abandoned by the Attorney General in the course of an ex officio claim may be excepted from the general costs of the claim[5].

It has been held that costs of persons who, on public grounds, give advice to the Attorney General to secure the appointment of fit persons as charity trustees, are not allowed out of the charity funds[6].


1    This does not of itself make the Crown a party to the proceedings so as to give the court discretion to order costs as between subjects: see the Administration of Justice (Miscellaneous Provisions) Act 1933 s 7(2) (as amended); and CROWN PROCEEDINGS AND CROWN PRACTICE vol 12(1) (Reissue) para 136. As to relators see further para 539 et seq ante. Relator proceedings are now rare in practice.

2    *A-G v Dove* (1823) Turn & R 328.

3    *A-G v Wyggeston Hospital* (1855) Seton's Judgments and Orders (6th Edn, 1901) 1290; *A-G v Dove* (1823) Turn & R 328. The court has a very wide discretionary jurisdiction to determine allocation of costs: see para 550 ante.

4    *A-G v Drapers' Co* (1841) 4 Beav 305; and see *Cockburn v Raphael* (1843) 12 LJCh 263.

5    *A-G v Ward* (1848) 11 Beav 203 at 208 per Lord Langdale MR.

6    *Re Gloucester Charities* (1853) 10 Hare, App I, iii, where prior to the appointment by the court of new trustees of a charity under the Municipal Corporations Act 1835 s 71 (repealed: see now the Municipal Corporations Act 1882 s 133), a public notice was issued inviting parties to lay before the Attorney General any objections or suggestions with reference to the proposed appointments.


**553. Costs of application for fiat.** The costs of obtaining the Attorney General's fiat before taking proceedings requiring it, such as a relator action[1], and the costs of proceedings before the Attorney General with reference to the withdrawal of his fiat pending an appeal, may be made costs in the claim[2].

Where an application is made to the Attorney General without the direction or sanction of the court, the court has no jurisdiction to order payment of the costs occasioned by it[3].

1 See para 541 ante. As to relators see further para 539 et seq ante. Relator proceedings are now rare in practice.
2 *A-G v Halifax Corpn* (1871) LR 12 Eq 262. The court has a very wide discretionary jurisdiction to determine allocation of costs: see para 550 ante.
3 *A-G v Harper* (1838) 8 LJCh 12, where certain persons, who were purchasers in good faith of an improvident lease of charity lands, presented a memorial to the Attorney General praying that the matter might be referred to the master to approve a proper lease.

## (ii) The Relator

**554. Relator's liability for costs.** As the relator is answerable for costs, he should be a person of substance[1]. He may be directed to give security for costs[2], but this is not done where he sues as claimant as well as relator[3].

When proceedings are unnecessary[4], or are instituted from improper motives, such as private revenge[5], or where wrong parties are joined[6], the court may order the relator to pay costs, or such part as is occasioned by his misconduct.

1 *A-G v Knight* (1837) 3 My & Cr 154. As to relators see further para 539 et seq ante. Relator proceedings are now rare in practice. The court has a very wide discretion to determine allocation of costs: see para 550 ante.
2 *A-G v Rochester Corpn* (1680) Shelford's Law of Mortmain (1836) 425.
3 *A-G v Knight* (1837) 3 My & Cr 154.
4 *A-G v Glegg* (1738) Amb 584 (where the relators were charged with costs on the dismissal of an information which sought specific performance of an agreement between three executors, trustees of a charity, giving each a right to nominate to a third part of the charity funds absolutely); *A-G v Parker* (1747) 3 Atk 576; *A-G v Smart* (1748) 1 Ves Sen 72 (information in contradiction to the charity rights as established by its charter); *A-G v Hartley* (1820) 2 Jac & W 353 at 370 per Lord Eldon LC (where an information was filed involving most expensive inquiries, containing gross imputations on the conduct of individuals and allegations not proved, upon which no relief was or could be given); *A-G v Earl of Mansfield* (1827) 2 Russ 501 at 538 per Lord Eldon LC (information containing unfounded charges against officers of a charity). See also *Southmolton Corpn v A-G* (1854) 5 HL Cas 1 at 39 per Lord St Leonards.
5 *A-G v Middleton* (1751) 2 Ves Sen 327 at 330 per Lord Hardwicke LC; *A-G v Bosanquet* (1841) 11 LJCh 43.
6 *A-G v Berry* (1847) 11 Jur 114.

**555. When costs denied to relator.** Where a relator totally fails in substantiating the case, no costs can be given to him; the utmost he can then claim is to be discharged without costs[1]. This rule is applied where a relator acts in good faith but in error with a view to protecting a charity[2], or with similar motives seeks to divert charitable funds to purposes not contemplated by the trust[3]. Even if his application is partially successful, the relator may not obtain his costs where the proceedings have been conducted with unnecessary expense[4].

1 *A-G v Oglander* (1790) 1 Ves 246. As to relators see further para 539 et seq ante. Relator proceedings are now rare in practice. The court has a very wide discretion to determine allocation of costs: see para 550 ante.

2   *A-G v Bolton* (1796) 3 Anst 820; and see *A-G v Bosanquet* (1841) 11 LJCh 43.
3   *A-G v Braithwaite* (1885) 2 TLR 56, CA.
4   *A-G v Cullum* (1836) 1 Keen 104, where no costs up to the hearing were given to the relators.


**556. Costs given to relator.** Where there is nothing to impeach the propriety of the proceedings and no special circumstances to justify a special order, the relator in charity proceedings which terminate successfully is entitled to his costs on the standard basis[1], and to be paid out of the charity estate the difference between the amount of those costs and the amount recovered from the defendant[2]. In special circumstances a relator may also be given his charges and expenses[3]. Again, even though costs may be refused him, he may be allowed money actually expended by him although without the sanction of the master, if in the result the expenditure has been of use to the charity[4].

A relator who, with the Attorney General's consent, proceeds by action when the relief desired might otherwise have been obtained, may be allowed his costs[5]. So also may costs be given to a relator who is changed before the hearing of the proceedings[6], or to a relator who acts in error but with the intention in good faith of benefiting the charity[7].


1   See para 551 note 5 ante.
2   *A-G v Berwick-upon-Tweed Corpn* (1829) Taml 239; *A-G v Kerr* (1841) 4 Beav 297. As to relators see further para 539 et seq ante. Relator proceedings are now rare in practice. The court has a very wide discretion to determine allocation of costs: see para 550 ante.
3   *A-G v Kerr* (1841) 4 Beav 297 at 303 per Lord Langdale MR; *A-G v Taylor* (1802) cited in 7 Ves 424; *A-G v Skinners' Co* (1821) Jac 629 at 630 per Lord Eldon LC; *A-G v Winchester Corpn* (1824) 3 LJOS Ch 64.
4   *A-G v Ironmongers' Co* (1847) 10 Beav 194.
5   *A-G v Biddulph* (1853) 22 LTOS 114. He may not be allowed costs where the Attorney General's sanction is not first obtained: *A-G v Holland* (1837) 2 Y & C Ex 683.
6   *A-G v Tyler* (1838) Coop Pr Cas 358.
7   *A-G v Bosanquet* (1841) 11 LJCh 43.


**557. When further parties allowed to intervene.** Where, owing to their peculiar character and position, relators are incapable of adequately representing and protecting the interests of all the objects of a charity, persons who are not parties to the proceedings may be allowed to intervene in the proceedings, on the understanding, however, that only one bill of costs will be allowed against the charity estate[1].


1   *A-G v Shore* (1836) 1 My & Cr 394. See also *Royal Society for the Prevention of Cruelty to Animals v A-G* (2001) Times, 13 February. As to relators see further para 539 et seq ante. Relator proceedings are now rare in practice. The court has a very wide discretion to determine allocation of costs: see para 550 ante.


### (iii) Charity Trustees


**558. Charity trustees' right to costs.** The rules with respect to the costs of trustees of charities are for the most part the same as those with respect to the costs of trustees for other purposes[1].

Thus, in general, charity trustees who have not been guilty of misconduct expect to be paid out of the trust funds all costs, charges and expenses properly incurred by them in the execution of or in connection with the trust[2]. In particular, under the Civil Procedure Rules, in every detailed assessment of a trustee's costs where he is or has been a party to any proceedings in that capacity and he is entitled to be paid his costs out of the proceedings of any fund which he holds in that capacity, costs are to be assessed on the indemnity basis[3]. If parties to proceedings who are ordered to pay the trustees' costs are unable to do so, the trustees may recoup themselves out of the charity funds or estate[4].

1   Shelford's Law of Mortmain (1836) 467; *Man v Ballet* (1682) 1 Vern 43 at 44 per Lord Nottingham LC; and see *A-G v Drummond* (1842) 3 Dr & War 162 at 163–164, where Sugden LC pointed out how in some ways charity trustees are more favoured than ordinary trustees. As to the costs of trustees generally see TRUSTS vol 48 (2000 Reissue) paras 798–805. The court has a very wide discretion to determine allocation of costs: see para 550 ante.
2   *A-G v Norwich Corpn* (1837) 2 My & Cr 406 at 424 per Lord Cottenham LC.
3   See CPR 48.4(1), (2); and PRACTICE AND PROCEDURE. As to the CPR see para 522 ante. As to the weight to be given to be given to cases concerning matters of civil procedure decided before 26 April 1999 (ie the date on which the CPR came into force) see para 522 ante.
4   *A-G v Lewis* (1845) 8 Beav 179.

**559. Charity trustees' liability for costs.** Where a succession of charity trustees has for a long period acted wrongly but innocently in the administration of the trust, the court may refuse to visit the error of their predecessors upon the present trustees by depriving the latter of their costs[1], but the court's discretion is guided by the circumstances of each case[2]. So, too, if trustees take steps promptly to remedy an innocent and accidental breach of trust, they will not be made to pay the costs[3].

Charity trustees ought not to be visited with costs because of the misapprehension of the Charity Commissioners as to the construction of a public statute[4].

In relation to an exempt charity[5], the court may give charity trustees the costs of a successful application to Parliament for an Act to regulate the charity, even though the application is made without the previous sanction of the court[6]; or of an unsuccessful application to which the court's consent has previously been given[7].

Where the court orders charity trustees to pay costs personally, they may not pay them out of the charity fund. If they do so they will be directed to refund the amount so misapplied[8].

1   *A-G v Drummond* (1842) 3 Dr & War 162 at 163 per Lord Sugden LC, where the trustees had in error allowed Unitarians to participate in a trust property confined to another body; *A-G v Caius College* (1837) 2 Keen 150, where, notwithstanding certain misapplications, the trustees and their predecessors had accumulated a large amount for the benefit of the foundation.
2   *Shore v Wilson* (1842) 9 Cl & Fin 355, HL, where the trustees in similar circumstances were not allowed their costs. The Charity Commissioners have power to advise charity trustees: see the Charities Act 1993 s 29; and paras 335–336 ante. As to the Charity Commissioners see paras 486–512 ante. The court has a very wide discretion to determine allocation of costs: see para 550 ante.
3   *A-G v Drapers' Co, Kendrick's Charity* (1841) 4 Beav 67.
4   *Moore v Clench* (1875) 1 ChD 447 at 450–451 per Jessel MR.
5   As to exempt charities see para 293 ante.
6   *A-G v Vigor, Downing College Case* (1805) cited in 2 Russ at 519 per Lord Eldon LC. Costs will not be given where the application is unsuccessful: *A-G v Earl of Mansfield* (1827) 2 Russ 501 at 519 per Lord Eldon LC. See also *Solicitor General for Ireland v Dublin Corpn* (1877) 1 LR Ir 166.

7   *Re Bedford Charity* (1857) 26 LJCh 613. The Charity Commissioners may give permission to trustees to promote a private Bill: see the Charities Act 1993 s 17(7); and para 301 ante.

8   See *A-G v Daugars* (1864) 33 Beav 621 at 624 per Romilly MR; and *A-G v Mercers' Co, Re St Paul's School* (1870) 18 WR 448. See para 397 note 2 ante.

**560. Charity benefited by breach of trust.** Where a breach of trust has been committed, the trustees may be refused the costs of an inquiry into the matter, even where the breach has benefited the charity, although the fact that the property has been improved may properly be taken into account in disposing of the costs[1].

1   *Solicitor-General v Bath Corpn* (1849) 18 LJCh 275 at 277 per Wigram V-C, distinguishing *A-G v Caius College* (1837) 2 Keen 150, where, in somewhat similar circumstances, costs were given to trustees who had innocently misapplied trust property to the advantage of the charity; *A-G v Armitstead* (1854) 19 Beav 584, where trustees greatly exceeded the estimate authorised by the court for erecting a building. Cf *Bartlett v Barclays Bank Trust Co Ltd (No 2)* [1980] Ch 515, [1980] 2 All ER 92, where gains made in breach of trust were set off against losses made in breach of trust: see TRUSTS vol 48 (2000 Reissue) para 980 et seq.

     The court has a very wide discretion to determine allocation of costs: see para 550 ante.

**561. Severance of defence in claim for breach of trust.** Where, in a claim against charity trustees charged with breaches of trust, one of the trustees severs his defence and adopts the view taken by the claimant, he may be allowed to recover his costs on the standard basis out of the charity property, the costs to be recovered over against the other trustees[1].

1   *A-G v Mercers' Co, Re St Paul's School* (1870) 18 WR 448. In this case costs were awarded against the other trustees on a party and party basis. This basis was abolished when RSC Ord 62 was reformed and recast by the RSC (Amendment) 1986, SI 1986/632, and recovery over may well now be on the standard basis. As to the basis of assessment see now CPR 44.4. As to the CPR see para 522 ante.

     The court has a very wide discretion to determine allocation of costs: see para 550 ante.

**562. Proceedings occasioned by trustees' misconduct.** If proceedings are rendered necessary by any particular instance of misconduct on the part of trustees, whether they be private individuals or a corporation[1], or by their general dereliction of duty, even where they have not acted corruptly[2], they must expect to pay the costs occasioned by their improper behaviour[3]. Thus they may be fixed with the costs of proceedings where they have claimed unsuccessfully to be entitled beneficially to property belonging to a charity[4], or have committed a breach of trust and acted in a spirit of animosity[5], or have wilfully suppressed evidence thereby obstructing the course of justice[6], or have negligently professed ignorance of matters which they might have ascertained from an examination of their documents[7]; or where they adopt a wrong mode of procedure[8]; or where, pending proceedings instituted for the purpose of having new trustees appointed, they appoint new trustees themselves and this appointment is subsequently set aside[9].

So, too, on being removed from the trusts on account of their misconduct, charity trustees may be ordered to pay the cost of vesting the trust property in the new trustees[10]. Again, where trustees of a religious congregation who refuse to retire on account of holding opinions incompatible with the terms of the trust are removed by the court, they may be made to pay the costs of appointing new trustees[11].

When proceedings are necessary to force charity trustees to comply with orders of the Charity Commissioners[12], the trustees must expect to pay the costs of the proceedings[13].

1   Eg an appointment of officials contrary to the terms of the trust: *Salop Town v A-G* (1726) 2 Bro Parl Cas 402, HL; *A-G v Lord Carrington* (1850) 4 De G & Sm 140.

2   *East v Ryal* (1725) 2 P Wms 284; *A-G v Stafford Corpn* (1740) Barn Ch 33.

3   *Haberdashers' Co v A-G* (1702) 2 Bro Parl Cas 370, HL (negligent trustees ordered to pay costs of original suit and part of those of the appeal); *A-G v Wilson* (1840) Cr & Ph 1; *A-G v Mercers' Co* (1833) 2 My & K 654 (where a corporation, trustee of a charity, which had failed to apply properly a number of charitable legacies, was ordered to pay the costs of an information filed against it, but not of the subsequent reference to the master to settle a scheme). The court has a very wide discretion to determine allocation of costs: see para 550 ante.

4   *A-G v Drapers' Co, Kendrick's Charity* (1841) 4 Beav 67; *A-G v Christ's Hospital* (1841) 4 Beav 73 (where trustees, who had for a long period administered charitable funds erroneously, on being called upon to administer them duly, unsuccessfully insisted on their own rights adversely to the charity); *A-G v Webster* (1875) LR 20 Eq 483 at 492 per Jessel MR (where the trustees disregarded the opinion of their own counsel that the property was charitable, but the Attorney General, by whom this was an ex officio information, did not press the costs against the trustees personally); *Re St Stephen, Coleman Street, Re St Mary the Virgin, Aldermanbury* (1888) 39 ChD 492 (a test case instituted by trustees claiming that certain property was not charitable). See also *A-G v Brewer's Co* (1717) 1 P Wms 376; *A-G v Gibbs* (1847) 1 De G & Sm 156 (affd 2 Ph 327); *A-G v Mercers' Co, Re St Paul's School* (1870) 18 WR 448.

5   *A-G v Stroud* (1868) 19 LT 545.

6   *Hertford Corpn v Hertford Poor* (1713) 2 Bro Parl Cas 377, HL.

7   *A-G v East Retford Corpn* (1833) 2 My & K 35; revsd without affecting this point (1838) 3 My & Cr 484. In *Solicitor-General v Bath Corpn* (1849) 18 LJCh 275 at 277 per Wigram V-C, it was suggested that the court might be compelled to fix charity trustees with constructive notice of a document which they had innocently failed to disclose.

8   *Ludlow Corpn v Greenhouse* (1827) 1 Bli NS 17 at 93, HL.

9   *A-G v Clack* (1839) 1 Beav 467.

10  *Coventry Corpn v A-G* (1720) 7 Bro Parl Cas 235 at 237–238, HL; *Ex p Greenhouse* (1815) 1 Madd 92 at 109 per Plumer V-C.

11  *A-G v Murdoch* (1856) 2 K & J 571. They will not be made to pay costs where they retire voluntarily, though whether they will receive them is a question for the court's discretion, and may depend upon the circumstances of their retirement: *A-G v Murdoch* supra at 573 per Wood V-C.

12  As to the enforcement of orders of the Commissioners see para 494 ante. As to the Charity Commissioners see paras 486–512 ante.

13  Cf *Re St Brides', Fleet Street, Church or Parish Estate* (1877) 35 ChD 147n; affd [1877] WN 149, CA; *Re Gilchrist Educational Trust* [1895] 1 Ch 367.

**563. Mistaken application for scheme.** Where, having paid a fund into court and thereby discharged themselves from the office of trustees, charity trustees prepared an application to the court for a scheme to administer the charity, to which the Attorney General refused his fiat, the trustees were not allowed the costs of the abortive application, although they might have been given their costs in connection with an application by the Attorney General for the same purpose[1].

1   *Re Poplar and Blackwall Free School* (1878) 8 ChD 543. The court has a very wide discretion to determine allocation of costs: see para 550 ante.

**564. Proceedings to obtain accounts.** As it is the duty of charity trustees to render accounts without application to those to whom they are accountable, they are liable to the costs of proceedings to compel an account, even if in the result the charity proves to be indebted to the trustees. However, if the accounts show that the trustees are not debtors to the trust, no subsequent costs on either side are likely to be given[1]. So, too, trustees refusing to render accounts to the Charity Commissioners[2] may be ordered to pay the costs of an order for committal[3].

1   *A-G v Gibbs* (1847) 2 Ph 327. The court has a very wide discretion to determine allocation of costs: see para 550 ante.
2   As to the Charity Commissioners see paras 486–512 ante.
3   *Re Gilchrist Educational Trust* [1895] 1 Ch 367.

**565. Trustees allowed costs.** Trustees who are made claimants in proceedings without their consent are allowed their costs of having their names struck out[1].

Where unjustifiable proceedings are taken against trustees of a charity, the claimant may be ordered to pay the trustees' costs on the standard basis, so that the charity fund may be preserved intact[2].

When the official custodian for charities[3] has been made a party to legal proceedings the claimants have been ordered to pay his costs[4].

1   *A-G v Maryatt* (1838) 2 Jur 1060. The court has a very wide discretion to determine allocation of costs: see para 550 ante.
2   *Edenborough v Archbishop of Canterbury* (1826) 2 Russ 93 at 112 per Lord Eldon LC; *A-G v Cuming* (1843) 2 Y & C Ch Cas 139 at 155 per Knight Bruce V-C; *Andrews v Barnes* (1888) 39 ChD 133, CA. See *A-G v Holland* (1837) 2 Y & C Ex 683, where an information, which contained false charges against the existing trustees of culpable mismanagement, was in part dismissed with costs, though the earlier part of the information was successful. See para 551 note 5 ante.
3   As to the official custodian for charities see para 273 et seq ante.
4   *Re Church Patronage Trust, Laurie v A-G* [1904] 1 Ch 41 at 51 per Buckley J, where the plaintiffs failed in their summons and were ordered to pay the costs of the Official Trustee of Charity Lands (now replaced by the official custodian for charities).

**566. Where property forfeited.** Where, owing to a breach of a condition by charity trustees, part of the charity property is held to be forfeited, the trustees are not entitled to their costs of an unsuccessful appeal against the decision, the only fund out of which those costs would be payable being no longer in their possession[1].

1   *A-G v Grainger* (1859) 7 WR 684. The court has a very wide discretion to determine allocation of costs: see para 550 ante.

### (iv) Costs in relation to Charitable Gifts by Will

**567. Costs of construction claim.** As a rule the costs of a claim for contruction occasioned by obscurity in a will, for example to determine whether a particular charitable bequest is valid[1], are payable out of the testator's residuary personal estate[2]; but there is no absolute right to costs out of the estate, and the causing of unnecessary expense is discouraged by withholding costs[3]. Costs of an administration action are included in the words 'testamentary expenses', a direction as to which is often included in a will[4].

If a dispute arises between persons claiming a charitable legacy and persons claiming the residue as to whether the legacy is or is not payable, the costs of the litigation are payable out of the estate[5]. An executor cannot relieve the residue of its proper burden by paying a disputed charitable legacy into court[6].

1   *Kirkbank v Hudson* (1819) 7 Price 212 at 222 per Lord Richards CB; *A-G v Hinxman* (1820) 2 Jac & W 270 at 278 per Plumer MR; *Giblett v Hobson* (1833) 5 Sim 651 at 662 per Shadwell V-C (affd (1834) 3 My & K 517); *Daly v A-G* (1860) 11 I Ch R 41.

2   *Philpott v President and Governors of St George's Hospital, A-G v Philpott* (1857) 6 HL Cas 338 at 374 per Lord Wensleydale; *Wilson v Squire* (1842) 13 Sim 212; *Daly v A-G* (1860) 11 I Ch R 41 at 49; and see EXECUTORS AND ADMINISTRATORS vol 17(2) (Reissue) para 746 et seq.

3   See *Re Amory, Westminster Bank Ltd v British Sailors' Society Inc at Home and Abroad* [1951] 2 All ER 947n (costs withheld); *Re Daysh, Dale v Duke of Richmond and Gordon* (1951) 1 TLR 257 per Wynn-Parry J, where the costs were allowed in the particular circumstances of the case. Costs may also be disallowed where they are incurred in preferring hopeless claims: see para 569 note 1 post. The court has a very wide discretion to determine allocation of costs: see para 550 ante.

4   *Penny v Penny* (1879) 11 ChD 440.

5   *A-G v Lawes* (1849) 8 Hare 32 at 43 per Knight Bruce V-C.

6   *Re Birkett* (1878) 9 ChD 576 at 581 per Jessel MR.


**568. Dispute as to legacy severed from estate.** If executors admit a legacy to be payable and sever it from the estate, and a dispute afterwards arises between the persons to whom or to some of whom the legacy belongs, and the court has to decide to whom it belongs, the legacy bears the cost[1]. Thus, where executors have appropriated a charitable legacy and divided the residue, the costs of proceedings to secure the legacy must be paid out of it[2]. The mere fact that executors have set apart a sum to meet the legacy, if payable, does not constitute a severance[3].

An admission by an executor of assets for the payment of a charitable legacy extends to an admission of assets for the payment of costs to secure payment of the legacy, if the court thinks fit to direct them[4].

1   *A-G v Lawes* (1849) 8 Hare 32 at 43 per Knight Bruce V-C; *Re Lycett, Riley v King's College Hospital* (1897) 13 TLR 373 (ambiguous bequest to charitable institution wrongly described). The court has a very wide discretion to determine allocation of costs: see para 550 ante.

2   *Governesses' Benevolent Institution v Rusbridger* (1854) 18 Beav 467.

3   *A-G v Lawes* (1849) 8 Hare 32.

4   *Philanthropic Society v Hobson* (1833) 2 My & K 357.


**569. Charities claiming bequest.** Where a testator occasions difficulty to his executors in administering his estate by misdescribing a charitable institution which he intends should receive a legacy, and more than one institution claims the legacy, the costs even of the unsuccessful claimants, on the standard basis, notwithstanding the opposition of the residuary legatees, are often directed to be paid out of the estate; but where in the court's opinion a claim is hopeless and not made in good faith, the unsuccessful claimant may be ordered to pay his own costs, and in some cases may be ordered to pay the costs of other parties[1].

1   *Re Clarke, Clarke v St Mary's Convalescent Home* (1907) 97 LT 707; and cf *Re Lycett, Riley v King's College Hospital* (1897) 13 TLR 373, where the costs were made payable out of the legacy, presumably on the ground that it had been severed from the estate. Farwell J stated that a society which appeared in court to support a claim which was not admitted must not expect as of right to be paid its costs out of the estate, and might in certain events have to pay costs: *Re Millington* (1932) Times, 14 January referred to in *Re Preston's Estate, Raby v Port of Hull Society's Sailors' Orphans' Homes* [1951] Ch 878, [1951] 2 All ER 421 (costs of claimants not allowed after a point in the proceedings where it had become clear that the claims were hopeless); *Re Vernon's Will Trusts, Lloyds Bank Ltd v Group 20 Hospital Management Committee (Coventry)* [1972] Ch 300n, [1971] 3 All ER 1061n (where (although this does not appear from the report) the second defendant was not allowed its costs out of the estate). See also para 578 post.
   The court has a very wide discretion to determine allocation of costs: see para 550 ante.
   In practice, proceedings can often be avoided by an approach to the Treasury Solicitor to discover what view would be taken by the Attorney General were the matter to come before the court, and, if a firm view is given to act on that basis. This is an inexpensive way of dealing with the misdescription of charities in a will and apparent cases of initial failure where a cy-près scheme may be made by the Charity Commission if all concerned agree. As to the cy-près doctrine see para 201 et seq ante. As to the Treasury Solicitor see CONSTITUTIONAL LAW AND HUMAN RIGHTS vol 8(2) (Reissue) para 541.

**570. Costs in administration claim.** Where the next of kin[1] are made parties to a claim for administration relating to a charity and raise no improper point, they are as a rule, though not as of right[2], allowed their costs on the standard basis, even where their claim does not succeed[3], and they may be allowed charges and expenses as well[4].

The rule that the costs of an administration action were payable out of residue generally, and not primarily out of a lapsed share, applied when that share was given to a charity and lapsed[5], but the rule seems to have been superseded[6].

1   Most of the cases referred to in notes 2–5 infra are cases in which it was the heir at law who was made a party. The principle must apply in just the same way to persons entitled under the Administration of Estates Act 1925 s 46 (as amended): see EXECUTORS AND ADMINISTRATORS vol 17(2) (Reissue) para 619 et seq. If the heir at law brought an unnecessary suit, the costs were directed to be paid out of the real estate: *Leacroft v Maynard* (1791) 1 Ves 279.
2   *Whicker v Hume* (1851) 14 Beav 509 at 528 per Romilly MR (where the heir was only given party and party costs); *Aria v Emanuel* (1861) 9 WR 366; *Wilkinson v Barber* (1872) LR 14 Eq 96 at 99 (next of kin).
3   *A-G v Haberdashers' Co* (1793) 4 Bro CC 178; *Currie v Pye* (1811) 17 Ves 462; *A-G v Kerr* (1841) 4 Beav 297 at 299; *James v James* (1849) 11 Beav 397 (heir at law cases); *Gaffney v Hevey* (1837) 1 Dr & Wal 12 at 25; *Carter v Green* (1857) 3 K & J 591 at 608; *Lewis v Allenby* (1870) LR 10 Eq 668 (next of kin cases).
4   *A-G v Haberdashers' Co* (1793) 4 Bro CC 178; *A-G v Kerr* (1841) 4 Beav 297. The court has a very wide discretion to determine allocation of costs: see para 550 ante.
5   *Blann v Bell* (1877) 7 ChD 382; contra, *Taylor v Mogg* (1858) 27 LJCh 816; and see *Linley v Taylor* (1859) 1 Giff 67.
6   See the Administration of Estates Act 1925 s 34(3), Sch 1 Pt II para 1, whereby, as regards solvent estates, property of the deceased undisposed of by will becomes primarily liable, subject to the retention of a fund to meet pecuniary legacies, for testamentary and administration expenses; but this is subject to any contrary provision in the will. See also EXECUTORS AND ADMINISTRATORS vol 17(2) (Reissue) para 417.

### (v) Payment and Apportionment of Costs Payable out of Charity Funds

**571. Costs charged on estates or income.** A charge[1] of the whole or part of the charity estates may be ordered for the payment of costs. Sometimes the payment of costs may be directed out of the income of a charity fund[2].

It has been held that, where proceedings are taken in respect of one only of several gifts belonging to a charity, the costs should in the first instance fall on the property which is the subject of the proceedings; but a different provision may be made if justice to the relator or the interests of the charity require it[3].

1   *A-G v Atherstone School Governors* (1833) Shelford's Law of Mortmain 477; *A-G v Bishop of St David's* (1849) Seton's Judgments and Orders (7th Edn, 1912) 1269; *Re Lambeth Charities* (1850) Seton's Judgments and Orders (7th Edn, 1912) 1247; *A-G v Archbishop of York* (1853) 17 Beav 495; *A-G v Murdoch* (1856) 2 K & J 571. The court might possibly order a sale of part of the charity estates for the same purpose under its general power to authorise a sale of charity lands: *A-G v Newark-upon-Trent Corpn* (1842) 1 Hare 395; *A-G v Nethercoat* (1840) cited in 1 Hare 400. As to mortgages generally see MORTGAGE.
2   *A-G v Smythies* (1853) 16 Beav 385, where the costs of an application by a new master of a hospital for payment of the income of a fund in court was held payable out of the income. It was held that where a charitable corporation is ordered to pay costs, and it is entitled to a fund representing the proceeds of sale of part of its property, the party to whom the costs are payable may charge them upon that fund: *A-G v Thetford Corpn* (1860) 8 WR 467.
    The court has a very wide discretion to determine allocation of costs: see para 550 ante.
3   *A-G v Kerr* (1841) 4 Beav 297 at 303 per Lord Langdale. As to relators see further para 539 et seq ante. Relator proceedings are now rare in practice.

**572. Apportionment of costs.** The costs of settling one scheme for a number of charities are apportioned rateably, though primarily they may be made payable out of a fund not belonging to all the charities[1]. Where a charity includes two classes of estates, both of which are the subject of proceedings, the costs of establishing a scheme for the regulation of one estate only are borne by that estate[2]. Similarly, where several distinct charities are vested in the same set of trustees, the costs of proceedings relating to one charity alone must be borne entirely by that charity[3].

1   *Re Stafford Charities* (1858) 26 Beav 567. For a form of order apportioning costs see *Re Saffron Walden Charity* (1857) Seton's Judgments and Orders (7th Edn, 1912) 1250. The court has a very wide discretion to determine allocation of costs: see para 550 ante.
2   *A-G v Skinners' Co* (1827) 2 Russ 407 at 446 per Lord Eldon LC.
3   *A-G v Grainger* (1859) 7 WR 684.

### (vi)  Costs where Charity Land is Compulsorily Acquired

**573. Costs on compulsory acquisition.** Where land belonging to a charity is compulsorily acquired under the provisions of the Compulsory Purchase Act 1965[1], and the compensation is paid into court under those provisions[2], the High Court may order[3] the acquiring authority to pay the costs, including all reasonable charges and expenses, of or incurred in consequence of the purchase of the land[4], of the investment of the compensation in court or of its reinvestment in the purchase of other land[5], and of all proceedings relating to orders for those matters except such as are occasioned by litigation between adverse claimants[6].

Where the legal estate in the land is vested in the official custodian for charities[7], and the compensation has been fixed, the official custodian is under no obligation to receive the compensation so as to relieve the acquiring authority from the cost of payment into court and investment[8].

1 As to sales under compulsory purchase powers see para 358 ante; and COMPULSORY ACQUISITION OF LAND.

2 See the Compulsory Purchase Act 1965 s 2, Sch 1 para 6(2); and COMPULSORY ACQUISITION OF LAND vol 8(1) (Reissue) para 156.

3 The power does not apply where payment into court was necessitated by wilful refusal to accept the money or convey the property, or wilful neglect to make a good title: see ibid s 26(1); and COMPULSORY ACQUISITION OF LAND vol 8(1) (Reissue) para 148.

4 See ibid s 26(2)(a), (3); and COMPULSORY ACQUISITION OF LAND vol 8(1) (Reissue) para 159.

5 See ibid s 26(2)(b), (3); and COMPULSORY ACQUISITION OF LAND vol 8(1) (Reissue) para 148. As to when the costs of more than one application for reinvestment in land are allowed see s 26(4); and COMPULSORY ACQUISITION OF LAND vol 8(1) (Reissue) para 148.

6 See ibid s 26(3)(d); and COMPULSORY ACQUISITION OF LAND vol 8(1) (Reissue) para 159. The court has a very wide discretion to determine allocation of costs: see para 550 ante.

7 As to the official custodian for charities see para 273 et seq ante.

8 Cf *Re Leeds Grammar School* [1901] 1 Ch 228.

**574. Costs of payment out of compensation or dividends on it.** An application by charity trustees for the transfer to the account of the official custodian for charities[1] of a fund paid into court and invested in government securities is regarded as an application for the payment of money out of court, and the acquiring authority is liable for the costs of the application[2]. After the fund has been paid or transferred to the official custodian, the costs of the subsequent reinvestment are not payable by the acquiring authority[3].

The acquiring authority is not liable for costs where the dividends arising from a fund in court have been ordered to be paid to existing trustees of a charity and a fresh application to the court is rendered necessary owing to the appointment of new trustees[4].

Where, after land belonging to a charity has been compulsorily acquired[5] and the usual order for investment of the compensation and payment of the dividend to the then trustees of the charity has been made, the constitution of the charity is altered by a scheme, the acquiring authority may be directed to pay the cost of an application for payment out of part of the fund to cover the expenses of the new scheme[6]. Again, where in such a case an application is made to sanction a scheme applying the compensation cy-près and for payment out to trustees to carry out the scheme, the costs, so far as they are increased by the necessity for a scheme, may be excepted from the costs payable by the acquiring authority[7].

1 As to the official custodian for charities see para 273 et seq ante.

2 *Re Bristol Free Grammar School Estates* (1878) 47 LJCh 317; *Re Bishop Monk's Horfield Trust* (1881) 43 LT 793; *Re Rector and Churchwardens of St Alban's, Wood Street* (1891) 66 LT 51. See *Re London, Brighton and South Coast Rly Co* (1854) 18 Beav 608. The court has a very wide discretion to determine allocation of costs: see para 550 ante.

3 *Re Bishop Monk's Horfield Trust* (1881) 43 LT 793.

4 *Re Andenshaw School* (1863) 1 New Rep 255. It is otherwise where the charity has been reconstituted under a scheme: *Re Shakespeare Walk School* (1879) 12 ChD 178; cf *Re St Paul's Schools, Finsbury* (1883) 52 LJCh 454.

5 As to the compulsory acquisition of land see para 573 ante; and COMPULSORY ACQUISITION OF LAND.

6 *Re Shakespeare Walk School* (1879) 12 ChD 178; *Re Wood Green Gospel Hall Charity, ex p Midddlesex County Council* [1909] 1 Ch 263. As to the direction of schemes see para 170 et seq ante.

7 *Re St Paul's Schools, Finsbury* (1883) 52 LJCh 454.

## (vii) Miscellaneous Provisions as to Costs

**575. Assessment on order of Charity Commissioners.** The Charity Commissioners[1] may order that a solicitor's bill of costs for business done for a charity[2], or for charity trustees[3] or trustees for a charity, be assessed, together with the costs of the assessment, by a costs officer in such division of the High Court as may be specified in the order, or by the costs officer of any other court having jurisdiction to order the assessment of the bill[4]. On any such order the assessment must proceed, and the costs officer has the same powers and duties, and the costs of the assessment must be borne, as if the order had been made, on the application of the person chargeable with the bill, by the court in which the costs are assessed[5]. If the bill has already been paid, an order may not be made under this provision unless the Commissioners think it contains exorbitant charges[6]. No such order may be made where the solicitor's costs are not subject to an assessment on an order of the High Court by reason either of an agreement as to his remuneration or of the lapse of time since payment of the bill[7].

1   As to the Charity Commissioners see paras 486–512 ante.
2   For the meaning of 'charity' see para 1 ante.
3   For the meaning of 'charity trustees' see para 1 note 10 ante.
4   Charities Act 1993 s 31(1). In practice, the Charity Commission does not exercise its power to order assessment of a solicitor's bill of costs. The Law Society has a procedure in non-contentious business whereby on the application of a party it can issue a remuneration certificate.
5   Ibid s 31(2).
6   Ibid s 31(3).
7   Ibid s 31(3). As to the relevance of lapse of time see in particular the Solicitors Act 1974 s 70; and SOLICITORS vol 44(1) (Reissue) para 229.

**576. Costs on the standard basis.** In matters of equitable jurisdiction the court has power to order an unsuccessful litigant to pay the costs of the claim on the standard basis[1]. In many cases costs have been allowed out of a charity fund to all parties[2], or to some of them[3].

1   *Andrews v Barnes* (1888) 39 ChD 133, CA. The court has a very wide discretion to determine allocation of costs: see para 550 ante.
2   *A-G v Carte* (1746) 1 Dick 113; *Moggridge v Thackwell* (1803) 7 Ves 36 at 69, 88 per Lord Eldon LC; *Bishop of Hereford v Adams* (1802) 7 Ves 324 at 332 per Lord Eldon LC; *Mills v Farmer* (1815) 1 Mer 55; *Gaffney v Hevey* (1837) 1 Dr & Wal 12 at 25; *Wickham v Marquis of Bath* (1865) LR 1 Eq 17 at 25 per Romilly MR; *Re Cardwell, A-G v Day* [1912] 1 Ch 779 at 784 per Warrington J (where the costs of all parties were directed to be paid out of three charitable funds in proportion to their respective values).
3   *A-G v Stewart* (1872) LR 14 Eq 17.

**577. Interest on costs.** Although interest is recoverable[1] on costs which one party is ordered to pay to another, it is not recoverable on costs directed to be raised out of a charity estate[2], unless the court in the exercise of its discretion as to costs so directs[3].

1   See the Judgments Act 1838 ss 17, 18 (both as amended); Administration of Justice Act 1970 s 44; Judgment Debts (Rate of Interest) Order 1993, SI 1993/564. See the non-charity case *Taylor v Roe* [1894] 1 Ch 413. As to interests on judgment debts expressed in currencies other than sterling, see

Administration of Justice Act 1970 s 44A (added by the Private International Law (Miscellaneous Provisions) Act 1995 s 1(1)).

2   *A-G v Nethercote* (1841) 11 Sim 529.

3   *A-G v Bishop of St David's* (1849) Seton's Judgments and Orders (7th Edn, 1912) 1269 (and see Seton's Judgments and Orders (6th Edn, 1901) 1290 for the form of order), where 4% interest was given. This rate might now be 8%, which is the rate applicable under the Judgments Act 1838 s 17 (amended by the Civil Procedure Acts Repeal Act 1879 s 2, Schedule, Pt I; the Statute Law Revision (No 2) Act 1888; the Judgment Debts (Rate of Interest) Order 1993, SI 1993/564, art 2; the Civil Procedure (Modification of Enactments) Order, SI 1998/2940, art 3).

The court has a very wide discretion to determine allocation of costs: see para 550 ante.

**578. When costs allowed out of charity funds.**   The costs of making an unsuccessful application to the court in a charity matter may be given out of the charity funds, if there are substantial grounds for the application, although it may be induced by private interest[1], or even if the grounds of the application are based in good faith on a misconception of law[2]. The costs of vexatious proceedings[3], or of proceedings taken under an inappropriate procedure[4], are not allowed out of the charity funds. In some cases unsuccessful applications in charity matters are dismissed without costs[5].

Where an unnecessary party, by setting up a claim, renders service of process upon him necessary, costs will not be paid to him out of the charity funds[6]. Where a person who is not personally interested in a charity attends proceedings before a master, he will not be given his costs out of the charity funds[7] unless he can show that the charity is likely to derive benefit from his attendance[8].

Even though it is the court's duty in charity cases to grant the proper relief, whether it has been asked or not[9], the question of costs may depend upon the form of the application[10].

1   *Re Storie's University Gift* (1860) 2 De GF & J 529.
2   *Re Betton's Charity* [1908] 1 Ch 205 at 212 per Swinfen Eady J. The court has a very wide discretion to determine allocation of costs: see para 550 ante.
3   *Re Chertsey Market, ex p Walthew* (1819) 6 Price 261, where there was great delay in bringing forward charges of breach of trust against the representatives of deceased trustees, and the proceedings were accordingly held vexatious.
4   *Re Phillipott's Charity* (1837) 8 Sim 381. The summary procedure on petition provided by the Charities Procedure Act 1812 (Romilly's Act; repealed by the Charities Act 1960 ss 28(9), 48(2), Sch 7) was held to be appropriate only for simple cases: *Ludlow Corpn v Greenhouse* (1827) 1 Bli NS 17, HL.
5   *A-G v Stewart* (1872) LR 14 Eq 17 at 25 per Malins V-C.
6   *Re Shrewsbury School* (1849) 1 Mac & G 85.
7   *Re Shrewsbury Grammar School* (1849) 1 Mac & G 324 at 334 per Lord Cottenham LC.
8   *Re Shrewsbury Grammar School* (1849) 1 Mac & G 324 at 335 per Lord Cottenham LC.
9   As to this principle, which is in practice now obsolete, see para 525 note 2 ante.
10  *A-G v Hartley* (1820) 2 Jac & W 353 at 369 per Lord Eldon LC. See also para 525 ante.

**579. Co-defendant liable for trustee defendants' costs.** Where the Attorney General takes proceedings on behalf of a charity and there are two sets of defendants, namely the trustees of the charity and another party who, in the event, is adjudged liable to pay the costs, the court may direct the defendant so liable to pay the costs of the trustees directly instead of ordering the trustees' costs to be paid out of the charity funds and afterwards to be repaid by that defendant[1].

1   *A-G v Chester Corpn* (1851) 14 Beav 338 at 341. See also *A-G v Mercers' Co, Re St Paul's School* (1870) 18 WR 448 at 450 per James V-C, and the non-charity cases of *Rudow v Great Britain Mutual Life Assurance Society* (1881) 17 ChD 600 at 608, CA, per Jessel MR, and *Sanderson v Blyth Theatre Co* [1903] 2 KB 533, CA.

    The court has a very wide discretion to determine allocation of costs: see para 550 ante.

**580. Costs of proceedings to set aside lease.** As a rule the costs of proceedings to set aside an improvident lease of charity lands are paid by the lessee[1]; but the costs of setting aside a lease at an undervalue made in pursuance of a direction in a will which the court holds to be void as a perpetuity may be directed to be paid by the lessor[2].

1   *A-G v Lord Hotham* (1823) Turn & R 209 at 220–222 per Plumer MR. The court has a very wide discretion to determine allocation of costs: see para 550 ante.

2   *A-G v Greenhill* (1863) 33 Beav 193, where the costs were awarded on what is now the standard basis.

**581. Costs of appeals.** There must be a substantial ground for an appeal by defendants in a charity suit to exempt them from payment of costs if the appeal is unsuccessful[1]. As a rule, in the case of appeals, costs of all parties should not be given out of the charity funds, as such a practice tends to encourage groundless appeals[2].

1   *A-G v Rochester Corpn* (1854) 5 De GM & G 797. The court has a very wide discretion to determine allocation of costs: see para 550 ante.

2   *Bruce v Deer Presbytery* (1867) LR 1 Sc & Div 96 at 98, HL, per Lord Cranworth.

# INDEX

# Charities

**References are to paragraph numbers; superior figures refer to notes**

**References are to paragraph numbers; superior figures refer to notes**

**References are to paragraph numbers; superior figures refer to notes**

CHARITY—*continued*
  failure of object. *See under* CHARITABLE
    PURPOSE
  financial year—
    *meaning*, $210n^3$, $309n^4$
    first, $309n^4$
    rating purposes, $373n^6$
    subsequent, $309n^4$
  fund raising—
    charitable institution, for. *See* FUND
      RAISING
    house to house. *See* HOUSE TO HOUSE
      COLLECTION
    national lottery. *See* NATIONAL LOTTERY
    non-charitable trading company, by, 5
    public. *See* PUBLIC CHARITABLE
      COLLECTION
  grant to, by Charities Board, 454
  gross income: meaning, $210n^2$
  hospital. *See under* CHARITABLE
    CORPORATION
  income tax provisions. *See under* taxation
    *below*
  inheritance tax, 380
  inquiries—
    expenses, 498
    offences, 499
    power to institute, 497
  institution—
    *meaning*, 1, $419n^2$
    carrying on trade, 11
    fund raising for. *See under* FUND RAISING
    not for profit, examples, $377n^{17}$
    subject to control of High Court, 1
  jurisdiction over—
    Charity Commissioners', 489
    county court's, 485
    Crown's—
      charitable corporation,
        visitatorial, 456, 461, 471
      charitable trusts, protector of, 456
      general, without trust, 457
    High Court's—
      charitable gift, need for, 480
      charity regulated by statute, 482
      circumstances for exercise of, 483
      enforcement of trusts, 477
      extent, 478
      general charitable jurisdiction, 1, $224n^8$
      limits, 479
      royal charter, where, 481
      special remedies, and, 484
    visitor's. *See under* ELEEMOSYNARY
      CORPORATION
  land—
    boundaries of, 386
    disposition of. *See* disposition of land *above*
    fraudulent possession, 393

CHARITY—*continued*
  land—*continued*
    void lease or conveyance, possession
      under, 392
  law of mortmain, repeal of, 75, 76
  legacy, payment to, 383
  legislation, $1n^1$
  local—
    *meaning*, $180n^{10}$
    index—
      contents, 296
      inspection, 296
      power to maintain, 295
    review of—
      power to carry out, 297
      scope of, 298
    scheme extending area, 209
  lottery, national. *See* NATIONAL LOTTERY
  mismanagement, Commissioners' powers
    as to, 503
  mortgage of land. *See under* disposition of
    land *above*
  name change—
    circumstances requiring, 287
    company name, 288
    effect, 287
  nuisance, constituting, 73
  offence by body corporate, 515
  official custodian. *See* OFFICIAL CUSTODIAN
    FOR CHARITIES
  parochial. *See* PAROCHIAL CHARITY
  permanent endowment: meaning, $283n^3$
  principal address, disclosure of, $323n^5$
  private—
    association or perpetual institution, 55
    individual, benefit of, 53
    monument or tomb, 54
    nature of, 52
  proceedings. *See* CHARITY PROCEEDINGS
  protection of, by Charity Commissioners. *See*
    *under* CHARITY COMMISSIONERS
  public appeal, failure of purpose, 166–169
  public benefit. *See under* CHARITABLE
    PURPOSE
  purpose. *See* CHARITABLE PURPOSE
  rating—
    chargeable day: meaning, $373n^6$
    chargeable financial year: meaning, $377n^{29}$
    discretionary relief—
      conditions, 377
      grant of, 378
      revocation of decision, 378
      rural settlement condition, 377
      scope, 377
    excepted hereditament: meaning, $377n^{13}$
    mandatory relief—
      chargeable amount for occupied
        hereditament, 373

CHARITY—*continued*
  rating—*continued*
    mandatory relief—*continued*
      establishment of right, 372
      scope, 371
      unoccupied hereditament, 376
    occupation by charity: meaning, 374
    rateable value: meaning, $373n^7$
    registered charity, presumption
      regarding, 374
    wholly or mainly used for charitable
      purposes: meaning, 375
  receiver and manager—
    appointed person: meaning, $505n^2$
    Commissioners' power to
      appoint, 504, 505
    provision of security by, 504
    removal, 505
    remuneration, 505
    reports by, 506
  recreational. *See* RECREATIONAL CHARITY
  register of. *See under* registration *below*
  registered—
    meaning—
      annual return provisions, $326n^1$
      fund raising provisions, $424n^3$
  registration—
    appeal as to, 292
    change of name—
      company name, 288
      general principles, 287
    charity excepted by order or regulations:
      meaning, $283n^2$
    copies of register entries, 282
    duty to apply for, 284
    effect, 1, 289
    entry in register, 282
    entry in suspense, 292
    exceptions to requirement, 283
    exempt charities, 283, 293
    information, duty to supply, 285, 291
    inspection of register, 282
    lack of, effect, 1
    local index. *See under* local *above*
    lotteries, 294
    objection to, 290
    presumption arising from, 289
    publication of status, 286
    refusal of, effect, 289
    removal from register, 282, 290
  regulations and orders, 517
  relief of poverty. *See under* CHARITABLE
    PURPOSE
  religious. *See* RELIGIOUS CHARITY
  rentcharge—
    purchase of land subject to, 387
    recovery—
      proceedings for, 388
      time for, 390

CHARITY—*continued*
  rentcharge—*continued*
    release of, 348
    uncertainty as to land charged, 389
  restrictive covenant, established in
    breach of, 74
  scheme. *See* CHARITABLE SCHEME; CY-PRÈS
    SCHEME
  Secretary of State, transfer of functions, 513
  shops, 5
  small—
    *meaning*, 210
    modification of objects, 211
    modification of trusts, powers, 138
    transfer of property, 210
    very small, capital expenditure by, 212
  special case charity: meaning, $312n^2$
  special trust: meaning, $210n^2$
  stamp duty, 381
  statutory, schemes for administration,
    specified classes, 176
  superstitious uses—
    *meaning*, 56
    Act of Uniformity 1558 . . 56
    masses for the dead, gifts for, 57
    religious toleration and, 56
  taxation—
    capital gains tax, 380
    corporation tax, 379
    exemption—
      capital gain, 380
      Gift Aid scheme, 379
      payments between charities, 379
      Schedule A, under, 379
      Schedule D, under, 379
      Schedule F, under, 379
      stamp duty, 381
      transfers of value, 380
    income taxation, 379
    inheritance tax, 380
    non-qualifying expenditure:
      meaning, $379n^{12}$
    qualifying expenditure: meaning, $379n^{11}$
    rating. *See* rating *above*
    stamp duty, 381
    VAT, 382
  trading by or on behalf of, 5
  trust. *See* CHARITABLE TRUST
  trustees. *See* CHARITY TRUSTEES
  trusts: meaning, $210n^5$
  VAT, 382
  visitor. *See under* ELEEMOSYNARY
    CORPORATION
  war, former fund raising provisions, 417
CHARITY COMMISSIONERS
  advice—
    consequences of acting on, 336
    given negligently, 335

**References are to paragraph numbers; superior figures refer to notes**

**References are to paragraph numbers; superior figures refer to notes**

CHARITY TRUSTEES—*continued*
accounts—
annual audit or examination—
access to books, etc, 319, 502
auditor ceasing to hold office, 317
auditor's communications with Charity
Commissioners, 317
Charity Commissioners
ordering, 313, 502
circumstances requiring, 313
dispensing with requirements, 320
exempt and excepted charities, 324
expenses, 313
independent examiner: meaning, 313n[9]
information and explanations, right to
obtain, 319, 502
regulations, 314
report by auditor, 315, 316, 502
report by independent examiner, 318
report on receipts and payments basis, 316
supplementary provisions, 314
annual report—
contents, 322, 323
documents to be attached, 321
duty to prepare, 321
duty to preserve, 321n[7]
exempt and excepted charities, 324
information required in, 323
public inspection, 325
statutory requirements, 322
transmission to Charity
Commissioners, 321
annual returns of registered charities, 326
annual statement—
duty to prepare, 308
preparation principles, 310
prescribed form and content, 310
special case charity, 312
statutory requirements, application of, 309
auditor. *See under* annual audit or
examination *supra*
balance sheet, duty to sign, 310n[5]
copies of, 325
duty to keep records, 307
ex gratia payment: meaning, 311n[24]
exempt and excepted charities, 324
financial year. *See* CHARITY (financial year)
fixed assets: meaning, 311n[26]
fund: meaning, 310n[14]
income reserves: meaning, 323n[17]
independent examiner. *See under* annual
audit or examination *supra*
institution or body corporate connected
with charity: meaning, 311n[9]
most recent: meaning, 325n[6]
notes to, information required in, 311
preservation of records, 307, 321n[7], 324
proceedings to obtain, costs of, 564

CHARITY TRUSTEES—*continued*
accounts—*continued*
public inspection, 325
refusal to render, costs where, 564
restricted fund: meaning, 311n[15]
statement of recommended practice
('SORP'), 310, 311
unrestricted fund: meaning, 311n[15]
advice—
Commissioners'—
consequences of acting on, 336
written application for, 335
proper—
concerning investment, 362
concerning mortgage of charity land, 346
annual statement of accounts. *See under*
accounts *above*
appointment—
Charity Commissioners, by—
jurisdiction, 265
general powers, 507
mismanagement or misconduct, following, 503
practice, 266
court, by—
future appointments, provision for, 264
inherent jurisdiction, 261
number of vacancies, 263
Trustee Act 1925, under, 262
donor's failure to appoint, on, 246
express powers, under—
court's powers, 255
evidence of vesting, 257
strict and directory powers, 254
vesting of property in new trustees, 256
initial, 246, 247
new—
acting while disqualified, 250
disqualification grounds, 249
general principles, 248
number, 253
qualification under trust instrument
necessary, 251
religious opinions, 252
stamp duty, exemption from, 381
statutory powers, under—
church trust, 259
parochial charity, 260
religious or educational society, 259
Trustee Act 1925 . . 258
audit of accounts. *See under* accounts *above*
authorisation of dealings by Charity
Commissioners—
acts which may not be authorised, 333
agricultural charge, 334
directions as to expenditure, 331
general power, 330
transactions prohibited by disabling Acts,
332

---

**References are to paragraph numbers; superior figures refer to notes**

REVERTER—*continued*
  trust in relation to land arising under—
    *continued*
      Charity Commissioners' schemes—
        *continued*
        order establishing, 66
        relevant land: meaning, 64n[6]
        churchwardens: meaning, 63n[6]
        general principles, 63
        land: meaning, 63n[1]
        minister: meaning, 63n[6]
        parish: meaning, 63n[6]
        relevant enactment: meaning, 63n[1]
SALE OF LAND
  charity land. *See under* CHARITY (disposition of land)
SECRET TRUST
  creation, 72
  existence of, requisites establishing, 72
SECRETARY OF STATE
  *meaning*, 513
  charitable scheme, order amending, 184
  fund raising regulations, 426
  National Lottery distributing bodies, control by, 447
  public charitable collections, power to make regulations, 441
  sex discrimination in charitable instrument, order removing, 15, 405
SECRETARY OF STATE FOR EDUCATION AND EMPLOYMENT
  educational trusts, powers as to, 403, 513
  religious education trust, powers as to, 404, 513
SERVICE (DOCUMENTS)
  Charity Commissioners' orders and directions, 493
  charity trustees, etc, on, 342
  control of fund raising, relating to, 425
  public charitable collection, relating to, 440
SEX DISCRIMINATION
  *meaning*, 15n[11]
  charitable instrument, in, 15
  educational charity, in, 15
STAMP DUTY
  charity—
    appointment of trustee, 381
    conveyance etc for charitable purposes, 381

TOMB
  gift for repair, etc, 52
TRANSFER OF VALUE
  charity, to, 380
TRUST
  benevolent purposes, for, 4
  charitable purposes, for. *See* CHARITABLE TRUST
TRUSTEE
  charity. *See* CHARITY TRUSTEES
UNIVERSITY
  Commissioners' powers, 466
  eleemosynary corporation. *See* ELEEMOSYNARY CORPORATION
  qualifying institution—
    *meaning*, 466n[10]
    appropriate: meaning, 466n[13]
    staff member, dismissal—
      good cause, 466n[15]
      redundancy, 466n[14]
USAGE
  charitable trust, presumption of, from, 104, 105
  extrinsic evidence rule, in construction of trust instrument, 103
VALUE ADDED TAX
  charity, general principles, 382
VISITOR
  charities, of. *See under* ELEEMOSYNARY CORPORATION
  Inns of Court, jurisdiction over, 459
VOLUNTARY HOSPITAL
  *meaning*, 512n[1]
  committee of management: meaning, 512n[1]
  paying patients, Charity Commissioners' authorisation as to, 512
VOLUNTARY ORGANISATION
  *meaning*, 295n[5]
  power to maintain local charity index, 295
VOLUNTARY SCHOOL
  maintenance of, endowment for, 400
  trust deed: meaning, 400n[1]

**References are to paragraph numbers; superior figures refer to notes**

# Words and Phrases